INSECT DEFENSES

SUNY Series in Animal Behavior
JERRAM BROWN, EDITOR

Final instar caterpillar of the oxytenid moth *Oxytenis naemia* Druce on its food plant *Isertia Haenkeana* (Rubiaceae), near Gamboa, Panama. It rests on the upper surface of the leaf and resembles a rolled up dead leaf that has fallen from above. Younger caterpillars of this species are bird-dropping mimics. See Chapter 1 for further details. (Courtesy Malcolm Edmunds, Lancashire Polytechnic, United Kingdom)

INSECT DEFENSES

Adaptive Mechanisms and Strategies of
Prey and Predators

EDITED BY
DAVID L. EVANS AND JUSTIN O. SCHMIDT

State University of New York Press

Published by
State University of New York Press, Albany

For information, address State University of New York
Press, State University Plaza, Albany, N.Y. 12246

Library of Congress Cataloging-in-Publication Data

Insect defenses.

    (SUNY series in animal behavior)
    Includes index.
    1. Arthropoda—Behavior. 2. Insects—Behavior.
3. Animal defenses.   I. Evans, David L., 1945–
II. Schmidt, Justin O., 1947–   III. Series.
QL34.8.I57   1990   595.7′053   89-12311
ISBN 0-88706-896-0
ISBN 0-7914-0616-4 (pbk.)

10 9 8 7 6 5 4 3 2 1

Contents

Part 1. Evolution of Major Defensive Ensembles

Part 2. Predatory Strategies and Tactics

Part 3. Predation Prevention: Avoidance and Escape Behaviors

Part 4. Predation Prevention: Chemical and Behavioral Counterattack

List of Figures

Plate 12.1

1 Cephalothoracic defensive glands of *Leiobunum* sp. (Opiliones) **2** Internal view of *Leiobunum* sp. gland **3** *Leiobunum* gland opening **4** Defensive posture of *Glomeris conspersa* millipede **5** *G. conspersa*, segmental glands **6** Close-up of *G. conspersa* gland **7** Adult *Podisus maculiventris* metathoracic gland **8** *P. maculiventris* nymph abdominal glands **9** Ventral prothoracic defensive gland in the notodontid caterpillar *Schizura unicornis* **10** Internal view of *S. unicornis* gland 294

Plate 12.2

11 Tenebrionid beetle performing a head stand **12** *Romalea guttata* regurgitating **13** Defensive defecation by *R. guttata* **14** Larva of the chrysomelid beetle *Blepharida rhois* with sticky fecal shield **15** Larva of the chrysomelid beetle *Cassida* showing forked anal appendage that holds the defensive shield **16 & 17** Use of fecal shield in *Cassida* **18** Thrips with anal defensive droplet **19** Turret-like abdominal tip of thrips *Bagnalliella yuccae* 300

Plate 12.3

20 Defecation and autohemorrhaging in the meloid beetle *Megetna cancellata* **21** Autohemorrhaging by the chrysomelid beetle *Pyrrhalta luteola* **22** Defensive froth from cervical glands of a New Guinean arctiid moth **23** Poisonous spines of the saddleback caterpillar *Sibine stimulea* (Limacodidae) **24** Stinging spines of the buck moth caterpillar *Hemileuca maia* (Saturniidae) **25** *Papilio polyxenes* everting its osmeterium **26** Female vinegaroon *Mastigoproctus giganteus* aiming sensory tail (and defense gland) **27** Desert millipede *Orthoporus ornatus* exuding defensive secretion 304

Plate 12.4

28 & 29 Rectal diverticulum of the silphid beetle *Silpha americana* **30** Everted defensive glands of the melyrid beetle *Malachius aeneus* **31** The

List of Tables

PART 1

Evolution of Major Defensive Ensembles

Justin O. Schmidt

Defense and predation are not minor elements in the evolution of organisms; they are paramount for the survival of most species. A poor predator will rapidly perish and a less than maximally efficient predator will produce fewer progeny than its more effective conspecifics. Likewise, a prey individual with poor defenses is likely to pass fewer genes to subsequent generations. Thus, evolution plays a key role in the dynamics of predator-prey relationships. The manners in which prey have adapted to avoid predators are some of the most striking examples of evolution. These evolutionary adaptations may be exhibited as bizarre body shapes, including a resemblance to inedible bird feces, appearing like a dangerous predator, or producing dangerous spines and venoms. These adaptations may also take the form of altered behaviors which result in exhibitions of bold conspicuousness or in secretive and unobtrusive movement. The value of a majority of these adaptations can be comprehended almost exclusively in defensive terms. Indeed, what reproductive or physiological value could be imagined for an immature organism to appear like a bird dropping? Not only are many structures and activities of prey oriented toward defense, but they often are produced at a net physiological cost to the organism and, as a consequence, probably result in a lowered reproductive rate or capacity. The rich arena of survival and predator-prey interactions that so fascinates biologist and laypersons alike is the result of evolution.

In this section the authors focus on some of the overriding principles governing the evolution of many predator-prey systems. Edmunds presents evolutionary scenarios of how the major means of defense—crypsis and unobtrusive behavior—probably evolved. In contrast, Guilford details how the opposite strategy—appearing conspicuous and aposematic—might have evolved. Sakaluk explores the outcome of two often contrastingly different selection forces—sexual selection and natural selection—and how these forces interact. These three chapters provide a theoretical foundation upon which to build an understanding of many specific examples of how both prey and predators live and survive in nature.

CHAPTER 1

The Evolution of Cryptic Coloration

MALCOLM EDMUNDS

Introduction

Crypsis is the color resemblance of an animal to its background so that predators (or other animals) have difficulty in distinguishing it. Grasshoppers, caterpillars, and bugs are often green and thus harmonize in color with the leaves on which they rest and feed. Other grasshoppers and crickets that live among sparse vegetation are brown and so are camouflaged when resting on bare soil. Such insects are camouflaged to the human eye, and it is reasonable to suppose that they are similarly protected against insectivorous predators. The survival value of crypsis has been tested by several experiments using wild predators. Di Cesnola (1904) tethered green and brown mantids (*Mantis religiosa*) to green and brown vegetation. Over a period of eighteen days wild birds progressively ate all those mantids that differed in color from their background, but those that matched their background survived. Beljajeff (1927) repeated the experiment and also found that the conspicuous mantids suffered the heaviest predation. Similar experiments have been carried out on grasshoppers and other insects using a variety of birds and chameleons as predators (summarized by Cott 1940; Ergène 1951, 1953), and these too showed heaviest predation on conspicuous prey and least predation on cryptic prey.

With such stringent selective pressures it is not difficult to see how cryptic colors have evolved. Any individual with a slightly better color match to its background than its fellows will be less likely to be found and eaten, and so more likely to reproduce and propagate its genes in the next generation. Ergène (1950b) found several different color forms of the grasshopper *Oedipoda miniata* in Turkey, each restricted to a geographical region with a particular soil type similar to its own color. Any race that moved too far from its birthplace would presumably be more conspicuous and hence suffer more predation than the local cryptic race.

Evolution of Predators Capable of Finding Cryptic Prey

Once a prey insect has become cryptic, selection will favor those of its predators that are still able to find it. Precisely how predators recognize prey is not easy to determine, and there has been comparatively little rigorous experimentation on this matter (summarized by Robinson 1969b). We do not even know how much prey recognition is innate and how much is the result of discrimination learning. There is no doubt that crypsis is a defense against visually orientated predators, but whereas some predators recognize prey only when it moves, others are able to detect motionless, cryptic prey. How they may do this can sometimes be deduced from the counter-adaptations of the prey, so the argument is presented here in circular fashion, but sometimes there is also experimental evidence. Predators appear to have evolved the following ways of finding cryptic prey.

RECOGNITION OF PREY BY VENTRAL SHADOW

Because sunlight normally comes from above, and because insects typically have a body that is rounded in cross section, the lower surface of the insect is likely to be in shadow and so appear darker than the upper surface. A predator could therefore detect such an insect by means of its darker, lower surface (Cott 1940; Edmunds 1974).

RECOGNITION OF PREY BY BODY OUTLINE AND APPENDAGES

It seems probable that predators recognize insect prey by its characteristic body contour or by such features as head, wings, and legs. Robinson (1973a) glued heads and legs of stick insects in various positions to twigs and observed the behavior of predatory primates (the rufous-naped tamarin, *Saguinus geoffroyi*). He found that twigs were most often attacked if they had a head attached or if they had legs sticking out, but were usually ignored if the legs were closely aligned to the twig. He also showed that tamarins attacked shapes arranged in the form of a resting moth more often than similar shapes arranged to form a circle.

The eye may also be a prey recognition feature: some of the most convincing evidence for this theory comes from a study of the function of false eyespots on butterflies' wings. Carpenter (1941) studied beak marks on butterfly wings which indicated that the insect had survived seizure by a bird. He observed that many of these attacks were directed at the eyespots rather than at the body. This work has been extended by Robbins (1980, 1981) who found significantly more beak marks on butter-flies with dummy heads on their wings than on butterflies without dummy heads. This, together with other experiments, indicates that attacks were directed at the apparent head, and that attacks in this region often enabled the insect to escape. Blest (1957) observed the way in which birds attacked mealworms. Most pecks are normally directed at the head end, but if one end is painted brown, pecks are directed more at the painted end, and if one end is white with a black eyespot, that part receives the most pecks of all. Many lycaenid butterflies have dummy antennae and eyes on the hindwings. This fact further suggests that predators direct their attacks at the head and eyes of their prey, and therefore that eyes may be a feature by which predators recognize prey (summarized by Cott 1940; Wickler 1968; Edmunds 1974).

Thus it seems likely that insectivorous mammals, birds, and lizards use similar visual cues for the detection of cryptic prey. The precise cues involved will depend on the type of insect: Edmunds (1972) has suggested that birds recognize praying mantids by the head and foreleg profile in the "praying" posture, by the wings, and by the legs.

RECOGNITION OF PREY BY ACQUISITION OF A SEARCHING IMAGE

A predator may at first be quite unable to find cryptic prey (such as geometrid caterpillars or moths on bark), but after a time it accidentally finds one, and then quickly "learns" to find all of the others, presumably because it has a mental picture or searching image of the prey (Ruiter 1952; Kettlewell 1955). The phrase *searching image* was coined by L. Tin-bergen (1960) to explain the behavior of individual great tits (*Parus major*) of concentrating on one or two species of caterpillar prey for a while and then abruptly switching to another species which may be equally com-mon but was previously ignored. The concept of 'searching image' (or 'search image') was further explored experimentally by Croze (1970) and

Dawkins (1971), while Lawrence and Allen (1983) give a useful review of the use and misuse of the term. Dawkins' (1971) experiments clearly demonstrated that domestic chicks can improve their ability to detect cryptic prey with experience, while Pietrewicz and Kamil (1979, 1981) reached similar conclusions for the blue jay (*Cyanocitta cristata*) when presented with images of the cryptic moths *Catocala relicta* and *C. retecta*. These and other experiments purporting to demonstrate searching images are reviewed critically by Guilford and Dawkins (1987) who conclude that the case for the occurrence of search images remains unproven: each example cited could be explained by variation in search rate. My guess is that while some predators may improve their detection of prey by changes in search rate, others probably do form search images.

FINDING PREY BY AREA-RESTRICTED SEARCH

Predators may also find cryptic prey by changing their searching behavior as a result of experience, for example, by concentrating the search in a particular area or in a particular place which was previously found to contain prey (Croze 1970). There are numerous examples of this behavior; for example, black-capped chickadees (*Parus atricapillus*) concentrate their search on particular species of tree on which they have previously found caterpillars (Heinrich and Collins 1983).

FINDING PREY BY DETECTION OF ARTIFACTS

Predators may also find cryptic prey by searching for artifacts caused by the prey. Heinrich and Collins (1983) describe how black-capped chickadees concentrate their search on leaves that show evidence of caterpillar damage. Naturalists who have searched for large caterpillars (e.g., *Smerinthus ocellata, Cerura vinula*) on sand dunes quickly learn that one way to locate the cryptic insect is to search for frass on the sand beneath the food plant, and then to look directly above this for the caterpillar. It is not known if this technique is used by any natural predators.

DETECTION OF PREY ON AN INAPPROPRIATE BACKGROUND

Predators that are quite unable to find cryptic prey when it rests on its normal background may nevertheless be able to get sufficient food by finding those individuals that rest in the "wrong" place, such as green insects resting on bark or brown insects on green leaves.

DETECTION OF PREY WHEN IT MOVES

Some predators appear to recognize and attack prey only when it moves. Praying mantids, for example, orientate toward, stalk, and strike at flies only after they have seen them move. Naturalists who have experienced the tropical forest will also be familiar with the many "sit and wait" avian predators, including trogons and puffbirds in the Neotropics and kingfishers and shrikes in the Old World. These birds rest motionless for long periods and pounce when a previously cryptic or concealed insect or lizard moves on the ground or in vegetation. Lizards, too, appear to recognize prey when it moves.

Prey Responses to Predators That Can Find Cryptic Prey

As predators have evolved means of finding cryptic prey, so selection has favored those prey which have evolved further ploys to counter the predator's improved hunting strategy.

COUNTERSHADING

In response to predators that detect cryptic prey by its ventral shadow, many green and brown caterpillars and grasshoppers have evolved countershading such that the lower surface of the body is paler than the upper. The pale lower surface, together with the natural ventral shadow, now matches in hue the sides and upper surface so that the entire insect appears to be flattened and uniformly colored instead of a three-dimensional object. The caterpillar of the eyed hawkmoth (*Smerinthus ocellata*), which normally rests upside down on the stems and petioles of willows (*Salix* spp.), has reversed countershading (Cott 1940). It is about the size and shape of a man's finger, but because of its countershading, it is very difficult to see in its characteristic resting position. The view that countershading reduces the probability of one animal being detected by another has been widely accepted for almost a century, but Kiltie (1988) has recently pointed out that the theory lacks rigorous experimental proof.

DISRUPTIVE COLORATION

The evolution of disruptive coloration is a prey response to predators that recognize cryptic prey by its body outline or by such features as head, legs, or eyes. Good examples are bark-resting moths with patches of dark and pale color. On a tree trunk the eye sees these meaningless patches of bold color rather than the outline of the moth. Full-grown caterpillars of *Papilio demodocus* have bold marks of black on a green body; on a leafy background, these marks obscure the true outline of the insect. A classic example is the resting buff tip moth (*Phalera bucephala*), which resembles a lichenose, broken twig (Cott 1940.)

The theory of disruptive coloration relies on several principles which are clearly outlined by Cott (1940). First, it is essential for the animal to be on a background of mixed rather than uniform color. Then the strongly contrasting color marks on the prey become more noticeable than the true body outline, but since they have no more meaning to an observer than the rest of the mixed color in the environment, the animal escapes detection. Second, the color marks must not coincide with bodily features, otherwise they could merely make an insect more obvious to a predator. In *Papilio demodocus* one black band on the caterpillar appears to cut the body in half. Stripes of dark and pale brown cross the body and flexed legs of some grasshoppers and appear unbroken from abdomen to femur, thereby concealing the large hindleg which might otherwise be a prey recognition feature for a predator. Cott calls these "coincident disruptive patterns." Eyes may be similarly concealed by bold stripes that pass across thorax, head, and eye. Third, disruptive colors may be even more effective if one of the colors blends with part of the background.

Silberglied et al. (1980) tried to test the effectiveness of disruptive coloration in the palatable Neotropical butterfly *Anartia fatima*, which is black with a bold white stripe across both wings. Platt and Brower (1968) had previously suggested that this pattern is disruptive and hence improves the chances of survival of the insect. Silberglied and his co-workers marked and released butterflies in Panama, some of which had the white stripe painted black. Contrary to expectation, there was no difference in survival between experimental and control groups, and no evidence of any other differences in predation or attempted predation. These results suggest the white stripe is not disruptive, but must have some function unrelated to camouflage. However, Waldbauer and Sternburg (1983) have pointed out that the experimentally painted *Anartia* closely resemble blackish-brown species of *Parides* (Papilionidae) which are common at the release site in Panama. These *Anartia* may, therefore, have gained protection through Batesian mimicry to *Parides* which equalled the protection of the controls gained through disruptive coloration. So the experiment does not disprove the theory of disruptive coloration. It does, however, suggest that we need to be more cautious in ascribing a disruptive camouflage function to color markings, and that we need to be more careful in designing experiments to test the theory.

SPECIAL RESEMBLANCE

Another solution to predators finding cryptic prey is for the prey insect to develop a specific resemblance to part of its environment, such as twigs or leaves. This development can lead to the evolution of grass and stick mimics with long bodies of similar dimensions to blades of grass or twigs, or to the evolution of flattened forms that rest on tree trunks or on leaves. Stick mimics include geometrid caterpillars, stick insects, and praying mantids such as *Heterochaeta(=Stenovates)*, *Danuria*, and *Angela*; grass mimics include grasshoppers (*Cannula*) and praying mantids (*Pyrgomantis*); bark mimics include many geometrid and noctuid moths, heteropterans like *Dysodius* and *Ceratozygum*, and the mantids *Tarachodes* and *Theopompella*; green leaf mimics include leaf insects (*Phyllium*), tettigonids (*Mimetica*), and mantids (*Choerododis*); and brown dead-leaf mimics include the butterfly *Kallima* and the mantid *Phyllocrania* (Robinson 1969a,b; Cott 1940; Edmunds 1972, 1974; Silberglied and Aiello 1980). These extreme forms of crypsis have sometimes been considered as examples of Batesian mimicry (Edmunds 1974), but Vane-Wright (1980) argues that they are properly cryptic because they produce signals which are of no interest to a predator, whereas mimics produce signals which are of interest to a potential predator. Vane-Wright's paper stimulated several responses on the distinction between crypsis and Batesian mimicry (Edmunds 1981; Cloudsley-Thompson 1981; Robinson 1981; Rothschild 1981; Endler 1981; Vane-Wright 1981). Two points from this discussion are of importance here: first, stick mimics and similar extreme adaptations have undoubtedly evolved from fairly normal cryptic ancestors. An initial stage in the evolution of flattened forms may have been the development of lateral body flanges or hairs which obscure lateral shadow (Cott 1940). Robinson (1969b 1973b) has outlined the possible ways by which stick- and leaf-mimicking phasmids have evolved, and Edmunds (1972) has done the same for stick-, bark-, grass-, and leaf-mimicking praying mantids. Second, stick and leaf mimics differ from typically cryptic insects in one important respect: if placed on a neutral background such as a sheet of paper, a stick mimic still looks like a stick, whereas a simply cryptic insect immediately looks like an insect (Robinson 1969b, 1981). Cott doubtless faced the same dilemma of how to classify these animals when he wrote his classic *Adaptive Coloration in Animals* (1940), and perhaps he came to the most sensible conclusion by erecting a special category which he called "special resemblance." Animals which exhibit a special resemblance to sticks, leaves, and so forth have extreme morphological and behavioral adaptations that perfect the resemblance, for example, the elongated body and the resting posture of the stick-mimicking mantid genera *Angela, Danura,* and *Heterochaeta* (Robinson 1969a; Edmunds 1972, 1974), or the jagged outline to the flattened abdomen of the bark-mimicking bug *Dysodius* (Silberglied and Aiello 1980), which breaks up the outline and conceals any lateral shadow.

There are many more examples of special resemblance among insects. The tenebrionid beetle *Cossyphus* from East Africa resembles a winged seed (Cloudsley-Thompson 1977), and the full-grown caterpillar of *Oxytenis naemia* from Panama is a detritus mimic resting on the upper surface of leaves and resembling a dead, rolled-up leaf that has fallen from above (Nentwig 1985; personal observation). Its front end is flattened, and the marks further back give the illusion of a leaf that is partially rolled. The color and pattern varies so that some caterpillars resemble dead brown leaves and others resemble green and brown dying leaves. A more bizarre special resemblance is the habit of some caterpillars of resting on the upper surface of leaves, fully exposed to predators, but resembling a bird's excrement. Possibly these evolved from detritus mimics that already rested on the upper surface of leaves, or else from brown rather than green caterpillars that rested on stems and branches. If one such individual remained on the leaf, and because of some slight resemblance to a bird dropping survived better than its fellows that moved back to the large branches, the habit and the more perfect mimicry could have evolved. Bird dropping mimicry only seems to work for small caterpillars: *Oxytenis naemia, Papilio* spp., and *Apatele alni* all have bird dropping mimics when small but the final instars are quite different. *Oxytenis* becomes a polymorphic rolled-leaf detritus mimic, *Papilio* spp. usually become cryptic green or green and black, and *Apatele alni* becomes either aposematic or mimetic yellow and black (Nentwig 1985; Edmunds 1974; Ward 1979). The African *Trilocha kolga,* however, changes from a black and white bird dropping when small to a dark brown mimic of a bird or lizard feces when large (Edmunds 1974).

SPACING OUT

The prey response to predators that hunt by forming a searching image (or by varying their searching rate) is to be spaced out so that the chances of a predator encountering a second prey before the learned search image has waned are small. The selective advantage of spacing out was demonstrated experimentally by Tinbergen et al. (1967) and by Croze (1970) using wild birds and baited eggs or pastry prey. Spacing is probably equally effective against predators that hunt by a learned area-restricted search strategy: if a predator has searched many suitable places without success, its area-restricted search behavior may wane and it will search elsewhere or in other places. Croze (1970) also demonstrated this fact experimentally with wild birds as predators.

Spacing out is achieved in a variety of ways (summarized by Croze, 1970 and Edmunds 1974). Poplar hawkmoths (*Laothoe populi*) lay one or two eggs and then fly some distance before laying further eggs; a species of stick insect (*Carausius* sp.) catapults eggs one at a time up to one meter distant; some geometrid caterpillars "balloon" on silk like young spiders, and also tend to be most active and aggressive when close together so that they quickly disperse; Camberwell beauty caterpillars (*Vanessa antiopa*) are gregarious and probably aposematic, but just prior to pupation they move off in different directions so that the cryptic pupae are scattered; and nymphs of some praying mantids have a special display whose function seems to be to prevent individuals from getting too close to one another. Spacing out is an obvious defense against some predators, but its disadvantage is that the population must be low. The behavior and population of any cryptic insect will be a compromise between the conflicting selection pressures favoring sparse and dense populations.

POLYMORPHISM

One way by which a cryptic prey can occur at higher density yet not suffer increased predation from predators which hunt with the aid of a searching image is for the population to become polymorphic for color. Each predator would then have to learn a specific searching image for each of the morphs in the population. Croze (1970), using wild crows as predators (*Corvus corone*), found that trimorphic prey suffered less predation than monomorphic prey at the same density. Conversely, trimorphic prey could occur at a higher density then monomorphic prey for the same level of predation. Note that the development of cryptic polymorphism can be predicted from the search image theory, but it is not likely to evolve in response to predators that improve their detection of prey by varying their search rate (Guilford and Dawkins 1987).

Polymorphism is widespread in insects and may be either genetically or environmentally controlled. Caterpillars of *Papilio demodocus*,

Bupalus piniarius, and probably *Herse convolvuli* occur in two or more genetically determined color forms (Clarke et al. 1963; den Boer 1971; Edmunds 1974). Similar polymorphisms occur in some moths (Kettlewell 1973) and the homopteran *Philaenus spumarius* (Owen and Wiegert 1962; Halkka et al. 1980). Industrial melanism is a form of genetically controlled polymorphism that occurs in many species of moths (Kettlewell 1973) and also in psocids (Popescu et al. 1978) and *Philaenus spumarius* (Lees et al. 1983; Lees and Dent 1983). Environmentally controlled polymorphisms occur in many grasshoppers and praying mantids (Ergène 1950a; Otte and Williams 1972; Rowell 1971; Edmunds 1972, 1976) and also in some caterpillars (Poulton 1885, 1886; Grayson and Edmunds 1989; Greene 1989). Environmentally induced polymorphisms may also give the opportunity for an individual to change color. The most detailed studies of environmentally determined polymorphism in insects have been on pupae of various butterflies which can be either green or brown depending on conditions perceived by the caterpillar at a critical time shortly before pupation.

For species of both *Pieris* and *Papilio* it appears that a complex of environmental factors are involved in determining pupal color, including photoperiod, light, temperature, humidity, and texture of substrate (Smith 1978, 1980; Owen 1971; Hazel and West 1979, 1983; West and Hazel 1979; Sims 1983; Sims and Shapiro 1983). In *Papilio polytes* a short photoperiod induces caterpillars to produce brown pupae which diapause. These conditions occur naturally in autumn, and because the pupae will overwinter on brown vegetation, there is obvious cryptic advantage in having brown pupae. However, in long photoperiod conditions pupae are green on smooth surfaces and brown on rough ones. This also makes ecological sense, since green leaves typically have smooth surfaces, and stems and twigs are usually brown and rough. Similar results were obtained with *Battus philenor, Papilio polyxenes,* and *Pieris rapae,* although the specific factors determining pupal color vary in each species. Experiments on *Papilio polyxenes* by Hazel (1977) and on *Eurytides marcellus* by Hazel and West (1982) indicate that individual caterpillars in the population differ in their genetic tendency to produce either green or brown pupae, and that the mean of individual responses to a standard set of conditions can be modified by selection. Clarke and Sheppard (1972) had earlier shown that it is possible to alter the choice of pupation site in *Papilio polytes* by selection, so it is not difficult to envisage how pupal polymorphism and its determination by environmental cues have evolved. The survival of diapausing pupae on different substrates using natural predators has been studied by West and Hazel (1982), but comparable studies on green and brown pupae in the summer have not been undertaken.

ELIMINATION OF ARTIFACTS

The prey response to predators that hunt for caterpillars by searching for evidence of damaged leaves is to conceal the damage. Some large caterpillars do this by chewing through the petiole so that the leaf falls off; by eating a smooth edge to the leaf so that if differs little in shape from an intact leaf (Heinrich 1979; Heinrich and Collins 1983); or by resting on the chewed edge so that the caterpillar's body mimics the missing piece of leaf (personal observation of caterpillars in Panama). By contrast, aposematic caterpillars often leave a partially eaten leaf in tatters so that the damage is very obvious. Small geometrid caterpillars are probably too small to smooth off partially chewed leaves in this way, but they regularly move from one leaf or twig to another so that damage is not necessarily a sign that a caterpillar is nearby.

BACKGROUND CHOICE

A cryptic insect that rests on the "wrong" background will no longer be cryptic and is liable to be found by predators. The prey response to this problem is to develop a preference for resting on a particular type of background on which the animal is most cryptic. In Colorado, red and greenish grey morphs of the grasshopper *Circotettix rabula* have a preference for resting on a background similar to their own color. Gillis (1982) found that by painting red round the eyes of green grasshoppers he could reverse the preference, so for this species it seems that substrate color matching is achieved by a visual comparison of part of the body with the background. Green and brown morphs of other grasshoppers and praying mantids also often show clear preferences for resting on backgrounds of similar color to themselves (summarized by Edmunds 1974), although it is not always known how this color matching is achieved. Painting part of the eyes of green *Miomantis paykullii* black caused them to switch their preferred background from green to brown. It may be that the nature of the pigment in the eyes of the two color forms differs, and this difference gives rise to their different preferences.

Nocturnal moths also have pronounced preferences for resting by day on surfaces which match their wing color in reflectance (Boardman et al. 1974): dark species prefer to rest on black rather than white, and pale species which normally rest among dead grass prefer white to black surfaces. Kettlewell and Conn (1977) summarized earlier work on resting site selection by moths, and further showed that for several polymorphic species the melanic and the typical forms have different preferences. For *Biston betularia* they showed that typical moths preferred to rest on brown tree trunks, whereas melanic moths preferred to rest on trunks coated with a soot suspension. However, this choice of background is often far from efficient, since 40 to 45 percent of some species rested on an inappropriate background. This percentage is surprising in view of the demonstration of the selective elimination of noncryptic morphs of moths on nonmatching backgrounds (Kettlewell 1956, 1973; Bishop 1972; Lees and Creed 1975). For most of these species it is not known how the background matching is achieved. Sargent (1969) experimented with two species of moth in which the resting posture of the insect with relation to striations on the bark was critical in determining whether or not it was cryptic. He found that for *Melanolophia canadaria* choice of the most cryptic resting posture was achieved by tactile rather than visual cues, but for *Catocala ultronia* the resting posture was innate and quite unaffected by either the tactile or visual characteristics of the surface.

COLOR CHANGE

An alternative prey response to predation of individuals that rest on the "wrong" background is to change color so as to match the new background. Although color change in cephalopods, chameleons, and some fish can be rapid, in most insects the stimulus for color change needs to be present over a prolonged period of time, and the change itself usually coincides with a molt (summarized by Edmunds 1974).

Many species of grasshopper and praying mantid can change from green to brown (or vice versa) when they molt (Ergène 1950a; Edmunds 1974), and it appears to be some quality of the incident radiation perceived by the insect that induces color change (Rowell 1971; Jovancic 1960; Edmunds 1974). In the grasshopper *Syrbula admirabilis* and the mantid *Miomantis paykullii*, however, humidity is more important than light in determining the color the insect will become at its next molt (Otte and Williams 1972; Edmunds 1974). For two species of mantid Edmunds (1974, 1976) was able to show that the factors that determine color change (humidity for *Miomantis paykullii* and light for *Sphodromantis lineola*) are so related to the mantids' habitats and ways of life that the majority of individuals of both species are likely to be well camouflaged.

Some hawkmoth caterpillars can also change color. Caterpillars of *Smerinthus ocellata* and *Laothoe populi* can become either yellow-green or grey-green depending on the quality of light in which they were reared, and in the field this ability results in most caterpillars matching the color of their food plant to give excellent crypsis Grayson and Edmunds 1989; (Edmunds and Grayson, unpublished observations).

Limitations of Crypsis

Since crypsis is of such clear selective advantage, it is legitimate to ask what stops the evolution of ever more perfect forms of crypsis. The answer must be that the requirements for efficient crypsis conflict with other essential activities of the animal. For a palatable prey, successful crypsis requires that it remain motionless, but then it cannot feed. Since an insect may have some predators or parasites that find it by nonvisual senses, selection will favor any individuals that can grow and reproduce as rapidly as possible so that the chances of being found and eaten are reduced. For such an insect the selection pressure to be motionless may be less important than the selection pressure to feed as rapidly as is physiologically possible. The structural and behavioral requirements for efficient crypsis are likely to conflict with the requirements for efficient feeding, reproduction, dispersal, and secondary defense, and examples of this conflict have been discussed by Edmunds (1974). The evolution of crypsis described here is but one part of the interaction between predators and prey, and it is this complete interaction that determines the precise cryptic adaptations of any particular prey insect.

Summary

Crypsis is the color resemblance of an animal to its environment, and cryptic insects are less likely to be found by predators than are noncryptic insects. Predators have evolved a variety of ways of finding cryptic prey: recognition of key features of the prey (ventral shadow, legs); acquisition of a searching image or area-restricted search behavior; detection of prey artifacts; detection of prey individuals on the wrong background; and detection of movement. As a response to these predator hunting strategies, cryptic prey insects have evolved counterdefenses:

I am grateful to Dr. Janet Edmunds for her critical discussion of this paper.

countershading; disruptive coloration; special resemblance; spacing out; polymorphism; elimination of artifacts; choice of appropriate background; and color change. The interaction of predators and prey is dynamic and constantly being modified by natural selection, but there are limitations to the perfection of crypsis because adaptations for crypsis may conflict with other essential activities of the animal.

References

Beljajeff, M.M. 1927. Ein Experiment über die Bedeutung der Schutzfärbung. *Biol. zbl.,* 47: 107–113.

Bishop, J.A. 1972. An experimental study of the cline of industrial melanism in *Biston betularia* (L.) (Lepidoptera) between urban Liverpool and rural north Wales *J. Anim. Ecol.,* 41: 209–243.

Blest, A.D. 1957. The function of eyespot patterns in the Lepidoptera. *Behaviour,* 11: 209–256.

Boardman, M., Askew, R.R., and Cook, L.M. 1974. Experiments on resting site selection by nocturnal moths. *J. Zool., Lond.,* 172: 343–355.

Carpenter, G.D.H. 1941. The relative frequency of beak-marks on butterflies of different edibility to birds. *Proc. Zool. Soc. Lond.,* 111(A): 223–231.

Clarke, C.A., Dickson, C.G.C., and Sheppard, P.M. 1963. Larval color pattern in *Papilio demodocus. Evolution,* 17: 130–137.

Clarke, C.A., and Sheppard, P.M. 1972. Genetic and environmental factors influencing pupal colour in the swallowtail butterflies *Battus philenor* (L.) and *Papilio polytes* L. *J. Ent., A,* 46: 123–133.

Cloudsley-Thompson, J.L. 1977. The genus *Cossyphus* (Col., Tenebrionidae): a striking instance of protective resemblance. *Entomologist's Mon. Mag.,* 113: 151–152.

————. **1981.** Comments on the nature of deception. *Biol. J. Linn. Soc.,* 16: 11–14.

Cott, H.B. 1940. *Adaptive Coloration in Animals.* London, Methuen, 508 pp.

Croze, H. 1970. Searching image in carrion crows. *Z. Tierpsychol.,* supplement 5, 1–86.

Dawkins, M. 1971. Perceptual changes in chicks: another look at the 'search image' concept. *Anim. Behav.,* 19: 566–574.

den Boer, M.N. 1971. A colour polymorphism in caterpillars of *Bupalus piniarius* (L.) (Lepidoptera: Geometridae). *Neth. J. Zool.,* 21: 61–116.

di Cesnola, A.P. 1904. Preliminary note on the protective value of colour in *Mantis religiosa. Biometrika,* 3: 58–59.

Edmunds, M. 1972. Defensive behaviour in Ghanaian praying mantids. *Zool. J. Linn. Soc.,* 51: 1–32.

————. **1974.** *Defence in Animals: A Survey of Anti-Predator Defences.* Harlow, Longman, 357 pp.

————. **1976.** The defensive behaviour of Ghanaian praying mantids with a discussion of territoriality. *Zool. J. Linn. Soc.,* 58: 1–37.

————. **1981.** On defining 'mimicry'. *Biol. J. Linn. Soc.,* 16: 9–10.

Endler, J.A. 1981. An overview of the relationships between mimicry and crypsis. *Biol. J. Linn. Soc.,* 16: 25-31.

Ergène, S. 1950a. Untersuchungun über farbanpassung und farbwechsel bei *Acrida turrita. Z. vergl. Physiol.,* 32: 530-551.

_____. **1950b.** Wählen Heuschrecken ein homochromes Milieu? *Dt. Zool. Z.,* 1: 122-132.

_____. **1951.** Hat homochrome Färbung Schutzwert? *Dt. Zool. Z.,* 1: 187-195.

_____. **1953.** Weitere Untersuchugen über die biologische Bedeutungder Schutzfärbung. *Mitt. Zool. Mus. Berl.,* 29: 127-133.

Gillis, J. 1982. Substrate colour-matching cues in the cryptic grasshopper *Circotettix rabula rabula* (Rehn & Hebard). *Anim. Behav.,* 30: 113-116.

Grayson, J., and Edmunds, M. 1989. The causes of colour and colour change in caterpillars of the poplar and eyed hawkmoths *(Laothoe populi* and *Smerinthus ocellata). Biol. J. Linn. Soc.,* 37: 263-279

Greene, E. 1989. A diet-induced developmental polymorphism in a caterpillar. *Science,* 243: 643-646.

Guilford, T., and Dawkins, M.S. 1987. Search images not proven: a reappraisal of recent evidence. *Anim. Behav.,* 35: 1838-1845.

Halkka, O., Vilbaste, J., and Raatikainen, M. 1980. Colour gene allele frequencies correlated with altitude of habitat in *Philaenus* populations. *Hereditas,* 92: 243-246.

Hazel, W.N. 1977. The genetic basis of pupal colour dimorphism and its maintenance by natural selection in *Papilio polyxenes* (Papilionidae: Lepidoptera). *Heredity,* 38: 227-236.

Hazel, W.N., and West, D.A. 1979. Environmental control of pupal colour in swallowtail butterflies (Lepidoptera: Papilioninae): *Battus philenor* (L.) and *Papilio polyxenes* Fabr. *Ecol. Ent.,* 4: 393-400.

_____. **1982.** Pupal colour dimorphism in swallowtail butterflies as a threshold trait: selection in *Eurytides marcellus* (Cramer). *Heredity,* 49: 295-301.

_____. **1983.** The effect of larval photoperiod on pupal colour and diapause in swallowtail butterflies. *Ecol. Ent.,* 8: 37-42.

Heinrich, B. 1979. Foraging strategies of caterpillars: leaf damage and possible predator avoidance strategies. *Oecologia,* 42: 325-337.

Heinrich, B., and Collins, S.L. 1983. Caterpillar leaf damage, and the game of hide-and-seek with birds. *Ecology,* 64: 592-602.

Jovancic, L. 1960. Genèse des pigments tégumentaires et leur rôle physiologique chez la mante religieuse et chez d'autres espèces animales. *Mus. Hist. Nat., Beograd.,* 1-114.

Kettlewell, H.B.D. 1955. Recognition of appropriate backgrounds by the pale and black phase of Lepidoptera. *Nature, Lond.,* 175: 943–944.

—————. **1956.** Further selection experiments on industrial melanism in the Lepidoptera. *Heredity,* 10: 287–301.

—————. **1973.** *The Evolution of Melanism: The Study of a Recurring Necessity.* Oxford, Clarendon, 423 pp.

Kettlewell, H.B.D., and Conn, D.L.T. 1977. Further background-choice experiments on cryptic Lepidoptera. *J. Zool. Lond.,* 181: 371–376.

Kiltie, R.A. 1988. Countershading: universally deceptive or deceptively universal? *TREE,* 3: 21–23.

Lawrence, E.S., and Allen J.A. 1983. On the term 'search image'. *Oikos,* 40: 313–314.

Lees, D.R., and Creed, E.R. 1975. Industrial melanism in *Biston betularia:* the role of selective predation. *J. Anim. Ecol.,* 44: 67–83.

Lees, D.R., and Dent, C.S. 1983. Industrial melanism in the spittle bug *Philaenus spumarius* (L.) (Homoptera: Aphrophoridae). *Biol. J. Linn. Soc., 19: 115–129.*

Lees, D.R., Dent, C.S., and Gait. P.L. 1983. Geographic variation in the colour pattern polymorphism of British *Philaenus spumarius* (L.) (Homoptera: Aphrophoridae). *Biol. J. Linn. Soc.,* 19: 99–114.

Nentwig, W. 1985. A tropical caterpillar that mimics faeces, leaves and a snake (Lepidoptera: Oxytenidae: *Oxytenis naemia*). *J. Res. Lepidoptera,* 24: 136–141.

Otte, D., and Williams, K, 1972. Environmentally induced color dimorphisms in grasshoppers *Syrbula admirabilis, Dichromorpha viridis* and *Chortophaga viridifasciata. Ann. Ent. Soc. Am.,* 65: 1154–1161.

Owen, D.F. 1971. Pupal color in *Papilio demodocus* (Papilionidae) in relation to the season of the year. *J. Lepidopt. Soc.,* 25: 271–274.

Owen, D.F., and Wiegert, R.G. 1962. Balanced polymorphism in the meadow spittlebug, *Philaenus spumarius. Am. Nat.,* 96: 353–359.

Pietrewicz, A.T., and Kamil, A.C. 1979. Search image formation in the Blue Jay (*Cyanocitta cristata*). *Science,* 204: 1332–1333.

Pietrewicz, A.T., and Kamil, A.C. 1981. Search images and the detection of cryptic prey: an operant approach. In: *Foraging behaviour. Ecological, Ethological and Psychological Approaches* (Ed: A.C. Kamil & T.D. Sargent), pp. 311–331. New York: Garland STPM Press.

Platt, A.P., and Brower, L.P. 1968. Mimetic versus disruptive coloration in intergrading populations of *Limenitis arthemis* and *astyanax* butterflies. *Evolution,* 22: 699–718.

Popescu, C., Broadhead, E., and Shorrocks, B. 1978. Industrial melanism in *Mesopsocus unipunctatus* (Müll.) (Psocoptera) in northern England. *Ecol. Ent., 3: 209–219.*

Poulton, E.B. 1885. The essential nature of the colouring of phytophagous larvae (and their pupae); with an account of some experiments upon the relation between the colour of such larvae and that of their food-plants. *Proc. R. Soc.,* 237: 269–315.

_____. **1886.** A further enquiry into a special colour-relation between the larva of *Smerinthus ocellatus* and its food-plants. *Proc. R. Soc.,* 243: 135–173.

Robbins, R.K. 1980. The lycaenid "false head" hypothesis: historical review and quantitative analysis. *J. Lepidopt. Soc.,* 34: 194–208.

Robbins, R.K. 1981. The "false head" hypothesis: predation and wing pattern variation of lycaenid butterflies. *Am. Nat.,* 118: 770–775.

Robinson, M.H. 1969a. The defensive behaviour of some orthopteroid insects from Panama. *Trans. R. Ent. Soc. Lond.,* 121: 281–303.

_____. **1969b.** Defenses against visually hunting predators. In *Evolutionary Biology* 3, eds. T. Dobzhansky, M.K. Hecht, and W.C. Steere, pp. 225–259. New York, Meredith Corporation.

_____. **1973a.** Insect anti-predator adaptations and the behavior of predatory primates. *Actas Congr. IV Latinamericano Zool.,* 2: 811–836.

_____. **1973b.** The evolution of cryptic postures in insects, with special reference to some New Guinea tettigoniids (Orthoptera). *Psyche,* 80: 159–165.

_____. **1981.** A stick is a stick and not worth eating: on the definition of mimicry. *Biol. J. Linn. Soc.,* 16: 15–20.

Rothschild, M. 1981. The mimicrats must move with the times. *Biol. J. Linn. Soc.,* 16: 21–23.

Rowell, C.H.F. 1971. The variable coloration of acridid grasshoppers. *Adv. Insect. Physiol.,* 8: 146–198.

Ruiter, L. de 1952. Some experiments on the camouflage of stick caterpillars. *Behaviour,* 4: 222–232.

_____. **1959.** Some remarks on problems of the ecology and evolution of mimicry. *Archs. néerl. Zool.,* 13, suppl.: 351–368.

Sargent, T.D. 1969. Behavioural adaptations of cryptic moths. II. Experimental studies on bark-like species *J. N.Y. Ent. Soc.,* 77: 75–79.

Silberglied, R., and Aiello, A. 1980. Camouflage by integumentary wetting in bark bugs. *Science,* 207: 773–775.

Silberglied, R.E., Aiello, A., and Windsor, D.M. 1980. Disruptive coloration in butterflies: lack of support in *Anartia fatima. Science,* 209: 617–619.

Sims, S.R. 1983. The genetic and environmental basis of pupal colour dimorphism in *Papilio zelicaon* (Lepidoptera: Papilionidae). *Heredity,* 50: 159–168.

Sims, S.R., and Shapiro, A.M. 1983. Pupal colour dimorphism in California *Battus philenor:* pupation sites, environmental control and diapause linkage. *Ecol. Ent.,* 8: 95–104.

Smith, A.G. 1978. Environmental factors influencing pupal colour determination in Lepidoptera. I. Experiments with *Papilio polytes, Papilio demoleus* and *Papilio polyxenes. Proc. R. Soc. B,* 200: 295–329.

————. **1980.** Environmental factors influencing pupal colour determination in Lepidoptera. II. Experiments with *Pieris rapae, Pieris napi* and *Pieris brassicae. Proc. R. Soc. B,* 207: 163–186.

Tinbergen, L. 1960. The natural control of insects in pinewoods. *Archs. Néerl. Zool.,* 13: 259–379.

Tinbergen, N., Impekoven, M., and Franck, D. 1967. An experiment on spacing-out as a defence against predation. *Behaviour,* 28: 307–321.

Vane-Wright, R.I. 1980. On the definition of mimicry. *Biol. J. Linn. Soc.,* 13: 1–6.

————. **1981.** Only connect. *Biol. J. Linn. Soc.,* 16: 33–40.

Waldbauer, G. P., and Sternburg, J.G. 1983. A pitfall in using painted insects in studies of protective coloration. *Evolution,* 37: 1085–1086.

Ward, P. 1979. *Colour for Survival.* London, Orbis, 120 pp.

West, D.A., and Hazel, W.N. 1979. Natural pupation sites of swallowtail butterflies (Lepidoptera: Papilioninae): *Papilio polyxenes* Fabr., *P. glaucus* L. and *Battus philenor* (L.). *Ecol. Ent.,* 4: 387–392.

————. **1982.** An experimental test of natural selection for pupation site in swallowtail butterflies. *Evolution,* 36: 152–159.

Wickler, W., 1968. *Mimicry in Plants and Animals.* London, Wiedenfeld and Nicholson, 255 pp.

The Evolution of Aposematism

TIM GUILFORD

What is Aposematism?

In 1871, Charles Darwin wrote that he had become puzzled by the bright colors of many insect larvae (Darwin 1871). Although the beauty of adult butterflies might be attributable to sexual selection, that of their larvae obviously could not. He had posed the problem of their explanation to Wallace. Wallace reasoned that "distastefulness alone would be insufficient to protect a larva unless there were some outward sign to indicate to its would-be destroyer that his contemplated prey would prove a disgusting morsel, and so deter him from attack" (Wallace 1867, p. 1xxx). It is from Wallace's solution that the theory of aposematic or warning coloration has developed. Potential prey animals that have acquired some form of defense so as to be unpalatable (or, more generally, unprofitable) to predators benefit by advertising that defense. In Darwin's words, "It would be highly advantageous to a caterpillar to be instantaneously and certainly recognized as unpalatable by all birds and other animals. Thus the most gaudy colors would be serviceable, and might have been gained by variation and the survival of the most easily-recognized individuals" (Darwin 1871, pp. 499–500). The term *aposematic coloration* was later coined by Edward Poulton in his pioneering work of 1890, and defined as "an appearance which warns off enemies because it denotes something unpleasant or dangerous; or which directs the attention of an enemy to some specially defended, or merely non-vital part; or which warns off other individuals of the same species" (Poulton 1890, chart following page 339). The first part of Poulton's definition is that now generally equated with the theory of warning coloration. It is here that the interesting and more recently controversial evolutionary problems lie.

As we shall see, prey animals employ a variety of warning signals to advertise a variety of defenses. Not all are visual. Aposematism may include warning sounds and odors, and perhaps even vibrational and electrical signals (Brower 1984; Cott 1940; Edmunds 1974; Eisner and Grant 1981; Endler 1986; Guilford et al. 1987; Kay et al. 1989; Malcolm 1986; Rothschild 1961, 1985). It is possible that visual aposematic signals may make use of emitted light (in the form of bioluminescence) as well as reflected light (Grober 1988; but see Guilford and Cuthill 1989; Grober 1989). But most work has concentrated on the concept of warning coloration, and is this the subject that I will consider in most detail.

The Theory of Aposematic Coloration

The term *aposematism* is used to describe a common phenomenon in nature: the coincidence between conspicuous coloration and unpalatability in potential prey animals (e.g., Cott 1940; Edmunds 1974; Grober 1988; Malcolm 1986; Wiklund and Järvi 1982). Its incidence is especially well reviewed in Cott 1940 (see also Edmunds 1974; Owen 1980; Poulton 1890; Rothschild 1985). Although most obvious in insects and other terrestrial arthropods, where it has been best studied, the phenomenon finds notable examples among the molluscs (e.g., nudibranchs), amphibians (e.g., dendrobatid frogs, and the fire salamander, *Salmandra salmandra*), reptiles (e.g., coral snakes), and even perhaps mammals (e.g., the North American skunk, *Spilogale putorius*) (Cott 1940; Owen 1980). Possible examples exist among holothurians and other echinoderms, polychaete worms, cnidarians (Cott 1940), and even plants and fungi (Edmunds 1974). The question of whether brightly colored coral reef fish are actually conspicuous on their natural background is still unanswered. Birds also demonstrate the phenomenon (Baker and Parker 1979; Cott 1947), as do their eggs (Cott 1964). But although aposematism is used to describe this phenomenon, it is really a theory purporting to *explain* the phenomenon (see also Guilford 1988; Sillén-Tullberg 1985b). Theory-laden terms are often used in description, and there is nothing in principle wrong with that. But we should be careful to understand what the theory expects, and whether the evidence available lives up to that expectation and justifies using the theory to describe. We must look closely. Until very recently, the evidence in favor of the theory of warning coloration was of two kinds.

The first kind is comparative, and involves an accumulation of examples of conspicuously colored unpalatable prey (e.g., Carpenter 1921; Cott 1940; Poulton 1887, 1890). It is really just a verification of the existence of the coincidence between conspicuousness and unprofitability—the very *phenomenon* that the *theory* was proposed to explain. Of course, if there were no alternative explanations for the phenomenon, then this would not be a problem. But there are. For example, consider the following. A species that is well defended against predators may be more responsive to sexual selection for bright coloration because there is little or no counterbalancing selection due to predation on conspicuous forms (e.g., Guilford 1988; Krebs 1979; Poulton 1890 also make a similar suggestion). Alternatively, species that evolve bright coloration through sexual selection (or other pressures unrelated to defense, such as thermoregulation) may be forced to pay the price of defensive adaptations secondarily, because of their increased encounter frequency with predators. In both cases we expect to see the evolution of a coincidence between unpalatability and conspicuous coloration even if predators could not learn to recognize that coloration as a warning (Guilford 1988). Clearly, the phenomenon is not of itself good evidence for the explanatory theory.

The second kind of evidence comes from learning studies in which predators acquire conditioned aversions to brightly colored unpalatable prey (e.g., Brower 1958a,b,c; Cott 1940; Gittleman and Harvey 1980; Gittleman et al. 1980; Malcolm 1986; examples reviewed in Shettleworth 1972 and Edmunds 1974). This looks like good evidence. However, we must now be very cautious. If the theory of aposematism is to be merely a description of what conspicuous coloration in unpalatable prey does, then these experiments are indeed good evidence in its favor. They demonstrate that predators can learn to interpret conspicuous colors as warning signals. But if aposematism is to be an adaptive explanation, telling something of the selective advantages of conspicuous coloration, then we will need more (see Gittleman and Harvey 1980; Guilford 1988; Roper and Wistow 1986; Roper and Redston 1987). Of the many consequences a trait may have, only some will affect the adaptive status of that trait, by generating selective effects. That predators learn to avoid conspicuously colored unpalatable prey indicates that an effect of the coloration is to act as a warning signal. But predators can also learn to avoid cryptically colored unpalatable items (Papageorgis 1975; Gittleman and Harvey 1980; Gittleman et al. 1980). If warning coloration has the sense merely that it is coloration interpreted by predators as a warning signal, then cryptic coloration in unpalatable prey (e.g., the buff tip moth, *Phalera bucephala*) should also be considered warning coloration (although Rothschild 1981 considers this a crepuscular aposematic moth). However, warning coloration has a second sense that implies selective advantage. In this adaptive sense, conspicuous colors are considered warning colors not just because they are used to warn predators, but because they are especially good at it: because they are better than their cryptic alternatives. On the issue of which sense is meant by the term *warning coloration*, the literature is rarely explicit (e.g., Coppinger 1969). And, as suggested above, most of the evidence reported in favor of the theory does not address this distinction either. Yet most authors clearly imply that the theory is an adaptive explanation (e.g., Darwin 1871; Cott 1940; Edmunds 1974; Guilford 1988; Mallet and Singer 1987; Owen 1980; Poulton 1890; Wallace 1867), and it is with this sense that I use it from now on. What, then, is the evidence in favor of the adaptive theory of warning coloration?

We come to a third kind of evidence—evidence that there is something special about conspicuousness. Perhaps the first experiment to demonstrate this fact was that of Gittleman and Harvey (1980), who showed that domestic chicks (*Gallus gallus*) more readily learned to avoid eating quinine-flavored crumbs if these crumbs contrasted with the background. The results of other experiments are more equivocal because of failure to control for differences other than just the relative conspicuousness of the prey, such as color (Gibson 1974, 1980; Schuler 1985; Schuler and Hesse 1985) or resemblance to previously experienced palatable prey (Gibson 1974, 1980; Sillén-Tullberg 1985a,b), or because by the end of the experiment the conspicuous prey had still failed to show an overall selective advantage (Gittleman et al. 1980; Papageorgis 1975). However, Roper and Wistow (1986) have recently demonstrated that chicks learn more effectively to avoid eating unpalatable crumbs that contrast with the background, and Roper and Redston (1987) also show that chicks pecking at unpalatable beads learn more effectively to avoid the conspicuous ones. This finding confirms Gittleman and Harvey (1980)'s earlier result. There is something special about conspicuousness. We may now be clear that the adaptive theory of warning coloration can explain the evolution of conspicuous colors that are selectively advantageous when advertising unpalatability to predators. There are, however, some distinctions upon which experimental evidence of this kind will not allow us to make a judgement. Demonstrating selective advantage does not distinguish *adaptation* from *preadaptation* (or "exaptation"—Gould and Vrba 1982). It does not tell us whether a conspicuous pattern evolved from a very different ancestral state (e.g., crypsis) under the pressure of selection towards a warning function, or whether that selective pressure was secondarily imposed (by, for example, the arrival of new predators) on a pattern that happened to be preadapted to a warning role but had originally evolved for some other function. In practice, most features that we recognize as adaptations will be a combination of both. In both cases we are dealing with adaptation, but in the first the selection pressures identified are those responsible for previous change, and in the second they are those responsible for stabilization. Furthermore, demonstrating selective advantage does not imply that this advantage is the coloration's sole function. Other selective pressures may have coincidentally promoted the pattern, or may themselves have become secondarily imposed (aposematic colors might be used in courtship). However, neither the problem of multiple function, nor that of preadaptation, are unique to aposematism.

How Do Warning Colors Work?
—Evolutionary Implications

Many animal species, it seems, have countered the dangers of predation by evolving qualities unprofitable to predators and conspicuous signals designed to advertise that unprofitability. But this is a simplified notion. We must look more closely at exactly what is meant by "advertisement," for here we will find evolutionary implications. We must look more closely at how warning colors work.

It is commonly held that warning colors have evolved to be memorable to predators (e.g., Gittleman and Harvey 1980; Harvey and Greenwood 1978; Leimar et al. 1986; Sillén-Tullberg 1985a). In other words, a conspicuous color pattern is selectively advantageous because predators more readily form associations between it and the unpleasant consequences of attacking prey, than they would do if the pattern were not conspicuous. It is in the acquisition of learned aversions that conspicuousness is seen to be especially effective in its advertising role. But why evolve conspicuousness for such a role? Three hypotheses are followed (often implicitly) in the literature, and I characterize them here (see also Guilford 1986, 1988; Roper and Redston 1987; Sillén-Tullberg 1985a; Turner 1984). I also explore some interesting subdivisions within the three hypotheses, and attempt to assess the evidence bearing on each. This is not always easy, for much of the evidence is indirect, tentative, and fails to distinguish between the various mechanistic subdivisions, or even

between the three hypotheses themselves. A fourth hypothesis, concerned primarily not with the acquisition of learned aversions but with
their use once acquired, is also then discussed.

HYPOTHESIS 1

*Conspicuousness in an animal's color pattern enables predators to learn more
readily to associate that pattern with unpalatability* (Rettenmeyer 1970; Turner
1975a). The best evidence for this hypothesis is provided by experiments
using domestic chicks and artificial prey (Gittleman and Harvey 1980;
Roper and Wistow 1986; Roper and Redston 1987), and Gittleman and
Harvey suggest two mechanisms which may account for the effectiveness
of conspicuousness. (a) Conspicuous prey are captured at an initially
higher rate, which increases the effectiveness of each prey encounter in
inducing learned avoidance. (b) Conspicuousness itself is more easily
associated with unpalatability, irrespective of prey capture rate. I deal
with these in turn, before articulating a number of other variants of
hypothesis 1.

Conspicuousness Increases Capture Rate
         Mathews (1977) suggested that if a predator were to take large
numbers of a mildly toxic prey type in rapid succession, then toxin levels
might build up sufficiently to induce an aversion not otherwise associated
with that prey. Mathews similarly considered that "frustration" might
reach a threshold beyond which an "avoidance image" could form if the
frequency of contact between predator and prey individuals of a given
aspect was high enough. Mathews's discussion is concerned mainly with
build-up of toxin or frustration, but his "contact frequency model" is consistent with a memorability effect of contact rate—a pattern becoming
more memorable if it "saturates" the predator's recent experience. There
is direct evidence for the effect of toxin dosage on preceived palatability
by birds. The classic experiments of Lincoln Brower and his associates
(e.g., Brower 1969; Brower et al. 1967; Brower and Glazier 1975; Brower and
Moffitt 1974) indicate that below a certain dosage, cardenolides (heart
toxins sequestered by larval *Danaus plexippus* and ingested by adult
Cyanocitta cristata bromia—blue jays) are unlikely to cause emesis. Brower
observes that insects containing individual toxin levels below this threshold "could serve as an emergency ration during periods of food shortage,
provided that the birds ate successive individuals at a sufficiently slow
rate" (Brower 1969, p. 25). It seems plausible that conspicuousness could

increase contact rate (e.g., Gittleman and Harvey 1980; Smith 1974), and that this is why unpalatable animals have evolved conspicuousness as an aposematic strategy.

Gregariousness, by bringing similar prey together, could also increase contact rate (Smith 1974; Tinbergen et al. 1967), and is common among apparently aposematic insects (Harvey and Greenwood 1978) in their eggs (reviewed in Stamp 1980), larvae (Edmunds 1974; Harvey 1983; Rettenmeyer 1970; Sillén-Tullberg et al. 1982; Vulinec, this volume), and adult stages (Calvert et al. 1979; Linsley et al. 1961; Mallet 1986a,b,c; Rettenmeyer 1970; Sillén-Tullberg et al. 1982; Turner 1975b). Perhaps gregariousness functions to enhance a naive predator's noxious experience in the same way as conspicuousness, and so makes future avoidance more effective. Another curious possibility brings the concepts of conspicuousness and gregariousness yet closer together. Just as conspicuousness increases rate of capture, it is likely to cause temporal clumping in the diet. Conspicuous prey are usually detected before cryptic prey (Dawkins 1970; Endler 1986; Guilford and Dawkins 1987), and this detection can lead to a feeding run. Gregariousness may do the same as conspicuousness by shrinking a predator's search time between subsequent detections. Since not all prey defenses are immediately acting (see Brower 1984; Poulton 1887; Rothschild 1961; Turner 1984), a predator may only suffer from a previous ingestion after moving on to a new prey individual. Thus it may be the pattern of the latter individual that becomes associated with the noxious effect. Wouldn't a sensible predator be expected to think back to its earlier encounters when forming the association? Not necessarily, for not all defenses have delayed action. Even a sophisticated predator could not be sure that the effect it was experiencing was a delayed one. The point here is that clumping (whether through conspicuousness, gregariousness, or even synchronous emergence or activity) would increase the chance that both the individual causing the noxious effect, and the individual most recently associated with its onset, would be of the same type. The risk of the predator remembering the wrong pattern would be minimized (though this cannot explain the results of experiments in which only single prey types are presented: e.g., Gittleman and Harvey 1980; Roper and Wistow 1986; Roper and Redston 1987). So, how likely is it that aposematism has evolved because it increases initial contact frequency with naive predators? It is difficult to judge, but a closer look at how predators and prey actually interact shows that it cannot be the whole story. Although multiple trial learning is well documented (e.g., Cott 1940, p. 283; Gittleman and Harvey 1980; Malcolm 1986; Poulton 1887; Rothschild 1962), some predators learn to avoid apparently aposematic prey in a single trial (e.g., Brower et al. 1970 and references therein; Lane and Rothschild 1956; Mostler, quoted in Blest 1963). More important, the prey may be released alive, and even apparently unharmed, by naive birds (Linsley et al. 1961; Schuler and Hesse 1985; Wiklund and Järvi 1982; see also Rettenmeyer 1970), demonstrating that an individual's defenses can be immediately and amply effective. In these cases at least, increasing contact rate becomes irrelevant, so conspicuousness must be special for some other reason.

We have now reached the source of a recent evolutionary controversy. If an individual is defended so well that it immediately, and without serious injury, repels even a naive predator's first attack, then it is easy to see why possessing a memorable new advertising coloration could be of selective advantage in deterring that same predator from future attacks. It would be favored, at least partially, by individual selection. But if a predator only learns after several trials, those prey first encountered would be sacrificing themselves for the benefit of later survivors. A new aposematic morph would seem to be behaving altruistically. I discuss the individual selection–kin selection controversy in detail later, but we should bear in mind here that some of the mechanisms by which conspicuousness may achieve its effectiveness imply that some kind of selection for altruism be a prerequisite for the evolution of aposematism, and others imply that there is a strong individually selected component.

Conspicuousness Per Se is More Memorable

The second suggestion of Gittleman and Harvey (1980) is that conspicuousness is itself a quality more readily associated with unpalatability. There seems to be no evidence unequivocally in favor of this hypothesis although experiments have been misinterpreted in its support (e.g., Mathews's 1977 report of Gibson 1974). However, two recent experiments come very close. Roper and Wistow (1986) found that chicks learned more effectively to avoid unpalatable crumbs if the crumbs were presented on an off-white contrasting background (though they did not control completely for the faster ingestion of conspicuous crumbs, or for prior feeding experience: the chicks may already have learned that crumbs on a matching background were palatable). Though this second difficulty still remains in the study of Roper and Redston (1987), it is unlikely to account for their main result that conspicuous coloration is associated with noxious experience more easily (and for longer) than is cryptic coloration. In this experiment chicks were allowed only a single peck at a noxious bead, so encounter rate was controlled for.

Retrospective Learning Effects and Backward Conditioning: Thinking Back and Looking Forward

A third reason why conspicuousness may be especially memorable concerns retrospective learning effects. Turner (1984) considers that distinctive coloration may help a predator recall which of a sequence of previously ingested prey was responsible for delayed noxious consequences. Mathews had previously attempted to explain the conspicuous, high-density forms of insects such as locusts by supposing that ingestion of large numbers of normally palatable prey may cause a predator sickening (see contact rate model above) that is retrospectively associated with "the most contrastingly coloured individuals in its recent diet" (Mathews 1977, p. 216). Certainly, in aversion learning in particular, even a long delay between presentation of the conditioned stimulus (CS) and the unconditioned stimulus (US) will not stop associative conditioning (see Staddon 1983), and we can hypothesize that a *conspicuous* CS will be less interfered with by other intervening CSs during this delay. So it is indeed possible that, of those previously ingested prey items eligible as candidate causes of a delayed noxious experience, the most conspicuous will be singled out by the predator for association.

This suggestion is biologically distinct from the "contact rate" and "clumping in the diet" models described above, in which predators make an aversive association with the color pattern of whichever item was being handled at the time noxiousness was detected. Here the association is made retrospectively with the color pattern of a previously ingested item. However, in stressing the distinction I have bared its weakness. It is worth pursuing the point a little further.

When an aversive association with a color pattern is made by a predator, it can happen in one of two ways (or a combination of both). The predator must have an image of the prey it thinks caused the effect, and this can either be a real visual image of an uneaten item, or a remembered image of an item recently consumed. Which it will be depends on how quickly the prey's defenses act—something that again bears on the question of whether aposematism is altruistic or individually beneficial. A delayed-action toxin (one that is stored well inside the body, for example) is less likely to be individually beneficial and more likely to require the remembered image than, for example, the use of surface irritants, spines, or a sting. An example of the combination might be the image of what a prey item had looked like, before partial ingestion, reconstructed from the uneaten remains (predators may partially consume insects during aversion learning: e.g., Swynnerton 1919). Consider the remembered image.

Even cases of single-trial learning with complete ingestion must involve some kind of remembered image simply because unpalatability is manifested after ingestion—however soon. This looks suspiciously like retrospective learning, and yet it occurs in a single trial. Indeed, such retrospective association is a common part of ordinary associative conditioning. Association between a US (e.g., the unpalatable experience) and a CS (e.g., the color pattern) usually declines in strength as delay-of-reinforcement time increases. This is true both when the CS precedes and when it follows the US, but the strongest links are formed if the CS slightly precedes the US (Staddon 1983). In nature, effects follow their causes, so this is hardly surprising. But it does mean that probably *most* of the hypotheses of mechanism accounting for a putative increased memorability for conspicuousness will include some sort of retrospective effect. However, it is not just the *memory* of the color pattern that is important (rather than a real visual image), but the fact that it is the pattern of a *previous* prey item. This distinction is important where a series of items are rapidly consumed before the onset of aversive reaction (Turner 1984), and where there is ambiguity as to which item caused the reaction. Turner points out that conspicuousness (or "distinctness") may *reduce* this ambiguity. Mathews points out that conspicuousness may be used to *exploit* it.

The second method of association is with a real visual image (not a memory): perhaps the uneaten remains of a partially ingested prey item (Vermeij 1982), or a prey item the predator "spat out" or sampled without ingestion. Here it is unclear why conspicuousness should help the predator choose which object to associate with the noxious experience, for the choice is obvious. But where there is ambiguity, just as with the retrospective effects described above, it may help. If the predator has irreversibly ingested a prey item, and been punished, it may look around at objects close by for clues as to the cause. So, rather than thinking back to what might have been the cause, a predator might look forward, and avoid possible sources of similar danger in the future. Conspicuous prey might attract the predator's attention in such a way as to be more likely to become so avoided. Edmunds has suggested a similar effect for gregariousness: "The advantage of gregariousness is that if a predator tastes one caterpillar the visual impact of many others may speed up the process of learning to associate color with inedibility" (Edmunds 1974, p. 63). Although we lack direct evidence, the phenomenon of "backward conditioning" (a CS becomes paired with a preceding US: Keith-Lucas and Guttman 1975; Tait and Saladin 1986), and the fact that a CS-US association can be interfered with by events following the US (Staddon 1983), show that animals do attend to events that occur after punishment.

To summarize, conspicuousness may act retrospectively by increasing the prominence of previously ingested unpalatable items, or by becoming the focus of avoidance learning by attracting the attention of an already punished predator.

Conspicuousness Provides Frequent Reminders Without Attack

It has been suggested that repeated sightings alone may reinforce an already existing association between an aposematic pattern and the unpleasant consequences of ingestion (Brower et al. 1963; Edmunds 1974; Harvey and Greenwood 1978; Rettenmeyer 1970), providing a mechanism by which conspicuousness proved to be especially memorable (Harvey et al. 1982). Conspicuous prey will be seen more often, so if merely sighting prey inhibits extinction of an aversive association, then conspicuousness should facilitate this inhibition. However, when we look for evidence for this intriguing and plausible idea we find the literature unclear. But Brower et al. (1963) equate the idea with the "general principle of animal behaviour known as secondary reinforcement," and attribute its discovery to Swynnerton (e.g., Swynnerton 1915a). Harvey et al. (1982) also believe that secondary reinforcement could provide a mechanism. However, it is not at all clear *how* secondary (or conditioned) reinforcement helps. Conditioned stimuli can successfully reinforce behavior on which the presentation of the CS is contingent (Mackintosh 1974). However, where the original US was a reward, extinction occurs very quickly if the US is no longer paired with the CS. The effectiveness of a CS as a conditioned reinforcer is closely linked to its association with the US. If this pairing is lost, the CS loses its effectiveness as a secondary reinforcer. What, then, if the US is a punishment (as in the ingestion of unpalatable prey)? Avoidance reactions which occur at the onset of a signal known to warn of an impending electric shock can indeed take a long time to extinguish when the shock is no longer administered. But extinction does occur, and little evidence suggests that it does so *more slowly* if the CS is presented frequently (although see the disturbing experiments of Solomon et al. 1953). Indeed, Kamin at al. (1963) reported results implying that a warning signal is significantly less aversive for animals who have completed more rather than fewer consecutive successful avoidance responses. This finding suggests that if a predator frequently encounters and avoids familiar unpalatable prey, the aversive association should wane *more quickly*. Furthermore, even if the association extinguished more slowly (per encounter) with frequent encounters, this fact would not necessarily compensate for the increased risk (per unit time) consequent on the high encounter rate.

Conspicuousness Aids Observational Learning

By observing others feeding (not necessarily conspecifics—see Rothschild and Ford 1968), a predator may acquire useful knowledge about the relative acceptabilities of various prey. "Brightly colored prey are more likely to be observed in the diet of another predator than are cryptic prey" (Harvey et al. 1982, p. 716), so by being conspicuous an unpalatable prey may mediate more effective avoidance learning by ensuring that its lesson reaches a larger audience (Edmunds 1974; Harvey et al. 1982; Rettenmeyer 1970; Turner 1975a). Considerable evidence demonstrates that observing others performing or learning various tasks is effective at enhancing acquistion rate or response accuracy (e.g., Alcock 1969; Davies 1973; John et al. 1968; Palameta and Lefèbvre 1985; Tarpy 1982). Although some workers have failed to find that birds, by observation alone, will learn to avoid unpalatable items (e.g., Klopfer 1959), Mason and Reidinger (1982) showed that if red-winged blackbirds (*Ageliaus phoeniceus*) were sickened by intubation with methiocarb after eating food paired with a colored card, observer birds would avoid food paired with a card of the same color. It is also possible that animals not only learn by observing, but actively teach others (e.g., Swynnerton 1915b; Bonner 1980). The hypothesis is plausible, but merely demonstrating that observational learning occurs does not demonstrate that conspicuousness increases its effectiveness. I know of no evidence demonstrating the latter, crucial point.

HYPOTHESIS 2

Predators more readily associate unpalatability with specific colors or patterns which just happen to be usually conspicuous (e.g., Harvey and Paxton 1981a; Rothschild 1984, 1985; Sillén-Tullberg 1985a; Turner 1984). This second hypothesis concerns the memorability of specific colors or patterns themselves, with conspicuousness really no more than a potentially deleterious side effect, since it may attract naive predators. As with hypothesis 1, this memorability might be general, causing easy association with either punishing or rewarding experiences. Rothschild states that attributes such as "bright red, black-and-yellow alternating stripes, and white spots on a black ground" are "alerting signals" that have "memory-stimulating qualities" (Rothschild 1984, p. 317; see also Kaye et al 1989; Rothschild 1985). Willson and Melampy (1983) provide tentative evidence that bicolored fruit displays are better attractants of avian frugivores. Or the memorability could be specific to nasty consequences.

What is the evidence that this is the adaptive feature of aposematic patterns?

Direct evidence remains tentative, for there are usually alternative explanations. Bisping et al. (1974) demonstrated that goldfish more easily associated a delayed electric shock with a red light than with a green one of similar intensity. However, it could have been contrast (in this case with the reflected color of the background) that improved the signal's effectiveness. A similar criticism applies to Gibson's 1974 and 1980 experiments with finches and artificial prey (see also Turner 1984). Sillén-Tullberg (1985a) comes close to finding an effect of color per se, but prior feeding experience was not controlled for (also Sillén-Tullberg 1985b). However, circumstantial evidence may exist.

We are looking for a bias in the efficiency with which predators learn about the value of prey. Within hypothesis 2 we are looking particularly for a bias contingent on color or pattern, but we might equally extend the analysis to degree of conspicuousness (Hypothesis 1) or novelty (hypothesis 3). Although direct evidence from learning studies with confounding mechanisms controlled for is lacking, indirect evidence may be accessible. For a bias or predisposition to exist in learning efficiency, a difference in prior expectation must also, presumably, exist. These "priors" may become apparent before a proper learning study is completed, or even outside the context of learning. Such priors could range from innate preferences (e.g., Fischer et al. 1975; Hailman 1964) to innate aversions (Caldwell and Rubinoff 1983; Smith, S.M. 1975, 1977). They might be visible as hesitations during feeding (Schuler and Hesse 1985), or as fright reactions to certain stimuli (reviewed in Edmunds 1974). In a sense it is difficult to see how animals could *not* show priors of some sort, for the limitations of their sensory apparatus will necessarily introduce such biases. If an animal cannot distinguish a particular color from its background, then that color will be of no use as a CS in that context. Stimuli that cannot be sensed cannot be conditioned. Indeed, conditioning is sometimes used to *determine* sensory capacities (Kreithen and Keeton 1974a,b,c). Cryptic animals exploit constraints in the sensory systems of predators by adopting color patterns that are difficult to detect (Endler 1984, 1986, 1988; Guilford and Dawkins 1987). In reducing detectability the bias may be obvious. In increasing memorability it is not so.

However, differences between stimuli from different modalities in their associability are shown by the phenomenon of *cue-consequence specificity,* in which certain consequences appear to "belong" to certain types of cues (Garcia and Koelling 1966, 1967; Domjan 1980; but see Archer and

Sjöden 1982; reviewed in Domjan 1983). For example, rats more readily associate the taste of a solution with induced illness, quail the color (Wilcoxon et al. 1971; but see Gillette et al. 1980). Asymmetries might also occur between elements of a single quality such as color either as a product of sensory constraints or as prior expectations linked to particular stimuli. Male sticklebacks show strong innate reactions to red objects (Tinbergen 1952), reactions which, though adaptively related to the problems of defending territories against intruding males, might coincidentally lead to expectations concerning potential food that was red. Schuler and Hesse (1985) claim to have found an *adaptive* predisposition in domestic chicks: an apparently innate hesitancy to eat black and yellow banded (versus green) prey (see also Roper, 1990; Roper and Cook, in press), an aversion which seemed, in a later experiment (Schuler 1985), to be translated into readiness to form associations with unpalatability. Schuler's work is particularly rigorous, but still two problems are pertinent. First, although the chicks in these experiments were encountering their first ever orally ingested food, they had no doubt had experience of unrewarded pecking at inedible objects and might therefore already have built up prior expectations applicable to the two prey types. The second problem relates to an interpretation of these results under the "specific colors or patterns" hypothesis (hypothesis 2). The problem is itself twofold. First, these results are equally consistent with hypothesis 1: the special effect of the black and yellow banding may have been due to its conspicuousness against the background, not to anything specific about the pattern. Schuler has effectively refuted the novelty hypothesis (hypothesis 3) as an explanation, but he has not separated conspicuousness and pattern per se (or the effect of a specific color within the pattern). But there is a more fundamental difficulty here: this is my second point, and it is a general one. Patterns containing more than one color will produce their own internal color boundaries. If these boundaries are of high contrast, they will promote conspicuousness. So it is conceivable that although a specific pattern is more memorable to predators, it is the internally generated conspicuousness that makes it so.

Careful work needs to be done on the memorability of specific colors or patterns. For example, hypothesis 2 predicts that stimuli should not lose their special memorability (where it exists) even if they are neither more novel (hypothesis 3) nor more conspicuous (hypothesis 1, and also hypothesis 4) than their alternatives. Furthermore, the conspicuousness of such colors or patterns could have no advantage in defense but might still attract naive predators. Selection would, where possible, act against it, so we should not be surprised to find aposematic animals also using *crypsis* as a strategy if suitably colored habitats were available (see also Harvey and Paxton 1981a). Examples of animals cryptic on brightly colored backgrounds are known (e.g., Owen 1980), and may be common on coral reefs, but less is known about their palatability. Some red Eolid molluscs are both well defended and cryptic on their hydroid backgrounds (Edmunds 1966).

Many of the mechanistic variants discussed under hypothesis 1 might also apply here too. Specific colors or patterns might enhance observational learning. Their effects on memorability might act retrospectively. But, in contrast with hypothesis 1, there are no obvious reasons why this should be so. Whereas it is easy to see how conspicuousness could aid observational learning (for example), it is not so for specific colors or patterns. This is why I have left hypothesis 2 (and hypothesis 3) limited in articulation.

HYPOTHESIS 3

Predators more readily associate unpalatability with coloration that is different from that for which they normally hunt (Edmunds 1974; Harvey and Greenwood 1978; Shettleworth 1972; Turner 1975a; a similar suggestion was made by Wallace 1867). Edmunds stated the hypothesis like this: "if an animal is evolving aposematic coloration there will be fewer individuals lost by predators sampling them if they have a novel (and hence conspicuous) colour than if they have a colour with which the predators are familiar (such as green or brown)" (Edmunds 1974, p. 66). We may dub this the "novelty hypothesis." However, we should immediately note that novelty can be of two kinds. The first, and that implicit in Turner's (1975a) formulation of the hypothesis, is that of a predator having no previous association with a color pattern: *novelty of association*. Since a predator's usual experience of cryptic prey will be that they are palatable, cryptic colors will have prior expectations of reward associated with them. If the predator generalized to new patterns, this generalization could retard avoidance learning of cryptic unpalatable prey. Unpalatable prey should be conspicuous to avoid generalization and to exploit novelty of association.

The second kind of novelty is *novelty of detection*. Some colors (or patterns) may simply be rare in a predator's environment, so when they are detected they may be attended to with special interest, and might therefore facilitate aversion learning. Since the most novel colors will be those furthest removed from the greens, browns, and greys of the environment's non-animal material (and of the palatable prey animals hiding on that material), these are likely to be the conspicuous ones. Of course, for conspicuous colors novelty of detection will aid the acquisition of any association (and novelty of association may aid only the acquisition of associations with unpalatability).

Although she did not distinguish between these two kinds of novelty, Shettleworth (1972) showed that chicks learned more effectively to avoid punishing water (either shocked or quinine flavored) if it was of an unfamiliar color. The novelty effect is well demonstrated in taste-aversion learning (e.g., Best and Batson 1977; Channell and Hall 1981; Domjan 1980, 1983; Elkins 1973; Kalat and Rozin 1973; Mackintosh 1983; Staddon 1983) and odor-aversion learning (Domjan 1980). But again, these experiments also frequently confound the two kinds of novelty. Indeed, for certain types of stimuli, detection cannot really occur without some kind of reinforcing consequence. Tastes are contingent on ingestion (if only as far as the mouth or beak), and the consequences of ingestion are rarely irrelevant. So detection always leads to association with a consequence, and the two kinds of novelty converge in a way not so for visual stimuli. Many studies suggest that predators treat palatable prey (or other ingesta) with hesitation (even fear) if they are novel in some way (e.g., Brower 1984; Coppinger 1969, 1970; Domjan 1980; Hogan 1965; Rabinowitch 1968, 1969; Vaughan 1983; Wallman 1979). It is also possible to train animals to be neophobic to visual stimuli (Schlenoff 1984, for birds) or tastes (Best and Batson 1977; Domjan 1980, for rats).

In many contexts preexposure to a CS reduces speed of learning (and increases rate of extinction) when that CS is eventually paired to a US. This "stimulus familiarization effect" (Siegel 1971) occurs for both punishing and rewarding USs, so it demonstrates the importance of novelty of detection as distinct from novelty of association. Exploiting predator response to novelty may indeed have been an important selective force in the evolution of warning colors.

These three hypotheses, then, assume that the advantage of conspicuousness lies in improving the ability of predators to acquire and maintain aversive associations (through whatever mechanism). A fourth hypothesis suggests that conspicuousness may exploit a different kind of limitation in the predator's brain: limitation in the ability to use information about prey once it has already been acquired.

HYPOTHESIS 4

Conspicuousness reduces recognition errors in experienced predators (Guilford 1986, 1987, 1989 a). The "detection distance hypothesis" stems from the notion that conspicuousness may increase the distance from which predators detect prey. Of the conspicuous coloration of a caterpillar observed by Bates, Darwin reported, "Hence it caught the eye of any one who passed by, even at a distance of many yards, and no doubt that of every passing bird" (Darwin 1871, p. 499). Although increased detectability is usually seen as a complication in the evolution of warning coloration (e.g., Harvey et al. 1982), it may in fact serve an essential purpose by increasing the minimum time between detection and potential capture. Predators are likely to make mistakes in the identification of prey that they have already learned are unpalatable. They are more likely to do so, it is arguable, the less time they have for viewing their prey. So why should predators cut short their viewing time? One reason is that if most prey are palatable, then valuable time is actually wasted in taking care of effect "perfect" identification. By cutting short the time spent in the identification of familiar prey, predators will often save time, and rarely incur penalty. Time saved by making hasty decisions may be especially valuable to small homeotherms when it is cold (or whenever risk-prone behavior is expected: e.g., Caraco et al. 1980; Stephens 1981; Barnard and Brown 1985a; Barnard et al. 1985; Stephens and Krebs 1986), or when foraging brings predation risk (e.g., Dill and Fraser 1984). When prey are mobile or can elicit escapes reactions (Gibson 1974, 1980; Thompson 1973), or where there are competitors for the same food resource (Barnard and Brown 1918, 1985b; Barnard et al. 1983; Dill and Fraser 1984), making hasty decisions may avoid missing prey altogether. Conspicuousness in unpalatable prey may increase the time predators are obliged to spend viewing prey during approach before being able to capture them, and so may reduce recognition errors by allowing predators to realize their mistakes and abort attacks. Predators will not stumble upon, and hastily attack, conspicuous prey. This extra time may also be advantageous in reducing confusion with Batesian mimics. So far the detection distance hypothesis remains largely untested, but Guilford (1986) demonstrated that domestic chicks, given a choice between familiar palatable and differently colored familiar unpalatable items, made significantly fewer mistakes if they were given more time to view, but not to attack, the prey. Guilford (1989 a) also showed that great tits *(Parus major)* would abort attack flights to unprofitable prey, using information about the prey gathered during flight alone, although an improvement with distance was not demonstrated. It is conceivable, then, that conspicuousness could increase detection distance—and hence viewing time in a hurrying predator—and so reduce the risk of mistaken attacks on prey that the predator has already learned are unpalatable (an effect that would operate throughout the predator's foraging life).

Increasing detection distance may also encourage the acquisition of learned aversions. If the naive predator fully ingests a novel prey item before any noxious consequence arrives, then the only information it has to go on may be the image it recalls of the prey in the moments before capture. A longer look during approach may give a better image, and so make an acquired aversive association more accurate, or more likely. However, predators generally react with hesitation towards unfamiliar prey, and this fact argues against a role for increased detection distance itself increasing viewing time in encounters with novel prey. But what if the prey is not *recognized* as novel? Then, by increasing detection distance, conspicuousness may make the chance of such recognition more likely, and so allow the predator to exercise its caution towards the novel stimulus. The two would interact. This point has implications for the natural selection of aposematism. If conspicuousness makes a prey's defenses more likely to work on a predator's very first encounter (by inducing hesitancy and attentiveness), then a more prominent role may be attributed to individual selection, rather than selection for altruism (see below).

Other predictions can be made. In a recent "family model" for the evolution of warning coloration, Harvey et al. suggest "that the aposematic form must not be too readily detected" (Harvey et al. 1982, p. 717). Within their model this is correct, but in hypothesis 4, because increased detectability is the function of conspicuous coloration, and not just an unfortunate consequence, the opposite prediction is made. Similarly, the detection distance hypothesis seems to conflict with the notion of "crypsis at a distance" (Edmunds 1974; Endler 1978; Harvey et al. 1982; Järvi et al. 1981a; Papageorgis 1975; Rothschild 1964, 1981), one hypothesis that allows an escape from the Harvey et al. dilemma. Indeed, the detection distance hypothesis predicts that warning colors should not work well if hidden until the predator is close. Unpalatable prey should not use "startle coloration" to advertise unpalatability: startle-colored animals should be palatable (Guilford 1987).

The Natural Selection of Aposematism

Having looked closely at the sort of aposematic mechanisms that have evolved in unpalatable prey, we must now consider the selective conditions favoring them. Although controversy surrounds the natural selection of aposematism, some of the more problematic issues can now be clarified. The first concerns the question of whether or not aposematism is favored by individual selection, and whether kin selection is a prerequisite for its evolution (Brower 1984; Courtney 1984; Harvey and Greenwood 1978; Grober 1988; Harvey and Paxton 1981a,b; Järvi et al. 1981a,b; Leimar et al. 1986; Mallet 1986b; Mallet and Singer 1987; Rothschild 1985; Shettleworth 1984; Sillén-Tullberg 1985b; Sillén-Tullberg and Bryant 1983; Turner et al. 1984; Waldman and Adler 1979). The source of this controversy stems from Fisher (1930, revised edition 1958), who puzzled as to how natural selection could favor the evolution of unpalatability in prey that were so vulnerable to predators as to be likely to die after being attacked. Individuals could not profit from being defended themselves, but only by being associated with a predator's previous experience with similarly defended individuals. Fisher suggested that the gregarious habit of many larvae could provide a solution because members of aggregations are likely to be similarly unpalatable because of their close kinship. This solution is close to what is now known as "kin selection" (Hamilton 1964; Maynard Smith 1964), for Fisher reasoned that "the selective potency of the avoidance of brothers will of course be only half as great as if the individual itself were protected" (Fisher 1958, p. 178). Unpalatability could be favored because the death of one individual caused the protection of neighboring siblings who, by virtue of their common ancestry, are uncommonly likely to share the gene for unpalatability. It is *proximity* which gives the predator the cue by which the altruistic protection of relatives is mediated. This much is uncontroversial, although the degree to which kin selection is important in the evolution of unpalatability is an empirical question. As Fisher himself well realized, it is only certain forms of defense that require kin selection in this way: those that fail to deter a naive predator on first encounter, such as delayed-action toxins (e.g., Brower 1984). Defenses that allow an individual personally to survive attack may be individually selected (though they too might help relatives): defenses such as nonsuicidal stings, bites, urticating or inedible hairs, tough bodies, escape reactions, or even noxious chemicals (see chapters by Whitman and Blum, and Schmidt, this volume) if they are fast acting and can be secreted in time to save the victim. However, a defense may be favored by individual selection only if its net action is to cause the bearer to have more offspring. So we must consider costs as well as benefits. Much unpalatability involves merely the storage of plant natural products found in the food (e.g., sequestration of cardenolides by the monarch butterfly (Brower

1984), and iridoid glycosides (Bowers, this volume) and pyrrolizidine alkaloids (McLain 1984) by other insects). Even so, hidden costs may exist (e.g., search costs on adults choosing suitably toxic plants for oviposition; see also Brower 1969). Where unpalatability involves special defensive structures or behavior, the costs are more obvious. Although in many cases unpalatability may be individually selected, "the effect of selection on gregarious larvae...provides an alternative which will certainly be effective in a usefully large class of cases" (Fisher 1958, p. 178). The two may of course work in combination.

However, unpalatability is rarely found alone; it is usually in conjunction with defensive advertisement. So we cannot simply test the effectiveness of a prey's unpalatability by observing the reaction of naive predators, because it will be confounded with the effects of aposematic coloration (e.g., Wiklund and Järvi 1982). Nature does not make our task easy. Yet, as Harvey and Paxton (1981a) argue, it is important to view the evolution of these two traits separately because the conditions favoring their natural selection are quite different. So, what of the evolution of warning coloration, the second component of the aposematic strategy? Let us consider first the evolution of warning coloration in a species that has already acquired unpalatability (by whatever means).

INDIVIDUALLY BENEFICIAL WARNING COLORATION IN ALREADY UNPALATABLE SPECIES

For individual selection to be a correct description of the selective conditions favoring warning coloration in an already unpalatable species, the benefits from being warningly colored must go to the individual bearing the coloration, causing it to have more children than it would have had if it were (say) cryptic. This benefit could be mediated in two ways. First, conspicuousness might induce some special reaction from naive predators. The strongest reaction would be total avoidance, either through innate aversion to certain patterns, or to a general avoidance of novel patterns. Neither of these are likely. Although innate avoidance reactions are known (Caldwell and Rubinoff 1983; Smith, S. M. 1975, 1977), it is most probable that they are themselves specialist adaptations evolved in response to already existing aposematic prey. It is difficult to see how such innate avoidance reactions could be general constraints in the perceptual systems of predators, existing independently of any relationship with aposematic prey and forming the basis for the prey's evolutionary response. They are not general, and may not exist in species rarely encountering the appropriate prey (Smith, S. M. 1980). Furthermore, if such reactions were general, it is difficult to see why aposematic animals should be unpalatable at all. As for avoidance of novelty, this does not last. Predators will eventually attack new prey as they become familiar. But weaker responses to warning colors could help provide a basis for individual selection. If a naive predator were more cautious towards conspicuously colored prey, then he might allow the prey's defenses time to operate more fully. Wiklund and Järvi (1982) demonstrated that conspicuous unpalatable prey are treated with caution by naive birds, and that they become avoided without apparent injury (also Sillén-Tullberg 1985a; Schuler and Hesse 1985; Roper 1990; Roper and Cook, in press). Warning colors could be favored by individual selection because they enhance the effectiveness of a prey's own unpalatability in any particular encounter.

So far I have said nothing about predators remembering the warning color pattern. But if warning colors are remembered more readily, or used more effectively, then there is a second way in which individual benefit may accrue: a prey individual that survives attack by a naive predator may be protected more effectively in future encounters with the same predator.

These two possibilities are considered in a model by Sillén-Tullberg and Bryant (1983). And it seems likely that they do play a part in the natural selection of warning coloration at least in prey with immediately effective defenses. But Sillén-Tullberg and Bryant do not distinguish between learned avoidance due to previous encounters with the same individual (individual benefit) and to previous encounters with other similarly colored individuals (altruistic benefit). Demonstrating that individual selection can operate does not necessarily make it a sufficient description of the conditions favoring the evolution of warning coloration (see also Järvi et al. 1918a; Sillén-Tullberg 1985b). To see why, we must consider the altruistic element of warning coloration in an already unpalatable species.

ALTRUISTIC WARNING COLORATION IN ALREADY UNPALATABLE SPECIES

Two disadvantages exist for a new conspicuous mutant in a population of unpalatable cryptic prey. First, conspicuousness invites detection. Second, being conspicuous means being rare, and hence being of a form with which predators have no prior aversive association. This of course is not a problem unique to conspicuous forms, and indeed it may not be a problem at all where predators avoid novel prey (Sillén-Tullberg and Bryant 1983). But together these two disadvantages may mean that predators attack a number of new conspicuous morphs before these start to have an advantage over their cryptic counterparts. The advantage to being warning colored is frequency dependent (or locally density dependent), and disadvantageous at very low abundance (though the exact nature of the frequency dependence itself depends on the model of predator memory assumed—see Guilford 1988). So how does a conspicuous warning color ever get started in a population? Again, Fisher notes that aposematism is common in insects with a gregarious habit (also Harvey 1983), and his suggestions are taken to imply that, as with unpalatability, the evolution of warning coloration is favored by kin selection. Some authors have claimed that kin selection must be invoked to account for the evolution of warning coloration (Harvey and Greenwood 1978)—a position sometimes considered to be the general consensus (Engen et al. 1986; Järvi et al. 1981a).

Others have claimed that kin selection may be involved, but not necessarily or exclusively (Courtney 1984; Engen et al. 1986; Harvey and Paxton 1981a; Järvi et al. 1918a; Leimar et al. 1986; Mallet and Singer 1987; Rothschild 1985; Roper and Redston 1987; Sillén-Tullberg and Bryant 1983; Turner 1984; Waldman and Adler 1979). Present agreement now appears to be that the relative balance of kin selection and individual selection is the problem at issue (Harvey and Paxton 1981a; Järvi et al. 1981b), and that this is an empirical problem (Järvi et al. 1981b; Wiklund and Järvi 1982; Engen et al. 1986). Here is the root of the confusion, once described as a raging controversy (Rothschild 1985), and still persisting (e.g., Engen et al. 1986; Grober 1988; Leimar et al. 1986; Roper and Redston 1987). The confusion concerns the necessary equation of warning color altruism with kin selection.

It is useful to consider warning coloration in an already unpalatable species as having an altruistic element, because when one individual is attacked by a predator it is likely to have fewer children as a consequence. But other similarly colored individuals will be protected thereby, and so will produce more children in the future. Indeed, it is primarily as a result of this altruism that warning coloration works at all, for it is through the predator's ability to learn from experience and generalize by pattern to other individuals that members of a population become protected. However, it is an unusual form of altruism, and one which classical kin selection does not adequately describe. In classical kin selection (Hamilton

1964; Maynard Smith 1964), altruism is favored between relatives because they are uncommonly likely to share altruism genes. The "ancestral relatedness" (Grafen 1985) of members of the class of individuals to whom altruism is directed provides an estimate of the increased probability, over and above the population average, that those individuals will share an identical copy of the donor's gene for altruism. It is this increased probability that must be weighed against the cost of altruism, and that, if high enough, allows kin-selected altruism to evolve. The important insight in classical kin selection was that kinship provides a readily identifiable rule for "recoginizing" the presence of other copies of altruism genes. Kin recognition may be very simple. In the evolution of unpalatability, it may be mediated through the ability of predators to use proximity as a cue by which to avoid subsequent encounters with nasty prey. It is simple, but clumsy. In classical kin selection members of a class of relatives become targets for altruism regardless of their actual genotype. Hence, within a class of relatives, those who do and those who do not actually carry copies of the gene for altruism are not distinguished. However, for warning color altruism there is a more reliable cue for the identification of other copy-carriers, because the benefits from the death or injury of one individual go to other similarly colored individuals. Even within a class of relatives, altruism will be directed towards other altruists. Guilford (1985, 1988) argues that "green beard selection" better describes the selective conditions because, in a way similar to the "green beard genes" of Dawkins (1976, after Hamilton 1964), altruism is reliably directed to other individuals carrying copies of the same gene, regardless of their ancestral relatedness (Queller 1984 provides a different, game-theoretic analysis of similar problems; see also Guilford 1989 b). The existence of green beard genes is considered unlikely (Alexander and Borgia 1978; Dawkins 1976, 1979; Hamilton 1964; Michod and Anderson 1979; Nunney 1985; Ridley and Grafen 1981), because in their original formulation they seem to require the pleiotropic expression of (a) a conspicuous label (hence the "green beard"), (b) the ability to recognize others with the label, and (c) the tendency to be selectively altruistic to those others. Furthermore, they would seem to be vulnerable to "cheating": individuals with the label, but not the tendency to be altruistic, would receive but not donate altruism, and would therefore do much better. But in an interesting sense, warning colors avoid both problems. First, the three complicated requirements are met almost fortuitously, for it is the predator, through conditioning, that both mediates the "recognition" of, and allows altruism to be donated towards, other warningly colored individuals. Second, in an already unpalatable species, where unpalatability is favored regardless of coloration, warning coloration cannot be cheated. An individual cannot receive altruism from others without being similarly conspicuous and therefore risking the same danger of attack from naive predators. The benefits cannot be gained without the risk (discussed in Guilford 1985, 1988, 1989 b).

The important point is that warning coloration will spread not because *kin* are protected, but because those with *similar phenotypes* will be (Guilford 1988 argues that this idea is compatible with a more unified explanation—see Grafen 1985—using Hamilton's rule and a phenotypic measure of relatedness). The confusion which stems from Fisher's comment is that even though kin selection may not be important in the evolution of warning coloration in an unpalatable species, family gregariousness may be, but for a different reason which has to do with density dependence. The benefit to being warning colored depends on the number of similarly colored individuals likely to be encountered by the local predator population. If a conspicuous mutant individual arises on its own, it may never survive to reproduce. If it arises among many others, then local predators may become sufficiently educated to allow the operation of the warning color's inherent memory advantage. Family gregariousness is the most obvious way in which individuals with a new conspicuous phenotype may group together and allow this threshold to be overcome.

Family gregariousness may thus be important to the initial viability of traits with density-dependent benefit and a threshold for favorability, because it produces local abundance of similar phenotypes (not because of kin selection). This notion is compatible with the "family model" for the evolution of warning coloration of Harvey et al. (1982) (erroneously described as a kin selection model by Leimar et al. 1986).

If initial viability is the only problem, then chance events may also allow a new mutation to drift above the threshold density required for favorability. Mallet and Singer (1987) stress the importance of drift as a mechanism in the evolution of warning coloration, and show how frequency-dependent selection can be involved in the slow shift of color morph clines in Heliconiid butterfiles. The importance of frequency-dependence is further considered in a game-theoretic model by Leimar et al. (1986). They also find that "structure" in a population can destabilize crypsis in favor of aposematism, but that this structure may become unimportant when aposematism is common and reaches stability (Guilford 1985). However, they do not distinguish the different effects of family grouping.

THE JOINT EVOLUTION OF UNPALATABILITY
AND WARNING COLORATION

So far we have looked at two simple sets of selective conditions: the evolution of unpalatability, where favorability does not depend on coloration; and the evolution of warning coloration in an already unpalatable species. We must consider now the condition where unpalatability is only favored if prey are conspicuous, and conspicuousness is only favored if prey are unpalatable. Green beard selection remains relevant because altruism is again directed towards other altruists even within ancestral relatedness classes. Again, the local abundance of similar phenotypes is likely to be important in initial viability, because benefits will be density dependent. But if unpalatability is not favored independently of coloration, and is only beneficial if advertised, then cheats (conspicuously colored but not unpalatable) will prosper at the expense of conspicuously colored individuals who *do* pay the cost of unpalatability. Kin selection *may* therefore be involved, because like-colored relatives of an altruist are less likely to be cheats than like-colored nonrelatives. This of course depends on localization of protection (through territoriality, or the use by predators of proximity cues as well as color).

THE NATURAL SELECTION OF APOSEMATISM: A SYNTHESIS

We have now seen that a correct description of the selective conditions favoring the evolution of aposematism can be complicated, and may depend on many factors. Let us summarize some of the issues.

There is an important distinction to be made between the evolution of warning coloration and the evolution of the unpalatability it advertises (Harvey and Paxton 1981a). The conditions favoring unpalatability themselves affect the conditions favoring warning coloration. For example, unpalatability may be individually selected or kin selected. Individual selection must be part of the evolutionary description if, by being unpalatable, an individual has increased chances of survival (to produce more children) after encounters with naive predators—in other words, if the defense is immediately effective. There is evidence that this is likely in some cases, but not in all (Malcolm 1986). Classical kin selection must be part of this description if predators learn to avoid kin—who, because of their high ancestral relatedness, are uncommonly likely to share the gene for unpalatability—after encounters with unpalatable individuals. This is likely to occur where prey populations are viscous (and predators are locally restricted), and especially where prey form family groups and predators use proximity as an avoidance cue. So, if unpalatability is costly to produce and not immediately effective, then kin selection may be required to stop cheating. Families that contain palatable cheats will not be avoided by predators using the proximity cue. But even if the unpalatability is individually beneficial, kin-selected benefits may also accrue in family-grouped species. In such instances both individual selection and kin selection are necessary in the description of selective conditions.

We must also consider warning coloration's effect on the conditions favoring unpalatability. The selective conditions favoring unpalatability depend on how warning colors work. For example, predator hesitancy towards conspicuous patterns (whether because of their novelty of association, novelty of detection, or conspicuousness per se) may allow a relatively slow acting defense nevertheless to become individually beneficial (e.g., Schuler and Hesse 1985; Roper and Cook in press). An unpalatable trait previously requiring kin selection could, with the subsequent evolution of aposematic coloration, lose this requirment. Secondary loss of gregariousness would be feasible if some other force, like sibling competition, favored it (see Harvey and Paxton 1981b; Järvi et al. 1981b). If conspicuousness functions in the use of learned aversions only, or acts on memorability only after attack, and so does not affect a naive predator's initial reaction, then it will not so influence the selective status of unpalatability. However, if conspicuousness operates by increasing initial capture rate, then it may decrease the individually beneficial, but increase the kin-beneficial, element of unpalatability.

Once warning coloration has evolved, predators may use specific color cues to recognize unpalatable individuals, rather than proximity (and hence family). This switch removes the operation of kin selection in its role as a check against cheats. Since we can fairly assume that the presence of warning coloration leaves the population "better protected," even the individual benefits of being unpalatable are reduced. It may now be possible for automimicry to evolve, to the point where there is a stable equilibrium between palatable and unpalatable individuals when the cost of being unpalatable balances the increased personal risk associated with not being so (for discussions of automimicry, see Brower et al. 1967; Brower et al. 1970; Gibson 1984; Pough et al. 1973). Similarly, the conditions are set for the evolution of Batesian mimicry. As with automimicry, it is only if the predators stop using proximity (whether this is caused by the education of locally restricted predators, or the actual use of proximity as a cue) that "cross-species" cheating becomes possible. So just as family grouping may reduce—through kin selection—the possibility of auto-mimicry, it may also reduce the effectiveness of Batesian mimics. In fact, any sort of intraspecific aggregation will reduce vulnerability to Batesian mimicry, but family grouping is an obvious mechanism. Batesian mimicry should be less likely to evolve where potential model species form family groups. The evolution of warning coloration also sets the conditions for the evolution of Mullerian mimicry, and of innate avoidance reactions.

So much for the evolution of unpalatability, but what can we conclude about the natural selection of warning coloration itself? We have seen that by either inducing hesitation, or protecting the same individual in subsequent encounters, the evolution of conspicuous coloration is likely to have an individually selected component, and may even reach favorability because of it. However, there are good reasons to suspect that the sharing of protection between individuals with similar phenotypes is what contributes most greatly to a warning color gene's success. If predators generalize between individuals at all, then individual selection cannot be a sufficient description of the evolution of aposematism (contra Sillén-Tullberg and Bryant 1983; Wiklund and Järvi 1982). Although kin selection is usually considered the driving force behind the evolution of altruistic warning coloration, I argue that, in already unpalatable species at least, "green beard selection" provides a better description because it stresses the importance of benefit directed towards individuals with similar phenotypes rather than simply ancestral relatives.

Despite this, family grouping may be important because of warning coloration's frequency- or density-dependent benefits—allowing a local abundance to build up sufficiently to overcome initial inviability (see also Axelrod and Hamilton 1981; Guilford 1989 b). Other ways of overcoming initial inviability include grouping with Mullerian mimics (Guilford 1988), and genetic drift through chance events (Mallet and Singer 1987). The question of initial inviability depends on which warning color mechanism is operating, for it is directly linked to a lack of individual benefit. Again, we cannot ignore the mechanistic relationship between prey defense and predator psychology.

One further complication arises if unpalatability and warning coloration are only favored jointly, for kin selection may be required to stop the spread of palatable cheats. Kin-selected benefit might be mediated through the predator's ability to learn a combination of color and proximity cues, or it might work through the locally restricted activity of territorial predators even if they generalized to all similarly colored prey individuals, as long as the prey population was viscous. Again, it seems likely that green beard selection, and the local abundance effects of family grouping, will operate in the joint evolution of unpalatability and warning coloration.

Conclusion

In reviewing warning color mechanisms I hope that I have shown how closely bound is the strategy of aposematism to the complexities of predator psychology. I have chosen to view this interaction in a particular way, by asking what it is about predator psychology that aposematism has evolved to exploit. The predator is seen as an environment to which prey have adapted. This is just one approach; Schuler and Hesse (1985), for example, are more concerned with the other side of the coevolutionary process, and interpret their findings in terms of specific adaptations in the predator for dealing with aposematic prey. A balance is ultimately required, but the approach used here can clearly be fruitful.

I have shown that the details of predator-prey interactions are essential to an understanding of the evolution of aposematism. For example, if conspicuousness works by increasing initial ingestion rate, then clearly some form of altruistic selection (probably green beard selection rather than kin selection) will be prominent. Problems of initial viability will follow, and may mean that warning coloration only becomes established in family-grouped species, or those that group with Mullerian mimics. Initial viability is much less of a problem if conspicuousness functions by causing hesitation in naive predators (perhaps by exploiting neophobia), and by allowing the prey's defenses to become fully effective before ingestion otherwise leads to injury or death. Furthermore, a prominent role would be played by individual selection.

I thank Christine Nicol, Marian Stamp Dawkins, John Endler, Innes Cuthill, Paul Harvey, Andrew Read, Justin Schmidt, Malcolm Edmunds, Sue Healy, and an anonymous referee for their helpful comments. This work was carried out while I held the Drapers' Company Junior Research Fellowship at St. Anne's College, Oxford. I dedicate it to Diggory.

References

Alcock, J. 1969. Observational learning by fork-tailed flycatchers (*Muscivora tyrannus*). *Anim. Behav. 17:652-658.*

Alexander, R. D., and G. Borgia. 1978. Group selection, altruism and the levels of organization of life. *Ann. Rev. Ecol. Syst.* 9:449-474.

Archer, T., and P-O. Sjöden. 1982. Higher-order conditioning and sensory preconditioning of a taste aversion with an Exteroceptive CS₁. *Q. J. Exp. Psychol.* 34(B):1-12.

Axelrod, R., and W. D. Hamilton. 1981. The evolution of cooperation. *Science* 211:1390-1396.

Baker, R. R., and G. A. Parker. 1979. The evolution of bird coloration. *Phil. Trans. Roy. Soc.* 287 (B):63-130.

Barnard, C. J., and C. A. J. Brown. 1981. Prey size selection and competition in the common shrew (*Sorex araneus* L.). *Behav. Ecol. Scoiobiol.* 8:239-243.

————. **1985a.** Risk-sensitivity in foraging common shrews (*Sorex araneus* L.). *Behav. Ecol. Sociobiol.* 16:161-164.

————. **1985b.** Competition affects risk-sensitivity in foraging shrews. *Behav. Ecol. Sociobiol.* 16:379-382.

Barnard, C. J., C. A. J. Brown, and J. Gray Wallis. 1983. Time and energy budgets and competition in the common shrew (*Sorex araneus* L.). *Behav. Ecol. Sociobiol.* 13:13-18.

Barnard, C. J., C. A. J. Brown, A. I. Houston, and J. M. McNamara. 1985. Risk-sensitive foraging in common shrews: an interruption model and the effects of mean and variance in reward rate. *Behav. Ecol. Sociobiol.* 18:139-146.

Best, M. R., and J. D. Batson. 1977. Enhancing the expression of flavor neophobia: some effects of the ingestion-illness contingency. *J. Exp. Psychol.: Animal Behaviour Process* 3:132-143.

Bisping, R., U. Benze, P. Boxer, and N. Longo. 1974. Chemical transfer of learned colour discrimination in goldfish. *Nature* (Lond.) 249:771-773.

Blest, A. D. 1963. Longevity, palatability and natural selection in five species of new world Saturniid moth. *Nature* (Lond.) 197:1183-1186.

Bonner, J. T. 1980. *The Evolution of Culture in Animals.* Princeton University Press, Princeton, New Jersey.

Brower, J. V. Z. 1958a. Experimental studies of mimicry in some North American butterflies. Part I. The Monarch, *Danaus plexippus,* and the Viceroy, *Limenitis archippus archippus. Evolution* 12:32-47.

————. **1958b.** Experimental studies of mimicry in some North American butterflies. Part II. *Battus philenor* and *Papio troilus, P. polyxenes* and *P. glaucus. Evolution* 12:123-136.

_____. **1958c.** Experimental studies of mimicry in some North American butterflies. Part III. *Danaus glippus berenice* and *Limenitis archippus floridensis. Evolution* 12:273–285.

Brower, L. P. 1969. Ecological chemistry. *Sci. Am.* 220(1):22–29.

_____. **1984.** Chemical defences in butterflies. In R. I. Vane Wright, and P.R. Ackery (eds.), *The biology of butterflies.* Symp. Roy. Ent. Soc. Lond., 11:109–134. Academic Press, London.

Brower, L. P., and S. C. Glazier. 1975. Localization of heart poisons in the monarch butterfly. *Science* 188:19–25.

Brower, L. P., and C. M. Moffitt. 1974. Palatability dynamics of cardenolides in the monarch butterfly. *Nature* (Lond.) 249:208–283.

Brower, L. P., J. V. Z. Brower and C. T. Collins. 1963. Experimental studies of mimicry. 7. Relative palatability and Mullerian mimicry Neotropical butterflies of the subfamily Heliconiinae. *Zoologica* 48:65–84.

Brower, L. P., F. H. Pough, and H. R. Meck. 1970. Theoretical investigations of automimicry. I. Single trial learning. *Proc. Natn. Acad. Sci. U.S.A.* 66:1059–1066.

Brower, L. P., W. N. Ryerson, L. L. Coppinger, and S. C. Glazier. 1967. Ecological chemistry and the palatability spectrum. *Science* 161:1359–1351.

Caldwell, G. S., and R. W. Rubinoff. 1983. Avoidance of venomous sea snakes by naive herons and egrets. *Auk* 100:195–198.

Calvert, W. H., L. E. Hedrick, and L. P. Brower. 1979. Mortality of the monarch butterfly (*Danaus plexippus* L.): avian predation at five overwintering sites in Mexico. *Science* 204:847–851.

Caraco, T., S. Martindale, and T. S. Whittam. 1980. An empirical demonstration of risk-sensitive foraging preferences. *Anim. Behav.* 28:820–830.

Carpenter, G. D. H. 1921. Experiments on the relative edibility of insects, with special reference to their coloration. *Trans. R. Ent. Soc. Lond.* 54:1–105.

Channell, S., and G. Hall. 1981. Facilitation and retardation of discrimination learning after exposure to the stimuli. *J. Exp. Psychol.: Animal Behaviour Processes* 7:437–446.

Coppinger R. P. 1969. The effect of experience and novelty on avian feeding behavious with reference to the evolution of warning coloration in butterflies. *Behaviour* 35:45–60.

_____. **1970.** The effect of experience and novelty on avian feeding behaviour with reference to the evolution of warning coloration in butterflies. II. Reactions of naive birds to novel insects. *Am. Nat.* 104:323–335.

Cott, H. B. 1940. *Adaptive Coloration in Animals.* Methuen, London.

_____. **1947.** The edibility of birds: illustrated by five years' experiments and observations (1941–1946) on the food preferences of the hornet, cat and man; and considered with special reference to the theories of adaptive coloration. *Proc. Zool. Soc. Lond.* 116:371 –524.

_____. **1964.** Palatability of birds and eggs. In A. L. Thompson (ed.), *A New Dictionary of Birds,* pp. 589–591. Nelson, London.

Courtney, S. P. 1984. The evolution of egg clustering by butterflies and other insects. *Am. Nat.* 123:276–281.

Darwin, C. 1871. *The Descent of Man and Selection in Relation to Sex.* 2nd ed. John Murray, London.

Davies, J. M. 1973. Imitation: a review and critique. P. P. G. Bateson and P. H. Klopfer (eds.), *Perspectives in Ethology,* vol. 1. Plenum Press, New York, London.

Dawkins, M. 1970. The mechanism of hunting by 'searching image' in birds. D. Phil. Thesis, Oxford.

_____. **1979.** Twelve misunderstandings of kin selection. *Z. Tierpsychol.* 51:184–200.

Dawkins, M., and R. Dawkins. 1976. *The Selfish Gene.* Oxford University Press, Oxford.

Dill, L. M., and A. H. G. Fraser 1984. Risk of predation and the feeding behaviour of juvenile coho salmon (*Oncorhynchus kisutch*). *Behav. Ecol. Sociobiol.* 16:65–71.

Domjan, M. 1980. Ingestional aversion learning: unique and general processes. *Adv. Study Behav.* 11:275–336.

_____. **1983.** Biological constraints on instrumental and classical conditioning: implications for general process theory. *Psychol. Learn. Motiv.* 17:215–277.

Edmunds, M. 1966. Protective mechanisms in the Eolidacea (Mollusca Nudibranchia). *J. Linn. Soc. (Zool.)* 46:27–71.

_____. **1974.** *Defence in Animals: A Survey of Anti-predator Defences.* Longman, Harlow, Essex.

_____. **1987.** Color in opisthobranchs. *Am. Malacol. Bull.* 5:185–196.

Eisner, T. and R. P. Grant 1981. Toxicity, odor aversion, and "olfactory aposematism." *Science* 213:476.

Elkins, R. L. 1973. Attenuation of drug-induced bait shyness to a palatable solution as an increasing function of its availability prior to conditioning. *Behav. Biol.* 9:221–226.

Endler, J. A. 1978. A predator's view of animal colour patterns. *Evol. Biol.* 11:319–364.

_____. **1984.** Progressive background matching in moths, and a quantitative measure of crypsis. *Biol. J. Linn. Soc.* 22:197–231.

_____. **1986.** Defense against predators. In M. E. Feder and G. V. Lauder (eds.), *Predator-Prey Relationships. Perspectives and Approaches from the Study of Lower Vertebrates*, pp. 109–134. Chicago University Press, Chicago, London.

_____. **1988.** Frequency-dependent predation, crypsis, and aposematic coloration. *Phil. Trans. Roy. Soc. B.* 319:505–523.

Engen, S., T. Järvi, and C. Wiklund. 1986. The evolution of aposematic coloration by individual selection: a life-span survival model. *Oikos* 46:397–403.

Fischer, G. J., G. L. Morris, and J. P. Rusham. 1975. Color pecking preferences in white leghorn chicks. *J. Comp. Physiol. Psychol.* 88:402–406.

Fisher, R. A. 1958. The genetical theory of natural selection. 2nd ed. Dover, New York.

Garcia, J., and R. A. Koelling. 1966. Relation of cue to consequence in avoidance learning. *Psychonom. Sci.* 4:123–124.

_____. **1967.** A comparison of aversions induced by X-rays, toxins, and drugs in the rat. *Radiat. Res. Supl.* 7:439–450.

Gibson, D. O. 1974. Batesian mimicry without distastefulness. *Nature* 250:77–79.

_____. **1980.** The role of escape in mimicry and polymorphism: I. The response of captive birds to artificial prey. *Biol. J. Linn. Soc.* 14:201–214.

_____. **1984.** How is automimicry maintained? In R. I. Vane-Wright and P. R. Ackery (eds.), *The Biology of Butterflies*. Symp. Roy. Ent. Soc. Lond. 11:163–165. Academic Press, London.

Gillette, K., G. M. Martin, and W. P. Bellingham. 1980. Differential use of food and water cues in the formation of conditioned aversions by domestic chicks (*Gallus gallus*). *J. Exp. Psychol.: Animal Behaviour Processes* 6:99–111.

Gittleman, J. L., and P. H. Harvey. 1980. Why are distasteful prey not cryptic? *Nature* (Lond.) 286:149–150.

Gittleman, J. L., P. H. Harvey, and P. J. Greenwood. 1980. The evolution of conspicuous coloration: some experiments in bad taste. *Anim. Behav.* 28:897–899.

Gould, S. J., and E. S. Vrba. 1982. Exaptation—a missing term in the science of form. *Paleobiol.* 8:4–15.

Grafen, A. 1985. A geometric view of relatedness. *Oxf. Sur. Evol. Biol.* 2:28–89.

Grober, M. S. 1988. Brittle-star bioluminescence functions as an aposematic signal to deter crustacean predators. *Anim. Behav.* 36:493–501.

_____. **1989.** Bioluminescent aposematism: a reply to Guilford and Cuthill. *Anim. Behav.* 37:341–343.

Guilford, T. C., and I. Cuthill. 1989. Aposematism and bioluminescence. *Anim. Behav.* 37:339–341.

Guilford, T. 1985. Is kin selection involved in the evolution of warning coloration? *Oikos* 45:31–36.

————. **1986.** How do warning colours work: Conspicuousness may reduce recognition errors in experienced predators. *Anim. Behav.* 34:286–288.

————. **1987.** Aposematism. D. Phil. Thesis, Oxford.

————. **1988.** The evolution of conspicuous coloration. *Am. Nat.* 131: *S7–S21*

————. **1989 a.** Studying warning signals in laboratory. In R. J. Blanchard, P. F. Brain, D. C. Blanchard and S. Parmigiani (eds.), *Ethoexperimental Approaches to the Study of Behaviour.* pp. 87-103 Kluwer Academic Dordrecht.

————. **1989 b.** Evolutionary stability and the laboratory assessment of behaviour: the role of the go-between. In R. J. Blanchard, P. F. Brain, D. C. Blanchard and S. Parmiagiani (eds.), *Ethoexperimental Approaches to the Study of Behaviour.* pp. 644-656 Kluwer Academic Dordrecht.

Guilford, T. C., and I. Cuthill. 1989. Aposematism and bioluminescence. *Anim. Behav.* 37:339–341.

Guilford, T., and M. S. Dawkins. 1987. Search images not proven: a reappraisal of recent evidence. *Anim. Behav.* 35:1838-1845.

Guilford, T., C. J. Nicol, M. Rothschild, and B. P. Moore. 1987. The biological roles of pyrazines: evidence for a warning odour function. *Biol. J. Linn. Soc.* 31:113-128.

Hailman, J. P. 1964. Coding of the colour preference of the gull chick. *Nature* (Lond.) 204:710.

Hamilton, W. D. 1964. The genetical evolution of social behaviour. 1 and 2. J. *Theoret. Biol.* 7:1-52.

Harvey, P. H. 1983. Why some insects look pretty nasty. *New Scientist,* January 6th. 26–27.

Harvey, P. H., and P. J. Greenwood. 1978. Anti-predator defence strategies: some evolutionary problems. In J. R. Krebs and N. B. Davies (eds.), *Behavioural Ecology: An Evolutionary Approach.* Blackwell, Oxford.

Harvey, P. H., and R. J. Paxton. 1981a. The evolution of aposematic coloration. *Oikos* 37:391-393.

————. **1981b.** On aposematic coloration: a rejoinder. *Oikos* 37:395–396.

Harvey, P. H., J. J. Bull, M. Pemberton, and R. J. Paxton. 1982. The evolution of aposematic coloration in distasteful prey: a family model. *Am. Nat.* 119:710–719.

Hogan, J. A. 1965. An experimental study of conflict and fear: an analysis of behaviour of young chicks toward a mealworm. Part I. The behaviour of chicks which do not eat the meal-worm. *Behaviour* 25:45–97.

Houston, A. I., and J. M. McNamara. 1985. The choice of two prey types that minimises the probability of starvation. *Behav. Ecol. Sociobiol.* 17:135-141.

Järvi, T., B. Sillén-Tullberg, and C. Wiklund. 1981a. The cost of being aposematic. An experimental study of predation on larvae of *Papilio machaon* by the great tit *Parus major. Oikos* 36:267-272.

_____. **1981b.** Individual versus kin selection for aposematic coloration: a reply to Harvey and Paxton. *Oikos* 37:393-395.

John, E. R., P. Chesler, F. Bartlett, and I. Victor. 1968. Observational learning in cats. *Science* 159:1489-1491.

Kalat, J. W., and P. Rozin. 1973. 'learned safety; as a mechanism in long-delay taste-aversion learning in rats. *J. Comp. Physiol. Psychol.* 83:198-207.

Kamin, L. J., C. J. Brimer, and A. H. Black. 1963. Conditioned suppression as a monitor of the CS in the course of avoidance training. *J. Comp. Physiol. Psychol.* 56:497-501.

Kaye, H., N. J. MacKintosh, M. Rothschild, and B. P. Moore. 1989. Odour of pyrazine potentiates an association between environmental cues and unpalatable taste. *Anim. Behav.* 37:563-568.

Keith-Lucas, T., and N. Guttman. 1975. Robust single-trial delayed backward conditioning. *J. Comp. Physiol. Psychol.* 88:468-476.

Klopfer, P. H. 1959. Social interactions in discrimination learning with special reference to feeding behaviour in birds. *Behaviour* 14:282-299.

Krebs, J. 1979. Bird colours. *Nature* (Lond.) 282:14-16.

Kreithen, M. L., and W. T. Keeton. 1974a. Detection of changes in atmospheric pressure by the homing pigeon, *Columba livia. J. Comp. Physiol.* 89:73-82.

_____. **1974b.** Detection of polarised light by the homing pigeon, *Columba livia. J. Comp. Physiol.* 89:83-92.

_____. **1974c.** Attempts to condition homing pigeons to magnetic stimuli. *Columba livia. J. Comp. Physiol.* 91:355-362.

Lane, C., and M. Rothschild. 1956. Preliminary note on insects eaten and rejected by a tame shama (*Kittacincia malabarica* Gm.), with the suggestion that in certain species of butterflies and moths females are less palatable than males. *Entomol. Monthly Mag.* 93:172-179.

Leimar, O., M. Enquist, and B. Sillén-Tullberg. 1986. Evolutionary stability of aposematic coloration and prey unprofitability: a theoretical analysis. *Am. Nat.* 128:469-490.

Linsley, E. G., T. Eisner, and A. B. Klots. 1961. Mimetic assemblages of sibling species of lycid beetles. *Evolution* 15:15-29.

Mackintosh, N. J. 1974. *The Psychology of Animal Learning.* Academic Press, London.

_____. **1983.** *Conditioning and Associative Learning.* Oxford University Press, Oxford.

Malcolm, S. B. 1986. Aposematism in a soft-bodied insect: a case for kin selection. *Behav. Ecol. Sociobiol.* 18:387–393.

McLain, D. K. 1984. Coevolution: Mullerian mimicry between a plant bug (Miridae) and a seed bug (Lygaeidae) and the relationship between host plant choice and unpalatability. *Oikos* 43:143–148.

Mallet, J. 1986a. Hybrid zones of *Heliconius* butterflies in Panama and the stability and movement of warning colour clines. *Heredity* 56:191–202.

_____. **1986b.** Dispersal and gene flow in a butterfly with home range behavior: *Heliconius erato* (Lepidoptera: Nymphalidae). *Oecologia* 68:210–217.

_____. **1986c.** Gregarious roosting and home range in *Heliconius* butterflies. *Nat. Geog. Res.* 2:198–215.

Mallet, J., and M. Singer. 1987. Individual selection, kin selection, and the shifting balance in the evolution of warning colours: the evidence from butterflies. *Biol. J. Linn. Soc.* 32:337–350.

Mason, J. R., and R. F. Reidinger. 1982. Observational learning of food aversions in red-winged blackbirds (*Agelaius phoeniceus*). *Auk* 99:548–554.

Mathews, E. G. 1977. Signal-based frequency-dependent defense strategies and the evolution of mimicry. *Am. Nat.* 111:213–222.

Maynard Smith, J. 1964. Group selection and kin selection. *Nature* (lond.) 201:1145–1147.

Michod, R. E., and W. W. Anderson. 1979. Measures of genetic relationship and the concept of inclusive fitness. *Am. Nat.* 114:637–647.

Nunney, L. 1985. Group selection, altruism, and structured-deme models. *Am. Nat.* 126:212–230.

Owen, D. 1980. *Camouflage and Mimicry.* Oxford University Press, Oxford.

Palameta, B., and L. Lefèbvre. 1985. The social transmission of a food finding technique in pigeons: what is learned? *Anim. Behav.* 33:892–896.

Papageorgis, C. 1975. Mimicry in Neotropical butterflies. *Am. Sci.* 63:522–532.

Pough, F. H., L. P. Brower, H. R. Meck, and S. R. Kessel. 1973. Theoretical investigations of automimicry: multiple trial learning and the palatability spectrum. *Proc. Natn. Acad. Sci. U.S.A.* 70:2261–2265.

Poulton, E. B. 1887. The experimental proof of the protective value of colour and markings in insects in reference to their vertebrate enemies. *Proc. Zool. Soc. Lond.* 1887:191–274.

_____. 1890. *The Colours of Animals. Their Meaning and Use.* Especially considered in the case of insects. Kegan Paul, Trench, Trubner, London.

Queller, D. C. 1984. Kin selection and frequency dependence: a game theoretic approach. *Biol. J. Linn. Soc.* 23:133-143.

Rabinowitch, V. E. 1968. The role of experience in the development of food preferences in gull chicks. *Anim. Behav.* 16:425-428.

_____. 1969. The role of experience in the development and retention of seed preferences in zebra finches. *Behaviour* 33:222-236.

Rettenmeyer, C. W. 1970. Insect mimicry. *Ann. Rev. Entomol.* 15:43-74.

Ridley, M., and A. Grafen. 1981. Are green beard genes outlaws? *Anim. Behav.* 29:954-955.

Roper, T. J. 1990. Responses of domestic chicks to artificially coloured insect prey: effects of previous experience and background colour. *Anim. Behav. 39: 466-73.*

Roper, T.J., and S. E. Cook. In press. Responses of chicks to brightly colored insect prey. *Behaviour.*

Roper, T. J., and S. Redston. 1987. Conspicuousness of distasteful prey affects the strength and durability of one-trial avoidance learning. *Anim. Behav.* 35:739-747.

Roper, T. J., and R. Wistow. 1986. Aposematic colouration and avoidance learning in chicks. *Quarterly J. Exp. Psychol.* 38:141-149.

Rothschild, M. 1961. Defensive odours and Mullerian mimicry among insects. *Trans. Roy. Entomol. Soc. Lond.* 113:101-121.

_____. 1964. An extension of Dr. Lincoln Brower's theory on bird predation and food specificity, together with some observations on bird memory in relation to aposematic colour patterns. *Entomologist* 97:73-78.

_____. 1981. The mimicrats must move with the times. *Biol. J. Linn. Soc.* 16:21-23.

_____. 1984. Aide memoire mimicry. *Ecol. Entomo.* 9:311-319.

_____. 1985. British aposematic lepidoptera. In J. Heath and A. Maitland Emmet (eds.), *The Moths and Butterflies of Great Britian and Ireland,* 2:9-62. Harley, Colchester, Essex, England.

Rothschild, M., and B. Ford 1968. Warning signals from a starling *Sturnus vulgaris* observing a bird rejecting unpalatable prey. *Ibis* 102:328-330.

Schlenoff, D. H. 1984. Novelty: a basis for generalisation in prey selection. *Anim. Behav.* 32:919-921.

Schuler, W. 1985. A predisposition for learning to avoid warningly coloured prey. Poster presented at the 19th Ethological Conference, Toulouse, France. (Abstract in Proceedings, page 341).

Schuler, W., and E. Hesse. 1985. On the function of warning coloration: a black and yellow pattern inhibits prey-attack by naive domestic chicks. *Behav. Ecol. Sociobiol.* 16:249–255.

Shettleworth, S. J. 1972. The role of novelty in learned avoidance of unpalatable prey by domestic chicks. *Anim. Behav.* 20:29–35.

————. **1984.** Learning and behavioural ecology. In J. R. Krebs and N. B. Davies (eds.), *Behavioural Ecology: An Evolutionary Approach.* 2nd ed., pp. 170–194. Blackwell, Oxford.

Siegel, S. 1971. Latent inhibition and eyelid conditioning. In A. H. Black and W. F. Prokasy (eds.), *Classical Conditioning.* New York: Appleton-Century-Crofts.

Sillén-Tullberg, B. 1985a. The significance of coloration per se, independent of background, for predator avoidance of aposematic prey. *Anim. Behav.* 33:1382–1384.

————. **1985b.** Higher survival of an aposematic than a cryptic form of a distasteful bug. *Oecologia* 67:411–415.

Sillén-Tullberg, B., and E. H. Bryant. 1983. The evolution of aposematic coloration in distasteful prey: an individual selection model. *Evolution* 37:993–1000.

Sillén-Tullberg, B., C. Wiklund, and T. Järvi. 1982. Aposematic coloration in adults and larvae of *Lygaeus equestris* and its bearing on mullerian mimicry: an experimental study on predation on living bugs by the great tit *Parus major. Oikos* 39:131–136.

Smith, J. N. M. 1974. The food searching behaviour of two European thrushes II: the adaptiveness of the search patterns. *Behaviour* 49:1–61.

Smith, S. M. 1975. Innate recognition of coral snake pattern by a possible avian predator. *Science* 187:759–760.

————. **1977.** Coral-snake pattern recognition and stimulus generalisation by naive great kiskadees (Aves: Tyrannidae). *Nature* (Lond.) 365:535–536.

————. **1980.** Responses of naive temperate birds to warning coloration. *Am. Midl. Nat.* 103:346–352.

Solomon, R. L., L. J. Kamin, and L. C. Wynne. 1953. Traumatic avoidance learning: the outcome of several extinction procedures with dogs. *J. Abnormal Social Psychol.* 48:291–302.

Staddon, J. E. R. 1983. *Adaptive Behaviour and Learning.* Cambridge University Press, Cambridge.

Stamp, N. E. 1980. Egg deposition patterns in butterflies: why do some species cluster their eggs rather than deposit them singly? *Am. Nat.* 115:367–380.

Stephens, D. W. 1981. The logic of risk-sensitive foraging preferences. *Anim. Behav.* 29:628–629.

Stephens, D. W., and J. R. Krebs. 1986. *Foraging Theory.* Princeton University Press, Princeton, New Jersey.

Swynnerton, C. F. M. 1915a. *Proc. Ent. Soc.* 1915, p. xlii.

_____. **1915b.** Birds in relation to their prey: experiments on wood hoopoes, small hornbills, and a babbler. *J. S. Afr. Ornithol. Union,* December:32-108.

_____. **1919.** Experiments and observations bearing on the explanation of form and colouring, 1908-1913. *J. Linn. Soc.* 33:203-385.

Tait, R. W., and M. E. Saladin. 1986. Concurrent development of excitatory and inhibitory associations during backward conditioning. *Anim. Learn. Behav.* 14:133-137.

Tarpy, R. M. 1982. *Principles of Animal Learning and Motivation.* Scott, Foresman and Co., Glenview, Illinois.

Thompson, V. 1973. Spittlebug polymorphism for warning colour. *Nautre* (Lond.) 242:126-128.

Tinbergen, N. 1952. The curious behaviour of the stickleback. *Sci. Am.* 187(12):22-26.

Tinbergen, N., M. Impekoven, and D. Franck. 1967. An experiment on spacing-out as a defence against predation. *Behaviour* 28:307-327.

Turner, J. R. G. 1975a. A tale of two butterflies. *Nat. Hist.* 84:28-37.

_____. **1975b.** Communal roosting in relation to warning colour in two Helicoiine butterflies (Nymphalidae). *J. Lepidopterists' Soc.* 29:221-226.

_____. **1984.** Mimicry: the palatability spectrum and its consequences. In R. I. Vane-Wright and P. R. Ackery (eds.), *The Biology of Butterflies.* Symp. Roy. Ent. Soc. Lond. 11:141-161. Academic Press, London.

Turner, J. R. G., E. P. Kearney, and L. S. Exton. 1984. Mimicry and the Monte Carlo predator: the palatability spectrum and the origins of mimicry. *Biol. J. Linn. Soc.* 23:247-268.

Vaughan, F. A. 1983. Startle responses of blue jays to visual stimuli presented during feeding. *Anim. Behav.* 31:385-396.

Vermeij, G. J. 1982. Unsuccessful predation and evolution. *Am. Nat.* 120:701-720.

Waldman, G. & K. Adler. 1979. Toad tadpoles associate preferentially with siblings. *Nature* (Lond.) 282:611-613.

Wallace, A. R. 1867. *Proc. Ent. Soc.* March 4th :lxxx-lxxxi

Wallman, J. 1979. A minimal visual restriction experiment: preventing chicks from seeing their feet affects later responses to mealworms. *Dev. Psychobiol.* 12:391-397.

Wiklund, C., and T. Järvi. 1982. Survival of distasteful insects after being attacked by naive birds: a reappraisal of the theory of aposematic coloration evolving through individual selection. *Evolution* 36:998-1002.

Wilcoxon, H. C., W. B. Dragoin, and P. A. Kral. 1971. Illness-induced aversions in rat and quail: relative salience of visual and gustatory cues. *Science* 171:826–828.

Willson, M. F., and M. N. Melampy. 1983. The effect of biocolored fruit display on fruit removal by avian frugivores. *Oikos* 41:27–31.

Sexual Selection and Predation: Balancing Reproductive and Survival Needs

Scott K. Sakaluk

Introduction

If a sexually reproducing animal is to leave any offspring, it must acquire a mate and at the same time avoid being eaten by predators. The selection pressures shaping these two biological imperatives might at first appear to be mutually exclusive; indeed, in recent overviews of behavioral ecology, sex and predation are usually accorded separate treatments (e.g., Krebs and Davies 1984; Sibly and Smith 1985). Numerous morphological, physiological, and behaviorial traits have, of course, arisen as a response to *natural selection* imposed through predation—these defensive adaptations are the focus of much of this volume. But to what extent does predation influence the evolution of *sexually selected* traits—traits which have arisen because of the advantages which they confer on individuals in the competition for mates (Darwin 1871)? In this chapter I address this question, examining the role of predation in the evolution of arthropod mating systems. In so doing, I provide a framework within which the major categories of reproductive behavior can be arranged and the influence of predation on each systematically addressed.

Darwin (1859, 1871) introduced his theory of sexual selection to account for differences between males and females with respect to traits not directly involved in copulation and not readily explained in terms of increased survival advantage (i.e., natural selection). Such traits include sexual dissimilarities in size, strength, coloration, weaponry, and signaling behavior, and are referred to as "secondary sexual characters." Darwin proposed that these characters had evolved (1) because of the advantage they conferred on individuals in the struggle for mates (*intrasexual selection*) and/or (2) because of preferences exerted by individuals of the opposite sex (*intersexual selection*). Darwin was well aware that secondary sexual characters could incur an increased risk of predation for their bearers. Indeed, he invoked this risk to explain why the expression of a sexually selected trait is almost invariably delayed until an individual is of breeding age; in an immature animal, a sexually selected trait confers no mating advantage but still imparts the same cost to survival.

Although Darwin (1871) correctly identified the proximate mechanisms of sexual selection (intrasexual competition and intersexual mate choice), he could not adequately explain why sexually selected traits are more often expressed in males than in females. Trivers (1972), building on eariler work by Bateman (1948) and Williams (1966), provided the definitive answer: males compete for discriminating females in the majority of animal species because of a fundamental difference in *parental investment* by the sexes. Generally, females contribute more to the survival of offspring than do males, both in terms of the initial gametic investment and in the subsequent care of offspring. The most important implication of this disparity in parental investment is that male reproductive success is limited only by the number of eggs that males are able to fertilize. Females, on the other hand, are limited strictly by the number of eggs they are able to produce and become a limiting resource for which males are expected to compete. Females are predicted to be more discriminating in their choice of mates because they have more to lose in terms of future reproduction by mating with a genetically incompatible or inferior mate.

An important prediction from Trivers's (1972) analysis is that *as male parental investment is decreased relative to that of females, male survival should also decrease.* The rationale for this prediction is as follows. When a male does not invest parentally, his reproductive success is potentially far greater than that of a female, but only if he outcompetes other males. Noninvesting males are committed to traits that increase their competitive ability (e.g., increased aggressiveness, mobility, and size), but which also increase their probability of dying, either through direct conflict with other males or through greater exposure to predators. Simply stated, noninvesting males should take substantially more risks than females in acquiring mates because the reproductive payoffs to males are potentially far greater. Conversely, when male parental investment approaches that of females, a male's potential reproductive success is reduced and there is no longer a premium on competitive mechanisms and their concomitant risks. Thus for species in which parental investment by males is negligible, adult sex ratios should be biased in favor of females and approach unity only as male parental investment approaches female investment (Trivers 1972).

Trivers's (1972) hypothesis relating sexual differences in "risk taking" to parental investment will be a recurring theme in this discussion of predation and its importance in the evolution of sexually selected traits. I will review the predation risks associated with pair formation and mating and determine if this particular cost of mating (Daly 1978) is routinely associated with one or the other sex. Because female parental investment normally exceeds that of males, a basic prediction will be that risks involved in mating should normally be incurred by males. When the mating activities of females appear to expose them to danger from predators, we will look to see whether conspecific males are at even greater risk or if this is a species in which male parental investment approximates female investment.

Exploitation of Sexual Signals

For a communication system to evolve, it must have positive fitness effects on both the signaler and the receiver (Alcock 1984). This is certainly true of sexual signals, which serve to bring animals of the same species and opposite sex together for mating. Nonetheless, existing systems can be exploited by other animals which benefit at the expense of the legitimate participants. In arthropods, this exploitation usually involves the interception of sexual signals by predators, "illegitimate" receivers for whom the information was not intended. A less common means of exploitation involves "illegitimate" signalers, predators which broadcast misinformation to capture unwary prey (Otte 1974). In the following subsections I assess the risks associated with each mode of sexual communication (acoustic, chemical, and visual), and show that when such risks are substantial, they are usually incurred by the males.

ACOUSTIC COMMUNICATION

Acoustic signals are a particularly effective means of communication because such signals can be transmitted quickly, detected at long range, employed at night, and readily localized; these same characteristics render acoustic signaling modes particularly vulnerable to interception by predators (Alcock 1984). In the acoustic Orthoptera (crickets, katydids, and grasshoppers) and cicadas (Homoptera: Cicadidae), insects especially well known for their loud calls, it is normally the males which produce the species-specific signals that function in pair formation. Males also bear a heavy cost in the form of acoustically orienting predators which use the calls to locate potential prey. For example, calling male field crickets, *Gryllus integer* (Orthoptera: Gryllidae), are found by acoustically orienting parasitoid flies, *Euphasiopteryx ochracea* (Diptera: Tachinidae), which kill the males within about one week (Cade 1975, 1971, 1981a). Even before the males die, their calling time and mate-attracting ability is drastically reduced as a consequence of fly parasitism (Cade 1984). Tachinid flies are attracted to the calls of other hosts, including southeastern field crickets (Walker 1986), katydids (Burk 1982), and mole crickets (Fowler and Kochalka 1985; Mangold 1978), and sarcophagid flies, *Colcondamyia auditrix*, exhibit phonotaxis to their hosts, calling male cicadas (Soper et al. 1976). Vertebrate predators known to locate prey acoustically include domestic cats (Walker 1964), toads (Walker 1979), birds (Bell 1979; Moore 1973), lizards (Sakaluk and Belwood 1984), and bats (Belwood and Morris 1987; Tuttle and Ryan 1981; Tuttle et al. 1985).

Selection pressures imposed through predation appear to have had a profound influence on the subsequent evolution of acoustic communication systems. One simple but effective adaptation is the cessation of signaling when acoustically orienting predators are nearby. This tactic is employed both by katydids and sound-producing moths, which cease calling upon hearing the cries of echolocating bats (Spangler 1984). More fundamental evolutionary responses include reduced calling times (e.g., Cade 1975, 1979, 1981a; Cade and Wyatt 1984; Morris and Beier 1982), the use of less intense courtship calls once females have been attracted (Alexander 1962), the use of alternative signaling modalities (e.g., Bell 1980a,b; Morris 1980), and the total loss of calling in some groups (Otte 1977). A particularly convincing example of these effects has recently been presented by Belwood and Morris (1987) with respect to the calling behavior of Neotropical katydids. Forest-dwelling katydids are heavily predated by foliage-gleaning bats, which exploit the calls of male katydids as prey-finding cues. Belwood and Morris (1987) demonstrated that the song duty cycles (proportion of time spent calling) of the forest katydids were markedly reduced. Moreover, they showed that these species rely heavily on tremulation, substrate transmitted signals used in short-range communication with females. In contrast, species living in clearings (secondary growth areas) where bat predators are absent display the high-duty cycles which are characteristic of katydids worldwide.

CHEMICAL COMMUNICATION

Chemically mediated sexual signals are transmitted less quickly and are generally more difficult to localize than are acoustic signals. Although these characteristics make pair formation more difficult, they also reduce the risks of exploitation by predators (Alcock 1984). Perhaps this is why in the chemical communication systems of moths it is usually the female that is the active signaler and the male that fulfils the mate-locating role (Greenfield 1981). In moths, unlike acoustic insects, it is probably less dangerous to produce signals than it is to fly throughout the habitat in search of mates (see Fullard, this volume). Nonetheless, there are several documented examples of predators using the pheromones of insects to locate potential prey. Wood et al. (1968) showed that the male sex pheromone of a bark beetle, *Ips confusus* (Coleoptera: Scolytidae), attracts predaceous clerid and ostomid beetles under field conditions. Subsequently, a variety of predators and parasites have been identified which use bark beetle pheromones to locate the beetles as prey (Dixon and Payne 1980 and references). In another insect, the southern green stink bug, *Nezara viridula* (Hemiptera: Pentatomidae), the male produces a sex pheromone which, in addition to attracting conspecific females, attracts parasitic tachinid flies (Mitchell and Mau 1971). Harris and Todd (1980) showed that as a consequence of the male's signaling behavior, male stink bugs are parasitized in the field significantly more often than are females.

Perhaps the most bizarre example of chemical warfare by a predator involves the bolas spider, *Mastophora dizzydeani* (Araneidae). Bolas spiders capture prey by swinging a sticky ball at passing insects. The ball is attached at the end of a vertical line which in turn is secured to a horizontal line; if a prey adheres to the ball, the spider descends the vertical line to feed on it. The spider also acts as an illegitimate signaler, releasing a volatile odor which mimics the pheromone of female fall armyworms, *Spodoptera frugiperda* (Lepidoptera: Noctuidae). Male moths attracted to the odor are subsequently ensnared by the spider (Eberhard 1977, 1980).

VISUAL COMMUNICATION

A major disadvantage to visual signals is that they can be blocked entirely by physical barriers; this is why, perhaps, they are rarely employed in long-range sexual communication (Cade 1985). One notable exception is the "fireflies" (Coleoptera: Lampyridae), beetles which possess light-emitting organs used in the production of bioluminescent sexual displays. Males fireflies cruise throughout the habitat at night emitting their species-specific flash patterns. Sexually receptive females perched in the vegetation respond by emitting a flash reply. Males orient to the flashes of receptive females and copulate with them on the vegetation (Lloyd 1971).

Predators also use the bioluminescent signals of firefly prey as cues in attack guidance, although this behavior has been demonstrated only recently. Lloyd and Wing (1983) showed that predatory female *Photuris* fireflies exploit the signal emissions of other species to locate fireflies as prey. *Photuris* females also employ another remarkable predatory tactic: they mimic the flash responses of the females of other species to lure the males as prey (Lloyd 1975, 1984a). These femmes fatales have had an important evolutionary effect both on the subsequent evolution of their own species' sexual signals (Lloyd 1984b) and on the flash patterns of their prey. With respect to the former, Lloyd (1980) showed that some *Photuris* males mimic the sexual signals of other species to attract hunting femmes fatales of their own species as mates!

Other Risky Precopulatory Behaviors

In his excellent review of the evolutionary effects of predation on sexually signaling males, Burk (1982) categorized those aspects of male sexual behavior which render males vulnerable to predation. A list of risky precopulatory activities, modified after Burk (1982), runs as follows: conspicuous mating displays, lack of accurate discrimination, mate-searching behavior, territorial defense, aggregation behavior, and risky prenuptial obligations. Two of the major causes of increased vulnerability, conspicuous sexual displays and aggressive mimicry, have been dealt with in the preceding section. In this section I consider the remaining risk categories.

MATE SEARCHING

In searching for mates, individuals of one sex (usually males) are often more mobile than individuals of the other and thereby incur a greater risk of predation through increased conspicuousness. For example, adult sex ratios of dictynid spiders are often skewed heavily in favor of females, and Jackson and Smith (1978) hypothesized that these ratios arise as a consequence of the nomadic behavior of males. Males spend much of their time wandering in search of receptive females, and are thus more vulnerable to visually hunting predators than are female dictynids remaining in their webs. The predation risk to a male spider does not end with his finding the web of a female conspecific. Jackson (1976) observed predatory gnaphosid spiders in the field occupying the nests of female salticid spiders, *Phidippus johnsoni*. Fang marks on the remains of female *P. johnsoni* within the nests indicated that they had been preyed on by the gnaphosids, which subsequently remained in the nests of their prey. Male *P. johnsoni* entering such nests to court conspecific females may also fall prey to the resident gnaphosids.

Predation costs accruing to mate-searching behavior have also been invoked to explain the differential mortality of the sexes in spider crabs, *Inachus phalangium* (Crustacea: Decapoda). Individuals of this species reside within the stinging tentacles of sea anemones, which protect the crabs from predators. Males, however, often leave these protective confines, traveling among the sea anemones in search of mates; as a consequence of this behavior, males suffer a higher mortality risk. The cost of mate searching apparently has selected for the capacity in males of learning the positions and spawning times of females within male patrol areas. Such learning allows the males to minimize the transit time between potential mates (Diesel 1986).

Predation risks arising through mate-searching behavior will not result in biased sex ratios if they are balanced by risks incurred through reproductive behaviors exhibited solely by the nonsearching sex. For example, male damselflies, *Enallagma hageni* (Odonata: Coenagrionidae), spend much of their time flying in search of mates and, as a consequence, suffer heavy mortality from dragonflies and web-building spiders. Female damselflies avoid this mate-searching cost but when submerging to deposit their eggs, incur a comparable risk of predation by frogs, giant waterbugs, and other aquatic predators (Fincke 1982).

The increased mobility of males in searching for mates need not be the only cause of male-biased mortality. In the checkerspot butterfly, *Euphydrayas editha*, significantly fewer females than males were found trapped in spider webs (Moore 1987). Such a result could hypothetically be explained by a greater flight activity of males. However, Moore (1987) showed experimentally that males were far more likely to be trapped by webs containing dead conspecifics than they were by webs devoid of *E. editha* carcasses. Her results indicate that males attempt to copulate with anything resembling a teneral female, including the dead bodies of male and female *E. editha*. Male-biased mortality in this species is not therefore a consequence of greater mobility of males, but rather a result of the apparent lack of male discrimination in mate location behavior.

A final example of the risks involved in mate searching concerns predation on tick-tock cicadas, *Cicadetta quadricincta* (Homptera: Cicadidae), by wed-building spiders. Gwynne (1987) found significantly more male than female cicadas trapped in spider webs, and determined that the sex ratio of captured individuals was not merely a reflection of the overall population sex ratio. Pair formation in *C. quadricincta* involves timbaling by the male (the vibration of a "tymbal" within the male's abdomen causing sound to be produced), an acoustic response by the female produced through a wing-flicking behavior, and the subsequent phonotaxis of the male to the female. The active movement of the male to the female during pair formation is apparently responsible for the higher rate of predation on males by web-building spiders.

TERRITORIAL DEFENSE

In addition to actively searching for mates, males of various species obtain matings by maintaining territories, areas from which other males are actively excluded and which often contain resources important to females. Like active mate searching, however, territorial defense is not without its risks of predation. For example, in digger wasps, *Philanthus* spp. (Hymenoptera: Sphecidae), males establish territories for the purpose of mating and frequently make territorial flights. Such flights not only render the males more conspicuous to predators, but also entail the investigation of intruders, which occasionally turn out to be predatory robber flies (Diptera: Asilidae). Gwynne and O'Neill (1980) showed that significantly more male than female *Philanthus* fall prey to robber flies. Territorial *Philanthus parkeri* leave the territory when predators including female *P. basilaris* and robber flies enter the territorial area (Evans and O'Neill 1988). A similar cost to territorial defense has been implicated in the dragonfly, *Plathemis lydia* (Odonata: Libellulidae). In this species, males defend territories around ponds at sites that are favored by females for oviposition. However, males most successful at defending favored sites may be at the greatest risk of predation because of the aggregation of predators, such as frogs, in the same areas where female *P. lydia* oviposit (Koenig and Albano 1985).

MATING SWARMS

Another common means of mate acquisition in insects involves mating swarms, aggregations of males formed solely for the purpose of mating. Although most common in the Diptera, swarms are widespread throughout the Insecta, occurring in eight orders (Sullivan 1981). Adaptive benefits of two types have been ascribed to swarming behavior (reviewed in Sullivan 1981): (1) swarms are more apparent to spatially dispersed females than are males displaying alone, and (2) females compare prospective suitors before mating, making it adaptive for males to advertise near competitors (see Alexander 1975). Regardless of their adaptive significance, swarms are also conspicuous to a plethora of predators, including bats, birds, and predatory insects, which have been selected to exploit these convenient concentrations of food items. Once again it is the males that bear the brunt of this predation strategy, with females avoiding such risks except for the short time they are in the mating swarm. In at least one group of insects, the Hawaiian *Drosophila*, the predation pressure on clumped males apparently has been responsible for a dramatic shift in mating strategy (Spieth 1974). Unlike the non-Hawaiian species, Hawaiian *Drosophila* do not mate on or at their food sites. Rather, males set up territories in vegetation adjacent to food sites. Speith (1974) argued that predation was particularly intense on the Hawaiian fauna, and that the shift to defense of territories concealed in dense vegetation was an adaptive response to this selection pressure. Similar selection pressures have been invoked to explain nocturnal swarming of tropical mayflies (Ephemeroptera) at sites remote from larval habitats (Edmunds and Edmunds 1980).

MATE CANNIBALISM

In addition to the greater risk taking by males in obtaining mates, once a male has located a prospective mate, he may face an additional predation risk from his intended. Returning to digger wasps, we have already seen that males, through their territorial flights, expose themselves to visually hunting predators such as robber flies (Gwynne and O'Neill 1980; Evans and O'Neill 1988). Evans and O'Neill (1988) summarized the known data and report that female *Philanthus basilaris* occasionally provision their nests with the males of the species. They observed sixteen interactions involving predatory attempts by females on males, six of which resulted in the female successfully immobilizing her would-be mate by stinging him. All six predated males were smaller than any of the ten males that escaped; thus being territorial *and* small appears to be especially disadvantagous (Evans and O'Neill 1988).

Spiders are particularly well known for the cannibalism of males by their mates. Although cannibalism does sometimes occur, consumption of the male by the female is by no means an inevitable consequence of mating (Austad and Thornhill 1986; Breene and Sweet 1985; Christenson 1984; Jackson 1979, 1980). In several species, males employ specialized reproductive tactics during the courtship sequence which allow them to escape the voracious females (Christenson 1984; Jackson 1980). In the black widow spider, *Latrodectus mactans* (Araneae: Theridiidae), one of the more notorious of the cannibalistic species, males often escape previous mates and succeed in inseminating additional females (Breene and Sweet 1985). The male uses an escape mechanism which involves cutting portions of the female's web, thus disorienting the female during a predatory attack. The males also spin a "bridal veil," which may delay the female long enough after mating to allow the male to drop out of range (Breene and Sweet 1985; Ross and Smith 1979).

PRENUPTIAL OBLIGATIONS

As a prelude to mating, males of a variety of species are obliged to provide the female with a courtship food gift before the female will consent to mating (Quinn and Sakaluk 1986; Thornhill 1976a; Zeh and Smith 1985). In the scorpionfly, *Hylobittacus apicalis* (Mecoptera: Bittacidae), the courtship food gift consists of a prey item which the male obtains prior to attracting a female. The female feeds on the prey item while *in copula*. If the nuptial gift is too small and/or unpalatable, the female terminates the copulation and flies away before the male has transferred a full complement of sperm (Thornhill 1976b). To satisfy the demands of females and their own nutritional requirements, males fly throughout the foliage in search of prey. As a consequence of this searching behavior, males often become trapped by web-building spiders, the most important cause of mortality in bittacids (Thornhill, 1978, 1979). In *H. apicalis,* this mortality is significantly male biased: in 357 cases of spider predation observed over six years, males were the victim 69 percent of the time (Thornhill 1979). Evidence that this bias is due to the sexual asymmetry in time spent hunting is provided by *Bittacus strigosus,* a species in which courtship feeding by males does not occur. In this species, both males and females engage equally in hunting, and mortality of the sexes is similar (Thornhill 1979).

Male-biased predation is also widespread in the panorpid scorpion-flies (Thornhill 1978, 1981). Like males of *H. apicalis, Panorpa* males provide females with dead arthropods as nuptial food gifts. The provision of such gifts entails considerable foraging by males and, inevitably, a higher risk of predation.

FEMALE RISK TAKING

Female arthropods are not entirely immune to the predation risks posed by sex-related activities. In the firefly, *Photinus collustrans* (Coleoptera; Lampyridae), females are flightless and inhabit burrows in the soil. Virgin females leave the burrow to mate and otherwise remain near its entrance, but mated females usually never leave the burrow (Wing 1984, 1988). Flying male *P. collustrans* signal for about a twenty-minute period each night, beginning about twenty minutes after sunset. Virgin females outside their burrows flash in response to signaling conspecifics and thereby enable males to find them (Wing 1984). The responses of females may also be detected by predators, however, and Wing (1988) demonstrated an increased mortality of females outside their burrows relative to those remaining inside. Predators implicated in this differential mortality included lycosid spiders, ants, and toads.

An interesting example of sex-biased predation on females has been documented by Gwynne and Dodson (1983). In their study of predation by digger wasps, *Palmodes laeviventris* (Hymenoptera: Sphecidae), on Mormon "crickets," *Anabrus simplex* (Orthopetera: Tettigoniidae), Gwynne and Dodson (1983) excavated nineteen wasp nests to determine the sex ratio of prey. They found a sex ratio of thirty females to four males, differing significantly from the 1:1 sex ratio observed in a nearby aggregation of Mormon crickets. Gwynne and Dodson (1983) provided two hypotheses to account for the strong bias towards female prey: (1) wasps may prefer female Mormon crickets as prey because females are heavier than males and represent a larger food source for the developing brood, and (2) females are more mobile than males and may be more apparent to hunting wasps. The latter explanation may at first seem to conflict with Trivers's hypothesis regarding parental investment and differential risk taking by the sexes. But as is the case for most biological constructs, it is the exception which proves the rule. It turns out that *A. simplex* is one of the few insect species in which male parental investment may actually exceed female investment. At mating, male *A. simplex* transfer a large nutritious spermatophore which accounts for about 20 percent of a male's body weight, and which subsequently is consumed by the female. Gwynne (1980) showed that as a consequence of this huge paternal investment, a sex role reversal, in which female compete for access to choosy males, accompanies the reversal in risk taking by the sexes.

Female-biased predation may also occur in another orthopteran, the decorated cricket, *Gryllodes supplicans* (Gryllidae). Sakaluk and Belwood (1984) observed Mediterranean house geckos, *Hemidactylus tursicus*, which occur in Florida within the same microhabitat as *G. supplicans*, positioned close to the burrows of calling male *G. supplicans*. Captive geckos readily consumed crickets in the laboratory, and the feces of field-collected geckos contained cricket as well as other insect remains. Sakaluk and Belwood (1984) hypothesized that the geckos were using the calls of male *G. supplicans* to locate crickets as prey. They tested their hypothesis by releasing captured geckos, one at a time, in the center of a circular concrete platform, and recording the exits of geckos from the arena in relation to a sound source positioned several meters away. The sound source was a speaker which broadcast the previously recorded *G. supplicans* calling song or the calling song of the spring peeper, *Hyla crucifer*, as a control. The results of this experiment are shown in figure 3.1. Geckos exhibited a significant phonotactic response to playback of the cricket calling song, but showed no response to playback of the control sound. Thus it would appear, superficially at least, that calling male *G. supplicans* are at risk of predation to acoustically orienting geckos.

However, the geckos face two serious obstacles in exploiting male *G. supplicans* as prey: (1) the entrances of cricket burrows are physically too small to allow passage of a gecko (Sakaluk and Belwood 1984), and (2) male *G. supplicans* spend approximately 95 percent of their time within protected shelters, minimizing their exposure to potential predators (Sakaluk 1987). Sakaluk and Belwood (1984) proposed that geckos might still benefit by remaining near the burrows of sheltered male crickets, because this proximity would allow geckos to intercept sexually receptive female crickets orienting to the calling males. Sakaluk and Belwood (1984) termed this predatory strategy "satellite predation," and although their case was entirely inferential, suggested that female *G. supplicans* face a substantial predation risk simply by responding to the calls of males.

Interestingly, *G. supplicans* is a species like that of the Mormon "cricket" in which males make a large parental investment in the form of a

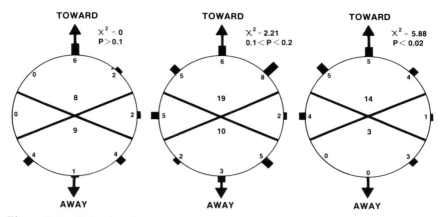

Figure 3.1   Exit of geckos from an arena during playback of sounds.

spermatophylax, a specialized portion of the spermatophore which is eaten by the female after mating (Sakaluk 1984). The mating system of *G. supplicans* could, perhaps, be taken as further support of the theory relating differential risk taking of the sexes to parental investment (Trivers 1972): spermatophore investment by male *G. supplicans* is large relative to that of other crickets (Sakaluk 1985) and, until recently, *G. supplicans* has been the only gryllid in which a *female* risk taking has been implicated. However, L. Simmons (University of Liverpool, personal communications) recently observed *H. tursicus* geckos in Spain employing the same satellite predator tactic to obtain cricket prey of a different species, *Gryllus bimaculatus*. In *G. bimaculatus*, the male does not provide the female with a nutritious spermatophylax but instead transfers a spermatophore which consists solely of a small sperm ampulla (Simmons 1986). Thus, the proposed relationship between spermatophore investment and differential risk taking by the sexes must remain tenuous until further species have been examined.

Copulation and Predation Risk

In addition to ancillary sexual activities, the act of copulation might itself increase the risk of predation to mating individuals through increased conspicuousness and/or reduced maneuverability of mating pairs. A heightened risk of predation should select for a decrease in both the duration and frequency of copulations; there are, however, few studies which bear on this hypothesis. It might also seem reasonable that predation on coupled individuals would be sexually nonspecific, that is, both the male and female would share equally in the risk. For example, White (1983) documented an interesting case of ants, *Formica podzolica* (Hymenoptera: Formicidae), preying on copulating black flies, *Prosimulium mixtum/fuscum* (Diptera: Simuliidae). The female black flies were observed dragging their copulating partners behind them along the ground. Ants crossing the trails of such pairs detected the flies (presumably by some olfactory cue) and were able to track them. Upon locating coupled flies, the worker ant usually killed only one of the pair. In so doing, the ants showed no preference with respect to the sex of their victim.

Copulating beetles may also fall prey to ants. Gwynne and Rentz (1983) observed male buprestid beetles, *Julodimorpha bakewell* (Coleoptera), attempting to copulate with discarded beer bottles. The shiny brown color and tubercles at the base of the bottles closely resembled the elytra of the beetle, and the males apparently mistook such bottles as females. Ants (*Irodomyrmex discolors*) were observed attacking the beetles and biting at the soft portions of the males' genitalia. Thus, the frustrated beetles endured not only the thwarting of their sexual advances, but paid a heavy mortality cost for their indiscriminate mating.

An increased risk of predation to mating pairs, in addition to selecting for fewer and shorter copulations, may influence the evolution of other aspects of copulatory behavior. Spieth (1974) argued that the specialized copulatory behavior exhibited by the Hawaiian *Drosophila* (Diptera: Drosophilidae), absent from non-Hawaiian species, arose largely as a consequence of the unusually intense predation pressure on the Hawaiian fauna. Such behavior includes a copulatory quiescence in which flies, once coupled, become entirely immobile, reacting not even to disturbance from other conspecifics. In addition, males perform a cataleptic behavior in which the male drops to the substrate immediately following copulation and remains motionless for several minutes. Behaviors such as these presumably reduce the conspicuousness of mating *Drosophila* to honey-creeper birds, flycatchers, and muscoid flies, potential predators which occupy the same habitats as those occupied by the Hawaiian dropsophiloids.

Contrary to expectation, there are a variety of ways in which mating can actually confer *increased* survival on its participants. These have been reviewed by Sivinski (1983) and include (1) intimidation of a predator confronted with a seemingly larger and more unwieldy prey item, (2) confusion of the predator arising through the separation of an apparently single prey object, (3) physical shielding of one individual by the other in the mating pair, (4) pooling of defenses such as noxious secretions, and (5) amplification of aposematic colors, visual signals which warn of distastefulness. The two studies documenting such beneficial effects both show (1) a sexual asymmetry in benefits derived (individuals of one sex gained more in terms of increased survival than individuals of the other) and (2) lengthy copulations of several hours or more.

The first of these studies concerns predation on stick insects, *Diapheromera veliei* (Phasmatodea: Heteronemiidae), by avian predators. Coupling in this species lasts from 3 to 136 hours in the laboratory. Sivinski (1980) suggested that one adaptive benefit derived through extended matings in *D. veliei* is the pooling of chemical defenses. This stick insect has two important secondary defenses which it uses upon being discovered by a predator: it regurgitates an unpleasant-tasting substance after being handled roughly, and/or it reflex bleeds, leaking distasteful hemolymph (insect blood) from between various body segments. Sivinski (1980) tested his hypothesis by placing stick insects on a bush in an enclosure containing two Mexican jays, *Aphelocoma ultramarina*. The results of his experiment are shown in table 3.1. Male survival of single individuals did not differ significantly from those in pairs, but female survival was significantly ehanced by copulation. Sivinski (1980) suggested that females are protected in matings because males mount females dorsally and are therefore in the more vulnerable position with respect to avian predators. However, insofar as copulation duration is entirely under male control, this empirical finding posed an interesting problem: why do males remain coupled with females, sacrificing additional mating opportunities, if their own survival is not increased? Sivinski's (1980, 1983) studies suggested two independent possibilities, neither of which has been discounted: (1) survival of a male's future offspring is increased through the shielding of his mate from avian predators and (2) a male prevents his mate from engaging in additional copulations and thereby avoids competition from the sperm of other males for the fertilization of her eggs (Parker 1970, 1984).

The second study relating copulation to increased protection from predators concerns wheelbugs, *Arilus cristatus* (Hemiptera: Reduviidae), and their prey, milkweed beetles, *Tetraopes tetraophthalmus* (Coleoptera: Cerambycidae). In the milkweed beetles, members of both sexes engage in numerous matings, and copulations are prolonged, lasting up to three hours (McCauley and Lawson 1986). Mark-recapture studies in the field have shown that males are more mobile than females, primarily because males are more heavily involved in mate-searching behavior (Lawrence

Table 3.1. The outcomes of bird attacks on single and mating stick insects, *Diapheromera veliei* (from Sivinski 1980, slightly modified).

	Number attacking	Number surviving	Percent surviving
Males			
Single	21	8	38
Mating	15	9	60[1]
Females			
Single	25	6	24
Mating	15	11	73[2]

[1]X^2 test, $p > .1$.
[2]X^2 test, $p < .005$.

1982; McCauley et al. 1981). This greater mobility of male milkweed beetles renders them more susceptible to predation by the wheelbug, which acts as a "sit and wait" predator. The wheelbug impales its prey on its proboscis and sucks out the body fluids. In a study in which male milkweed beetles made up 52 percent of the live population, 77 percent of individuals found killed by wheelbugs were males (McCauley and Lawson 1986). Thus, as we have seen in the previous section, males bear the brunt of predation risks through their greater mate-searching activity. However, McCauley and Lawson (1986) demonstrated that copulation provides a measure of protection to males because pairs are less mobile than individual males. In their laboratory experiment, they placed two wheelbugs in cages with ten male beetles, ten females bettles, or five male and five female beetles. Not unexpectedly, mortality was significantly higher in the all-male cages than in the all-female cages. However, the mortality of males and females in the mixed cages was about equal and significantly less than that in the all-male cages. McCauley and Lawson (1986) concluded that sexual and natural selection can interact in complex ways; the males' success in finding mates paradoxically increases their chances of survival.

Predation and the Evolution of Alternative Mating Tactics

Alternative mating tactics are mutually exclusive behavioral options, adopted by individuals of the same species, which function in the acquisition of mates (Dominey 1984). For example, some males may defend territories to obtain exclusive access to a small subset of females, whereas others eschew territorial defense in favor of searching a wider area for single females. These particular alternatives are commonly observed in dragonfly mating systems (Waltz and Wolf 1984). The extent to which alternatives are expressed will depend on the costs: benefits ratio associated with each tactic. Because predation risks may vary across mating tactics, predation may in fact contribute to the origin and maintenance of behavioral alternatives. Although data to test this hypothesis are scarce, studies by Cade (1975, 1979, 1980, 1981a, 1981b) and Thornhill (1979, 1981) point to an important role for predation in the evolution of alternative male mating tactics.

In the field cricket, *Gryllus integer,* the majority of males establish territories from which they call and attract females. Alternatively, some males call very little or not at all, but instead position themselves near calling males and intercept the phonotactically attracted females (Cade 1975, 1979, 1980). Such males avoid the energetic costs of calling, but the energy conserved alone is not enough to offset the apparent decrease in mating success accompanying the "satellite" tactic. However, satellite males also gain an increased survival advantage through the avoidance of acoustically orienting parasitoids, tachinid flies which frequently parasitize and ultimately kill males (Cade 1975, 1979, 1980).

A comparison of *G. integer* with species in which calling males do not attract acoustically orienting parasitoids suggests that the survival advantage accruing to satellite males has been an important factor favoring their evolution (Cade and Wyatt 1984). Such species include *G. pennsylvanicus, G. veletis,* and *Teleogryllus africanus,* and in these crickets, satellite males are uncommon. In addition, the calling times of males in each of these species are normally distributed, suggesting that calling duration has been subject to strong stabilizing selection (Cade and Wyatt 1984). In contrast, the distribution of calling times in *G. integer* is strongly skewed to the right and the individual variability in calling time is significantly greater (compare distributions in figure 3.2). Cade (1986b) found significant additive genetic variance underlying calling time in *G. integer* and conclude that fluctuating selection, in the form of parasitoid flies, was responsible for the maintenance of the alternative mating tactics.

Predation may have also played a role in the evolution of alternative mating behaviors in scorpionflies. We have already seen how males of *Hylobittacus apicalis* incur appreciable predation risks by flying throughout the habitat in search of nuptial prey with which to feed females. However, some male *H. apicalis* adopt female postures and behaviors to deceive prey-holding males into surrendering their courtship food gifts. These

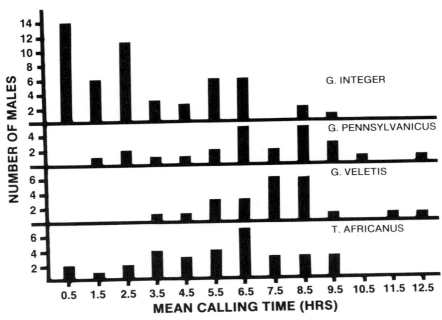

Figure 3.2   Frequency distributions of mean calling times per day of male *Gryllus interger, G. veletis,* and *Teleogryllus africanus* in the laboratory.

"transvestites" use the stolen prey to successfully obtain copulations and thus avoid the risks associated with finding their own nuptial prey (Thornhill 1979). The benefits derived from female mimicking are likely to be negatively frequency dependent (i.e., negatively correlated with the proportion of hunting males in the population), thus providing a mechanism by which the two alternative tactics could be maintained indefinitely over evolutionary time.

A final example which relates predation to the evolution of alternative mating tactics concerns the male-mimicking behavior of female damselflies, *Ischnura ramburi* (Odonata: Coenagrionidae). This species, like many other odonates, exhibits a sex-limited female dimorphism in which one morph is cryptically colored (heteromorph) and the other closely resembles the more colorful male (andromorph). Andromorphs not only look like males but, once mated, frequently perform malelike behaviors in subsequent interactions with males. Robertson (1985) showed that andromorphs engage in about half as many copulations as do hetermorphs and consequently experience a greater reproductive success: copulations in *I. ramburi* are unusually long, and andromorphs have more time for feeding, egg maturation, and oviposition, which otherwise would be lost in excessive copulations. Like the males, however, andromorphs are more visible to potential predators, and Robertson (1985) argued that this frequency-independent risk could perhaps balance the reproductive advantage of the andromorph.

Predation and the Evolution of Mate Choice

If some males afford females greater protection during mating than others, then females should choose as mates those males who, all else being equal, offer the best chance of survival. If females do indeed make such adaptive mate choices, then the trait which renders the male a better protector will become sexually selected. Borgia's (1981) study of mate choice in the dung fly, *Scatophaga stercoraria* (Diptera: Scatophagidae), is to my knowledge the only experimental test of this hypothesis. Female dung flies choose larger males as mates by actively moving toward such males on dung pats. Borgia (1981) argued that this female preference was adaptive because (1) larger males are better able to protect females from the copulatory attempts of other males, thereby reducing the possibility of physical injury to their mates, (2) protection from other males also reduces the time required by females for completion of copulation and oviposition, and (3) larger males are better able to fly with their mates and thereby escape predation. Borgia (1981) experimentally tested the last of these three putative benefits by disturbing mating pairs with his hand, recording whether the pair flew, and subsequently capturing the flies and measuring the wing length of each. The results of his experiment are shown in figure 3.3 and can be summarized as follows: small males are unable to fly with females of any size, intermediate-sized males have difficulty flying with larger females, and large males are able to fly with females of all sizes. Borgia (1981) concluded that females paired with larger males were more likely to escape capture by aerial predators such as wagtails.

Males may also reduce predation risks by being selective of their mates. In the amphipod crustacean, *Gammarus pulex*, there is size assortative mating with large males mating with large females in a size ratio of about 1.3:1 (Birkhead and Clarkson 1980). Positive assortative mating in amphipods is brought about by a complex interplay of various factors, including male-male competition (Elwood et al. 1987; Ward 1983, 1984), male choice (Adams and Greenwood 1985; Elwood et al. 1987; Ward 1984), female choice (Ward 1984), and drag constraints on male swimming performance (Adams and Greenwood 1983, 1985; Naylor and Adams 1987).

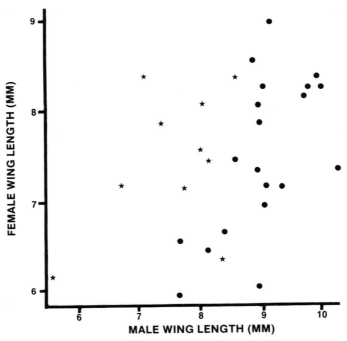

Figure 3.3 Ability of paired male *Scatophaga stercoraria* to fly
with females of different sizes.

The relative importance of each of these factors is a matter of some dispute
(see Adams and Greenwood 1987; Greenwood and Adams 1987; Ward
1987). Nonetheless, in at least some field situations (e.g., streams), males
pair with smaller, less fecund females even though larger females are
available for mating (Adams and Greenwood 1985). This apparently maladaptive mating preference can be explained in terms of the ability of
males to swim with females in fast flowing water. As current flow is
increased, the ability of males to maneouver effectively with larger
females is severely curtailed (Adams and Greenwood 1983, 1985; Naylor
and Adams 1987). A male whose swimming performance is hampered by
too large a mate risks not only being swept downstream, but also
increases his vulnerability to aquatic predators (Adams and Greenwood
1985). Ward (1986) showed that male *G. pulex* in mating pairs are more
vulnerable to fish predation than are unpaired males. Thus, although
males should optimally mate with the largest, most fecund females, their
choices may be environmentally constrained by the dangers of swimming
with such females (Adams and Greenwood 1985).

Summary

In the majority of animal species, males contribute far less to the survival of offspring than do females; consequently, males can increase their reproductive success merely by increasing their number of mates. Trivers (1972) proposed that noninvesting males should take substantially more risks than females in acquiring mates because the reproductive payoffs to males are potentially far greater. Thus the survival of males should be reduced relative to that of females when male parental investment is negligible.

An increased risk of predation is associated with a variety of sexual activities, including sexual signaling, mate-searching behavior, territorial defense, swarming, and the act of copulation itself. A review of arthropod mating systems shows that when such risks are substantial, they are usually incurred by males. In the majority of these species, males invest little more than sperm in the survival of offspring. The comparative evidence, therefore, strongly supports Trivers's hypothesis. The sexual asymmetry in predation risks should also lead to adult sex ratios which are biased in favor of females. Data to test this prediction are sparse, but where they exist, the corollary is supported.

Predation has been an important mitigating factor in determining which sex adopts an active-signaling versus a mate-searching role. In addition, it has had a profound influence on the evolution of other aspects of arthropod mating systems. These include the frequency and duration of copulations, the timing and location of sexual activity, signal structure, alternative mating tactics, and mate choice.

During the initial stages of writing this paper, I was supported by a Natural Sciences and Engineering Research Council of Canada postdoctoral fellowship. Additional support was provided by the Department of Biological Sciences, Illinois State University. I thank M.C. Sakaluk for helpful comments on the manuscript, S.R. Wing for kindly providing a copy of a manuscript in press and C.F. Thompson for assisting in the preparation of the figures. I also thank J.O. Schmidt for the invitation to contribute to this volume and for supplying the topic.

References

Adams, J., Greenwood, P. J. 1983. Why are males bigger than females in precopula pairs of *Gammarus pulex? Behav. Ecol. Sociobiol.* 13: 239–241.

_____. **1985.** Environmental constraints on mate choice in *Gammarus pulex* (Amphipoda). *Crustaceana* 50: 45–52.

_____. **1987.** Loading constraints, sexual selection and assortative mating in peracarid Crustacea. *J. Zool.* (Lond.) 211: 35–46.

Alcock, J. 1984. *Animal Behavior: An Evolutionary Approach* (third edition). Sunderland, Mass.: Sinauer Associates.

Alexander, R.D. 1962. Evolutionary change in cricket acoustical communication. *Evolution* 16: 443–467.

_____. **1975.** Natural selection and specialized chorusing behavior in acoustical insects. In *Insects, Science, and Society,* ed. D. Pimentel, 35–77. New York: Academic Press.

Austad, S.N., Thornhill, R. 1986. Female reproductive variation in a nuptial-feeding spider, *Pisaura mirabilis. Bull. Brit. Arachnol. Soc.* 7: 48–52.

Bateman, A.J. 1948. Intra-sexual selection in *Drosophila. Heredity* 2: 349–368.

Bell, P.D. 1979. Acoustic attraction of herons by crickets. *J. N.Y. Ent. Soc.* 87: 126–127.

_____. **1980a.** Multimodal communication by the black-horned tree cricket, *Oecanthus nigricornis* (Walker) (Orthroptera: Gryllidae). *Can. J. Zool.* 58: 1861–1868.

_____. **1980b.** Transmission of vibrations along plant stems: implications for insect communication. *J. N.Y. Soc.* 88: 210–216.

Belwood, J.J., Morris, G.K. 1987. Bat predation and its influence on calling behavior in neotropical katydids. *Science* 238: 64–67.

Birkhead, T.R., Clarkson, K. 1980. Mate selection and precopulatory guarding in *Gammarus pulex. Z. Tierpsychol.* 52: 365–380.

Borgia, G. 1981. Mate selection in the fly, *Scatophaga stercoraria:* female choice in a male-controlled system. *Anim. Behav.* 29: 71–80.

Breen, R.G., Sweet, M.H. 1985. Evidence of insemination of multiple females by the male black widow spider, *Latrodectus mactans* (Araneae, Theridiidae). *J. Arachnol.* 13: 331–335.

Burk, T. 1982. Evolutionary significance of predation on sexually signaling males. *Fla. Ent.* 65: 90–104.

Cade, W.H. 1975. Acoustically orienting parasitoids: fly phonotaxis to cricket song. *Science* 190: 1312–1313.

_____. **1979.** The evolution of alternative male reproductive strategies in field crickets. In *Sexual Selection and Reproductive Competition in Insects,* ed. M.S. Blum, N.A. Blum, 343–379. New York: Academic Press.

————. **1980.** Alternative male reproductive behaviors. *Fla. Ent.* 63: 30–45.

————. **1981a.** Field cricket spacing, and the phonotaxis of crickets and parasitoid flies to clumped and isolated cricket songs. *Z. Tierpsychol.* 55: 365–375.

————. **1981b.** Alternative male strategies: genetic differences in crickets. *Science* 212: 563–564.

————. **1984.** Effects of fly parasitoids on nightly calling duration in field crickets. *Can. J. Zool.* 62: 226–228.

————. **1985.** Insect mating and courtship behaviour. In *Comprehensive Insect Physiology, Biochemistry, and Pharmacology,* vol. 9, *Behaviour,* ed. G.A. Kerkut, L.I. Gilbert, 591–619. Oxford: Pergamon Press.

Cade, W.H., Wyatt, D.R. 1984. Factors affecting calling behaviour in field crickets, *Teleogryllus* and *Gryllus* (age, weight, density, and parasites). *Behaviour* 88: 61–75.

Christenson, T.E. 1984. Alternative reproductive tactics in spiders. *Am. Zool.* 24: 321–332.

Daly, M. 1978. The cost of mating. *Am. Nat.* 112: 771–774.

Darwin, C. 1859. *On the Origin of Species.* London: John Murray.

————. **1871.** *The Descent of Man, and Selection in Relation to Sex.* London: John Murray.

Diesel, R. 1986. Optimal mate searching strategy in the symbiotic spider crab *Inachus phalangium* (Decapoda). *Ethology* 72: 311–328.

Dixon, W.N., Payne, T.L. 1980. Attraction of entomophagous and associate insects of the southern pine beetle to beetle- and host tree-produced volatiles. *J. Georgia Ent. Soc.* 15: 378–389.

Dominey, W.J. 1984. Alternative mating tactics and evolutionarily stable strategies. *Am. Zool.* 24: 385–396.

Eberhard, W.G. 1977. Aggressive chemical mimicry by a bolas spider. *Science* 198: 1173–1175.

————. **1980.** The natural history and behavior of the bolas spider *Mastophora dizzydeani* sp. n. (Araneidae). *Psyche* 87: 143–169.

Edmunds, G.F., Edmunds, C.H. 1980. Predation, climate, and emergence and mating of mayflies. In *Advances in Ephemeroptera Biology.,* ed. J.F. Flannagan, K.E. Marshall, 277–285. New York: Plenum Press.

Elwood, R., Gibson, J., Neil, S. 1987. The amorous *Gammarus:* size assortative mating in *G. pulex. Anim. Behav.* 35: 1–6.

Evans, H.E., O'Neill, K.M. 1988. *The Natural History and Behavior of North American Beewolves.* Ithaca, NY: Comstock Publishing Associates.

Fincke, O.M. 1982. Lifetime mating success in a natural population of the damselfly, *Enallagma hageni* (Walsh) (Odonata: Coenagrionidae). *Behav. Ecol. Sociobiol.* 10: 293–302.

Fowler, H.G., Kochalka, J.N. 1985. New record of *Euphasiopteryx depleta* (Diptera: Tachinidae) from Paraguay: attraction to broadcast calls of *Scapteriscus acletus* (Orthoptera: Gryllotalpidae). *Fla. Ent.* 68: 225–226.

Greenfield, M.D. 1981. Moth sex pheromones: and evolutionary perspective. *Fla. Ent.* 64: 4–17.

Greenwood, P.J., Adams, J. 1987. Sexual selection, size dimorphism, and a fallacy. *Oikos* 48: 106–108.

Gwynne, D.T. 1981. Sexual difference theory: Mormon crickets show role reversal in mate choice. *Science* 213: 779–780.

_____. **1987.** Sex-biased predation and the risky mate-locating behavior of male tick-tock cicadas (Homoptera: Cicadidae). *Anim. Behav.* 35: 571–576.

Gwynne, D.T. Dodson, G.N. 1983. Nonrandom provisioning by the digger wasp, *Palmodes laeviventris* (Hymenoptera: Sphecidae). *Ann. Ent. Soc. Am.* 76: 434–436.

Gwynne, D.T., O'Neill, K.M. 1980. Territoriality in digger wasps results in sex biased predation on males (Hymenoptera: Sphecidae, *Philanthus*). *J. Kansas Ent. Soc.* 53: 220–224.

Gwynne, D.T., Rentz, D.C.F. 1983. Beetles on the bottle: male buprestids mistake stubbies for females (Coleoptera). *J. Aust. Ent. Soc.* 22: 79–80.

Harris, V.E., Todd, J.W. 1980. Male-mediated aggregation of male, female and 5-th instar southern green stink bugs and concomitant attraction of a tachinid parasite, *Trichopoda pennipes. Ent. Exp. Appl.* 27: 117–126.

Jackson, R.R. 1976. Predation as a selection factor in the mating strategy of the jumping spider *Phidippus johnsoni* (Salticidae, Araneae). *Psyche* 83: 243–255.

_____. **1979.** Comparative studies of *Dictyna* and *Mallos* (Araneae, Dictynidae) II. The relationship between courtship, mating, aggression and cannibalism in species with differing types of social organization. *Revue Arachnol.* 2: 103–132.

_____. **1980.** Cannibalism as a factor in the mating strategy of the jumping spider *Phidippus johnsoni* (Araneae, Salticidae). *Bull. Brit. Arachnol. Soc.* 5: 129–133.

Jackson, R.R., Smith, S.E. 1978. Aggregations of *Mallos* and *Dictyna* (Araneae, Dictynidae): population characteristics. *Psyche* 85: 65–80.

Koenig, W.D., Albano, S.S. 1985. Patterns of territoriality and mating success in the white-tailed skimmer *Plathemis lydia* (Odonata: Anisoptera). *Am. Midl. Nat.* 114: 1–12.

Krebs, J.R., Davies, N.B., eds. 1984. *Behavioral Ecology: An Evolutionary Approach.* Oxford: Blackwell Scientific Publications.

Lawrence, W.S. 1982. Sexual dimorphism in between and within patch movements of a monophagous insect: *Tetraopes* (Coleoptera: Cerambycidae). *Oecologia* 53: 245–250.

Lloyd, J.E. 1971. Bioluminescent communication in insects *Ann. Rev. Ent.* 16: 97–122.

_____. **1975.** Aggressive mimicry in *Photuris* fireflies: signal repertoires by femmes fatales. *Science* 187: 452–453.

_____. **1980.** Male *Photuris* fireflies mimic sexual signals of their females' prey. *Science* 210: 669–671.

_____. **1984a.** Occurrence of aggressive mimicry in fireflies. *Fla. Ent.* 67: 368–376.

_____. **1984b.** Evolution of a firefly flash code. *Fla. Ent.* 67: 228–239.

Lloyd, J.E., Wing, S.R. 1983. Nocturnal aerial predation of fireflies by light-seeking fireflies. *Science* 222: 634–635.

McCauley, D.E., Lawson, E.C. 1986. Mating reduces predation on male milkweed beetles. *Am. Nat.* 127: 112–117.

McCauley, D.E., Ott, J.R., Stine, A., McGrath, S. 1981. Limited dispersal and its effect on population structure in the milkweed beetle *Tetraopes tetraophthalmus. Oecologia* 51: 145–150.

Mangold, J.R. 1978. Attraction of *Euphasiopteryx ochracea, Corethrella* sp. and gryllids to broadcast songs of the southern mole cricket. *Fla. Ent.* 61: 57–61.

Mitchell, W.C., Mau, R.L. 1971. Response of the female southern green stink bug and its parasite, *Trichopoda pennipes,* to male stink bug pheromones. *J. Econ. Ent.* 64: 856–859.

Moore, S.D. 1987. Male-biased mortality in the butterfly *Euphydryas editha:* a novel cost of mate acquisition. *Am. Nat.* 130: 306–309.

Moore, T.E. 1973. Acoustical communication in insects. In *Introductory Entomology,* ed. V.J. Tipton, syllabus: 307–323, plus tape and slides. Provo, Utah: Brigham Young University Press.

Morris, G.K. 1980. Calling display and mating behaviour of *Copiphora rhinoceros* Pictet (Orthoptera: Tettigoniidae) *Anim. Behav.* 28: 42–51.

Morris, G.K., Beier, M. 1982. Song structure and description of some Costa Rican katydids (Orthoptera: Tettigoniidae) *Trans. Am. Ent. Soc.* 108: 287–314.

Naylor, C., Adams, J. 1987. Sexual dimorphism, drag constraints and male performance in *Gammarus duebeni* (Amphipoda). *Oikos* 48: 23–27.

O'Neill, K.M., Evans, H.E. 1981. Predation on conspecific males by females of the beewolf *Philanthus basilaris* Cresson (Hymenoptera: Sphecidae). *J. Kansas Ent. Soc.* 54: 553–556.

Otte, D. 1974. Effects and functions in the evolution of signaling systems. *Ann. Rev. Ecol. Syst.* 5: 385–417.

_____. **1977.** Communication in Orthoptera. In *How Animals Communicate,* ed. T.A. Sebeok, 334–361. Bloomington: Indiana University Press.

Parker, G.A. 1970. Sperm competition and its evolutionary consequences in the insects. *Biol. Rev.* 45: 525-567.

_____. **1984.** Sperm competition and the evolution of animal mating strategies. In *Sperm Competition and the Evolution of Animal Mating Systems.* ed. R.L. Smith, 1-60. New York: Academic Press.

Quinn, J.S., Sakaluk, S.K. 1986. Prezygotic male reproductive effort in insects: why do males provide more than sperm? *Fla. Ent.* 69: 84-94.

Robertson, H.M. 1985. Female dimorphism and mating behaviour in a damselfly, *Ischnura ramburi:* females mimicking males. *Anim. Behav.* 33: 805-809.

Ross, K., Smith, R.L. 1979. Aspects of the courtship behavior of the black widow spider, *Latrodectus hesperus* (Araneae: Therididdae), with evidence for the existence of a contact sex pheremone. *J. Arachnol.* 7: 69-77.

Sakaluk, S.K. 1984. Male crickets feed females to ensure complete sperm transfer. *Science* 223: 609-610.

_____. **1985.** Spermatophore size and its role in the reproductive behaviour of the cricket, *Gryllodes supplicans* (Orthoptera: Gryllidae). *Can. J. Zool.* 63: 1652-1656.

_____. **1987.** Reproductive behaviour of the decorated cricket, *Gryllodes supplicans* (Orthoptera: Gryllidae): calling schedules, spatial distribution, and mating. *Behaviour* 100: 202-225.

Sakaluk, S.K., Belwood, J.J. 1984. Gecko phonotaxis to cricket calling song: a case of satellite predation. *Anim. Behav.* 32: 659-662.

Sibly, R.M., Smith, R.H., eds. 1985. *Behavioural Ecology: Ecological Consequences of Adaptive Behaviour.* Oxford: Blackwell Scientific Publications.

Simmons, L.W. 1986. Female choice in the field cricket *Gryllus bimaculatus* (De Geer). *Anim. Behav.* 34: 1463-1470.

Sivinski, J. 1980. The effects of mating on predation in the stick insect *Dipheromera veliei* Walsh (Phasmatodea: Heteronemiidae). *Ann. Ent. Soc. Am.* 553-556.

_____. **1983.** Predation and sperm competition in the evolution of coupling durations, particularly in the stick insect *Diapheromera veliei.* In *Orthopteran Mating Systems: Sexual Competition in a Diverse Group of Insects,* ed. D.T. Gwynne, G.K. Morris, 147-162. Boulder, Col.: Westview Press.

Soper, R.S., Shewell, G.E., Tyrell, D. 1976. *Colcondamyia auditrix* Nov. sp. (Diptera: Sarcophagidae), a parasite which is attracted by the mating song of its host, *Okanagana rimosa* (Homoptera: Cicadidae). *Can. Ent. 108: 61-68.*

Spangler, H.G. 1984. Silence as a defense against predatory bats in two species of calling insects. *Southwest. Nat.* 29: 481-488.

Speith, H.T. 1974. Mating behavior and evolution of the Hawaiian *Drosophila.* In *Genetic Mechanisms of Speciation in Insects,* ed. M.J.D. White, 94–101. Sydney: Australia and New Zealand Book Co.

Sullivan, R.T. 1981. Insect swarming and mating. *Fla. Ent.* 64: 44–65.

Thornhill, R. 1976a. Sexual selection and paternal investment in insects. *Am. Nat.* 110: 153–163.

─────. **1976b.** Sexual selection and nuptial feeding behavior in *Bittacus apicalis* (Insecta: Mecoptera). *Am. Nat.* 110: 529–548.

─────. **1978.** Some arthropod predators and parasites of adult scorpionflies (Mecoptera). *Environ. Ent.* 7: 714–716.

─────. **1979.** Adaptive female-mimicking behavior in a scorpionfly. *Science* 205: 412–414.

─────. **1981.** *Panorpa* (Mecoptera: Panorpidae) scorpionflies: systems for understanding resource-defense polygyny and alternative male reproductive efforts. *Ann. Rev. Ecol. Syst.* 12: 355–386.

Trivers, R.L. 1972. Parental investment and sexual selection. In *Sexual selection and the Descent of Man: 1871–1971,* ed. B. Campbell, 136–179. Cambridge: Harvard University Press.

Tuttle, M.D., Ryan, M.J. 1981. Bat predation and the evolution of frog vocalizations in the neotropics. *Science* 214: 677–678.

Tuttle, M.D., Ryan, M.J., Belwood, J.J. 1985. Acoustical resource partitioning by two species of phyllostomid bats (*Trachops cirrhosus* and *Tonatia sylvicola*). *Anim. Behav.* 33: 1369–1371.

Walker, T.J. 1964. Experimental demonstration of a cat locating orthopteran prey by the prey's calling song. *Fla. Ent.* 47: 163–165.

─────. **1979.** Calling crickets (*Anurogryllus arboreus*) over pitfalls: females, males, and predators. *Environ. Ent.* 8: 441–443.

─────. **1986.** Monitoring the flights of field crickets (*Gryllus* supp.) and a tachinid fly (*Euphasiopteryx ochracea*) in north Florida. *Fla. Ent.* 69: 678–685.

Waltz, E.C., Wolf, L.L. 1984. By Jove:: Why do alternative mating tactics assume so many different forms? *Am. Zool.* 24: 333–343.

Ward, P.I. 1983. Advantages and a disadvantage of large size for male *Gammarus pulex. Behav. Ecol. Sociobiol.* 14: 69–76.

─────. **1984.** The effects of size on the mating decisions of *Gammarus pulex* (Crustacea, Amphipoda). *Z. Tierpsychol.* 64: 174–184.

─────. **1986.** A comparative field study of the breeding behaviour of a stream and a pond population of *Gammarus pulex* (Amphipoda). *Oikos* 46: 29–36.

_____. **1987.** Sexual selection and body size in *Gammarus pulex:* a reply to Greenwood and Adams. *Oikos* 48: 108–109.

White, D.J. 1983. Predation of *Prosimulium mixtum/fuscum* (Diptera: Simuliidae) copulating pairs by *Formica* ants (Hymenoptera: Formicidae). *J. N.Y. Ent. Soc.* 91: 90–91.

Williams, G.C. 1966. *Adaptation and Natural Selection.* Princeton, N.J.: Princeton University Press.

Wing, S.R. 1984. Female monogamy and male competition in *Photinus collustrans* (Coleoptera: Lampyridae). *Psyche* 91: 153–160.

_____. **1988.** Cost of mating for female insects: risk of predation in *Photinus collustrans* (Coleoptera: Lampyridae). *Am. Nat.* 131: 139–142.

Wood, D.L. Browne, L.E., Bedard, W.D., Tilden, P.E. Silverstein, R.M., Rodin, J.O. 1968. Response of *Ips confusus* to synthetic sex pheromones in nature. *Science* 159: 1373–1374.

Zeh, D.W., Smith, R.L. 1985. Paternal investment by terrestrial arthropods. *Am. Zool.* 25: 785–805.

PART 2

Predatory Strategies and Tactics

David L. Evans

To survive and reproduce, predators must successfully discover and obtain prey. To do so they must not only possess the physical attributes necessary to catch and overcome prey, but they must also possess a complement of strategies and behaviors for optimizing the size and number of prey caught. Some predators, such as aardvarks, pangolins, echidnas, and tamanduas have become extreme specialists that feed on only one specialized type of prey, in this case termites and ants. Other predators, such as common shrews, coyotes, and toads, are broad generalists that feed on almost any large or small animal that they can capture and overpower. Many predators exhibit prey preferences somewhere between these two extremes—they specialize in catching certain classes and sizes of prey preferentially to others. Common examples of predators with intermediate breadths of food niches include some orb-weaving spiders that specialize on flying insects of certain size ranges and of general taxonomic categories, and sand wasps such as the beewolves that prey only on bees and some other Hymenoptera.

To be successful, predators must have effective strategies for locating appropriate prey and tactics for capturing and consuming the prey once found. These strategies often are evolutionarily tailored to specific situations. Spiders, for example, are a group frequently neglected as a significant selection force in biological systems. This may be a consequence of the general misbelief that predation by spiders is largely a matter of chance. As discussed by Uetz this often is not the situation. Spiders select site locations for webs, web sizes, shapes, and stickiness, to mention a few variables that affect the nature and rate of prey capture.

Robinson views the whole area of predation and prey strategies from a different perspective. As a result of the evolutionary events occurring during the proverbial "cat-and-mouse" game played by predators and prey, selection pressure strongly favors the development of predator memory and intelligence. He cogently argues that, especially in the moist tropics, those predators that have greater intelligence will be more successful and will pass more genes to subsequent generations. Thus, environmental complexity is the cradle of intelligence in predators.

Birds are among the most studied and best understood of predators. They are diurnally active, have extremely keen eyesight, and are warm blooded, fast, and agile. Schuler discusses birds and the clear input they have on prey distribution and prey antipredator adaptations.

Prey Selection in Web-Building Spiders and Evolution of Prey Defenses

George W. Uetz

Introduction

Spiders have long been known to be among the major predators of insects. They are generally thought to be polyphagous in their diet, and studies have shown that most spiders feed on a wide variety of prey. For this reason, their importance as controlling influences on insect populations has been debated (Riechert 1974b; Riechert and Lockley 1984), and they have been largely ignored as potential pest control agents. The polyphagous habits of spiders might also suggest that they are incapable of putting any significant selection pressure on insect populations, and thus, they should contribute only diffusely to the development of antipredation strategies of insects. But the variety of behaviors exhibited by insects for avoiding or escaping from spider webs also suggests that predation by web-building spiders is an important selective force.

As part of the symposium on insect defense strategies, I was asked to consider the role of spiders in the evolution of insect antipredator strategies. This is not an easy task, because the literature is widely scattered and often does not directly address the question. Recently, a number of excellent reviews on aspects of spider web building and predatory strategies have appeared, and readers are directed to them for greater detail than is possible here (Riechert and Luczak 1982; Stowe 1986; Nentwig 1987). This review will mainly concern the web-building spiders, since more is known about their prey choices, and they appear to figure more prominently in the evolution of insect antipredator defense. In order to understand insect defenses against spiders, it will first be necessary to examine several aspects of spider prey selection and to find potential points of contact between spiders and their prey. In this way, it should be possible to see how spiders exert predation pressure on insect populations and how insects might evolve strategies to avoid or escape predation by spiders. Second, I will examime the prey selection process for an orb-weaving spider, *Microthena gracilis,* which has been the subject of research by several of my students and myself. Finally, I will consider some recent examples of studies of ploy and counterploy in the evolution of insect defenses against spiders.

Prey Selection in Web-Building Spiders

The effectiveness of spiders as predators of insects and the role of spiders in shaping insect antipredation strategies depend greatly on the degree to which spiders possibly can and actually do specialize on prey types. Web-building spiders are "sit-and-wait" predators, and would not be expected to exhibit much prey specialization. Once a suitable location is found and a web constructed, the spider remains stationary, waiting for prey. Optimal foraging theory predicts that web-building spiders should specialize in habitat, not prey type, and that their dietary choices should be guided by opportunism alone. Some workers have even viewed these spiders as passive filter feeders, consuming prey in proportion to the numbers hitting the web. However, recent research has shown that many spiders, especially web builders, exhibit considerable dietary specialization (see Riechert and Luczak 1982; Stowe 1986; Nentwig 1987).

It would appear, at least at first, that web-building spiders would have little choice in determining what kinds of insects fall into their webs. A closer look reveals that they have a great deal of control over what they catch, since the type of prey captured may be influenced by web location, web structure, and prey attack strategies. It is obvious that, in each of these cases, the degree of precision with which spiders select their prey may determine the intensity of selection pressure on insect populations. If enough members of these populations fall prey to spiders as the result of some aspect of web location or web structure, for example, then there should be sufficient impetus for the evolution of defense strategies on the part of the insects.

The prey selection process in web-building spiders can be separated into three distinct phases: (1) selection of web site and construction of a web; (2) waiting for prey to be caught in the web (in this phase, the web is, in a sense, passively selecting the prey for the spider); and, (3) attack and capture of prey caught in the web. In each of these phases, opportunities exist for spiders to make choices and thus narrow the range of prey types captured. If this process does occur, then these phases also represent points of contact in the evolutionary struggle between predator and prey populations where opportunities for insects to evolve means of escaping predation may lie.

WEB SITE SELECTION

Criteria used by spiders in choosing sites for webs include aspects of the physical environment (temperature, moisture, solar radiation, wind), the architecture of the web site (vegetation structure, availability of supports, retreats, etc.), and the availability of prey. Exactly how spiders assess the quality of a web site is not completely understood, although there is evidence that they use a variety of cues to guide them in the process, including the activity of prey insects or cues that might indicate that activity.

Studies of web site selection by spiders have revealed that many spiders have remarkably precise microhabitat preferences, and many species show strong associations with vegetation types or particular plant species (Barnes 1955; Duffey 1962, 1966; Luczak 1963; Riechert and Reeder 1972). In most of these studies, the most important criterion mentioned is the structure of the vegetation, which raises an important question: is the architecture of a web site a proximate cue to an important limiting factor like microclimate or prey availability, or is it a limiting factor in itself (see Uetz 1989)? There are many examples in the literature in which the architecture of a particular web site clearly relates to the structure of the web itself (Duffey 1966; Riechert and Cady 1984; Riechert and Gillespie 1986). Certain webs can only "fit" into spaces surrounded by a particular configuration of structural supports like branches or leaves. However, in some cases, proximate cues provided by vegetation structure may indicate the degree of stability of web anchor supports in the wind (Eberhard 1971). In still other cases, the presence of flowering vegetation may influence pollinator activity, and thereby indicate a high prey availability site (Riechert 1976; Riechert and Gillespie 1986).

Many workers have viewed the web site selection process as one of trial and error on the part of the spider: spiders locate webs at random, then stay or leave (or survive or die at a site) depending on success at prey capture (Riechert and Gillespie 1986). When web-building spiders locate in a site that provides them with an abundance of prey, they stay for longer periods of time (Gillespie 1981; Hodge 1984, 1987). Turnbull (1964) found that cobweb spiders abandon webs after a day or two if the rate of prey capture is too low, and "search" for prey by rebuilding webs elsewhere. Released into a vacant room, all the spiders wound up in areas with higher success rates (around a window where insects were drawn to light) and remained there. Similarily, others have reported an "aggregational response" of spiders (Readshaw 1973) by which numerous spider webs accumulate in areas of exceptionally high prey density around lights or other prey-rich locations like garbage dumps (Dabrowska-Prot et al. 1973; Heiber 1984; Rypstra 1983, 1984; Burgess and Uetz 1982). The amount of time a spider waits for prey at a site before abandoning it varies, since web-building spiders differ in their energetic investment in webs depending on the type of web they build. Janetos 1982a,b compared the "giving-up time" for orb weavers (Araneidae) and sheet line weavers (Linyphiidae), and found that orb weavers abandoned web sites sooner than did the linyphiids, a behavior which he attributes to the smaller silk investment that orb weavers have in their webs. Since orb weavers economize on silk—in the design of the web, and by ingestion of the web at the end of a day (web proteins are resorbed and reused)—they can become more active foragers by relocating webs whenever prey availability declines.

The most comprehensive studies of web site selection by spiders are those of a desert funnel web spider, *Agelenopsis aperta,* done by Susan Riechert (Riechert et al. 1973; Riechert and Tracy 1975; Riechert 1974a, 1976). She has shown this process to be complicated, involving the interplay of a variety of factors. Choice of microhabitat for these spiders involves a compromise—balancing the constraints of the thermal environment and the availability of insect prey. In many sites, prey are available, but the thermal environment limits the amount of time the spider can spend on the web. Spiders may get around this constraint by changing web orientation, thereby reducing solar exposure and increasing the amount of time spent on the web, which results in greater access to prey (see also Biere and Uetz 1981). Spiders may also exercise an alternative choice by locating a web in a higher prey availability site and by spending less time on the web.

Turnbull (1964) asserts that the search for prey by web-building spiders is essentially random with respect to the prey. Since a spider cannot determine prey availability until it builds a web, it cannot assess the quality of a web site until it has already been chosen. Once "rewarded" with prey, however, the spiders' search behavior becomes nonrandom, and is concentrated around the area of the web. Riechert (in Riechert and Luczak 1982) disagrees; she has found that agelenid spiders can actually assess the prey availability of sites before building a web—by monitoring the vibrations of insects hovering in the air around flowers, dung, and so forth. This view is also supported by Frederick Barth and his colleagues (Barth 1982; Hergenroder and Barth 1983a,b; Reissland and Gorner 1985), whose studies of sensory systems of spiders have shown them capable of such prey detection.

Although specializations for web site are common in spiders, it is not clear to what extent they contribute to specialization on prey. Studies of spider prey, either with artificial spider webs and other sticky traps or with direct observation, have shown that specific microhabitats may support a reduced range of prey types and sizes (Robinson and Robinson 1970; Uetz and Biere 1980; Chacon and Eberhard 1977; Nentwig 1983). For example, Riechert and Cady (1984) have demonstrated that web-building spiders occupying different microhabitats only inches apart on sandstone cliff faces in the Cumberland Mountains of Tennessee have access to very different prey. Species building webs in crevices on the cliff face itself (*Achaearanea tepidariorum,* a theridiid, and *Coelotes montanus,* an agelenid) catch mainly crawling insects like crickets and beetles. Orb weavers (*Araneus cavaticus*) building webs attached to the overhanging ledges just off the cliff face capture mainly Lepidoptera, which flutter in the vicinity of the cliff face below the ledges, but never touch the surface. An even more extreme example of this phenomenon may be seen among the spiders that selectively locate their webs in sites that are emergence or transit routes for insects, such as trails leading to and from ant colonies, animal burrows, tree holes, or pitcher plants. The question is whether the choice of these habitats is guided by a preference, on the part of the spider, for the prey species found in those sites. It is well known that black widow spiders (*Latrodectus mactans*) once were very common in outhouses and built webs beneath the seat hole, where calliphorid and muscid flies emerged from the septic pit below. Undoubtedly the limited breadth of diet in these spiders was to a large extent determined by the location of their web. However, it is not known whether the choice of habitat in these spiders was determined by the availability of those specific prey insects.

In a few cases, it has been demonstrated that some spiders selectively locate their webs in microhabitats which provide a specific kind of prey. *Tetragnatha montana,* an orb weaver found in Poland and eastern Europe, feeds mainly on mosquitoes (Dabrowska-Prot and Luczak 1968; Dabrowska-Prot et al. 1968; Luczak 1970). Both the habitat choice (herb stratum of wet alder forests) and the diel activity pattern of this species are closely tied to the occurrence and activity of the preferred prey. An ant specialist, *Steatoda fulva* (Theridiidae), builds its web at the entrances to ant mounds. Höldobler (1970) noted that changes in web location by this spider were associated with ant usage of that particular entrance: when ants very quickly ceased using the entrance in response to spider predation, the spiders moved to another. *Dinopis longipes,* an ogre-faced spider (Dinopidae) from tropical forests in Panama, has "portable" webs, which are held between the tarsi of the first two pairs of legs. According to Robinson (1977b) these spiders hang suspended on silk lines above leaf-cutter ant trails and drop their webs onto the unsuspecting ants below, thereby sweeping individual ants off their feet (and avoiding attack by the other colony members).

In many studies of the community organization of web-building spiders, it has been suggested that coexistence among species within a guild or between guilds is facilitated by interspecific differences in prey utilization (Enders 1974; Uetz et al. 1978). Apparently, a combination of aspects of spider foraging—microhabitat, web location, web structure, spider morphology, and behavior—interact, resulting in species specializing to some degree on different prey sizes or taxa, which serves to reduce competition (Luczak 1963; Kajak 1965; Uetz et al. 1978; Olive 1980). However, inferences from studies of coexisting species are not supported by recent experimental studies. Several attempts to provide evidence of competition or differential prey utilization in coexisting spider species have failed (Horton and Wise 1983; Wise and Barata 1983; Wise 1984). Further study is needed to understand the relationship of web location and habitat choice with prey selection in spiders.

It is clear that in most habitats insects have to contend with an array of spider predators. Despite the differences in the locations of spiders' webs, from the victims' point of view they have much in common —they are, after all, traps for insects, and it is easy to see how adaptations to avoid spider webs might come about. At this primary point of contact between spiders and their prey, it is probable that selection pressure from predation is diffuse, and a more generalized antipredation strategy on the part of insects would seem to be the most effective. Insects capable of detecting or recognizing spider silk and of avoiding webs altogether will, for the most part, escape being eaten by spiders. Obviously, it has also been incumbent on many spiders to make their webs less detectable, more efficient prey traps. This ploy and counterploy nature of insect defensive adaptations to spider webs leads to a consideration of the next point of contact between predator and prey—the capture of insects by the webs of spiders.

CAPTURE OF INSECTS BY SPIDER WEBS

A number of studies have examined the prey captured by spiders and/or their webs, and many have compared the captured prey with the insects available in the environment (Bilsing 1920; Turnbull 1962; Cherrett 1964; Kajak 1965; Robinson and Robinson 1970, 1973; Riechert and Tracy 1975; Chacon and Eberhard 1980; Uetz and Biere 1980; Olive 1980; Nentwig 1980, 1983; Shelly 1983; Riechert and Cady 1984). The most common way such comparisons are made is by observation of actual prey captures (or examination of prey in webs) and the "potential prey" captured by traps that in some way mimic spider webs (sticky traps, windowpane traps, etc.). Although there is disagreement about what kind of trapping method most accurately assesses the prey actually available to spiders (see Uetz and Biere 1980; Chacon and Eberhard 1980), all these studies suggest that the range of prey taken by spiders demonstrates some degree of selectivity. Most insect groups are underrepresented, and a select few are overrepresented in spider captures when compared to those potentially available for capture. Specificity in prey captured may relate to either prey size or taxa, or both, and varies between as well as within spider taxa.

An important question that many of these studies have addressed concerns the role of the spiders' web in the selection of prey, and why some prey insects are trapped more or less efficiently than others. Most workers agree that the process by which insects fall prey to spiders in their webs is neither random nor passive. For two reasons, the webs of spiders capture a nonrandom, select subsample of the insects that contact them: (1) insects vary in their ability to avoid webs or to escape from them once caught; and (2) web design and function favor capture of specific prey types and sizes.

To a large extent, the probability of encounter of a spider web by an insect will be determined by the perceptual abilities and behavior of the insect (Turnbull 1960; Riechert and Luczak 1982; Craig 1986). Many insects, particularly the Diptera and Hymenoptera, have a combination of good eyesight and flight navigation skills that allows them to detect and avoid webs. Many workers have reported seeing these insects change course rapidly to avoid encounter with webs (Turnbull 1960; Rypstra 1979), or skillfully fly through the threads (Turnbull 1960; Nentwig 1982). It has been suggested that many spiders' nocturnal web-building behavior, particularly in the tropics, is an adaptation to compensate for the visibility of webs in daytime (Rypstra 1979, 1982). Rypstra (1982) compared the efficiency of three different web types (tangle webs, sheet webs, and orb webs) at capturing approaching *Drosophila.* She found that thread density affected both the visibility of the web and the retention of prey. Densely meshed webs (tangle webs) effectively detained flies once contacted but were more visible and thus were more frequently avoided. Orb webs were less visible yet highly effective at detaining insects because of the combination of lower thread density and the adhesive properties of the web. Recent work by Catherine Craig and her colleagues (Craig et al. 1985; Craig 1986) has suggested that the optical properties of some orb webs tend to reduce visibility, especially in low-light and varying background conditions. One of the most important visual cues enabling well-sighted insects to avoid spider webs is background contrast. The tendency of orb webs to oscillate at low wind velocities may obscure contrast by moving the web in and out of the insects visual plane of focus, reducing detection. Craig (1986, 1987) and Rypstra (1982) point out that there may be trade-offs between visibility reduction and impact absorption properties of webs (i.e., stronger, impact-absorbing webs are more visible, and less visible webs tend to be more fragile), and that these properties have influenced the evolution of diverse foraging strategies in araneoid spiders (see Stowe 1986; Shear 1986).

Once the web is contacted, the probability of capture or escape will be influenced by a number of characteristics of the insect and properties of the web. Nentwig (1982, 1987) has conducted a comprehensive survey of insects' escape from spider webs; in his surveys he has considered the flight speed of insects, their impact energy upon encountering an orb web (Araneidae), and their subsequent behavior if ensnared. He found that larger, heavier insects (such as Coleoptera, Hymenoptera, Orthoptera) could crash through webs without being captured. Most of the escaping insects exhibited a combination of behavioral and morphological means of extricating themselves. Many smaller Coleoptera, Hymenoptera, and Brachycera were highly active, and most were capable of struggling free within five seconds. Nematocera, Orthoptera, and many Heteroptera alternated brief periods of active struggling with long pauses of inactivity, in this way avoiding triggering the spider's predatory behavior. Some prey (Bibionidae, Rhagionidae, Coccinellidae, Curculionidae, Chrysomelidae) took an alternative strategy, feigning death, which for many was reasonably effective. Nentwig also examined the importance of wing size and morphological structure on entanglement in webs. In general, larger-winged, lighter-bodied insects (Tipulidae, Chrysopidae, Chironomidae,

Odonata) were easily entangled and retained by webs, and were therefore more likely to fall prey to spiders. In contrast, some larger-winged insects possess wing surface characteristics like fatty oils (Blattidae) and wing scales (Lepidoptera, Trichoptera) that make possible a quick escape from the adhesive threads in spider webs. The capacity of moths and butterflies to escape from spider webs as the result of wing scales has also been demonstrated by Eisner et al. (1964). From these studies, as well as from Craig's work (1986, 1987), it can be seen that all insects are not equally likely to be caught by spiders in their webs, and that this inequality may contribute in part to apparent specialization by spiders on certain prey types. It also represents varying degrees of success of adaptations on the part of insects to avoid predation by spiders.

The structure of spiders' webs may also contribute a degree of passive selectivity for prey, and many consider the differences in web types among spider families to be adaptations for the capture of specific prey types (Riechert and Luczak 1982; Stowe 1986; Nentwig and Heimer 1987). It has been suggested that the evolution of differences in web structure among spiders is a means of reducing competition by fostering differences in prey utilization (Bristowe 1941; Kaston 1966; Kullmann 1972; Levi 1978). The degree to which even slight differences in the fine structure and orientation of webs can influence prey captured is evident in the experimental studies of Chacon and Eberhard (1980), who used artificial sticky monofilament nylon web traps of different thread densities, orientations, and amounts of adhesive. They found that all of these aspects of web design influenced the types of prey captured. A number of studies have demonstrated that different web types capture different prey, although most have been conducted under somewhat limited circumstances, in widely different habitats, and at different times (Turnbull 1960; Kajak 1965; Dabrowska-Prot and Luczak 1968; Robinson and Robinson 1970, 1973). Few studies actually provide a comparison of species with different web structures in the same microhabitats at the same time. Riechert and Cady (1984) found differences in prey types captured by orb weavers (Araneidae), sheetline weavers (Agelenidae), and cobweb weavers (Therididdae), but these differences were more attributable to web location and prey behavior than to web structure itself. Wise and Barata (1983) compared two orb weavers (*Mecynogea lemniscata* and *Metepeira labyrinthea*) whose webs are grossly different in overall structure and orientation yet which occupy nearly identical microhabitats. They found no significant differences in the size or taxa of prey captured by these species, from which they conclude that web structural differences between species have little effect on differences in prey utilization. Uetz et al. (1978), however, compared the prey captured by two syntopic, congeneric orb weavers (*Argiope aurantia* and *A. trifasciata*) and found them to show differences in prey attributable to web structure differences. These two very similar species, which differ only slightly in web placement but show marked differences in web mesh size, feed on significantly different sizes of prey (the species with the larger mesh web feeds on the largest prey). These findings are supported by experimental studies with artificial sticky web traps of identical size, but different mesh size, located side by side in the same habitats (Hartsock 1983). Coarse-mesh webs, with monofilament lines three millimeters apart, consistently trapped and retained significantly larger insects than fine-mesh webs with lines one millimeter apart.

Obviously, the structure of spider webs varies among species and higher taxa, and to some extent this variation may contribute to specialization on different prey types. Typically, selection might be expected to favor insects avoiding, slipping through, or breaking through webs if they functioned only as passive aerial filters. But another set of factors may come into play when the dynamic properties of webs are considered. There is evidence that the structural properties of webs relating to thread density may affect not only filtering, but also impact resistance, allowing in some cases for the capture of heavier or stronger prey (Eberhard 1986). Aspects of web structure may also allow the selective trapping of insects with certain flight characteristics. Orb webs with extensible sticky threads and flexible radii tend to move slightly in the wind, trapping hovering flies that normally would avoid capture (Craig et al. 1985). Webs of finer mesh in general would appear to trap smaller insects, but may also selectively retain certain larger prey sizes for a long enough time for the spider to attack (Uetz and Biere 1980; Uetz and Hartsock 1987). A number of studies of unusually modified web types, particularly among the orb-weaving families (Araneidae, Uloboridae, and Theridiosomatidae) and the Theridiidae in the American tropics, suggest that many spiders have evolved unique web designs adapted for the capture of specific prey types or for countering the defenses of insects against spider webs (Robinson and Robinson 1975; Robinson 1977b; Eberhard 1975, 1980; Lubin et al. 1978; Lubin and Dorugl 1982; Eberhard 1986; Stowe 1986; Shear 1986; Lubin 1986). These will be discussed in a later section of this paper.

CAPTURE OF INSECTS ON THE WEB BY SPIDERS

The capture of insects by spiders on the web is also a nonrandom process; that is, spiders have the ability to choose whether or not to attack, ignore, or reject prey caught in their webs. Behavioral choices made by spiders, at this level of contact are made on the basis of prey size, activity, and palatability, and are guided by the constraints of optimal foraging rules (Riechert and Luczak 1982). When a generalized sequence of spider prey capture behavior (Riechert and Luczak 1982) is examined, there are clearly several stages at which selection is known to occur. The behavioral strategies of insects which affect the choices exercised by spiders at these points will influence their chances of escape.

The first choice a spider has when a potential prey item becomes ensnared in the web is whether or not to begin the prey capture sequence. The web provides information about the prey—its size, its location in the web, its level of activity, and perhaps other information, in the form of vibrations (Suter 1978; Barth 1982). It is probable that the properties of these vibrational stimuli influence the decisions made by spiders (Suter 1978). If the information provided by vibrations suggests that the prey item is of an acceptable size and poses no danger, spiders at this point may proceed to locate and approach the prey. However, if the insect is too large or too active, the spider may retreat from it. If, on the other hand, the insect is very small or inactive, the spider may ignore it. There are several examples in the literature of how spiders use the information obtained from web vibrations to make decisions about prey approach and attack behavior (Robinson and Olazarri 1971; Jackson 1977; Riechert and Luczak 1982; Reissland and Gorner 1985). In most cases the degree of discrimination shown at this point is variable, and spiders will respond with predatory behavior to a fairly wide range of vibration frequencies (Suter 1978; Barth 1982; Hergenroder and Barth 1983a,b). In one case—the social spider *Mallos gregalis*—specialization is extreme. Burgess (1975) has shown that only vibration frequencies within the range of those produced by an ensnared muscid fly will elicit the predatory behavior of these spiders, which appear to be specialists on dipterans.

It is easy to see that this point in the predatory sequence provides many opportunities for insect antipredation strategies. Many insects, especially the Lepidoptera, have the capacity to escape from the web before the spider begins an attack sequence, and others use a number of strategies to avert capture by avoiding triggering the predatory response of the spider. Nentwig (1982) found that a number of insect groups charactreristically feign death when ensnared by spider webs. This strategy precludes a quick escape, but may "buy time" for the insect by increasing the chance that the spider will ignore a nonstruggling prey item. Some insects, upon becoming caught in a web, alternate long periods of inactivity with brief, violent struggling to free themselves. It is thought that this strategy capitalizes on the fact that in many cases only prolonged, low-amplitude vibrational stimuli provoke an attack by the spider (Hoffmaster and Hays 1977; Nentwig 1982).

Once the spider has determined that the prey are of sufficient size and pose no threat, the next steps in the predatory sequence—orientation, location, and approach—are taken. These may occur in rapid succession (often in less than one second), and the first physical contact with the prey is made. Spiders initially palpate prey with one or more pairs of legs to gain a variety of information about the prey. Spiders may make several choices at this point. If the prey are heavily armored or potentially dangerous, they may be cut out of the web. Depending on the size and activity level of the prey, spiders may use a "bite attack" or a "wrap attack" (Robinson et al. 1969). Smaller prey, or prey with a high probability of escape (e.g., scale-winged insects like Lepidoptera) are usually bitten first, and larger and more active prey are immobilized by wrapping them with silk. Robinson (1969) and Robinson and Olazarri (1971) have shown that orb weavers in the genera *Argiope* and *Nephila* can detect the presence of scales on wings of lepidopterans and change their attack strategy accordingly.

The palatability of insects is usually determined when the first bite is delivered. The chemical defenses of insects against predators come into play at this point, and work with variable success against spiders (Eisner 1965; Carrel and Eisner 1984; Nentwig 1987). Spiders have been observed to quickly reject unpalatable insects, drop them from the web, and groom their chelicerae to remove the toxic defense secretions (Robinson and Robinson 1973). Studies with *Nephila clavipes* (L.) (Vasconcellos-Neto and Lewinson 1984) have shown that spiders discriminate between a number of palatable and unpalatable species of butterflies, releasing distasteful species unharmed. Spiders must recognize distastefulness by chemical cues. The presentation of lepidopteran models and mimics shows that visual cues are not involved, and that there is no indication of learning in this process. Since spiders release unpalatable butterflies unharmed but immediately bite and kill others, the selection pressure for chemical as well as visual warning of distastefulness would be strong. Recent studies by Nentwig (1987) have suggested that previous experience with poisoned prey may influence acceptance or rejection of distasteful items, and that spiders may develop "tolerance" for certain toxins. The abilities of spiders to detect, avoid, or tolerate the chemical defenses of insects are not well understood, and represent a topic of potential research.

The constraints on spider decision making at this point involve the balance between the cost of handling the prey item and the return in biomass from the investment of energy in its capture. Turnbull (1973) suggests that the size range of prey attacked by spiders is set at the lower end of the range by a minimum amount of biomass needed to "justify" the energy expended, and at the upper end of the range by limits to handling, probability of escape, and danger to the spider. The profitability of capture will thus determine how much a spider will specialize on particular prey types. If among the prey available some species are easier to capture and/or subdue, or in some way are more likely to provide a high reward for the energy expended, they should be preferred over others (which should be ignored or rejected unless the hunger level dictates otherwise). Nentwig and Wissel (1986) and Nentwig (1987) have demonstrated that spiders trend to capture prey less than or equal to their own size more often than larger insects, with preference maxima between 50 and 80 percent of the spider's size. Departures from this trend include crab spiders and jumping spiders, which tend to capture prey 200 to 300 percent of their size, and social spiders, whose cooperative attack behavior enables them to subdue prey many times their size (Nentwig 1985b; 1987). Riechert (in Riechert and Luczak 1982) has shown that *Agelenopsis* rejects a total of 20.8 percent, and ignores 11.3 percent, of all potential prey, primarily on the basis of profitability factors mentioned above. She also has found that the majority of these "decisions" are made early in the prey capture sequence, and suggests that selection should favor discrimination among prey before much energy is expended in the capture process.

These constraints on spider foraging may also mean that opportunities for insects to escape predation should occur with greater frequency early in the process. The probability of escape would appear to decrease as the spider expends more time and energy in trying to capture the prey. Turnbull (1973) suggests that prey will rarely escape a "determined" attack by a spider.

Prey Selection in Micrathena gracilis

For the past several years, my students (J. Michael Biere and Scott Hartsock) and I have collected data on a spider species which will serve to illustrate the degree of prey selectivity in orb weavers. *Micrathena gracilis* is a common orb weaver (Araneidae) occurring in the eastern deciduous forest region of North American. *Micrathena* occurs solely in large open spaces in the forest understory, where it is exposed to diversity of flying insect prey.*M. gracilis* builds a small (20 centimeter diameter) orb within a relatively large frame (often 1.5 to 2 meters across). This fact suggests that these spiders have a large energy expense in their webs but should have a low encounter probability for all but the most abundant of prey. In addition, *Micrathena* is slow moving and almost clumsy, and usually takes more than three seconds to reach a prey item in its web. Since most insects can escape entanglement in that time (Nentwig 1982), prey capture efficiency should also be low. This species is thus uniquely suited to provide a conservative test of a null hypothesis regarding prey selectivity, because its characteristics suggest that opportunistic predation and extreme generalization of diet are an appropriate strategy.

In an earlier study (Uetz and Biere 1980), the prey caught in several types of web-mimicking traps (windowpane, sticky screen, artificial sticky web) and in a sweep net were compared with prey captured by spiders. It was clear from these data that *M. gracilis* was not taking prey in the proportions encountered. The spiders appear to capture larger flies and hymenopterans at far greater frequencies than they are potentially available. Biere then constructed artificial sticky webs, with size and thread density indentical to that of *M. gracilis,* and hung them in the forest next to live spiders. For several days he sat nearby, watching the insects that flew into and escaped from the natural and artificial webs. He found that both webs retained a different size array of insects than they encountered, and that from this array spiders selected only the largest insects (Uetz and Biere 1980).

FIELD OBSERVATIONS OF PREY CAPTURE

Scott Hartsock's M.S. research also addressed the selectivity question, by examining the fate of insects that encounter the web of *M. gracilis.* Observation of *Micrathena* in the field permitted a comparison of the prey captured by the spider with potential prey items made available to the spider by its web within the forest understory. Because the spider was present, these observations allowed a test of the hypothesis that *Micrathena* actively attacks insects of all size classes sticking to its web in proportion to their rate of encounter.

Adult, female *Micrathena* were observed for a total of 77 web hours (number of webs x hours observed) between 1 August and 10 September 1981. After locating the web(s), the observer sat on a stool 1 to 1.5 meters from the web(s). This distance allowed close observations of even the smallest insects striking the web, but was far enough away so as not to disturb the spider or to attract or repel insects (insect repellent was not worn during observations). Observations took place between 0800 hours and 1800 hours and lasted from one to two hours at a time. Up to three webs could be observed at once if they were clumped within 1 to 2 meters of one another.

When an insect struck the web, its length (estimated by holding a millimeter scale close to the web) and taxon were recorded. The insect's "fate" in the web was then followed. It should be noted that the "fate" of insects already present in the web at the beginning of the observation period was not recorded. This precaution prevented the researcher from overestimating the number of small insects that actually came in contact with webs (larger insects may have contacted the web and escaped while the smaller ones were trapped and remained in the web—and the observer had no way of knowing the former unless he or she was present). An insect that struck any part of the orb was recorded as a HIT. An insect that was retained by the web longer than three seconds was called a STICK (after Rypstra 1981). Any insect that left the web at any time under its own power was termed an ESCAPE. An escape could occur at a number of different points along the predation sequences (see figures 4.1 and 4.2). An ATTACK occurred if the spider came in contact with the insect, usually with its two front legs. An IGNORE was recorded when the spider made no contact with the insect even though it may have oriented itself toward and plucked at the insect in the web. A CAPTURE was recorded when the spider actually had control of the insect in its chelicerae. If the spider voluntarily discarded the insect, a REJECT was recorded. If the spider wrapped the prey item in silk after capture, a WRAP was recorded. Finally, if it fed on the insect during the observation period, a FEED was entered.

Of the 133 insects observed to strike webs, 118 stuck to the web for at least three seconds (for an initial web capture efficiency of 88.7 percent). Of these 118 insects, 66 were actively attacked by the spider, 44 were ignored, and 8 escaped before a "decision" was made. Of those 66 insects actively attacked, 54 were captured, 5 were rejected, and 7 escaped due to mishandling. A total of 38 insects escaped at some point in the predatory sequence (figure 4.1), leading to an overall web capture efficiency of 71.4 percent.

COMPARISON OF PREY CAUGHT BY WEB VERSUS BY SPIDER

A comparison can be made of the insects captured by the web and those captured by a web-mimicking artificial sticky web trap (modified from a design reported by Uetz and Biere 1980). This comparison will

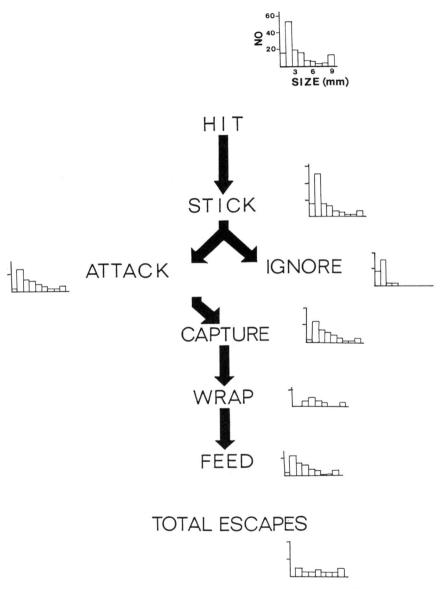

Figure 4.1 The predation sequence of *Micrathena gracilis*.

Table 4.1. Web Selectivity (E_w) Values for Prey Types and Sizes Caught in Webs of *Micrathena gracilis*

	Caught in Spider Web		Caught in Sticky Trap		E_w
	No.	r_i	No.	p_i	
Taxon					
Diptera	89	.669	268	.355	+.307
Hymenoptera	20	.150	338	.448	−.498
Coleoptera	5	.038	48	.064	−.255
Homoptera	4	.030	43	.057	−.310
Thysanoptera	-	.000	21	.028	−1.00
Psocoptera	-	.000	11	.015	−1.00
Hemiptera	-	.000	8	.011	−1.00
Lepidoptera	-	.000	1	.001	−1.00
Other (Unident.)	-	.000	17	.023	−1.00
Size (MM)					
0-2	56	.475	600	.795	−.252
2-4	32	.271	138	.183	+.194
4-6	16	.136	13	.017	+.778
6-8	4	.034	2	.003	+.838
8+	10	.085	2	.003	+.932

reveal if the web of the spider contributes to dietary selectivity. Data from Hartsock's observations and from web traps placed nearby while observations were being made were analyzed using an index of dietary specialization—the "Electivity" index of Ivlev (1961):

$$E = \frac{r_i - p_i}{r_i + p_i}$$

where r_i = proportion of item *i* taken, and p_i = proportion of item *i* available. Values for this index range from + 1.0 (highly preferred to –1.0 (least preferred). For this comparison, the catches of the artificial webs were assumed to estimate the proportions of prey available in each size class or taxon considered.

Results of this comparison indicate that the webs of *Micrathena gracilis* are selective and show electivity for Diptera sized greater than 2 millimeters (table 4.1). However, the majority of insects hitting and then sticking to the web are quite small—53 percent (70 of 133 hits) are 2 millimeters or less in length; and 59 percent (67 of 116 sticks) of the insects sticking to the web are less than 2 millimeters. Therefore, well over half of the insects which encounter the web (and thus available as potential prey

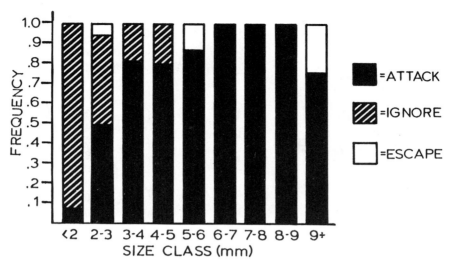

Figure 4.2 Size-frequency distribution of insects attacked or ignored by *Micrathena,* showing the increased frequency of attacks on larger-sized insects.

items) are small insects containing very little biomass per insect. Larger insects are much rarer, but they contain far more biomass per individual. Since the electivity index measures the degree to which prey are preferred in comparison to their availability, the results of the comparison between the web and the trap suggest that the web selectively retains larger prey. This conclusion is supported by the observation that escapes occur in nearly the same proportion for all size classes except for the smallest and the very largest (figure 4.2). Escapes by very small insects (1 to 3 millimeters) can be attributed to almost instantaneous escape after contact with the web. It is possible that these insects are not very fast fliers, but are strong enough to pull free of the web before the chance of attack. On the other hand, 75 percent of the insects larger than 9 millimeters escaped before being attacked, with 50 percent of these insects escaping within three seconds of hitting the web. This is probably due to their faster flight velocities and strength (see Nentwig 1980).

Consequently, *Micrathena* was presented with a preselected array of potential prey items to attack. The spiders were observed to attack a greater proportion of larger insects than smaller ones (figure 4.2). A comparison of prey taken by the spiders with those taken by the web shows evidence of high selectivity (table 4.2). The Ivlev index values are highest for Diptera in the middle range of size classes (4 to 8 millimeters).

The frequency of insects attacked or ignored in each class versus insects sticking in each size class shows that *Micrathena* is not attacking (or ignoring) insects in each size class with the same frequency in which they are encountered. A Kolmogorov-Smirnov test of the difference in the frequency distributions across size classes of those insects sticking to the web and those being attacked by the spider indicates a significant difference (p < .001) in the frequency of attacks by size class. This difference suggests that the spider is ignoring the smaller, more abundant insects sticking to the web and is preferentially attacking the larger yet rarer, insects between 3 and 9 millimeters (table 4.2).

Table 4.2. Spider Selectivity (E_s) Values for Prey Types and Sizes Caught by *Micrathena gracilis*

	Captured By Spider		Caught In Web		E_s
	No.	r_i	No.	p_i	
Taxon					
Diptera	41	.759	89	.669	+.670
Hymenoptera	10	.185	20	.150	−.567
Coleoptera	2	.037	5	.038	−.013
Homoptera	1	.019	4	.030	−.224
Size (MM)					
0-2	20	.370	56	.475	−.124
2-4	16	.296	32	.271	+.044
4-6	13	.241	16	.136	+.279
6-8	2	.037	4	.034	+.042
8+	3	.056	10	.085	−.206

Even though the spider is ignoring a disproportionately higher number of small prey, it is not omitting a large amount of biomass from its diet by doing so. If all of those insects that were ignored were consumed, they would constitute approximately 15 percent of the total biomass available to the spider. It is also probable that the spider consumes these insects at night when it takes down its web (if the insects do not escape during the day). The spider may therefore reap this collective caloric benefit without actively attacking each small insect striking its web during the day. In energetic terms, attacking these smaller insects may cause the spider to expend more energy than it would gain from them, as well as increase its exposure to predation (Schoener 1969). By "wasting its time" with small prey, a spider may even reduce its readiness to capture a more profitable prey type striking another part of the web. *Micrathena* appears to concentrate its efforts on those size classes where the frequency of available biomass is the greatest, not where the frequency of prey is the greatest. This species forages in an optimal manner, by selecting the size classes and taxon that provide the spider with the most energetic reward, given its availability (Uetz and Hartsock 1987).

The predatory sequence of *Micrathena gracilis* (figure 4.2) makes clear that throughout the sequence the spider is presented with many more small insects than it is with large insects. After the web has restrained an insect, the spider will either attack it or ignore it. It has been shown that the spider attacks insects larger than 3 millimeters with a significantly higher frequency that it does those smaller than 3 millimeters, which are ignored most of the time. The term *ignore* implies that the spider actually makes a choice of what it attacks, which is what is implied in this study, and the term has been used by other arachnologists (e.g., Olive 1980; Riechert and Luczak 1982). During the course of observations, spiders did appear to choose whether or not to attack certain insects, most probably on the basis of some sort of vibrational stimuli. For example, the spider was often seen orienting toward the impact area of a small insect with the web, plucking the radii in that area, and even advancing a few millimeters toward the insect, but not attacking it. The impact of the insect may have been enough of a vibrational stimulus to initiate the attack sequence, but the lack of vibration after impact indicated either a very small prey item or no prey item. Suter (1978) found that the impact stimulus was important in initiating the attack behavior of *Cyclosa turbinata*, another forest-dwelling orb weaver. This particular species may be capable of detecting the mass of an insect by its impact vibration, which could be, according to Suter, "a mechanism for discerning the insect's relative food value." This same mechanism could be operating in *Micrathena*.

Riechert and Luczak (1982) suggest that three parameters regarding profitability should be important in the spider's decision to consume (attack) or ignore the prey item: prey type, prey size, and level of hunger. Observations of other species indicate that orb weavers are able to discriminate between prey and alter their attack behavior accordingly. *Argiope argentata* (Robinson and Olazarri 1971) and *Nephila maculata* (Robinson and Robinson 1973, 1976) have been shown to alter their approach to different sizes of prey, moving slowly to larger prey items and quickly to smaller types. For example, *Nephila clavipes* shows a bite-and-back-off behavior only on larger, probably more dangerous prey types (Robinson and Mirick 1971). Both *Argiope argentata* and *A. aemula* discriminate between prey types by using a primitive bite-wrap attack sequence for relatively innocuous but fast-escaping prey, such as Lepdoptera, and a more advanced wrap-bite behavior for stronger, more dangerous prey such as Orthoptera, Coleoptera, and Odonata (Robinson 1969; Robinson and Olazarri 1971; Robinson and Robinson 1976). This innate behavior allows these species to secure prey in such a way as to prevent quick escapes and/or minimize the risk of injury (Robinson and Robinson 1976; Robinson, Mirick, and Turner 1969). *Cyclosa turbinata,* however, exhibits the opposite behavior (Suter 1978), as does *Microthena.* These species are not subjected to the many large, dangerous prey types that the afore-mentioned tropical forest or meadowland species may encounter. Most of the potential prey of both these species are small Hymenoptera and Diptera (as seen in availability estimates in table 4.1), and they pose little threat to the spiders. *Microthena* exhibits the more primitive bite-wrap behavior pattern, which suggests that it should be more efficient in attacking fast-escaping but relatively harmless prey. Prey size is probably a more important criterion in prey selectivity for this species than is prey type. The hunger level of the spider may also play an important role in what the spider may choose to attack, but it is a difficult parameter to control in observational field studies such as this. Spiders are often sub-jected to severe food shortages (Olive 1982) and may switch from being a specialist to a generalist, that is, accept a less preferred prey item because of the paucity of preferred prey types (Pulliam 1974; Emlen 1966).

The degree of selectivity shown by *Microthena gracilis* is surely not as precise as that shown by many of the prey specialists mentioned earlier. However, any specialization should be risky for a spider with its attri-butes, and in this case the risky strategy has paid off, providing this species with an apparently optimal diet. If other web-building spiders, particularly the orb weavers, show similar degrees of specialization in their diets, it is easy to see why certain groups of insects (such as Diptera, Lepidoptera) show adaptations for avoiding or escaping spider webs. The selection pressure put on these insects by spider predation may not be as intense as it would be in a two-species predator-prey system, but it has undoubtedly contributed to the evolution of defensive behavior.

Ploy and Counterploy: Web-Building Spiders and Their Prey

Several recent studies have provided evidence of coevolutionary relationships between spiders and their prey. It is not surprising that two groups of insects that figure prominently in the prey of spiders—Diptera and Lepidoptera—have evolved defenses against being eaten by spiders. What is surprising is that spiders have responded in kind, demonstrating in some cases behaviors that overcome or outwit these defenses.

THE SPIDER AND THE FLY

The common image of a helpless fly trapped in a spider web may not be as accurate as it seems. Apparently, some flies caught in spider webs can use behavioral strategies which give them access to certain avenues of escape. Hays (1976) found that *Musca domestica* uses bouts of intense activity, interspersed with long periods of immobility, as a means of getting around the prey detection and attack behavior sequence of orb weavers. Hoffmaster and Hays (1977) used a simulation model to examine the probability of escape for a fly using different behaviors, and to predict an optimal behavior strategy. The results of this model suggest that flies in spider webs are behaving in a manner suited to increase the probability of escape, and this behavior may vary with the circumstances. The fierce struggle may increase the chance of breaking free, but it must be short enough not to trigger an advance by the spider. The interval between bouts of struggling must also be long enough for the spider to return to a preimpact behavior state. The success of this strategy depends on the ability of the fly to assess the impending behavior of the spider by sensing vibrations in the web. Ironically, flies are able to use the same kind of mechanism spiders use in detecting prey—web vibration—as information critical to their choice of an escape strategy.

A number of species of gall gnats (Cecidomyidae) are associated with spider webs, and can exploit them as both a well-protected resting site and as a source of food (Eberhard 1980). Often, large numbers of these flies will rest on the nonsticky web strands of orb weavers, out of the range of predatory ants and wandering spiders that search twigs and foliage for prey. By remaining motionless as they hang on the silk threads, they do not trigger the predatory behavior of the resident spider. If the spider moves, the flies swiftly release their grip on the line and fly away. Many of these flies are kleptoparasites, stealing unattended prey from the spiders' webs (Sivinski and Stowe 1980). Some spiders have been able to exploit the web exploiters' behavior as a means of getting a meal. A number of Uloborid and Theridiid spiders spin a "web" consisting of a single thread, which is laid out in the vegetation. When flies come to rest upon the thread, the spider slowly pulls the line closer and closer, until it can quickly grab a fly (Eberhard 1979, 1980, 1981; Lubin and Dorugl 1982). There is some evidence that some of these webs contain chemical substances (perhaps pheromone mimics) which actually attract files to land on them (Eberhard 1981).

Two recent studies have demonstrated that flies of the family Tephritidae mimic the agonistic display of jumping spiders as a means of escaping predation by them (Mather and Roitberg 1987; Green et al. 1987). Flies from the two tephritid species studied (*Rhagoletis zephyria* Snow; *Zonosemata vittigera* [Coquillet]) have striped markings on their wings which resemble legs of jumping spiders when held at an angle perpendicular to the substratum or when moved in a waving display. Observations of the salticid spider *Salticus scenicus* (Clerck) stalking *Rhagoletis* (Mather and Roitberg 1987) revealed that spiders cease predatory behavior and run away from flies performing wing displays, much as spiders avoid conspecifics after leg-waving displays. Other flies (*Musca*) and *Rhagoletis* with experimentally ink-blackened wings were attacked as prey. Greene et al. (1987) found similar results in their study of *Zonosemata* and *Phidippus apacheanus.* They experimentally transplanted unmarked wings (from *Musca*) onto *Zonosemata,* and striped (*Zonosemata*) wings onto *Musca* (which does not display to jumping spiders). These experiments showed that both the wing pattern and the wing-waving display are necessary for effective mimicry. Tephritid flies with housefly wings and houseflies with or without striped (tephritid) wings are captured as prey, but displaying tephritids were avoided by jumping spiders. Identical experiments also demonstrated that wing markings and displays do not protect *Zonosemata* from other predatory species (nonsalticid spiders, assassin bugs, mantids, or lizards). These elegant experimental studies demonstrate a high degree of specificity in the evolution of behaviors used in predator evasion by insects, underscoring the importance of spiders as selective agents in some cases.

SPIDERS AND MOTHS

Earlier in this manuscript, reference was made to the role of scales on the wings of lepidopteran and trichopteran insects in allowing escape from the sticky threads of orb webs (Eisner et al. 1964; Eisner 1965). There is interesting evidence that some spiders may have evolved behaviors to offset the effect of these defensive scales. A number of orb weavers, particularly in the genus *Argiope,* show an innate discrimination between scale-winged insects and those without scales (Robinson 1969; Robinson 1976).

This discriminating ability allows them to change their attack strategy when they contact the prey—from a wrap-first to a bite-first behavior—and this change decreases the chance of the moth or butterfly escaping (Robinson and Robinson 1976).

Several orb weavers build a type of web that deviates remarkably from the web structure typical of this group and allows them to capture scale-winged insects. Webs of *Scoloderus, Eustala,* and several other orb weavers make a "ladder" web, (figure 4.3) with vertical extensions of the sticky orb above or below the circumference of the circular catching orb (Robinson and Robinson 1972; Eberhard 1975; Robinson 1977b; Stowe 1986). When a moth strikes the web, it slides down the ladder, leaving scales behind on the sticky silk, until enough are removed that the moth becomes ensnared (Stowe 1986; C.S. Hieber, personal communication). The prey of these species consists largely of nocturnal moths.

One of the most spectacular examples of spider-moth coevolution is seen among "bolas" spiders of the genus *Mastophora* (Eberhard 1977, 1980; Stowe 1986). These orb weavers do not build sticky webs. Instead, they dangle a drop of sticky adhesive at the end of a single silk line held by one leg, swinging it at prey insects (figure 4.4). When the sticky adhesive ball contacts a prey insect, even a scale-winged moth, it sticks, allowing the spider to descend the line, paralyze the prey, and feed. However, the prey of some *Mastophora* consists entirely of male moths of the fall army-worm *Spodoptera frugipera* (Eberhard 1977). This specificity is the result of the release of a volatile chemical substance by the spider (*Mastophora dizzydeani*) which mimics the sex attractant pheromone of female army-worm moths and several other species, drawing male moths into "pitching" range (Stowe et al. 1987).

ARANEOPHAGY: SPIDERS ARE OFTEN THEIR OWN WORST ENEMIES

Among the recent examples of predatory specialization by spiders are found a set of fascinating araneophagic species—spiders that eat other spiders. Several species from a number of families are known to use a variety of tactics to capture spiders. Theridiid spiders of the genus *Argyrodes* are usually described as kleptoparasites which steal prey from webs of other spiders, but recent studies have shown them to invade webs and feed upon the resident (Wise 1982; Larcher and Wise 1985; Whitehouse 1986). Pirate spiders (Family Mimetidae) use aggressive mimicry in their capture of spiders, by producing vibratory stimuli on webs, thereby inducing a predatory response of the resident. When the

Figure 4.3 The "inverted ladder" web of *Scoloderus cordatus,* a nocturnal moth specialist. Moths flying into the upper portion of the web fall down its 70 cm length, losing scales as they fall and ending up ensnared at the bottom where the spider waits. (Photo by Mark Stowe, used with permission.

Figure 4.4   A bolas spider, *Mastophora basaccata,* showing the suspended droplet of sticky glue on a single silk line. These spiders use aggressive chemical mimicry to lure male moths as prey. (Photo by Mark Stowe, used with permission).

spider moves out to capture the "prey," it is itself captured by the mimetid (Jackson and Whitehouse 1986). Aggressive mimicry using vibration to lure spiders to their deaths has been seen in a number of recent studies of spiders from other families as well, including the Pholcidae (Jackson and Brassington 1987; Jackson and Rowe 1987), Gnaphosidae (Jarman and Jackson 1986) and the Salticidae (Jackson and Hallas 1986a).

A recent set of studies by Robert Jackson and colleagues (Jackson and Blest 1982a, b; Jackson and Hallas 1986a, b), concern a behaviorally complex and aberrant group of jumping spiders in the genus *Portia* (see Jackson 1986). These spiders are unique among the salticids because they build capture webs, and show a high degree of predatory versatility. In addition to capturing insects on their own webs, *Portia* may invade the webs of other spider species and be kleptoparasitic, or capture and eat the occupant of the web. *Portia* shows a number of behaviors associated with araneophagic habits—specialized movements of the legs and palps, which create vibrations which mimic the struggles of ensnared insects. These spiders may also prey upon other jumping spider species (which have excellent vision) aided by their cryptic morphology and slow stalking abilities.

Trade-Offs in Evolution of Foraging Specialization

Although many spiders are polyphagous in their prey choices, the research reviewed here has pointed out that some species can specialize on prey to varying degrees. An important question that has been addressed rarely in spiders has to do with the obvious trade-off between a generalized predatory strategy and specialization: if predators use specialized behaviors that increase efficiency but limit the range of prey they can capture, does this compensate for a reduction in availability of prey? Jackson and Hallas (1986c) tested the hypothesis that a "Jack-of-All-Trades is the Master of None" by examining prey capture efficiency of different *Portia* species. Compared to other salticids, *Portia* were less efficient in capturing insects, which would support the hypothesis. However, within the genus *Portia,* the "Jack-of-all-trades" species, *P. fimbriata,* was more efficient as a predator of web-building spiders than its congeners. These seemingly contradictory results may arise from the fact that although *Portia* shows predator versatility by feeding on insects and spiders, it has evolved a set of extremely specialized vibration-mimicking behaviors that increase its ability to capture web-building spiders.

Conclusions

There appears to be a sizeable amount of evidence that some spiders do exert enough selection pressure on insect populations to cause the evolution of specific antipredator behaviors. The prey-specific behaviors of spiders and the antispider defense strategies of insects are best known from studies of tropical species. However, it is probable that common temperate species may show the same kinds of adaptations if we look closely enough. The behavioral interactions between spiders and their prey are often complex, and there is considerable diversity in these behaviors. This wide variety of behavior, as well as the potential for predator-prey interaction between these two arthropod groups, suggests that spider predation is an important force in the evolution of insect anti-predator behavior.

References

Barnes, R.D. 1955. The spider population of the abstract broomsedge community of the southeastern Piedmont. *Ecology* 35:25–25.

Barth, F.G. 1982. Spiders and vibratory signals: sensory reception and behavioral significance, chap. 3. *In:* P.N. Witt and J.S. Rovner, Eds., *Spider Communication: Mechanisms and Ecological Significance,* 67–122. Princeton, N.J.: Princeton University Press.

Biere, J.M., and G.W. Uetz. 1981. Web orientation in the spider *Micrathena gracilis* (Wzlckenaer) (Araneae: Araneida). *Ecology* 61:1121–1132.

Bilsing, S.W. 1920. Quantitative studies in the food of spiders. *Ohio. J. Sci.* 20:215–260.

Bristowe, W.S. 1941. *The Comity of Spiders,* vol. 2. London: Ray Society.

Burgess, J.W. 1975. The sheet web as a transducer, modifying vibration signals in social spider colonies of *Mallos gregalis. Neurosci. Abstr.* 1:557.

Burgess, J.W., and G.W. Uetz. 1982. Social spacing strategies in spiders. In: P.N. Witt and J.S. Rovner, Eds., *Spider Communication: Mechanisms and Ecological Significance,* 317–351. Princeton, N.J.: Princeton University Press.

Carrel, J.E., and T. Eisner. 1984. Defense mechanisms of arthropods. Spider sedation induced by defensive chemicals of millipede prey. *Proc. Nat. Acad. Sci.* 81(3):806–810.

Chacon, P., and W.G. Eberhard. 1980. Factors affecting numbers and kinds of prey caught in artificial spider webs, with considerations of how orb webs trap prey. *Bull Brit. Arachnol. Soc.* 5:29–38.

Cherrett, J.M. 1964. The distribution of spiders on the Moor House Nature Reserve, West-Morland. *J. Anim. Ecol.* 33:26–48.

Craig, C.L. 1986. Orb-web visibility: the influence of insect flight behaviour and visual physiology on the evolution of web designs within the Araneoidae. *Anim. Behav.* 34:54–68.

————. 1987. The ecological and evolutionary interdependence between web architecture and web silk spun by orb weaving spiders. *Biol. J. Linn. Soc.* 30:135–162.

Craig, C.L., A. Okuba, and V. Andreasen. 1985. Effect of spider orb web and insect oscillations on prey interception. *J. Theor. Biol.* 115:201–211.

Dabrowska-Prot, E. 1970. Influence of spiders on the behaviour of mosquito populations. *Ekol. Pol. A.* 26:531–537.

Dabrowska-Prot, E., and J. Luzak. 1968. Spiders and mosquitoes of the ecotone of alder forest (Carici elongatae-Alnetum) and oakpine forest (Pino-Quercetum). *Ekol. Pol.* 16:461–483.

Dabrowska-Prot, E., J. Luczak, and K. Tarwid. 1968. The predation of spiders on forest mosquitoes in field experiments. *J. Med. Entomol.* 5:252–256.

Dabrowska-Prot, E., J. Luczak, and Z. Wojcik. 1973. Ecological analysis of two invertebrate groups in the wet alder wood and meadow ecotone. *Ekol. Pol.* 21:753–812.

Duffey, E. 1962. A population study of spiders in limestone grassland: the field-layer fauna. *Oikos* 13:15–34.

_____. **1966.** Spider ecology and habitat structure (Arach., Araneae). *Senckenbergiana Biol.* 47:45–49.

Eberhard, W.G. 1971. The ecology of the web of *Uloborus diversus* (Araneae: Uloboridae). *Ocecologia* 6:328–342.

_____. **1975.** The "inverted ladder" orb web of *Scoloderus* sp. and the intermediate orb of *Eustala* (?) sp. Araneae: Araneidae. *J. Nat. Hist.* 9:93–106.

_____. **1977.** Aggressive chemical mimicry by a bolas spider. *Science* 198:1173–1175.

_____. **1979.** *Argyrodes attenuatus* (Theridiidae): a web that is not a snare. *Psyche* 86:407–413.

_____. **1980.** The natural history and behavior of the bolas spider *Mastophora dizzydeani* sp. n. (Araneidae). *Psyche* 87:143–169.

_____. **1981.** The single line web of *Phoroncidia studo* Levi (Araneae, Theridiidae): a prey attractant? *J. Arachnol.* 9:229–232.

_____. **1986.** Effects of orb-web geometry on prey interception and retention. In: W.A. Shear, Ed., *Spiders: Webs, Behavior and Evolution,* 70–100. Stanford, Calif: Stanford University Press.

Eisner, T. 1965. Defensive spray of a phasmid insect. *Science* 148(3672):966–968.

Eisner, T., R. Alsop, and G. Ettershank. 1964. Adhesiveness of spider silk. *Science* 146: 1058–1061.

Eisner, T., and J. Dean. 1976. Ploy and counterploy in predator-prey interactions: orb-weaving spiders versus bombardier beetles. *Proc. Nat. Acad. Sci.* 73:1365–1367.

Emlen, J.M. 1966. The role of time and energy in food preference. *Am. Nat.* 100:611–617.

Enders, F. 1974. Vertical stratification in orb-web spiders (Araneidae: Araneae) and a consideration of other methods of coexistence. *Ecology* 55:317–328.

Gillespie, R.G. 1981. The quest for prey by the web building spider *Amaurobius similis* (Blackwell). *Anim. Behav.* 29:953–954.

Greene, E., L.J. Orsak, and D.W. Whitman. 1987. A tephritid fly mimics the territorial displays of its jumping spider predators. *Science* 236:310–312.

Greenstone, M.H. 1984. Determinants of web spider species diversity: vegetation structural diversity vs. prey availability. *Oecologia* 62:299–304.

Hartsock, S.P. 1983. The influence of web structure and web placement on prey capture in orb-weaving spiders. Master's Thesis, University of Cincinnati, Cincinnati, Ohio.

Hays, H.E. 1976. Responses of the housefly, *Musca domestica,* to webs of the spiders *Argiope aurantia* and *Argiope trifasciata. Diss. Abst.* 37(04):1522-1525.

Hieber, C.S. 1984. Orientation and modification of the web to wind and light by the spiders *Araneus diadematus* and *Araneus gemmaides* (Araneae: Araneidae). *Z. Tierpsychol.* 65: 250-260.

Hergenroder, R., and F.G. Barth. 1983a. The release of attack and escape behavior by vibratory stimuli in a wandering spider *(Cupiennius salei* Keys). *J. Comp. Physiol.* 152:347-358.

_____. **1983b.** Vibratory signals and spider behavior: how do the sensory inputs from the eight legs interact in orientation? *J. Comp. Phusiol.* 152:361-371.

Hodge, M.A. 1984. Macro- and microhabitat selection by the spiny orb weaving spider *Micrathena gracilis* (Walckenaer) (Araneae: Araneidae). Master's Thesis, University of Georgia, Athens.

_____. **1987.** Factors influencing web site residence time of the orb-weaving spider, *Microthema gracilis. Psyche* 94:363-371.

Hoffmaster, D.K. and H.E. Hays. 1977. Simulation of predatory interactions: spiders and flies. *Proc. Penn. Acad. Sci.* 51:131-133.

Holldobler, B. 1970. *Steatoda fulva* Theridiidae), a spider that feeds on harvester ants. *Psyche* 77:202-207.

Horton, C.C., and D.H. Wise. 1983. The experimental analysis of competition between two syntopic species of orb-web spiders (Araneae: Araneidae). *Ecology* 64:929-944.

Ivlev, V. 1961. *Experimental Ecology of the Feeding of Fishes.* New Haven, Conn.: Yale University press.

Jackson, R.R. 1977. Comparative studies of *Dictyna* and *Mallos* (Araneae: Dictynidae) III. Prey and predatory behavior. *Psyche* 84:267-280.

Jackson, R.R. 1986. Web-Building, Predatory versatility, and the evolution of the Salticidae. pp. 232-268. In W.A. Shear, Ed., *Spiders: Webs, Behavior, and Evolution* Stanford, Calif: Stanford University Press.

Jackson, R.R., and A.D. Blest. 1982a. The biology of *Portia fimbriata,* a web-building jumping spider (Araneae, Salticidae) from Queensland: utilization of webs and predatory versatility. J. Zoll., Lond. 196:255-293.

_____. **1982b.** The distances at which a primitive jumping spider, *Portia fimbriata,* makes visual discriminations. *J. Exp. Biol.* 97:441-445.

Jackson, R.R. and S.E. Hallas. 1986a. Predatory versatility and intraspecific interactions of spartaeine jumping spiders (Aranea: Salticidae): *Brettus adonis, B. cingulatus, Cyrba algerina,* and *Phaecius* sp indet. *New Zealand J. Zool.* 13:491-520.

_____. **1986b.** Comparative biology of *Portia africana, P. albimana, P. labiata* and *P. schultzi,* araneophagic, web-building jumping spiders (Araneae: Salticidae): utilization of webs, predatory versatility, and intraspecific interactions. *New Zealand J. Zool.* 13:423-429.

_____. **1986c.**Capture efficiencies of web-building jumping spiders (Araneae: Salticidae); is the jack-of-all-trades the master of none? *J. Zool. Lond.* 209:1–7

Jackson, R.R. and M.E.A. Whitehouse. 1986. The biology of New Zealand and Queensland pirate spiders (Araneae, Minetodae): aggressive mimicry, araneophagy and prey specialization. *J. Zool. Lond. 210:279–303.*

Janetos, A.C. 1982a. Active foragers vs. sit-and-wait predators: a simple model. *J. Theor. Biol.* 95:381–385.

Janetos, A.C. 1982b. Foraging tactics of two guilds of web-spinning spiders. *Behav. Ecol. Sociobiol.* 10:19–27.

Jarman, E.A.R. and R.R. Jackson, 1986. The biology of *Taeria erebus* (Araneae, Gnaphosidae), an araneophagic spider from New Zealand: silk utilization and predatory versatility. *New Zealand J. Zool.* 13:521–541.

Kajak, A. 1965. An analysis of food relations between the spiders *Araneus cornutus* Clerck and *Araneus quadratus* Clerck and their prey in meadows.

Kaston, B.J. 1966. Evolution of the web. *Nat. Hist. Mag.* 75:26–34.

Kullmann, E. 1972. Evolution of social behavior in spiders (Araneae: Eresidae and Theridiidae). *Am. Zool.* 12:419–426.

Larcher, S.F. and D.H. Wise. 1985. Experimental studies of the interactions between a web-invading spider and two host species. *J. Arachnol.* 13:45–59.

Levi, H.W. 1978. Orb-webs and phylogeny of orb-weavers. *Symp. Zool. Soc. Lond.* 42:1–15.

Lubin, Y.D. 1986. Web building and prey capture in the Uloboridae. pp. 132–171. *In* W.A. Shear, Ed., *Spiders: Webs, Behavior, and Evolution* Stanford University Press.

Lubin, Y.D., and S. Dorugl. 1982. Effectiveness of single-thread webs as insect traps: sticky trap models. *Bull. Brit. Arachnol. Soc.* 5:399–407.

Lubin, Y.D., W.G. Eberhard, and G.G. Montgomery. 1978. Webs of *Miagrammopes* (Araneae: Uloboridae) in the neotropics. *Psyche* 85:1–23.

Luczak, J. 1963. Differences in the structure of communities of web spiders in one type of the environment as a result of interspecies competition. *Ekol. Pol.* 14:233–244.

_____. **1980.** Behaviour of spider populations in the presence of mosquitoes. *Ekol. Pol.* 31: 625–634.

Luczak, J., and E. Dabrowska-Prot. 1966. Experimental studies on the reduction of the abundance of mosquitoes by spiders. I. Intensity of spider predation on mosquitoes. *Bull. Acad. Polonaise Sci. Cl. II.* 14:315–320.

Mather, M.H., and B.D. Roitberg. 1987. A sheep in wolf's clothing: tephritid flies mimic spider predators. *Science* 236:308–310.

Nentwig, W. 1980. The selective prey of linyphiid-like spiders and of their space webs. *Oecologia* 45:236–243.

————. 1982. Why do only certain insects escape from a spider's web? *Oecologia* 53: 412–417.

————. 1983. The prey of web-building spiders compared with feeding experiments (Araneae: Araneidae, Linyphiidae, Plolcidae, Agelenidae). *Oecologia* 56:132–139.

————. 1985. Prey analysis of four species of tropical orb-weaving spiders (Araneae: Araneidae) and a comparison with araeids of the temperate zone. *Oecologia* 66:580–594.

————. 1985b. Social spiders catch larger prey: a study of *Anelosimus eximius* (Araneae: Theridiidae). *Behav. Ecol. Sociobiol.* 17:79–85.

————. 1987. The prey of spiders. *In:* W. Nentwig, Ed., *Ecophysiology of Spiders*, 249–263. Berlin: Springer-Verlag.

Nentwig, W., and C. Wissel. 1986. A comparison of prey lengths among spiders. *Oecologia* 68: 595–600.

Nentwig, W., and S. Heimer. 1987. Ecological aspects of spider webs. *In:* W. Nentwig, Ed., *Ecophysiology of Spiders*, 211–225. Berlin: Springer-Verlag.

Olive, C.W. 1980. Foraging specializations in orb-weaving spiders. *Ecology* 61:1133–1144.

————. 1982. Behavioural response of a sit and wait predator to spatial variation in foraging gain. *Ecology* 63(4):912–920.

Pulliam, H.R. 1974. On the theory of optimal diets. *Am. Nat.* 108:59–75.

Readshaw, J.L. 1973. The numerical response of predators to prey density. *In:* Hughes, Ed., *Quantitative Evaluation of Natural Enemy Effectiveness. J. Applied Biol.* 10:342–351.

Reissland, A., and P. Gorner. 1985. Trichobothria. *In:* F.G. Barth, Ed., *Neurobiology of Arachnids*, 138–161. Berlin: Springer-Verlag.

Riechert, S.E. 1974a. The pattern of local web distribution in a desert spider: mechanisms and seasonal variation. *J. Anim. Ecol.* 43:733–746.

————. 1974b. Thoughts on the ecological significance of spiders. *Bioscience* 24:352–356.

————. 1976. Web site selection in the desert spider *Agelenopsis aperta. Oikos* 27:311–315.

Riechert, S.E., and A.B. Cady. 1984. Patterns of resource use and tests for competitive release in a spider community. *Ecology* 64(4):899–913.

Riechert, S.E., and W.G. Reeder. 1972. Effects of fire on spider distribution in Southwestern Wisconsin prairies. *Proc. Second Midwest Prairie Conf.* 73–90.

Riechert, S.E., and R. Gillespie. 1986. Habitat choice and utilization in the web-building spiders. *In:* W.A. Shear, Ed., *Spiders: Webs, Behavior and Evolution*, 23–48. Stanford, Calif.: Stanford University Press.

126   REFERENCES

Riechert, S.E., and T. Lockley. 1984. Spiders as biological control agents. *Ann. R. Ent.* 29: 299–320.

Riechert, S.E., and J. Luczak. 1982. Spider foraging: behavioral responses to prey. *In:* P.N. Witt and J.S. Rovner, Eds., *Spider Communication: Mechanisms and Ecological Significance.* 353–385. Princeton, N.J.: Princeton University Press.

Riechert, S.E., W.G. Reeder, and T.A. Allen. 1973. Patterns of spider distribution (*Agelenopsis aperta* [Gertsch]) in desert grassland and recent lava bed habitats, South-Central New Mexico. *J. Anim. Ecol.* 42:19–23.

Riechert, S.E., and C.R. Tracy. 1975. Thermal balance and prey availability; bases for a model relating web-site characteristics to spider reproductive success. *Ecology* 56:265–285.

Robinson, M.H. 1969. Predatory behavior of *Argiope argentata* (Fabricius). *Am. Zool.* 9:161–173.

_____. 1970. Insect anti-predator adaptations and the behavior of predatory primates. *Act. IV Congr. Latin. Zool.* 2:811–836.

_____. 1975. The evolution of predatory behaviour in araneid spiders. *In:* G. Bearends, C. Beer, and A. Manning, Eds., *Function and Evolution in Behaviour: Essays in Honour of Professor Niko Tinbergen, F.R.S.,* 292–312. Oxford: Clarendon Press.

_____. 1977a. Symbioses between insects and spiders: an association between lepidopteran larvae and the social spider *Anelosimus eximius* (Araneae: Theridiidae). *Psyche* 83:225–232.

_____. 1977b. Tropical spinners. *New Scientist* 76:552–554.

_____. 1982. Courtship and mating behavior in spiders. *Ann. Rev. Ent.* 27:1–20.

Robinson, M.H., and B. Robinson. 1970. Prey caught by a sample population of the spider *Argiope argentata* (Araneae: Araneidae) in Panama: a year's census data. *Zool. J. Linn. soc.* 49:345–358.

_____. 1971. The predatory behavior of the ogre-faced spider *Dinopis longipes* F. Cambridge. *Am. Midl. Nat.* 85:85–96.

_____. 1972. Techniques for the observation of spider behavior. *Bull. Brit. Arachnol. Soc.* 4:58–59.

_____. 1973. Ecology and behavior of the giant wood spider *Nephila maculata* (Fabricius) in New Guinea. *Smithsonian Contributions to Zoology* 149:1–76.

_____. 1975. Evolution beyond the orb web: the web of the araneid spider *Pasilobus* sp, its structure, operation and construction. *Zool. J. Linn. Soc.* 56:301–314.

_____. 1976. Discrimination between prey types: an innate component of the predatory behavior of Araneid spiders. *Z. Tierpsychol.* 41:266–276.

Robinson, M.H., and H. Mirick. 1971. The predatory behavior of the golden-web spider *Nephila clavipes. Psyche* 78:123–139.

Robinson, M.H., and J. Olazarri. 1971. Units of behavior and complex sequences in the predatory behavior of *Argiope argentata* (Fabricus) (Araneae: Araneidae). *Smithsonian Contributions to Zoology* 65:1-36.

Robinson, M.H., H. Mirick, and O. Turner. 1969. The predatory behavior of some araneid spiders and the origin of immobilization wrapping. *Psyche* 76:487-501.

Robinson, M.H., and C.E. Valerio. 1977. Attacks on large or heavily defended prey by tropical salticid spiders. *Psyche* 84:1-10.

Rypstra, A.L. 1979. Foraging flocks of spiders, a study of aggregate behavior in *Cyrtophora citricola* Forskal (Araneae: Araneidae) in west Africa. *Behav. Ecol. Sociobiol.* 5:291-300.

_____. **1981.** The effect of kleptoparasitism on prey consumption and web relocation in a Peruvian population of the spider *Nephila clavipes. Oikos* 37:179-182.

_____. **1982.** Building a better insect trap: an experimental investigation of prey capture in a variety of spider webs. *Oecologia* 52:31-36.

_____. **1983.** The importance of food and space in limiting web-spider densities: a test using field enclosures. *Oecologia* 59:312-319.

_____. **1984.** A relative measure of predation on web-spiders in temperate and tropical forests. *Oikos* 43:129-132.

Schoener, T.W. 1969. Models of optimal size for solitary predators. *Am. Nat.* 103:277-313.

Shear, W.A., Ed., 1986. *Spiders: Webs, Behavior and Evolution.* Stanford Calif.: Stanford University Press. pp. 492.

Shelly, T.E. 1983. Prey selection by the neotropical spider *Alpaida tuonabo* with notes on web-site tenacity. *Psyche* 90:123-133.

Sivinski, J. and M. Stowe. 1980. A kleptoparasitic cecidomyiid and other flies associated with spiders. *Psyche* 87(3-4):337-343.

Stowe, M.K. 1986. Prey specialization in the Araneidae. pp. 101-131 *In:* W.A. Shear, Ed., *Spiders: Webs, Behavior and Evolution.* Stanford, Calif.: Stanford University Press.

Stowe, M.K., J.H. Tumlinson, and R.R. Heath. 1987. Chemical mimicry: bolas spiders emit components of moth prey species sex pheromones. *Science* 236:964-967.

Suter, R.B. 1978. *Cyclosa turbinata:* Prey discrimination via web-borne vibrations. *Behav. Ecol. Sociobiol.* 3:283-296.

Turnbull, A.L. 1960. The prey of the spider *Linyphia triangularis* (Clerck) (Araneae, Linyphiidae). *Can. J. Zool.* 38:859-873.

_____. **1962.** Quantitative studies of the food of *Linyphia triangularis* Clerck (Araneae: Linyphiidae). *Can. Ent.* 94:1233-1249.

_____. **1964.** The search for prey by a web-building spider *Achaearanea tepidariorum* (C.L. Koch) (Araneae, Theridiidae). *Can. Ent.* 96:568-579.

_____. **1973.** Ecology of the true spiders (Araneomorphae). *Ann. Rev. Ent.* 18:305–348.

Uetz, G.W. 1989. Habitat structure and spider foraging. *In:E.* D. McCoy, S. A. Bell, Eds., *The Physical Arrangement of Objects in Space.* London: Chapman and Hall. (in press).

Uetz, G.W., and J.M. Biere. 1980. Prey of *Micrathena gracilis* (Walckenaer) (Araneae: Araneidae) in comparison with artificial webs and other trapping devices. *Bull. Brit. Arachnol. Soc.* 5:101–107.

Uetz, G.W., and S.P. Hartsock. 1987. Prey selection in an orb weaving spider: *Micrathena gracilis* (Araneae: Aranethdae). *Psyche* 94:103–116.

Uetz, G.W., A.D. Johnson, and D.W. Schemske. 1978. Web placement, web structure, and prey capture in orb-weaving spiders. *Bull. Brit. Arachnol. Soc.* 4:141–148.

Vasconcellos-Neto, J., and T.M. Lewinson. 1984. Discrimination and release of unpalatable butterflies by *Nephila clavipes,* a neotropic orb-weaving spider. *Ecol. Ent.* 9:337–344.

Whitehouse, M.E.A. 1986. The foraging behaviours of *Argyrodes antipodiana* (Theridiidae), a klepto parasitic spider from New Zealand. *New Zealand J. Zool.* 13:151–168.

Wise, D.H. 1982. Predation by a commensal spider, *Argyrodes trigonum,* upon its host: an experimental study. *J. Arachnol.* 10:111–116.

Wise, D.H. 1984. The role of competition in spider communities: insights from field experiments with a model organism. *In:* D.R. Strong, Jr., D. Simberloff, L.G. Abele, A.B. Thistle, Eds., *Ecological Communities:* 42–53. Princeton, N.J.: Princeton University Press.

Wise, D.H., and J.L. Barata. 1983. Prey of two syntopic spiders with different web structures. *J. Arachnol.* 11:217–281.

CHAPTER 5

Predator-Prey Interactions, Informational Complexity, and the Origins of Intelligence

Michael H. Robinson

The Germans...also developed a most ingenious paint for their U-boats to camouflage them against infra-red as well as against visible light. If a normal grey-painted ship, which is thus camouflaged well against typically grey sea, is viewed by infra-red it still looks grey but the sea looks blackish. They therefore had to make a paint which looked grey to the human eye, but blackish to the infra-red viewer. They achieved this. (Jones 1979, 410–411.

Introduction

There have been a number of attempts in the last few years to provide a biological and evolutionary background for the evolution of intelligence in animals (for example, Beck 1980; Humphrey 1976; Jolly 1966; Moynihan 1976; Robinson 1979; and Sagan 1977). A much earlier treatment of complex learning in animals by Rensch (1950, 1967) is full of insights. In addition, the issues of concept formation, consciousness, and animal awareness have been raised as legitimate concerns of biologists in general and of behavior students in particular (the whole field was sparked into life by Griffin 1976; see also 1984, and Crook 1980). Although intelligence and the above-used related terms are difficult to define, general agreement exists on the range of phenomena that they describe. In evolutionary terms, one can ask what morphological, anatomical, and behavioral characteristics accompanied the evolution of intelligence and related phenomena; this is the approach of Sagan (1977). It is an interesting question, but a more fundamental problem concerns the situations in which intelligencelike properties were likely to have contributed to fitness (or to have acquired *survival value,* to use a less fashionable term). This approach has been adopted by Jolly (1966), Humphrey (1976), Robinson (1979), and Moynihan (1976). Of these, Moynihan's is the most comprehensive review and assumes that a plethora of factors was involved. Humphrey assumes that intelligence arose to allow primates to cope with the complexities of social interactions.

In this chapter I argue that mental processes akin to those subsumed under the term *intelligence* probably evolved when the ability to process complex information allowed animals to exploit resources unavailable to other animals. Thus it is argued that the tropical rain forest was the cradle of intelligence, since it, by virtue of its extreme range of species diversity and interspecific interactivity, offers the greatest information complex of all terrestrial habitats (Robinson 1977 reviews an extensive literature illustrating the interspecific complexity found in tropical rain forest and coral reef ecosystems). Furthermore, it is argued that the context of interspecific behavior provided the most opportunity for exploiting the capacity to process complex information, particularly with respect to obtaining food.

This hypothesis implies a rejection of the contrary view that it is in the context of social interactions, within species behaviors, that the ability to process complex information first arose. The main argument against the function of intelligence being primarily intraspecific (i.e., social) is that selection has favored the evolution of a circumscribed number of unambiguous social signals that facilitate information processing by recipients (displays are displays because they are ritualized). The social context is thus a relatively simple one vis-à-vis information. Moynihan (1970) has emphasized that the total content of display repertories is remarkably constant across wide taxonomic spectra and over a range of degrees of sociality. On the other hand, the continuing arms race between predators and prey has increased, and continues to do so, the greatest complexity of signals generated by most potential prey other than those depending on aposematism.

I came to this view of the origins of intelligence as a consequence of a long-term interest in both sides of the predator-prey interaction (see Robinson 1969a,b and particularly 1970). In reviewing the defensive adaptations of a range of tropical insects, this paper provides evidence of the generation of information complexity. This complexification can lead, logically, to two major evolutionary pathways for predators: either the path of increasing specialization or the development of complex information-processing capacities. In short, it is argued that intelligence could have begun its evolution as a means of exploiting the considerable resources potentially available to a sophisticated tropical entomophage. Of course, detecting the presence of organisms that have evolved complex anti-predator adaptations is only part of the information-processing task involved in food finding. Most organisms also have to "know" where and when to search. This knowledge may involve an extensive stored memory map and a scanning of clock and calendar information. And food finding is not the only aspect of interspecific activity in which the tropical animal is potentially confronted by a vast array of information that can be used in a way that has great survival value. Many predators are also potential prey and need appropriate defensive behaviors. These defenses may use considerable quantities of information (for instance, topographic details of home ranges for escape routes and refuges, specialized responses to specific predators, and so on; to be discussed). Animals may also need to store and process information about shelter from climatic variables and care of injuries and wounds. In addition, I have been reminded (J. E. Bannerman, in litt.) that animals may use plants for self-medication against diseases and parasites. They would choose those containing appropriate secondary compounds. Such compounds are undoubtedly numerous and diverse in tropical plants. If such self-medication is widespread, the discriminations involved could be under particularly intense selection pressures and would require the processing of complex information.

At this stage it is appropriate to consider two ways in which information can be acquired from the environment. It can either be acquired "phylogenetically," in the lifetime of the species, or in the lifetime of the individual. Lorenz's treatment of this issue (1965) is a very important one. There is little doubt that many animals are hard-wired to be highly successful in niches that require relatively small amounts of information processing. For instance, an animal that feeds on only moving insects may (and probably does) require a smaller program of food-finding information than one that can find motionless insects. On the other hand, the more complex the environment, the more there will be niches for animals that can use a wider range of information. Thus a tendency seems to have occurred in the evolutionary process toward increase in brain size and more individual nongenetic storage of information (see Jerison 1970). These matters are dealt with in the following treatment, although not as extensively as they merit. Finally, in considering how animal information-processing systems might operate, I will review some possible functions of consciousness.

Prey Detection versus Defenses

Studies of the cues used in prey recognition, whether this is the principal focus or merely an incidental part, lag far behind other studies of the ethology of predation. For instance, only around 8 percent of Curio's (1976) review of predation behavior deals with prey recognition per se. This relative neglect is not due to the fact that the subject lacks intrinsic interest. For example, food finding has been most heavily studied in birds. Many specialized entomophages are birds, yet we know little about how they recognize prey. Tinbergen (1963) has stressed our ignorance: "We know that yound birds have, at the start, a very open mind with regard to food; they respond to an enormous variety of objects, edible and inedible alike, and learn to confine themselves to those they find edible. My suggestion is that we have as yet no more than the faintest idea of the kinds of things such birds learn when young." There are some exceptions—see, for instance, Greenberg (1984)—but this statement is still esentially true. In the absence of direct studies, it is tempting to make inferences about the behavior of predators from the presumed antipredator adaptations of their prey. This kind of deduction is often both logical and useful. Thus anyone encountering the submarine painted in the manner described at the head of this paper would be able to deduce that the predator had, in this case, detectors capable of operating in visible and in infra-red light. Similarly, if the so-called stealth bomber is ever built, an examination of its structure could lead to the deduction that radiodetection devices (radar) exist. Examples of successful deduction of function from structure are readily found in the literature on recent military intelligence operations (see Jones 1979 for intricate examples). There are perils, however, in deducing function from structure. Wood-Mason, in 1878, published a description of a phasmid that he claimed was specialized for aquatic life. It has a flattened body, with a concave undersurface fringed with hair, and flattened limbs. All these adaptations are found in mayfly larvae that live in streams, where they are aquatic adaptations. However, in the case of *Prisopus berosus*, they are adaptations to profile concealment when the insect is in its concealment posture; see figure 16 in Robinson 1969a.

Despite these problems, there are good examples of verified deductions of function from structure in relation to insect defensive systems. Color-matching camouflage, countershading, Batesian mimicry, and aposematism have all had their deduced functions subjected to experimental testing. (Rather than cite a plethora of references, I refer the reader to Edmunds 1974, Curio 1976 and other chapters in this volume.) A particularly interesting example of such deduction concerns the function of eyelike markings in Lepidoptera. These have long been regarded as startle devices when large and very similar to the vertebrate eye, and as deflection devices when small and generalized (Blest 1957). Blest was able to show, experimentally, that the startle effect was greatest when the resemblance to an eye was closest.

A number of major visual defenses are still, to my knowledge, untested. These include outline-concealing structures (see figure 5.1), obliterative patterning, flash coloration, and behaviors such as dash and freeze locomotion, to name but a few. It is probable that obliterative patterning (disruptive coloration) has been tested in its military applications. My own studies of the mimetic postures of stick- and leaf-mimicking insects (1969a,b, 1970, 1973, 1981a), including data on more than fifty species of phasmids from Papua New Guinea that are as yet unpublished because of the impossibility of obtaining species identifications, have led me to certain conclusions about predator behavior. These can be summed up very simply: the insects have elaborate and complex devices that apparently serve to conceal structures that are typical of insects in particular and many arthropods in general. The structures concealed are segmentation, legs, heads, antennae, and often wings. The concealment of these structures occurs in some phasmids that are not specialized stick and leaf mimics and could have preceded the evolution of such mimicry even though it now enhances the disguise. Functionally such concealment could have evolved in cryptic insects to enhance their crypticity and could then been a preadaptation to plant mimicry (disguise). This arguement is presented in detail in Robinson (1969a,b), and other examples are cited by Edmunds (1974). A revised outline of how stick and leaf mimicry could have evolved is shown in figures 5.2–5.6.

Merely looking at the visually operating systems of primary defense found in terrestrial arthropods allows us to make some guesses about how prey detection abilities could operate in predators. Thus the existence of color-matching camouflage, diurnal immobility, disruptive patterning, and countershading suggests that visually hunting predators can recognize prey by their shape. A huge literature in experimental psychology suggests that animals can learn to respond to a considerable catalog of shapes or patterns. Humans also have an impressive ability to do this (Haber 1970); it is a right-brain function. However, a predator responding to the shape of a prey organism in the tropics would be confronted with an enormous array of specific learning tasks. It could encounter a

Figure 5.1 Profile of the neotropical tettigoniid *Acanthodis curvidens* (Stal). This has both concealing coloration and a posture that tend to conceal its outline. The inset shows the head of the leaf-tailed gecko *Uroplates fimbriata* which also rests on trees and has profile concealing devices such as the irregular-edged fringe on the ventral surface. This, shown enlarged, breaks up the dividing line between the lizard and its substrate. (Photo M. H. Robinson).

THE ORIGINS OF INTELLIGENCE

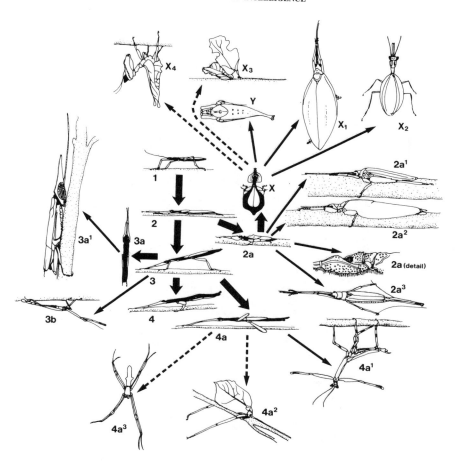

Figure 5.2   The evolution of stick- and leaf-mimicry in the insect Order Phasmida and convergent postures found in other arthropods. The central grouping of insects with solid black bodies connected by broad arrows is the phasmid element of the diagram. The other figures show anatomically and/or posturally convergent forms. Explanation in the Appendix at the end of the chapter.

multitude of species. (Recent studies of tropical forest insects in the canopy, by Erwin [1982, 1983], have suggested that the estimate of the total number of insect species in the world needs upgrading from 1.5 million to as much as 30 million; most of these are in the tropics.) Furthermore, the hunting pressure of predators may have tended to accentuate differences

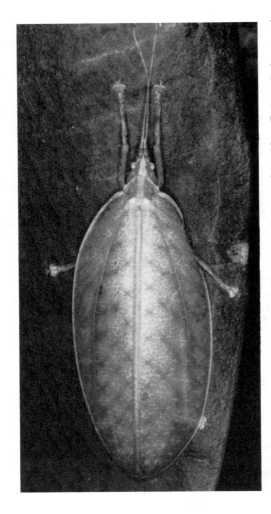

Figure 5.3 The tettigoniid *Acauloplacella immunis* Brunner, from New Guinea, in its cryptic posture. The wings are flattened so that they tent over most of the intermediate and posterior legs and touch the leaf surface, producing a very low profile. Note the position of the anterior legs (compare with X_1 on Figure 5.2). (Photo M. H. Robinson).

Figure 5.4   The Australian preying mantis *Neomantis australis* (Saussure and Zehntner) which has a permanently flattened posture for the wings, this is essentially similar to that shown in Figure 5.3. (Compare with X_2 on Figure 5.2). (Photo M. H. Robinson).

between appearances by apostatic selection (Clark 1969), thereby increasing the learning task confronting predators by producing aspect diversity (Rand 1967, Rickleffs and O'Rourke 1975). Species diversity and aspect diversity combine to produce massive informational complexity. To treat this kind of complexity there are at least two conceivable mechanisms. One is to store information about all the prey that are encountered and have an efficient system of reviewing the stored information (see later, for comments on this possibility). The other is to group the information into subsets and act on these subsets; this is the process of stimulus generalization or nonverbal concept formation. I am inclined to think that predators may have an impossible task if they rely on individual recognition of prey types. Scanning the floppy disk of memory could be an impossibly complex operation when the data base is massive. It would help to be able to recognize some general characteristics of subsets of the general assemblage of prey. To do this would require the beginnings of intelligence. What are some of the possible bases for subsets?

Possible Simplifying Mechanisms

One, of course, is the recognition of the insect "taxonomically" by

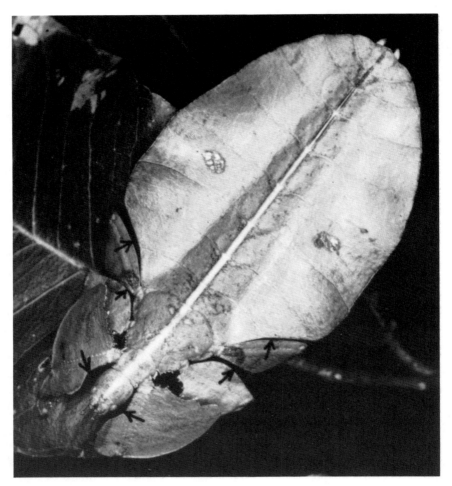

Figure 5.5   Leaf insect from New Guinea, note the huge gauntlet-like dilated and flattened femora (arrowed) of all six legs. The arrows show the direction in which the legs move to form the resting outline shown in X of Figure 5.2. (Photo M. H. Robinson).

its diagnostic parts. This possibility is suggested by the extreme modifications for concealing these parts (which are discussed above, and illustrated in figures 5.2–5.6). There is, so far, little evidence that this is how prey recognition works. However, I have carried out some experiments the results of which are at least suggestive (Robinson 1970). These experiments show that some predators can use the presence of heads or legs to find otherwise concealed prey. There are also experiments that show that

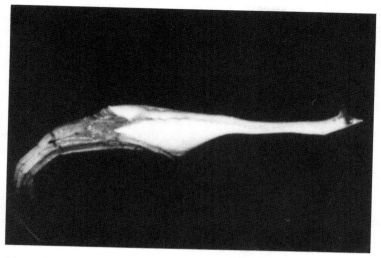

Figure 5.6   The orb-web spider *Arachnura melanura*. This sits at the center of its web with all its legs folded against themselves or the margins of the body. Legs I and II project forward, legs III and IV fold against the body. The spider is bright yellow and flower-like. (Photo M. H. Robinson).

even creatures with such small brains as jumping spiders (Salticidae) respond to leglike projections on models when attacking prey (Drees 1952). And a number of birds show head recognition in the manipulation of prey. A further possibility is that predators may respond to the bilateral symmetry of insect prey. Cryptic patterns on the wings of moths are invariably bilaterally symmetrical. The use of symmetry as a detection device can be easily demonstrated in human subjects confronted with photographs of cryptic insects. It would provide an almost universal cue in the detection of immobile cryptic prey because the developmental processes of insects seem to rigidly produce symmetricality of patterning. Significantly, military camouflage patterns avoid this symmetry; see comparison in figure 5.7. Elegant experiments by Delius and Nowak (1982) have shown that pigeons can learn to recognize symmetry and make discriminations between patterns that are based on symmetry. It has also been shown that pigeons can solve inversion problems at least as well as humans (Hollard and Delius 1982).

Thus it is possible that predators may have an *averbal taxonomic ability* (named after Koehler's 'averbal counting ability' concept; see Rensch 1950) and also an *averbal symmetry discrimination*. These abilities, it can be argued, could imply complex mental phenomena. If it turns out that visually hunting predators can store and review large numbers of bits of information, in a "directory of prey shapes," which is not impossible, then they will prove to have an information-processing system that could be an important adjunct or precursor of induction.

It has been suggested, for two reasons, that orangutans may be intelligent (Galdikas 1978). One reason is that, although they are the least social of the great apes, they have to store social information for long periods between encounters. I do not find this argument very convincing. On the other hand, the fact that they may have a sense of 'averbal botanic tzxonomy' to cope with a plethora of plants is suggestive. (For comments on orangutan intelligence, see also Maple 1980.)

Other Complex Information-Processing Tasks

Food finding is not the only situation that could evoke the evolution of intelligence. I suggested earlier that there were a number of interspecific tasks that faced many animals and were of great survival importance. In many of these cases the ability to store, review, and "abstract" complex information could be crucial to success. Admittedly animals can be well adapted in tropical forest niches without apparently using this information, but its existence opens up the possibility that a better animal would have a greater evolutionary potential. In these cases, reviewed below, conventional learning paradigms may be inapplicable—animals may need new types of plastic behavior to exploit the new opportunities to the full. A case in point involves the acquisition of detailed familiarity with a home range (familiarity with a territory may be a similar phenomenon, worth consideration at length, but omitted here for space considerations). Many mammals show detailed familiarity with the topography and contents of their home range. This knowledge can be of value to them in locating food and in the urgent situation of finding escape routes and refuges when pursued, or confronted, by a predator. It is not clear that the kind of learning involved in this kind of information acquisition fits any conventional paradigms. The learning of maze layouts by rats, which were merely given maze experience without extraneous reinforcement, was called "latent learning" by Hinde (1966). He has since pointed out some of the problems involved in this kind of categorization but argues that "place learning" could best be explained in cognitive rather than stimulus-response terms (Hinde 1970). Mackintosh (1983) remarks of these phenomena that "the topic of maze learning has shown a marked revival in recent years, partly due to the suggestion that such learning depends on the establishment of a cognitive map of the rat's environment." Bernard (1983) still uses the term *latent learning,* citing a 1930 experiment as an example, but states that "a detailed geographical knowledge of the home area could be crucial in escaping from predators." It seems to me that this kind of conventionally unrewarded learning is of great interest. There is a dearth of field studies on the extent to which free-living animals use a cognitive map. Many observations suggest that they do. It is tempting to speculate, by introspection, that some kind of mental reward may accompany such types of learning. The possibility that some kinds of locality learning may be of survival value only in the context of extremely rare events is raised by the use of water holes by baboons in East Africa. This rare use may occur during droughts that may be many, many years apart. Here the old members of a troop prove their usefulness as repositories of knowledge (Altmann and Altmann 1970). The occurrence of rare climatic events even in purportedly stable, humid tropics (Rand and Rand 1982) suggests that animals could gain survival advantages from long-term knowledge of resource distribution.

Lorenz (1981) has argued that exploratory behavior plays an important part in the kinds of mental cartography described above, and some classic treatments suggest that curiosity is an important appetitive behavior. The linkage or parallel of exploration to play is also a link to intelligence.

Tool use by animals (Beck 1980, Griffin 1984) may be another instance where intelligence may immediately confer an adaptive advantage. Insight learning may give an opportunity to exploit resources that are out of reach or otherwise unavailable. The classic experiments of Kohler (1957) are still cited as examples, although Goodall's chimpanzee termite-catching behavior (1968) may have arisen this way.

Animals also have to cope with climatic variables that affect the distribution of food supplies. Species that range widely to exploit resources that are localized in space and time could benefit from having a capacity for learning phenological sequences of flowering, fruiting, and leafing, for instance. Using a calendar of biological seasonality would be as useful as possessing a cognitive map of resource distribution. Knowledge thus acquired could guide an animal to flowers, fruits, and new leaves or to the animals (insects perhaps) that feed on them. Of course, simple trial and error patrolling would achieve the same end, but could involve the expenditure of a great deal more energy. A calendar would be more efficient.

Figure 5.7   Photograph of a sphinx moth showing symmetrical markings and a delta-winged bomber showing asymmetrical camouflage markings (moth photo M. H. Robinson, aircraft courtesy of National Air and Space Museum, Smithsonian Institution).

Most animals face the possibility, in their lives, of experiencing injuries or wounds. Predators, in particular, because of their extreme reliance on maximum efficiency in capturing prey, cannot afford debilitating injuries. They must therefore not only learn what organisms are edible but also what organisms they should not attack. The avoidance learning of distasteful and dangerous organisms may be simplified by the evolution of warning coloration by prey organisms. On the other hand, the existence of Batesian mimicry and other kinds of false warning coloration means that a "simplistic" response to aposematism could result in a predator ignoring a whole range of potentially edible organisms. Although there has been extensive research showing that predators learn to generalize aversive responses to aposematic prey, there have been few studies of whether sophisticated predators can learn to detect deception. I suspect that such discrimination will eventually be discovered. My own studies suggest that tamarins (small monkeys) are not fooled by eye markings and startle displays, although birds are (Robinson 1966, Blest 1957). Furthermore, there is a whole range of insects that bring stings and other weapons into play only as secondary defense, and the alpha predator needs to be able to discriminate between these and harmless look-alikes. It is in the tropics that by far the greatest number of kinds of potential prey could either be dangerous or be falsifying information (lying) about their dangerousness. Thus the need for intelligent behavior in detecting food is likely to be paralleled by a similar need in determining sources of danger. One of the most intriguing aspects of animal behavior is the care of injuries and wounds. This care is of immediate adaptive value. As far as I know, it has not been studied by ethologists; it should be possible to do so without inflicting pain and injury on experimental animals.

This brief review suggests that the beginnings of tendencies to process complex information, through systems of complex learning and cognition, could provide a whole series of adaptive windows for the possessor in fields other than food finding. This idea raises the question of the evolution of consciousness—does it have some relationship to information processing?

Consciousness

Mayr (1982) has argued that consciousness is undefinable and, by implication, not susceptible to discussion or study: "As far as consciousness is concerned, it is impossible to define it ... therefore detailed discussion is impossible." Griffin (1984) ranges over a whole series of attributes of consciousness without approaching a single satisfactory definition. Crook (1980) also uses a multicomponent definition.

To avoid definitional problems, it is perhaps appropriate to consider particular aspects of consciousness. Thus there is the question of "memory awareness," as it might be called. One introspectively available datum is that only a small portion of the memory store is available to our minds at any one time. It is as if a huge memory store (nonconscious) were scanned and the appropriate piece of information were brought onto the screen of the mind for conscious viewing. The impossibility of being simultaneously aware of the entire contents of a memory store suggests one major function of consciousness. It allows for an ordered review of the information that is necessary for action. It is difficult to imagine any other mechanism that could allow a selective review of stored information in animals. To the computer enthusiast, reading off the sequential content of a ROM provides a bewildering succession of information. The brain does not consciously work that way. Information is not presented in massive successional series. The extensive content of the nonconscious visual memory banks is nicely illustrated by the act of reviewing a box of color slides from, say, twenty years ago. Despite the enormous volume of visual experiences that have occupied the twenty intervening years, most people will recall all the scenes on a roll of film and be able to add verbal detail to describe them (I owe this illustration to Balkeslee 1980). This is, coldly considered, an amazing feat. Lorenz (1981) has drawn attention to a similar phenomenon: "It borders on the miraculous the way in which gestalt perception can abstract configurations of distinctive features from a chaotic background of accidental stimulus data, and then retain these over the years." It is interesting that for most people sights are retained in greater profusion than sounds and smells. We may be impinging on a device that once served our predatory past. Perhaps consciousness is not the problem; perhaps nonconsciousness is really the important adaptation. Without it all animals could be in a state of constant information shock, overwhelmed by the simultaneous input of countless bits of stored data.

Conclusion

If intelligence is a response to information processing in an information-rich environment, this may have been only its originating function. Just because the adaptive steps to higher learning conferred advantages in enabling the possessor to exploit new resources, there is no need to assume that this was the only function. In postulating the origins of intelligence, we have merely described an interspecific climate that favored the start of an evolutionary porgression. The milieu of increasing social complexity may then have added its synergism to that of interspecific complexity. Humphrey (1976) and Jolly (1966) have perhaps identified a later stage of the evolutionary progression.

I have suggested elsewhere (Robinson 1977, 1981b) that there is a fundamental difference between tropical biology in complex habitats (rain forests and coral reefs) and the biology of all other regions. I have characterized this difference as being reflected in the utter complexity of the biotic component of the habitat. The suggestion made throughout this paper is that one way of coping with biotic complexity is for some animals to have a capacity for plastic behavior and for individuals to store, process, and adaptively reorganize information during their lifetimes (in contradistinction to the phylogenetic processing of information involved in preprogrammed behaviors.) When animals that evolved in information-rich environments later moved into relatively simple ones, those that had evolved sophisticated cognition and intelligence may have had a surplus capacity. This release from pressures of survival may have been analogous in many ways to infancy in higher mammals. It could have been a period in which mental exploration and intellectual play were possible for the first time. It could have been the point at which abstract thought had its first flowering. It may have happened when our ancestors moved from the information-rich forests into the savannas.

APPENDIX: The Evolution of Stick- and Leaf-Mimicry in the Phasmids and Covergent Postures in Other Arthropods

The argument is simply that, from a relatively generalized ancestor (figure 5.1), adaptations for profile concealment in cryptic postures led to apparent elongation. These adaptations included extension of legs I in front of the head (which incidentally concealed its structure and the antennae) and posterior extension of legs II and III apposed to the body as shown in figure 5.2. This concealed the legs and profile. Together these behaviors enhanced the stick-like appearance of the resting insect. A further step would be to become increasingly flattened (as in element 2a and detail: this is the insect *Prisopus berosus*, referred to in the text, that was once assumed to be aquatic). Dorso-ventral flattening could be a pre-adaptation to leaf-mimicry as in X. Once the insect became elongate and had appropriate leg postures, the next evolutionary step could be the one to stand-alone stick mimicry shown in element 3. Once this is achieved, the insect is no longer cryptic but a true mimic and can be protected from predators by its resemblance to the inedible rather than merging with a background. Disguise is substituted for concealment. Element 3a is the total stick position assumed by many phasmids after dropping from a substrate—all legs are folded against the body. Stages 4 and 4a are a further enhancement of stick posture 3. They involve either structural concealment or structural and postural concealments of other legs in a stick-with-branches position. The insect shown in element 4a is illustrated in detail by Robinson 1969a.

Around the central block of phasmids the other drawings show similar postures and structures found in other arthropod groups, $2a^1$ and $2a^2$ are tettigoniid resting postures that exactly parallel that shown in 2a. Element $2a^1$ is the tettigoniid shown in Figure 5.1 while element $2a^2$ is a tettigoniid from Asia (see Robinson 1977 for details). Element $2a^3$ is another tettigoniid that assumes an essentially similar posture to 2a but which rests on flat rather than curved surfaces (from Robinson 1969b). Elements $4a^1$, $4a^2$ and $4a^3$ show leg concealment postures in which legs become branches associated with a stick or leaf. Element $4a^1$ is a West African mantid that assumes a stick-with-branches position (from Robinson 1966), $4a^2$ is a dead leaf katydid (from Robinson 1969a) and $4a^3$ is the spider *Dinopis rufipes* which hangs from vegetation with its legs grouped into four stick-like units (original, from a color slide). Element 3b is a stick posture found in stick-like mantids which involves the protraction of both legs I in a similar manner to that shown in 3. Element $3a^1$ shows the grass dwelling mantid *Pyrgomantis pallida* in its resting posture which is essentially similar to 2 and 3a but with the anterior legs folded beneath the thorax and very closely apposed to it (original from a color slide).

Elements X_1, X_2 two insects, a tettigoniid and mantid respectively, that are at a stage that could lead to the evolution of leaf mimicry. Both have broadly flattened wings that are leaf-like and cover the body and parts of the legs. Compare with figures 5.3 and 5.4. Elements X_3 and X_4 are functionally leaf mimicks, with complex leg concealment postures (see Robinson 1969a for details). Element Y the orb-weaving spider *Arachnura melanura* that is a flower mimic with a complex mimetic posture involving leg concealment and specialized form (compare with figure 5.6).

References

Altmann, S.A., and J. Altmann. 1970. *Baboon Ecology. U. of Chicago Press. Chicago.*

Beck, B.B. 1980. *Animal Tool Behavior.* Garland Press. N.Y.

Bernard, C.J. 1983. *Animal Behaviour.* Croom Helm. London.

Blakeslee, T.R. 1980. *Right Brain.* Doubleday, N.Y.

Blest, A.D. 1957. The function of eyespot patterns in Lepidoptera. *Behaviour* 11:209–256.

Clark, 1969. The evidence for apostatic selection. *Heredity* 17:319–345.

Crook, J.H. 1980. *The Evolution of Human Consciousness.* Clarendon Press. Oxford.

Curio, E. 1976. *The Ethology of Predation.* Springer-Verlag. New York.

Delius, J.D., and B. Nowak. 1982. Visual Symmetry Recognition by Pigeons. *Psych. Research* 44:199–212.

Dress, O. 1952. Untersuchungen über die angeborenen Verhaltensweisen bei Springspinnen (Salticidae). *Z. Tierpsychol.* 9:169–207.

Edmunds, M. 1974. *Defence in Animals.* Methuen. London.

Erwin, T.L. 1982. Tropical forests: their richness in coleoptera and other arthropod species. *The Coleopterists' Bulletin* 36:74–75.

Erwin, T. 1983. Beetles and other insects of tropical forest canopies at Manaus, Brazil, sampled by insecticidal fogging. In *Tropical Rain Forest: Ecology and Management,* S.L. Sutton T.C. Whitmore, and A.C. Chadwick, eds., pp. 59–75. Blackwell Scientific Publications, Edinburgh.

Galdikas, B. 1978. Orangutans and Hominid Evolution. In *Spectrum,* S. Udin, ed., pp. 287–309, Jakarta: Dian Rakyat.

Goodall, J. van Lawick. 1968. Behaviour of free-living chimpanzees of the Gombe Stream area. *Anim. Behav. Monogr.* 1:165–311.

Greenberg, R. 1984. Neophobia in the foraging site selection of a Neotropical migrant bird: an experimental study. *Proc. Natl. Acad. Sci., USA* 81:3778–3780.

Griffin, D. 1976. *The Question of Animal Awareness.* Rockefeller University Press. N.Y.

————. 1984. *Animal Thinking.* Harvard University Press. Cambridge.

Haber, R.N. 1970. How we remember what we see. *Scientific American* 222(5):104–112.

Hinde, R.A. 1966. *Animal Behaviour.* McGraw-Hill. New York.

————. 1970. *Animal Behaviour.* 2nd ed. McGraw-Hill. Tokyo.

Hollard, V.D., and J.D. Delius. 1982. Rotational Invariance in Visual Pattern Recognition by Pigeons and Humans. *Science* 218:804–806.

Humphrey, N. 1976. The social function of intellect, in *Growing Points in Ethology*. Ed. P.P.G. Bateson and R.A. Hinde, 303–317. Cambridge University Press. N.Y.

Jerison, H.J. 1970. Brain evolution: new light on old principles. *Science* 170:1224–1225.

Jolly, A. 1966. Lemur social behavior and primate intelligence. *Science* 153:501–506.

Jones, R.V. 1979. *Most Secret War.* Hodder and Stoughton. London. 410–411.

Kohler, W. 1957. *The Mentality of Apes.* Penguin Books. United Kingdom.

Lorenz, K. 1965. *Evolution and Modification of Behavior.* Methuen & Co. London.

_____. 1981. *The Foundations of Ethology.* Simon and Schuster. N.Y.

Mackintosh, N.J. 1983. *Gneral Principles of Learning in Animal Behaviour.* 3rd ed. T.R. Halliday and P.J.B. Slater. Blackwell Scientific Publications. Oxford.

Maple, T.L. 1980. *Orang-utan Behavior.* Van Nostrand. N.Y.

Mayr, E. 1982. *The Origins of Biological Thought.* Harvard University Press. Cambridge.

Moynihan, M.H. 1970. The control, suppression, decay, disappearance and replacement of displays. *J. Theor. Biol.* 29:85–112.

_____. 1976. *The New World Primates.* Princeton University Press. Princeton, N.J.

Rand, A.S. 1967. Predator-prey interactions and the evolution of aspect diversity. *Atas. Simp. Biota Amazonica* 5:73–83.

Rand, A.S., and W.M. Rand. 1982. Variation in rainfall on Barro Colorado Island, in: *The Ecology of a Tropical Forest.* Ed. E.G. Leigh, A.S. Rand, and D.M. Windsor, 47–59. Smithsonian Institution Press. Washington, D.C.

Rensch, B. 1950. *Evolution above the Species Level.* Columbia. N.Y.

_____. 1967. Evolution of brain achievements, in: *Evolutionary Biology* I. 26–28, Appleton, Century, Crofts, N.Y.

Rickleffs, R., and K.O. O'Rourke. 1975. Aspect diversity in moths: a temperate-tropical comparison. *Evolution* 29:313–324.

Robinson, M.H. 1966. Anti-predator adaptations of stick- and leaf-mimicking insects. D. Phil. thesis, Oxford. Clarendon Library.

_____. 1969a. Defenses against visually hunting predators. *Evolutionary Biology III.* Appleton, Century, Crofts. N.Y.

————. **1969b.** The defensive behaviours of some orthopteriod insects from Panama. *Trans. Roy. Ent. Soc. Lond.* 121:281–303.

————. **1970.** Insect anti-predator adaptations and the behavior of predatory primates. *Act. IV Congr. Latin. Zool.* 2:811–836.

————. **1973.** The evolution of cryptic postures in insects, with special reference to some New Guinea tettigoniids (Orthoptera). *Psyche* 80:159–165.

————. **1977.** Is tropical biology real? *Tropical Ecology* 19:30–50.

————. **1979.** Informational complexity in tropical rain forest habitats and the origins of intelligence. *Actas del IV Simposium Internacional de Ecologia Tropical* 1:148–168.

————. **1981a.** A stick is a stick and not worth eating: on the definition of mimicry. *Biol. J. Linn. Soc. Lond.* 16:1–6.

————. **1981b.** Existe realmente la biologia tropical? *Academia Panamena de Medicina y Cirugia* 6 (1):13–45.

Sagan, C. 1977. *The Dragons of Eden.* Random House. N.Y.

Tinbergen, N. 1963. On aims and methods in ethology. *Z. Tierpsychol.* 20:410–433.

Wood-Mason, J. 1878. Preliminary notes on a species of Phasmidae apparently possessing all the structural arrangements needed both for aerial and aquatic respiration. *Ann. Mag. Nat. Hist.* 5:101–102.

Avian Predatory Behavior and Prey Distribution

Werner Schuler

Our present knowledge of the predatory behavior of insectivorous birds stems from investigations of the prey they eat, from precise descriptions of food brought to the young in relation to prey available in the habitat, from the comparison of search paths of individual birds to the distribution of their main prey, and from theoretical concepts. The first of these concepts, L. Tinbergen's (1960) search image hypothesis, was soon rivalled by Royama's (1970) profitability hypothesis and optimal foraging theory. The most important contribution of the latter is the introduction of gain in energy and time costs as criteria for the foraging bird. They can determine where it searches, how long it stays there, and whether it eats a prey found. Prey species can exploit the predatory behavior of birds by various adaptations. Since birds are flexible in their predatory behavior the value of these adaptations is not a fixed one but depends on the size, frequency, temporal and spatial distribution of the prey species in question, on the species and number of predators present, and on the availability of alternative prey for them.

During the twenties biologists still disputed enthusiastically whether cryptic coloration protects an animal against predators (Heikertinger 1928, 1930). Karl Peter (1930) set out to decide the wordy debate by means of an experiment. He collected one and a half thousand young caterpillars of *Inachis io* (Nymphalidae) and liberated them on their foodplant near his institute. After the larvae would have grown and pupated he planned to score at first how well each pupa matched to its surroundings and to find out later on whether pupae with good similarity, i.e. well camouflaged ones, survived at a higher rate than others. The larvae grew well, but Peter could not demonstrate the proof intended because his experiment failed. Even when searching with his colleagues for several days they did not find a single pupa! He knew certainly that these caterpillars which live gregariously on stinging nettle disperse just before pupation. However he had underestimated their migratory abilities considerably. There are data on this for *Nymphalis antiopa* another Nymphalid species: Forty-five caterpillars sitting together on a small birch tree dispersed over an area of about 2.5 hectares (6.2 acres; Besemer and Meeuse 1938).

Peter's failure demonstrates impressively the relationship between adaptive coloration and the distribution of prey species: Conspicuously colored insects such as the larvae of *Inachis* often live gregariously, whereas crytic ones such as its pupae are mostly solitary. Since we conceive cryptic as well as aposematic coloration as adaptations to predators hunting by sight, we can assume that the appropriate distributions, too, have to do with defense of predators. We suppose that they increase the protective value of those colorations or, the other way round, that they decrease the hunting success of their predators. From this follows the idea that the hunting success of predators is influenced generally by the distributions of their prey species.

In the present contribution I will discuss this idea. I will at first describe factors which influence the behavior of foraging birds and then point out how prey animals can take advantage of this influence to reduce the predator pressure impinging on them. Principally I will restrict myself to insectivorous birds and their prey, although the considerations and conclusions are valid also for other predators and other prey, if the respective circumstances are taken into account and can partially be applied to granivorous and frugivorous species and their food.

Methods for Studying the Food and Foraging Behavior of Insectivorous Birds

The foraging behavior of insectivorous birds can not be followed easily. If one accompanies for instance, a tame chicken searching a meadow for food one can occasionally see that it has preyed upon a small arthropod or bitten off a piece of a leaf, often, however, one cannot decide whether it has taken something or has only pecked against a blade of grass. With wild birds direct observation is even more difficult. To analyse their foraging behavior one has therefore to choose cases which can be observed easily and has additionally to make use of indirect evidence and of experimental investigations.

The analysis of crop and gizzard contents tells us what a bird has eaten, provided we are able to determine the prey from their more or less intact remains. Accordingly, we owe a great deal of our knowledge of the food of bird species to this method. However, since each individual bird can be inspected only once, statements about differences in food selection by the same individual at different times and their dependence on the type and amount of food available and other factors are rather impeded. This is also valid for the more sparing procedures, for which the birds are not killed but only caught, and released, after the content of their crop, gizzard or gut has been made accessible by means of an emetic (Zach and Falls 1976) or enema (Brensing 1977). In contrast to these procedures methods which do not interfere with the freeliving bird's life and behavior provide the opportunity for repeated examination of the same individual and thus yield more detailed data on the dynamics of food selection. Such methods are the analysis of pellets and feces as well as the collection of the food brought by parent birds to their dependent young.

Many bird species regurgitate food remains as pellets. If this is done regularly at the same place, such as by owls, pellets may easily be collected and examined. This method applies also to some insectivorous birds: Fry (1984) measured the food of bee-eaters quantitatively by placing sheets of cloth beneath their perches and thus collecting the pellets produced at short intervals by these birds.

In some cases the feces of birds contain remains which give astonishingly precise information on their diet. Davies (1977b) isolated from the droppings of wagtails (*Motacilla spp.*) well-preserved wings of flies, by means of which he could analyse the frequency, size, and genus of the flies eaten.

The food given to nestling birds by their parents can be registrated by direct observation (L. Tinbergen 1960), photographically (Royama 1970, J. Tinbergen 1981) or by means of neck collars (Kluijver 1933). For the latter method a collar (which impedes swallowing, but not breathing) is fitted to the neck of the nestling for some time. The investigator can remove the food from the nestling's gullet, just as Chinese fishermen take fish caught by tame cormorants wearing a metal ring around their necks (Egremont and Rothschild 1979). Here the food of the nestlings can be preserved and analysed later on. In contrast photographical registration and direct observation demand a thorough knowledge of possible prey species, since these must be identified while the parent bird holds them in its beak.

Provided the prey of a bird is known, precise information on its food selection is still lacking. This can be gained by comparing the food eaten to that available. Therefore we must know the prey present in the habitat. If prey is not distributed equally, and this is rarely so even in habits appearing rather homogenous at first sight, its distribution as well as the search path of the predator must be known. The finest study on this topic was carried out by Joost Tinbergen (1981) on European starlings (*Sturnus vulgaris* L.) on the Dutch island of Schiermonikoog (having a tree-less, easily observable terrain, and rather monotonous prey fauna). He recorded simultaneously the prey brought in by individual starlings, their search path and the distribution of their main prey. By means of this nearly perfect description he was able to demonstrate an unexpectedly precise memory for places in starlings and to determine significant results on their foraging decisions. We shall return to these findings later.

Our present knowledge about the predatory behavior of birds is, however, not only based upon as precise as possible descriptive data but also on a series of ethological and ecological concepts used in interpreting them. The development of these concepts and the appertaining experimental evidence mirrors the development of behavioral ecology as an independent branch of biological science.

The first concept of this type was the search image hypothesis of Lukas Tinbergen (1960). In a large scale investigation he compared the supply of arthropods in a Dutch pine forest to the food brought in by great tits (*Parus major* L.) to their nestlings. If the tits took prey at random, one would have expected a linear relation between density of each prey type in the habitat and its frequency in the nestlings' diet. Actually he found prey types of low and of high density less frequently in the diet than expected and types of medium density more frequently. He attributed the underrepresentation of high density prey to a possible tendency for a varied diet in the tits, such as that known from rats which are given a choice of several different foodstuffs *ad libitum*. More important for us is his interpretation of the change from underrepresentation to overrepresentation of a prey at the transition from low to medium densities. Tinbergen assumed that a bird which finds a particular prey type several times by chance forms a search image for it, i.e. learns to find it more easily. Experiments of de Ruiter (1952) had indicated such perceptive changes. He offered stick-like caterpillars (*Biston betularia* L.) together with sticks of the same size to jays (*Garrulus glandarius* L.) and chaffinches (*Fringilla coelebs* L.). The birds ignored the caterpillars at first, but if they detected the first one by chance, for instance by stepping upon it, they soon found the others by pecking at sticks as well as at stick-capterpillars. Later on some of the jays learned to detect the larvae by sight alone. These experiments show why the protection of a well camouflaged insect depends on its distribution. If a bird finds a first one by chance and pecks subsequently at all similar objects, it will quickly detect other ones sitting nearby. If, however, the next one is far away, the bird will stop pecking at inedible objects after a while. Even those birds which have learned to differentiate between similar objects and the camouflaged insect by only looking at them, will stop searching for it, if the distance between individuals of this prey is long enough.

The idea, that spacing out is an important attribute of camouflage in the same way as selection of an appropriate background or immobility (see Edmunds, this volume), was first described by Niko Tinbergen and tested by him and his coworkers (N. Tinbergen et al. 1967). They offered to wild crows (*Corvus corone* L.) hens' eggs painted to be cryptic either at large or at small distances between eggs. They found that the crows were less successful with eggs spaced out. The reason for this was that the crows searched in the vicinity of the first egg found. This "area concentrated search" is found in various predators that search for more than one prey per hunting trip, e.g. predatory mites (Kaiser 1983), ladybirds and their larvae (Murakami and Tsubaki 1984), birds (Smith 1974a, b). The concentration on the vicinity of the place of the first success is accomplished by a reduction of walking speed and an increase in rate and/or degree of turns.

Investigations on the search image hypothesis were subsequently carried out by Croze (1970) with carrion crows (*Corvus corone* L.) in the field and by Dawkins (1971a, b) in the laboratory. (For search images in human visual perception see Neisser ([1967]). Croze found that crows can search for a specific prey type after one or two reinforcements and that they are nearly as successful when searching for three different types simultaneously as when looking for only one. However, their hunting success was influenced by other factors additionally. They searched an area thoroughly on which they had been offered prey several times but completely ignored adjacent places. Such interfering variables were excluded by Dawkins in her carefully controlled experiments with chicks searching for colored grains on different backgrounds. She found evidence for the perceptive changes postulated by the search image hypothesis, but also for short terms alterations in choice behavior which she attributed to shifts of attention. Finally, Pietrewicz and Kamil (1979, 1981) by testing blue jays (*Cyanocitta cristata*) with operant conditioning techniques, Lawrence (1985a, b) by experimenting with European blackbirds (*Turdus merula*) in the field, and Gendron (1986) by training bobwhite quails (*Colinus virginianus*) to search for cryptic food in the laboratory all seemed to prove beyond doubt that birds can form a search image. This evidence has recently been criticized by Guilford and Dawkins (1987).

In any case, even the definite proof for search image formation in birds, will not mean that a search image caused the increase of prey types in the nestling food of tits at medium densities observed by Lukas Tinbergen (1960). As Dawkins (1971a) has pointed out this effect could be also produced by alterations in the tits' searching or accepting behavior, such as by concentration on a profitable place or by increase in acceptability of a prey. Other authors have labelled various alterations of behavior resulting in the prevalence of one prey in the diet as search image. But this term should be used only for the perceptive changes named by it originally (Lawrence and Allen 1983).

Royama (1970), who similarly to Likas Tinbergen compared the arthropod supply within the territories of great tits to the food they brought to their nestlings explained the overabundance of certain prey types at medium densities by his profitability hypothesis. He assumed that the tit regularly patrols the different places where food can be found, such as trees and bushes, thereby staying at each place as long as its search is successful. He hypothesized that the tit gives up searching after having found nothing for a certain period which he called 'giving up time'. This behavioral mechanism results in searching most of the time at profitable places. Thereby prey species concentrated at these places appear more often in the diet than it corresponds to their overall density within the territory.

Smith and Sweatman (1974) tried to weigh the two hypotheses by observing the directions of arriving and departing great tits feeding their young. They found that tits returning to the nestbox after a short trip (i.e. probably from a profitable place) started the next one mostly in the old direction, indicating the old place. In contrast to this they changed direction after having searched for a longer time. These findings fit to the assumption of a giving up time. Series of feedings brought from one direction consisted of different prey species. This conforms readily to Royamas' conception of concentration on profitable places whereas the search image hypothesis can explain it only by supplementary assumptions, for instance that the tits used several different searching images simultaneously.

The facts thus favoured the profitability hypothesis more than the search image concept. During the following years the profitability hypothesis was strengthened even more, since its basic assumption forms also the basis of the optimal foraging theory, which was developed at that time.

This theory starts from the assumption that natural selection has preferred those types which produced more offspring than others because they utilized their food optimally either by eating more during the time available for searching and feeding (intake maximizers) or by gathering the necessary amount of food as fast as possible, thereby saving time for other activities relevant for survival or reproduction such as vigilance for predators or courtship (time minimizers). Applying the optimal foraging theory to a specific problem is done in three steps (Schoener 1971). First, a currency must be chosen, that is, the parameter to be optimized. This is often energy uptake per unit of time or a proportional measure. Second, the limitations of the system must be determined, such as the frequency, size and energy content of the prey types and the searching and handling time which the predator needs for finding, catching and eating. The third step is the derivation of an optimal solution for the problem under the conditions given. Subsequently this solution has to be compared to the predator's actual behavior. If both agree well, the behavior is better understood than before. Thus Davies (1977b) was able to explain the choice of wagtails (*Motacilla alba* L.) among dungflies (Scatophagidae) of different sizes. If the optimal solution and the behavior of the predator do not conform, not all the important limitations of the system have been considered—provided the mathematics of the derivation were correct. Then arises the question: What additional factor(s) must be taken into account.

If there are prey animals of the same quality but of different sizes a conclusion follows from the consideration of the predator's time expenditure, which has been derivated by several different authors almost simultaneously (see Pyke et al. 1977, p. 141): The predator should accept only types which yield a large gain in energy per unit of foraging time and should ignore all the rest. If, for instance, there is a large and a small prey type, the predator should eat the large one exclusively as long as its gain in energy per foraging time is greater than with the small one. Only when the large type is so rare that this gain is reduced to the amount of the small one should the predator accept the small prey. Whether the small prey is eaten should therefore depend only on the frequency of the larger. This sounds surprisingly at first, but it becomes plausible if one considers a prey so tiny and tedious to eat, that the predator becomes hungry while eating it, whereas it could become satiated by searching for a rarer but larger prey.

Krebs and his co-workers (Krebs et al. 1977) tested this prediction with great tits which were offered half and whole mealworms on a conveyor belt. They found an astonishingly fast change from accepting to rejecting the small prey when they increased the frequency of the large one. Nevertheless, the transition was not as immediate and the rejection of the small prey not as complete as predicted. Several authors have put forward a series of reasons, why such partial preferences might exist, e.g. mistaking one prey type for the other or a response to random fluctuations of the larger prey's frequency (see Krebs and McCleery 1984, McNamara and Houston 1987).

The time which a bird needs to get to a place where it can find food, (a "patch") is part of its time costs. Especially, the time necessary for flying to the next patch, the "travel time," should influence the decision as to when to leave the present one, where prey is depleted gradually making the search increasingly more time consuming. If the travel time is short, an expensive search does not pay from the viewpoint of gain in energy per unit of time, but it may do so with a long travel time. According to Charnov et al. (1976) the predator should stop searching in a patch exactly when the gain in energy per unit time has fallen to the mean value obtainable within the territory (marginal value theorem). In a territory in which the distances between patches are large, this marginal value is low and in this case the predator should stay longer within each patch than in a habitat in which, other things being equal, distances between patches and therefore travel times are smaller. This prediction was tested by Cowie (1977) in the laboratory. His tits could find pieces of mealworms in boxes filled with saw-dust which were fastened to the branches of artificial trees. The boxes contained equal numbers of prey, but had two different types of lids, which required different amounts of time. Thus different travel times were represented by different times needed to get to the prey. The results conformed to the expectation qualitatively: The tits searched longer in each box if they had to spend more "travel" time. Cowie was able to achieve a quantitative agreement between his theoretical model and data when he subtracted the energy necessary for the various activities of the tit from its gross gain in energy, i.e. by considering the net gain only.

The marginal value theorem can be applied also to a bird which carries food to his nest for feeding young (central place foraging), since in this case travel time is also important and the growing costs of an increasing load size correspond to those for searching in a gradually depleted patch (Orians and Pearson 1978). One prediction of this model is that a bird should take a bigger load size if it has to search at greater distances from the nest. This was confirmed qualitatively by Carlson & Moreno (1981) for wheatears (*Oenanthe oenanthe* L.) and by Bryant & Turner (1982) for house martins (*Delichon urbica* L.). Kacelnik (1984) developed a more sophisticated model which takes into account that load size increases stepwise for a given prey type and confirmed it quantitatively for starlings in the field to which he offered mealworms.

Andersson (1978) showed that according to the theory of central place foraging the bird should search preferably in the vicinity of its nest. The search effort and, therefore, the predator pressure exerted by the bird should decrease with increasing distance from the nest and the size of the feeding territory should depend on prey density. Both predictions could be confirmed for whinchats (*Saxicola rubetra* L.), the territories of which were supplemented in part of the experiments with a great number of dishes containing mealworms (Andersson 1981).

The idea that time costs influence the decisions of foraging birds was applied by Erichsen et al. (1980) and Houston et al. (1980) to searching for cryptic prey. They showed that tits which were offered pieces of mealworms inside opaque pieces of drinking straws as a cryptic prey, accepted or rejected that depending on the frequency of inedible objects looking similarly. Thus time necessary for sorting out inedible objects (which was rather long here, since each item had to be picked up and carried to a perch for close inspection) influenced the decision to search for a cryptic prey.

The experiments on optimal foraging theory mentioned so far began with constant conditions since the experimental birds were accustomed to the conditions in question for some time before testing. However factors such as prey density are rarely constant in the field. Therefore, Royama (1970) has assumed that tits patrol all patches in their territories to find out changes in profitability. Krebs et al. (1978) designed an experiment to test whether tits could make an optimal choice between two sources of food, the profitability of which they did not know before. Initially the tits altered between both sources. After some time they specialized on the more profitable one. The duration of the initial testing phase corresponded well to the theoretical model developed for this problem. Similarly Lima (1985) demonstrated that starlings can learn to discriminate between patches of different profitability by sampling. The theory which deals with the problem of how a predator can adjust to a fluctuating food supply is called stochastic foraging theory (see Krebs and McCleery 1984).

In the experiments of Krebs et al. (1978) and Lima (1985) the birds had to determine the higher reward rate. This problem has been studied intensively by experimental psychologists using pigeons and rats which had to choose between different schedules of variable interval reinforcement. Since the basic idea of these experiments is the same as that in experiments testing the choice of patches differing in profitability, both can be treated using the same or very similar theoretical models. Moreover both approaches can profit from their respective results (Shettleworth 1984). Thus both Dow and Lea (1987) and Shettleworth et al. (1988) have recently shown that pigeons can make an optimal or near optimal choice between food sources fluctuating in various ways, and have analyzed, what cues and behavioral rules the birds use for achieving their appropriate solution.

It is obvious at this point that the experiments on optimal and stochastic foraging have reached a degree of abstraction in their theoretical models as well as in their experimental procedures that one can doubt whether they are adequate to field conditions. The protagonists of the theory meet doubts of this type by noting that the hitherto existing models are simplistic but can be developed by incorporating more factors, so that in future it will become possible to make even quantitative predictions for complicated natural systems (Krebs et al. 1981). Some factors have been incorporated into the models already. For instance, the readiness of the bird to take a higher or lower risk depending on its hunger state (Caraco et al. 1980), or the necessity of vigilance for predators (Milinski and Heller 1978). Sceptics will continue to doubt the possibility of quantitative predictions for complex systems. They are supported by the study of first order difference equations (May 1976) and by the results of 'chaos' physics (Lauterborn and Meyer-Ilse 1986) which demonstrate that even simple systems cannot be predicted exactly if non-linear processes are involved.

Zach illustrates the possibilities and limitations of a treatment of foraging problems by means of optimality theory. On the one hand the behavior of northwestern crows (*Corvus caurinus*), which select whelks (*Thais lamellosa*) on the shore and open them by dropping them from some height, can be predicted quantitatively including the size of whelk selected, height of flight, and rate of dropping (Zach 1979). On the other hand the searching behavior of the ovenbird (*Seiurus aurocapillus*) on the forest floor obviously cannot be treated in this way, since the density and quality of its prey varies over space and time to such degree, that neither a researcher nor a bird seems to be able to measure all the factors necessary for an optimal choice (Zach and Falls 1979, Zach and Smith 1981).

Moreover, birds sometimes do not make an optimal choice even under simple conditions. This was attributed to the influence of additional factors (Draulans 1984), to optimization of intake on a seasonal rather than on a daily basis (Dill 1978), or to a strategy different from optimizing intake (Inglis and Ferguson 1986).

However, we should emphasize the advantages of the theoretical approach rather than being too sceptical. Its most important merit is the introduction of time and energy costs as a criterion for foraging decisions. Without this one would assume that the question of whether the spotted flycatcher (*Muscicapa striata*) preys upon bumble-bees (*Bombus spec.*) depends only on its ability to deal with bees' stinging apparatus. However, considering time and energy costs Davies (1977a) could demonstrate that it preys upon these insects only when other ones, which it can handle more easily, are not flying because of low ambient temperature. A further merit of the theoretical approach is the fact that it has stimulated investigations which demonstrated abilities of birds not expected, such as the ability to differentiate between prey types or patches differing in profitability. Finally without quantitative models we cannot understand how several factors interplay quantitatively.

The concentration of the theory on functional aspects allows us on the one hand to produce foraging models that can be applied to predators as different as sea stars (Campbell 1983) and birds. On the other hand most authors have neglected the mechanisms governing the predators' behavior. As we can learn from 'chaos' physics simple deterministic prosesses may be involved even if the output of a system cannot be predicted quantitatively (Lauterborn and Meyer-Ilse 1986; Werner Lauterborn, personal communication). It is assumed generally that the predator does not measure all the variables incorporated into a model directly but rather uses rules of thumb to achieve an approximately optimal choice. An example is Royama's (1970) giving up time, which means "stop searching in a place when you have found nothing for a certain amount of time," as a measure of profitability. Only recently behavioral mechanisms have been incorporated into foraging models for bees (Cheverton et al. 1985, Schmid-Hempel et al. 1985) whereas birds seem still to be thought of measuring energy uptake only by rules of thumb such as intake rate or size of prey. However, the findings that starlings prefer sugar solutions probably because their energy concent (Schuler 1983), that they are able to choose the food containing more energy in the form of sugar or fatty oil (Schuler 1987), and that drinking sugar solution influences subsequent eating behavior (Zinner 1985), indicate that birds can measure energy uptake more directly. Further research on foraging mechanisms will probably demonstrate a wealth of possible solutions for the functional problems of foraging achieved by different species.

In the laboratory one can adjust testing conditions to the problem and theory to be examined. Thereby factors which are important for a bird may be neglected. In the field, on the other hand, important variables often cannot be measured as accurately as necessary. Joost Tinbergen (1981) succeeded in combining the advantages of both approaches in an almost ideal manner by choosing an easily observable system and by making intense efforts to measure the decisive variables. As mentioned earlier he measured prey distributions, search paths and the food brought to the young by starlings. On a pasture the food brought in consisted of more than 90% leatherjackets (larvae of the crane fly *Tipula paludosa* Meigen). Thus the system could be treated in the first approximation as a one-prey system. After having found the larvae for one feeding quickly, the starlings returned to the old place for searching with a precision more accurate than the measure of 1 meter, which Tinbergen had choosen. If they had needed more time for collecting they often continued their search at a new place. By this behavior the starlings utilized the areas of high prey density more intensively. Principally this conforms to the choice of profitable patches, however who could have thought that a free-living bird can adjust so quickly and so precisely to the more profitable ranges within a habitat appearing to our eyes as a monotonuous area?

Tinbergen's starlings occasionally flew to a more distant saltmarsh from where they brought in caterpillars of a noctiud moth (*Cerapteryx graminis*). From an energetic point of view this was a rather unprofitable prey, because it required long flying and searching times. Choice experiments showed that starlings decidedly preferred caterpillars to leatherjackets if both were easily accessible. Moreover nestlings fed too much leatherjackets may suffer from very wet droppings fouling their nests and feathers, with possible fatal consequences (Kluijver 1933). Therefore Tinbergen assumed that the adult starlings searched for leatherjackets only because they could supply energy by this easily obtainable food, and that they supplemented it by high quality caterpillars to avoid damage to their young.

According to this hypothesis starlings which were given for some time additional nestlings searched for leatherjackets exclusively, since they could not meet the increased demands otherwise. Starlings with nestboxes near the saltmash did not gather them at all, since the cater-pillars were for them not only a high-quality prey but also, because of short flying times, a profitable one. Tinbergen thus demonstrated that two currencies existed for the starlings according to which they optimized their search for food. Thereby, as in human economics, the values of the currencies were not fixed but adjusted to the respective demands.

These field studies demonstrated the importance of prey quality (see also Goss-Custard 1977), whereas, as we have seen, for laboratory experiments researchers usually abstracted from prey quality, offering larger and smaller or easily and not easily accessible prey of the same kind.

Here arises the question of how many prey types a bird discrimin-ates. From the few studies of the ontogeny of food selection in birds one can conclude that a naive youngster starts from some predispositions about general properties of its prey and subsequently learns which objects are edible and which of these are profitable prey (Kear 1985). But does an experienced bird know each species of its arthropod prey or distinguishes it only cross categories such as "flies," "caterpillars" or "bugs"? The latter seems more probable, since birds generalize experience from one species to similarly looking others they never have seen before (Coppinger 1969). However, if we recall that J. Tinbergen's (1981) starlings obviously had a thorough knowledge of the location, distribution and quality of at least two prey species and that pigeons can remember at least 100 (Delius 1985), 320 (Vaughan and Green 1984) or even 625 (Juan Delius, personal communication) different visual patterns, we must admit that birds may possibly have a much more detailed knowledge of their prey.

Experiments with warningly colored insects gave conflicting evi-dence on this point. Black and red colored insects of about the same size were either treated as different prey (Sillen-Tullberg et al. 1982) or as one type (Evans et al. 1987). Apart from the fact that different bird species were involved, the possibility exists that young birds tend to generalize where-as older ones are more inclined to discriminate because of their accumul-ated experience (Evans et al. 1987). However, the question, whether a bird discriminates between prey types is not only a matter of its state of experience or its discriminative abilities, since starlings, which had shown before that they could discriminate almost identical prey types, made use of this ability or not depending on the alternative prey they were given (Schuler 1974). So further research is necessary not only to find out what birds really learn about their insect prey, but also under what conditions they make use of their discriminative capacities.

From all the conceptions and facts described above it follows that the behavior of a foraging bird is determined on the one hand by its own properties and on the other hand by the quality, size, frequency and distribution of its prey. In which way a given species behaves in a given habitat can only be established by a detailed etho-ecological analysis. Nevertheless some general rules can be formulated:

1. The bird should search for food at a time and in a place, when and where it can gather its prey at as low a cost as possible.

2. The bird should select those prey species which can fulfill its requirements at the lowest expense in time and energy.

3. The bird's requirements refer primarily to energy uptake but also to prey quality which probably means the supply of nutrients and vitamins as well as the avoidance of damage by poisonous or noxious species.

The foraging behavior of the individual bird can additionally be influenced by the behavior of conspecifics and non-conspecifics. Birds of its own as well as of other species may attract it to or exclude it from a feeding site. Competition between species is often diminished by specialization on different food types or habitats, especially when food is scarce (Lack 1971), sometimes by defending interspecific territories (Leisler et al. 1983). Competition with conspecifics can be reduced by establishing territories. This is only feasible if the food supply is not fluctuating too much. Otherwise colonial breeding and flock feeding may be a better life-style (Horn 1968). According to the concept of economic defendability (Brown 1964) a territory should only be defended if the benefits gained exceed the costs of defense. This is normally the case at a medium or moderately high food supply. With lower supplies costs may be higher than benefits, and at very high levels benefits may be gained without defense. The best evidence for this concept comes from nectar feeding birds for which the value of a territory seems to be given at each moment by the number of flowers and their nectar production. Insect eating birds do not respond as quickly to short term fluctuations of their food since long term benefits of a territory are more important for them (see Davies and Houston [1984] for a review.)

How Can Prey Insects Evade Foraging Birds?

Insect eating birds exert selection pressures which favor variations in their prey species reducing the rate of predation. By this process of variation and selective predation a wide range of adaptations can be shaped. One group of characters diminishes the probability of an attack by birds. A prey species may develop cryptic coloration or shift its activity to places or periods where and when birds search little or at all. Another group of adaptations reduces the success of an attack: A prey may drop itself from its foodplant as soon as it perceives the vibrations caused by a perching bird, it may jump off, or may simply have a body coloration inhibiting prey-attack by the respective bird species (Schuler and Hesse 1985). These and other examples out of nature's wealth in defensive adaptations are treated lucidly in the other chapters of this book.

The concepts and facts discussed in this chapter suggest that additionally all features reducing the profitability of a prey for birds may reduce predator pressure. This can be achieved, first, by increasing the necessary searching time per individual prey item, e.g. by spacing out, second, by increasing the necessary handling time, e.g. by having hard elytra which the bird must remove before swallowing or by hiding under a tough web, or third by reducing the predator's gain, e.g. by having a small body mass.

There are constraints which hold for the evolution and function of all defensive adaptations. Such adaptations may not have been evolved in each species for which they might be useful, and they do not protect against all predators. We can illustrate this by means of a partly hypothetical example. As mentioned earlier leatherjackets live on grassland in the upper layers of the soil and are preyed upon by starlings. A phenotype in which the larva retreats only a few centimeters deeper into the soil, would totally exclude this predator. The trait could only be evolved firstly when the proper variations arise, and secondly if the alteration in live-style would be compatible to vital requirements such as oxygen uptake. The trait having evolved would exclude many other predators, too, but not specialists (waders probing the soil with long bills or digging mammals such as moles). Nevertheless its bearers would replace other phenotypes, since they would survive and therefore reproduce at a higher rate than others.

Our considerations remain speculative in many respects, partly because our knowledge is rather incomplete and partly because the effectiveness of most adaptations depends on many variables. More precise statements can be made if the ecology of only one species is considered, the periodical cicadas being a famous example (Lloyd and Dybas 1966). As nymphs they live underground, i.e. out of the reach of birds, for many years; then, as adults they appear in one short season in vast numbers, only few of which birds can utilize; and finally they "disappear" again for many years, making adaptations on the predators' side impossible.

Nevertheless, an important conclusion from our discussion of avian predatory behavior is, that we cannot look at isolated defensive features of prey animals since their effectiveness depends firstly on other properties of the species in question, such as its size, frequency distribution over space and time, and secondly on properties of the ecosystem such as the species and number of predators present and the alternative prey available for them. Moreover, we must keep in mind, that the same feature may have other functions in other species (see Kettlewell 1973 for melanism in different species of butterflies). On the other hand we can assume, that under natural conditions many adaptations are much more effective against birds than in laboratory tests, in which the experimental birds have only very limited possibilities to change over to another maybe more profitable prey or feeding place.

I am very grateful to Dr. David Evans and Dr. Justin Schmidt for inviting me to write this chapter and for editorial efforts including improvement of my English, to Dr. Ellen Deusser-Schuler for critically reading and discussing the manuscript, and to Gisela Vogel for typing German and English drafts.

References

Andersson, M. 1978. Optimal foraging area: size and allocation of search effort. *Theor. Pop. Biol.* 13: 397-409.

_____. **1981.** Central place foraging in the whinchat (*Saxicola rubetra*). *Ecology* 62: 538-544.

Besemer, A.F.H., Meeuse, B.J.D. 1938. Rouwmantels. *Levende Nat.* 43: 1-12.

Brensing, D. 1977. Nahrungsökologische Untersuchungen an Zugvögeln in einem südwest-deutschen Durchzugsgebiet während des Wegzuges. *Vogelwarte* 29: 44-56.

Brown, J.L., 1964. The evolution of diversity in avian territorial systems. *Wilson Bull.* 76: 160-169.

Bryant, D.M., Turner, A.K. 1982. Central place foraging by swallows (Hirundinidae): the question of load size. *Anim. Behav.* 30: 845-856.

Campbell, D.B. 1983. Foraging behavior of the sea-star *Asterias forbesi. Am. Zool. 23: 881.*

Caraco, T., Martindale, S., Whitham, T.S. 1980. An empirical demonstration of risk-sensitive foraging preferences. *Anim. Behav.* 28: 820-830.

Carlson, A., Moreno, J. 1981. Central place foraging in the wheatear (*Oenanthe oenanthe*): an experimental test. *J Anim. Ecol.* 50: 917-924.

Charnov, E.L., Orians, G.H., Hyatt, K. 1976. Ecological implications of resource depression. *Am. Nat.* 110: 247-259.

Cheverton, J., Kacelnik, A., Krebs, J.R. 1985. Optimal foraging: constraints and currencies. *Fortschr. Zool.* 31: 109-126.

Coppinger, R.P. 1969. The effect of experience and novelty on avian feeding behavior with reference to the evolution of warning coloration in butterflies. I. *Behaviour* 35: 45-58.

Cowie, R.J. 1977. Optimal foraging in great tits (*Parus major*). *Nature, Lond.* 268: 137-139.

Croze, H. 1970. Searching image in carrion crows. *Z. Tierpsychol. Beih.* 5: 1-86.

Davies, N.B. 1977a. Prey selection and the search strategy of the spotted flycatcher (*Musciapa striata*), a field study on optimal foraging. *Anim. Behav.* 25: 1016-1033.

_____. **1977b.** Prey selection and social behaviour in wagtails (Aves: Motacillidae). *J. Anim. Ecol.* 46: 37-57.

Davies, N.B., Houston, A.I. 1984. Territory economics. In *Behavioural Ecology,* ed. J.R. Krebs, N.B. Davies, 148-169. 2nd ed. Oxford: Blackwell.

Dawkins, M. 1971a. Perceptual changes in chicks: another look at the 'search image' concept. *Anim. Behav.* 19: 566-574.

————. **1971b.** Shifts of 'attention' in chicks during feeding. *Anim. Behav.* 19: 575–582.

Delius, J.D. 1985. Cognitive processes in pigeons. In *Cognition, Information Processing and Motivation,* ed. G. d'Ydewalle, 3–18. Amstrdam: Elsevier.

de Ruiter, L. 1952. Some experiments on the camouflage of stick caterpillars. *Behaviour* 4: 222–232.

Dill, L.M. 1978. An energy-based model of optimal feeding territory size. *Theor. Popu. Biol.* 14: 369–429.

Dow, S.M., Lea, S.E.G. 1987. Sampling of schedule parameters by pigeons: tests of optimizing theory. *Anim. Behav.* 35: 102–114.

Draulans, D. 1984. Suboptimal mussel selection by tufted ducks *Aythya fuligula:* test of a hypothesis. *Anim. Behav.* 32: 1192–1196.

Egremont, P., Rothschild, M. 1979. The calculating cormorants. *Biol. J. Linn. Soc.* 12: 181–186.

Erichsen, J.T., Krebs, J.R., Houston, A.I. 1980. Optimal foraging and cryptic prey. *J. Anim. Ecol.* 49: 271–276.

Evans, D.L., Castoriades, N., Badruddine, H. 1987. Warning signal generalization in young predators. *Ethology* 74: 335–345.

Fry, C.H. 1984. *The Bee-eaters.* Calton England, Poyser.

Gendron, R.P. 1986. Searching for cryptic prey: evidence for optimal search rates and the formation of search images in quail. *Anim. Behav.* 34: 898–912.

Goss-Custard, J.D. 1977. The energetics of prey selection by redshank, *Tringa totanus* (L.), in relation to prey density. *J. Anim. Ecol.* 46: 1–19.

Guilford, T., Dawkins, M.S. 1987. Search images not proven: a reappraisal of recent evidence. *Anim. Behav.* 35: 1838–1845.

Heikertinger, F. 1928. Über das Mimikryproblem und seine Schwesterprobleme. *Internat. Congr. Entomol., Ithaca* 2: 821–831.

————. **1930.** Über "transformative Schutzfärbung" und ihre wissenschaftliche Begründung. *Biol Zentralbl.* 50: 193–219.

Horn, H.S. 1968. The adaptive significance of colonial nesting in the Brewer's blackbird (*Euphagus cyanocephalus*). *Ecology* 49: 682–694.

Houston, A.I., Krebs, J.R., Erichsen, J.T. 1980. Optimal prey choice and discrimination time in the great tit (*Parus major L.*). *Behav. Ecol. Sociobiol.* 6: 169–175.

Inglis, I.R., Ferguson, N.J.K. 1986. Starlings search for food rather than eat freely available, identical food. *Anim. Behav.* 34: 614–617.

Kacelnik, A. 1984. Central place foraging in starlings. I. Patch residence time. *J. Anim. Ecol.* 53: 283–299.

Kaiser, H. 1983. Small scale spatial heterogeneity influences predation success in an unexpected way: model experiments on the functional response of predatory mites (Acarina). *Oecologia* 56: 249–256.

Kear, J. 1985. Food selection. In *A Dictionary of Birds.* ed. B. Campbell, E. Lack, 224–234: Cafton England: Poyser.

Kettlewell, B. 1973. *The Evolution of Melanism.* Oxford: Clarendon.

Kluijver, H.N. 1933. Bijdrage tot de biologie en de ecologie van den Spreeuw (*Sturnus vulgaris vulgaris* L.) gedurende zijn voortplantingstijd. *Verslagen Mededeelingen Plantenziekten-kundigen Dienst Wageningen* 69: 1–145.

Krebs, J.R., Erichsen, J.T., Webber, M.I., Charnov, E.L. 1977. Optimal prey selection in the great tit (*Parus major*). *Anim. Behav.* 25: 30–38.

Krebs, J.R., Kacelnik, A., Taylor, P. 1978. Test of optimal sampling by foraging great tits. *Nature, Lond.* 275: 27–31.

Krebs, J.R., Houston, A.I., Charnov, E.L. 1981. Some recent developments in optimal foraging. In *Foraging Behavior.* ed. A.C. Kamil, T.D. Sargent, 3–18. New York: Garland.

Krebs, J.R., McCleery, R.H. 1984. Optimization in behavioural ecology. In *Behavioral Ecology,* ed., J.R. Krebs, N.B. Davies, 91–121. 2nd ed. Oxford: Blackwell.

Lack, D. 1971. *Ecological Isolation in Birds.* Oxford: Blackwell.

Lauterborn, W., Meyer-Ilse, W. 1986. Chaos. *Phys. unserer Zeit* 17(6): 177–187.

Lawrence, E.S. 1985a. Evidence for search image in blackbirds (*Turdus merula* L.): short term learning. *Anim. Behav.* 33: 929–937.

————. **1985b.** Evidence for search image in blackbirds (*Turdus merula* L.): long term learning. *Anim. Behav.* 33: 1301–1309.

Lawrence, E.S., Allen, J.A. 1983. The term search image. *Oikos* 40: 313–324.

Leisler, B., Heine, G. Siebenrock, K.H. 1983. Einnischung und interspezifische Territorialität überwinternder Steinschmätzer (*Oenanthe isabellina, O. oenanthe, O. pleschanka*) in Kenia. *J. Ornithol.* 124: 393–413.

Lima, S.L. 1985. Sampling behavior of starlings foraging in simple patchy environments. *Behav. Ecol. Sociobiol.* 16: 135–142.

Lloyd, M., Dybas, H.S. 1966. The periodical cicada problem. I. Population ecology. *Evolution* 20: 133–149.

McNamara, J.M., Houston, A.I. 1987. Partial preferences and foraging. *Anim. Behav.* 35: 1084-1099.

May, R.M. 1976. Simple mathematical models with very complicated dynamics. *Nature* 261: 459-467.

Milinski, M., Heller, R. 1978. Influence of a predator on the optimal foraging behaviour of stickle-backs (*Gasterosteus aculeatus* L.). *Nature, Lond.* 275: 642-644.

Murakami, Y., Tsubaki, Y. 1984. Searching efficiency of the lady beetle *Coccinella septempunctata* larvae in uniform and patchy environments. *J. Ethol.* 2: 1-6.

Neisser, U. 1967. *Cognitive Psychology.* New York: Appleton-Century-Crofts.

Orians, G.H. Pearson, N.E. 1978. On the theory of central place foraging. In *Analysis of Ecological Systems,* ed. D.F. Horn, 155-177. Columbus: Ohio State University Press.

Peter, K. 1930. Über die Bedeutung der Schutztracht. *Biol. Zentralbl.* 50: 19-25.

Pietrewicz, A.T., Kamil, A.C. 1979. Search image formation in the blue jay (*Cyanocitta cristata*). *Science,* 204: 1332-1333.

_____. **1981.** Search images and the detection of cryptic prey: an operant approach. In *Foraging Behavior,* ed. A.C. Kamil, T.D. Sargent, 311-331. New York: Garland.

Pyke, G.H., Pulliam, H.R., Charnov, E.L. 1977. Optimal foraging: a selective review of theory and tests. *Q. Rev. Biol.* 52: 137-154.

Royama, T. 1970. Factors governing the hunting behaviour and selection of food by the great tit (*Parus major* L.). *J. Anim. Ecol.* 39: 619-668.

Ruiter, L. de. 1952. Some experiments on the camouflage of stick caterpillars. *Behaviour.* 222-232.

Schmid-Hempel, P., Kacelnik, A., Houston, A.I. 1985. Honeybees maximize efficiency by not filling their crop. *Behav. Ecol. Sociobiol.* 17: 61-66.

Schoener, T.W. 1971. Theory of feeding strategies. *Ann. Rev. Ecol. Syst.* 2: 369-404.

Schuler, W. 1974. Die Schutzwirkung künstlicher Batesscher Mimikry abhängig von Modellähnlichkeit und Beuteangebot. *Z. Tierpsychol.* 36: 71-127.

Schuler, W. 1983. Responses to sugars and their behavioural mechanisms in the starling (*Sturnus vulgaris* L.). *Behav. Ecol. Sociobiol.* 13: 243-251.

Schuler, W. 1987. *Untersuchungen zur Bedeutung der unmittelbaren Erfahrung und des Lernens in Funktionskreis Nahrung beim Star.* Habilitationsschrift. University of Göttingen. 284 pp.

Schuler, W., Hesse, E. 1985. On the function of warning coloration: a black and yellow pattern inhibits prey-attack by naive domestic chicks. *Behav. Ecol. Sociobiol.* 16: 249-255.

Shettleworth, S.J. 1984. Learning and behavioural ecology. In *Behavioural Ecology,* ed. J.R. Krebs, N.B. Davies, 170–194. 2nd ed. Oxford: Blackwell.

Shettleworth, S.J., Krebs, J.R., Stephens, D.W., Gibbon, J. 1988. Tracking a fluctuating environment: a study of sampling. *Anim. Behav.* 36: 87–105.

Sillén-Tullberg, B., Wiklund, C., Järvi, T. 1982. Aposematic coloration in adults and larvae of *Lygaeus equestris* and its bearing on Müllerian mimicry: an experimental study on predation on living bugs by the great tit (*Parus major* L.). *Oikos* 39: 131–136.

Smith, J.N.M. 1974a. The food searching behavior of two European thrushes. I. Description and analysis of the search paths. *Behaviour* 48: 276–302.

————. **1974b.** The food searching behaviour of two European thrushes. II. The adaptedness of the search patterns. *Behaviour* 49: 1–61.

Smith, J.N.M., Sweatman, H.P.A. 1974. Food-searching behaviour of titmice in patchy environments. *Ecology* 55: 1216–1232.

Tinbergen, J.M. 1981. Foraging decisions in starlings (*Sturnus vulgaris* L.). *Ardea* 69: 1–67.

Tinbergen, L. 1960. The natural control of insects in pine woods. I. Factors influencing the intensity of predation by songbirds. *Arch. Neerl. Zool.* 13: 265–336.

Tinbergen, N., Impekoven, M., Franck, D. 1967. An experiment on spacing out as defense against predation. *Behaviour* 28: 307–321.

Vaughan, W., Greene, L.L. 1984. Pigeon visual memory capacity. *J. Exp. Psychol. Anim. Behav. Processes* 10: 256–271.

Zach, R. 1979. Shell dropping: decision-making and optimal foraging in northwestern crows. *Behaviour* 68: 106–117.

Zach, R. Falls, J.B. 1976. Bias and mortality in the use of tartar emetic to determine the diet of ovenbirds (Aves: Parulidae). *Can. J. Zool.* 54: 1599–1603.

————. **1979.** Foraging and territorialty of male ovenbirds (Aves: Parulidae) in a heterogeneous habitat. *J. Anim. Ecol.* 48: 33–52.

Zach, R., Smith, J.N.M. 1981. Optimal foraging in wild birds? In *Foraging Behavior,* ed. A.C. Kamil, T. D. Sargent, pp. 95–109. New York: Garland.

Zinner, D. 1985. *Untersuchungen zur Frage der Ontogense von Geschmacksreaktionen und zum Einfluss frühkindlicher Erfahrung auf die Nahrungswahl des Stars (Sturnus vulgaris L.).* Göttingen: Diplomarbeit.

PART 3

Predation Prevention:
Avoidance and Escape Behaviors

David L. Evans

From the perspective of a prey animal, the best defenses against predators are often to avoid detection and, if detected, to escape. Obviously, total avoidance of predator detection is the perfect defense. But even in the best of circumstances, this is almost impossible. Moreover, avoidance of detection usually conflicts with other interests of the organism, such as feeding, reproducing, and dispersing. Thus an evolutionary trade-off between predator avoidance and other needs must occur. After discovery by a predator, or even the approach of a predator to a distance that makes escape difficult, a prey animal often selects escape as the next line of defense.

Within the realm of avoidance and escape are unveiled some of the most fascinating and intricate of animal interactions: interactions often exquisitely subtle and complex. Lederhouse focuses on specific and highly evolved systems used by one group of organisms, caterpillars, in one aspect of defense, the avoidance of detection. This study illustrates both the subtleties and the morphological and behavioral complexity necessary for this one aspect of defense to be effective.

A little investigated means of defense is use of phenology—the timing of events and activities in the life cycle of a prey organism. By having a shorter or longer life cycle or reproductive phase, a prey organism can dramatically improve its chances of successfully passing its genes to subsequent generations while ensuring that the abilities of its progeny to do likewise are maximized. Evans develops this concept of phenology and explores its value as a defense.

Some of the most interesting predator-prey relationships are those resulting from the long coevolution of specialist predators and their speialized prey. A case in point as eloquently presented by Fullard involves predatory bats and their moth prey. This predator-prey interaction is based almost entirely on the use of ultrasonic echolocating sounds by bats to detect prey and the ability of many moth species to hear the ultrasonic cries of bats in time to take appropriate action.

CHAPTER 7

Avoiding the Hunt: Primary Defenses of Lepidopteran Caterpillars

Robert C. Lederhouse

Introduction

The most effective antipredator adaptations of a potential prey avoid the elicitation of capture attempts by its predators. Such prey individuals save the energetic costs of interacting with predators and the risks of injury or death. These antipredator adaptations have been categorized as primary defense mechanisms (Robinson 1969) and operate whether a predator is nearby or not (Kruuk 1972; Edmunds 1974). The variety of these mechanisms is considerable, but cryptic coloration and mimicry have received disproportionate emphasis for well over a century (Bates 1864; Müller 1879; Poulton 1887; Thayer 1909; Cott 1940; Owen 1980). This is understandable given the intricacies of these resemblances and our own reliance on vision. Here I hope to provide more even treatment of the diversity of primary defense mechanisms.

Secondary defense mechanisms are those that come into play after a prey has detected a predator in its vicinity (Edmunds 1974). A common assumption is that primary defenses are passive and secondary ones are active. This generalization fails in both regards. Active primary defenses include building a retreat or reducing evidence of feeding (Heinrich 1979). Passive secondary mechanisms include armored body surfaces, distasteful exteriors, and playing dead. Most animals escape predation through a combination of primary and secondary mechanisms. These are continuously being adjusted through evolutionary time as a result of the antagonistic coevolutionary relationship between prey and their predators (Futuyma and Slatkin 1983).

In deference to other chapters in this volume, I have largely limited this one to primary defenses. However, I have considered some secondary mechanisms where they directly contribute to overall understanding. The specific examples in this review have been drawn mainly from lepidopteran larvae. The taxonomic and ecological diversity within this taxon has allowed this focus to reflect the bias of my experience yet permits a framework broadly applicable to other insects. The abundant terminology for defense mechanisms (Pasteur 1982) has been used in conflicting and confusing ways. I have tried to eliminate unnecessary jargon wherever possible. A number of mechanisms and the examples supporting them are speculative. So many of these have been considered obviously adaptive that little or no experimental verification has been conducted. This is particularly true of visual mechanisms such as the resemblance to bird droppings (but see Evans 1985). I have tried to present experimental support where it is available.

Primary mechanisms can be grouped by the mode in which they function. Prey capture attempts are reduced or eliminated if the predator and prey rarely come into direct contact. This category of predator escape has rarely been considered in reviews of defense mechanisms (Robinson 1969; Edmunds 1974; but see Curio 1976). It includes temporal and spatial separation as well as protective feeding modes and the use of retreats. A second category is detection avoidance, which is generally referred to as "crypsis." Crypsis is divided into eucrypsis, in which the organism blends into a general undefined background (Robinson 1969) and mimesis, in which the organism resembles a specific but usually inanimate object such as a leaf, twig, or animal dropping (Pasteur 1982). The third category involves advertisement of unsuitability as a prey item. The advertisement may be backed up by chemical or physical protection, as in aposematism, or based on resemblance to a protected organism, as in Batesian mimicry.

Avoiding Direct Contact

PREDATOR-PREY ALLOPATRY

Predator avoidance can occur from micro- or macrohabitat separation. A number of butterflies locate larval host plants but oviposit on dead vegetation or the ground nearby (Singer et al. 1971). Predators or parasitoids that search the larval hosts are not likely to find these eggs. The caterpillars of a number of species regularly commute considerable distances from feeding sites to resting sites (Young 1972; Heinrich and Collins 1983). Caterpillars of *Morpho peleides limpida* show pronounced vertical movements associated with feeding. Larvae in the last three instars commute from resting sites near the ground to feeding sites in the uppermost one-third of the host plant, a distance of about sixty centimeters (Young 1972). Zebra swallowtail caterpillars regularly rest off of pawpaw hosts when not feeding (Damman 1986). In Jamaica, larvae of the hawkmoth *Erinnyis ello* avoided wasp predation by resting on trunks of their host plants but risked greater predation by lizards which did not forage on the leaves (Curio 1970). Buckmoth caterpillars, *Hemileuca lucina*, moved from exposed sites to shaded mature foliage as the result of wasp predation (Stamp and Bowers 1988).

When caterpillars have completed their larval feeding, many wander considerable distances before selecting pupation sites (West and Hazel 1979, Young et al. 1986). This behavior effectively separates them from their larval hosts. I have observed mass movements in gregariously feeding *Nymphalis milberti* and *N. antiopa*. This phenomenon has also been reported for *Pieris brassicae* (Baker 1970). Such behavior reduces the density of pupae in any given area. Lower density might reduce or prevent the formation of search images for the pupae by generalist predators (West and Hazel 1982).

The monarch, *Danaus plexippus*, may evade high parasitoid mortality by migrating northward (Urquhart 1960). Parasitoids are the major cause of mortality in a sedentary population of its close relative *Danaus chrysippus* in Africa (Edmunds 1976). In the monarch, the frequency of parasitoids increases from generation to generation during the year in a particular area. In 1980, third-generation monarch larvae in northern New Jersey had a 32 percent parasitism rate mainly from tachinid larvae. Earlier, second brood larvae in northern New Jersey had a 5 percent rate, and second brood larvae from central New York that developed nearly synchronously with New Jersey third-generation larvae had a 3 percent rate (Lederhouse, unpublished data).

PHYSICAL BARRIERS

A number of lepidopteran larvae feed inside shoots and stems as borers, between layers of leaves as miners, or inside galls. These are frequently viewed as feeding specializations resulting from competition with other herbivorous insects. However, another obvious advantage of these feeding modes is the barrier of plant tissue between the larva and its potential predators (Price et al. 1986). Indeed, this may be the primary advantage for borers feeding on nutritionally limiting xylem tissue. Baker (1970) demonstrated higher suvivorship of fourth and fifth instar larvae of *Pieris rapae* on cabbage than on brocolli or kale. These caterpillars were protected from predation by feeding inside cabbage heads rather than exposed on the flat leaves of the other hosts. Certain predators such as woodpeckers and some parasitoids such as ichneumonids are specialized in overcoming plant tissue barriers. Nevertheless, many generalized predators are excluded by these feeding mechanisms.

Caterpillars of many species build protective retreats frequently using silk and plant parts (Rawlins 1984). The retreats usually provide a barrier to predator access to the caterpillar and may be spatially separated from feeding sites and provide a cryptic appearance. Young lavae of the pyralid, *Omphalocera munroei,* pulled together mature leaves of pawpaw and tied them together with silk (Damman 1987). Tied leaves sheltered communal feeding larvae. Older larvae feed singly in leaf rolls. Both shelter types reduced predation by wasps.

Avoiding Detection

EUCRYPSIS

Eucrypsis is defined as a blending of an organism into a nonspecific background (Robinson 1969). This mechanism depends on homochromy, a matching of color. In herbivorous caterpillars, greens and browns are most commonly seen, although caterpillars that feed on inflorescences often blend with the color of the flowers. As noted by early investigators of cryptic coloration (Poulton 1887; Thayer 1909), an organism must appear flat to blend effectively with the background. Organisms with uniform homochromy appear three-dimensional because of light and shadow. Countershading makes a three-dimensional object appear flat. If the surface toward the incident light is darker than the surface usually in shadow, typical lighting will give the entire surface a uniform appearance. In caterpillars, the surface which is usually upward during feeding or resting is the darker one (Ruiter 1956; but see Evans 1986). Caterpillars of *Colias edusa* actually orient to light intensity to maximize the effectiveness of their countershading (Cott 1940). In many sphingid larvae, two areas are countershaded differently and separated by a light contrasting line to produce two apparently flat surfaces.

Although countershading makes a cylindrical caterpillar appear flat, its outline may be detectable from the shadows where it attaches to the substrate or from imperfect homochromy against a varied background. Some *Catocala* caterpillars have flattened bodies and rest with their length closely pressed against twigs or bark. Larvae such as *Catocola nupta* have fleshy papillae and others have rows of hairs along the junction of their bodies with the substrate (Cott 1940). Some geometrid caterpillars that resemble twigs have fleshy protuberances where they contact the branches on which they rest (Poulton 1887). These projections neutralize the shadow that would indicate where body and substrate join. Such shadow reduction decreases detection of the outline of larvae.

Disruptive coloration also decreases the apparency of an animal's outline. Boldly patterned caterpillars may appear obvious against uniform backgrounds. However, against mottled backgrounds, particularly in bright sun, bold patterns break up body shape. *Clemensia albata* larvae blend with their algal hosts, but a disruptive stripe across the body disguises its outline (McCabe 1981). Caterpillars of *Papilio machaon, P. polyxenes, P. oregonius,* and close relatives blend with sun-dappled vegetation because of a disruptive pattern of green and black with yellow, orange, or red spots (Järvi et al. 1981; Lederhouse, personal observations).

DEMONSTRATED VALUE OF EUCRYPSIS

In southern Africa, the last instar of *Papilio demodocus* has two morphs (Clarke et al. 1963). In that area the species feeds on citrus and umbellifers such as fennel. The polymorphism is determined by a single genetic locus plus some modifers and is maintained by differential survival of larvae on the different hosts. One form blends well with the unbellifer hosts and the other with citrus foliage. Predation, primarily by birds, eliminates larvae that do not match their background.

In Jamaica, the hawkmoth *Errinyis ello* has four color morphs in the last larval instar (Curio 1970). The green morph blends well with the leaves of its host, *Poinsettia,* but still suffers high mortality by *Polistes* wasps. All caterpillars resting on trunks of the host escape wasps, but mismatched color morphs are preferentially eaten by *Anolis* lizards. Brown morphs survive best. The advantages of blue and green-gray morphs were not demonstrated, but they may be related to avian predation (Curio 1970).

Caterpillars of the geometrid *Bupalus piniarius* are usually green, but up to 3 percent are yellow (Boer 1971). Birds mainly took the yellow morph unless conditioned with green larvae to build up a search image. Vespid wasps showed a strong preference for green caterpillars. By smearing twigs with hemolymph, Boer (1971) showed that wasps searched much more around the hemolymph of green larvae. This olfactory preference for green larvae by wasps offset higher predation on less cryptic yellow larvae by birds. Both morphs were maintained in the population.

MIMESIS

Potential prey may avoid attack by resembling something in the typical environment of the predator that the predator views as inedible. Such a resemblance is termed mimesis (Pasteur 1982). Prey look like specific plant parts such as leaves or twigs, animal droppings, carcasses, or pebbles. Caterpillars of various families resemble twigs. This appearance is particularly well developed in the Geometridae. Caterpillars frequently resemble bird droppings, particularly in early instars. This resemblance is widespread in the genus *Papilio*.

The effectiveness of mimesis also depends on other factors, such as a caterpillar's posture, immobility, and population density (L. Brower 1958). Stick caterpillars present stretched postures sometimes aided by silk threads. Larvae that look like bird droppings often rest with a curved body. Nocturnal feeding is the general rule in these species. Small larvae that must feed more frequently often show a flash and freeze behavior pattern. To fully benefit from mimesis, individuals must be sparse; otherwise predators may develop search images (Tinbergen 1960).

DEMONSTRATED VALUE OF MIMESIS

In an experiment by Ruiter (1952), birds that were familiar with twigs in their environment did not discover twiglike geometrid caterpillars despite searching eagerly for prey. The stick caterpillars were only attacked if they moved or if a bird inadvertently stepped on them. However, after finding a caterpillar, a bird searched for more and could distinguish a caterpillar from all but the most sticklike caterpillars. This ability of predators to discriminate provides a continuing selective pressure favoring improved mimesis on the part of the caterpillar.

ELIMINATING EVIDENCE OF PRESENCE

Lepidopterists seeking caterpillars frequently search for characteristic foraging damage or accumulated frass. When these signs are found, the host foliage nearby is carefully searched. It has been suggested that visually hunting predators might locate insect prey in similar ways (Thurston and Prachuabmoh 1971). Heinrich and Collins (1983) showed experimentally that chickadees used leaf damage to locate caterpillars. Caterpillars make their feeding damage less obvious by eating entire leaves, producing smooth edges or symmetrical damage, or clipping the petioles of partially consumed leaves and dropping them to the ground (Heinrich 1979). Larvae also perform hygenic removal of frass from their feeding sites (Usher 1984).

A caterpillar behavior that may reduce cues to the caterpillar's existence is the consumption of the egg chorion by newly hatched larvae. Although this action may conserve nutrients for the caterpillar, it also removes evidence of its location. Young swallowtail caterpillars resemble bird droppings, and this resemblance might be compromised if an empty egg shell were nearby.

A close examination of the behavior of tiger swallowtail caterpillars, *Papilio glaucus*, reveals the flexibility of responses that reduce the evidence of foraging (Lederhouse et al. 1984; unpublished data). Their foraging behavior depended on their age and on which host they were feeding. The larvae were too small to eat entire leaves in the first two instars and incapable of clipping petioles until the end of the second instar. They fed on the margins of leaves, producing damage with relatively smooth edges regardless of the host species. By the third instar, their behavior varied from host to host. On large-leafed hosts such as tuliptree, *Liriodendron tulipifera*, or sassafras, *Sassafras albidum*, caterpillars chewed through the petioles of partially consumed leaves, dropping them to the substrate. Petiole clipping was most likely just before a larva molted, a period of relative defenselessness. The proportion of leaf consumed increased from about 50 percent in young third instars to greater than 95 percent in fifth instars. In fact, many final instar larvae consumed entire tuliptree leaves and did not need to clip petioles. On smaller-leafed wild black cherry, *Prunus serotina*, caterpillars were capable of eating entire leaves in earlier instars and petiole clipping was much less common. On compound-leafed white ash, *Fraxinus americana*, smaller larvae removed all tissue on one side of the midrib of a single leaflet. Larger larvae ate entire leaflets. Since ash leaves naturally vary in the number of leaflets, it is unlikely that predators could detect the loss of individual leaflets. Thus regardless of the host species, the tiger swallowtail caterpillars acted to mimimize the cues available to searching predators. Caterpillars of the related black swallowtail feeding on umbellifer herbs also produced smooth or symmetrical damage (Codella and Lederhouse 1984).

Certain parasitoids use caterpillar feces as olfactory cues to locate their hosts (Vinson 1984). Accumulations of frass can also alert predators to the location of the larva. Hygenic behavior has been noted in several species. Some hesperiids can eject feces up to one meter (Frohawk 1913). Some insects throw frass with their mandibles; this behavior occurs in *Pieris rapae* (Usher 1984) and in both *Papilio polyxenes* and *P. glaucus* larvae (Lederhouse, unpublished observations). Usher (1984) demonstrated that the braconid parasitoid *Cotesia glomerata* searched significantly longer where frass or extracts of frass of *Pieris rapae* had been applied.

Advertising Unsuitability

APOSEMATISM

Organisms protected from predators often advertise their protection. This warning is termed "aposematism" and usually involves color, although sound and smell may be involved as well. The caterpillar antipredator protection that backs up the warning is primarily caused by hairiness, spininess, distastefulness, or toxicity. Warning color is characterized by repetitive patterns of bold colors, particularly black with yellow, orange, or red. Both vertebrate and invertebrate predators can learn to associate prey patterns with unpleasant experiences (Brower 1958a,b,c; Boyden 1976; Berenbaum and Miliczky 1984).

The effectiveness of aposematic color in caterpillars has been demonstrated for both experienced and naive vertebrate predators. In some experiments, great tits, *Parus major*, collected from areas outside the normal range of the swallowtail, *Papilio machaon*, initially attacked the swallowtail caterpillars (Järvi et al. 1981). The typical response of a tit was to drop the caterpillar after seizing the larva in its beak. The birds rapidly learned to avoid the caterpillars after experiencing their apparent distastefulness. Rarely were the caterpillars injured, even during the bird's learning period. Similar results occurred using hand-reared individuals of four bird species (Wiklund and Järvi 1982). Aposematic caterpillars of both *P. machaon* and *Pieris brassicae* were tested. About 90 percent of the larvae survived the learning period of the birds, and the birds learned to avoid the caterpillars. These studies demonstrate not only the efficacy of the aposematic coloration but also that it could evolve by individual selection, since caterpillars frequently survive the learning process of the predator.

Two aposematic species could benefit from a shared appearance if predators learned to avoid a single warning pattern with less total death of aposematic caterpillars than if predators learned two different patterns. Although this phenomenon may not be considered mimicry since no dupe is fooled (Pasteur 1982), the concept of Mullerian mimicry is widely understood but less well documented than Batesian mimicry (Benson 1972; Huheey 1984; Evans et al. 1987). Caterpillars of *Battus philenor* and *Parnassius* species may be Mullerian mimics of certain millipedes (Scott 1986).

BATESIAN MIMICRY

If an aposematic larva can benefit from advertising its unsuitability, a palatable caterpillar would benefit by mimicking an aposematic one. Certainly the selective advantage of Batesian mimicry has been demonstrated experimentally for a wide range of organisms (Brower 1958a,b,c; Brower and Brower 1962; Platt et al. 1971; Boyden 1976; Huey and Pianka 1977; Sternberg et al. 1977; Jeffords et al. 1979; Brodie and Brodie 1980; Evans and Waldbauer 1982; Bowers 1983). The relative frequency and importance of Batesian and Mullerian mimicry for lepidopteran larvae are poorly understood, for several reasons. The palatability and protection of many caterpillars are unknown, and resemblances to other species may be due to factors other than mimcry, such as crypsis, thermal considerations, or phylogenetic relationships. Nevertheless, some caterpillars clearly are mimics.

The larvae of several species resemble snakes (Curio 1965). The caterpillar of *Leucorampha ornatus* combines a dilated triangular thorax with eyespots and serpentine movements to be a convincing snake mimic to human eyes (Robinson 1969). However, the effect on predators has not been determined. The larvae of at least eight *Papilio* species in North America have rather intricate eyespots on their enlarged, usually green thoraces. These caterpillars also have been considered snake mimics (Scott 1986), although there are no small poisonous green snakes that are sympatric with the swallowtails. An alternative suggested by S. B. McDowell (personal communication) is that these caterpillars are actually treefrog mimics. Treefrogs are generally unpalatable and rest with their legs drawn tight to the body. Green treefrogs are sympatric with many of the swallowtail species. The lateral two-tone coloration and resting posture of the caterpillars present a similar appearance. Perhaps *P. troilus* larvae are the best treefrog mimics, with their poorly developed second set of "eyespots" actually mimicking frog tympana.

Integrating Mechanisms

Most caterpillars have a diverse arsenal of defensive adaptations. These may function simultaneously or sequentially and reflect evolutionary responses to different functional subsets of potential predators. For example, a single coloration or pattern may function in more than one way, especially if color-blind predators are important. In a similar fashion, the larvae of *Papilio machaon* appear cryptic from a distance (Järvi et al. 1981). The striped green and black pattern with orange spots blends with the sun-dappled, multipinnate leaves of the umbellifer hosts. The black stripes create a disruptive effect. However, avian predators quickly learn to associate this pattern with the distastefulness of the larvae. At close quarters, the pattern functions as a warning pattern. Clearly, an aposematic pattern need not advertise the presence of the caterpillar to all potential predators to be effective (Järvi et al. 1981). Similar patterns are seen for caterpillars of a number of related swallowtails. The snakelike caterpillars generally are cryptic from a distance. Fuller understanding of prey colors, patterns, or even behavior may depend on determining the multiple functions an adaptation serves.

Caterpillars commonly undergo changes in color or pattern as they grow larger during larval development. Last instar larvae of *Hyloicus pinastri* replace the green striped pattern that protects them when resting on pine needles with a mottled brown design. In the final instar, they rest on the bark of twigs much more than on needles (Herrebout et al. 1963). Most species undergo extreme changes in color and pattern as they get larger. The new patterns may be cryptic, mimetic, or aposematic. Many species of *Papilio* are bird dropping mimics only during the first two or three instars (Klots 1951): perhaps there is a limit on how large a convincing dropping mimic can get.

Conclusion

The focus of this chapter has been on avoiding potential predators. However, the secondary defenses that come into play after detection of caterpillars are as diverse and effective as are the primary defenses. These may range from playing dead (Rawlins 1984) to dropping from the host-plant (Baker 1970) to relying on urticating hairs, distasteful exteriors, or defensive glands (Järvi et al. 1981; Damman 1986; Stamp 1986).

Primary defenses of lepidopteran larvae are truly varied. Although much emphasis and interest has been applied to crypsis, mimesis, and mimicry, population attributes that reduce direct contact between caterpillars and their potential predators may be as important for many species. Although many of the more spectacular adaptations have engendered "just-so" adaptive stories, experimental demonstrations of their efficacy are limited. Well-designed experimental studies and perceptive field observations are required if we hope to make substantial progress in understanding the role of diverse primary defense mechanisms in reducing predation.

References

Baker, R.R. 1970. Bird predation as a selective pressure on immature stages of the cabbage butterflies, *Pieris rapae* and *P. brassicae. J. Zool., Lond.* 162: 43–59.

Bates, H.W. 1864. *The Naturalist on the River Amazons.* John Murray, London, Reprinted, Univ. California Press, Berkeley, 1962.

Benson, W.W. 1972. Natural selection for Mullerian mimicry in *Heliconius erato* in Costa Rica. *Science* 176: 936–939.

Berenbaum, M.R., and E. Miliczky. 1984. Mantids and milkweed bugs: efficacy of aposematic coloration against invertebrate predators. *Am. Midl. Natur.* 111: 64–68.

Boer, M.H. den 1971. A colour polymorphism in caterpillars of *Bupalus piniarius* (L.) (Lepidoptera: Geometridae). *Neth. J. Zool.* 21: 61–116.

Bowers, M.D. 1983. Mimicry in North American checkerspot butterflies: *Euphydryas phaeton* and *Chlosyne harrisii* (Nymphalidae). *Ecol. Ent.* 8: 1–8.

Boyden, T.C. 1976. Butterfly palatability and mimicry: experiments with *Ameiva* lizards. *Evolution* 30: 73–81.

Brodie, E.D., Jr., and E.D. Brodie III. 1980. Differential avoidance of mimetic salamanders by free-ranging birds. *Science* 208: 181–182.

Brower, J. vZ. 1958a. Experimental studies of mimicry in some North American butterflies. Part I. The monarch, *Danaus plexippus,* and the viceroy, *Limenitis archippus archippus. Evolution* 12: 32–47.

_____. **1958b.** Experimental studies of mimicry in some North American butterflies. Part II. *Battus philenor* and *Papilio troilus, P. polyxenes* and *P. glaucus. Evolution* 12: 123–136.

_____. **1958c.** Experimental studies of mimicry in some North American butterflies. Part III. *Danaus gilippus berenice* and *Limenitis archippus floridensis. Evolution* 12: 273–285.

Brower, L.P. 1958. Bird predation and foodplant specificity in closely related procryptic insects. *Am. Nat.* 92: 183–187.

Brower, L.P., and J. vZ. Brower. 1962. The relative abundance of model and mimic butterflies in natural populations of the *Battus philenor* mimicry complex. *Ecology* 43: 154–158.

Clarke, C.A., C.G.C. Dickson, and P.M. Sheppard. 1963. Larval color pattern in *Papilio demodocus. Evolution* 17: 130–137.

Codella, S.G., and R.C. Lederhouse. 1984. Foraging strategy and leaf damage patterns of black swallowtail caterpillars, *Papilio polyxenes. Bull. New Jersey Acad. Sci.* 29: 37.

Cott, H.B. 1940. *Adaptive Coloration in Animals.* Methuen, London.

Curio, E. 1965. Die schlangenmimikry einer sudamerikanischen schwarmerraupe. *Natur und Museum* 95: 207–211.

————. **1970.** Validity of the selective coefficient of a behaviour trait in hawkmoth larvae. *Nature* 228: 382.

————. **1976.** *The Ethology of Predation.* Springer-Verlag, Berlin.

Damman, H. 1986. The osmaterial glands of the swallowtail butterfly *Eurytides marcellus* as a defence against natural enemies. *Ecol. Entomol.* 11: 261–265.

————. **1987.** Leaf quality and enemy avoidance by the larvae of a pyralid moth. *Ecology* 68: 88–97.

Edmunds, M. 1974. *Defence in Animals.* Longman Inc., New York.

————. **1976.** Larval mortality and population regulation in the butterfly *Danaus chrysippus* in Ghana. *Zool. J. Linn. Soc. Lond.* 58: 129–145.

Evans, D.L. 1985. The defensive ensembles of two palatable moths. *J. Lepidopt. Soc.* 39: 43–47.

————. **1986.** Anti-predatory autecology in the geometrid larvae of *Larentia clavaria pallidata. Ent. Exp. Appl.* 40: 209–214.

Evans, D.L., N. Castoridaes, and H. Badruddine. 1987. The degree of mutual resemblance and its effect on predation in young birds. *Ethology* 74: 335–345.

Evans, D.L., and G.P. Waldbauer. 1982. Behavior of adult and naive birds when presented with a bumblebee and its mimic. *Z. Tierpsychol.* 59: 247–259.

Frohawk, F.W. 1913. Fecal ejection in hesperids. *Entomologist* 49: 201–202.

Futuyma, D.J., and M. Slatkin. 1983. *Coevolution.* Sinauer Associates, Sunderland, Mass.

Heinrich, B. 1979. Foraging strategy of caterpillars: leaf damage and possible predator avoidance strategies. *Oecologia* 42: 325–337.

Heinrich, B., and S.L. Collins. 1983. Caterpillar leaf damage, and the game of hide-and-seek with birds. *Ecology* 64: 592–602.

Herrebout, W.M., P.J. Kuyten, and L. de Ruiter. 1963. Observations on colour patterns and behaviour of caterpillars feeding on scots pine. *Archs. Neerl. Zool.* 15: 315–357.

Huey, R.B., and E.R. Pianka. 1977. Natural selection for juvenile lizards mimicking noxious beetles. *Science* 195: 201–202.

Huheey, J.E. 1984. Warning coloration and mimicry. Pp. 257–297. in W.J. Bell and R.T. Carde (eds.), *Chemical Ecology of Insects.* Chapman and Hall, London.

Järvi, T., B. Sillén-Tullberg, and C. Wiklund. 1981. The cost of being aposematic. An experimental study of predation on larvae of *Papilio machaon* by the great tit *Parus major. Oikos* 36: 267–272.

Jeffords, M.R., J.G. Sternburg, and G.P. Waldbauer. 1979. Batesian mimicry: field demonstration of the survival value of pipevine swallowtail and monarch color patterns. *Evolution* 33: 275–286.

Klots, A.B. 1951. *A Field Guide to the Butterflies.* Houghton Mifflin, Boston.

Kruuk, H. 1972. *The Spotted Hyaena.* Univ. of Chicago, Chicago.

Lederhouse, R.C., B.E. Lippe, and D.W. Grossmueller. 1984. Petiole clipping behavior maintains crypticity in tiger swallowtail caterpillars, *Papilio glaucus. Bull. New Jersey Acad. Sci.* 29: 37.

McCabe, T.L. 1981. *Clemensia albata,* an algal feeding arctiid. *J. Lepidopt. Soc.* 35: 34-40.

Müller, F. 1879. *Ituna* and *Thyridia.* Kosmos 5: 100-108. (English translation, R. Meldola, *Ituna* and *Thyridia:* a remarkable case of mimicry in butterflies, *Proc. Ent. Soc. Lond.* 1879: xx-xxix.

Owen, D. 1980. *Camouflage and Mimicry.* Univ. of Chicago, Chicago.

Pasteur, G. 1982. A classificatory review of mimicry systems. *Ann. Rev. Ecol. Syst.* 13: 169-199.

Platt, A.P., R.P. Coppinger, and L.P. Brower. 1971. Demonstration of the selective advantage of mimetic *Limenitis* butterflies presented to caged avian predators. *Evolution* 25: 692-701.

Poulton, E.B. 1887. The experimental proof of the protective value of colour and markings in insects in reference to their vetebrate enemies. *Proc. Zool. Soc. Lond.* 1887: 191-274.

Price, P.W., G.W. Fernandes, and G.L. Waring. 1987. Adaptive nature of insect galls. *Environm. Entomol.* 16: 15-24.

Rawlins, J.E. 1984. Mycophagy in Lepidoptera. Pp. 382-423 in Q. Wheeler and M. Blackwell (eds.), *Fungus-Insect Relationships.* Columbia University Press, New York.

Robinson, M.H. 1969. Defenses against visually hunting predators. *Evol. Biol.* 3: 225-259.

Ruiter, L. de 1952. Some experiments on the camouflage of stick caterpillars. *Behaviour* 4: 222-232.

————. 1956. Countershading in caterpillars. *Archs. Neerl. Zool.* 11: 285-341.

Scott, J.A. 1986. *The Butterflies of North America.* Stanford University Press, Stanford, Calif.

Singer, M.C., P.R. Ehrlich, and L.E. Gilbert. 1971. Butterfly feeding on lycopsid. *Science* 172: 1341-1342.

Stamp, N.E. 1986. Physical constraints of defense and response to invertebrate predators by pipevine caterpillars (*Battus philenor:* Papilionidae). *J. Lepid. Soc.* 40: 191-205.

Stamp, N.E. and M.D. Bowers. 1988. Direct and indirect effects of predatory wasps (*Polistes* sp.:Vespidae) on gregarious caterpillars (*Hemileuca lucina:*Saturniidae). *Oecologia* 75: 619-624.

Sternberg, J.G., G.P. Waldbauer, and M.R. Jeffords. 1977. Batesian mimicry: selective advantage of color pattern. *Science* 195: 681-683.

Thayer, G.H. 1909. *Concealing-coloration in the Animal Kingdom.* MacMillan, New York.

Thurston, R., and O. Prachuabmoh. 1971. Predation by birds on tobacco hornworm larvae infesting tobacco. *J. Econ. Ent.* 64: 1548–1549.

Tinbergen, L. 1960. The natural control of insects in pine woods. I. Factors influencing the intensity of predation by songbirds. *Archs. Neerl. Zool.* 13: 265–336.

Urquhart, F.A. 1960. *The Monarch Butterfly.* University of Toronto Press, Toronto.

Usher, B.F. 1984. Housecleaning behavior of an herbivorous caterpillar: selective and behavioral implications of frass-throwing by *Pieris rapae* larvae. Dissertation, Cornell Univ., Ithaca, N.Y. 120 pp.

Vinson, S.B. 1984. Parasitoid-host relationship. Pp. 205–233 in W.J. Bell and R.T. Carde (eds.), *Chemical Ecology* Chapman and Hall, London.

West, D.A., and W.N. Hazel 1979. Natural pupation sites of swallowtail butterflies (Lepidoptera: Papilioninae): *Papilio polyxenes* Fabr., *P. glaucus* L. and *Battus philenor* (L.). *Ecol. Ent.* 4: 387–392.

——————. **1982.** An experimental test of natural selection for pupation site in swallowtail butterflies. *Evolution* 36: 152–159.

Wiklund, C., and T. Järvi. 1982. Survival of distasteful insects after being attacked by naive birds: a reappraisal of the theory of aposematic coloration evolving through individual selection *Evolution* 36: 998–1002.

Young, A.M. 1972. Adaptive strategies of feeding and predator-avoidance in the larvae of the neotropical butterfly, *Morpho peleides limpida* (Lepidoptera: Morphidae). *J.N.Y. Entomol. Soc. 80: 66–82.*

Young, A.M., M.S. Blum, H.H. Fales, and Z. Bian. 1986. Natural history and ecological chemistry of the neotropical butterfly *Papilio anchisiades* (Papilionidae). *J. Lepid. Soc.* 40: 36–53.

CHAPTER 8

Phenology as a Defense:
A Time to Die, A Time to Live

David L. Evans

Introduction

Phenology is the study of natural events in relation to other physical or biological happenings. In terms of population biology, we could think of it as distribution through time. Just as spatial distribution is an important consideration in population studies of cryptic organisms (Tinbergen 1960), also should temporal distribution be considered important. Hence, investigations including time-based density should be as inherently useful as the more usual topographical analyses. Organisms may use temporally-based distribution as one type of technique to reduce the probability of predation, that is, as a defensive technique. How might timing events help to protect an organism?

There are several basic patterns that can be used, but at the outset some general observations on the variability of the risk of death through predation might be appropriate. Predatory efficiency will increase in those species for which learning plays an important role in hunting and killing (but see Smith 1977; Schuler and Hesse 1985). On the other hand, where hunting techniques are largely genetically acquired, those individuals with superior capturing methods will clearly prevail and pass on their attributes to future generations thereby creating greater predator pressure (Zach and Falls 1978). Successfully escaping prey may also desert an area after attempted predation, thus causing low prey densities

(Duggins 1983). Many species of predators are more likely to recognize and to attack weaker animals (Kruuk 1972). Therefore, predator pressures will change as different classes of prey are removed and no new recruitments appear in those prey groups during a given time unit. Ontological events (Brown 1984), learning (Arnold 1978), or specialized resource availability may enhance effective escape. Play and other types of exploratory behavior (Fagan 1983) and higher metabolic requirements are often linked to early development in mammals and birds. All types of prey with specialized defensive techniques (see Evans and Maier 1987) are especially threatened by such young investigative animals, since young predators will pick up all sorts of things that an older animal will either ignore as low probable profit (such as sticks, stones, or cryptics; Evans 1983) or avoid (such as aposematics or Batesian mimics; Evans and Waldbauer 1982).

Clearly, steady state predation models are too simplistic. However, developmental events in and physiological constraints on the predator can create windows in time which a potential prey item can exploit and therefore live in comparative safety. It is possible to divide such antipredatory adaptations in phenology into two major types based on the regularity of their appearance: acyclic and cyclic.

ACYCLIC PHENOLOGY

Acyclic phenologies, in order to be effective as aids in the defense against predation, must be unpredictable. If there is a synchronous appearance of many prey of a certain type, then an additional advantage may accrue: predator satiation. This phenomenon occurs when so many palatable items appear in such a short time that the local predator community can only process a small proportion of the prey. Furthermore, since the prey are only available for a brief time, the predator population will not be able to respond reproductively quickly enough to take advantage of the resource. There may be enough time to encourage an initial reproductive effort in the predators which, will in turn only result in a subsequent catastrophic crash as the resource vanishes. Predator satiation as a defense has been observed in animals (Dybas and Lloyd 1974) and plants (Janzen 1971). To the predator, these are unpredictable resource islands in the matrix of time. Obviously, semelparous (big bang reproduction) organisms are more predisposed to this defensive mode than are itereoparous (reproducing continuously or at intervals throughout one's life) organisms.

CYCLIC PHENOLOGIES

Annual Cycles

Semelparity may also be preadaptive in a protective system which Rothschild (1981) has called "historical mimicry." Briefly stated, this defensive technique occurs where Batesian mimics (according to the original form of the paradigm; Waldbauer and Sheldon 1971) are found at certain times in greater numbers than their sympatric models. Initially such a temporal distribution might seem illogical, since if the mimics are found in greater population densities than the model then it might be profitable for a predator to switch its attacks to all forms similar to the mimic and model (Bates 1862; Edmunds 1974; but see Alcock 1970). However, the paradigm specifies that this greater abundance occur only after the predators have been dissuaded by an earlier annual majority of models. Waldbauer and Sheldon (1971) showed that dipterous mimics of aculeate (Hymenoptera) models were more frequent than the aposematics in the spring before naive avian insectivores usually fledged. I should note that fledgling phenology itself is in concert with general insect abundance. Without alternative prey, birds would have to be totally undescriminating or die. The young birds would then become independent and attack various types of prey, learning of the relative noxiousness of various insects. These newly independent birds would then learn to avoid the stinging insects and would remember their unpleasant experiences until the following spring. At that time they would have the best chance of encountering large numbers of mimics, which they would avoid. Figure 8.1 summarizes these concepts. This model requires that continued sampling by predators be uncommon (see Brower 1958; Evans 1984; Evans et al. 1987), and has relatively little impact upon fitness. There exists a body of evidence that adult birds remember their unpleasant encounters with noxious prey for periods of at least several months (Mostler 1935; Rothschild 1964; Evans and Waldbauer 1982; Evans 1984). Waldbauer and associates subsequently confirmed that similar phenological defenses appeared with mimicry groups in several different environments (Waldbauer and Sheldon 1971; Waldbauer et al. 1977; Waldbauer and La Berge 1985). A similar phenomenon may be at work in the seasonal distribution of the long-lived salamander, *Desmognathus ochrophaeus* (Brodie 1981). In order for differential predation to be effective as a selective factor in these seasonal phenomena, it is necessary that young predators be more likely than adults to attack mimics. In an experiment using hand-reared avian insectivores and adults of the same species, mistnetted as they returned from their winter migration, it was possible to

FIELD OBSERVATIONS:

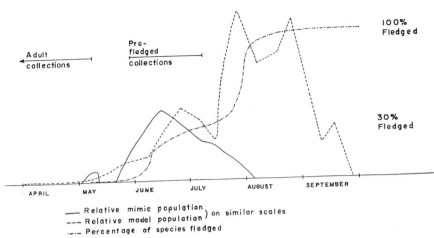

Figure 8.1   A generalized model showing the relative phenologies of model, mimic, and fledglings.

show that young birds were much more dangerous to bumblebee mimics (and bumblebee workers) than the adults (Evans 1978; Evans and Waldbauer 1982) (see figure 8.1).

Naturally, larger population densities of mimics could represent a threat to individual models and the members of the population's Mullerian ring. Increased contact with many positively reinforced stimuli may make it difficult to later associate that same signal with punishment (Mason and Reidinger 1983). Hence, more models will die if they are present at the same time as their mimics. Therefore, a seemingly successful adaptation for the model is to delay its appearance to avoid high frequencies of mimics (Bobisud 1978; Huheey 1980). Reproductive forms of social Hymenoptera are normally safely within their colonies when temperate fledglings are exploring their environment (see chapter 15 of this volume). Queen bumblebees and some vespid wasps are exposed earlier when only the older birds are present. The reproductive forms of these eusocial species survive to generate more offspring, and some daughters (coinciding in appearance with naive insectivores) die to educate the young predators, which will then avoid kin, conspecifics, and mimics (Brower and Brower 1965; Evans and Waldbauer 1982). Death by predation is frequent (stings are not terribly effective against bird beaks but there is distastefulness, however (Mostler 1935; Evans and Waldbauer 1982). There is a large, separate argument about the role of kin selection in the evolution of aposematism (see McLain 1984; Wiklund and Sillén-Tullberg 1985; Evans et al. 1986a; Evans 1987; Grober 1988). Many aposematic forms are also either inactive or hidden during cold periods. Poulton (1908) suggested that these may not be apparent at that time because that is the period when resident endothermic insectivores will be hungriest but still active. In any case, ectotherms, hibernators, some cachers, and migrators will present considerably less risk in temperate winters to aposematics.

Other types of distribution in annual cycles used as a defense are less striking but none the less significant. They normally escape our notice because they are part of the routine background. The analog of historical mimicry as discussed above clearly can be extended to cryptics. Many defensive strategies typically adapted in Batesian mimicry have their parallel in cryptic prey. As long as there is a definite annual cycle of exploratory predators whose foraging behavior can change, there is an adaptive advantage in being inactive, anachoretic, or otherwise unavailable at the time. Pine trees (I apologize for using an occasional non-arthropod example in my attempt at being reductionist) in boreal forests shed their seeds in the winter apparently to take advantage of the general lack of granivores. There are still problem animals (such as Clark's nutcracker) but these are lower in density than the entire summer granivore guild.

An animal example of this annual phenological defense is found in the cryptic, palatable larvae of *Larentia clavaria pallidata* (Lepidoptera: Geometridae) (Evans 1986). These caterpillars are active only from December to March (missing the fall migration of yearling and adult insectivores) in coastal Lebanon and usually pupate before the spring arrival of migrants returning to nesting homes in Europe and northern Asia. As with many other examples, purely physiological factors also play a role in the phenology because the larval food plant, *Althaea setosa* (Bristly hollyhock), has younger, more nutritious leaves at that time.

The phenology of the color forms of a species may also be affected by predation. In these cases protection from predation is enhanced by the ability to measure time. Some cryptic forms are highly specialized (that is, having special resemblance), conforming only to a particular habitat (Evans and Maier 1987). In contrast, some cryptics (such as bird dung mimics) are "go anywhere" organisms (Evans 1985). The specialist cryptics (the term camouflage has been used confusingly in the past and should probably be avoided) will have their fate more closely linked to and limited by the extent of their environment. Habitat backgrounds change predictably, seasonally in temperate, polar, and even tropical situations (Fuseini and Kumar 1975). These cycles are predicted by sensing the change in the length of the photoperiod. Cryptic animals then make their physiological preparations to match the new backgrounds. Examples of creatures which can accommodate these changes include a green [sic] lacewing, *Crysopa carnea,* several mantids (see chapter 1 of this volume), and the willow ptarmigan. Adults of the multivoltine *C. carnea* eclosing in the North Temperate spring are green but those which emerge in the fall are brown. *C. carnea* lives in broadleafed forests but many of its relatives are confined to coniferous woods. The later species, not surprisingly, do not exhibit any seasonal color change. Willow ptarmigans, long-lived arctic grouse, molt their brown feathers in the fall, making way for new white feathers. The opposite molt occurs in the spring. The molting usually occurs in patches, presumably because the environment does not suddenly become completely brown or totally white on a dependable basis. The color changes in both groups of animals have the photoperiod as the proximal cause. A possible additional benefit of color change is that the likelihood of a predator learning to search for one color form is reduced, a kind of seasonal apostatic selection. Seasonal form change as a defense is different from other phenological techniques only becaues members of the same species are present for longer periods of the year.

Daily Phenologies

It is frequently possible to determine that predation plays an important role as the ultimate cause of a circadian rhythm. Many species of cryptic, palatable caterpillars feed on leaves at night in one place but retreat to refugia, where they have not been feeding, to hide during the day (Heinrich 1979). With this behavior, they escape foraging insectivorous birds which seek out leaf damage as a cue in locating their prey (Heinrich and Collins 1983). On the other hand, distasteful larvae forage diurnally and move away from feeding sites only when the area is no longer useful.

One sometimes encounters motionless, cryptic arthropods during the day. While this catylepsy may have been elicited by the signals produced by the observer's approach (Evans 1983), some insects never move when there is bright light (Rotheray 1986). Movement is an easy clue that an organism is not (for example) a dead stick. A similar defensive ensemble occurs in prey species of orb-weaving spiders which remove their webs during the day (Edmunds and Edmunds 1983). A similar situation can be found with some vertebrates. Cushing (1985) found that estrous deer mice, the most apparent form of the rodent (because of behavioral and possibly pheromonal differences), are more active in the evening than their most significant predator, the least weasel. The hunter's activity cycle is fairly predictable, so the females are able to feed and go about their other functions with lower risk early in the evening.

Many animals in marine and aquatic habitats where animals are primarily active in areas of high resource availability only at times when the risk of encountering hunters is lowest (Hughes 1969; Levinton 1971; Hill et al. 1987; Clark and Levy 1988). I will use a well documented example from fish in order to illustrate a related principle which seems to be at work in most arthropods as well. Power (1984) found that the larger, more threatened (by visually hunting predators) armored catfish (Loricariidae) ventured into shallow waters only at night to feed on the abundant algae because wading birds and other predators were inactive in the dark. As in numerous species of reef and beach crustaceans, the potential prey were able to forego eating for long periods of time because of the lower cellular respiratory requirements typical of ectotherms. Ectothermy is a physiological refuge from metabolic demands.

Conversely, ectothermy can be a hinderance for cryptic animals. Many ectotherms, including arthropods, exhibit behavioral thermoregulation (Stevenson 1985). Principal among these is simply resting in a sunny spot (Evans et al. 1986b). Unfortunately, bright light makes the visual hunt that much easier even on closely matching backgrounds. Hence, there may be conflicting selective forces which govern phenologies.

Circadian phenomena have been well documented in the zooplankton (primarily larval crustaceans). These creatures migrate vertically throughout a twenty-four-hour cycle, and are found at lower depths during the day (Zaret and Suffern 1976). Visually hunting predators such as fish and adult crustaceans find it much more difficult to see these small animals against the darker background of the deep water (Woodbury 1986). For an interesting exception to this very frequently observed behavior in fresh water zooplankton, see Sih (1982).

Dry sand dunes represent a terrestrial metaphor for water and ammiophiles exhibit a daily pattern exactly analogous to that shown in wetter situations. This constitutes a phenological defense since visually hunting predators will easily find surface-active prey whenever there is sufficient light to hunt. The phenomenon has been demonstrated in lizards, spiders, and antlions (Wagner 1979, Cloudsley-Thompson 1983, and Cain 1987 respectively). While the extreme temperature fluctuations so typical of sand dunes is a contributing factor, the role of predation in selecting for this activity pattern is clear. The general and widespread application of the principles of phenology as defense is obvious.

Finally, it is frequently suggested that the generally nocturnal adaptations of mammals (good hearing and olfaction but poor color vision) arose as a response to predator pressure upon the ancestral late Therapsida. The Archosauria had begun their long dominance of the daylight world and were, if the fossil evidence of large, probably bird-like eyes and fearsome talons can be trusted, relentless and efficient visual hunters. Nocturnal activity patterns seem to have been the only viable option (McLoughlin 1980). Hence, nocturnal phenology as a defense against predation has had an impact in our own ancestral line.

Phenology is Not Always the Key

Clearly, the activity cycles of predators have an important selective force in the shaping of phenologies. However, some studies, while investigating this explanation, have found no time cycle occuring in response to variable predatory pressure (Sih 1982, Heads and Lawton 1985). Gilinsky (1984) found no advantage in a phenological defense in the macroinvertebrates in lake studies but that spatial heterogeneity provided refugia in that habitat. If there are sufficient (that is, capable) defenses to protect an organism from attack, then there is no adaptive advantage in having yet another. Other, nonexclusive explanations for the lack of certain adaptations include developmental constraints (Maynard Smith 1982) and the lack of the relevant genetic material. The inability to express a character (even when related organisms exhibit the phenotype) may be due to a gene being lost, completely changed by mutation, or normally repressed.

Looking Ahead

I suggest that the use of time as a refuge in predator avoidance, rather than being a rare characteristic, is an under-researched phenomenon. Part of the fault lies in the failure to think in terms of gaps, slots, islands, or windows of opportunity (or vulnerability) in the fourth dimension. There is at least one other source of this failure: lack of empirical work. Too few modern studies have investigated the temporal relationships between predator and prey. It is time to do so.

References

Alcock, J. 1970. Punishment levels and the response of blackcapped chickadees (*Parus atricapillus*) to three kinds of artificial seeds. *Anim. Behav.* 18: 592–599.

Arnold, S.J. 1978. The evolution of a special class of modifiable behaviors in relation to environmental pattern. *Am. Nat.* 112: 415–427.

Bates, H.W. 1862. Contributions to an insect fauna of the Amazon Valley Lepidoptera: Heliconidae. *Trans. Linn. Soc., Lond.* 23: 495–566.

Bobisud, L.E. 1978. Optimal time of appearance of mimics. *Am. Nat.* 112: 962–994.

Brodie, E.D. 1981. Phenological relationships of model and mimic salamanders. *Evolution* 35: 988–994.

Brower, J.V.Z. 1958. Experimental studies of mimicry in some North American butterflies. I. *Danaus plexippus* and *Limenitis archippus archippus. Evolution* 12: 32–47.

Brower, J.V.Z. and L.P. Brower. 1965. Experimental studies of mimicry. 8. Further investigations of honeybees (*Apis mellifera*) and their Dronefly mimics (*Eristalis* spp.). *Am. Nat.* 99: 173–188.

Brown, J.A. 1984. Parental care and the ontogeny of predator-avoidance in two species of centarchid fish. *Anim. Behav.* 32: 43–119.

Cain, M.L. 1987. Prey capture behavior and diel movement of *Brachynemurus* (Neuroptera: Myremeleontidae) antlion larvae in south central Florida. *Fla. Entomol.* 70: 397–400.

Clark, C.W. and D.A. Levy. 1988. Diel migrations by juvenile sockeye salmon and the antipredation window. *Am. Nat.* 131: 271–290.

Cloudsley-Thompson, J.L. 1983. Desert adaptations in arachnids. *in* Proceedings of the 9th international congress of Arachnology, Panama. W.G. Eberhard, T.D. Lubin, B.C. Robinson (eds.). Smithsonian Institution Press. Washington. pp 292–32.

Cushing, B.S. 1985. Estrous mice and vulnerability to weasel predation. *Ecology* 66: 1976–1978.

Duggins, D.O. 1983. Starfish predation and the creation of mosaic patterns in a kelp dominated community. *Ecology* 64: 1610–1619.

Dybas, H.S. and M. Lloyd. 1974. The habits of 17-year periodical cicadas (Homoptera: Cicadidae: *Magicicada* spp.). *Ecol. Monogr.* 44: 279–324.

Edmunds, J. and M. Edmunds. The defensive mechanisms of orb weavers (Araneae: Arnaeidae) in Ghana, West Africa. in Proceedings of the 9th international congress of Arachology, Panama. W.G. Eberhard, T.D. Lubin, B.C. Robinson (eds.). Smithsonian Institution Press. Washington. pp 292–32.

Edmunds M. 1974. Defence in animals. Longman, Harlow, Essex, U.K.

Evans, D.L. 1978. Strategies for survival. Ph.D. Thesis, Univ. Ill.

_____. **1983.** Relative defensive behavior of some moths and the implications to predator-prey interactions. *Entomol. Exp. Appl.* 33: 103–111.

_____. **1984.** Reactions of some adult passerines to *Bombus pennsylvanicus* and its mimic *Mallota bautias. Ibis* 126: 50–58.

_____. **1985.** The defensive ensembles of two palatable moths. *J. Lep. Soc.* 39: 43–47.

_____. **1986.** Anti-predatory autecology in the geometrid larvae of *Larentia clavaria pallidata. Entomol. Exp. Appl.* 40: 209–214.

_____. **1987.** Tough, harmless cryptics could evolve into tough, nasty aposematics: an individual selectionist model. *Oikos* 48: 114–115.

Evans, D.L., N. Castoriades, and H. Baddrudine. 1986b. Cardenolides in the defense of *Caenocoris nerii. Oikos* 46: 325–329.

Evans, D.L., H.K. Evans, A.A. Sfeir. 1986b. Possible thermoregulation in the buprestid beetel, *Capnodis tenebrionis. Am. Zool.* 26: 86.

Evans, D.L., N. Castoridaes, and H. Baddrudine. 1987. The degree of mutual resemblance and its effect on predation in young birds. *Ethology* 74: 335–345.

Evans, D.L. and C.T. Maier. 1987. Hatitat constancy and defenses against predation. *Am. Zool.* 27: 426.

Evans, D.L. and G.P. Waldbauer. 1982. Behavior of adult and naive birds when presented with a bumblebee and its mimic. *Z. Tierpsychol.* 59: 247–260.

Fagen, R.M. 1981. Animal play behavior. Oxford University Press, Inc., New York.

Fuseini, B.A. and Kumar, R. 1975. Ecology of cotton stainers (Heteroptera: Pyrrhocoridae) in southern Ghana. *Biol. J. Linn. Soc., Lond.* 7: 113–146.

Gilinsky, E. 1984. The role of predation and spatial heterogeneity in determining benthic community structure. *Ecology* 65: 455–468.

Grober, M.S. 1988. Brittle-star bioluminescense functions as an aposematic signal to deter crustacean predators. *Anim. Behav.* 36: 493–501.

Heads, P.A. and J.H. Lawton. 1985. Bracken, ants and extrafloral nectaries. III. How insect herbivores avoid ant predators. *Ecol. Entomol.* 10: 29–42.

Heinrich, B. 1979. Foraging strategies of caterpillars, leaf damage, and possible predator avoidance strategies. *Oecologia* 42: 325–337.

Heinrich, B. and S.L. Collins. 1983. Caterpillar leaf damage and the game of hide-and-seek with birds. *Ecology* 64: 592–602.

Hill, L., A.R. Schmidt, and D. Rittschof. 1987. Vertical and horizontal movements of hard clams *Mercenaria mercenaria. Am. Zool.* 27: 192.

Hughes, R.N. 1969. A study of feeding in *Scrobicularia plana. J. Mar. Biol. Assn., U.K.* 49: 805–824.

Huheey, J.E. 1980. The question of synchrony or "temporal sympatry" in mimicry. *Evolution* 34: 614–616.

Janzen, D.H. 1971. Escape of *Cassia grandis* L. beans from predators in time and space. *Ecology* 52: 964–979.

Kruuk, H. 1972. The spotted hyena. Univ. Chi. Press.

Levinton, J.S. 1971. Control of Tellicanean (Mollusca: Bivalva) feeding behavior by predation. *Limnol. oceanog.* 16: 660–662.

McLain, D.K. 1984. Coevolution: Mullerian mimicry between a plant bug (Miridae) and a seed bug (Lygaeidae) and the relationship between host plant choice and upalatability. *Oikos* 43: 143–148.

McLoughlin, J.C. 1980. Synapsida: A new look into the origin of mammals. Viking Press: New York.

Mason, R.T. and R.F. Reidinger. 1983. Generalization of and effects of pre-exposure on color avoidance learning by redwinged blackbirds (*Agelaius phoeniceus*). *Auk* 100: 461–468.

Maynard Smith, J. 1982. Evolution and the theory of games. Cambridge Univ. Press: Cambridge, U.K.

Mostler, G. 1935. Beobachtungen zur Frage der Wespenmimikry. *Z. Morphol. Oekol. Tiere* 29: 382–454.

Poulton, E.B. 1908. Essays on evolution. Oxford Univ. Press.

Power, M.E. 1984. Depth distributions of armored catfish: Predator-induced resource avoidance. *Ecology* 65: 523–528.

Rotheray, G.E. 1986. Colour, shape and defence in aphicophagous syrphid larvae (Diptera). *Zool. J. Linn. Soc.* 88: 201–216.

Rothschild, M. 1964. A note on the evolution of defensive and repellent odors of insects. *Entomologist* 97: 276–280.

————. **1981.** The mimicrats must move with the times. *Biol. J. Linn. Soc.* 16: 21–23.

Schuler, W. and E. Hesse. 1985. On the function of warning coloration: a black and yellow pattern inhibits prey-attack by naive domestic chicks. *Behav. Ecol. Sociobiol.* 16: 249–255.

Sih, A. 1982. Foraging strategies and the avoidance of predation by an aquatic insect, *Notonecta hoffmanii. Ecology* 63: 786–796.

Smith, S.M. 1977. Coral-snake pattern recognition and stimulus generalisation by naive great kiskadees (Aves: Tyrannidae). *Nature 265: 535–536.*

Stevenson, R.D. 1985. The relative importance of behavioral and physiological adjustments controlling body temperature in terrestrial ectotherms. *Am. Nat.* 126: 362–386.

Tinbergen, L. 1960. The natural control of insects in pine woods. I. Factors influencing the intensity of predation by songbirds. *Archs. Neerl. Zool.* 13: 265–343.

Wagner, F.H. 1979. Wildlife of the desert. Chanticleer Press, Inc., New York.

Waldbauer, G.P. and W.E. LaBerge. 1985. Phenological relationships of wasps, bumblebees, their mimics and insectivorous birds in Northern Michigan. *Ecol. Entomol.* 10: 99–110.

Waldbauer, G.P. and J.K. Sheldon. 1971. Phenological relationships of some aculeate hymenoptera, their dipteran mimics, and insectivorous birds. *Evolution* 25: 371–382.

Waldbauer, G.P., J.G. Sternburg, and C.T. Maier. 1977. Phenological relationships of wasps, bumblebees, their mimics, and insectivorous birds in an Illinois sand area. *Ecology* 58: 583–591.

Wiklund, C. and B. Sillén-Tullberg. 1985. Why distasteful butterflies have aposematic larvae and adults, cryptic pupae: Evidence from predation experiments on the Monarch and the European Swallowtail. *Evolution* 39: 1155–1158.

Woodbury, P.B. 1986. The geometry of predator avoidance by the blue crab, *Callinectes sapidus* Rathbun. *Anim. Behav.* 34: 28–37.

Zach, R. and J.B. Falls. 1978. Prey selection by captive ovenbirds (Aves: Parulidae). *J. Anim. Ecol.* 47: 943–957.

Zaret, J.M. and J.S. Suffern. 1976. Vertical migration in zooplankton as a predator avoidance mechanism. *Limn. ocean.* 21: 804–813.

The Sensory Ecology of Moths and Bats: Global Lessons in Staying Alive

James H. Fullard

Moths of a variety of families possess simple tympanic organs (ears) which detect the echolocation signals of sympatric, insectivorous bats (see Agee 1967, 1969; and Roeder 1967, 1974 for a review). Moth ears are polyphyletic in origin, appearing on the head (Sphingoidea), thorax (Noctuoidea) or abdomen (Geometroidea). They are, however, similar in the limited neural base servicing the tympanal membrane. The total number of acoustically receptive neurons per ear ranges from one to four. Although simply constructed, these ears provide a substantial survival ability to the moths that own them, and it appears that their possession is the norm rather than the exception. During times of high bat activity in both temperate and tropical localities, the incidence of auditive (those with ears) moth species captured can reach up to 95 percent of the total moth fauna (personal observation).

Moths use their ears to mediate a set of defensive behaviors that act to reduce the chance of detection by approaching bats. These responses can be categorized as either primary or secondary (Robinson 1966; Edmunds 1974) (table 9.1) and are related to the perceived distance of the approaching bat (Roeder 1967). Distant bats (giving faint acoustic signals) elicit coordinated avoidance flight, a primary response intended to remove the moth from "echo earshot" of the bat. Secondary responses such as flight cessation are directed to closer bats (giving intense acoustic stimulation) and are intended as "last-ditch" evasion maneuvers. Primary responses are performed before the bat has detected the echo from its intended prey and probably account for the moth's maximum chances for survival.

Table 9.1. Categories of Moth Flight Defense with Examples

I. Primary Defense	II. Secondary defense
a. Negative phonotaxis:	**a. Evasive flight**
Geometrids	(also refer to primary defense)
Noctuids	*Heliothis virescens*[1]
Heliothis zea	*Halysidota* spp.[6]
Ostrinia nubialis[1]	*Estigmene acrea*[6]
Trichoplusia ni[2]	*Feltia subterranea*[1]
Celerio lineata[3]	*Pseudaletia unipuncta*[1]
Phoesia tremula[4] (Surlykke 1984)	*Prodenia ornithogalli*[1]
Lymantria dispar[5] (Baker and Cardé 1977)	*Spodoptera frugiperda*[1] (Agee 1969)
	b. Sound production
	Halysidota tessellaris[6] (Dunning and Roeden 1965)
	Cycnia tenera[6] (Fullard et al. 1979)
	c. Flight cessation
	Cycnia tenera[6]

[1]*Pyralidae*
[2]*Noctuidae*
[3]*Sphingidae*
[4]*Notodontidae*
[5]*Lymantriidae*
[6]*Arctiidae*

A moth's interaction with a hunting bat is a problem in sensory ecology. The moth should be able to (1) accurately monitor its acoustic environment and respond only to sounds that represent hunting bats and, (2) distinguish these sounds from irrelevant (nonpredatory) ones (such as chorusing insects). In turn, to successfully prey on auditive moths, bats should structure their echolocation signals so as to mimimize their acoustic conspicuousness. The bat-moth situation is convenient in that only one modality, sound, forms the sensory basis for the behavioral interaction. This fact greatly reduces the complexity of the relationship and offers a valuable opportunity to study the precise evolutionary pressures acting on this system.

Roeder (1970) observed a close spectral match (syntony [Fullard 1987a]) between moth auditory sensitivities and the echolocation frequencies of sympatric, insectivorous bats in the New England location where he worked. Moths in this part of the world are exposed to a relatively limited fauna of insectivorous bats. Ontario, where our studies are

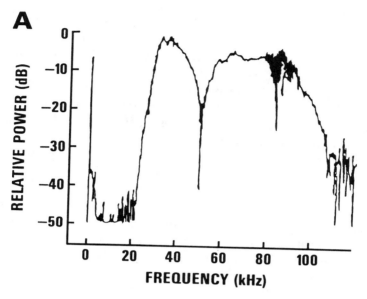

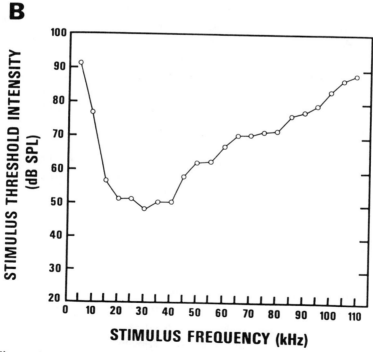

Figure 9.1 (A) Frequency spectrum of *Eptesicus* and (B) auditory threshold curves of its moth prey.

centered, has only nine species, two of which, *Myotis lucifugus* and *Eptesicus fuscus*, form the greatest proportion of the total bat community (Fullard et al. 1983). These two species emit similar echolocation signals with peak frequencies (maximally intense spectra) at 41 kHz (*M. lucifugus*) and 29 kHz (*E. fuscus*). As a result, moths in this area have ears with greatest sensitivities at frequencies ranging broadly from 25 to 50 kHz (figure 9.1; Fullard and Barclay 1980). This syntony suggests that a strong selective pressure is acting on the physiological design of moth ears to maximize their auditory efficiency as bat detectors.

In these studies, we assume that moth ears function primarily to alert their owners to the calls of hunting bats. Evidence exists, however, that some Lepidoptera produce sounds as part of their social interactions (butterflies: Darwin 1894; agaristid moths: Bailey 1978; pyralid moths: Spangler et al. 1984, Gwynne and Edwards 1986; noctuid moths: Surlykke and Gogola 1986; arctiid moths: Conner, 1987). Presumably, these species use ears for detecting the sounds of conspecifics. These examples, however, are exceptional (pheromones form the most common avenue of lepidopteran intersexual communication) and imply that social communication represents a secondary function for moth ears. Acoustically active moths may use their ears, already tuned to the echolocation calls of bats, for the detection of conspecific signals (Surlykke and Gogola 1986). What acoustic cues these moths use to discriminate between potential mates and hungry bats, however, are presently unknown. Regardless of the secondary purposes for tympanic organs, moths do use them extensively for the detection and evasion of bats, and this critically important function should remain even in the presence of additional requirements. If bat predation forms the heaviest evolutionary pressure influencing the physiological design of most moth ears, we can make two predictions about the sensory relationships between moths and sympatric predatory bats.

PREDICTION 1:
MOTHS SHOULD POSSESS EARS DESIGNED TO DETECT THE MAXIMUM
ARRAY OF PERTINENT PREDATORS

Since bats are both most numerous and diverse in equatorial regions, one would expect moths in the tropics to have ears that are more sensitive over a wider range of frequencies than moths in temperate areas, which possess fewer echolocating bat species. However, even when exposed to diverse faunas, moths should only be influenced by bats that form a real and substantial predatory threat. Many echolocating bats do not prey heavily on insects (e.g., sanguivorous vampires), and their signals should not contribute to the total selection pressure acting on the auditory characteristics of sympatric moths.

PREDICTION 2:
THIS RELATIONSHIP CAN BE EXPLOITED

Since a large moth constitutes a substantial meal, it is reasonable to predict that some bats will have developed echolocation signals that are, in some way, acoustically mismatched (i.e., inconspicuous) to the ears of sympatric moths. Echolocation mismatching could occur in three ways. (1) The bat could send calls too short to be discriminated against background noise, (2) calls with frequencies outside of the tuning of the moth's ear, or (3) calls too faint to be adequately detected by the moth. Bats emitting these signals would therefore be "cheaters" in the acoustically matched predator-prey relationship existing in that habitat and should be able to increase their intake of moth prey. This would happen provided that their population numbers (i.e., predation pressures) would not exceed a threshold that would cause sympatric moth ears to become tuned to the new acoustic selection pressure.

This evolutionary "arms race" between moths and bats can therefore be examined either from the moth's perspective of maximizing the bat detection ability of its ears, or from the bat's perspective of minimizing the acoustic conspicuousness of its echolocation signals. Figure 9.2 illustrates the acoustic features of echolocation pulses that bats can physically manipulate to hypothetically reduce their detectability to auditive moths. Table 9.2 lists the bat species whose described echolocation signals place them in one or more of these categories.

The Moths' Perspective

PROBLEM 1:
INCONSPICUOUS ECHOLOCATION FREQUENCY

As described above, bats in southeastern Ontario emit signals with principal frequencies between 25 and 50 kHz (see figure 9.1). Although energy in the form of harmonics exists at higher values, it is weaker in power and of less use to the moth. As figure 9.2 suggests, bats with calls that fall either below or above the best frequencies of sympatric moths

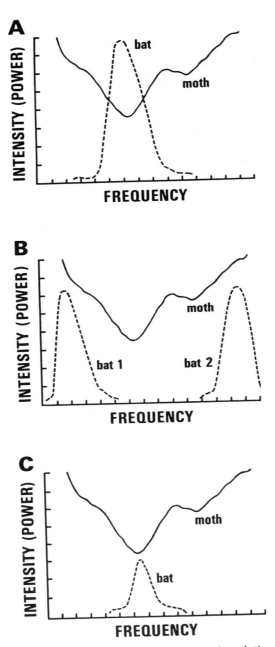

Figure 9.2 The hypothetical acoustic relationships between the ears of moths and the signals of sympatric bats.

Table 9.2. Insectivorous Bats That Emit Hypothetically Inconspicuous Echolocation Signals*

I. Inconspicuous frequency

a. Low frequency**

Otomops martiensseni[1]: 13 kHz

Tadarida fulminans[1]: 17 kHz

Tadarida aegypticaca[1]: 18 kHz

Tadarida ansorgei[1]: 17.8 kHz

Tadarida chapini[1]: 20.5 kHz

Tadarida nigeriae[1]: 17 kHz
(Zimbabwe) (Fenton and Bell 1981)

Tadarida macrotis[1]: 21 kHz
(Arizona) (Fenton and Bell 1981)

Euderma maculatum[2]: 10.9
(British Columbia) (Fenton and Bell 1981)

b. High frequency

Cloeotis percivali[3]: 212 kHz

Hipposideros ruber[3]: 138 kHz

Rhinolophus denti[4]: 110 kHz

Kerivoula argentata[2]: 90–118 kHz
(Zimbabwe) (Fenton and Bell 1981)

Rhinolophus lander[4]: 100.6 kHz
(Côte d'Ivorie)
(Fenton and Fullard 1979)

Hipposideros cafer[3]: 130–160 kHz
(Kenya, Uganda, Nigeria)

Asellia tridens[3]: 115–121 kHz
(Egypt)

Micronycteris hirsuta[5]: 105–110 kHz

Micronycteris megalotis[5]: 105–110 kHz
(Panama) (Belwood 1988)

II. Inconspicuous intensity

a. Low intensity***

Nycteris macrotis[6]

Hipposideros ruber [3]
(Côte d'Ivoire)
(Fenton and Fullard 1979)

Nycteris woodi[6]

Nycteris thebaica[6]

Kerivoula argentata[2]
(Zimbabwe) (Fullard and Thomas 1981)

Glossophaga soricina[5]

Artibeus jamaicensis[5]

Uroderma bilobatum[5]

Carollia perspicillata[5]
(Panama) (Griffin 1958)

Mimon crenulatum[5]

Micronycteris hirsuta[5]

Micronycertis megalotis[5]

Tonatia sylvicola[5]
(Panama) (Belwood and Fullard in preparation)

---

*This table assumes an average moth sensitivity tuned to 20–50 kHz, with best frequency threshold of 30–40 dB.

**Value reported is of peak (maximum power) frequency.

***Intensity determined qualitatively, units not given.

[1]Molossidae
[2]Vespertilionidae
[3]Hipposideridae
[4]Rhinolophidae
[5]Phyllostomatidae
[6]Nycteridae

have a theoretical advantage in approaching these insects. Roeder (1970) found that the moths he studied in the northeastern United States detect flying bats at distances of 30 to 40 meters. This is considerably further than the 3- to 4-meter distance at which bats are first aware of the echoes returning from the moths, and gives these insects a significant advantage in initiating their primary defenses. By emitting calls of mismatched (allotonic: Fullard 1987a) frequencies, however, bats can effectively reduce their respective maximum detection distance (MDD), that is, the distance at which they are first detected by moths (Fenton and Fullard 1979), without sacrificing signal intensity. MMDs for given frequencies can be predicted from a moth's auditory sensitivity, a bat's initial signal intensity, and the atmospheric attenuation rates of the sounds (Griffin 1971; Lawrence and Simmons 1982). For example, to an average moth in Ontario (Fullard and Barclay 1980), a bat could reduce its MDD from 40 meters to 3 meters by emitting a signal with its peak energy centered at 80 kHz rather than 30 kHz. This reduced MDD would then allow the bat, with its greater flight speed, to increase the likelihood of capturing the moth before the insect had a chance to initiate secondary flight responses. A counterselective pressure to this tactic, however, is the greater attenuation rates of high frequencies, which make these echolocation calls less effective over long distances. At the other end of the echolocation acoustic spectrum, the long wavelengths of frequencies too low to be adequately detected by moths provide little echo information about small items, and bats employing these calls would be restricted to hunting large prey. Considering these limitations, one would expect to find bats emitting allotonic calls in habitats where the resident density of insect prey is sufficiently high to compensate for their echolocation's reduced acoustic efficiency. We find that wherever we have recorded bats, the standard average echolocation peak frequency (the echolocation assemblage peak: Fullard 1982; Fullard and Belwood 1988) falls between 25 and 50 kHz, probably as a compromise to these acoustic constraints. Nevertheless, there are bats which do use allotonic frequencies (table 9.2) and it is the presence of these species that places special predation pressures on sympatric moths.

Although North America has served as a good starting point for these investigations, it offers only a limited diversity of bats. Testing the predictions outlined above requires the more complex bat faunas typically encountered in the tropics (Novick 1977). Africa, with its diverse bat communities and accompanying echolocation strategies, serves as a natural laboratory for examining these interactions. Moths from two areas, Côte d'Ivoire and Zimbabwe, were studied to determine if they possess ears physiologically adapted to the increased diversity of bats with which they must cope (Fullard 1982, 1987a). Auditory examinations of moths caught in these areas were done with portable electrophysiological equipment that monitored the auditory nerve responses to synthetic sounds covering the frequencies emitted in the echolocation signals of bats. The moth tympanic preparation, even in field conditions, is a simple one to execute and, when properly maintained, gives reliable neurological activity for hours.

From these studies we have determined that the total auditory sensitivity of tropical moths is significantly higher than that found in temperate species. This increase lies primarily in the low (less than 25 kHz) and high (greater than 80 kHz) frequency ranges (figure 9.3). Sensitivity differences are less pronounced in middle frequencies, suggesting that this range is syntonic with the heaviest predation pressure for both temperate and tropical moths. Presumably, at these frequencies, all moths respond with the maximum sensitivity of which their ears are physiologically capable. Figure 9.4 compares the acoustically generated predation pressure confronting moths from temperate, subtropical, and tropical habitats. In Africa, allotonic low frequencies are emitted primarily by molossid bats, and allotonic high frequencies are produced mainly by small hipposiderid bats (table 9.2). Since these bats are common in the African sites studied, it is likely that they, and their echolocation signals,

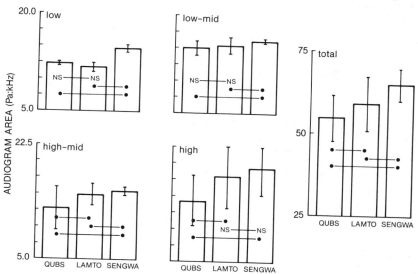

Figure 9.3 Comparisons of the auditory characteristics of moths analyzed in North America, Côte d'Ivoire, and Zimbabwe.

form a significant (but not primary) component of the total selection pressure acting on the moths' sensitivities. As a result, moths sympatric with these bats have physiologically responded by reducing their auditory thresholds to deal with these additional predation pressures. High-frequency sensitivity is particularly evident in moths from Papua New Guinea. There, moths exhibited the greatest auditory sensitivity of any moth tested to date, with most of the individuals tested readily responding to stimulus frequencies higher than 100 kHz. New Guinea, like Africa, possesses many species of hipposiderids that echolocate at high frequencies (Grinnell and Hagiwara 1972).

A major problem in interpreting the data gathered from these study sites is to determine the precise predation potential that each bat contributes. For example, the large African insectivorous bat, *Hipposideros commersoni*, echolocates at 62 kHz (Fenton and Bell 1981) and at first appears to be somewhat allotonic to the auditory characteristics of sympatric moths. This bat, however, feeds primarily on large beetles (Vaughan 1977) and probably does not contribute to the total predation pressure operating upon sympatric moth ears. In general, the feeding preferences of bats are difficult to document (Fenton 1983), and bats whose diets include a wide variety of insects may contribute different predation pressures depending on their nightly and/or seasonal feeding habits. Bat foraging behavior changes in response to factors such as prey availability (Buchler 1976), community composition (Fenton and Thomas 1980; Husar 1975), and reproductive status (Belwood and Fenton 1976). Certain moth defenses phenologically reflect these shifts (Fullard 1977; Fullard and Barclay 1980), and their precise relationship to the sympatric bat fauna is difficult to determine.

One remedy to the problems encountered in high-diversity habitats was to examine the sensory relationships between bats and moths in two Nearctic sites containing only slightly different levels of bat diversities (Fullard et al. 1983). Audiograms from moths in Ontario were compared to those from moths of British Columbia (figure 9.5). Although both groups of insects have similar best frequencies (20 to 40 kHz), western moths possess significantly greater sensitivities in the 30- to 75-kHz range. We feel that these increased secondary sensitivities reflect the higher acoustic diversity of bats in this area and in particular the presence of *Myotis evotis*, a vespertilionid that echolocates with an uncharacteristically high (for North American bats) predominant frequency of 63 kHz. This bat is moderately common in the area we studied and has been reported

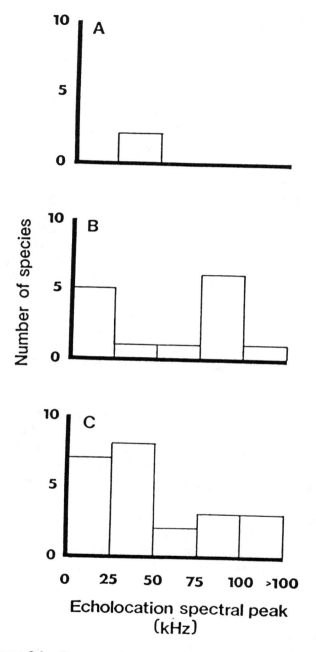

Figure 9.4 A survey of the echolocation types which are potentially present to moths from Ontario, Côte d'Ivoire, and Zimbabwe.

to feed on moths (Black 1974; Husar 1975). It appears that even between similar Nearctic sites there exists sufficient differences in bat faunas to place unique predation pressures on sympatric moths and thereby to give rise to adaptive auditory specifications. Recent studies (Barclay, personal communication) now suggest that *M. evotis* may prey on moths part of the time by listening to them as they rustle in the leaves and uses its echolocation system for detecting objects in its way rather than the insect itself. If this is the case, having ears tuned to the calls of this bat may tell the moth to stop moving and thereby deny the attacking bat its acoustic cues. Alternatively, preliminary evidence suggests that gleaning echolocation signals are undetectable by moths and *M. evotis* may be another 'cheater' (at least when in its gleaning mode).

Although simpler than those encountered in tropical sites, the bat faunas of Canada still present a confounding array of foraging strategies. Islands, with their depauperate faunas, offer a solution to this problem (Fullard 1984a; Surlykke 1986). One of these sites, Kauai (Hawaii), is further unique in that it possesses only one species of bat, the Hawaiian hoary bat, *Lasiurus cinereus semotus,* and allows for a precise quantification of predator and prey interactions.

All of the moths examined (Noctuidae and Geometridae) on Kauai possess neurologically functional ears, broadly tuned from 15 to 50 kHz. Observations of interactions between moths and the hoary bat further demonstrated that the moths elicit a complete set of antibat evasive flight maneuvers. It appears that this island bat actively hunts moths and preferentially includes them in its diet (Belwood and Fullard 1984). This dietary specialization has also been described for populations of the North American subspecies of *L. cinereus* (Black, 1972, 1974)—but see Whitaker and Tomich (1983), who argue that this bat is more of a feeding generalist on the island of Hawaii. It seems that the Hawaiian hoary bat, as the sole representative chiropteran in this particular ecosystem, presents enough predation potential to sustain physiologically functional ears and appropriate behavioral responses in sympatric moths. A surprising aspect of the auditory characteristic of Kauaian moths is the significantly greater sensitivity to low (less than 20kHz) frequencies compared with that measured in moths from either Ontario of Zimbabwe, areas with higher bat fauna diversities. This low-frequency sensitivity appears to be related to the total vocal repertoire of foraging *L. c. semotus.*

The Hawaiian hoary bat, like its North American relative, is a strong-flying, aggressive bat that routinely hunts in areas of considerably variable concentrations of insects (Belwood and Fullard 1984). During

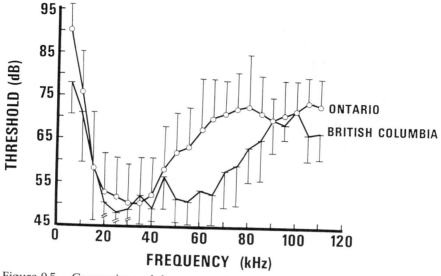

Figure 9.5   Comparison of the averaged audiograms from moths analyzed in south-central British Columbia, Canada, and southeastern Ontario, Canada.

windy or cold nights, when insects are scarce, bats often engage in active pursuit of one another, presumably as a territorial response to drive intruders from an already scant prey base. As the bats chase one another, they emit loud chirps that can be readily heard by human ears up to 20 meters away. Subsequent acoustic analyses of these social signals revealed them to be short, echolocation-like calls with peak frequencies centered at 9.8 kHz (hence the human audibility). They are commonly heard during foraging bouts and are reliable acoustic indicators of aggregations of hunting bats. I suggest that our ears are not the only ones capable of hearing these sounds. The low-frequency sensitivity of Kauaian moth ears should allow these insects to exploit *L. c. semotus's* social behavior to avoid congregations of hungry bats. The tuning of moth ears to bat sounds other than typical echolocation signals would be more likely in a habitat of low total bat diversity, such as Hawaii, where moths have no other acoustic selection pressure. Zimbabwe moths are also faced with bat-originated, low-frequency sounds (table 9.2, figure 9.4), but presumably these species do not constitute enough of a threat to result in increased moth sensitivities. Confronted with only one echolocating bat, Kauaian moth ears may have been physiologically freed to be tuned to an additional source of acoustic information, the social sounds of this predator. If the moths on Kauai use the social calls of *L. c. semotus* to elicit their defensive behavior, it would represent a novel example of an insect prey eavesdropping on the social interactions of their predators in contrast to the more conventional deceptive predator strategy (e.g., predacious fireflies (Lloyd 1981).

PROBLEM 2:
INCONSPICUOUS ECHOLOCATION INTENSITY

Moths face additional pressures from bats that echolocate with low intensities or mismatched frequencies (figure 9.2). By reducing the emitted intensities of its signals while increasing its own auditory sensitivity and/or relying on other sensory modalities such as vision, a bat may approach auditive moths before the insects initiate evasive maneuvers. Faint echolocation calls would elicit primary moth responses appropriate to a bat further away than it actually was. Bats which emit low-intensity calls ("whispering" bats [Griffin 1958]) were originally believed to exist only in the Neotropics as members of the New World leaf-nosed family, Phllostomidae, but recent studies have indicated that this characteristic may be widespread among other bat families.

We have looked at these questions at the Smithsonian Tropical Research Institute's field station on Isla Barro Colorado (BCI) in the Republic of Panama. BCI is well suited for this work because it is extensively studied and houses a particularly rich fauna of bats. It has fifty-four species of bats exhibiting every known foraging specialty (Gardner 1977), and the island is particularly rich in "whispering" phllostomids (Belwood 1988; Fullard and Belwood 1988).

On BCI, I first noticed a diverse array of moths belonging to the family Notodontidae. Since these moths possess only one peripheral neuron per ear, the fewest of any moth (Eggers 1919; Roeder 1974; Surlykke 1984), they would seem particularly ill-suited for this part of the world. Adaptations, however, have evolved in some of these moths (Fullard 1984b). Two large notodontids, *Antaea lichyi* and *Hapigia curvilinea,* posses external cuplike projections directed laterally from their tympanic recesses (figure 9.6) which bear a striking resemblance to the external apparatus of mammalian ears. Mammals have features in their external ears: the pinnae, which act to assist sound localization by providing acoustic shadows, and the conchae, hornlike tubes leading to the tympanic membranes which concentrate incoming sounds by acting as tuned resonators (Yost and Nielson 1977). The question was posed, did the external structures on the ears of these moths serve similar auditory functions as those found in mammalian ears?

To see if the cups aid in sound localization, auditory thresholds were measured in *Hapiqia curvilinea* as the preparation was rotated through 360° relative to a speaker broadcasting stimulus tones of 10 or 30 kHz. As figure 9.7 ilustrates, the moth exhibits reduced directionality in its polar auditory sensitivity when it is deprived of its external cups. This fact suggests that the cups function as pinnae acting to increase the moth's directional hearing. This increased directionality is probably of little practical use to the moth considering the large acoustic shadow that the insect's body presents to the sound wavelengths in the bat's echolocation calls. Payne et al. (1966) demonstrated a similar phenomenon in noctuid moths, which presumably do not possess these structures. This acoustic shadowing is a valuable factor in the moths' ability to bilaterally localize the position of an echolocating bat.

The second hypothesis, that the cups act as high-frequency auditory enchancers, was tested by comparing auditory sensitivity response curves to stimuli of 5 fto 150 kHz in individual *H. curvilinea* with intact or ablated membranous cups (figure 9.7). The resultant audiograms indicate that removal of the membranous cups renders the insects less sensitive to frequencies of 70 kHz and higher. This effect was also seen when the cups were blocked and the access to the tympanic membrane partially occluded so that it resembled the structure of conventional moth ears. In all individuals tested, the auditory sensitivity was totally abolished to frequencies above 115 kHz when these structures were interfered with.

These experiments suggest that the structures have acoustic properties similar to those of mammalian pinnae and conchae, increasing both these insects' ability to localize sounds and their sensitivity to allotonic frequencies. Two questions remain: why do only notodontid moths appear to have these adaptations, and which bats are the structures designed to detect?

BCI notodontids, with their single auditory neuron, had the poorest ears tested; their ears were significantly less sensitive than those of either two-celled (auditory) noctuoids or the four-celled geometroids. As a result, faint bats or those echolocating outside the conventional 25- to 40 kHz bandwidth would have a considerable advantage in approaching these particular moths. By possessing external structures which increase their sensitivity to frequencies above 70 kHz, these insensitive notodontids may have overcome their neurologically imposed auditory limitations.

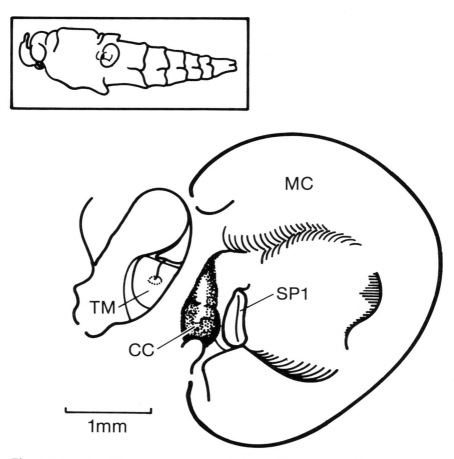

Figure 9.6   Ear of the Panamania notodontid moth, *Antaea lichyi.*

Although it is not clear why more neurons should increase the ear's sensitivity, peripheral interaction among the auditory cells in noctuid moths has been suggested (Coro and Pérez 1983; Suga 1961), and overall sensitivity may be one of those effects.

Whatever the physiological mechanisms involved, Neotropical moths have ample reason to detect allotonic sounds. Present analyses of the echolocation calls of Panamanian bats, reveal that a considerable number of species pitch their signals higher than 70 kHz (table 9.2). From studies with prerecorded echolocation signals of BCI bats (Fullard 1987b) it appears that the auditory adaptations of Neotropical notodontids are

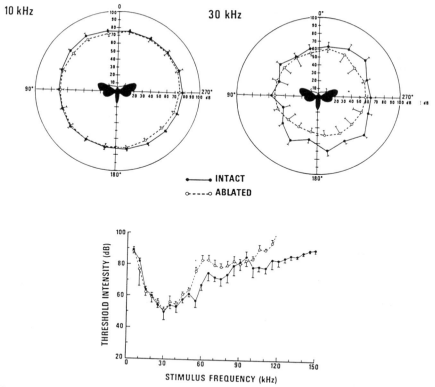

Figure 9.7 Directional sensitivity plots and audiograms of the notodontid *Hapigia curvilinea*.

designed for the better detection of allotonic phyllostomid bats, some of which are moth-eaters (Belwood 1988).

Other acoustic problems exist for Neotropical moths. Many of the high-frequency echolocating bats on BCI are also "whispering" bats that are able to glean their prey from the surface of foliage. Substrate gleaning is accompanied by certain specializations in the bat's echolocation design, particularly in the emitted intensities of its calls. The carnivorous false vampire bat, *Megaderma lyra,* often ceases signal emission during the terminal stages of its approach, possibly to deny its auditive prey (e.g., rodents) an acoustic forewarning of the attack (Fieldler 1979; Fieldler et al. 1980). On BCI the bat *Trachops cirrhosus* orients to the mating calls of its prey, the frog *Physalaemus pustulosus,* to glean it from ponds of water (Tuttle and Ryan 1981). Other phyllostomids may use similar acoustic techniques to hunt singing cicadas (Bonaccorso 1979) or katydids (Belwood and Morris

1987). Substrate-gleaning bats, listening for the sounds of prey, present profound problems to a fluttering moth as it warms up in preparation for flight. Werner (1981) demonstrated a clinging response in stationary, North American moths to acoustic stimulation resembling bat echoloca-tion calls and argued that this response renders the insects less conspic-uous to gleaning bats. Another antibat defense may be to reinvade the daytime hours and to avoid bats altogether. BCI offers a selection of moths to choose from to address these possibility. I have looked at the auditory physiology and behavior of the uraniid moth, *Urania fulgens,* a diurnal species that is occasionally very common in Panama during its migratory flights (Smith 1983). These moths spend their nights roosting in groups under palm fronds (N.G. Smith, personal communication) and would seem, at first, to be safe from bats. Nocturnal dormancy, however, does not completely protect them from predation by phyllostomids, since their wing remains have been found in roosts used by the substrate gleaners, *Tonatia silvicola* and *Micronycteris* spp. (Belwood, personal communication). It would seem, therefore, that even roosting diurnal moths require some form of bat alert. *U. fulgens,* in addition to possessing a pair of sensitive abdominal tympanic organs, which may be used to ward off the attacks of crepuscular bats (cf. gypsy moths: Baker and Cardé 1977; Cardone and Fullard 1987) also reveals a response which may afford it protection against gleaning bats. By monitoring a thoracic nerve trunk in this moth, I isolated receptors within a branch innervating the insects's hind wing that responded to air movement across the wing. These sensors may function in the flying insect as air speed indicators, but it is tempting to speculate that these cells might also monitor the wing beats of a gleaning bat as it hovers before its intended prey. Preliminary experiments with resting *U. fulgens* suggest that when the moth is stimulated with air puffs, it responds by dropping from its roost. This may be a nonauditory defense against bats and could represent a possible tactic for inauditive moths (e.g., Saturniidae).

The Bats' Perspective

Since moths form a substantial portion of the diets of many bats (Belwood and Fullard 1984; Black 1972, Fenton and Thomas 1980, Goldmand and Henson 1977), selection should favor those individuals emitting calls with reduced acoustic conspicuousness (figure 9.2). I was first exposed to this possibility in Côte d'Ivoire (Fenton and Fullard 1979), where we flew different bats in a laboratory in which a moth ear prep-aration had been positioned. We found that low-intensity and/or very-high-frequency echolocators elicited considerably less auditory nerve activity than did bats emitting signals with a more conventional (i.e., 30-to 50kHz, high-intensity) acoustic structure. In a subsequent study in Zimbabwe (Fullard and Thomas 1981), we measured the relative distances that different bats could fly before a moth tympanic preparation detected them. The Zimbabwean savannah's rich faunal diversity allowed us to test fourteen species of insectivorous bats representing four families, and our initial suspicion about the relatively poor detectability of low-intensity/high-frequency echolocation signals was quantitatively sup-ported by the results of these studies. Species that emitted intense, mid-frequency signals were easily detected up to 5 meters by the moths' ears as the bats flew anywhere in the lab. Certain very large bats were unwilling to fly in the room but could be induced to freely echolocate as they hung from one's finger. These bats readily activated the moth's tympanic organs at distances up to 23 meters. Included in this high-detectability category was the large beetle feeder, *Hipposideros commersoni*. When the smaller, agile hipposiderids and nycterids were flown in the room, they achieved much shorter distances before the moths' ears registered their presence. *Hipposideros ruber* flew to within 50 centimeters of the tympanal preparation before any discernible auditory activity was observed. From the bat's viewpoint, this distance provides an enormous improvement over the 30- to 40-meter distances that Roeder observed in his North American studies and could give these particular African bats a considerable advantage in approaching their auditive prey.

Whether or not these experimental observations translate into real improvements in foraging success is still speculative. One bat that is par-ticularly tempting as a test for this hypothesis is the African hipposiderid *Cloeotis percivali*, which echolocates with an astoundingly high frequency of 212 kHz (Fenton and Bell 1981). There is little chance that a sympatric, auditive moth could detect the calls of *C. percivali*, and this bat may have rendered itself acoustically "invisible." Not surprisingly, *C. percivali* has been described as feeding almost exclusively on moths (Whitaker and Black 1976). At the present we lack direct evidence that these theoretically inconspicuous echolocators actually do enjoy greater success at catching auditive moths when compared to the more typical echolocating species with which they compete and that these preferences actually represent long-term (i.e., evolutionary) shifts in feeding strategies (Fenton 1983).

Summary

It is apparent that moths make considerable use of their simple auditory organs for increased survival odds against the attacks of predatory, echolocating bats. The situation which exists from the unimodality of the sensory interactions between bats and moths has allowed a close examination of the ecological and evolutionary factors that act on the precise structure of this fascinating relationship. We are now investigating the questions which remain in this story: for example, why do some moths (i.e., saturniids, lasiocampids) not appear to possess ears, and how do these insects cope with bats? Also, there are the short-range (secondary) defenses of moths, such as flight cessation and, of particular interest, sound production (Arctiidae, table 9.1), which remain to be explained. The exact defensive function of sound production in arctiid moths is presently unknown, and the existing theories of aposematism (Carpenter 1938; Dunning 1968; Dunning and Roeder 1965) or jamming/protean display (Webster and Brazier 1968; Fullard et al. 1979) are subjects of debate (Miller 1983). The simplicity in the ear of a moth and the adaptive behavior which it governs are key players in one of the most parsimonious predator-prey relationships ever discovered and remain subjects which continue to stimulate the activity of nervous systems considerably (and presumably) more complex than their own.

Numerous individuals have contributed in one way or another to this research, and I thank them for their assistance and or advice. They are M.B. Fenton, G.K. Morris, R.M.R. Barclay, D.W. Thomas, G.P. Bell, S.K. Sakaluk, C.L. Furlonger, R. Kunz (Canada): J.D. Pye (England): A. Surlykke (Denmark): J.A. Simmons (U.S.A.): E. and R. Rice, J.C.E. Riotte (Hawaii): R. Vuattoux (Côte d'Ivoire): D.H.M. Cumming (Zimbabwe); and J.J. Belwood (Hawaii, Panama). I thank the following for permission to use their facilities: Queen's University, University of British Columbia (Canada): LAMTO Research Station (Côte d'Ivoire), Sengwa Wildlife Research Area (Zimbabwe); Wau Ecology Institute (Papua New Guinea); 150th Air National Guard (Kauai); and the Smithsonian Tropical Research Institute (Panama). I particularly thank J.J. Belwood for her patient help in the field and her comments on the manuscript. These studies were funded by grants from the following: National Geographic Society, University of Toronto, Natural Sciences and Engineering Research Council of Canada, and Sigma Xi, to whom I extend my gratitude for their continued support.

References

Agee, H.R. 1967. Response of acoustic sense cell of the bollworm and tobacco budworm to ultrasound. *J. Econ. Ent.* 60: 366–369.

_____. **1969.** Responses of flying bollworm moths and other tympanate moths to pulsed ultrasound. *Ann. Ent. Soc. Am.* 62: 801–807.

Bailey, W.J. 1978. Resonant wing system in the Australian whistling moth *Hecatesia* (Agarasidae (*sic.*), Lepidoptera). *Nature* 272: 444–446.

Baker, T.C., and R.T. Cardé. 1977. Disruption of gypsy moth male sex pheromone behavior by high frequency sound. *Environ. Ent.* 7: 45–52.

Belwood, J.J. 1988. Foraging behavior, prey selection and echolocation in phyllostomine bats (Phyllostomidae). In *Animal Sonar,* ed. P. E. Nachtigall and P.W.B. Moore. New York: Plenum.

Belwood, J.J., and M.B. Fenton. 1976. Variation in the diet of *Myotis lucifugus* (Chiroptera: Vespertilionidae). *Can. J. Zool.* 54: 1674–1678.

Belwood, J.J., and J.H. Fullard. 1984. Echolocation and foraging behaviour in the Hawaiian hoary bat, *Lasiurus cinereus semotus. Can. J. Zool.* 62: 2113–2120.

Belwood, J.J., and G.K. Morris. 1987. Bat predation and its influence on calling behavior in Neotropical katydids. *Science.* 238: 64–67.

Black, H.L. 1972. Differential exploitation of moths by the bats *Eptesicus fuscus* and *Lasiurus cinereus. J. Mammal.* 53: 598–601.

_____. **1974.** A north temperate bat community: structure and prey populations. *J. Mammal.* 55: 128–157.

Bonaccorso, F.J. 1979. Foraging and reproductive ecology in a Panamanian bat community. *Bull. Fla. State Mus.* 24: 359–408.

Buchler, E.R. 1976. Prey selection by *Myotis lucifugus* (Chiroptera: Vespertilionidae). *Am. Nat.* 110: 619–628.

Cardone, B. and J.H. Fullard. 1987. Auditory characteristics and sexual dimorphism in the gypsy moth. *Physiol. Ent.* 13: 9–14.

Carpenter, G.D.H. 1938. Audible emission of defensive frothby insects: with appendix on the anatomical structures concerned in a moth, by H. Eltringham. *Proc. Zool. Soc. Lond. A* 108: 243–252.

Conner, W.E. In 1988. Ultrasound: its role in the courtship of the arctiid moth, *Cycnia tenera. Experientia* 43: 1029–1031.

Coro, F., and M. Pérez 1983. Peripheral interaction in the tympanic organ of a moth. *Naturwissenhaften* 70: 99–100.

Darwin, C. 1894. *The Descent of Man, and Selection in Relation to Sex.* London: John Murray.

Dunning, D.C. 1968. Warning sounds of moths. *Z. Tierpsychol.* 25: 129–138.

Dunning, D.C., and K.D. Roeder. 1965. Moth sounds and the insect-catching behavior of bats. *Science* 147: 173–174.

Edmunds, M. 1974. *Defence in Animals.* New York: Longman.

Eggers, F. 1919. Das thoracale bitympanale Organ einer Gruppe der Lepidoptera Heterocera. *Zool. Jb. (Anat.)* 41: 273–376.

Fenton, M.B. 1983. Echolocation, insect hearing, and feeding ecology of insectivorous bats. In *Ecology of Bats,* ed. T.H. Kunz. New York: Plenum.

Fenton, M.B., and G.P. Bell. 1981. Recognition of species of insectivorous bats by their echolocation calls. *J. Mammal.* 62: 223–243.

Fenton, M.B., and J.H. Fullard. 1979. The influence of moth hearing on bat echolocation strategies. *J. Comp. Physiol.* 132: 77–86.

Fenton, M.B., and D.W. Thomas 1980. Dry-season overlap in activity patterns, habitat use, and prey selection by sympatric African insectivorous bats. *Biotropica* 12: 81–90.

Fieldler, J. 1979. Prey-catching with and without echolocation in the Indian false vampire (*Megaderma lyra*). *Behav. Ecol. Sociobiol.* 6: 155–160.

Fieldler, J., J. Habersetzer, and B. Vogler. 1980. Hunting strategies and echolocating preformance of bats—quantitative behavioral laboratory analysis. In *Animal Sonar Systems,* ed. R.G. Busnel and J.F. Fish. New York: Plenum.

Fullard, J.H. 1977. Phenology of sound-producing arctiid moths and the activity of insectivorous bats. *Nature* 267: 42–43.

_____. 1982. Bat echolocation assemblages and their effects on moth auditory systems. *Can. J. Zool.* 60: 2572–2576.

_____. 1984a. Acoustic relationships between tympanate moths and the Hawaiian hoary bat, *Lasiurus cinereus semotus. J. Comp. Physiol.* 155: 795–801.

_____. 1984b. External auditory structures in two species of Neotropical notodontid moths. *J. Comp. Physiol.* 155: 625–632.

_____. 1987a. Sensory ecology and neuroethology of moths and bats: interactions in a global perspective. In *Recent Advances in the Study on Bats,* ed. M.B. Fenton, P.A. Racey, and J.M.V. Rayner. Cambridge: Cambridge University Press. pp 244–272.

_____. 1987b. Adaptive function of auditory enhancers in the Neotropical moth, *Antaea lichyi* (Lepidoptera: Notodontidae). *Can. J. Zool.* 65: 2042–2046.

Fullard, J.H. and R.M.R. Barclay. 1980. Audition in spring species of arctiid moths as a possible response to differential levels of insectivorous bat predation. *Can. J. Zool.* 58: 1745–1750.

Fullard, J.H., and J.J. Belwood. 1988. The echolocation assemblage: acoustic ensembles in a Neotropical habitat. In *Animal Sonar,* ed. P.E. Nachtigall and P.W.B. Moore. New York: Plenum.

Fullard, J.H., M.B. Fenton, and C.L. Furlonger. 1983. Sensory relationships of moths and bats sampled from two Nearctic sites. *Can. J. Zool.* 61: 1752–1757.

Fullard, J.H., M.B. Fenton, and J.A. Simmons. 1979. Jamming bat echolocation: the clicks of arctiid moths. *Can. J. Zool.* 57: 647–649.

Fullard, J.H., and D.W. Thomas. 1981. Detection of certain African insectivorous bats by sympatric, tympanate moths. *J. Comp. Physiol.* 143: 363–368.

Gardner, A.L. 1977. Feeding habits. In *Biology of Bats of the New World Family Phyllostomatidae, Part II.* Tex. Tech. Mus. Spec. Publ. Lubbock: Texas Tech. Press.

Goldman, L.J., and O.W. Henson, Jr. 1977. Prey recognition and selection by the constant frequency bat, *Pteronotus p. parnellii. Behav. Ecol. Sociobiol.* 2: 411–419.

Griffin, D.R. 1958. *Listening in the Dark.* New Haven, Conn.: Yale Univ. Press.

————. **1971.** The importance of atmospheric attenuation for the echolocation of bats (Chiroptera). *Anim. Behav.* 19: 55–61.

Grinnell, A.D., and S. Hagiwara. 1972. Adaptation of the auditory system for echolocation: studies of New Guinea bats. *Z. vergl. Physiol.* 76: 41–81.

Gwynne, D.W., and E.D. Edwards. 1986. Ultrasound production by genital stridulation in *Syntonarcha iriatis* (Lepidoptera: Pyralidae): long distance signalling by male moths? *Zool. J. Linn. Soc.* 88: 363–376.

Husar, S.L. 1975. Behavioral character displacement: evidence of food partitioning in insectovprpus bats. *J. Mammal.* 57: 331–338.

Lawrence, B.D., and J.A. Simmons. 1982. Measurements of atmospheric attenuation at ultrasonic frequencies and the significance for echolocation by bats. *J. Acoust. Soc. Am.* 71: 585–590.

Lloyd, J.E. 1981. Mimicry in the sexual signals of fireflies. *Sci. Am.* 245: 138–145.

Miller, L.A. 1983. How insects detect and avoid bats. In *Neuroethology and Behavioral Physiology,* ed. F. Huber and H. Mark. Berlin: Springer-Verlag.

Novick, A. 1977. Acoustic orientation. In *Biology of Bats,* ed. W. Wimsatt (vol 3.). New York: Academic.

Payne, R.S., K.D. Roeder, and J. Wallman. 1966. Directional sensitivity in the ears of noctuid moths. *J. Exp. Biol.* 44: 17–31.

Robinson, M.H. 1966. *Anti-predator Adaptations in Stick- and Leaf-mimicking Insects.* Ph.D. Thesis, Oxford University.

Roeder, K.D. 1967. *Nerve Cells and Insect Behavior.* Cambridge, Mass.: Harvard.

_____. **1970.** Episodes in insect brains. *Am. Sci.* 58: 378-389.

_____. **1974.** Acoustic sensory responses and possible bat evasion tactics of certain moths. In *Proceedings of the Canadian Society of Zoologists Annual Meeting,* ed. M.D.B. Burt 71-78. Ottawa: National Research Council of Canada.

Smith, N.G. 1983. Population irruptions and periodic migrations in the day-flying moth, *Urania fulgens.* In *The Ecology of a Tropical Forest,* ed. E.G. Leigh, Jr., A.S. Rand, and D.M. Windsor. Washington, D.C.: Smithson. Inst. Press.

Spangler, H.G., M.D. Greenfield, and A. Takessian. 1984. Ultrasonic mate calling in the lesser wax moth. *Physiol. Entomol.* 9: 87-95.

Suga, N. 1961. Functional organization of two tympanic neurons in noctuid moths. *Jap. J. Physiol.* 11: 666-667.

Surlykke, A. 1984. Hearing in notodontid moth: a tympanic organ with only a single auditory neurone. J. Exp. Biol. 113: 323-335.

_____. **1986.** Moth hearing in the Faeroe Islands, an area without bats. *Physiol. Ent.* 11: 221-225.

Surlykke, A., and M. Gogola. 1986. Stridulation and hearing in the noctuid moth *Thecophora fovea* (Tr.). *J. Comp. Physiol.* 159: 267-273.

Tuttle, M.D., and M.J. Ryan. 1981. Bat predation and the evolution of frog vocalizations in the Neotropics. *Science* 214: 667-678.

Vaughan, T.A. 1977. Foraging behavior of the giant leaf-nosed bat (*Hipposideros commersoni*). *E. Afr. Wildl. J.* 15: 237-249.

Webster, F.A., and O.J. Brazier. 1968. Experimental studies on echolocation mechanisms in bats. *Aero. Med. Res. Lab., Air Force Sys. Com., Wright-Patterson AFB, Ohio* AMRL-TR—67-192.

Werner, T.K. 1981. Responses of nonflying moths to ultrasound: the threat of gleaning bats. *Can. J. Zool.* 59: 525-529.

Whitaker, J.O., Jr., and H.L. Black. 1976. Food habits of cave bats from Zambia, Africa. *J. Mammal.* 57: 199-204.

Whitaker, J.O., Jr., and P.Q. Tomich. 1983. Food habits of the hoary bat, *Lasiurus cinereus,* from Hawaii. *J. Mammal.* 64: 151-152.

Yost, W.A., and D.W. Nielsen. 1977. *Fundamentals of Hearing.* New York: Holt, Rinehart and Winston.

PART 4

Predation Prevention:
Chemical and Behavioral Counterattack

Justin O. Schmidt

Whenever a predator succeeds in overcoming prey strategies designed to prevent detection and attack, and prey escape is not a reasonable possibility, the prey must resort to its last defense—counterattack. Prey can fight back in a variety of ways. These range from psychological attack, to discharging noxious odors and tastes, to physically damaging or killing the predator. The exact counterattack, or combination of counterattack measures, depends upon the structural limitations of the prey and the situation in which the prey finds itself. Many palatable prey have no, or little, possibility of physically counterattacking; however, they do sometimes have well-developed measures for psychological counterattack. Perhaps the best known of these ploys is the startle reflex. Underwing moths are masters at startle. As elucidated by Sargent, the instantaneous flashing in the face of a predator of the brightly colored, and normally hidden, hind wings often intimidates and surprises the predator, allowing the moth to escape.

The saying "united we stand" is often as true for arthropods as it is for humans. An individual prey is often an easy target for a hungry predator; but if many individuals of that prey species stand together in an aggregation, their survival chances are greatly improved. Vulinec, in a refreshing approach, details the subtleties, and not so subtleties, of how aggregation acts as defense both before and after predator attack.

Chemical warfare is developed to the extreme in the arthropods. There are acids, aldehydes, ketones, quinones, terpenes, alkaloids, plus an almost innumerable diversity other compounds available for organisms to spray onto, daub onto, or vaporize near potential predators. As magnificently illustrated by Whitman, Blum, and Aslop, arthropods are the masters of the animal world in the use of chemicals to blunt predator attacks. The effectiveness of these allomones, in turn, allows their possessors to exploit a plethora of other avoidance and defensive measures, often in beautiful and bizarre ways.

In contrast to the active approaches of startle, aggregation, and allomonal release, some arthropods utilize more passive means of chemically defending themselves. Instead of emanating allomones, these animals sequester or synthesize highly toxic compounds that are then stored in their body tissues. These toxic compounds, when ingested by a predator, cause sickness or death. Although appearing passive, these chemical defenses are, as described by Bowers, one of the most effective and powerful of all known counterattack measures.

Vertebrate predators pose a particularly difficult problem for arthropods. Vertebrate size, strength, and speed and agility give them an immense advantage over usually much smaller arthropod prey. In addition to the many ways addressed earlier that arthropod prey can fight back, some arthropods possess another, and particularly effective defense—a venomous sting. Venoms are used defensively to hurt, damage, or even kill vertebrate predators. Venoms are uniquely suited for this role because they are delivered by means of the biological equivalent of the syringe through a predator's skin and into the susceptible body tissues. The theoretical and actual effectiveness of this ultimate prey counterattack, as illustrated by the ants, wasps and bees, is presented by Schmidt.

Social insects are faced with different problems vis-á-vis defense than most other arthropods. Social insect colonies are long-lived, nutrient-rich, collections of individuals and their progeny that often remain in one nest location and cannot readily flee to escape. These problems are especially acute for primitive social wasp species which often do not have available the outright physical and chemical counterattack potential of highly evolved social species, yet which have many of the same risks as their more highly social relatives. Starr presents a fascinating and detailed account of how primitively social wasps survive despite the mélange of predators in their environment.

CHAPTER 10

Startle as an Anti-Predator Mechanism, with Special Reference to the Underwing Moths, (Catocala)

Theodore D. Sargent

Startle is a widely recognized, though relatively poorly understood, antipredator mechanism. Unlike crypsis, aposematic coloration, and most cases of mimicry, startle is a transitory phenomenon, involving abrupt behavior changes on the part of prey organisms and often instantaneous responses on the part of predators. The ephemeral nature of the behaviors involved may explain why there has been so little experimental work in this area.

Numerous presumed startle devices have been described (Cott 1940; Edmunds 1974), and in many cases the correlation of morphological features and behavior provides convincing, though indirect, evidence for a startle function (e.g., the display of conspicuous structures only upon disturbance). However, experimental confirmation of this function is usually lacking. On the other hand, there is some observational evidence that certain startle displays may deter or delay predator attacks on at least some occasions.

Crane (1952) and Maldonado (1970) have observed that some monkeys, birds, and lizards will not attack mantids that have adopted conspicuous display postures. Yet Edmunds (1972) has noted that certain mammalian predators will attack displaying mantids and that the display itself seems to elicit these attacks. These different observations point out the obvious fact that startle displays may not always be effective. Rather, they may serve to deter only some predators, and then only in some circumstances.

Careful experimentation involving appropriate controls (i.e., individuals who do not exhibit the startle device in question) has rarely been attempted. An exception, however, is provided by Blest's studies (1957) on the responses of birds to various eyespot patterns. In one case, Blest presented both normal peacock butterflies (*Inachis io*) and individuals with the prominent eyespots rubbed from their wings to yellow buntings, and found that the birds exhibited significantly more escape responses to the normal butterflies than to the altered ones. In another experiment, Blest placed mealworms on a box and displayed various illuminated patterns under these mealworms when yellow buntings, chaffinches, and great tits alighted on the box. Under these circumstances, circular patterns elicited more escape responses than did linear patterns, and the closer the circular patterns approached the appearance of vertebrate eyes, the more effective they were in eliciting escape.

The only other experimental studies of startle are those involving *Catocala* moths and avian predators (primarily blue jays), which will be described later in this paper. The results of these experiments, like those of Blest, indicate that startle devices may be effective as antipredator mechanisms. However, we have yet to obtain quantitative evidence that any startle device enhances the survival (fitness) of individuals displaying it, as opposed to individuals who do not, in a natural population that is exposed to normal predation.

Terminology and Definitions

The study of startle has been plagued by uncertainty as to precisely what kinds of stimuli and responses are appropriately included under the heading *startle*. There does seem to be agreement that startle is a secondary defense, involving behaviors that a prey organism initiates only after a primary defensive mechanism (usually crypsis) has failed to prevent discovery of disturbance by a predator (Edmunds 1974; Robinson 1969a,b). There also seems to be agreement that the function of a startle display is to interfere in some way with the predator's completion of attack. Beyond this, however, there is considerable confusion as to what constitutes the essential features of a startle display, and why these features are effective in deterring predator attack.

STARTLE STIMULI

Many authors have stresed the apparently threatening or intimidating aspects of startle stimuli. Edmunds (1974), for example, uses the

Table 10.1. Potential bases of the startle effect.

Attribute	Description	Presumed response
Novelty	New, unknown	Avoidance
Rarity	Scarce, infrequent	Rejection
Conspicuousness	Intense, striking	Alarm
Anomaly	Unexpected, out of context	Surprise
Threat	Dangerous, aversive	Fear

NOTE: See text for fuller descriptions.

term *deimatic* ("frightening") to describe startle displays in general. Such a restriction seems inappropriate to me, however, because there are a number of stimulus characteristics that could induce "startle," and a number of internal emotional states that might underlie a startle response (table 10.1).

Novelty and rarity are two potentially important characteristics of some startle stimuli. Unfortunately, these terms are sometimes used rather loosely and their meanings confounded. I take *novelty* to mean "new" (never previously encountered) and *rarity* to mean "scarce" (infrequently encountered). Technically, then, a novel stimulus ceases to be novel after a single encounter, though some authors have used the term to describe a stimulus not previously encountered by their experimental subjects, even though it is presented over and over during the course of their experiments (Coppinger 1969, 1970). Novelty is also sometimes used to describe "unusual" stimuli, but I would advise against using the term in this way, and would suggest that the term *conspicuous* (see below) may often be more appropriate.

I would also advise against the use of two additional terms that are sometimes used to describe new or rarely encountered stimuli: *unfamiliar* and *odd*. To me, unfamiliarity is an imprecise concept that has strongly subjective overtones, and oddity has been used traditionally to describe stimuli that differ from the normal in situations where several stimuli (prey items) are simultaneously visible to an experimental subject (Kaufman 1973; Landeau and Terbough 1986; Muller 1968, 1971, 1972, 1975; Ohquchi 1981). Oddity, in this sense, (1) lacks a temporal dimension, (2) may attract rather than deter predation, and (3) may be confounded with conspicuousness as a stimulus attribute (Curio 1976). Because of these connotations, oddity seems generally inappropriate as a description of most startle stimuli.

These semantic matters aside, there is no doubt that both novel and rare food items are avoided by many animals (Allen 1976; Allen and Clarke 1968; Carroll et al. 1975; Coppinger 1969, 1970; Domjan 1977; Hogan 1965; Rabinowitch 1968, 1969), and that the conservatism in diet selection that this avoidence reflects is often adaptive. This being the case, it seems reasonable to suppose that prey exhibiting startle stimuli that are novel or rare may sometimes be avoided or rejected on these grounds. It seems unlikely, however, that any startle mechanism could operate on the basis of novelty or rarity alone, since neither of these attributes would exist if the prey species involved were to become common.

Conspicuousness, like novelty and rarity, is a relative stimulus characteristic (Ruper and Redston 1987; Sillén-Tullberg 1985). It is not, however, a frequency-based trait, and is therefore more difficult to define in quantitative terms. Generally, conspicuous stimuli are simply described as "striking," "dramatic," or "bold." In most cases, these stimuli exhibit the characteristics of high intensity (e.g., bright, loud) and strong contrasts (e.g., abrupt light-dark boundaries). Such stimuli seem to elicit reflexlike protective reactions in animals (withdrawal or avoidance), much like the human response to a loud noise or sudden flash of bright light (Sokolov, 1960). Given that abrupt and intense stimuli are often associated with real danger (e.g., predator attacks), then initial withdrawal from them seems appropriate and adaptive. Ultimately, if the stimulus is not associated with real danger, then a predator may learn not to respond to it (i.e., habituate) —a matter we will consider in detail later.

Unfortunately, conspicuousness is rarely the only attribute of a startle stimulus. Thus, in some experimental studies conspicuous stimuli are also novel or rare (Coppinger 1969, 1970), and in others they may be threatening, or at least mimic threatening stimuli (Blest 1957). The only study to my knowledge in which conspicuousness and novelty have been varied independently is that of Schlenoff (1983, 1985), who presented a novel, nonconspicuous stimulus to blue jays who had habituated to a conspicuous stimulus. In this case, the novel stimulus failed to elicit startle responses, suggesting that conspicuousness (or at least some attribute other than novelty) is indeed an important property of some startle devices.

Several interpretations as to the internal (motivational) basis for the avoidance of conspicuousness have been advanced. Many authors simply assume that all startle stimuli evoke fear, and that conspicuousness simply contributes to that response (Curio 1976; Edmunds 1974). In this view, fear results in behaviors (e.g., escape) that are incompatible with attack (Curio 1976; Hogan 1965). Other authors, using a more neurophysiological approach, suggest that prey attributes like conspicuousness produce high arousal levels in predators, and that these high arousal levels inhibit attack (Berlyne 1960; Coppinger 1969, 1970; Sillén-Tullberg 1985). Finally, some authors have stressed the confusion or uncertainty that conspicuous displays might engender and the hesitation to attack that would result (Chance and Russell 1959; Driver and Humphries 1970; Humphries and Driver 1967, 1970). Clearly there is uncertainty in our understanding of conspicuousness and the responses it produces, and a need for rigorous experimental work in this area is obvious.

Anomaly is another potentially important characteristic of some startle stimuli, and like most of those discussed to this point may act in combination with others to produce a startle effect. Anomaly is usually described with terms or phrases like *unexpected* or *out-of-context*, and the predator reaction is assumed to be one of surprise or puzzlement rather than one of fear. The concept was first advanced by Sargent (1968) in describing cases among *Catocala* moths where two or more species with very similar cryptic forewings have strikingly different hindwings (figure 10.1). It was suggested that birds come to associate certain forewing and hindwing patterns on the basis of experiences with them, and that unexpected forewing and hindwing associations would induce startle. Schlenoff (1983, 1985) has obtained experimental evidence to support this suggestion by varying the forewing and hindwing combinations of *Catocala* models presented to caged blue jays (see more details later). However, it remains questionable whether the concept of anomaly is applicable to any startle system other than that of the *Catocala*.

Finally, some startle stimuli may indeed be threatening or fear inducing. And in some cases the threat may be "honest advertising," as in the hissing of certain snakes, which signals a very real capacity to deliver a dangerous bite. In other cases, the threat may be entirely "bluff," as in the hissing of harmless snakes, hole-nesting birds, and certain insects (mantids, beetles, etc.) (Buchler et al. 1981; Masters 1979). Of course, whether a threat is real or bluff will depend on the predator involved in any particular case. As Edmunds (1974) has said, "There is not always a clear-cut distinction between a warning display and a bluff display."

A number of classic startle displays are clearly cases of Batesian mimicry. For example, the large, paired eyespots exhibited by various

Figure 10.1   Examples of *Catocala* species with similar forewings but dissimilar hindwings.

butterflies and moth upon disturbance are often remarkable representations of vertebrate eyes (figure 10.2), but cannot conceivably signal real danger to their predators. The same seems true of the snakelike appearance and behavior of certain lepidopteran larvae (e.g., the sphingid, *Panacra mydon*) (Morrell 1969).

The question as to whether predator responses to such mimetic stimuli are innate or acquired (i.e., learned by each individual predator through prior experiences with the models involved) is not easily resolved. There is evidence for learned avoidance (aversive conditioning and stimulus generalization) in some well-studied cases of primary Batesian mimicry (e.g., toads to honeybees and their dronefly mimics: Brower and Brower 1962; birds to the monarch and viceroy butterflies: Brower 1958). On the other hand, there is also evidence for innate avoidance responses to certain kinds of stimuli (e.g., motmots and kiskadees to the coral snake banding pattern: Smith 1975, 1977; see also Schuler and Hesse 1985). In most cases, however, the issue remains in doubt. Thus, Blest (1957) concluded that birds have innate avoidance responses to large eyespots, but Copponger (1969, 1970) has criticized that interpretation, pointing out that a general avoidance of novel (or conspicuous) stimuli could

Figure 10.2   Hindwing eyespot patterns in several moth species from Leverett, Massachusetts.

also account for Blest's experimental results. Further studies in this area are certainly called for, but they must involve careful control of the experiences of the predators and a full appreciation of the variety of stimulus characteristics that might elicit startle responses.

In summary, the essential features of a startle stimulus are (1) that it be presented after a primary defensive strategy has failed to prevent discovery or to deter attack by a predator, and (2) that it disrupt ongoing predator behavior such that the probability of successful attack is reduced. Stimuli that exhibit these features are usually novel, rare, conspicuous, anomalous and/or threatening as well, and it is these latter attributes that seem to trigger the responses of predators that interfere with attack. Further work is needed, both to define these various stimulus attributes and to determine the extent to which each, acting singly or in combination, plays a role in any specific case.

STARTLE RESPONSES

Startle responses are often described in terms of an emotional state that the startle stimulus is presumed to evoke. Thus, terms like *fear, surpise,* and *confusion* are frequently encountered in the startle literature. Unfortunately, these terms are sometimes treated as explanations, and this anthorpomorphic tendency obscures the fact that startle responses are behavioral outcomes of any internal changes being assumed.

Generally, an effective startle stimulus must induce either a hesitation (delay) in a predator's attack, or some alternative behavior that is incompatible with ongoing attack (e.g., withdrawal, crouching, vocalizing, etc.). Such behaviors are certainly consequences of neurophysiological events that are triggered by exposure to the startle stimulus (Eaton 1984). However, given the complexity of these internal events and our relative ignorance regarding them in naturalistic situations, it seems best at present to focus attention on observable behaviors rather than on presumed emotional responses.

In some cases where behavioral responses to startle stimuli have been described, retreat and escape are evident (e.g., birds responding to mantid displays [Maldonado 1970] and eysepot patterns [Blest 1957], and an assumption of underlying fear may be justified. Other cases are not so easily interpreted, however, (e.g., crest raising and vocalizations of blue jays in response to *Catocala* models: Schlenoff 1983, 1985).

Some workers, in an effort to obtain an objective and quantitative assessment of startle responses, have not described behaviors per se, preferring instead to record delays or hesitations (whatever their behavioral bases) in attacking a startle stimulus (Vaughn 1981, 1983). This approach has merit in certain experimental situations, but it also emphasizes the fact that there has been very little careful description of the behavioral responses of predators to startling stimuli. Until such descriptive work has been done, it will not be possible to specify a set of behaviors that can be defined as startle responses.

Although the key to the adaptive significance of startle is undoubtedly provided by the fact that a predator's attack is delayed or averted by exposure to the stimulus in question, our understanding of the mechanisms involved must await further behavioral and physiological work.

Habituation

From a predator's point of view, a startle response yields benefits only so long as it enables the predator to avoid some sort of dangerous or unpleasant stimulation (i.e., some sort of negative reinforcement). If, however, a startle stimulus is not signaling real danger (e.g., attack) or unpleasantness (e.g., noxious taste), and the predator is losing out on opportunities to feed on perfectly palatable prey, then the costs of its startle response may become substantial. Given these circumstances, it is not surprising to find that predators possess a mechanism which enables them to reduce or eliminate such costs. This mechanism is, of course, the simple learning process we know as habituation.

Habituation has been defined as, "the relatively permanent waning of a response as a result of repeated stimulation which is not followed by any kind of reinforcement" (Thorpe 1956). A capacity for this kind of learning seems nearly universal among animals, and an enormous literature has accumulated on the subject, from studies at virtually every phylogenetic level and from both physiological and behavioral perspectives (Hinde 1954b, 1961, 1970; Melzack 1961; Nice and ter Pelkwijk 1941; Peeke and Herz 1973a,b). However, despite the great diversity in subjects, methods, and levels of analysis employed in habituation studies, there does seem to be general agreement on a series of characteristics that describe this learning process (Petrinovich 1973; Thompson and Spencer 1966). The most relevant of these characteristics from our point of view (i.e., in terms of interactions between predators and prey in startle contexts) are the following:

1. Habituation proceeds as a negatively exponential function of the number of stimulus presentations;

2. Withholding a stimulus to which habituation has occurred leads to recovery of the original response;

3. Habituation is more rapid the less intense the stimulus involved;

4. Subjects tend to generalize from the stimulus to which they have habituated to other similar stimuli, exhibiting habituation to those stimuli as well;

5. Presentation of a novel stimulus interferes with the habituation process ("dishabituates").

If we apply these characteristics to the startle situation, we can conclude that habituation will proceed most rapidly (i.e., benefit the predator) when startle stimuli are (1) abundant, (2) of low intensity, and

(3) similar to one another. Conversely, habituation will proceed most slowly (i.e., benefit the prey) when startle stimuli are (1) rare, (2) of high intensity, and (3) dissimilar with respect to one another.

Thus, the characteristics of habituation lead us to expect certain characteristics in prey that rely on startle devices. First, since habituation strength increases with increasing presentation of the stimulus, we would expect prey that use startle to be dispersed in space and of solitary habits. In the *Catocala,* at any rate, this expectation seems to be met, since collectors often note that these moths occur singly on trees (except in the most dramatic outbreak situations (Sargent 1976). Second, since habituation is more rapid to less intense stimuli, we would expect startle stimuli to be intense (conspicuous). In the *Catocala,* again, we see this expectation met by the bold, contrasting colors and patterns of their hindwings. (One of my current graduate students, Victoria A. Ingalls, has shwon experimentally that colored stimuli with bold black bands are more effective in eliciting startle from blue jays then are solid, unbanded colors.) Finally, since stimulus generalization occurs during habituation, and very different stimuli interfere with habituation (i.e., cause dishabituation), we would expect to see striking differences in the startle stimuli that a predator might encounter at any one time. And again, the *Catocala* provide good examples, particularly with respect to the co-occurrence of achromatic and chromatic hindwings among closely related species (Sargent 1969a; Sargent 1978, 1981a,b, 1982).

In summary, habituation seems to be the most effective countermeasure available to predators whose startle responses lead to the loss of edible prey items that are using a startle defense. On the other hand, the characteristics of habituation, although undoubetly adaptive overall, do allow for some further strategic countermeasures by the prey. These countermeasures would include adaptations that (1) reduce the encounter rate with predators, (2) increase the intensity of the startle stimuli themselves, and (3) increase the diversity of the startle stimuli to which the predators are exposed.

The Catocala *Startle System*

Catocala moths make up a large North Temperate genus of noctuid moths, including over one hundred North American species (Hodges et al. 1983). These moths frequent deciduous woodlands, and forty or more species may occur together at any one locality (Sargent 1976). Most of the

Figure 10.3   Representative *Catocala* species exhibiting different types of hindwings.

species have barklike cryptic forewings, and all are characterized by boldly patterned and often colorful hindwings that remain concealed beneath the forewings when the moths are at rest (figure 10.3). The crysis of the *Catocala* has been studied in detail, both with respect to behavioral attributes of the moths themselves (Keiper 1968; Sargent 1966, 1968, 1969b,c, 1973a; Sargent and Keiper 1969), and with respect to the perceptual and behavioral responses of their avian predators (Pietrewicz 1977; Pietrewicz and Kamil 1977, 1979, 1981).

The hindwings of the *Catocala* have long been assumed to function as startle devices, though convincing evidence to support that assumption has only recently been acquired. It has also been suggested that *Catocala* hindwings may serve other antipredator functions. They might, for example, be aposematic devices that signal some degree of unpalatability of these moths to predators. However, a large-scale study of the relative acceptability of various butterflies and moths to birds coming to a feeding tray (MacLean, et al. 1989) (table 10.2) places *Catocala* nearly at the top of the list of acceptable lepidopteran prey to common woodland birds (blue jays, titmice, chickadees, and nuthatches). It is also possible that *Catocala* hindwings are very generalized mimetic structures, possessing colors and patterns that are often associated with noxious or unpalatable prey (e.g., black; or reds and yellows, banded with black) (Cott 1940; Edmunds 1974; Rettenmeyer 1970). Here again, however, the high acceptability of these moths to birds (table 10.2) argues against such an interpretation. Finally, it has been suggested that *Catocala* hindwings may play a role in the court-ship and mating behaviors of the moths themselves (Sargent 1972, 1976, 1981a). This suggestion is based on the observation that hindwing pat-terns within each *Catocala* species are remarkably uniform. There is, however, no direct evidence to support the suggestion, and it should be noted that chemical signals (pheromones) seem to provide the primary cues for species and mate recognition in most noctuids (Kaae et al. 1973).

The first line of evidence to support a startle function for *Catocala* hindwings was acquired in a study of beak damage patterns found on the wings of wild-caught specimens (Sargent 1973b). These damage patterns were compared with those inflicted on *Catocala* by captive birds in an avi-ary, and it was concluded that certain characteristic damage patterns (especially crisp beak imprints) (figure 10.4) resulted when birds loosened their grip on moths they had just captured. Subsequent work has con-firmed these earlier findings, indicating that *Catocala* are subject to heavy avian predation, but that many individuals are able to survive after being captured by a bird (table 10.3). (In this regard, it is interesting to note that I have yet to find crisp beak imprint damage on any large barklike moths other than *Catocala*, despite examining hundreds of specimens from light trap collections over many years.)

More direct evidence for a startle function of *Catocala* hindwings has been acquired through the recent experimental studies of two of my graduate students. Vaughn (1981, 1983) devised an experimental appara-tus which presented caged blue jays with a series of stations requiring manipulations which resemble the sequence of events involved in captur-ing a *Catocala* in the field. Essentially, the apparatus consisted of a board with twenty-four wells into which rewards (mealworm pieces) could be placed. Each well was covered with a masonite flap ("moth forewing") that could be pushed aside to reveal a colored cardboard disc ("moth hindwing") which the bird had to remove in order to obtain the food reward below. By varying the colors of the discs, and using latencies to remove them as an index of startle, Vaughan was able to demonstrate that both novel and rare colors induced startle, and that the responses to rare

Table 10.2. The relative acceptability of various Lepidoptera to wild birds coming to a feeding tray in Leverett, Massachusetts (1982–1985).

Groups	Number of species	Number of individuals	Percent taken
Butterflies			
Hesperiidae	2	16	75
Satyridae	4	42	57
Pieridae	3	124	56
Papilionidae	3	51	53
Nymphalidae	14	115	50
Danaidae	1	17	35
Moths			
Notodontidae	14	53	98
Catocala	23	169	98
Lasiocampidae	5	79	95
Sphingidae	15	77	94
Noctuidae	88	887	94
Lymantriidae	3	72	86
Saturniidae	3	76	82
Geometridae	22	259	71
Arctiidae	14	229	70
Drepanidae	3	28	46

NOTE: The basic procedure involved presenting six dead (frozen-thawed) insects for a fifteen minute period and recording each insect that was taken away by a bird during that interval (see MacLean et al. 1989).

colors were frequency dependent (i.e., the rarer a color was, the greater the startle elicited). In all cases, Vaughan's birds habituated rather quickly, though it is important to remember that his subjects encountered twenty-four discs in approximately ten minutes—an encounter rate that is presumably much higher than any that birds would have with *Catocala* in the field.

Table 10.3. Incidence of Type III bird damage (crisp beak imprints) on *Catocala* specimens taken in two Robinson traps in Amherst, Massachusetts (1979).

Specimens	Numbers	Type III damage Numbers	Percent
Chromatic *Catocala*	1,369	47	3.4
Achromatic *Catocala*	149	6	4.7
TOTALS	1,518	53	3.5

SOURCE: Data courtesy Frank A. Vaughan and T.D. Sargent.

Figure 10.4   Specimen of *Catocala ultronia* exhibiting Type III damage.

In order to more closely approximate actual prey items, Schlenoff (1983, 1985) devised an "artificial *Catocala*" model (figure 10.5). These triangular-shaped, cardboard "moths" were inserted into openings in a board, and when they were pulled from these openings, their plastic hindwings (painted to resemble *Catocala* hindwings) would suddenly expand from beneath the forewings. Each "moth" had a pinyon nut "body" affixed to its underside, so that her subjects (blue jays) were rewarded directly, as is the case upon successful capture and handling of a *Catocala* in nature. Schlenoff also developed a direct behavioral assessment of startle, rather than using the latency criterion of Vaughan. She observed, for example, whether or not the jays raised their crests, uttered alarm calls, flew to the far side of the cage, dropped the prey item and so forth, and devised a three-step ranking of startle intensity.

Like Vaughan, Schlenoff demonstrated that novel and rare hindwings elicited strong startle responses, and that jays will habituate to repeated presentations of any one stimulus. In her experiments, however, habituation often took many days (up to three weeks), presumably because her subjects encountered fewer moths (eight, as opposed to twenty-four, in each session) and her startle stimuli were more intense (patterned and moving, as opposed to uniform and stationary). Schlenoff also demonstrated that novelty alone may not elicit startle responses, since jays

Figure 10.5 Examples of the artificial *Catocala* models devised by Schlenoff.

that had habituated to a *Catocala* pattern (e.g., red and black, banded hindwings) did not then startle to a novel, though inconspicuous pattern (e.g., uniform, gray hindwings). This result suggests that conspicuousness (i.e., the stimulus properties of high intensity and strongly contrasting elements) is an important attribute of *Catocala* hindwings in terms of eliciting startle.

Finally, Schlenoff has also provided the first experimental evidence that anomaly may play a role in eliciting some startle responses. By using model moths with different forewing markings, she could control the relationships between forewing and hindwing patterns, and so determine the effect of a newly encountered forewing-hindwing pairing on her subjects. Thus, for example, if uniform gray forewings were always associated with black hindwings, and forewings with distinctive black markings were always associated with red and black, banded hindwings, then she could present these pairings until her subjects had habituated to both hindwing types. At this point, she could switch the forewing-hindwing associations, such that the uniform gray forewings were now paired with the banded hindwing pattern and the distinctively marked forewings were now paired with the black hindwing pattern. When this was done, her subjects showed startle responses to the familiar hindwings in their new forewing contexts.

This experimental demonstration of the effectiveness of anomalous stimuli in eliciting startle lends credence to the suggestion that hindwing diversity among otherwise similar *Catocala* species serves such a function in nature (Sargent 1969a, 1973b, 1976, 1978, 1981a,b, 1982). (It might also be noted that MacLean (1984) has supported the anomaly suggestion regarding *Catocala* hindwing diversity, though his conclusion is based on a multivariate analysis of the population and life history traits of these moths.)

References

Allen, J.A. 1976. Further evidence for apostatic selection by wild passerine birds—9:1 experiments. *Heredity* 36:173–180.

Allen, J.A., Clarke, B. 1968. Evidence for apostatic selection by wild passerines. *Nature, Lond.* 220:501–502.

Barnett, S.A. 1958. Experiments on "neophobia" in wild and laboratory rats. *Brit. J. Psychol.* 49:195–201.

Berlyne, D.E. 1960. *Conflict, Arousal and Curiosity.* New York: McGraw-Hill.

Blest, A.D. 1957. The funtion of eyespot patterns in the Lepidoptera. *Bahaviour* 11:209–256.

Brower, J.V.Z. 1958. Experimental studies of mimicry in some North American butterflies. Part 1. The Monarch, *Danaus plexippus,* and Viceroy, *Limenitis archippus archippus. Evolution* 12:32–47.

Brower, J.V.Z., Brower L.P. 1962. Experimental studies of mimicry. 6. The reaction of toads (*Bufo terrestris*) to honeybees (*Apis mellifera*) and their dronefly mimics (*Eristalis vinetorum*). *Am. Nat.* 96:297–307.

Buchler, E.R., Wright, T.B., Brown, E.D. 1981. On the functions of stridulation by the passalid beetle *Odontotaenius disjunctus* (Colepotera: Passalidae). *Anim. Behav.* 29:483–486.

Carroll, M.E., Dinc. H.I., Levy, C.J., Smith, J.C. 1975. Demonstrations of neophobia and enhanced neophobia in the albino rat. *J. Comp. Physiol. Psychol.* 89:457–467.

Chance, M.R.A., Russell W.M.S. 1959. Protean displays: a form of allaesthetic behavior. *Proc. Zool. Soc. Lond.* 132:65–70.

Coppinger, R.P. 1969. The effect of experience and novelty on avian feeding behavior with reference to the evolution of warning coloration in butterflies. Part I. Reactions of wild caught adult blue jays to novel insects. *Behavious* 35:45–60.

———. **1970.** The effect of experience and novelty on avian feeding behavior with reference to the evolution of warning coloration in butterflies. II. Reactions of naive birds to novel insects. Am. Nat. 104:323–35.

Cott, H.B. 1940. *Adaptive Coloration in Animals.* London: Methuen. 508 pp.

Crane, J. 1952. A comparative study of the innate defensive behavor in Trinidad mantids (Orthoptera, Mantoidea). *Zoologica, N.Y.* 37:259–293.

Curio, E. 1976. *The Ethology of Predation.* Berlin: Springer-Verlag. 250 pp.

Domjan, M. 1977. Attenuation and enhancement of neophobia for edible substances. In *Learning Mechanisms in Food Selection,* ed. L.M. Baker, M.R. Best, M. Domjan, pp. 151–179. Waco, Tex.: Baylor Univ. Press.

Driver, P.M., Humphries, D.A. 1970. Protean displays as inducers of conflict. *Nature, Lond.* 226:1968–1969.

Eaton, R.C., ed. 1984. *Neural Mechanism of Startle Behavior.* New York: Plenum. 363 pp.

Edmunds, m. 1972. Defensive behavior in Ghanaian praying mantids. *Zool. J. Linn. Soc.* 51:1–32.

_____. **1974.** *Defence in Animals: A Survey of Anti-Predator Defences.* Essex: Longman. 357 pp.

Hinde, R.A. 1954a. Factors governing the changes in strength of a partially inborn response, as shown by the mobbing behavior of the chaffinch (*Fringilla coelebs*). I. The nature of the response, and an examination of its course. *Proc. Roy. Soc., Ser. B* 142:306–331.

_____. **1954b.** Factors governing the changes in strength of a partially inborn response, as shown by the mobbing behavior of the chaffinch (*Fringilla coelebs*). II. The waning of the response. *Proc. Roy. Soc., Ser. B* 142:331–358.

_____. **1961.** Factors governing the changes in strength of a partially inborn response, as shown by the mobbing behavior of the chaffinch (*Fringilla coelebs*). III. The interaction of short-term and long-term incremental and decremental effects. *Proc. Roy. Soc., Ser. B* 153:398–420.

_____. **1970.** Behavioural habituation. In *Short-term Changes in Neural Activity and Behaviour,* ed. G. Horn, R.A. Hinde, pp. 3–40. London: Canbridge Univ. Press.

Hodges, R.W., et al., eds. 1983. *Check List of the Lepidoptera of America North of Mexico.* London: Classey, Ltd., Wedge Entomol. Res. Found. 284 pp.

Hogan, J.A. 1965. An experimental study of conflict and fear: an analysis of behaviour of young chicks toward a mealworm. Part I. The behaviour of chicks which do not eat the mealworm. *Behaviour* 25:45–97.

Humphries, D.A., Driver, P.M. 1967. Erratic displays as a device against predators. *Science* 156:1767–1768.

_____. **1970.** Protean defence by prey animals. *Oecologia* 5:285–302.

Kaae, R.S., Shorey, H.H., McFarland, S.U., Gaston, L.K. 1973. Sex pheromones of Lepidoptera. XXXVII. Role of sex pheromones and other factors in reproductive isolation among ten species of Noctuidae. *Ann. Entomol. Soc. Am.* 66:444–448.

Kaufman, E.W. 1973. Was oddity conspicuous in prey selection experiments? *Nature, Lond.* 244:111–112.

Keiper, R.R. 1968. Field studies of *Catocala* behavior *J. Res. Lepid.* 7:113–121.

Landeau, L., Terborgh, J. 1986. Oddity and the "confusion effect" in predation. *Anim. Behav.* 34:1371–1380.

MacLean, D.B. 1984. Evaluation of population attributes and life history traits of Catocala (Lepidoptera: Noctuidae) by means of multivariate analysis. *Am. Midl. Nat.* 112:67–75.

MacLean, D.B., Sargent, T.D., MacLean, B.K. 1989. Discriminant analysis of lepidopteran prey characteristics and their effects on the outcome of bird-feeding trial. *Bio. J. Linn. Soc.* 36: 295–311.

Maldonado, H. 1970. The deimatic reaction in the praying mantis *Stagmatoptera biocellata*. *Z. Vergl. Physiol.* 68:60–71.

Masters, W.M. 1979. Insect disturbance stridulation: its defensive role. *Behav. Ecol. Sociobiol.* 5:187–200.

Melzack, R. 1961. On the survival of mallard ducks after "habituation" to the hawk-shaped figure. *Behavious* 17:9–16.

Morrell, R. 1969. Play snake for safety. *Animals* 12:154–155.

Mueller, H.C. 1968. Prey selection: oddity or conspicuousness? *Nature, Lond.* 217:92.

————. **1971.** Oddity and specific searching image more important than conspicuousness in prey selection. *Nature, Lond.* 233:345–346.

————. **1972.** Further evidence for the selection of odd prey by hawks. *Am. Zoll.* 12:656.

————. **1975.** Hawks select odd prey. *Science,* 188:953–954.

Nice, M.M., ter Pelkwijk, J.J. 1941. Enemy recognition by the song sparrow. *Auk* 58:195–214.

Ohquchi, O. 1981. Prey density and selection against oddity by three-spined sticklebacks. *Z. Tierpsychol. Supl.* 23:1–79.

Peeke, H.V.S., Herz, M.J., eds. 1973a. *Habituation.* Vol. I. Behavioral Studies. New York: Academic Press. 290 pp.

————. **1973b.** *Habituation.* Vol. II. Physiological Substrates. New York Academic Press. 216 pp.

Petrinovich, L. 1973. A species-meaningful analysis of habituation. In *Habituation: Behavioral Studies,* Vol. I., ed. H.V.S. Peeke, M.J. Herz, pp. 141–62. New York: Academic Press.

Pietrewicz, A.T. 1977. Search image formation in the blue jay (*Cyanocitta cristata*). Ph.D. Thesis. Univ. Massachusetts, Amherst, Mass. 96 pp.
Pietrewicz, A.T., Kamil A.C. 1977. Visual detection of cryptic prey by blue jays (*Cyanocitta cristata*). *Science* 195:580–582.

————. **1979.** Search image formation in the blue jay (*Cyanocitta cristata*). *Science* 204:1332–1333.

————. **1981.** Search images and the detection of cryptic prey: an operant approach. In *Foraging Behavior: Ecological, Ethological, and Psychological Approaches,* ed. A.C. Kamil, T.D. Sargent, pp. 311–331. New York: Garland.

Rabinowitch, V.E. 1968. The role of experience in the development of food preferences in gull chicks. *Anim. Behav.* 16:425–428.

————. **1969.** The role of experience in the development and retention of seed preferences in zebra finches. *Behaviour* 33:222–236.

Rettenmeyer, C.W. 1970. Insect mimicry. *Ann. Rev. Entomol.* 15:43–74.

Robinson, M.H. 1969a. Defenses against visually hunting predators. In *Evolutionary Biology,* III, ed. T. Dobzhansky, pp. 225–259. New York: Appleton-Century-Crofts.

Robinson, M.H. 1969b. The defensive behaviour of some orthopteroid insects from Panama. *Proc. Roy. Entomol. Soc. Lond.* 121:281–303.

Ruper T.J., Redston, S. 1987. Conspicuousness of distasteful prey affects the strength and durability of one-trail avoidance learning. *Anim. Behav.* 35:739–747.

Sargent, T.D. 1966. Background selections of geometrid and noctuid moths. *Science* 154: 1674–1675.

_____. **1968.** Cryptic moths: effects on background selections of painting the circumocular scales. *Science* 159:100–101.

_____. **1969a.** A suggestion regarding hindwing diversity among moths of the genus *Catocala* (Noctuidae). *J. Lepid. Soc.* 23:261–264.

_____. **1969b.** Behavioral adaptations of cryptic moths. II. Experimental studies on bark-like species. *J. N.Y. Entomol. Soc.* 77:75–79.

_____. **1969c.** Behavioral adaptations of cryptic moths. III. Resting attitudes of two bark-like species, *Melanolophia canadaria* and *Catocala ultronia. Anim. Behav.* 17:670–672.

_____. **1972.** Studies on the *Catocala* (Noctuidae) of southern New England. III. Mating results with *C. relicta* Walker. *J. Lepid. Soc.* 26:94–105.

_____. **1973a.** Behavioral adaptations of cryptic moths. VI. Furhter experimental studies on bark-like species. *J. Lepid. Soc.* 27:8–12.

_____. **1973b.** Studies on the *Catocala* (Noctuidae) of southern New England. IV. A preliminary analysis of beak-damaged specimens, with discussion of anomaly as a potential anti-predator function of hindwing diversity. *J. Lepid. Soc.* 27:175–192.

_____. **1976.** *Legion of Night: The Underwing Moths.* Amherst, Mass.: Univ. Massachusetts Press. 222 pp.

_____. **1978.** On the maintenance of stability in hindwing diversity among moths of the genus *Catocala* (Lepidoptera: Noctuidae). *Evolution* 32:424–434.

_____. **1981a.** On the achromatic *Catocala. J. Lepid. Soc.* 35:81–93.

_____. **1981b.** Antipredator adaptations of underwing moths. In *Foraging Behavior: Ecological, Ethological, and Psychological Approaches,* ed. A.C. Kamil, T.D. Sargent, pp. 259–284. New York: Garland.

_____. **1982.** Studies on the *Catocala* (Noctuidae) of southern New England. VI. The "paring" of *C. neogama* and *C. retecta. J. Lepid. Soc.* 36:42–53.

Sargent, T.D., Keiper, R.R. 1969. Behavioral adaptations of cryptic moths. I. Preliminary studies on bark-like species. *J. Lepid. Soc.* 23:1–9.

Schleidt, W.M. 1961. Reaktionen von Truthühnern auf fliegende Raubvögel und Versuche zur Analyse ihrer AAM's. *Z. Tierpsychol.* 18:534–560.

Schlenoff, D.H. 1983. The startle response of blue jays (*Cyanocitta cristata*) to *Catocala* (Lepidoptera: Noctuidae) prey models. Ph.D. Thesis Univ. Massachusetts, Amherst, Mass.

————. **1985.** The startle response of blue jays to *Catocala* (Lepidoptera; Noctuidae) prey models. *Animal Behav.* 33:1057–1067.

Schuler, W., Hesse, 1985. On the function of warning colouration: a balck and yellow pattern inhibits prey-attack by naive domestic chicks. *Behav. Ecol. Sociobiol.* 16:249–255.

Sullén-Tullberg, B. 1985. The significance of coloration per se, independent of background, for predator avoidance of aposematic prey. *Anim. Behav.* 33:1382–1384.

Smith, S.M. 1975. Innate recognition of coral snake pattern by a possible avian predator. *Science* 187:759–760.

————. **1977.** Coral snake pattern recognition and stimulus generalization by naive great kisdadees (Aves: Tyrannidae). *Nature, Lond.* 265:535–536.

Sokolov, E.N. 1960. Neuronal models and the orienting reflex. In *The Central Nervous System and Behavior,* ed. M.A.B. Brazier, pp. 187–276. New York: Joseph Macy, Jr. Found.

Thompson, R.F., Spencer, W.A. 1966. Habituation: a model phenomenon for the study of neuronal substrates of behavior. *Psychol. Rev.* 73:16–43.

Thorpe, W.H. 1956. *Learning and Instinct in Animals.* Cambridge; Mass.: Harvard Univ. Press. 493 pp.

Vaughan, F.A. 1981. An experimental investigation of the startle response, with reference to the adaptive significance of *Catocala* hindwings. Ph.D. Thesis. Univ. Massachusetts, Amherst, Mass. 97 pp.

————. **1983.** Startle responses of blue jays to visual stimuli presented during feeding. *Anim. Behav.* 31:385–396.

Collective Security:
Aggregation by Insects as a Defense

Kevina Vulinec

Although it increases apparancy, aggregation is used by a variety of prey animals as a protection against predation. A prey animal in an aggregation may be protected from predation by active mechanisms, passive mechanisms, or both. Active mechanisms include detection of predators, confusion of predators, and direct counterattack against predators. Passive mechanisms involve the statistical lowering of the risk of capture by cover seeking among group members, the swamping of predators, and the advertisement of a noxious quality. This paper reviews the theoretical and empirical work on these mechanisms of defense by prey aggregations.

The variety of contexts in which animal aggregations occur has encouraged the formation of exhaustive classifications. Deegener (1918) recognized one hundred different categories of animal aggregations (with names such as *sympatrogynopaedia* and *amphoterosynhesmia*). Other classifications were attempted by Alverdes (1927) and Wheeler (1930). Allee (1931) presented a simplified scheme based on two main divisions: associations, which were defined as loosely integrated, relatively unstable, and temporary systems formed by the reactions of individuals to environmental stimuli; and societies, which were defined as more closely integrated, more stable and permanent systems, primarily dependent on reactions of individuals to each other. In this chapter a distinction will only be made between social animals and gregarious animals. The terms *aggregation, clump, association, group,* and *cluster* will be used to refer to the latter. Gregariousness is defined as the tendency of an animal to aggregate with others such that the animals are in contact with one another, or are nearly so, and that the distribution of the animals in the local environment is extremely patchy. This definition does not include cyclical outbreaks of insect species unless they aggregate, aggregations formed solely for mating, or aggregations formed inadvertently because of an environmental stimulus.

Examples of aggregating insects can be found in many of the major orders (table 11.1). Although aggregation has been correlated with aposematic coloration (Pasteels et al. 1983), many gregarious insects are not brightly colored. It should be noted that, of the examples listed, many are aggregations that are not hidden, but are also not brightly or aposematically colored. A more thorough discussion and comparison of these examples is in the final section of this paper.

Predatory Methodology and Evolution of Prey Defenses

The efficacy of predatory mechanisms is a function of the type of prey consumed and the defenses that the prey animal employs (see, for example, Kidd and Mayer 1983; Green and Nunez 1986). Likewise, the specific defenses that a prey animal develops may be influenced by a number of factors, including its vulnerability to each phase of predation. The act of predation has been divided into (1) the recognition or detection phase, (2) the pursuit or escape phase, and (3) the subjugation or resistance phase (Holling 1966; Griffiths 1980; Vermeij 1982). In terms of energy conservation, a defense that operates against phase 1 would be optimal (Pasteels et al. 1983). Aggregations tend to be conspicuous, therefore, as a defense they are more effective against one of the other two phases. If the group is aposematic and the predators are experienced with them, aggregations tend to be conspicuous, therefore as a defense they are more effective during the first phase of predation. Learning, energy return, and predatory mode may all influence the evolution of prey aggregations.

There may be qualitative differences between predators in their ability to learn and remember (Holling 1965, 1966). If aggregation serves, like aposematism, to advertise a prey's noxious quality, this defense would be most profitably employed by those prey whose predators can learn (Brock and Riffenburgh 1960; Estes 1966). The formation of search images or other mechanisms of learning by a predator (Tinbergen 1960; Croze 1970; Dawkins 1971a, b), may be facilitated by aggregated animals, but only if the predator is rewarded (Neill and Cullen 1974; Milinski 1977a; Gillet et al. 1979). One model shows that modifiable behavior (learning) is

Table 11.1. A survey of gregarious insects.

GREGARIOUS INSECTS

SPECIES	LIFE STAGE	COLOR	HABITAT	NOXIOUS	REFERENCE
Collembola					
Hypogastura viatica	Adults & juveniles		H	?	Mertens & Bourgiognie 1977
Thysanoptera					
Hoplothrips karnyi	Adults & juveniles	Black	H	+	Bullington 1978
Batnalliella yuccae	Adults & juveniles	Dark	H	+	Howard *et al.* 1983
Orthoptera					
Ceuthophilus secretus	Adults & juveniles	Dark	H	?	Nagel & Cade 1983
Periplanata americana,	Adults & juveniles	Dark	H	+	Roth & Willis 1960
Blatta orientalis,					
Supella ium,					
Leucophaea maderae					
Homoptera					
Aphis fabae	Adults & juveniles	Dark	E	?	Ibbotson & Kennedy 1951
Schizolachnus pineti	Adults & juveniles	Dark	E	–	Kidd 1982
Hemiptera					
Blissus leucopterus	Overwintering adults	Black & white	H	+	Brues 1926
Oceopeltus famelicus	Nymphs	Black & orange	E	+	Carpenter 1921
Nezara viridula	Nymphs	Green	E	+	Lockwood & Story 1986
Dysdercus intermedius	Nymphs	Black & red	E	+	Youdeowei 1969, Blum 1981
Dysdercus superstitiosus	Nymphs	Pink & grey	E	±	Carpenter 1921
Halobates robustus	Adults & juveniles	Dark	E	?	Foster & Treherne 1980
Velia caprai	Adults & juveniles	Dark	E	+	Brönmark *et al.* 1984
Rhagovelia obesa	Adults & juveniles	Dark	E	–	Deshefy 1980
Roscius illustris	Adults	Black, orange, & red	E	–	Carpenter 1921

Table 11.1. (Cont'd.)

GREGARIOUS INSECTS

SPECIES	LIFE STAGE	COLOR	HABITAT	NOXIOUS	REFERENCE
Neuroptera					
Ascaloptynx furciger	Larvae		H	+	Henry 1972
Diptera					
Tipula simplex	Larvae		H	–	Hartman et al. 1978
Coleoptera					
Agonum, Brachinus, Calathus, Chlaenius, Bradycellus, Bembidion, Nebria	Adults	Mostly dark	H	+	Larochelle 1974, Garneau & Liard 1979, Lesage 1976
Scaphinotus interruptus, Scaphinotus sitatopuntatus, Scaphinotus ventricosus, Scaphinotus elevatus	Adults (immobile)	Dark	H	+	Kavanaugh 1977
Dineutus, Gyrinus	Adults	Dark	E	+	Hatch 1925
Stenotaurus rotundus	Diapausing adults	Black & red	E	?	Wolda & Denlinger 1984
Hippodamia convergens,	Overwintering adults	Black & red	H	+	Ewert & Chiang 1966, Lee 1980
Coleomegilla maculata	Adults	Yellow	E	–	Turchin 1987
Epilachna varivestis	Overwintering adults	Black & red	E	+	Brues 1926
Desoria glacialis	Adults	Black & red	E	+	Linsley et al. 1961
Chauliognathus profunds	Adults	Black & yellow or red	E	+	Linsley et al. 1961
Lycus loripes, Lycus fernandezi	Adults & larvae	Dark	H	–	Buchler et al. 1981
Odontotaenius disjunctus	Adults	Dark	E	?	Brues 1926
Hymenorus densus, Hymenorus obscurus	Adults	Bright green	E	+	Carpenter 1921
Aenidia sp.	Adults	Black & pinkish-orange	E	+	Carpenter 1921
Deacantha conifera, Exosoma ugandaensis	Adults	Dark	E	–	Carpenter 1921

Table 11.1. (Cont'd.)

Species	Observation	Color	Code	Note	Reference
Gastrophysa cyanea	Early instar larvae	Yellow & red	H	+	Blum et al. 1978
Galerucella luteola	Overwintering adults	Black & yellow	H	?	Brues 1926
Galerucella xanthomelaena	Adults & larvae	Black	E	?	Craighead 1949
Plagiodera versicolora	Larvae	Black	E	+	Wade & Breden 1986
Zophosis pterygomalis	Adults	Dark	H	+	Carpenter 1921
Tricoptera					
Dicosmoecus atripes	Overwintering larvae & pupae	Pale	H	?	Cotceitas 1985
Lepidoptera					
Anthanassa frisia frisia	Larvae	Black & yellow-green	H	(spines, hairs)	Chermock & Chermock 1947
Asterocampa clyton	Early instar larvae	Yellow, green, & white	E	?	Klots 1951
Euphydryas phaeton	Larvae in communal web	Black & orange	E	?	Klots 1951
Heliconius spp.	Adults at night	Black & orange, black & white	E	+	Jones 1931, Young 1978, Turner, 1975
Marpesia berania	Adults at night	Orange	E	?	Benson & Emmel 1973
Melitaea harrisii	First instar larvae	Black & orange	E	?	Klots 1951
Nymphalis antiopa	Larvae	Black, white, red	e	+	Heinrich 1979b
Nymphalis californica	Larvae (reported periodicity)	Black	E	(spiny)	Emmel & Emmel 1962
Nymphalis j-album	Larvae	Light green, black spines		?	Klots 1951
Nymphalis milberti	Larve	Black & greenish-yellow		(bristles)	Klots 1951
Phyciodes tharos		Black & yellow	E	?	Edwards 1877
Smyrna karwinskii	Adults, daytime	Black & orange-brown	H	?	Muyshondt 1973
Euchaetias egle	Larvae	Black, orange, white	?	(milkweed, dogbane)	Dethier 1959
Halisidota caryae	Larvae	Black & white	E	?	Craighead 1949
Hyphantria cunea	Larvae, communal webs	Green	E	-	Morris 1976
Anisota senatoria	Early instar larvae	Black & yellow	E	?	Craighead 1949
Malacosoma americana	Larvae, communal webs	Black & white	E	?	Craighead 1949
Ceratomia catapae	Early instar larvae	Green & yellow	E	?	Craighead 1949
Callosamia promethea	Early instar larvae	Black & yellow	E	?	Craighead 1949
Hemileuca maia	Larvae	Yellow & dark brown	E	?	Craighead 1949
Phosphila turbulenta	Larvae	Black & white	E	?	Craighead 1949

Table 11.1. (Cont'd.)

	Stage	Color	H/E	+/−	Reference
Agrotis infusa	Aestivating adults	Brown	(in caves)	?	Common 1952
Ichthyura inclusa	Larvae	Black & yellow	H	?	Craighead 1949
Datana sp.	Larvae	Black & yellow	E	?	Craighead 1949
Calocalpe undulata	Larvae	Black & yellow	H	?	Craighead 1949
Tetralopha asperatella	Larvae	Brown & yellow	H	?	Craighead 1949
Archips ceraivorana	Larvae	Black & yellow	H	?	Craighead 1949
Cameraria cicinnatiella	Larvae in leaf mines		H	?	Craighead 1949
Gracilaria syringella	Larvae in leaf mines	Pale yellow	H	?	Craighead 1949
Hymenoptera					
Perga sp.	Larvae	Black, brown (bristles)	E	+	Crane 1966
*Neodiprion*spp., *Diprion* spp.	Larvae	Yellowish green	E	+	Prop 1960
Trichiocampus viminalis, *Trichiocampus irregularis*	Larvae	Black & yellow	H	?	Craighead 1949
Pristiphora geniculata	Larvae	Black & greenish-white	E	?	Craighead 1949
Croesus latitarsus	Larvae	Black & yellow green	E	?	Craighead 1949
Blennocampa caryae	Larvae	Green & white	E	?	Craighead 1949
Acantholyda erythrocephala	Larvae, communal webs	Grey	H	?	Craighead 1949
Neurotoma inconspicula, *Neuratoma faciata*	Larvae, communal webs	Brown, changing to green	H	?	Craighead 1949
Chalybion caeruleum	Adults	Blue	E	+	Rau & Rau 1916
Melissodes obluqua	Adults	Black & yellow	E	+	Rau & Rau 1916

NOTE: This table presents examples of gregarious insects, the stage that aggregates, their color, whether the insects are normally found hidden (H) or exposed (E), and whether they are known to be noxious or distasteful (+) or are readily eaten (−). A (+) sign is not meant to imply that the species is never consumed by predators.

of advantage to a predator primarily when noxious prey and nonnoxious mimics are clumped (Arnold 1978).

Predators are expected to select larger prey, in an effort to maximize energy return, as the distance to the prey increases (Schoener 1969). Therefore, being in a group could increase a prey's risk from predation, since the predator may initiate pursuit of a group from a greater distance on the basis of its apparent size (Vine 1971). Prey clumping, however, tends to increase the amount of time a predator needs to locate prey by increasing the distance between available prey groups.

The formation of aggregations may be influenced by the type of predation the groups experience (see Stamp and Bowers 1988). A model of central-place foraging predicts that a predator, if unsuccessful, should leave a patch after a fixed time, and a predator foraging in variable patches should leave after an even shorter time. This idea implies that prey confronted with this kind of predation should aggregate (Green and Nunez 1986). Once a predator has detected a prey aggregation, phase 2 of a predator-prey encounter, the pursuit phase is initiated (Vermeij 1982). The odds favoring prey escape begin to lessen as predators change their hunting mode to accommodate grouped prey. For example, a coccinellid larva moves in a straight line along a leaf until it encounters and consumes an aphid, after which it turns. This behavior may increase its chances of finding another aphid because of the prey's tendency to be clumped (Banks 1957; Rowlands and Chapin 1978).

Two specific responses by predators to aggregated prey are of interest. One is the tendency of some predators to intensify a search in an area after finding a prey item there (Taylor 1977a; Yamasaki et al. 1978). Some braconid parasitoids stay near a colony of their prey larvae and visit them for several consecutive days to oviposit (Morris 1963). The second behavior is the wasteful killing of prey by some predators, such as damselfly naiads (Johnson et al. 1975). Both of these behaviors would seem to select against clumping, and in fact many vulnerable prey species do maintain dispersed populations (Keiper 1969; Robinson 1969; Price 1975). However, many predators will also avoid an immediate area after rejecting a food item (Taylor 1974), a behavior that could benefit aggregated distasteful prey.

Functions of Aggregation

In the last two decades, much interest —primarily theoretical—has been focused on the adaptive function of animal aggregations (see

Pulliam and Caraco 1984). Of the experimental studies that have been conducted, the majority have examined aggregations in vertebrates (Bertram 1980; Patridge 1980; Elgar and Catterall 1981, Thompson and Barnard 1983); however, several important studies have examined the physiological, foraging, reproductive, and defensive functions of aggregation in arthropods.

Physiological functions of insect aggregations can include water retention and thermoregulation. Aggregations of woodlice lose water more slowly and survive longer in dry air than do single individuals (Friedlander 1965), and stinkbug nymph aggregations mediate water retention and temperature, allowing nymphs to increase weight gain and decrease the duration of the first instar (Lockwood and Story 1986). The clustering of insect eggs reduces the surface area exposed to desiccation (Stamp 1980). Overwintering aggregations are thought to protect carabid and coccinellid beetles against water loss (Greenslade 1963; Thiele 1977; Lee 1980; Copp 1983). Honey bee and bumblebee colonies can actively regulate hive temperatures (Heinrich 1979a); however, most other aggregated insects do not thermoregulate (Copp 1983).

Animals in groups can often enhance the feeding rate of other individuals through imitation, social facilitation, and observational learning (Alcock 1969). By flushing prey, groups of predatory animals may increase each other's feeding rate (Rand 1953; Sih 1979). In insects, the feeding efficiency of one individual may be aided by conspecifics. Jack-pine sawfly larvae (*Neodiprion pratti banksianae*) have difficulty biting into pine needles. When one larva does break the outer covering, other larvae converge on the spot and the hole becomes enlarged, allowing may larve to feed. Ghent (1960) showed that isolated individuals of this species suffered an 80 percent mortality rate, whereas only 53 percent of grouped larvae died. Burnet moth larvae can exploit their food resources more efficiently when in groups (Tsubaki and Shiotsu 1982). The male maize weevil (*Sitophilus zeamais*) releases an attractant pheromone. Chewing through tough grain kernels requires more than one insect, and the pheromone functions to promote aggregations for this purpose (Walgenbach et. al. 1983).

Mating swarms are only temporary aggregations but may be at high risk from predation when they occur; however, little defensive behavior is seen in them (Lloyd and Dybas 1966a; Alcock 1987). For permanent aggregations, defense from predation seems to be the most universal function.

Aggregation as a Defense: Active Mechanisms

COUNTERATTACK AGAINST PREDATORS

Active avoidance of predation can be achieved by a group through one or more methods: counterattack, early detection, and predator confusion. A cooperative counterattack against potential predators, used to advantage by vertebrates (Altmann 1956; Kruuk 1972; Blancher and Robertson 1982) is rarely seen in nonsocial insects, possibly because the size differential between many predators and insect prey makes such a defense ineffective. In some cases aggression by an insect group may be used successfully against invertebrate predators. Many social insects use cooperative defense to deter both vertebrate and invertebrate predators, often aided by pheromonal communicatory systems. Group defense may have been one of the selective factors in the evolution of insect sociality (Michener 1958; Lin 1964; Michener and Kerfoot 1967; Seeley et al. 1982; Schmidt, this volume).

Some nonsocial insects also use counterattack against predation. First-instar larvae of the neuropteran *Ascaloptynx* aggregate above their egg shells in an overlapping fashion that exposes only the head and large jaws. Ants and other invertebrate predators stimulate a group response of head rearing and jaw snapping. A more intense disturbance results in the larvae dropping to the ground. This behavior suggests that group attack is effective against ants which can overpower single but not grouped larvae, but it may not be effective against larger predators and an alternative defense is necessary (Henry 1972; Cornell et al. 1987).

The effectiveness of chemical defenses may be enhanced by aggressive group behavior. Aggregated early-instar larvae of the leaf beetle *Gastrophysa cyanea* simultaneously evert their defensive glands when disturbed. These young larvae lack an additional gland that is present in the solitary later instars of this same species (Blum et al. 1978). Grouped sawfly larvae jerk their posterior and anterior ends up and down in sychrony while exuding a sticky substance from their mouthparts (Prop 1960; Tostowaryk 1972).

DETECTION OF PREDATORS

Animals in groups may have superior ability in the early detection of predators compared with solitary animals. This advantage of flocking

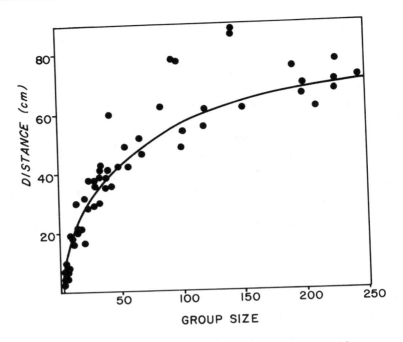

Figure 11.1   The relationship between the number of *Halobates robustus* individuals per aggregation and the distance at which a predator model elicited escapes behavior.

was suggested by Hamilton (1971), Vine (1971), and Pulliam (1973). Most experimental work on early predator detection has been done with birds, though insects have been the subject of a few recent studies. Treherne and Foster (1980, 1981, 1982) and Foster and Treherne (1980, 1982) examined the aggregation behavior of *Halobates robustus*, the ocean skater. The ocean skater is a hemipteran that lives on the surface of the ocean near man-groves and lava edges in the Galapagos. These insects are solitary feeders but remain in flotillas when not feeding (Foster and Treherne 1980). Although the flotillas also serve the purpose of mate location and selection (Foster and Treherne 1982), predator avoidance appears to be their primary function (Treherne and Foster 1982). The data (Treherne and Foster 1980) show that a predator model can get much closer to a single insect or small group than to a large group (figure 11.1). The encounter rate between individuals increases as the insects that have perceived danger move rapidly and randomly, and consequently bump into other individuals. Treherne and Foster called this phenomenon the "Trafalgar effect" because of its similarity to the series of signals sent between ships in Admiral Nelson's fleet before the battle of Trafaglar. A similar mechanism occurs in tightly clumped aggregations of Thysanura and the aphid *Schizolachnus pineti,* which use the disturbance of bodily contacts as a cue for approaching danger (Delany 1959; Kidd 1982). Aphids in small aggregations had a higher probability of being captured by syrphid larvae than those in large aggregations (Kidd 1982). In ocean skaters it was also found that the speed of transmission of avoidance behavior throughout the flotilla of ocean skaters (mean value = 59.9 cm/sec) exceeded that of an approaching predator model (8 cm/sec) (Treherne and Foster 1981). Although some predators move considerably faster than this, the speed of transmission still allows individuals that have not actually sighted the predator to escape.

Ocean skaters appear to use different defensive tactics with different predators (Treherne and Foster 1982). Fish predators can approach unseen from under the water. Aggregation by *Halobates robustus* gives protection from fish as a result of two factors: the probability of attack upon one individual is inversely related to the size of the group, and reduced capture success of fish predators is apparently due to the confusing movement of members of an agitated swarm. The insects also rely on the enhanced detection capabilities of aggregations and one of two flight behaviors, depending on group size. Groups of ten or fewer individuals disperse rapidly and synchronously when attacked, whereas groups larger than ten tend to remain aggregated but participated in confusing rapid movements. Other water-surface-dwelling insects that aggregate, such as the riffle bug *Rhagovelia obesa,* exhibit different group responses to different predators. This hemipteran disperses when confronted with an aerial predator, but remains aggregated and exhibits group movements when confronted with a slowly moving object under the water (Deshefy 1980).

Similar predator avoidance mechanisms are found in the water-surface-living beetle, *Dineutes horni* (Vulinec 1987; Vulinec and Kolmes 1987; Vulinec and Miller, in press). The predator detection and avoidance capabilities of these beetles vary directly with the size of aggregations (figure 11.2), and are accomplished by the increase in the number of eyes available for surveillance. This finding supports Pulliam's hypothesis of aggregation (1973). In addition, gyrinids use an early warning system similar to the "Trafalgar effect." Rather than relying on the contact of

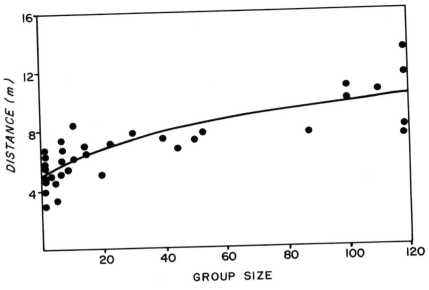

Figure 11.2   The relationship between the number of *Dineutes horni* individuals per aggregation and the distance at which a predator model elicited escape behavior.

rapidly moving bodies as a cue for escape, gyrinid beetles can feel the wave motion of other agitated members of the flotilla.

Some insects, such as the bug *Dysdercus intermedius* (Calam and Youdeowei 1968) and some aphids (Dixon and Stewart 1975; Montgomery and Nault 1977, Nault and Phelan 1984), use a conspecific's defensive substance as a dispersal or alarm pheromone. On the other hand, the grey pine aphid and the whirligig beetle, though possessing defensive chemicals, use bodily contacts and surface waves as sensory extensions in the early detection of predators (Kidd 1982; Vulinec and Miller, in press).

Aggregations that use early detection of predators as a defensive strategy might be expected to show an upper limit to group size. Whirligig beetle aggregations usually number less than two hundred individuals. Where larger aggregations are found, they tend to be subdivided into smaller groups (Heinrich and Vogt 1980). Like whirligig beetles, group size in the ocean skater peaks at approximately two hundred (Treherne and Foster 1982). These examples may reflect a maximum group size beyond which effective communication of a predator's proximity cannot occur.

CONFUSION OF PREDATORS

Many insects, when fleeing attack, describe an erratic path, and some even move erratically during undisturbed normal activities. This behavior has been termed "protean display" and is assumed to stimulate fright reactions in predators and to also reduce the predictability of prey location (Humphries and Driver 1967). Protean displays exhibited by groups of animals disorient predators with behaviors such as synchronous scattering, multiple lures, or deterrence (Humphries and Driver 1970). Sticklebacks will attack the densest part of a swarm of *Daphnia* only when very hungry (Heller and Milinski 1979), and *Daphnia* that stray from swarms have been shown to have an increased risk from fish predation (Milinski 1977a, b). Predation success on locust nymphs (*Schistocera gregaria*) has been diminished when the predator is presented with large groups of prey, a result attributed to confusion on the predator's part (Gillett et al. 1979).

Aggregation as a Defense: Passive Mechanisms

THE DILUTION EFFECT AND APPARANCY: MODELING THE BENEFITS OF AGGREGATION

Some authors have suggested that members of an aggregation might be protected by a dilution effect by which any individual has less chance of being attacked when it is surrounded by others than when it is alone, once the predator has located it. Williams (1964) proposed that an aggregation forms as a result of cover-seeking attempts of individuals: each attempts to place as many others as possible between itself and a predator. Hamilton (1971) explored this idea further. In his model, a frog on a one-dimensional circular pond can reduce its "domain of danger" by moving to a spot between its neighbors. This behavior will ultimately lead to a large clump of frogs on one side of the pond. Thus, gregarious behavior can result from a purely selfish motive. A consequence of this influx is that marginal animals are at risk (table 11.2); for example, aphids often bunch in the presence of a parasitoid, leaving the peripheral individuals vulnerable to attack (Klingauf and Sengonca 1970).

Vine (1971) proposed a model by which a group of prey animals are detected by a predator in two different situations: in case 1, as in Hamilton's model, a predator appears in the center of loosely clumped prey; in

Table 11.2. A synopsis of the different models that describe passive defense by aggregation.

Model	Behavior of Predator	Behavior of Prey	Other Defenses Necessary	Predictions of Model
Selfish herd (Hamilton 1971)	Emerges among prey.	Prey tighten up numbers as each attempts to achieve a central position.		Prey benefit most from a tight, circular flock.
Apparancy model (Vine 1971)	Approaches loose aggregation from outside original habitat, may or may not detect prey.	As above.		As above.
Increased apparancy model	Flocking of prey increases distance at which predator can detect animals.			Small flocks disadvantageous to prey; medium to large flocks advantageous.
Early detection model (Pulliam 1973)	Predator approaches from outside flock.	Intermittent surveillance by flock members.	Early detection and evasion of predator.	All flocking advantageous to prey.
Concealment model (Treisman 1975a)	Predator may not detect clumped prey.			If only one prey killed, more advantageous for prey to be clumped; if more killed, more advantageous to be solitary.
Evasion model (Treisman 1975a)	As above.		Early detection and evasion of predator.	Group formation better than random scattering.
Optimal economic model (Treisman 1975b)	Predator approaches from outside flock.	Decision making by each prey animal as to how much surveillance is needed based on group size.	Early detection and evasion of predator.	Finite upper limit to group size; predictable optimal number of watchers at any one time, and reactivity of watchers dependant on probability of predator being present.

Table 11.2. *(Con't.)*

Model	Behavior of Predator	Behavior of Prey	Other Defenses Necessary	Predictions of Model
Adaptive payoff model (Treisman 1975b)	Predator may or may not be present; if predator present, may not detect prey before they detect predator.	Optimal numbers of watchers of group size for particular conditions.	As above.	Animals of moderate density and subject to high levels of predation should be gregarious; animals of very low or very high density and subject to low predation should be scattered.
Gut size model (Taylor 1976)	Ambush predators can only hold certain number of prey in gut.	Mobile prey in clumps of various sizes.		Clumping almost always benefits prey and costs predators.
Gut size and detectability model (Taylor 1977b)	As above.	As above.	Crypsis or not.	Noncryptic prey always benefit from groups above a certain size; for cryptic prey aggregation is beneficial at high and low group size but not at intermediate; only when cryptic prey approach their maximum detectability does clumping become advantageous.
Nonzero sum game (Eschel 1978)	Attacks herd only if single prey not located.	Prey attempt to outmaneuver slowest prey.		Herd always benefits leaders, but it is still not beneficial for any animals to abandon lead.
Attack abatement model (Turner and Pitcher 1986)	Predator intake is constant.	No confusion effect, cooperative defense, information transfer.	Avoidance by spacing in local environment.	Avoidance and dilution benefit prey in combination only.

case 2, the predator detects the prey while it is still outside the boundaries of the group. (see table 11.2). Vine argued that Hamilton did not satisfactorily explore the second case, and that the tendency of animals to aggregate regardless of predator proximity requires further explanation. In case 2, a predator approaching from outside the group may not necessarily take a marginal animal. The optimal situation from the standpoint of the prey is detection of a predator from a distance and subsequent flight. Therefore, case 2 situations should select for good vision and flight abilities, attributes often found in prey animals that live in open habitats. Vine based his model on probabilities of detection, assuming that a predator would move to a new habitat if its scanning activity is unrewarded. The time a predator must scan the environment to detect prey is increased with clumping, possibly causing the predator to move elsewhere quickly. Security from both detection and pursuit for an individual within a group is increased by a more central position, which again will result in tightly packed aggregations. In a subsequent paper, Vine (1973) expanded his model to include the maximum distance at which a predator can just detect a group of prey. Both small and large groups will increase this distance, but this disadvantage is probably outweighed by the decrease in the probability of individuals being singled out when in a group.

Pulliam (1973) objected to the idea of marginal predation as a selective factor in the formation of groups. He argued that marginal animals which are more at risk than solitary animals will leave the flock, exposing new individuals. This behavior will eventually result in the disintegration of the group. Pulliam suggested that individuals in groups profit primarily by the increased probability of early predator detection.

Treisman (1975a) suggested that there are two basic mechanisms that explain the evolution of flocking in animals: enhanced detection of predators and concealment. He criticized Hamilton's model by stating that the genes for selfish behavior could not spread throughout the population. The advantage to an individual would decrease with an increase in the proportion of the gene in the population, since there would eventually be selection for behavior protecting other group members from selfish exploitation. His concealment model incorporated a decision process that affects whether a predator moves to a new area, based on the maximization of the ratio of prey detected and captured to the energy expended. This model predicts that it is advantageous for the prey to be clumped if only one prey is killed during a predator's attack. If more are killed it may be better to be solitary. Treisman also suggested that sessile organisms benefit little from aggregation unless there is an additional defense, such as chemical protection. Many insect eggs that are laid in clusters are also unpalatable (Stamp 1981), a finding that appears to support this suggestion.

In Treisman's evasion model, as in Pulliam's, animals in a group communicate their detection of a predator to one another; even if one is killed, all others will escape because of decreased reaction time. For animals that can evade a predator the least risk accrues to a compact group of animals. Individual risk will be much higher for scattered animals than for those in groups. Treisman concluded that if a prey's main defense is concealment, prey group configuration depends on the predator's mode. If predators hunt by olfaction, random scattering carries the lowest risk. If predators hunt by sight, prey grouping may be advantageous unless the prey, if discovered, will lose all their members to a predator, in which case grouping is never advantageous. If animals are able to evade a predator, group formation always yields the lowest risk per individual, especially if information is shared.

Treisman (1975b) further explored "economic" models or predator-prey interactions whereby animals make decisions about their own actions on the basis of the costs and benefits of that action. The values of the decisions are calculated by means of a payoff matrix. Individual animals can calculate how watchful each needs to be on the basis of its risk and the number of watchers in its group (optimal economic model), or each animal can maintain a level of watchfulness appropriate for a solitary animal (fixed payoff model), or animals can vary their responses according to the size of the group to which they belong (adaptive payoff model). This model predicts that only solitary prey or prey in small groups can vary their individual thresholds for responsiveness to a predator when there is an increase in the probability of a predator in the vicinity. For animals in large groups, it would be more advantageous to increase the number of watchers rather than to lower their response level, considering the costs of overresponding to nondangerous situations. Gregariousness should occur in animals of moderate density in a given area, which have high levels of predation and can evade predators effectively. Dispersed animals should be those with either very high or very low density and with ineffective or costly evasive capabilities.

Taylor (1976) considered situations in which a predator's attack on a group results in only one kill, if the attack is even successful, because of effective group defense of flight after disturbance. If the predator is an ambush predator, prey in groups benefit. As long as a predator can eat only a few prey at a time, prey will always benefit from being in a group, unless a predator's capture success increases with prey aggregation. With very large numbers of prey, however, prey will benefit even in this last case. Taylor considered only ambush predators, and concluded that the evolution of a predator's body size is dependent on the distribution of prey. The model predicts that prey clumping will almost always benefit prey but will be detrimental to predators. Because aggregation of prey will involve a decrease in the frequency of encounters between predator and prey, selection will favor an optimal predator gut size when prey aggregate. Increased gut size should allow a predator to benefit when attacking prey in groups, but the costs attendant with developing the larger size will also increase. The advantage prey enjoy in aggregation is a monotonically decreasing function of the ratio of the maximum rate of killing by the predator to the maximum rate of digestion. In a later publication, Taylor (1977a) amended his original model by including the increase in apparancy that would be associated with larger aggregations. This model predicts that aggregation will be beneficial for small and large groups but not for intermediate ones. The vulnerable group sizes fall between the point where crypsis loses its effectiveness and the point where animals are clumped and so infrequent that encounters with predators decrease significantly. Only when prey clumps approach their maximum apparancy to the predator does aggregation confer an advantage on them.

Eschel (1978) explained gregarious behavior in terms of a nonzero sum game in which two participants can choose from a range of strategies, all of which will give each participant a certain cost or payoff. At least one strategy will benefit both parties. The participants in this case consist of the predator and the individual prey animals, each prey differing in its speed of escape. The end result of the game is predation on the slowest prey. Since the predator will preferentially pursue single prey, the best strategy for the prey is to aggregate and then move in complicated patterns. This action serves to outmaneuver and expose the slowest prey, rather than evade the predator.

Turner and Pitcher (1986) formulated a model that combines the effects of avoidance (in this case, increased predatory search time) with the effects of dilution. The assumptions are (1) that there is no confusion or counterattack strategy, and no increased information acquisition by prey, (2) that prey are located either singly or a single clump in each "location," and (3) that the predator hunts until a certain quota of prey has been captured. This model uses an Evolutionary Stable Strategy approach to examine the probability of an individual that is solitary or a "joiner" being captured. Two situations are examined: the prey's risk of detection during the predator's search phase, and the prey's risk of capture during the predator's attack phase. These probabilities are calculated for prey that rely on dilution only, avoidance only, and both dilution and avoidance. This model predicts that prey groups must combine both avoidance and dilution effects to obtain a selective advantage from aggregation behavior. This combination is termed "attack abatement," and the model explains aggregative behavior without requiring any behavioral mechanisms such as confusion or early detection.

DILUTION COMBINED WITH OTHER DEFENSES

Some authors have assumed that protection is obtained by groups strictly from aggregation, without alternate or auxiliary defenses. With the increasing complexity of these models, however, other defenses, such as evasion or early detection of predators, are incorporated to explain the benefits of aggregation to individual prey animals. Virtually none of the insects surveyed (table 11.1) relies on the dilution effect alone for protection. Most rely on chemical defenses (Blum 1981; Pasteels et al. 1983), early detection and evasion (Treherne and Foster 1980, 1982; Vulinec and Miller, in press), or both. Evasive tactics by prey normally go well beyond the centripetal milling envisioned by Hamilton (1971). Prey evasion from a predatory encounter most often results in a smooth transition from groups to dispersed animals and back to groups (Heinrich and Vogt 1980; Treherne and Foster 1982).

Unfortunately, experimental studies of the effects of aggregated prey on predatory success have not kept pace with the theoretical modeling. A number of studies have shown that predators experience greater success at finding prey when the prey are clumped rather than solitary (Burnett 1958; Madden and Pimentel 1965; Croze 1970; but see Taylor 1977b). Prey that are easily located are not necessarily those that are easily taken. One study examined the effects of aggregation by the digger wasp *Crabo cribrellifer* on nest parasitism by the fly *Metopia campestris*. It was found that whereas the number of parasitic flies increased proportionally to wasp nest density, the probability of nest parasitism decreased with increasing nest density. It was suggested that increased activity around high-density nest sites may discourage nest parasites (Wcislo 1984). Nevertheless, no experimental studies have demonstrated that the dilution effect alone is used effectively by prey aggregations, except in the case of swamping.

DILUTION: SWAMPING OF PREDATORS

In one specialized situation an individual in an aggregation may be statistically protected without resorting to other defenses. This situation occurs during enormous emergences or outbreaks of a prey species. Periodical insects may have evolved their periodicity as a mechanism to avoid predation (Lloyd and Dybas 1966b; Bulmer 1977; Lloyd 1984). The local predators eat so many prey that they become satiated, and the majority of the prey survive long enough to reproduce (White et al. 1979; Karban 1982). The best-known example of a periodical insect is the periodical cicada (*Magicicada* sp.). Three species of this insect emerge in extremely high densities synchronously every seventeen years (or thirteen years in the south), but in different years depending on the region (Alexander and Moore 1958, 1962; Lloyd and Dybas 1966a, b). These cicada emergences swamp local predators. For example, in a small suburban yard where 158,054 cicadas emerged, mortality was heaviest due to faulty eclosion and not predation (White et al. 1979). When the density of cast skins per square meter was compared to the front wings recovered per square meter (a measure of the number eaten by birds), the density of adults increased (as measured by the cast skins), whereas the number of front wings recovered remained constant (Karban 1982; figure 11.3). Whereas nonperiodical cicada populations appear to be regulated by their predators, the periodical cicada has evolved an escape from the density-dependent effects of predation (Lloyd and Dybas 1966a). Seventeen (or thirteen) years is so long that any numerical response by predators is no longer possible.

Another periodical insect is the May beetle of Europe (*Melolontha* sp.), which has a life cycle of three to five years. In this case, two species enter the adult stage synchronously (Blumer 1977). Escape from natural predators is cited as the reason for outbreaks of pest species such as the nonperiodical cicada *Morgannia minuta* (Ito and Nagamine 1981). Although not strictly periodical, individuals of the migratory locusts of Africa enter the migratory phase at one time. Depending on whether a nymph is exposed in early life to high or low densities of other nymphs, it will develop into the gregarious or solitary phase, respectively, each with its own coloration, morphology, and behavior. The migratory phase is brightly colored and migrates in huge numbers, effectively swamping predators (Loher 1960).

Periodicity may also have its costs. If some periodical cicadas emerge in an off year, the density may not be great enough to swamp

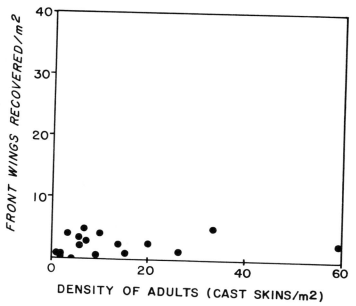

Figure 11.3   The relationship between the number of front wings recovered and the density of adult *Magicicada* species.

predators, and so none may live to reproduce (White and Lloyd 1979). If densities are too high in one place, cicadas may die from a delay in eclosion due to insufficient vertical perching places (White et al. 1979). Crowding is also thought to be detrimental to nymphs, which may explain why females are less apt to aggregate for oviposition during high densities (Simon et al. 1981).

The selective factors that led to both the long life cycle and the periodicity were most likely rare and isolated in time. Lloyd and Dybas (1966b) hypothesized a parasitoid with a life cycle of many years. This parasitoid exhibited a life cycle nearly in sychrony with the protoperiodical cicadas and exerted counterselection pressure favoring a longer life cycle in the cicadas. Eventually the life cycle of the cicadas outdistanced that of the parasitoid and its population became extinct. Once the population began to emerge synchronously, an individual that emerged in an off year will be less likely to reproduce, limiting the variability in life cycle length. According to Hoppensteadt and Keller (1976), periodicity will evolve if three conditions are met: (1) there is a very long developmental period, (2) predator populations are satiated, and (3) there is a limited number of feeding sites available underground that are filled by the earliest hatching nymphs. However, the unusual lack of an escape response in periodical cicadas may have also been the key to the evolution of periodicity. Because nonperiodical cicadas have efficient evasive defenses, they can maintain populations and reproduce even at low densities; it was not necessary for these insects to have high-density populations to swamp predators. Conversely, cicadas without effective defenses against predation need high densities to survive by swamping predators; therefore the evolution of periodicity was facilitated in these insects (Hoppensteadt and Keller 1976; Pasteels et al. 1983; Lloyd, 1984).

ENHANCED ADVERTISEMENT OF UNPALATABILITY

The hypothesis that aggregations of distasteful insects would enhance their aposematic coloration by "advertisement" has been proposed repeatedly (Eisner and Kafatos 1962; Benfield 1972; Wilson 1975, p. 43; Young 1978). An early observer (Carpenter 1921) suggested that one insect is not very conspicuous by itself; therefore more are needed to achieve an aposematic effect. It has been more recently asserted that gregariousness in aposematic insects increases the effectiveness of warning signals (Pasteels et al. 1983). That predators might learn to avoid an aposematic group more readily than a solitary aposematic individual has never been demonstrated. In some cases it has not even been shown that certain aggregated, aposematically colored species are distasteful to predators (Moynihan 1981). Moreover, many aposematic insects remain nonaggregating, for example, velvet ants (Manley and Taber 1978; Schmidt and Buchmann 1986) and certain swallowtail butterflies (Waldbauer and Sternburg 1975).

An alternative hypothesis for aggregation by distasteful species could be a pooling of defensive compounds, which does not need to depend on an explanation of enhanced advertisement. Insects that are able to exude or project chemicals would certainly benefit from an increase in sources. Bombardier beetles and other carabids (Greenslade 1963), thrips (Howard et al. 1983), coreid bugs (Aldrich and Blum 1978), and stinkbugs (Lockwood and Story 1986), are able to excrete chemical defenses to the outside. In these groups, an increase in secretions would be advantageous, and this increase can be achieved by aggregation.

In insects that have nonsecretory defensive compounds, the purpose of aggregation is less clear. Either advertisement by large numbers is more effective, or statistically an animal is better protected in a group: the selfish herd hypothesis. As detailed earlier, protection may be achieved because patchy dispersal will force a predator to search longer, and when the aggregation is found, sampling of one should be sufficient to convince a predator to avoid the others. Aggregations may become tightly clumped as group members attempt to be in a central position in the group, because peripheral individuals will be the first ones tasted by inexperienced predators.

If advertisement operates in nature, it should be amenable to experimental testing. Sessile organisms might constitute a good experimental subject, since no behavioral escape tactics would be present. Insect eggs are often distasteful and aposematic, and many of these eggs are clustered (Stamp 1980). The clustering of toxic eggs might produce an immediate advantage for prey by reducing the number of eggs taken by predators (Orians and Janzen 1974). Stamp (1980) suggests that a later advantage might then be obtained by the death of any parasitoid larvae in the developing egg. It remains to be demonstrated, however, whether a larger stimulus (more eggs) becomes established as a signal of toxicity to predators more quickly than a single aposematic egg. It is possible that the toxicity of clustered eggs may be a mechanism aimed at defeating parasitoids, rather than predators, since many parasitoids focus their oviposition activities on local aggregations (Burnett 1958; Hassel 1971; Taylor 1974). This hypothesis does not explain all egg clustering, since many species that cluster eggs also have gregarious larvae (Stamp 1980). Egg-clustering and larval gregariousness are more likely to evolve in species with unpalatable larvae (Sillén-Tullberg 1988). Additional factors that may influence egg clustering include foraging efficiency (Lyons 1962; Damman 1987), patchiness of the host plant, decrease in the desiccation of eggs (Stamp 1980), or fecundity constraints (Courtney 1984).

A number of butterfly species roost gregariously as adults (Benson and Emmel 1973; Muyshondt 1973; Muyshondt and Muhshondt 1974; Turner 1975; Young 1978), and could be considered sessile during this time. Most of these are unpalatable and aposematic (Turner 1975) (see table 11.1), and include (1) night-roosting aggregations, with repeated homing to the same roost; (2) nighttime aggregations of temperate grassland butterflies, which may result from high population densities, and (3) long-term aggregations during diapause, as in the monarch (Turner 1975). Turner (1975) suggested that communal night roosts will be found in tropical butterflies which are unpalatable, long-lived, have restricted home ranges, and reproduce slowly, and protection is conferred because a predator may sample one and leave the rest alone.

Two studies have attempted to examine predatory success on distasteful, aggregated, and nonsessile insects. In one, it was found that the effectiveness of chemical defenses varied with the species of predator. Adult ladybird beetles would not prey on any first-instar nymphs of the stinkbug *Nezara viridula*, but spined soldier bugs would. Predatory success by the soldier bug and certain ant species, however, decreased when the nymphs were aggregated (Lockwood and Story 1986). Another study showed that the distasteful Heteroptera *Velia caprai* suffered decreasing predation rates when presented to captive brown trout in increasing group sizes. This result was attributed to a predator's avoidance response being reinforced by a greater encounter rate with the prey (Brönmark et al. 1984). However, although the confusion effect and increased vigilance were rejected as explanations of this phenomenon, no data were presented to eliminate either of these mechanisms of group defense in *V. caprai*.

THE EVOLUTION OF GREGARIOUSNESS

Kin selection (Hamilton 1964) and intrademic group selection (Wade 1978; Wilson 1983) could have an influence on the selection of gregarious traits. Many of the lepidopteran larval aggregations are sibling groups. These insects are often distasteful and aposematic, and it is assumed that kin selection reinforces their gregariousness (Turner 1975). However, Sillén-Tullberg (1988) showed that, in butterflies, aposematism has never evolved after gregariousness. Because gregarious larvae are invariably related, this finding showed that individual selection is more important than kin selection in the evolution of warning coloration, and unpalatability (but not necessarily aposematism) may be a prerequisite for the evolution of gregarious behavior in Lepidoptera (Sillén-Tullberg 1988). In addition, aggregations in some insects may be composed of more than one species, as in whirligig beetles, which even form multigeneric aggregations (Hatch 1925; Istock 1966, 1967). Treisman's (1975b) model of the evolution of gregariousness predicts that the benefits from aggregation gained by group members will be independent of their genetic relationship. The advantages to individual group members need clarification particularly in the case of three categories of insect aggregations: (1) hidden aggregations, (2) conspicuous aposematic aggregations, and (3) conspicuous nonaposematic aggregations (see table 11.1).

Hidden aggregations, both aposematic and nonaposematic, are those that remain concealed during the time the insects are aggregated. This group includes the various carabid genera (Greenslade 1963; Larochelle 1974; LeSage 1976; Kavanaugh 1977; Graves and Graves 1978;

Garneau and Liard 1979), the ladybird beetles (Ewert and Chiang 1966; Lee 1980), and thrips (Bullington 1978). Butterfly larvae are occasionally found in hidden aggregations, for example, a larvae of *Anthanassa frisa frisa* (Chermock and Chermock 1947). All of these aggregations may be responding to environmental conditions (Kavanaugh 1977). Group formation may also be obligate, large numbers of individuals being necessary to temper an environmental stress (Copp 1983; Walgenbach et al. 1983). These concealed groups may be overwintering or estivating aggregations, and the individuals in them may exhibit slowed metabolic rates, as in ladybird beetles (Kavanaugh 1977). One common denominator appears to be the presence of defensive chemicals in these insects (Greenslade 1963; Copp 1983; Howard et al. 1983), or in the case of some butterfly larvae, spines and bristles (Chermock and Chermock 1947). Cockroaches, which tend to aggregate in inaccessible places, may be repellent to some predators (Roth and Willis 1960). It would be most efficient in terms of predator avoidance for the defensive compounds in these species to be apparent prior to an attack (Pasteels et al. 1983).

Aposematic and gregarious insects that make no effort to be concealed probably rely entirely on their chemical defenses for protection. Groups of gregarious butterflies that occur in plain sight, such as heliconiini, are good examples (Turner 1975; Young 1978). Generally, the bright colors are signals of distastefulness, and the clustering habit may advertise this distastefulness or may result in predators taking fewer samples (however, periodical cicadas, although brightly colored, are not distasteful to any predators). Chemical defense should be positively correlated with the probability of detection by a predator and negatively correlated with the existence of alternate defense mechanisms (Pasteels et al. 1983). This statement implies that chemical defenses may be energetically expensive, and in fact they are secondarily lost in some species, such as flea beetles (Pasteels et al. 1983). A number of palatable mimics, including other beetles and moths, are found in the aggregations of aposematic lycid beetles, which may be an indication of the protective nature of these aggregations. However, many of these mimics are also protected during the dispersed phase of the lycids (Linsley et al. 1961).

Life history characteristics are also hypothesized to be key factors in the evolution of these conspicuous aggregations. Communal roosting of butterflies should be found only in those species with a limited, learned home range; therefore, only long-lived and sedentary species should develop this characteristic. Slow, sustained reproduction because of limited resources could result in longevity, and low dispersal could lead to evolution of aposematism and unpalatability through kin selection (Turner 1975; but see Sillén-Tullberg 1988).

Nonaposematic insects that aggregate in conspicuous groups present a dilemma. Some of these may be distasteful, such as whirligig beetles (Benfield 1972) or *Velia caprai* (Brödnmark et al. 1984), but others are apparently not, such as ocean skaters (Foster and Treherne 1980) and grey pine aphids (Kidd 1982). It is apparent in these species that efficient escape behavior and early warning of predators remain the primary lines of defense. These insects exist in exposed habitats. Gregarious behavior may have evolved to facilitate early warning of predator approach.

Conclusion

Animal aggregations that persist longer than mating or foraging activities require probably provide group members with protection from predators. The mechanisms by which protection is obtained can be active or passive. Active mechanisms include counterattack, early detection of predators, and confusion of predators by erratic escape movements. Of these, the last two are most often employed, especially by nonsocial insects. Early detection and warning of predators, although the subject of theoretical work, has only recently been documented in insects. This behavior may be found to have more importance than previously thought, not only in insects that live in exposed habitats, but also in those that aggregate in more cryptic habitats.

Aggregating animals may also be protected passively, merely by being near another possible target for a predator. Much theoretical work has been generated from this hypothesis. As models are expanded to more closely reflect reality, additional defenses, such as evasion, early detection, or unpalatability, must be incorporated to ensure an aggregating animal's survival. Those organisms that are sessile and aggregated (such as insect eggs) must be protected chemically. The "selfish herd" seems to be an effective defense only when used by arthropods with enormous populations that emerge suddenly (such as periodical cicadas). Aggregation by prey may also increase the area a predator has to search to find prey, although this effect may be countered by predators using habitat cues (Taylor 1977a).

Noxious prey that are aposematic are often assumed to aggregate to advertise their unpalatability. A more parsimonious explanation is that protection is conferred because a predator will most likely not sample more than one of a group. This defense would be especially efficient in animals that concentrate their toxic chemicals in a less vulnerable but more prominent part of the body, such as the wings (Brower and Glazier 1975; see Bowers, this volume).

Aggregation works as a defense because it allows individual animals to gain protection from predators. It has evolved independently in many diverse taxa of insects, possibly as a result of habitat characteristics. Exposed habitats necessitate a greater vigilance. In addition, it seems that aggregation in insects is a secondary response to the presence of other defenses, often morphological (as spines or bristles) or chemical (Sillén-Tullberg 1988). When an insect combines aggregation with its defenses, it is able to exploit habitats not available to it before, such as the exposed surfaces of water or leaves. It is also possible that aggregation in exposed habitats evolved when chemical defenses were lacking or not effective. In these cases, aggregation allows early warning of predators and the asset of predator confusion during flight. Finally, aggregation as a dilution mechanism may evolve specifically because other defenses are lacking (Lloyd 1984).

I would like to thank Anne B. Clark, Thomas C. Kane, and Monte Lloyd for their comments on various versions of this manuscript. I also thank Jennifer Bolden-White, Marie Foglesong, Arthur Gray, JoAnn Norris, Amy Peterson, and Claude Richmond for their help. This project was supported by the Cincinnati Museum of natural History.

References

Alcock, J. 1969. Observational learning in three species of birds *Ibis* 3:303–321.

_____. **1987.** Leks and hilltopping in insects. *J. Nat. History* 21:319–328.

Aldrich, J.R. and M.S. Blum. 1978. Aposematic aggregation of a bug and formation of aggregation. Biotropica 10:58–61.

Alexander, R.D., and T.E. Moore. 1958. Studies on the acoustical behaviour of seventeen-year cicadas. *Ohio J. Sci.* 58:107–127.

_____. **1962.** The evolutionary relationships of 17-year and 13-year cicadas, and three new species (Homoptera, Cicadidae, *Magicicada*). *J. Misc. Pubs. Mus. Zool. Univ. Michigan* 121:1–59.

Allee, W.C. 1931. *Animal Aggregations: A Study in General Sociology.* The University of Chicago Press, Chicago.

Altmann, S.A. 1956. Avian mobbing behaviour and predator recognition. *Condor* 58:241–253.

Alverdes, F. 1927. *Social Life in the Animal World.* Harcourt, Brace and Co., New York.

Arnold, S.J. 1978. The evolution of a special class of modifiable behaviours in relation to environmental pattern. *Am. Nat.* 112:415–427.

Banks, C.J. 1957. The behaviour of individual coccinellid larvae on plants. *Brit. J. Anim. Behav.* 5:12–24.

Benfield, E.F. 1972. A defensive secretion of *Dineutes discolor* (Coleoptera: Gyrinidae). *Ann. Entomol. Soc. Am.* 65:1324–1327.

Benson, W.W., and T.C. Emmel. 1973. Demography of gregariously roosting populations of the nymphaline butterfly *Marpesia berania* in Costa Rica. *Ecology* 54:326–335.

Bertram B.C.R. 1980. Vigilance and group size in ostriches. *Anim. Behav.* 28:278–286.

Blancher P.J., and R.J. Robertson. 1982. Kingbird aggression: does it deter predators: *Anim. Behav.* 30:929–930.

Blum, M.S. 1981. *Chemical Defenses of Arthropods.* Academic Press, New York.

Blum, M.S., J.B. Wallace, R.M. Duffield, J.M. Brand, H.M. Fales, and E.A. Sokoloski. 1978. Chrysomelidial in the defensive secretion of the leaf beetle *Gastrophysa cyanea* Melsheimer. *J. Chem. Ecol.* 4: 47–53.

Brock, V.E., and R.H. Fiffenburgh. 1960. Fish schooling: a possible factor in reducing predation. *Jour. du Conseil, Conseil Permanent International pour l'Exploration de la mer* 25:307–317.

Brömark, C., B. Malmqvist, and C. Otto. 1984. Antipredator adaptations in a neustonic insect (*Velia caprai*). *Oecologia* 61:189–191.

Brower, L.P. 1969. Ecological chemistry. *Sci. Am.* 220 (No. 2):22–27.

Brower, L.P., and S.C. Glazier. 1975. Localizations of heart poisons in the Monarch butterfly. *Science* 188:19–25.

Brues, C.T. 1926. Remarkable abundance of a cistelid beetle with observations on other aggregations of insects. *Am. Nat.* 60:526–551.

Buchler, E.R., T.B. Wright, and E.D. Brown. 1981. On the functions of stridulation by the passalid beetle *Odontotaenius disjunctus* (Coleoptera: Passalidae). *Anim. Behav.* 29:483–486.

Bullington, S.W. 1978. A possible over-wintering aggregation of *Hoplothrips karnyi* (Hood) (Thysanoptera: Phlaeothripidae) on *Lenzites betulina* (Fr.) Fr. (Aphyllophorales: Polyporaceae). *Entomol. News* 89:174.

Bulmer, M.G. 1977. Periodical insects. *Am. Nat.* 3:1099–1117.

Burnett, T. 1958. Effect of host distribution on the reproduction of *Encarsia formosa* Gahan (Hymenoptera: Chalcidoidea). *Can. Entomol.* 60:179–191.

Calam, D.H., and A. Youdeowei. 1968. Identification and functions of secretion from the posterior scent gland of fifth instar larva of the bug *Dysdercus intermedius*. *J. Insect Physiol.* 14:1147–1158.

Carne, P.B. 1966. Primitive forms of social behaviour, and their significance in the ecology of gregarious insects. *Proc. Ecol. Soc. of Australia* 1:75–78

Carpenter, G.D.H. 1921. Experiments on the relative edibility of insects, with special reference to their coloration. *Trans. Entomol. Soc. Lond.* 1921:1–105.

Chermock, R.L., and O.D. Chermock. 1947. Notes on the life histories of three Floridian butterflies. *Can. Entomol.* 79:142–144.

Common, I.F.B. 1952. Migration and gregarious aestivation in the bogong moth *Agrotis infusa*. *Nature, Lond.* 170:981–982.

Copp, N.H. 1983. Temperature-dependent behaviours and cluster formation by aggregating ladybird beetles. *Anim. Behav.* 31:424–430.

Cornell, J.C., N.E. Stamp, and M.D. Bowers. 1987. Developmental change in aggregation, defense and escape behavior of buckmoth caterpillars, *Hemileuca lucina* (Saturniidae). *Behav. Ecol. Sociobiol.* 20:383–388.

Courtney, S.P. 1984. The evolution of egg clustering by butterflies and other insects. *Am. Nat.* 123:276–281.

Craighead, F.C. 1949. *Insect Enemies of Eastern Forests.* U.S. Dept. Agric. Misc. Publ. No. 657. U.S. Govt. Printing Office, Washington, D.C.

Croze, H. 1970. Searching image in carrion crows. *Z. Tierpsychol. Beih.* 5:1–85.

Damman, H. 1987. Leaf quality and enemy avoidance by the larvae of a pyralid moth. *Ecology* 68:88–97.

Dawkins, M. 1971a. Perceptual changes in chicks: another look at the "search image" concept. *Anim. Behav.* 19:566–574.

_____. **1971b.** Shifts of "attention" in chicks during feeding. *Anim. Behav.* 19:575–582.

Deegener, P. 1918. Die Formender Vergesellschaftung im Tierreiche. *Ein Systematisch-soziologischer Versuch.* Veit, Leipzig.

Delaney, M.J. 1959. Group formation in the Thysanura. *Anim. Behav.* 7:70–75.

Deshefy, G.S. 1980. Anti-predator behaviour in swarms of *Rhagovelia obesa* (Hemiptera: Veliidae). *Pan -Pac. Entomol.* 56:111–112.

Dethier, V.G. 1959. Egg-laying habits of Lepidoptera in relation to available food. *Can. Entomol.* 41:554–561.

Dixon, A.F.G., and W.A. Stewart. 1975. Function of the siphunculi in aphids with particular reference to the sycamore aphid *Drepansosiphum platanoides. J. Zool. Lond.* 175:279–289.

Edwards, W.H. 1877. History of *Phyciodes tharos,* a polymorphic butterfly. *Can. Entomol.* 9:1–10.

Eisner, T., and F.C. Kafatos. 1962. Defense mechanisms of arthropods. X. A pheromone promoting aggregation in an aposematic distasteful insect. *Psyche* 69:53–61.

Elgar, M.A., and C.P. Catterall. 1981. Flocking and predator surveillance in house sparrows: test of an hypothesis. *Anim. Behav.* 29:869–872.

Emmel, T.C., and J.F. Emmel. 1962. Ecological studies of Rhopalocera in a high Sierran community—Donner Pass, California. I. Butterfly associations and distributional factors. *J. Lep. Soc.* 16:23–44.

Eschel, I. 1978. On a pre-predator nonzero-sum game and the evolution of gregarious behaviour of evasive prey. *Am. Nat.* 112:787–795.

Estes, R.D. 1966. Behaviour and life history of the wildebeest (*Connochaetes taurinus* Burchell). *Nature* 212:999–1000.

Ewert, M.A., and H.C. Chiang. 1966. Effects of some environmental factors on the distribution of three species of coccinellidae in their micro habitat. In *Ecology of Aphidophagous Insects* (ed. I. Modek). Academia, Prague.

Foster, W.A., and J.E. Treherne. 1980. Feeding, predation, and aggregation behaviour in a marine insect, *Halobates robustus* Barber (Hemiptera: Gerridae), in the Galapagos Islands. *Proc. R. Soc. Lond.* 209:539–553.

_____. **1982.** Reproductive behavior of the oceanskater *Halobates robustus* (Hemiptera: Gerridae) in the Galapogos Islands. *Oecologia* 55:202–207.

Friedlander, C.P. 1965. Aggregation in *Oniscus asellus. Anim. Behav.* 13:342–346.

Garneau, R., and F. Liard. 1979. Coleopteres carabidae en hibernation dans une bille de bios. *Cordulia* 5:10.

Ghent, A.W. 1960. A study of the group-feeding behaviour of larvae of the jack pine swafly, *Neodiprion pratti banksianae* Roh. *Behaviour* 16:110–148.

Gillett, S.D., P.J. Hogarth, and F.E.H. Noble. 1979. The response of predators to varying densities of gregaria locust nymphs. *Anim. Behav.* 27:592–596.

Gotceitas, V. 1985. Formation of aggregations by overwintering fifth instar *Dicosmoecus atripes* larvae (Trichoptera). *Oikos* 44:313–318.

Graves, R.C., and A.C.F. Graves. 1978. An aggregation of *Scaphinotus elevatus* in Mississippi. *Cordulia* 4:13.

Green, R.F., and A.T. Nunez. 1986. Central-place foraging in a patchy environment. *J. Theor. Biol.* 123:35–43.

Greenslade, P.J. 1963. Further notes on aggregation in Carabidae (Coleoptera) with especial reference to *Nebria brevicollis* (F). *Entomol. Monthly Magazine* 99:109–114.

Griffiths, D. 1980. The feeding biology of ant-lion larvae: prey capture, handling, and utilization. *J. Anim. Ecol.* 49:99–125.

Hamilton, W.D. 1964. The genetical theory of social behaviour. I, II. *J. Theor. Biol.* 7:1–52.

————. **1971.** Geometry for the selfish herd. *J. Theor. Biol.* 31:295–311.

Hartman, M.J., J.A. Surfleet, and C.D. Hynes. 1978. Aggregation pheromone in the larvae of *Tipula simplex* Doane: mode of action and site of production. *Pan-Pac. Entomol.* 54:305–310.

Hassell, M.P. 1971. Mutual interference between searching insect parasites. *J. Anim. Ecol.* 35:473–486.

Hatch, M.H. 1925. An outline of the ecology of Gyrinidae. *Bull. Brook. Entomol. Soc.* 20:101–114.

Heinrich, B. 1979a. *Bumblebee economics.* Harvard University Press, Cambridge, Massachusetts.

————. **1979b.** Foraging strategies of caterpillars: leaf damage and possible predator avoidance strategies. *Oecologia* 42:325–337.

Heinrich, B., and F.D. Vogt 1980. Aggregation and foraging behaviour of whirligig beetles (Gyrinidae). *Behav. Ecol. Sociobiol.* 7:179–186.

Heller, R., and M. Milinski. 1979. Optimal foraging of sticklebacks on swarming prey. *Anim. Behav.* 27:1127–1141.

Henry, C.S. 1972. Eggs and repagula of *Ululodes* and *Ascaloptynx* (Neuroptera: Ascalaphidae): a comparative study. *Psyche* 79:1-22.

Holling, C.S. 1965. The functional response of predators to prey density and its role in mimicry and population regulation. *Mem. Entomol. Soc. Can.* 45:1-60.

_____. **1966.** The functional response of invertebrate predators to prey density. *Mem. Entomol. Soc. Can.* 48:1-86.

Hoppensteadt, F.C., and J.B. Keller. 1976. Synchronization of periodical cicada emergences. *Science* 194:335-337.

Howard, D.F., M.S. Blum, and H.M. Fales. 1983. Defense in thrips: forbidding fruitiness of a lactone. *Science* 220:335-337.

Humphries, D.A., and P.M. Driver. 1967. Erratic display as a device against predators. *Science* 156:1767-1768.

_____. **1970.** Protean defence by prey animals. *Oecologia* 5:285-302.

Ibbotson, A., and J.S. Kennedy. 1951. Aggregation in *Aphis fabae* (Scop.) 1. Aggregation on plants. *Ann. Appl. Biol.* 38:65-78.

Istock, C.A. 1966. Distribution, coexistence, and competition of whirligig beetles. *Evolution* 20:211-234.

_____. **1967.** Transient competitive displacement in natural populations of whirligig beetles. *Ecology* 48:929-937.

Ito, Y.I. and M. Nagamine. 1981. Why a cicada, *Mogannia munuta,* became a pest of sugarcane: an hypothesis based on the theory of 'escape.' *Ecol. Entomol.* 6:273-283.

Johnson, K.M., B.G. Arke, and P.H. Crowley. 1975. Modeling arthropod predation: wasteful killing by damselfly naiads. *Ecology* 56:10181-1093.

Jones, F.M. 1931. The gregarious sleeping habit of *Heliconius charithonea.* L. *Proc. Entomol. Soc. Lond.* 6:4-10.

Karban, R. 1982. Increased reproductive success at high densities and predator satiation for periodical cicadas. *Ecology* 63:321-328.

Kavanaugh, D.H. 1977. An example of aggregation in the *Scaphinotus* subgenus *Brennus* Motschulsky (Coleoptera: Carabidae: Cychrini). *Pan-Pac. Entomol.* 53:27-31.

Keiper, R.R. 1969. Behavioural adaptation of cryptic moths. IV. Preliminary studies on species resembling dead leaves. *J. Lepidop. Soc.* 23:205-210.

Kidd, N.A.C. 1982. Predator avoidance as a result of aggregation in the grey pine aphid, *Schizolachnus pineti. J. Anim. Ecol.* 51:397-412.

Kidd, N.A.C., and A.D. Mayer. 1983. The effect of escape responses on the stability of insect host-parasite models. *J. Theor. Biol.* 140:275-287.

Klingauf. F., and C. Sengonca. 1970. Koloniebildung von Roehrenblattaeusen (Aphididae) unter feindeinwirkung. (Effect of enemies on colony formation of aphids.) *Entomophaga* 15:359-377.

Klots, A.B. 1951. *A Field Guide to the Butterflies of North America, East of the Great Plains.* Houghton Mifflin Company, Boston.

Kruuk, H. 1972. *The Spotted Hyena: A Study of Predation and Social Behaviour.* Univ. of Chicago Press, Chicago.

Larochelle, A. 1974. Winter habits of carabid beetles (Coleoptera: Carabidae). *Great Lakes Entomol.* 7:143-145.

Lee, R.E., Jr. 1980. Physiological adaptations of Coccinellidae to supranivean and subnivean hibernacula. *J. Insect Physiol.* 26:135-315.

LeSage, L. 1976. Notes sur l'hibernation de quelques carabidae (Coleopteres) du sud-est du Quebec. *Cordulia* 2:123-125.

Lin. N. 1964. Increased parasitic pressure as a major factor in the evolution of social behaviour in halictine bees. *Insectes Sociaux* 11:187-192.

Linsley, E.G., T. Eisner, and A.B. Kloffs. 1961. Mimetic assemblages of sibling species of lycid beetles. *Evolution* 15:15-29.

Lloyd, M. 1984. Periodical cicadas. *Antenna* 8:78-91.

Lloyd, M., and H.S. Dybas. 1966a. The periodical cicada problem I. Population ecology. *Evolution* 20(2):133-149.

————. **1966b.** The periodical cicada problem. II. Evolution. *Evolution* 20:466-505.

Lockwood, J.A., and R.N. Story. 1986. Adaptive functions of nymphal aggregation in the southern green stink bug, *Nezara viridula* (L.) (Hemiptera: Pentatomidae). *Environ. Entomol.* 15:739-749.

Loher, W. 1960. The chemical acceleration of the maturation process and its hormonal control in the male of the desert locust. *Proc. R. Entomol. Soc. Lond.* Ser. B, 153:380-397.

Lyons, L.A. 1962. The effect of aggregation on egg and larval survival in *Neodiprion swainei* Middl. (Hymenoptera: Diprionidae). *Can. Entomol.* 94:49-58.

Madden, J.L., and D. Pimentel. 1965. Density and spatial relationships between a wasp parasite and housefly host. *Can. Entomol.* 97:1031-1037.

Manley, D.G., and S. Taber III. 1978. A mating aggregation of *Dasymutilla foxi* in southern Arizona. *Pan-Pac. Entomol.* 54:231-235.

Mertens, J., and R. Bourgoignie. 1977. Aggregation pheromone in *Hypogastrura viatica* (Collembola). *Behav. Ecol. Sociobiol.* 2:41-48.

Michener, C.D. 1958. The evolution of social behaviour in bees. *Proc. Tenth Int. Congr. Entomol., Montreal 1956* 2:441-447.

Michener, C.D., and W.B. Kerfoot. 1967. Nests and social behaviour of three species of *Pseudaugochloropis* (Hymenoptera: Halictidae). *J. Kans. entomol. Soc.* 40:214-232.

Milinski, M. 1977a. Do all members of a swarm suffer the same predation? *Z. Tierpsychol.* 45:373-388.

_____. **1977b.** Experiments on the selection by predators against spatial oddity of their prey. *Z. Tierpsychol.* 43:311-325.

Montgomery, M.E., and L.R. Nault. 1977. Comparative response of aphids to the alarm pheromone (E)-β-farnesene. *Entomol. Exp. Appl.* 22:236-242.

Morris, R.F. 1963. The effect of predator age and prey defense on the functional response of *Podisus maculiventris* Say to the density of *Hyphantria cunea* Drury. *Can. Entomol.* 95:1009-1020.

_____. **1976.** Relation of parasite attack to the colonial habit of *Hyphantria cunea*. *Can. Entomol.* 108:833-836.

Moynihan, M. 1981. The coincidence of mimicries and other misleading coincidences. *Am. Nat.* 117:372-378.

Muyshondt, A. 1973. Preliminary report on communal resting of *Smyrna karwinskii* adults (Nymphalidae). *J. Lepidop. Soc.* 27:15-16.

Muyshondt, A., and A. Muyshondt, Jr. 1974. Gregarious seasonal roosting of *Smyrna karwinski* adults in El Salvador (Nymphalidae). *J. Lepidop. Soc.* 28:224-229.

Nagel, M.G., and W.H. Cade. 1983. On the role of pheromones in aggregation formation in camel crickets, *Ceuthophilus secretus* (Orthoptera: Gryllacrididae). *Can. J. Zool.* 61:95-98.

Nault, L.R., and P.L. Phelan. 1984. Alarm pheromones and sociality in pre-social insects. In *Chemical Ecology of Insects* (eds. W.J. Bell and R.T. Carde). Sinauer Assoc.,Sunderland, Massachusetts.

Neill, S.R., St. J. Neill and J.M. Cullen. 1974. Experiments on whether schooling by their prey affects the hunting behaviour of cephalopods and fish predators. *J. Zool. Lond.* 172:549-569.

Orians, G., and D. Janzen. 1974. Why are embryos so tasty? *Am. Nat.* 108:581-590.

Partridge, B.L. 1980. The effect of school size on the structure and dynamics of minnow schools. *Anim. Behav.* 28:68-77.

Pasteels, J.M., J.C. Gregoire, and M. Rowell-Rahier. 1983. The chemical ecology of defense in arthropods. *Ann. Rev. Entomol.* 28:263-289.

Price, P.W. 1975 *Insect Ecology.* John Wiley and Sons, New York.

Prop, N. 1960. Protection against birds and parasites in some species of tenthredinid larvae. *Arch. Neerl. Zool.* 13:380-447.

Pulliam, R.H. 1973. On the advantages of flocking. *J. Theor. Biol.* 38:419–422.

Pulliam, R.H., and T. Caraco. 1984. Living in groups: Is there an optimal group size? Pp 122–147. In *Behavioral Ecology: An Evolutionary Approach,* 2nd Edition (eds., J.R. Krebs and N.B. Davies. Blackwell Scientific Publications, Great Britian.

Rand, A.L. 1953. Factors affecting feeding rates of *Anis. Auk* 70:26–30.

Rau, P., and N. Rau. 1916. The sleep of insects: an ecological study. *Ann. Entomol. Soc. Am.* 9:227–274.

Robinson, M.H. 1969. Defenses against visually hunting predators. *Evol. Biol.* 3:225–259.

Roth, L.M., and E.R. Willis. 1960. The biotic association of cockroaches. *Smithsonian Misc. Collections* 141:1–1470.

Rowlands, M.L.J., and J.W. Chapin. 1978. Prey searching behaviour in adults of *Hippodamia convergens* (Coleoptera: Coccinellidae). *J. Georgia Entomol. Soc.* 13:309–315.

Schmidt, J.O., and S.L. Buchmann. 1986. Are multillids scarce? (Hymenoptera: Mutillidae). *Pan-Pac. Entomol.* 62:103–104.

Schoener, T.W. 1969. Models of optimal size for solitary predators. *Am. Nat.* 103:277–313.

Schowalter, T.D. 1986. Overwintering aggregation of *Boisea rubrolineatus* (Heteroptera: Rhopalidae) in western Oregon. *Environ. Entomol.* 15:1055–1056.

Scott, J.A. 1974. Adult behaviour and po;ulation biology of *Poladryas minuta,* and the relationship of the Texan and Colorado populations (Lepidoptera: Nymphalidae). *Pan-Pac. Entomol.* 50:9–22.

Seeley, T.D., R.H. Seeley, and P. Akratanakul. 1982. Colony defense strategies of the honeybees in Thailand. *Ecol. Monog.* 52:43–63.

Sih, A. 1979. Stability and prey behavioural responses to predator density. *J. Anim. Ecol.* 48:79–89.

Sillén-Tullberg, B. 1988. Evolution of gregariousness in aposematic butterfly larvae: a phylogenetic analysis. *Evolution.* 42:293–305.

Simon, C., R. Karban, and M. Lloyd. 1981. Patchiness, density, and aggregative behavior in sympatric allochronic populations of 17-year cicadas. *Ecology.* 62:1525–1535.

Stamp, N.E. 1980. Egg deposition patterns in butterflies: why do some species cluster their eggs rather than deposit them singly? *Am. Nat.* 115:367–380.

—————. **1981.** Effect of group size on parasitism in a natural population of the Baltimore checkerspot *Euphydrya phaeton. Oecologia* 49:201–206.

Stamp, N.E., and M.D. Bowers. 1988. Direct and indirect effects of predatory wasps (*Polistes* sp.: Vespidae) on gregarious caterpillars (*Hemileuca lucina:* Saturniidae). *Oecologia* 75:619–624.

Taylor, R.J. 1974. Role of learning in insect parasitism. *Ecol. Monogr.* 44:89–104.

_____. 1976. Value of clumping to prey and the evolutionary response of ambush predators. *Am. Nat.* 110:13–29.

_____. 1977a. The value of clumping to prey. *Oecologia* 30:285–294.

_____. 1977b. The value of clumping to prey when detectability increases with group size. *Am. Nat.* 111:229–301.

Thiele, H.U. 1977. *Carabid Beetles in Their Environments.* Springer-Verlag, Berlin, Heidelberg, New York.

Thompson, D.B.A., and C.J. Barnard, 1983. Anti-predator responses in mixed-species associations of lapwings, golden plovers, and black-headed gulls. *Anim. Behav.* 31:585–593.

Tinbergen, L. 1960. The natural control of insects in pinewoods. I. Factors influencing the intensity of predation by songbirds. *Arch. Neerl. Zool.* 13:265–343.

Tostowaryk, W. 1972. The effect of prey defense on the functional response of *Podisus modestus* (Hemiptera: Pentatomidae) to densities of the sawflies *Neodiprion swainei* and *N. pratti banksianae* (Hymenoptera: Neodiprionidae). *Can. Entomol.* 104:61–69.

Treherne, J.E., and W.A. Foster. 1980. The effects of group size on predator avoidance in a marine insect. *Anim. Behav.* 28:1119–1122.

_____. 1981. Group transmission of predator avoidance in a marine insect: the Trafalgar effect. *Anim. Behav.* 29:911–917.

_____. 1982. Group size and anti-predator strategies in a marine insect. *Anim. Behav.* 30:536–542.

Treisman, M. 1975a. Predation and the evolution of gregariousness. I. Models for concealment and evasion. *Anim. Behav.* 23:779–800.

_____. 1975b. Predation and the evolution of gregariousness. II. An economic model for predator-prey interaction. *Anim. Behav.* 23:801–825.

Tsubaki, Y., and Y. Shiotsu. 1982. Group feeding as a strategy for exploiting food resources in the Burnet moth *Pryeria sinica. Oecologia* 55:12–20.

Turchin, P. 1987. The role of aggregation in the response of Mexican bean beetles to host-plant density. *Oecologia* 71:577–582.

Turner, J.R.G. 1975. Communal roosting in relation to warning colour in two heliconiine butterflies (Nymphalidae). *J. Lepidop. Soc.* 29:221–226.

Turner, G.F., and T.J. Pitcher. 1986. Attack abatement: a model for group protection by combined avoidance and dilution. *Am. Nat.* 128:228–240.

Vermeij, G.J. 1982. Unsuccessful predation and evolution. *Am. Nat.* 120:701–720.

Vine, I. 1971. Risk of visual detection and pursuit by a predator and the selective advantage of flocking behaviour. *J. Theor. Biol.* 30:405–422.

————. 1973. Detection of prey flocks by predators. *J. Theor. Biol.* 40:207–210

Vulinec, K. 1987. Swimming in whirligig beetles (Coleoptera: Gyrinidae): a possible role of the pygidial gland secretion. *Coleopterists Bull.* 41:151–153.

Vulinec, K., and S.A. Kolmes. 1987. Temperature, contact rates, and interindividual distance in whirligig bettles (Gyrinidae). *J.N.Y. Entomol. Soc.* 95:481–486.

Vulinec, K., and M.C. Miller. In press. Aggregation and predator avoidance with whirligig beetles (Coleoptera: Gyrinidae). *J.N.Y. Entomol. Soc.*

Wade, M.J. 1978. A critical review of the models of group selection. *Q. Rev. Biol.* 53:101–114.

Wade, M.J., and F. Breden. 1986. Life history of natural populations of the imported willow leaf beetle, *Plagiodera versicolora* (Coleoptera: Chrysomelidae). *Ann. Entomol. Soc. Am.* 79:73–79.

Waldbauer, G.P., and J.G. Sternburg. 1975. Saturniid moths as mimics: an alternative interpretion of attempts to demonstrate mimetic advantage in nature. *Evolution* 29:650–658.

Walgenbach, C.A., J.K. Phillips, D.L. Faustini, and W.E. Burkholder. 1983. Male-produced aggregation pheromone of the maize weevil, *Sitophilus zeamais,* and interspecific attraction between three *Sitophilus* species. *J. Chem. Ecol.* 9:831–841.

Wcislo, W.T. 1984. Gregarious nesting of a digger wasp as a "selfish herd" response to a parasitic fly (Hymenoptera: Sphecidae; Diptera: Sarcophagidae). *Behav. Ecol. Sociobiol.* 15:157–160.

Wheeler, W.M. 1930. Societal evolution. In *Human Biology and Racial Welfare* (ed. E.V. Cowdry). Hoeber, New York.

White, J., and M. Lloyd. 1979. 17-year cicadas emerging after 18 years: a new brood? *Evolution* 33:1193–1199.

White, J., M. Lloyd, and J.H. Zar. 1979. Faulty eclosion in crowded suburban periodical cicadas: populations out of control. *Ecology* 60:305–315.

Williams, G.C. 1964. Measurement of consociation among fishes and comments on the evolution of schooling. *Misc. Publs. Mus. Biol. Univ. Michigan* 2:349–384.

Wilson, D.S. 1983. The group selection controversy: history and current status. *Ann. Rev. Ecol. Syst.* 14:159–187.

Wilson, E.O. 1971. *The Insect Societies.* Harvard University Press, Cambridge, Massachusetts.

————. 1975. *Sociobiology.* Harvard University Press, Cambridge Massachusetts.

Wolda, H. and D.L. Denlinger. 1984. Diapause in a large aggregation of a tropical beetle. *Ecol. Entomol.* 9:217–230.

Yamasaki. M., Y. Hirose, and M. Takagi. 1978. Repeated visits of *Polistes Jadwigae* Dalla Torre (Hymenoptera: Vespidae) to its hunting site. *Jap. J. Appl. Entomol. Zool.* 22:51-55.

Youdeowei, A. 1969. The behaviour of a cotton stainer, *Dysdercus intermedius,* Distant (Heteroptera: Pyrrhocoridae) towards models and its significance for aggregation. *Anim. Behav.* 17:232-237.

Young, A.M. 1978. A communal roost of the butterfly *Heliconuis charitonius* L. in Costa Rican premontane tropical wet forest (Lepidoptera: Nymphalidae). *Entomol. News.* 89: 235-243.

CHAPTER 12

Allomones: Chemicals for Defense

Douglas W. Whitman, Murray S. Blum, David W. Alsop

Evolutionary theory argues that animals should invariably attempt to avoid capture by predators. Escape, however, is not always possible. Once seized by a predator, a prey has a variety of options available. For terrestrial arthropods, perhaps the most common countermeasure to predatory attack is chemical defense. Indeed, arthropods manifest an extraordinarily rich diversity of allomonal defensive systems. Included are glandular-derived secretions, anal and oral discharges, reflex bleeding, poisonous bites and stings (See Schmidt, this volume), and internal toxins. In some cases, chemical weapons are obtained from dietary sources (See Bowers, this volume). In this chapter we will examine those arthropods that biosynthesize their own defensive allomones.

Arthropods That Produce Defensive Compounds De Novo

Over half of all terrestrial arthropod orders contain species which use chemical deterrents (table 12.1). Among these, the most common form of chemical defense is glandular, a defense that is particularly well developed in the Hymenoptera (see Schmidt, this volume), Opiliones, Diplopoda, Isoptera, Hemiptera, and Coleoptera.

Opiliones (Phalangida), the so-called daddy longlegs, secrete a great variety of ketones and quinones from paired cephalothoracic defensive glands (figures 1, 2, 3) (Eisner, Alsop, and Meinwald 1978). Exudates are oozed, sprayed, or spread along specialized integumental grooves (Lawrence 1938; Bishop 1950; Juberthie 1961b; Blum and Edgar 1971; Duffield et al. 1981). In some cases the concentrated glandular contents are mixed with oral discharges, presumably to increase their volume. They are sometimes dabbed onto attackers with the legs (Juberthie 1961a; Eisner et al. 1971, 1977), and are highly effective in deterring a diversity of predators (Meinwald et al. 1971; Duffield et al. 1981).

The millipedes (Diplopoda), are well defended; the majority of species possess pairs of defensive glands (ozopores) on most body segments (figures 4-6, 27). When attacked, these armor-plated animals curl into a tight spiral with the head in the center, and discharge a diverse array of repellent substances (Eisner, Alsop, Hicks, and Meinwald 1978). Some species secrete benzoquinones or cresols, and others produce enough hydrogen cyanide and benzaldehyde to kill predators confined with them (Davenport et al. 1952; Eisner and Eisner 1965; Eisner, Alsop, and Eisner 1967; Duffey et al. 1977). Certain Golmerida discharge viscous proteinaceous secretions fortified with toxic and repellent alkaloids (Meinwald, Meinwald, and Eisner 1966). Ants and other small invertebrate predators can become entangled in these exudates, and a variety of large predators are deterred by their toxic properties (Schildknecht, Maschwitz, and Wenneis 1967; Eisner, Alsop, Hicks, and Meinwald 1978).

In termites (Isoptera) colony defense is usually relegated to a specialized soldier cast (Prestwich 1979, 1984; Deligne et al. 1982; Howse 1984). Soldiers are typically larger and more powerful than the workers, are attracted to the sites of disturbances, and exhibit varied chemical and mechanical weaponry. Some species jab or tear with sharp mandibles while squirting or dabbing enemies with toxic monoterpene hydrocarbons or ketones derived from the frontal gland (Moore 1969; Prestwich 1979, 1984; Blum et al. 1982; Quennedey 1984). Others, called "nasutes," squirt a sticky, entangling latex from nozzle-shaped heads (Nutting et al. 1974; Quennedey 1984). Many Apicotermitinae expel salivary secretions when attacked, and others, like six-legged grenades, perform the ultimate altruistic act. By violently contracting their abdomens, they actually explode, entangling invaders in the viscous ooze of their internal organs and blood (Noirot 1969; Sands 1982; Prestwich 1988).

The Hemiptera, or true bugs, secrete an incredible diversity of defensive substances when disturbed. Usually of low molecular weight and high volatility, these repellent compounds run the gamut from aldehydes, ketones, alcohols, acids, terpenes, and esters to short-chain hydrocarbons (Blum 1981; Staddon 1986; Aldrich 1988). Adults store these substances in paired metathoracic glands (figure 7), that open at metapleural grooves, sometimes associated with a specialized evaporative area (Remold 1962, 1963; Filshie and Waterhouse 1968, 1969; Carayon 1971;

Table 12.1. The occurrence of chemical defenses in terrestrial arthropod orders.

TYPES OF CHEMICAL DEFENSES

Class Order	None Known[1]	Internal toxin	Poisonous bite[2]	sting	Reflex bleeding	Enteric discharge	Glandular exudate
ARACHNIDA							
Scorpionida				X			
Pseudoscorpiones	X						
Opiliones							
Acari	X					X	X
Thelyphonida							
Schizomida	X						X
Amblypygida	X						
Palpigrada	X						
Ricinuleida	X						
Solpugia	X						
Araneida			X				X
CRUSTACEA							
Isopoda							
Decapoda	X						X
DIPLOPODA							
Polyxenida	X						
Glomeridesmida	X						
Glomerida							
Sphaerotheriida	X						X
Polydesmida							
Platydesmida							X
Polyzoniida							X
Chordeumida	X						X
Julida							
Spirobolida							X
Callipodida							X
Stemmiulida							X
Siphonophorida							X
Spirostreptida							X
CHILOPODA							
Scutigeromorpha			X				
Lithobiomorpha			X				
Scolopendromorpha			X				X
Geophilomorpha			X				X
							X
PAUROPODA	X						
SYMPHYLA	X						
INSECTA							
Protura	X						
Collembola							
Diplura	X						X
Thysanura	x						
Ephemeroptera							
Odonata	X						X
Orthoptera		X					
Dermaptera					X	X	X
							X

Table 12.1. *(Cont'd.)*

Class Order	None Known[1]	Internal toxin	Poisonous bite[2]	sting	Reflex bleeding	Enteric discharge	Glandular exudate
Dictyoptera							X
Isoptera						X	X
Embioptera	X						
Plecoptera					X		
Zoraptera	X						
Psocoptera	X						
Mallophaga	X						
Anoplura	X						
Thysanoptera						X	X
Hemiptera		X	X			X	X
Homoptera		X					X
Neuroptera						X	X
Coleoptera		X	X		X	X	X
Strepsiptera	X						
Mecoptera	X						
Trichoptera							X
Lepidoptera		X		X	X	X	X
Diptera		X	X			X	X
Siphonaptera	X						
Hymenoptera			X	X	X	X	X

[1]Anecdotal reports were not used.
[2]Administered with the mouthparts, fangs, or chelicerae.

Weatherston and Percy 1978b; Staddon 1979). In addition, many adults and larvae possess dorsal abdominal glands (figure 8) or produce potent salivary toxins that are effective vertebrate deterrents (Dupuis 1948; Edwards 1962); Schmidt 1982; Staddon 1986; Aldrich 1988).

Preeminent among chemically defended arthropods are the beetles (Coleoptera) (Weatherston and Percy 1978a; Dettner 1987). The number of species possessing chemical defenses and the great variety of defensive glands and compounds produced are extraordinary and document the virtuosity of the insects as allomonal chemists. Particularly well known are some species of darkling beetles (Tenebrionidae), that lower their heads and emit a quinonoid defensive secretion from paired abdominal glands when threatened (figure 11) (Meinwald et al. 1966; Eisner 1970; Tschinkel 1975a, b, c).

Ground beetles (Carabidae) produce a heterogeneous collection of hydrocarbons, aldehydes, phenols, quinones, esters, and acids in their paired pygidial glands (Eisner, Swithenbank, and Meinwald 1963; Moore and Wallbank 1968; Schildknecht et al. 1968; Blum 1981; Dettner 1987). However, certain species have taken chemical defense to its extreme.

Appropriately called "bombardier beetles," they generate 1,4-quinones by mixing hydroquinones, hydrogen peroxide, peroxidases, and catalases in an abdominal reaction chamber (figures 40, 41). The peroxides are decomposed by the catalases to liberate oxygen, and the hydroquinones are instantly oxidized by the peroxidases to 1,4-quinones. This hot (100° C) and toxic reaction mixture is explosively ejected from the abdomen as a vapor with a loud pop. A flexible abdominal turret allows the bombardier to discharge this cannonade directly into the face of an attacking predator (Schildknecht 1957; Eisner 1958a; Schildknecht and Holoubek 1961; Aneshansley et al. 1969).

Rove beetles (Staphylinidae) possess a diversity of abdominal glands which emit quinones, hydrocarbons, lactones, aldehydes, and esters (Brand et al. 1973; Wheeler et al. 1972; Gnanasunderam et al. 1981; Dettner and Schwinger 1986). When molested, these brachypterous beetles raise or twist their highly flexible abdomens, smearing their defensive exudates against their aggressors (Brand et al. 1973; Klinger and Maschwitz 1977; Gnanasunderam et al. 1981; Dettner and Schwinger 1982).

In leaf beetles (Chrysomelidae), both adults and larvae may be chemically protected. Paired thoracic and abdominal defensive glands in the latter generate various monoterpenes, aldehydes, esters, and organic acids (figures 47, 48) (Blum et al. 1972; Pasteels et al. 1984). In adults, thoracic and elytral glands secrete a rich diversity of defensive steroids characterized by the presence of a butenolide (Pasteels and Daloze 1977). Lampyrids, on the other hand, biosynthesize steriods that contain a pyrone ring (Meinwald et al. 1979). However, in terms of biosynthetic versatility, few insects rival adult Dytiscidae, which possess both prothoracic and pygidial glands. The prothoracic glands generate a multitude of defensive steroids, some of which are unique natural products (Schildknecht 1970; Miller and Mumma 1976; Fescemyer and Mumma 1983), and the pygidial glands produce various aromatic compounds (Schildknecht 1970; Dettner and Schwinger 1980).

Origins of Defensive Compounds

Arthropod defensive compounds are derived from a variety of sources, both glandular and nonglandular. These sources can be conveniently classified by their location within the body and by their overall functional morphology.

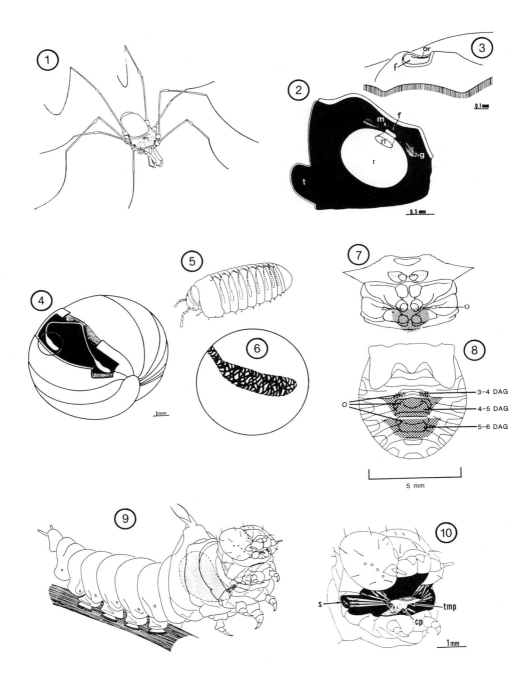

Plate 12.1

1 Paired cephalothoracic defensive glands (stippled) of *Leiobunum* sp. (Opiliones). **2** Internal view of *Leiobunum* sp. cephalothoracic gland (semidiagrammatic). Reservoir (r), neck of gland (n), paired muscles inserting on neck (g), paired muscles inserting on floor of opening (m), membranous floor of opening (f), eye-bearing turret (t). **3** *Leiobunum* sp. frontal view of gland opening prominence showing slit-like gland orifice (or) resting in saddle-shaped membrane (f). **4** Reaction of the glomerid millipede *Glomeris conspersa* to disturbance. The millipede coils into a tight sphere and discharges sticky droplets from paired segmental glands. **5** *G. conspersa*, showing the paired segmental glands and common middorsal gland openings. **6** *G. conspersa* gland showing the muscular covering which constricts the gland to effect secretion discharge. **7** Ventral thorax of an adult pentatomid stink bug, *Podisus maculiventris,* showing metathoracic gland (stippled) and paired gland openings (o). **8** Dorsal abdomen of a fifth-stage *P. maculiventris* nymph, showing various abdominal glands (stippled) and paired gland openings between tergites 3 and 4, 4 and 5, and 5 and 6. **9** Ventral prothoracic defensive gland in the notodontid caterpillar *Schizura unicornis,* showing basal and apical chambers (stippled) and their short tubular interconnection (crosshatched). Although in many species this gland is eversible, in *S. unicornis* it is not. **10** *S. unicornis.* Cutaway of neck region showing the muscles serving to help aim the defensive spray.

ENTERIC DISCHARGE

Many arthropods discharge their gut contents when molested (table 12.2). Grasshoppers and other Orthoptera "spit tobacco" (figure 12), and many sawfly larvae (Hymenoptera) and caterpillars regurgitate. These oral emissions are a complex blend of digestive enzymes, salivary secretions, and partially digested food. In some cases regurgitates are fortified with sequestered plant compounds or products of defensive glands. For example, *Neodiprion* and *Pseudoperga* sawfly larvae store pine terpenes and eucalypt oils, respectively, in modified gut diverticula and eject these materials when threatened (Eisner et al. 1974; Morrow et al. 1976). The regurgitates of notodontid and noctuid caterpillars often become contaminated with products from the ventral prothoracic gland (figures 9, 10), which is everted when the larvae are disturbed (Weatherston et al. 1979).

Other arthropods defecate when molested (figures 13, 20). Moths and butterflies accumulate their waste products (meconium) during pupation, and can forcefully expel them at predators during the short, vulnerable postecdysial period when the cuticle is soft and the wings are nonfunctional. Carrion beetles (Silphidae) have taken fecal defense one step further. They possess rectal glands which empty immediately anterior to the anal opening (figures 28, 29). In *Necrodes* the terpene products of this gland admixed with fecal fluid are sprayed at attackers (Eisner and Meinwald 1982; Eisner, Deyrup, Jacobs, and Meinwald 1986).

Instead of discarding their feces, some chrysomelid larvae attach it to their backs and use it like a shield to thwart the intentions of small predators (figure 14). Larvae of the leaf beetle *Cassida* possess a long forked appendage to which both feces and the cast off skins from earlier molts are attached (Eisner, van Tassell, and Carrel 1967). The highly flexible appendage can be maneuvered to effectively block attacks from any direction (figures 15, 16, 17).

Thrips are tiny, elongate insects which often aggregate and live in confined habitats, such as between flower petals. When attacked, they exude from their anus a droplet of defensive fluid which is held at the tip of the abdomen by a ring of long hairs (figures 18, 19). Possessing a highly flexible turret-like abdomen, the thrips can easily maneuver the droplet to counter attacks from any aspect (Howard et al. 1983). This defense is particularly effective in certain subcortical species which aggregate with their heads facing inward and their abdomens facing outward. Attacking predators such as ants are met with a phalanx of anal droplets which cannot be breached because of the narrow height of the habitat.

Table 12.2. Examples of terrestrial arthropods known to regurgitate or defecate when disturbed.

TAXON	REFERENCE
ARTHROPODS THAT REGURGITATE	
ARACHIDA	
OPILIONES	Eisner 1972; Eisner et al. 1977
INSECTA	
ORTHOPTERA	
Pyrgomorphidae	Kevan 1949
Acrididae	Curasson 1934; Freeman 1968; Uvarov 1977; Lymbery and Bailey 1980
Romaleidae	Eisner 1970; Whitman et al. 1985
Tettigoniidae	Personal observation
Gryllidae	Personal observation
Phyllidae	Robinson 1969
ISOPTERA	
Termitidae	Prestwich 1984
Cantharidae	Eisner et al. 1981
COLEOPTERA	
Chrysomelidae	Deroe and Pasteels 1982
Cantharidae	Eisner et al. 1981
LEPIDOPTERA	
Papilionidae larvae	Stamp 1986
Nymphalidae larve	Stamp 1984
Danaidae larvae	Brower 1984
Pyralidae larvae	Eisner, Jutro, Aneshansley, and Niedhauk 1972
Notodontidae larvae	Weatherston et al. 1986
Saturniidae larvae	Cornell et al. 1987
Lasiocampidae larvae	Peterson et al. 1987
HYMENOPTERA	
Diprionidae larvae	Eisner et al. 1974
Pergidae larvae	Morrow et al. 1976
Tenthredinidae larvae	Maxwell 1955; Prop 1960
Apidae	Fuller and Plowright 1986
DIPTERA	
Syrphidae larvae	Eisner 1972
ARTHROPODS THAT DEFECATE	
DIPLOPODA	
Numerous species	Eisner, Alsop, Hicks, and Meinwald 1978
INSECTA	
ORTHOPTERA	
Pyrgomorphidae	Kevan 1949
Acrididae	Personal observation
Romaleidae	Whitman et al. 1985
ISOPTERA	

Table 12.2 *(Cont'd).*

TAXON	REFERENCE
HEMIPTERA	
Lygaeidae	Games and Staddon 1973; Duffey 1977
Pyrrhocoridae	Youdeowei and Calam 1969
THYSANOPTERA	
Various families	Howard et al. 1983; Suzuki et al. 1986
NEUROPTERA	
Chrysopidae	Kennett 1948; LaMunyon and Adams 1987
COLEOPTERA	
Staphylinidae	Jefson et al. 1983
Meloidae	Figure 20
Silphidae	Schildknecht and Weis 1962; Eisner and Meinwald 1982
Chrysomelidae	Deroe and Pasteels 1982
LEPIDOPTERA	
Danaidae	Brower 1984
Arctiidae	Blum 1981
Notodontidae	Rothschild 1985; Weatherston et al. 1986
HYMENOPTERA	
Tenthredinidae	Smith 1970

INTERNAL TOXINS

Numerous terrestrial arthropods, particularly beetles, fortify their blood or internal organs with toxic or distasteful allomones. Because these compounds are stored inside the body, predators do not generally contact them until the body wall is broken, as occurs when the predator pierces the prey's integument. However, in some cases (e.g., Coccinellidae), these internal allomones may be externalized when blood is discharged reflexively (see below). The offensive compounds are often sequestered directly from the diet (see Bowers, this volume), while in other cases they are autogenously synthesized (table 12.3). Unlike the exocrine defenses which are generally highly volatile, internal allomones tend to be relatively nonvolatile, distasteful, vesicatory, or emetic compounds, which elicit predator distress only after the prey has been tasted or consumed.

AUTOHEMORRHAGE

Many insects bleed reflexively when attacked (table 12.4). Blister (Meloidae), leaf (Chrysomelidae), lycid (Lycidae), soldier (Cantharidae), lampyrid (Lampyridae), and lady beetles (Coccinellidae) emit allomone-fortified hemolymph from intersegmental membranes (figures 20, 21). On the other hand, the blood of some leaf beetles and stoneflies (Plecoptera) appears to lack noxious constituents, and is probably used as a physical entangling agent for small invertebrate predators (Blum 1981).

Some tiger (Arctiidae) and ctenuchid moths (Ctenuchidae) eject blood in admixture with cervical gland secretions (figure 22) (Rothschild 1985). *Eugaster* katydids autohemorrhage in response to visual stimuli and can accurately eject blood forty centimeters (Vosseler 1893). Other species of grasshoppers also produce defensive secretions containing blood cells (von Euw et al. 1967).

RESERVOIRLESS DEFENSIVE GLANDS

These glands consist of single or aggregated secretory cells that expel their products directly onto the body surface. There are no extra-cellular storage areas, although capacious intracellular reservoirs are sometimes seen. Examples are found in the hydrogen cyanide-secreting glands of *Asanada* and *Geophilus* centipedes (Jones et al. 1976; Maschwitz et al 1979) and in the elytral and pronotal glands of adult chrysomelid beetles (Deroe and Pasteels 1977; Daloze et al. 1986). Polistine wasps produce fatty acid esters in reservoirless sternal glands and apply these compounds by means of a sternal brush to the nest petiole, where they deter ants (Hermann and Dirks 1974; Jeanne et al 1983; Post et al. 1984).

The yellow or orange bitter-tasting liquids ejected by adult coccinellid beetles have long been considered to be examples of reflex bleeding (Table 12.4). It appears, however, that in at least some species, the substance is not blood, but a secretion produced by single and aggregated hypodermal gland cells (McIndoo 1916).

SPINES AND STINGING HAIRS

In some insects, single or aggregated secretory cells pour their products into or onto sharp barbed spines or hairs which pierce the skin of predators and release their toxic contents subcutaneously. This poison dart defense is particularly characteristic of lepidopterous larvae in the families Saturniidae (Quiroz 1978), Notodontidae (Quiroz 1978), Arctiidae (Frazer 1965; Rothschild 1985), Lymantriidae (de Jong and Bleumink 1977; Rothschild 1985), Lasiocampidae (Rothschild 1985; Quiroz 1978), Limacodidae, Megalopygidae, and others (Beard 1963; Pesce and Delgado 1971; Picarelli and Valle 1971; Kawamoto and Kumada 1984; Novak et al. 1987) (figures 23, 24). In some cases, urticating hairs are shed and embedded in

Plate 12.2

11 Tenebrionid beetle performing a headstand and emitting a droplet of defensive secretion in response to disturbance.   **12** Many grasshopper species, like this *Romalea guttata,* not only regurgitate crop contents when attacked but bite with sharp mandibles, contaminating the subcutaneous tissues of predators with potentially irritating substances and thereby increasing the defensive efficacy.   **13** Defensive defacation by *R. guttata.*   **14** Larva of the chrysomelid beetle *Blepharida rhois* with sticky moist fecal shield.   **15** Larva of the chrysomelid beetle *Cassida* showing forked anal appendage which holds the defensive shield.   **16 & 17** Larva of the chrysomelid beetle *Cassida* using shield composed of feces and cast-off skins to fend off forceps. **18** Thrips with anal defensive droplet.   **19** Turret-like abdominal tip of thrips *Bagnalliella yuccae,* showing the ring of hairs which holds the defensive droplet.

the cocoon, where they provide protection for the developing pupae. This defense is also found in the adults of some Saturniidae and Thaumetopoeidae, which, like the larvae, possess thick piles of urticating hairs. These "flechettes" are easily dislodged and produce dermatitus and respiratory discomfort in man and other animals (Lamy et al. 1984; Novak et al. 1987).

EVERSIBLE SACS

Some insects possess sac-like cuticle-lined invaginations of the body wall (table 12.5), which serve as storage areas for defensive substances produced by surrounding glands. When disturbed, the insect everts the sac by hemostatic pressure, releasing the stored defensive substances. Retractor muscles usually return the sac to its inverted position. Such glands are seen in the osmeteria of swallowtail butterfly larvae (figure 25), the ventral prothoracic glands of numerous moth caterpillars (figures 9, 10), the abdominal glands of lagriid beetles, and the paired thoracic and abdominal glands of some melyrid adults (figure 30) and chrysomelid larvae (figures 47, 48).

INTERNAL RESERVOIR GLANDS

The most common type of arthropod defensive gland consists of an internal, noneversible, cuticle-lined reservoir in which defensive secretions are stored (table 12.6, figures 26, 31-41). The exudates are produced in secretory cells lining or adjacent to the reservoir. In most cases, the reservoir opens through a narrow valved passage, and the insect expels the glandular contents by collapsing the reservoir by muscle action or hemostatic pressure. Defensive glands can exist as single, paired, or serially arranged organs, and can be found in nearly any part of an arthropod's body (table 12.6).

CUTICULAR CAVITIES

Certain zygaenid moth caterpillars store cyanoglucosides in cavities within the cuticle. Interestingly, no specialized secretory organells can be found; the secretion appears to enter the cavities via active transport across the lamellate cuticle. The secretion is discharged through cuticular weak areas as a result of increased pressure caused by muscular contraction of the entire body segment (Franzl and Naumann 1985).

The lygaeid *Oncopeltus fasciatus* sequesters cardiac glycosides from its diet and stores them in a vacuolated epidermal cell layer (dorsolateral

Table 12.3. Examples of terrestrial arthropods with autogenously derived internal toxins.

TAXON	TOXIC PRINCIPLE	REFERENCE
INSECTA		
COLEOPTERA		
Staphylinidae	Pederin	Matsumoto et al. 1968; Pavan 1975
Coccinellidae	Alkaloids	Pasteels et al. 1973; Eisner, Goetz, Aneshansley, Ferstandig-Arnold, and Meinwald 1986
Buprestidae	Buprestins	Brown et al. 1985; Moore and Brown 1985
Lycidae	Alkaloids	Moore and Brown 1981
Lampyridae	Steroids	Eisner, Wiemer, Haynes, and Meinwald 1978; Goetz et al. 1981
Meloidae	Cantharidin	Selander 1960; Capinera et al. 1985
Oedemeridae	Cantharidin	Kurosa and Watanabe 1958
Chrysomelidae	Anthraquinones Cardenolides Hydrogen cyanide	Howard, Blum, Jones, and Philips 1982; Howard, Phillips, Jones and Blum, 1982; Pasteels et al. 1984; Nahrstedt and Davis 1986
LEPIDOPTERA		
Pieridae	Pierin	Marsh and Rothschild 1974; Marsh et al. 1984
Nymphalidae, Zygaenidae, and fourteen other families	Hydrogen cyanide	Davis and Nahrstedt 1984; Witthohn and Naumann 1987
Geometridae	Histamine	Rothschild 1985
Arctiidae	Histamine Acetylcholine	Bisset et al. 1960; Rothschild 1985
Zygaenidae	Histamine	Marsh and Rothschild 1974; Muhtasib and Evans 1987
Yponomeutidae	Butenolide	Fung et al. 1988

space). Weak areas of the cuticle rupture when the insect is squeezed, releasing the secretion to the surface. Contamination of the haemolymph is prevented by a thick basal lamina (Scudder et al. 1986).

SALIVARY AND MANDIBULAR GLANDS

Numerous arthropods produce defensive substances from modified salivary or mandibular glands (table 12.7). Although many species

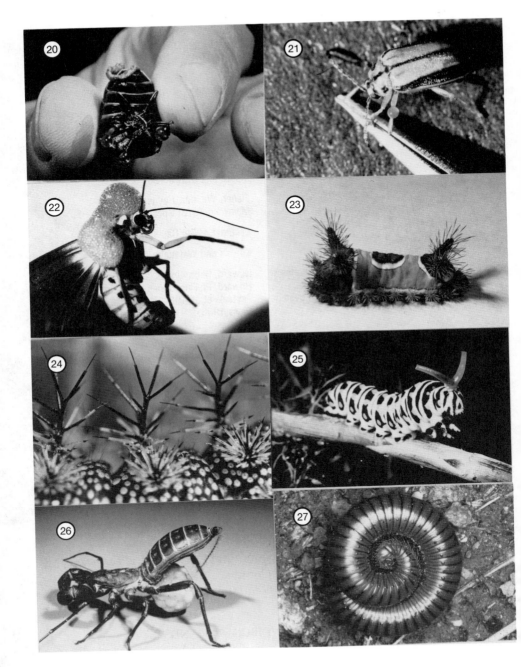

Plate 12.3

20 Defecation and autohemorrhaging in the meloid beetle *Megetna cancellata*. Contact with the cantharidin-containing blood can cause severe blistering and itching.   **21** Autohemorrhaging from the femo-tibial joints by the chrysomelid beetle *Pyrrhalta luteola*.   **22** Defensive froth from the paired cervical glands of a New Guinean arctiid moth. Foam is produced by mixing blood and air with the cervical secretion. **23** The saddleback caterpillar, *Sibine stimulea* (Limacodidae), showing poisonous spines.   **24** Closeup of the stinging spines of the buck moth caterpillar *Hemileuca maia* (Saturniidae).   **25** The papilionid caterpillar *Papilio polyxenes* everting its osmeterium.   **26** Female vinegaroon, *Mastigoproctus giganteus*, with eggs, aiming sensory tail (and defense gland) at camera.   **27** Desert millipede *Orthoporus ornatus* exuding droplets of defensive secretion.

Table 12.4. Examples of terrestrial arthropods that autohemorrhage when disturbed.

TAXON	LOCATION	ALLOMONE	REFERENCE
PLECOPTERA			
Pteronarcidae	Legs	None known	Benfield 1974
Peltoperlidae	Legs	None known	Benfield 1974
ORTHOPTERA			
Pyrgomorphidae	Abdominal gland	Histamine	Grassé 1937; von Euw et al. 1967
Tettigoniidae	Various	None known	Vossler 1893; Hingston 1927; Gurney 1947
HEMIPTERA			
Rhopalidae	Rostrum	Cyanogens	Aldrich et al. 1990
COLEOPTERA			
Chrysomelidae	Mouth, legs, and tubercles	Alkaloids	Wallace and Blum 1971; Deroe and Pasteels 1977, 1982; Howard, Blum, Jones, and Phillips 1982
Coccinellidae	Legs	Alkaloids	Hollande 1911; Happ and Eisner 1961; Kendall 1971; Eisner, Goetz, Aneshansley, Ferstandig-Arnold, and Meinwald 1986
Meloidae	Legs	Cantharidin	Selander 1960; Carrel and Eisner 1974
Lampyridae	Elytra and antennal sockets	Steriods	Williams 1917; Blum and Sannasi 1974
Lycidae	Wings	Alkaloids	Darlington 1938; Moore and Brown 1981
LEPIDOPTERA			
Zygaenidae	Thorax and tarsi	Histamine	Rothschild 1961a, 1985
Arctiidae	Tarsi and cervical gland	Histamine	Rothschild and Haskell 1966; Rothschild 1985
HYMENOPTERA			
Tenthredinidae larvae	Body	Unknown	Heads 1986

can inject salivary toxins directly with fangs, beaks, or probosci (spiders, hemipterans, flies), others dab, squirt, or spray their exudates onto aggressors, or simply allow the secretion to spread over their own bodies. For example, some reduviids spray enzyme-rich salivary secretions and

Table 12.5. Examples of terrestrial arthropods with eversible defense glands.

TAXON	GLAND	REFERENCE
ORTHOPTERA		
Acrididae	Prothoracic	Jannone 1939; Uvarov 1966; Schmidt et al. 1987
DICTYOPTERA		
Polyphagidae	Abdominal	Roth and Alsop 1978
COLEOPTERA		
Tenebrionidae, Lagriidae, and Alleculidae	Caudal	Roth 1945; Tschinkel 1969, 1975c; Dettner 1987
Staphylinidae	Pygidial	Jenkins 1957; Schildknecht 1970; Jefson et al. 1983; Dettner 1987
Elateridae	Pygidial	Bertkau 1882; Dettner 1987
Cantharidae	Lateral abdominal	Sulc 1949; Barth 1958
Malachiidae	Lateral abdominal and cervical	Klemensiewicz 1882
Chrysomelidae	Middorsal abdominal	Moore 1967
	Lateral thoracic and abdominal	Garb 1915; Patterson 1930; Hinton 1951; Pasteels et al. 1984; Dettner 1987
LEPIDOPTERA		
Papilionidae	Osmeterium	Eisner and Meinwald 1965; Crossley and Waterhouse 1969; Young et al. 1986
Larvae of various families	Ventral eversible	Peterson 1948; Marti and Rogers 1988
HYMENOPTERA		
Tenthredinidae larvae	Midventral abdominal	Yuasa 1922; Benson 1950; Maxwell 1955; Smith 1970; Boevé and Pasteels 1985
	Ventral thoracic	Yuasa 1922; Maxwell 1955
Tenthredinidae and Xyelidae larvae	Paired cervical	Yuasa 1922; Maxwell 1955
Cimbicidae larvae	Paired abdominal	Benson 1950

can accurately hit objects thirty centimeters away. Serious lesions can result when this secretion contacts the sensitive eyes of vertebrates (Edwards 1961, 1962).

Table 12.6. Examples of internal reservior defensive glands in terrestrial arthropods.

TAXON	GLAND	REFERENCE
ARACHNIDA OPILIONES Most families	Lateral prosomal	Juberthie 1961a, b; Eisner et al. 1977; Duffield et al. 1981; Eisner, Alsop, and Meinwald 1978
THELYPHONIDA	Postabdominal	Börner 1904; Kästner 1932; Werner 1935; Eisner et al. 1961; Eisner, Alsop, and Meinwald 1978
DIPLOPODA Most orders	Ozopore	Eisner, Hurst, and Meinwald 1963; Woodring and Blum 1963, 1965; Weatherston and Percy 1969; Eisner, Alsop, Hicks, and Meinwald 1978
INSECTA COLLEMBOLA Onychiuridae	Pseudocelli	Usher and Balogun 1966
EPHEMEROPTERA Limnephilidae	Sternal	Duffield et al. 1977
ORTHOPTRA Pyrgomorphidae	Middorsal abdominal	De Lotto 1950; Ewer 1957; Fishelson 1960; Qureshi and Ahmad 1970; Abushama 1972
Phasmatidae	Lateral pronotal	Scudder 1876; Moreno 1940; Grangrade 1964; Eisner 1965; Beier 1968
Phylliidae	Lateral pronotal	Robinson 1969
DICTYOPTERA Blattidae	Midventral abdominal	Stay 1957; Blum 1964; Waterhouse and Wallbank 1967; Maschwitz and Tho 1978; Roth and Alsop 1978; Brossut and Sreng 1980
	Paired tergal	Oettinger 1906; Konček 1924; Liang 1956; Roth and Alsop 1978; Brossut and Sreng 1980
ISOPTERA Most families	Frontal	Quennedey 1975, 1984; Quennedey and Deligne 1975; Prestwich 1979, 1984
Termitidae	Cibarial	Quennedey 1984; Prestwich 1984

Table 12.6 *(Con't.)*

TAXON	GLAND	REFERENCE

DERMAPTERA
  Forficulidae
	Paired dorso-
	  lateral abdominal
		Vosseler 1890; Eisner 1960

HEMIPTERA
  Most nymphs
	Middorsal
	  abdominal
		Remold 1962; Gupta 1964; Stein 1967;
		Calam and Scott 1969; Youdeowei and
		Calam 1969; Staddon 1979; Aldrich et al.
		1984; Gough et al. 1985; Staddon
		et al. 1987; Farine 1988

Most adults	Metathoracic	Gupta 1961; Remold 1962, 1963; Filshie and Waterhouse 1968; Carayon 1971; Staddon 1979; Aldrich et al. 1984; Staddon et al. 1987
HOMOPTERA Aphididae	Cornicles	Dixon 1958; Edwards 1966; Strong 1967; Lindsay 1969
NEUROPTERA Chrysopidae	Lateral prothoracic	McDunnough 1909
COLEOPTERA Dytiscidae	Prothoracic	Blunck 1912; Forsyth 1968; Schildknecht, Birringer, and Maschwitz 1967; Schildknecht, Siewerdt, Maschwitz 1967; Schildknecht et al. 1969
Most Adephaga	Pygidial	Forsyth 1968, 1970, 1972; Kanehisa and Murase 1977; Moore 1979; Dazzini- Valcurone and Pavan 1980; Balestrazzi and Dazzini-Valcurone 1985; Dettner 1987

Chrysomelidae
  larvae
	Thoracic and
	  abdominal
		Garb 1915; Wallace and Blum 1969;
		Eisner 1970; Pasteels et al. 1984

Chrysomelidae
  adults
	Thoracic and
	  elytral
		Deroe and Pasteels 1982;
		Pasteels et al. 1984

Tenebrionidae,
  Alleculidae,
  and Lagriidae
	Paired caudal	Roth 1945; Eisner et al. 1964;
		Kendall 1968, 1974; Tschinkel 1975c;
		Dettner 1987

	Paired prothoracic	Kendall 1968, 1974; Tschinkel 1975c; Detter 1987

Cantharidae
  larvae, pupae,
  and adults
	Lateral thoracic
	  and abdominal
		Payne 1916; Verhoeff 1917; Sulc 1949;
		Meinwald et al. 1968

Table 12.6 *(Con't.)*

TAXON	GLAND	REFERENCE
Staphylinidae	Dorsal abdominal	Jenkins 1957; Kistner and Pasteels 1969; Happ and Happ 1973; Araújo 1973, 1978; Dettner and Schwinger 1982; Dettner 1987
	Sternal abdominal	Klinger and Maschwitz 1977; Araújo 1978; Araújo and Pasteels 1987
Silphidae	Rectal diverticulum	Alsop 1970; Eisner and Meinwald 1982
Cerambycidae	Paired metasternal	Linsley 1959; Vidari et al. 1973
Scarabaeidae	Pygidial	Alsop 1970; Pluot-Sigwalt 1983
TRICHOPTERA Limnephilidae	Sternal abdominal	Duffield et al. 1977
LEPIDOPTERA Notodontidae larvae	Prothoracic	Detwiler 1922; Hintze 1969; Eisner, Kluge, Carrel, and Meinwald 1972; Pavan and Dazzini-Valcurone 1976; Weatherston et al. 1979
Arctiidae	Paired dorsal	Carpenter 1938; Dethier 1939; Rothschild 1985
HYMENOPTERA Tenthredinidae	Midventral abdominal	Maxwell 1955; Jonsson et al. 1988
Formicidae	Dufour's	Blum and Hermann 1978a; Maschwitz 1975; Buschinger and Maschwitz 1984
	Jessen's	Jessen et al. 1979; Buschinger and Maschwitz 1984
	Metapleural	Maschwitz 1974; Buschinger and Maschwitz 1984; Hölldobler and Engel-Siegel 1984
	Venom	Blum and Hermann 1978a; Buschinger and Maschwitz 1984; Schmidt 1986
	Janet's	Pavan and Ronchetti 1955; Kugler 1979

TRACHEAL GLANDS

Two insect groups have independently adapted their tracheal systems for defense. In Romaleinae grasshoppers, glandular cells lining the metathoracic tracheae secrete a mixture of phenols and quinones into the

Table 12.7. Examples of terrestrial arthropods that employ salivary or mandibular glands for defense. Arthropods that inject salivary venoms (i.e., spiders and centipedes) are not included.

TAXON	REFERENCE
ARACHNIDA	
ARANEIDA	
Scytodidae	Monterosso 1928; McAlister 1960
INSECTA	
ISOPTERA	
Mastotermitidae and Termitidae	Moore 1968; Noirot 1969; Quennedey 1975, 1984; Billen et al. 1989
DERMAPTERA	
Labiduridae	Blum 1981
HEMIPTERA	
Reduviidae	Edwards 1961, 1962
Veliidae	Andersen 1976
COLEOPTERA	
Cerambycidae	Moore and Brown 1971
LEPIDOPTERA	
Cossidae	Pavan and Dazzini-Valcurone 1976; Rothschild 1985
DIPTERA	
Syrphidae	Eisner 1972
HYMENOPTERA	
Formicidae	Maschwitz and Kloft 1971; Blum and Hermann 1978a,b; Bradshaw and Howse 1984; Buschinger and Maschwitz 1984
Multillidae	Fales et al. 1980
Apoidea	Cane and Michener 1983; Duffield et al. 1984; Roubik et al. 1987; Cane 1986

tracheal lumina (figures 42, 43). The secretion is stored behind closed spiracular valves, which are not used for respiration. When the grasshopper is disturbed, all spiracles but the metathoracic ones close, and the abdomen is compressed. The resulting hemostatic and pneumatic pressure forces air and secretion out through the narrow spiracular slit as a bubbly adherent froth, accompanied by a hissing noise (figure 44) (Whitman et al., unpublished).

A similar phenomenon occurs in the blaberid cockroach *Diploptera punctata,* in which a quinone-laden secretion is ejected from the second pair of abdominal spiracles with a hissing noise. Unlike the grasshopper

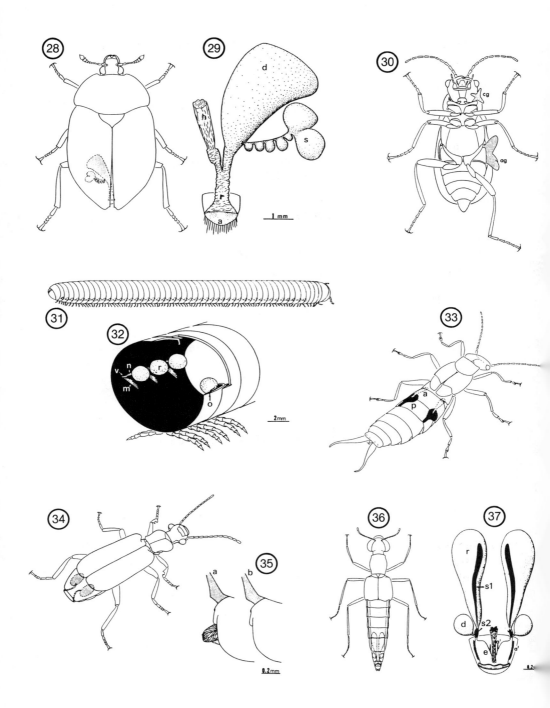

Plate 12.4

28 & 29 Rectal diverticulum of the silphid beetle *Silpha americana*, the presumed origin of the anal defensive secretion. Hind gut (h), main body of the diverticulum (d), smaller, multilobate diverticulum (s) extending from the main body, rectum (r), and the anus (a) attached to the underside of the last tergite. **30** The melyrid beetle *Malachius aeneus* with left cervical (cg) and left abdominal (ag) defensive glands everted. **31** The millipede *Narceus gordanus* showing location of lateral defensive glands, which occur on most body segments. **32** Internal view of *N. gordanus* showing defensive glands. Gland reservoir (r), gland duct (n), terminal valve (v), valve opener muscle (m), and location of external oriface (o). In this species, the secretion can be ejected up to a meter via increased hemolymph pressure. **33** The earwig *Forficula auricularia* showing anterior glands (a) opening at posterior edge of abdominal tergite III, and posterior glands (p) opening at posterior edge of abdominal tergite IV. **34** The location of the pygidial glands in the carabid *Helluomorphoides latitarsus*. **35** Outer edge of abdominal tergite VIII of *H. latitarsus* showing its appearance when (a) the gland is everted, and (b) when it is retracted. **36** Pygidial defensive glands of the rove beetle, *Stenus bipunctatus*. Glands can be partially everted and produce surface active secretions which rapidly propel the beetles across water. **37** Ventral view of *S. bipunctatus* glands, each of which consists of a capacious reservoir (r) and a smaller diverticulum (d), which communicate through a narrow neck region with a basal eversible pouch (e) possessing two apodemes (a^1, a^2) on which retractor muscles insert. Secretions originate from two distinct groups of secretory cells (s1, s2).

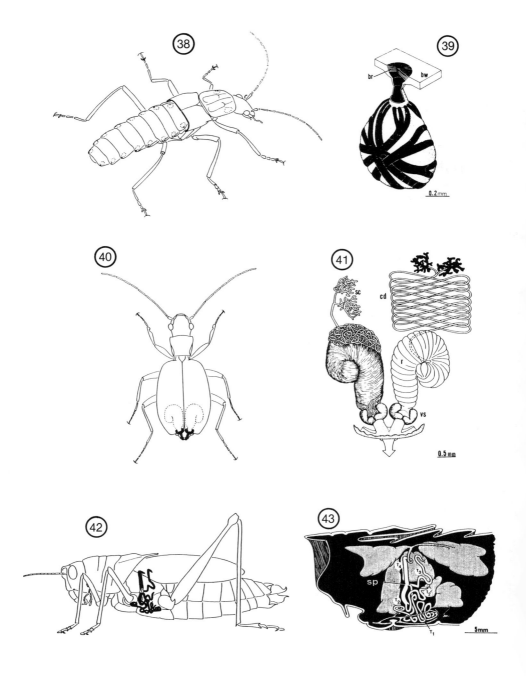

Plate 12.5

38 The soldier beetle *Chauliognathus lecontei* with wings cut away to expose abdominal glands which discharge dorsolaterally, and thoracic glands which open ventrally. **39** Detail of single *C. lecontei* abdominal gland. Surrounding muscles constrict gland reservoir to effect secretion discharge. Leakage of secretion prevented by a fringe of bristles (br) protruding inward from the external opening in the body wall (bw). **40** *Brachinus* sp. ground beetle showing location of paired pygidial glands. **41** Details of *Brachinus* pygidial glands. Left gland in natural state; right gland after potassium hydroxide-digestion. Hydrogen peroxide and hydroquinones produced by secretory cells (sc) are transferred via collecting ducts (cd) to muscle-covered reservoir (r). An instantaneous and highly exergonic reaction occurs when the contents of the reservoir are mixed with enzymes contained in a second chamber, the vestibule (vs), resulting in explosive discharge of hot by-products. **42** *Romalea guttata* metathoracic tracheal gland. **43** Internal view of *R. guttata* thoracic region showing location of various air sacs, glandular tracheae (T1, T2, T3, T4), and location of metathoracic spiracle (sp).

exudate, that of the cockroach is discharged as a broadly dispersed spray which presumably aids volatilization of the deterrent constituents (Eisner 1958b; Roth and Stay 1958; Roth and Alsop 1978).

CHEMICAL DEFENSE OF EGGS

Arthropod eggs are sometimes chemically defended. The protective allomones are acquired or produced by the female and are usually incorporated into the egg during its formation, or spread over its surface at the time of oviposition. The brightly colored eggs of some chrysomelid beetles contain ant-deterring oleic acid (Howard, Blum, Jones, and Phillips 1982), and some coccinellid eggs are fortified with alkaloids. The conspicuous egg clusters of other Chrysomelidae and some Lepidoptera are presumed to contain deterrent allomones (Hinton 1981; Howard, Blum, Jones, and Phillips 1982; Brower 1984). The egg rafts of the mosquito *Culex pipiens* possess on their upper end a lipoidal droplet which provides protection from ant predators (Hinton 1968). Female *Chauliognathus* soldier beetles have reproductive accessory glands rich in dihydromatricariate waxes. The waxes presumably coat the eggs, providing both antifeedant and bacteriostatic activity (Brown et al. 1988).

Among the more intriguing forms of egg defense are the deterrent barriers placed around egg clusters. Some insects cover their eggs with sticky or slimy exudates. *Chrysopa claveri* lacewings suspend their eggs at the ends of long stalks, fortified with sticky droplets (Eisner 1970). In certain owlflies (Neuroptera), fertile eggs are laid in clumps at the ends of dead twigs, and rings of smaller abortive eggs, termed "repagula," are laid a few millimeters below. The repagula are coated with a shiny liquid; when ascending ants contact these structures, they immediately and violently withdraw, sometimes falling to the ground (Henry 1972.)

Types of Defensive Compounds

Insects manufacture an extraodinarily diverse array of defensive compounds (table 12.8). Blum catalogued over six hundred in 1981, and the number has grown substantially since then. Although some are novel, most are natural products previously identified from other animals or plants. Generally, defensive substances released from glands are relatively low in molecular weight and are highly volatile. Included are normal alkanes, terpenes, alcohols, ketones, esters, aldehydes, organic acids, phenols, and quinones. These defensive compounds are usually secreted as blends, often containing both polar and nonpolar constituents.

In contrast to exocrine allomones, defensive compounds that fortify blood and internal organs are typically more complex. Included are steroids, tricyclic alkaloids, and complex amines (Blum 1981; Dettner 1987).

Although the compositions of defensive exudates were once considered to be species specific, we now know that a high degree of intraspecific variability occurs. Qualitative and quantitative differences in allomonal composition within individuals of a single species have been attributed to age, stage, sex, social caste, diet, season, geographic race, and past gland use (Wallbank and Waterhouse 1970; Tschinkel 1975a; Aldrich et al. 1978; Owen 1978; Brower et al. 1982, 1984; Goh et al. 1984; Jones et al. 1986, 1987, 1988; Scheffrahn et al. 1986; Young et al. 1986).

The Function of Defensive Substances

How do we know that purported defensive substances are indeed defensive? These materials could serve any number of biological functions or conceivably have no demonstrable role. Perhaps the compounds emitted by arthropods are by-products of other essential metabolic processes, and their discharge or occurrence in glands and other tissues represents excretion or storage excretion (Hottes 1928; Schildknecht and Weiss 1962; Blum 1981). Furthermore, since the products of exocrine glands are often complex mixtures, they could serve multiple roles (Blum 1974; Howse et al. 1977; Pasteels et al. 1983). In fact, what were believed to be primarily defensive exudates have been subsequently found to function parsimoniously as sexual (figure 45) (Hölldobler 1971; Whitman 1982; Peschke 1983; Post and Jeanne 1983), aggregation (Tannert and Hien 1973; Lockwood and Story 1985), alarm (Wheeler and Blum 1973; Maschwitz 1974; Löfqvist 1976; Howard, Blum, Jones, and Tomalski 1982; Buschinger and Maschwitz 1984; Lockwood and Story 1987), trail (Ritter et al. 1975; Buschinger and Maschwitz 1984), and territorial or spacing (Loconti and Roth 1953; Renner 1970) pheromones. These secretions also act as microbicides (Schildknecht 1970; Duffey 1977; Duffey and Blum 1977; Dettner 1985; Roncadori et al. 1985), wetting agents for aquatic beetles (Dettner

Table 12.8. Characteristic defensive compounds identified in terrestrial arthropods.

Taxon	Compound Class	Representative Compound
ARACHNIDA		
THELYPHONIDA	Carboxylic acid	Acetic acid
SCORPIONIDA		
Scorpionidae	Biogenic amine	Serotonin
OPILIONES		
Gonyleptidae	1,4-quinone	2,3-dimethyl-1,4-benzoquinone
Phalangiidae	Aliphatic ketone	4-methyl-3-hexanone
DIPLOPODA		
GLOMERIDA		
Glomeridae	Alkaloid	1-methyl-2-ethyl-4-(3*H*)-quinazolinone
JULIDA		
Julidae	1,4-quinone	2-methyl-1,4-benzoquinone
POLYDESMIDA		
Euryuridae	Aromatic aldehyde	Benzaldehyde
Polydesmidae	Aromatic acid	Benzoic acid
	Phenol	Phenol
	Aromatic nitrile	Benzoyl cyanide
INSECTA		
ORTHOPTERA		
Romaleidae	1,4-quinone	1,4-benzoquinone
Phasmidae	Monoterpene lactone	Nepetalactone
DERMAPTERA		
Forficulidae	1,4-quinone	1-ethyl-1,4-benzoquinone
ISOPTERA		
Mastotermitidae	1,4-quinone	2-methyl-1,4-benzoquinone
Rhinotermitidae	Hydrocarbon	Pentacosane
	Aliphatic ketone	1-tetradecen-3-one
	Nitkroalkene	1-nitro-1-pentadecene
Termitidae	Monoterpene hydrocarbon	α-pinene
	Diterpene hydrocarbon	Cembrene A
	Sesquiterpene hydrocarbon	α-selinene

Table 12.8 *(Con't.)*

Taxon	Compound Class	Representative Compound
DICTYOPTERA		
Blaberidae	1,4-quinone	1,4-benzoquinone
Blattidae	Monoterpene ketone	6-methyl-5-hepten-2-one
	Aliphatic aldehyde	2-methylene butanal
	Phenol	*p*-cresol
THYSANOPTERA		
Phlaeothripidae	Lactone	γ-decalactone
	1,4-quinone	Juglone
HOMOPTERA		
Aphididae	Sesquiterpene hydrocarbon	*E-B*-farnesene
HEMIPTERA		
Pentatomidae	Aliphatic hydrocarbon	Tridecane
	Aliphatic aldehyde	*E*-2-hexenal
Alydidae	Aliphatic aldehyde	4-oxo-*E*-2-hexenal
Coreidae	Aliphatic alcohol	1-hexanol
	Aliphatic ester	Hexyl acetate
	Aliphatic aldehyde	Hexanal
COLEOPTERA		
Dytiscidae	Steroid	Testosterone
	Aromatic aldehyde	*p*-hydroxybenzaldehyde
	Aromatic ester	Methyl *p*-hydroxybenzoate
Staphylinidae	Monoterpene aldehyde	Citral
	Lactone	γ-dodecaloctone
	Alkaloid	Actinidine
	Secondary amine	Pederin
Carabidae	Phenol	*m*-cresol
	Aromatic aldehyde	Salicylaldehyde
	Carboxylic acid	Methacrylic acid
Meloidae	Terpene anhydride	Cantharidin
Coccinellidae	Alkaloid	Coccinelline
Tenebrionidae	Alkene	1-undecene
	1,4-quinone	6-methyl-1,4-naphthoquinone
	Aromatic lactone	8-hydroxyisocoumarin
Gyrinidae	Sesquiterpene aldehyde	Gyrinidal
Chrysomelidae	Monoterpene lactone	Chrysomelidial
	1,4-quinone	1,8-dihydroxy-9,10-anthroquinone
	Steroid	Periplogenin

Table 12.8 *(Con't.)*

Taxon	Compound Class	Representative Compound
Cicindelidae	Aromatic nitrile	Mandelonitrile
LEPIDOPTERA		
Papilionidae	Carboxylic acid	Isobutyric acid
	Sesquiterpene hydrocarbon	Germacrene A
Notodontidae	Carboxylic acid	Formic acid
Arctiidae	Quartenary ammonium ester	Acetylcholine
Zygaenidae	Nitrile	Hydrogen cyanide
Cossidae	Aliphatic alcohol	Tetradecatrien-1-ol
HYMENOPTERA		
Vespidae	Biogenic amine	Norepinephrine
Multillidae	Aliphatic ketone	4-methyl-3-heptanone
Apidae	Aliphatic ketone	2-heptanone
Formicidae	Hydrocarbon	Pentadecane
	Aliphatic alcohol	3-octanol
	Aliphatic ketone	2-tridecanone
	Monoterpene lactone	Iridomyrmecin
	Furanosesquiterpene	Dendrolasin
	Alkyl sulfide	Dimethyldisulfide
	Alkaloid	2,6-dimethyl-3-ethylpyrazine
	Carboxylic acid	β-hydroxydecanoic acid
	Alkaloid	2-methyl-6-undecylpiperidine

and Schwinger 1980; Dettner 1985), and waterproofing agents, for cocoon silk (Latter 1897). Although venoms from stings and fangs are often used for both predation and defense (See Schmidt, this volume), this type of multiple functionality is rare for oozing or squirting glands. However, the silphid beetle *Ablattaria* uses its rectal defensive secretion aggressively when attacking snail prey (Heymons and von Lengerken 1932).

In spite of the many possible functions which these substances can have, an overwhelming body of evidence supports the contention that these compounds primarily serve antipredation roles. For the most part, arthropods release these substances only in direct response to disturbances, frequently aim them toward attackers, and often eject them only at that point on the body being stimulated. For example, millipedes usually discharge their ozopores only at those segments under attack (Blum and

Woodring 1962; Eisner and Eisner 1965; Woodring and Blum 1965; Eisner and Meinwald 1966). Response times can be astonishingly short. Bombardier beetles can eject their secretion just seventy-five milliseconds after being pinched (Dean 1979). Instead of waiting to be attacked, certain walking sticks (Eisner 1965), cockroaches (Maschwitz and Tho 1978), and lubber grasshoppers (Whitman, unpublished) preempt aggression by firing volleys of defensive substances. Bird-sized objects moving toward them can elicit discharge. Much like long-range artillery, *Orthocricus* millipedes, *Archiblatta* roaches, spitting reduviids, and *Schizura* caterpillars can accurately hit targets up to twenty to sixty centimeters away (Detwiler 1922; Edwards 1961, 1962; Woodring and Blum 1965; Maschwitz and Tho 1978; Weatherston et al. 1979). Other arthropods dab or smear defensive exudates directly onto their adversaries (figure 46) (Kennett 1948; Juberthie 1961a; Eisner and Meinwald 1965; Youdeowei and Calam 1969; Eisner et al 1971, 1974; Tschinkel 1975b; Jefson et al. 1983). For example, certain Hemiptera collect droplets of defensive secretion with their legs and apply them directly to their attackers (Remold 1962, 1963).

Not only are defensive substances judiciously conserved until needed, but when molestation ceases, they are sometimes withdrawn to be used again (Garb 1915; Prop 1960; Pasteels et al. 1984; Cornell et al. 1987). When attacked, larvae of willow-feeding chrysomelid beetles secrete droplets of odorous salicylaldehyde, but quickly resorb the secretion after the danger passes (figures 47, 48) (Wallace and Blum 1969; Pasteels et al. 1984). In lubber grasshoppers, most of the metathoracic secretion may be expelled during the first discharge. However, the insect can continue frothing for some time by passing air through the mass of ejected secretion that adheres to the metathoracic spiracles. Additional frothing and the continued production of the hissing noise that accompanies secretion ejection is ensured, because a certain amount of exudate is pulled back into the body through the spiracles with each postdischarge abdominal extension (Whitman et al., unpublished).

The antipredatory role for many of these exudates is further suggested by the fact that some of them appear to be highly adapted for specific relevant habitats or enemies. For example, most adephagous beetles secrete volatile hydrocarbons, esters, and quinones from paired abdominal pygidial glands. Although the aquatic Dytiscidae also possess pygidial glands, they have evolved additional prothoracic glands that produce a variety of steriods highly toxic to the fish and amphibian predators which share their habitat (Forsyth 1968; Schildknecht 1970; Miller and Mumma 1976; Dettner 1985).

Some terrestrial arthropods also appear to have adapted their secretions to function in specific defensive contexts. When attacked, *Pachycondyla harpax* ants fill their nest tunnels with an insecticidal froth and lay down strands of sticky exudate (Overal 1987). These defenses are presumably effective in preventing the movement of small predators through the narrow nest galleries.

The defensive nature of these exocrine and nonexocrine compounds is also supported by reports of their irritating qualities or toxicities (Eisner et al. 1961; Remold 1963; Eisner 1965, 1970; Eisner and Meinwald 1966; Blum and Hermann 1978b; Prestwich 1979; Blum 1981; Alexander 1984; Whelan and Weir 1987). Defensive exudates frequently contain highly volatile, low-molecular weight compounds which are extremely odorous (i.e., E-2-hexenal, salicylaldehyde) or very reactive (i.e., 1,4-benzoquinone) (Blum 1981). Other arthropods produce vesicating or irritating compounds that are powerful cytotoxins (e.g., formic acid, hydrogen cyanide) or are capable of producing painful lesions (e.g., cantharidin, pederin) (Whelan and Weir 1987). Some compounds may be targeted against specific enzymes (Howard and Mueller 1987). Nonexocrine defensive compounds, such as the alkaloids found in lady beetles and the cardenolides found in fireflies, produce pronounced emesis in vertebrate predators.

The strongest evidence that these substances are indeed defensive is that prey possessing them are rejected by predators (Marshall 1902; Swynnerton 1915, 1919; Jones, 1932, 1934; Carpenter 1941-42; Eisner and Meinwald 1966; Eisner 1970; Duffey 1977; Blum 1981; Wiklund and Järvi 1982; Rothschild 1985). A single encounter with a chemically defended insect is often sufficient to establish long-term aversion to subsequent attack (Brower 1969; Boyden 1976; Whitman et al., unpublished). As long as their defensive stores last, many arthropods continue to repel predators, but when exudates are depleted, they can quickly fall prey (Eisner 1958a, 1960, 1965; Blum and Woodring 1962; Eisner, Swithenbank, and Meinwald 1963; Blum and Sannasi 1974; Jones et al. 1976; Chow and Lin 1986; Damman 1986). Predators that ignore the warnings of chemically defended arthropods can suffer anosmia or be temporarily blinded, sickened, paralyzed, or even killed (figures 49-52) (Burtt 1947; Kennett 1948; Eisner 1958a, 1965, 1970; Remold 1963; Brower 1969). Short-term incapacitation renders predators more susceptible to attack from their own predators. At the least, the loss of gut contents during toxin-induced emesis and the temporary inability to forage reduce fitness.

HOW ALLOMONES FUNCTION TO DETER PREDATION

There is considerable uncertainty regarding the modes of action of arthropod allomones. This confusion partially reflects the great structural diversity of allomones possessed by this heterogeneous group. As this chapter has emphasized, arthropods produce a tremendous variety of defensive compounds that differ in their solubility, volatility and toxicity, in the manner in which they are applied, and in their qualitative and quantitative composition. As a consequence, only broad generalizations can be made regarding their modes of action.

Part of the confusion surrounding the modi operandi of arthropod defensive allomones arises from the great diversity of predators which attack arthropods. Included are fish, amphibians, reptiles, birds, mammals, and other arthropods. The various predatory groups exhibit different morphologies, physiologies, ecologies, and capacities to learn, and most importantly, use different sensory systems to find, subdue, and differentiate among prey. For example, an ant, a lizard, and a bird may all reject a given prey, but for very different reasons.

Further confounding our understanding of allomonal relationships is the complexity inherent in predator-prey interactions. A potential allomone might stimulate one or more of four possible predator sensory systems: (1) olfaction, (2) gustation, (3) the "general chemical sense," or (4) a variety of internal and external sense organs may be stimulated when the compound disables or makes the predator ill. The "general chemical sense" refers to those sensory systems, such as the trigeminal senses in vertebrates (Eisner and Meinwald 1966; Moncrieff 1967; Engen 1982; Wright 1982), which do not convey taste or smell qualities, but rather burning, itching, irritation, or pain (Keele and Armstrong 1964). Compounds capable of stimulating the general chemical sense include highly caustic and reactive substances such as acids and bases.

A variety of additional predator features, such as experience, physiological state, and innate (genetically determined) tendencies, can alter the way in which defensive allomones function. Prey attributes, such as the possession of acoustic, tactile, or visual aposematic features, or other defenses (i.e., powerful bites or kicks, hard exoskeletons, or defensive behaviors such as thanatosis or startle displays), also influence predator-prey allomonal relations (Pearson 1989).

In spite of the multitude of factors which impinge upon the predator-prey interface, it is generally accepted that defensive allomones function by harming or producing unpleasant sensations in predators.

How this occurs is debated. However, various studies suggest that naive predators can be repelled by odor, taste, or allomone-produced pain or disability, whereas experienced predators (ones that have had a previous contact with a given prey species) can also be repelled by odor, taste, or allomone-produced pain, but for different reasons than those influencing naive predators.

Contrary to what some authors have implied, it appears that certain predators can be repelled by prey odors the very first time they come into contact with a given prey (Eisner and Meinwald 1966; Eisner 1970; Blum et al. 1973; Kugler 1979; Howard et al. 1983; Jefson et al. 1983; Cane 1986). In fact, some natural volatile substances are so toxic that their vapors alone can kill or incapacitate (Davenport et al. 1952; Eisner and Eisner 1965; Eisner, Alsop and Eisner 1967; Read et al. 1970).

It is also apparent that naive predators can reject prey soley on the basis of taste (Blum and Sannasi 1974; Boyden 1976; Wiklund and Järvi 1982; Brower and Fink 1985). For example, naive birds often readily attack young, toxic *Romalea guttata* grasshoppers, but after biting the acridids, the birds will often reject them. Rejection in this case is most likely based on taste, since the young grasshoppers do not develop their odorous tracheal secretion until the third instar (Whitman et al., unpublished).

Evidence also suggests that rejection can be based on stimulation of the general chemical senses. Vertebrate predators which are sprayed in the eyes, nose, or other sensitive areas will sometimes drop their prey, tear, blink, or rub their mouths and noses through dirt, and show additional symptoms of pain and distress (Eisner and Meinwald 1966; Eisner 1970) (figure 52). Certainly, the immediate rejection of stinging prey following envenomization can only be explained by stimulation of pain sensors.

Once a predator has experienced a particular defended prey, a change may occur in the mechanism by which subsequent prey are rejected. Predators can learn through classical Pavlovian conditioning to associate previous neutral odors or tastes with the unpleasant consequence of attacking particular prey (Gustavson 1977). Thus, a prey-produced chemical signal which has a neutral quality for a naive predator may become highly repellent following an unpleasant experience (Eisner and Grant 1981; Brower 1984; Camazine 1985). Likewise, a tasteless, odorless substance which causes illness or distress in predators may facilitate aversion conditioning toward the prey's visual, tactile, or acoustic properties (Brower 1984).

The fact that predators can be conditioned against certain chemical signals opens the way for chemical-based Batesian mimicry (Eisner and Grant 1981). For example, honey bees, which are shunned by most predators because of their painful stings, liberate odorous isopentyl acetate when disturbed. The rove beetle *Creophilus maxillosus* not only looks and sounds like a wasp or bee when it flies, but, like honey bees, produces isopentyl acetate when attacked (Jefson et al. 1983).

Allomones may also function to reinforce Mullerian mimetic complexes. Rothschild (1961b) noted that numerous beetles, bugs, ants, butterflies, and moths which sting or contain potent internal toxins also emit odorous pyrazines. She suggested that these alkaloids function as aposematic signals, and that their occurrence in disparate groups represents convergent Mullerian mimicry (Rothschild et al. 1984; Rothschild 1985, 1986; Kaye et al. 1989).

Although it is generally accepted that arthropod defensive allomones function primarily by producing unpleasant sensations in predators, other mechanisms for their deterrent activities have been proposed. For example, some arthropods may escape predation through aggressive chemical mimicry. Many inquilines living in ant and termite colonies are believed to release substances which mimic those produced by their hosts (Kistner and Blum 1971; Whitman 1988). Although these guests feed at the colony's expense, they are tolerated because the hosts are unable to differentiate between them and colony members. Chemical mimicry may also function to protect the social wasp *Parachartergus aztecus,* which nests in ant-acacias. The *Pseudomyrmex* ants that guard these trees normally attack all insect invaders. However, they do not assail the *P. aztecus,* perhaps because the cuticular hydrocarbons of the wasp are almost identical to those of the ant (Espelie and Hermann 1988).

It has also been suggested that arthropods may produce cryptic odors in much the same way that they assume cryptic appearances. Thus, by smelling and tasting like its host plant, a prey would presumably escape attack by olfactorily oriented predators (Whitman 1988).

Other prey species may elude predators by disrupting or overstimulating predator chemical senses. Some arthropods exude incredibly complex allomonal blends, containing forty to fifty components (Duffey 1977; Jones et al. 1988). It is possible that these heterogenous secretions overwhelm the sensory capabilities of olfactorily oriented predators, allowing prey to escape under a "chemical smoke screen" (Blum and Brand 1972; Blum 1974, 1981; Duffey et al. 1977).

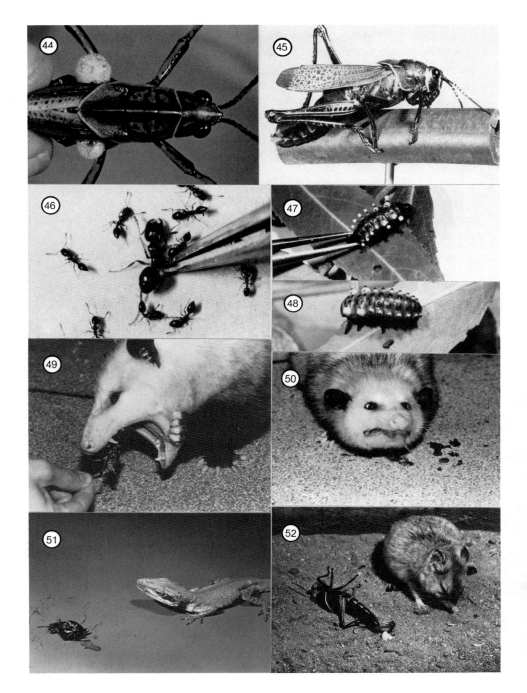

Plate 12.6

44 *Romalea guttata* tracheal defensive secretion. **45** Male *T. eques* attempting to copulate with a rubber tube to which female tracheal defensive secretion has been applied. **46** *Monomorium minimum* ants responding to the presence of a larger *Solenopsis invicta* ant by dabbing extruded droplets of venon. **47** Larva of the chrysomelid beetle *Chrysomela scripta* exuding salicylaldehyde-containing defensive secretions from thoracic and abdominal defensive glands in response to disturbance. **48** Same larva fifteen seconds after forceps have been removed; secretion has been drawn back into the glands. **49** A naive opossum, *Didelphis marsupialis,* eagerly attacking a chemically defended *Romalea guttata* grasshopper. **50** Same opposum regurgitating after consuming several *R. guttata.* **51** An *Anolis carolinensis* lizard which has just regurgitated a toxic *R. guttata* grasshopper. **52** A grasshopper mouse, *Onychomys torridus,* rubbing its nose and paws through dirt after being sprayed with *Taeniopoda eques* defensive secretion.

Finally, some semiaquatic insects secrete substances which may not harm or repel predators, but nevertheless aid in escape. Certain staphylinid beetles (Schildknecht et al. 1976) (figures 36, 37) and veliid ripple bugs (Andersen 1976) expell surface-active substances which lower the water tension and result in the rapid propulsion of the insect across the water.

It is clear that a great deal remains to be learned about the modes of action of arthropod defensive compounds. Certainly, the cataloguing of new allomones and allomonal sources will continue at a brisk pace, but the greatest future opportunities and advances will perhaps lie in understanding how defensive allomones function.

We thank K. Smith-Whitman for reviewing numerous editions of this chapter. The following kindly supplied photographs: J. Aldrich (figures 7, 8); E. Greene (figure 25); D. Howard (figures 14, 18, 19, 21, 46); L. Orsak (figure 22); and T. Wiewandt (figure 27). Figure 45 courtesy of Blackwell Scientific Publications.

References

Abushama, F.T. 1972. The repugnatorial gland of the grasshopper *Poecilocerus hieroglyphicus* (Klug). *J. Entomol.* (A) 47:95–100.

Aldrich, J.R. 1988. Chemical ecology of the Heteroptera. *Annu. Rev. Entomol.* 33:211–238.

Aldrich, J.R., Blum, M.S., Lloyd, H.A., Fales, H.M. 1978. Pentatomid natural products: chemistry and morphology of the III–IV dorsal abdominal glands of adults. *J. Chem. Ecol.* 4:161–172.

Aldrich, J.R., Carrol, S.P., Lusby, W.R., Thompson, M.J., Kochansky, J.P., Waters, R.M. 1990. Sapindaceae, cyanolipidis, and bugs. *J. Chem. Ecol.* 16: 199-210.

Aldrich, J.R., Kochansky, J.P., Lusby, W.R., Sexton, J.D. 1984. Semiochemicals from a predaceous stink bug, *Podisus maculiventris* (Hemiptera: Pentatomidae). *J. Wash. Acad. Sci.* 74:39–46.

Alexander, J.O. 1984. *Arthropods and Human Skin.* Springer, Berlin. 422 pp.

Alsop, D.W. 1970. *Defensive glands of arthropods: comparative morphology of selected types.* Ph.D. dissertation. Cornell Univ., Ithaca, New York. 378 pp.

Andersen, N.M. 1976. A comparative study of locomotion on the water surface in semiaquatic bugs (Insecta, Hemiptera, Gerromorpha). *Vidensk. Meddr dansk naturh. Foren.* 139:337–396.

Aneshansley, D.J., Eisner, T., Widom, J.M., Widom, B. 1969. Biochemistry at 100° C: explosive secretory discharge of bombardier beetles (*Brachinus*). *Science* 165:61–63.

Araújo, J. 1973. Morphologie et histologie de la glande pygidiale défensive de *Bledius spectabilis* Kr. (Staphylinidae, Oxytelinae). *C. R. Acad. Sci. Paris* 276D:2713–2716.

————. **1978.** Anatomie comparée des systèmes glandulaires de défense chimique des Staphylinidae. *Arch. Biol.* 89:217–250.

Araújo, J., Pasteeles, J.M. 1987. Ultrastructure de la glande défensive d'*Eusphalerum minutum* Kraatz (Coleoptera, Staphylinidae). *Arch. Biol.* (Bruxelles) 98:15–34.

Balestrazzi, E., Dazzini-Valcurone, M.L. 1985. Morphological and chemical studies on the pygidial defence glands of some Carabidae (Coleoptera). *Naturwissenschaften* 72:482–484.

Barth, R. 1958. Über die abdominalen Seitendrüsen von *Discodon cyanomelas* (Perty) (Coleoptera, Cantharidae, Silini). *Studia Entomol. N. S.* 1:487–495.

Beard, R.L. 1963. Insect toxins and venoms. *Annu. Rev. Entomol.* 8:1–18.

Beier, M. 1968. Phasmida. In *Handbuch der Zoologie,* M. Beier, ed., 4(2):1–56. De Gruyter, Berlin. 56 pp.

Benfield, E.F. 1974. Autohemorrhage in two stoneflies (Plecoptera) and its effectiveness as a defense mechanism. *Ann. Entomol. Soc. Am.* 67:739–742.

Benson, R.B. 1950. An introduction to the natural history of British sawflies (Hymenoptera Symphyta). *Trans. Soc. Brit. Entomol.* 10:45-142.

Bertkau, P. 1882. Über den Stinkapparat von *Lacon murinus* L. *Arch. Naturgesch.* 48:371-373.

Billen, J., Joyce, L., Leuthold, R.H. 1989. Fine structure of the labial glands in *Macrotermes bellicosus* (Isoptera, Termitidae) *Acta Zool.* 70:37-45.

Bishop, S.C. 1950. The life of a harvestman. *Nature Mag.* 276:264-267.

Bisset, G.W., Frazer, J.F.D., Rothschild, M., Schachter, M. 1960. A pharmacologically active choline ester and other substances in the Garden Tiger moth *Arctia caja* (L.). *Proc. Roy. Soc. Lond.* B 255-262.

Blum, M.S. 1964. Insect defensive secretions. Hex-2-enal-1 in *Pelmatosilpha coriacea* (Blattaria) and its repellent value under natural conditions. *Ann. Entomol. Soc. Am.* 57:600-602.

_____. **1974.** Deciphering the communicative Rosetta stone. *Bull. Entomol. Soc. Am.* 20: 30-35.

_____. **1981.** *Chemical Defenses of Arthropods.* Academic, New York. 562 pp.

Blum, M.S., Brand, J.M. 1972. Social insect pheromones: their chemistry and function. *Am. Zool.* 12:553-576.

Blum, M.S., Edgar, A.L. 1971. 4-Methyl-3-heptanone: identification and role in opilionid exocrine secretions. *Insect Biochem.* 1:181-188.

Blum, M.S., Hermann, H.R. 1978a. Venoms and venom apparatuses of the Formicidae: Myrmeciinae, Ponerinae, Dorylinae, Pseudomyrmecinae, Myrmicinae, and Formicinae. In *Handbuch der experimentallen Pharmakologie,* Vol. 48, Arthropod Venoms, S. Bettini, ed., 801-869. Springer-Verlag, Berlin. 977 pp.

_____. **1978b.** Venoms and venom apparatuses of the Formicidae: Dolichoderinae and Aneuretinae. In *Handbuch der experimentallen Pharmakologie,* Vol. 48, Arthropod Venoms, S. Bettini, ed., 871-894. Springer-Verlag, Berlin. 977 pp.

Blum, M.S., Sannasi, A. 1974. Reflex bleeding in the lampyrid *Photinus pyralis:* defensive function. *J. Insect Physiol.* 20:451-460.

Blum, M.S., Woodring, J.P. 1962. Secretion of benzaldehyde and hydrogen cyanide by the millipede *Pachydesmus crassicutis* (Wood). *Science* 138:512-514.

Blum, M.S., Brand, J.M., Wallace, J.B., Fales, H.M. 1972. Chemical characterization of the defensive secretion of a chrysomelid larva. *Life Sci.* 11:525-531.

Blum, M.S., Wallace, J.B., Fales, H.M. 1973. Skatole and tridecene: identification and possible role in a chrysopid secretion. *Insect Biochem.* 3:353-357.

Blum, M.S., Jones, T.H., Howard, D.F., Overal, W.L. 1982. Biochemistry of termite defenses: *Coptotermes, Rhinotermes* and *Cornitermes* species. *Comp. Biochem. Physiol.* 71B:731-733.

Blunck, H. 1912. Die Schreckdrüsen des *Dytiscus* und ihr Sekret. *Teil. Z. Wiss. Zool.* 100:493–508.

Boevé, J., Pasteels, J.M. 1985. Modes of defense in nematine sawfly larvae. Efficiency against ants and birds. *J. Chem. Ecol.* 11:1019–1036.

Börner, C. 1904. Beiträge zur Morphologie der Arthropoden. I. Ein Beitrag zur Kenntnis der Pedipalpen. *Zoologica* 42:1–174.

Boyden, T.C. 1976. Butterfly palatability and mimicry: Experiments with *Ameiva* lizards. *Evolution* 30:73–81.

Bradshaw, J.W.S., Howse, P.E. 1984. Sociochemicals of Ants. In *Chemical Ecology of Insects,* W.J. Bell, R.T. Cardé, eds., 429–473. Sinauer, Sunderland, Mass. 524 pp.

Brand, J.M., Blum, M.S., False, H.M., Pasteels, J.M. 1973. The chemistry of the defensive secretion of the beetle, *Drusilla canaliculata. J. Insect Physiol.* 19:369–382.

Brossut, R., Sreng, L. 1980. Ultrastructure comparée des glandes exocrines abdominales des Blattaria (Dictyoptera). *Int. J. Insect Morphol. Embryol.* 9:199–213.

Brower, L.P. 1969. Ecological Chemistry. *Sci. Am.* 220(2):22–29.

——————. **1984.** Chemical defence in Butterflies. In *The Biology of Butterflies,* R.I. Vane-Wright, P.R. Ackery, eds., 109–134. Academic, New York. 456 pp.

Brower, L.P., Fink, L.S. 1985. A natural toxic defense system: cardenolides in butterflies versus birds. *Ann. N.Y. Acad. Sci.* 443:171–188.

Brown, W.V., Jones, A.J., Lacey, M.L., Moore, B.P. 1985. The chemistry of buprestins A and B. Bitter principles of jewel beetles (Coleoptera: Buprestidae). *Aust. J. Chem.* 38:197–206.

Brown, W.V., Lacey, M.J., Moore, B.P. 1988. Dihydromatricariate-based triglycerides, glyceride ethers, and waxes in the Australian soldier beetle, *Chauliognathus lugubris* (Coleoptera: Cantharidae). *J. Chem. Ecol.* 14:411–423.

Burtt, E. 1947. Exudate from millipedes with particular reference to its injurious effects. *Trop. Dis. Bull.* 44:7–12.

Buschinger, A., Maschwitz, U. 1984. Defensive behavior and defensive mechanisms in ants. In *Defensive Mechanisms in Social Insects,* H.R. Hermann, ed., 95–150. Praeger, New York. 259 pp.

Calam, D.H., Scott, G.C. 1969. The scent gland complex of the adult cotton stainer bug, *Dysdercus intermedius. J. Insect Physiol.* 15:1695–1702.

Camazine, S. 1985. Olfactory aposematism: association of food toxicity with naturally occurring odor. J. Chem. Ecol. 11:1289–1295.

Cane, J.H. 1986. Predator deterrence by mandibular gland secretions of bees (Hymenoptera: Apoidea). *J. Chem. Ecol.* 12:1295–1309.

Cane, J.H., Michener, C.D. 1983. Chemistry and function of mandibular gland products of bees of the genus *Exoneura* (Hymenoptera, Anthophoridae). *J. Chem. Ecol.* 9:1525–1531.

Capinera, J.L., Gardener, D.R., Stermitz, F.R. 1985. Cantharidin levels in blister beetles (Coleoptera: Meloidae) associated with alfalfa in Colorado. *J. Econ. Entomol.* 78:1052–1055.

Carayon, J. 1971. Notes et documents sur l'appareil odorant méthathoracique des Hémiptères. *Ann. Soc. Entomol. Fr. N. S.* 7:737–770.

Carpenter, G.D.H. 1938. Audible emission of defensive froth by insects. *Proc. Zool. Soc. Lond.* A 108:243–252.

_____. 1941-42. Observations and experiments in Africa by the late C.F.M. Swynnerton on wild birds eating butterflies and the preference shown. *Proc. Linn. Soc. Lond.* 154:10–46.

Carrel, J.E., Eisner, T. 1974. Cantharidin: potent feeding deterrent to insects. *Science* 183:755–757.

Chow, Y.S., Lin, Y.M. 1986. Actinidine, a defensive secretion of stick insect, *Megacrania alpheus* Westwood (Orthoptera: Phasmatidae) *J. Entomol. Sci.* 21:97–101.

Coaton, W.G. 1971. Five new termite genera from South West Africa (Isoptera: Termitidae). *Cimbebasia* (A) 2:1–34.

Cornell, J.C., Stamp, N.E., Bowers, M.D. 1987. Developmental change in aggregation, defense and escape behavior of buckmoth caterpillars, *Hemileuca lucina* (Saturniidae). *Behav. Ecol. Sociobiol.* 20:383–388.

Crossley, A.C., Waterhouse, D.F. 1969. The ultrastructure of the osmeterium and the nature of its secretion in *Papilio* larvae (Lepidoptera). *Tissue and Cell* 1:525–554.

Curasson, G. 1934. Sur la toxicité de la sécrétion buccale des Sauterelles. *Bull. Acad. Vet. France* 7:377–382.

Daloze, D., Braekman, J.C., Pasteels, J.M. 1986. A toxic dipeptide from the defense glands of the Colorado beetle. *Science* 233:221–223.

Damman, H. 1986. The osmeterial glands of the swallowtail butterfly *Eurytides marcellus* as a defense against natural enemies. *Ecol. Entomol.* 11:261–265..

Darlington, P.J. Jr. 1938. Experiments on mimicry in Cuba, with suggestions for future study. *Trans. Roy. Entomol. Soc. Lond.* 87:681–695.

Davenport, D., Wootton, D.M., Cushing, J.E. 1952. The biology of the Sierra luminous millipede, *Luminodesmus sequoiae* Loomis and Davenport. *Biol. Bull.* 102:100–110.

Davis, R.H., Nahrstedt, A. 1984. Cyanogenesis in insects. In *Comprehensive Insect Physiology, Biochemistry and Pharmacology,* Vol 11, G.A. Kerkut, L.I. Gilbert eds., 635–654. Pergamon, Oxford.

Dazzini-Valcurone, M., Pavan, M. 1980. Glandole pigidiali e secrezioni difensive dei Carabidae (Insecta Coleoptera). *Pubbl. Ist. Entomol. Univ. Pavia* 1980 12:1–36.

Dean, J. 1979. Defensive reaction time of bombardier beetles: an investigation of the speed of a chemical defense. *J. Chem. Ecol.* 5:691–701.

de Jong, M.C.J.M., Bleumink, K. 1977. Investigative studies of the dermatitus caused by the larva of the brown tail moth, *Euproctis chrysorrhoea* L. (Lepidoptera, Lymantridae). IV. Further characterization of skin reactive substances. *Arch. Dermatol. Res.* 259:263–281.

Deligne, J., Quennedey, A., Blum, M.S. 1982. The enemies and defense mechanism of termites. In *Social Insects,* H.R. Hermann, ed., 2:1–67. Academic, New York. 491 pp.

De Lotto, G. 1950. Sulla presents di una ghiandola ripugnatoria in due Ortotteri del genera *Phymateus. Boll. Soc. Ital. Med. Sez. Eritrea.* 10:195–201.

Deroe, C., Pasteels, J.M. 1977. Defensive mechanisms against predation in the Colorado beetle (*Leptinotarsa decemlineata* Say). *Arch. Biol.* 88:289–304.

_____. **1982.** Distribution of adult defense glands in chrysomelids (Coleoptera: Chrysomelidae) and its significance in the evolution of defense mechanisms within the family. *J. Chem. Ecol.* 8:67–82.

Dethier, V.C. 1939. Prothoracic glands of adult Lepidoptera. *J.N.Y. Entomol. Soc.* 47:131–144.

Dettner, K. 1985. Ecological and phylogenetic significance of defensive compounds from pygidial glands of Hydradephaga (Coleoptera). *Proc. Acad. Nat. Sci. Philadelphia* 137:156–171.

_____. **1987.** Chemosystematics and evolution of beetle chemical defenses. *Annu. Rev. Entomol.* 32:17–48.

Dettner, K., Schwinger, G. 1980. Defensive substances from pygidial glands of water beetles. *Biochem. Syst. Ecol.* 8:89–95.

_____. **1982.** Defensive secretions of three Oxytelinae rove beetles (Coleoptera: Staphylinidae). *J. Chem. Ecol.* 8:1411–1420.

_____. **1986.** Volatiles from the defensive secretions of two rove beetle species (Coleoptera: Staphylinidae). *Z. Naturforsch.* 41c:366–368.

Detwiler, J.D. 1922. The ventral prothoracic gland of the red-humped apple caterpillar (*Schizura concinna* Smith & Abbot). *Can. Entomol.* 54:175–191.

Dixon, A.F.G. 1958. The escape responses shown by certain aphids to the presence of the coccinellid *Adalia decempunctata* (L.) *Trans. Roy. Entomol. Soc. Lond.* 110:319–334.

Duffey, S.S. 1977. Arthropod allomones: chemical effronteries and antagonists. In *Proc. XV Int. Congr. Entomol.,* 323–394. Entomological Society of America, College Park, Md. 824 pp.

Duffey, S.S., Blum, M.S. 1977. Phenol and guaiacol: biosynthesis, detoxication, and function in a polydesmid millipede, *Oxidus gracilis. Insect Biochem.* 7:57–65.

Duffey, S.S., Blum, M.S., Fales, H.M., Evans, S.L., Roncadori, R.W., Tiemann, D.L., Nakagawa, Y. 1977. Benzoyl cyanide and mandelonitrile benzoate in the defensive secretions of millipedes. *J. Chem. Ecol.* 3:101–113.

Duffield, R.M., Blum, M.S., Wallace, J.B., Lloyd, H.A., Regnier, F.E. 1977. Chemistry of the defensive secretion of the caddisfly *Pycnopsyche scabripennis* (Trichoptera: Limnephilidae). *J. Chem. Ecol.* 3:649–656.

Duffield, R.M., Olubajo, O., Wheeler, J.W., Shear, W.A. 1981. Alkylphenols in the defensive secretion of the nearctic opilinoid, *Stygnomma spinifera* (Arachnida: Opiliones). *J. Chem. Ecol.* 7:445–452.

Duffield, R.M., Wheeler, J.W., Eickwort, G.C. 1984. Sociochemicals of bees. In *Chemical Ecology of Insects,* W.J. Bell, R.T. Carde, eds., 387–428. Sinauer, Sunderland, Mass. 524 pp.

Dupuis, C. 1948. Données nouvelles sur la morphologie abdominale des Hémiptères Héteroptères et en particulier des Pentatomoidea. *C.R. XIII Int. Cong. Zool.* 471–472.

Edwards, J.S. 1961. The action and composition of the saliva of an assassin bug *Platymeris rhadamanthus* Gaerst (Hemiptera; Reduviidae). *J. Exp. Biol.* 38:61–77.

Edwards, J.S. 1962. Spitting as a defensive mechanism in a predatory reduviid. In *Proc. XI Int. Congr. Entomol.* (1960) 3:259–263.

Edwards, J.S. 1966. Defence by smear: supercooling in the cornicle wax of aphids. *Nature* 211:73–74.

Eisner, H.E., Alsop, D.W., Eisner, T. 1967. Defense mechanisms of arthropods. XX. Quantitative assessment of hydrogen cyanide production in two species of millipedes. *Psyche* 74:107–117.

Eisner, T. 1958a. The protective role of the spray mechanism of the bombardier beetle, *Brachynus ballistarius* lec. *J. Insect Physiol.* 2:215–220.

Eisner, T. 1958b. Spray mechanism of the cockroach *Diploptera punctata. Science* 128:148–149.

Eisner, T. 1960. Defense mechanisms of arthropods. II. The chemical and mechanical weapons of an earwig. *Psyche* 67:62–70.

Eisner, T. 1965. Defensive spray of a phasmid insect. *Science* 148:966–968.

Eisner, T. 1970. Chemical defense against predation in arthropods. In *Chemical Ecology,* E. Sondheimer, J.B. Simeone, eds., 157–217. Academic, New York. 336 pp.

Eisner, T. 1972. Chemical ecology: on arthropods and how they live as chemists. *Verh. Dtsch. Zool. Ges.* 65:123–137.

Eisner, T., Alsop, D., Hicks, K., Meinwald, J. 1978. Defensive secretions of millipedes. In *Arthropod Venoms,* S. Bettini, ed. 41–72, Springer-Verlag, Berlin. 977 pp.

Eisner, T., Alsop, D., Meinwald, J. 1978. Secretions of opilionids, whip scorpions and pseudoscorpions. In *Arthropod Venoms,* S. Bettini, ed. 87–99. Springer-Verlag, Berlin. 977 pp.

Eisner, T., Deyrup, M., Jacobs, R., Meinwald, J. 1986. Necrodols: anti-insectan terpenes from defensive secretion of carrion beetle (*Necrodes surinamensis*). *J. Chem. Ecol.* 12:1407–1415.

Eisner, T., Eisner, H.E. 1965. Mystery of a millipede. *Nat. History* 74:30–37.

Eisner, T., Goetz, M., Aneshansley, D., Ferstandig-Arnold, G., Meinwald, J. 1986. Defensive alkaloid in blood of Mexican bean beetle (*Epilachna varivestis*). *Experienta* 42:204–207.

Eisner, T., Grant, R. 1981. Toxicity, odor aversion, and "olfactory aposematism." *Science* 213:476.

Eisner, T., Hill, D., Goetz, M., Jain, S., Alsop, D., Camazine, S., Meinwald, J. 1981. Antifeedant action of Z-dihydromatricaria acid from soldier beetles (*Chauliognathus* spp.). *J. Chem. Ecol.* 7:1149–1158.

Eisner, T., Hurst, J.J., Meinwald, J. 1963. Defense mechanism of arthropods. XI. The structure, function, and phenolic secretions of the glands of a chordeumoid millipede and a carabid beetle. *Psyche* 70:94–116.

Eisner, T., Johnessee, J.S., Carrell, J., Hendry, L.B., Meinwald, J. 1974. Defensive use by an insect of a plant resin. *Science* 184:996–999.

Eisner, T., Jones, T.H., Hicks, K., Silberglied, R.E., Meinwald, J. 1977. Quinones and phenols in the defensive secretions of neotropical opilionids. *J. Chem. Ecol.* 3:321–329.

Eisner, T., Jutro, P., Aneshansley, D.J., Niedhauk, R. 1972. Defense against ants in a caterpillar that feeds on ant-guarded scale insects. *Ann. Entomol. Soc. Am.* 65:987–988.

Eisner, T., Kluge, A.F., Carrel, J.C., Meinwald, J. 1972. Defense mechanisms of arthropods. XXXIV. Formic acid and acyclic ketones in the spray of a caterpillar. *Ann. Entomol. Soc. Am.* 65:765–766.

Eisner, T., Kluge, A.F., Carrel, J.C., Meinwald, J. 1971. Defense of phalangid: liquid repellent administered by leg dabbing. *Science* 173:650–652.

Eisner, T., McHenry, F., Salpeter, M.M. 1964. Defense mechanisms of arthropods. XV. Morphology of the quinone-producing glands of a tenebrionid beetle (*Eleodes longicollis* Lec.). *J. Morph.* 115:355–400.

Eisner, T., Meinwald, J. 1966. Defensive secretions of arthropods. *Science* 153:1341–1350.

Eisner, T., Meinwald, J. 1982. Defensive spray mechanism of a silphid beetle (*Necrodes surinamensis*). *Psyche* 89:357–367.

Eisner, T., Meinwald, J., Monro, A., Ghent, R. 1961. Defence mechanisms of arthropods. I. The composition and function of the spray of the whipscorpion, *Mastigoproctus giganteus* (Lucas) (Arachnida, Pedipalpida). *J. Insect Physiol.* 6:272–298.

Eisner, T., Meinwald, Y.C. 1965. Defensive secretion of a caterpillar (*Papilio*). *Science* 150:1733–1735.

Eisner, T., Swithenbank, C., Meinwald, J. 1963. Defense mechanisms of arthropods. VIII. Secretion of salicylaldehyde by a carabid beetle. *Ann. Entomol. Soc. Am.* 56:37–41.

Eisner, T., van Tassell, E., Carrel, J.E. 1967. Defensive use of a "fecal shield" by a beetle larva. *Science* 158:1471–1473.

Eisner, T., Wiemer, D.F., Haynes, L.W., Meinwald, J. 1978. Lucibufagins: defensive steroids from the fireflies *Photinus ignitus* and *P. marginellus* (Coleoptera: Lampyridae). *Proc. Natl. Acad. Sci.* USA 75:905–908.

Engen, T. 1982. The Perception of Odors. Academic Press, New York. 202 pp.

Espelie, K.E., Hermann, H.R. 1988. Congruent cuticular hydrocarbons: biochemical convergence of a social wasp, an ant, and a host plant. *Biochem. Syst. Ecol.* 16:505–508.

Ewer, D.W. 1957. Notes on acridid anatomy. IV. The anterior abdominal musculature of certain acridids. *J. Entomol. Soc. S. Africa* 20:260–279.

Fales, H.M., Jaouni, T.,M. Schmidt, J.O., Blum, M.S. 1980. Mandibular gland allomones of *Dasymutilla occidentalis* and other mutillid wasps. *J. Chem. Ecol.* 6:895–903.

Farine, J.-P. 1988. The exocrine glands of *Dysdercus cingulatus* F. (Heteroptera: Pyrrhocoridae): morphology and function of adults' glands. *Annls. Soc. Entomol. Fr.* (N. S.) 24:241–256.

Fescemyer, H.W., Mumma, R.O. 1983. Regeneration and biosynthesis of dytiscid defensive agents (Coleoptera: Dytiscidae). *J. Chem Ecol.* 9:1449–1464.

Filshie, B.K., Waterhouse, D.F. 1969. The structure and development of a surface pattern of the cuticle of the green vegetable bug *Nezara viridula. Tissue and Cell* 1:367–385.

Filshie, B.K., Waterhouse, D.F. 1968. The fine structure of the lateral scent glands of the green vegetable bug *Nezara viridula* (Hemiptera, Pentatomidae). *J. Microscopic* 7:231–244.

Fishelson, L. 1960. The biology and behavior of *Poekilocerus bufonius* Klug, with a special reference to the repellent gland. *Eos. Rev. Espan. Entomol.* 36:41–62.

Forsyth, D.J. 1968. The structure of the defence glands in the Dytiscidae, Noteridae, Haliplidae and Gyrinidae (Coleoptera). *Trans. Roy. Entomol. Soc. Lond.* 120:159–182.

Forsyth, D.J. 1970. The structure of the defence glands of the Cicindellidae, Amphizoidae, and Hygrobiidae (Insecta: Coleoptera). *J. Zool. Lond.* 160:51–69.

Forsyth, D.J. 1972. The structure of the pygidial defence glands of Carabidae (Coleoptera). *Trans. Zool. Soc. Lond.* 32:249–309.

Franzl, S., Naumann, C.M. 1985. Cuticular cavities: storage chambers for cyanoglucoside-containing defensive secretions in larvae of a zygaenid moth. *Tissue and Cell* 17:267–278.

Frazer, J.F.D. 1965. The cause of urtication produced by larval hairs of *Arctia caja* (L.) (Lepidoptera: Arctiidae). *Proc. Roy. Entomol. Soc. Lond.* 40:96–100.

Freeman, M.A. 1968. Pharmacological properties of the regurgitated crop fluid of the African migratory locust, *Locusta migratoria* L. *Comp. Biochem. Physiol.* 26:1041–1049.

Fuller, G.A., Plowright, R.C. 1986. Nest defense by honey-daubing in the bumblebee *Bombus griseocollis* De Geer (Hymenoptera: Apidae). *Can. Entomol.* 118:479–480.

Fung, S.Y., Herrebout, W.M., Verpoorte, R., Fischer, F.C. 1988. Butenolides in small ermine moths, *Yponomeuta* spp. (Lepidoptera: Yponomeutidea), and spindle-tree, *Euonymus europaeus* (Celastraceae). *J. Chem. Ecol.* 14:1099–1111.

Games, D.E., Staddon, B.W. 1973. Composition of scents from the larva of the milkweed bug *Oncopeltus fasciatus. J. Insect Physiol.* 19:1527–1532.

Garb, G. 1915. The eversible glands of a chrysomelid larva, *Melasoma lapponica. J. Entomol. Zool.* 7:88–97.

Gnanasunderam, C., Butcher, C.F., Hutchins, R.F.N. 1981. Chemistry of the defensive secretions of some New Zealand rove beetles (Coleoptera: Staphylinidae). *Insect Biochem.* 11:411–416.

Goetz, M.A., Meinwald, J., Eisner, T. 1981. Lucibufagins. IV. New defensive steroids and a pterin from the firefly *Photinus pyralis* (Coleoptera: Lampyridae). *Experientia* 37:679–680.

Goh, S.H., Chuah, C.H., Tho, Y.P., Prestwich, G.D. 1984. Extreme intraspecific chemical variability in soldier defense secretions of allopatric and sympatric colonies of *Longipeditermes longipes. J. Chem. Ecol.* 10:929–944.

Gough, A.J.E., Hamilton, J.G.C., Games, D.E., Staddon, B.W. 1985. Multichemical defense of plant bug *Hotea gambiae* (Westwood) (Heteroptera: Scutelleridae). Sesquiterpenoids from abdominal gland in larvae. *J. Chem. Ecol.* 11:343–352.

Grangrade, G.A. 1964. The repugnatorial glands of *Necrosia sparaxes* (Phasmidae: Phasmida). *Current Sci.* (India) 23:717–718.

Grassé, P.P. 1937. L'hémaphorrhée, rejet-réflexe de sang et d'air par les acridiens phymatéides. *Séance. Acad. Sci. Paris* 204:65–67.

Gupta, A.P. 1961. A critical review of the studies on the so-called stink or repugnatorial glands of Heteroptera with further comments. *Can. Entomol.* 93:482–486.

Gupta, A.P. 1964. Musculature and mechanism of the nymphal scent-apparatus of *Riptortus linearis* H.S. (Heteroptera: Alydidae) with comments on the number, variation and homology of the abdominal scent glands in other Heteroptera. *Entomol. Soc. Wash.* 66:12–18.

Gurney, A.B. 1947. A new species of *Pristoceuthophilus* from Oregon, and remarks on certain special glands of Othoptera (Gryllacrididae; Rhaphidophorinae). *J. Wash. Acad. Sci.* 37:430–435.

Gustavson, C.R. 1977. Comparative and field aspects of learned food aversions. In *Learning Mechanisms in Food Selection,* M. Barker, M.R. Best, M. Domjan, eds., 23–44. Baylor Univ. Press, Waco Texas.

Happ, G.M., Eisner, T. 1961. Hemorrhage in a coccinellid beetle and its repellent effect on ants. *Science* 134:329–331.

Happ, G.M., Happ, C.M. 1973. Fine structure of the pygidial glands of *Bledius mandibularis* (Coleoptera: Staphylinidae). *Tissue and Cell* 5:215-231.

Heads, P.A. 1986. Bracken, ants and extrafloral nectaries. IV. Do wood ants (*Formica lugubris*) protect the plant against insect herbivores? *J. Anim. Ecol.* 55:795-809.

Henry, C.S. 1972. Eggs and repagula of *Ululodes* and *Ascaloptynx* (Neuroptera: Ascalaphidae): a comparative study. *Psyche* 79:1-22.

Hermann, H.R., Dirks, T.F. 1974. Sternal glands in polistine wasps: morphology and associated behavior. *J. Ga. Entomol. Soc.* 9:1-8.

Heymons, R.. von Lengerken, H. 1932. Studien über die Lebenserscheinungen der Silphini (Coleopt.). VIII. *Ablattaria laevigata* F. *Z. Morphol. Oekol. Tiere* 24:259-287.

Hingston, R.W.G. 1927. The liquid-squirting habit of oriental grasshoppers. *Trans. Entomol. Soc. Lond.* 75:65-68.

Hinton, H.E. 1951. On a little known protective device of some chrysomelid pupae (Coleoptera). *Proc. Roy. Entomol. Soc. Lond.* (A) 26:67-73.

Hinton, H.E. 1968. Structure and protective devices of the egg of the mosquito *Culex pipiens. J. Insect Physiol.* 14:145-161.

Hinton, H.E. 1981. *Biology of Insect Eggs,* Vol. I. Pergamon, New York.

Hintze, C. 1969. Histologische Untersuchungen am Wehrsekretbeutel von *Cerura vinula* L. und *Notodonta anceps* Goeze (Notodontidae, Lepidoptera). *Z. Morph. Tiere* 64:1-8.

Hollande, A.C. 1911. L'autohémorrhée ou le rejet du sang chez les insectes. *Arch. Anat. Micr.* 13:171-318.

Hölldobler, B. 1971. Sex pheromone in the ant *Xenomyrmex floridanus. J. Insect Physiol.* 17:1497-1499.

Hölldobler, B., Engel-Siegel, H. 1984. On the metapleural gland of ants. *Psyche* 91:201-224.

Hottes, F.C. 1928. Concerning the structure, function, and origin of the cornicles of the family Aphididae. *Proc. Biol. Soc. Wash.* 41:71-84.

Howard, D.F., Blum, M.S., Fales, H.M. 1983. Defense in thrips: forbidding fruitiness of a lactone. *Science* 220:335-336.

Howard, D.F., Blum, M.S., Jones, T.H., Phillips, D.W. 1982. Defensive adaptations of eggs and adults of *Gastrophysa cyanea* (Coleoptera: Chrysomelidae). *J. Chem. Ecol.* 8:453-462.

Howard, D.F., Blum, M.S., Jones, T.H., Tomalski, M.D. 1982. Behavioral responses to an alkylpyrazine from the mandibular gland of the ant *Wasmannia auropunctata. Insectes Sociaux* 29:369-374.

Howard, D.F., Phillips, D.W., Jones, T.H., Blum, M.S. 1982. Anthraquinones and anthrones: occurrence and defensive function in a chrysomelid beetle. *Naturwissenschaften* 69:91-92.

Howard, R.W., Mueller, D.D. 1987. Defensive chemistry of the flour beetle *Tribolium brevicornis* (LeC.): Presence of known and potential prostaglandin synthetase inhibitors. *J. Chem. Ecol.* 13:1707–1723.

Howse, P.E. 1984. Sociochemicals of termites. In *Chemical Ecology of Insects,* W.J. Bell, R.T. Cardé, eds., 475–519. Sinauer, Sunderland, Mass. 524 pp.

Howse, P.E., Baker, R., Evans, D.A. 1977. Multifunctional secretions in ants. In *Proc. VIIIth Int. Congr.* 44–45. IUSSI, Wageningen.

Jannone, G. 1939. Osservazioni sulla presenza, struttura e funzione d'una vescicola ghiandolare confinata nel protorace delle specie mediterrane del gen. *Acrotylus* Fieb., con particolare riguardo all' *A. insubricus* (Scop.) (Orthoptera: Acridiodea). *Boll. Lab. Zool., Portici* 31:41–62.

Jeanne, R.L., Downing, H.A., Post, D.C. 1983. Morphology and function of sternal glands in polistine wasps (Hymenoptera, Vespidae). *Zoomorphology* 103:149–164.

Jefson, M., Meinwald, J., Nowicki, S., Hicks, K., Eisner, T. 1983. Chemical defense of a rove beetle (*Creophilus maxillosus*). *J. Chem. Ecol.* 9:159–180.

Jenkins, M.F. 1957. The morphology and anatomy of the pygidial glands of *Dianous coerulescens* Gyllenhal (Coleoptera: Staphylinidae). *Proc. Roy. Entomol. Soc. Lond. (A) 32:159–167.*

Jessen, K., Maschwitz, U., Hahn, M. 1979. Neue Abdominal-drüsen bei Ameisen. II. Ponerini. *Zoomorphologie* 94:49–66.

Jones, C.G., Hess, T.A., Whitman, D.W., Silk, P.J., Blum, M.S. 1986. Idiosyncratic variation in chemical defenses among individual generalist grasshoppers. *J. Chem. Ecol.* 12:749–761.

Jones, C.G., Hess, T.A., Whitman, D.W., Silk, P.J., Blum, M.S. 1987. Effects of diet breadth on autogenous chemical defense of a generalist grasshopper. *J. Chem Ecol.* 13:283–297.

Jones, C.G., Whitman, D.W., Silk, P.J., Blum, M.S. 1988. Diet breadth and insect chemical defenses: A generalist grasshopper and general hypothesis. In *Chemical Mediation of Coevolution,* K. Spencer ed., 477–512. Academic Press, New York.

Jones, F.M. 1932. Insect coloration and the relative acceptability of insects to birds. *Trans. Roy. Entomol. Soc. Lond.* 80:345–385.

Jones, F.M. 1934. Further experiments on coloration and relative acceptability of insects to birds. *Trans. Roy. Entomol. Soc. Lond.* 82:443–453.

Jones, T.H., Conner, W.E., Meinwald, J., Eisner, H.E., Eisner, T. 1976. Benzoyl cyanide and mandelonitrile in the cyanogenetic secretion of a centipede. *J. Chem. Ecol.* 2:421–429.

Jonsson, S., Bergstrom, G., Lanne, B.S., Stensdotter, U. 1988. Defensive odor emission from larvae of two sawfly species, *Pristiphora erichsonii* and *P. wesmaeli. J. Chem. Ecol.* 14:713–721.

Juberthie, C. 1961a. Structure des glandes odorantes et modalitiés d'utilisation de leur sécrétion chez deux opilions cyphophthalmes. *Bull. Soc. Zool. France* 86:106–116.

Juberthie, C. 1961b. Structure et fonction des glandes odorantes chez quelques Opilions (Arachnida). *Verh. deutsche zool. Ges.* 55:533–537.

Kanehisa, K., Murase, M. 1977. Comparative study of the pygidial defensive systems of carabid beetles. *Appl. Entomol. Zool.* 12:225–235.

Kästner, A. 1932. Pedipalpi. In *Handbuch der Zoologie,* W. Kükenthal, T. Krumbach, eds., 3-II-1:1–76. De Gruyter, Berlin. 659 pp.

Kawamoto, F., Kumada, N. 1984. Biology and venoms of Lepidoptera. In *Handbook of Natural Toxins.* 2., A.T. Tu, ed., 291–330. Marcel Dekker, New York. 732 pp.

Kaye, H., MacKintosh, N.J., Rothschild, M., Moore, B.P. 1989. Odour of pyrazine potentiates an association between environmental cues and unpalatable taste. *Anim. Behav.* 37:563–568.

Keele, C.A., Armstrong, D. 1964. *Substances Producing Pain and Itch.* Edward Arnold, London. 399 pp.

Kendall, D.A. 1968. The structure of the defence glands in Alleculidae and Lagriidae (Coleoptera). *Trans. Roy. Entomol. Soc. Lond.* 120:139–156.

Kendall, D.A. 1971. A note on reflex bleeding in the larvae of the beetle *Exochomus quadripustulatus* (L.) (Col.:Coccinellidae). *Entomol. Lond.* 104:223–235.

Kendall, D.A. 1974. The structure of defence glands in some Tenebrionidae and Nilionidae (Coleoptera). *Trans. Roy. Entomol. Soc. Lond.* 125:437–487.

Kennett, C.E. 1948. Defense mechanism exhibited by larvae of *Chrysopa californica* Coq. (Neuroptera: Chrysopidae). *Pan. Pac. Entomol.* 24:209–211.

Kevan, D.K. 1949. Notes on East African bush locusts. *Bull. Entomol. Res.* 40:359–369.

Kistner, D.H., Blum, M.S. 1971. Alarm pheromone of *Lasius* (*Dendrolasius*) *spathepus* (Hymenoptera: Formicidae) and its possible mimicry by two species of *Pella* (Coleoptera: Staphylinidae). *Ann. Entomol. Soc. Am.* 64:589–594.

Kistner, D.H., Pasteels, J.M. 1969. A new tribe, genus, and species of termitophilous Aleocharinae (Coleoptera: Staphylinidae) from South-West Africa with a description of its integumentary glands. *Ann. Entomol. Soc. Am.* 62:1189–1202.

Klemensiewicz, S. 1882. Zur näheren Kenntnis der Hautdrüsen bei den Raupen und bei *Malachius. Verh. Zool.-Bot. Ges. Wien* 32:459–474.

Klinger, R., Maschwitz, U. 1977. The defensive gland of Omaliinae (Coleoptera: Staphylinidae). I. Gross morphology of the gland and identification of the scent of *Eusphalerum longipenne* Erichson. *J. Chem. Ecol.* 3:401–410.

Konček, S.K. 1924. Zur Histologie der Rückendrüse unserer einheimischen Blattiden. *Z. Wiss. Zool.* 122:311–321.

Kugler, C. 1979. Alarm and defense: a function for the pygidial gland of the myrmicine ant, *Pheidole biconstricta. Ann. Entomol. Soc. Am.* 72:532–536.

Kurosa, K., Watanabe, H. 1958. On the toxic substance of *Xanthochroa waterhousei* (Coleoptera: Oedemeridae). *Japan. J. Sanit. Zool.* 9:200-201.

LaMunyon, C.W., Adams, P.A. 1987. Use and effect of an anal defensive secretion in larval Chrysopidae (Neuroptera). *Ann. Entomol. Soc. Am.* 80:804-808.

Lamy, M., Pastureaud, M., Novak, F., Ducombs, G. 1984. Papillons urticants d'Afrique et d'Amérique du Sud. (g. *Anaphae* et g. *Hylesia*). *Bull. Soc. Zool. Fr.* 109:163-177.

Latter, O.H. 1897. The prothoracic gland of *Dicranura vinula* and other notes. *Trans. Lond. Entomol. Soc.* 1897:113-126.

Lawrence, R.F. 1938. The odoriferous glands of some South African harvest spiders. *Trans. Roy. Soc. South Afr.* 25:333-342.

Liang, C. 1956. The dorsal glands and ventral glands of *Periplaneta americana* (L.) (Blattidae: Orthoptera). *Ann. Entomol. Soc. Am.* 49:548-551.

Lindsay, K.L. 1969. Cornicles of the pea aphid, *Acyrthosiphon pisum;* their structure and function. A light and electron microscope study. *Ann. Entomol. Soc. Am.* 62:1015-1021.

Linsley, E.G. 1959. Ecology of Cerambycidae. *Annu. Rev. Entomol.* 4:99-138.

Lockwood, J.A., Story, R.N. 1985. Bifunctional pheromone in the first instar of the southern green stink bug, *Nezara viridula* (L.) (Hemiptera: Pentatomidae): its characterization and interaction with other stimuli. *Ann. Entomol. Soc. Am.* 78:474-479.

Lockwood, J.A., Story, R.N. 1987. Defensive secretion of the southern green stink bug (Hemiptera: Pentatomidae) as an alarm pheromone. *Ann. Entomol. Soc. Am.* 80:686-691.

Loconti, J.D., Roth, L.M. 1953. Composition of the odorous secretion of *Tribolium castaneum*. *Ann. Entomol. Soc. Am.* 46:281-289.

Löfqvist, J. 1976. Formic acid and saturated hydrocarbons as alarm pheromones for the ant *Formica rufa*. *J. Insect Physiol.* 22:1331-1346.

Lymbery, A., Bailey, W. 1980. Regurgitation as a possible anti-predator defensive mechanism in the grasshopper *Goniaea* sp. (Acrididae: Orthoptera). *J. Aust. Entomol. Soc.* 19:129-130.

Marsh, N., Rothschild, M. 1974. Aposematic and cryptic Lepidoptera tested on the mouse. *J. Zool. Lond.* 174:89-122.

Marsh, N., Rothschild, M., Evans, F. 1984. A new look at butterfly toxins. In *The Biology of Butterflies,* R.I. Vane-Wright, P.R. Ackery, eds., 135-139. Academic, New York. 429 pp.

Marshall, G.A.,. 1902. Five years' observations and experiments (1896-1901) on the bionomics of South African insects, chiefly directed to the investigation of mimicry and warning colours. *Trans. Entomol. Soc. Lond.* 1902:287-584.

Marti, O.G., Rogers, C.E. 1988. Anatomy of the ventral eversible gland of fall armyworm *Spodoptera frugiperda* (Lepidoptera: Noctuidae) larvae. *Ann. Entomol. Soc. Am.* 81:308-317.

Maschwitz, U. 1974. Vergleichende Untersuchungen zur Funktion der Ameisenmetathor-akaldrüse. *Oecologia* 16:303–310.

Maschwitz, U. 1975. Old and new chemical weapons in ants. Symposium IUSSI, Dijon, France, 41–45.

Maschwitz, U.W.J., Kloft, W. 1971. Morphology and function of the venom apparatus of insects —Bees, wasps, ants, and caterpillars. In *Venomous Animals and Their Venoms,* W. Bücherl, E.E. Buckley, eds., III:1–60. Academic, New York. 537 pp.

Maschwitz, U., Lauschke, U., Würmli, M. 1979. Hydrogen cyanide-producing glands in a scolopender, *Asanada* n. sp. (Chilopoda: Scolopendridae). *J. Chem. Ecol.* 5:901–907.

Maschwitz, U., Tho, Y.P. 1978. Phenols as defensive secretion in a Malayan cockroach, *Archiblatta hoeveni* Vollenhoven. J. Chem. Ecol. 4:375–381.

Matsumoto, T., Yanagiya, M., Maeno, S., Yasuda, S. 1968. A revised structure of pederin. *Tetrahedron Letters* 60:6297–6300.

Maxwell, D.E. 1955. The comparative internal larval anatomy of sawflies (Hymenoptera: Symphyta). *Can. Entomol.* 87 (suppl. 1):1–132.

McAlister, W.H. 1960. The spitting habit in the spider *Scytodes intricata* Banks (Family Scytodidae). *Tex. J. Sci.* 12:17–20.

McDunnough, J. 1909. Über den Bau des Darms und seiner Anhänge von *Chrysopa perla* L. *Arch. Naturgesch.* 75:313–360.

McIndoo, N.E. 1916. The reflex "bleeding" of the coccinellid beetle, *Epilachna borealis. Ann. Entomol. Soc. Am.* 9:201–223.

Meinwald, J., Kluge, A.F., Carrel, J.E., Eisner, T. 1971. Acyclid ketones in the defensive secretion of a daddy longlegs (*Leiobunum vittatum*) (Arachnida/Opiliones). *Proc. Nat. Acad. Sci.* USA 68:1467–1468.

Meinwald, J., Koch, K.F., Rogers, J.E. Jr., Eisner, T. 1966. Biosynthesis of arthropod secretions. III. Synthesis of simple *p*-benzoquinones in a beetle (*Eleodes longicollis*). *J. Am. Chem. Soc.* 88:1590–1592.

Meinwald, J., Meinwald, Y.C., Chalmers, A.M., Eisner, T. 1968. Dihydromatricaria acid: acetylenic acid secreted by soldier beetle. *Science* 160:890–892.

Meinwald, J., Wiemer, D.F., Eisner, T. 1979. Lucibufagins. 2. Esters of 12-oxo-2B,5B,11a-trihydroxybufalin, the major defensive steriods of the firefly *Photinus pyralis* (Coleoptera: Lampyridae). *J. Am. Chem. Soc.* 101:3055–3060.

Meinwald, Y.C., Meinwald, J., Eisner, T. 1966. 1,2-dialkyl-4(3H)-quinazolinones in the defensive secretion of a millipede (*Glomeris marginata*). *Science* 154:390–391.

Miller, J.R., Mumma, R.O. 1976. Physiological activity of water beetle defensive agents. I. Toxicity and anesthetic activity of steroids and norsesquiterpenes administered in solution to the minnow *Pimephales promelas* Raf. *J. Chem. Ecol.* 2:115–130.

Moncrieff, R.W. 1967. *The Chemical Senses.* Wiley, London. 760 pp.

Monterosso, B. 1928. Note araneologiche. Su la biologia degli scitodidi e la ghiandola glutinifera di essi. *Arch. Zool. Ital,* 12:63-124.

Moore, B.P. 1967. Hydrogen cyanide in the defensive secretions of larval *Paropsini* (Coleoptera: Chrysomelidae). *J. Aust. Entomol. Soc.* 6:36-38.

Moore, B.P. 1968. Studies on the chemical composition and function of the cephalic gland secretion in Australian termites. *J. Insect Physiol.* 14:33-39.

Moore, B.P. 1969. Biochemical studies in termites. In *Biology of Termites,* K. Krishna, F.M. Weesner, eds., 1:407-432. Academic, New York. 600 pp.

Moore, B.P. 1979. Chemical defense in carabids and its bearing on phylogeny. In *Carabid Beetles: Their Evolution, Natural History and Classification,* T.L. Erwin, G.E. Ball, D.R. Witehead, eds., 193-203. Junk, The Hague.

Moore, B.P., Brown, W.V. 1971. Chemical defence in longhorn beetles of the genera *Stenocentrus* and *Syllitus* (Coleoptera: Cerambycidae). *J. Aust. Entomol. Soc.* 10:230-232.

Moore, B.P., Brown, W.V. 1981. Identification of warning odour components, bitter principles and antifeedants in an aposematic beetle: *Metriorrhynchus rhipidius* (Coleoptera: Lycidae). *Insect Biochem.* 11:493-499.

Moore, B.P., Brown, W.V. 1985. The buprestins: bitter principles of jewel beetles (Coleoptera: Buprestidae). *J. Aust. Entomol. Soc.* 24:81-85.

Moore, B.P., Wallbank, B.E. 1968. Chemical composition of the defensive secretion in carabid beetles and its importance as a taxonomic character. *Proc. Roy. Entomol. Soc. Lond.* (B) 37:62-72.

Moreno, A. 1940. Glandulas odoriferas en *Paradoxomorpha* (Orthoptera: Phasmidae). *Notas Mus. de La Plata* 5:319-323.

Morrow, P.A., Bellas, T.E., Eisner, T. 1976. Eucalyptus oils in the defensive oral discharge of Australian sawfly larvae (Hymenoptera: Pergidae). *Oecologia* 24:193-206.

Muhtasib, H., Evans, D.L. 1987. Linamarin and histamine in the defense of adult *Zygaena filipendulae. J. Chem. Ecol.* 13:133-142.

Nahrstedt, A., Davis, R.H. 1986. (*R*)-Mandelonitrile and prunasin, the sources of hydrogen cyanide in all stages of *Paropsis atomaria* Coleoptera: Chrysomelidae. *Z. Naturforsch.* 41c: 928-934.

Noirot, C.H. 1969. Glands and secretions. In *Biology of Termites,* K. Krishna, F.M. Weesner, eds., 1:89-123. Academic, New York. 600 pp.

Novak, F., Pelissou, V., Lamy, M. 1987. Comparative morphological, anatomical and biochemical studies of the urticating apparatus and urticating hairs of some Lepidoptera: *Thaumetopoea pityocampa* Schiff., *Th. processionea* L. (Lepidoptera, Thaumetopoeidae) and *Hylesia metabus* Cramer (Lepidoptera, Saturniidae). *Comp. Biochem. Physiol.* 88A:141-146.

Nutting, W.L., Blum, M.S., Fales, H.M. 1974. Behavior of the North American termite *Tenuiro-stritermes tenuirostris,* with special reference to the soldier frontal gland secretion, its chemical composition and its use in defense. *Psyche* 81:167–177.

Oettinger, R. 1906. Über die Drüsentaschen am Abdomen von *Periplaneta orientalis* und *Phyllodromia germanica. Zool. Anz.* 30:338–349.

Overal, W.L. 1987. Defensive chemical weaponry in the ant *Pachycondyla harpax* (Formicidae: Ponerinae). *J. Entomol. Sci.* 22:268–269.

Owen, M.D. 1978. Venom replenishment, as indicated by histamine, in honeybee (*Apis mellifera*) venom. *J. Insect. Physiol.* 24:433–437.

Pasteels, J.M., Daloze, D. 1977. Cardiac glycosides in the defensive secretion of chrysomelid beetles: Evidence for their production by the insects. *Science* 197:70–72.

Pasteels, J.M., Deroe, C., Tursch, B., Braekman, J.C., Daloze, D., Hootele, C. 1973. Distribution et activitiés des alcaloides défensifs des Coccinellidae. *J. Insect Physiol.* 19:1771–1784.

Pasteels, J.M., Grégoire, J. -C., Rowell-Rahier, M. 1983. The chemical ecology of defense in arthropods. *Annu. Rev. Entomol.* 28:263–289.

Pasteels, J.M., Rowell-Rahier, M., Braekman, J.C., Daloze, D. 1984. Chemical defences in leaf beetles and their larvae: the ecological, evolutionary and taxonomic significance. *Biochem. Syst. Ecol.* 12:395–406.

Patterson, N.F. 1930. Studies on the Chrysomelidae - part I. The bionomics and morphology of the early stages of *Paraphaedon tumidulus* Germ. (Coleoptera, Phytophaga, Chryso-melidae). *Proc. Zool. Soc. Lond.* 1930:627–676.

Pavan, M. 1975. Sunto delle attuali conoscenze sulla pederina. *Pubbl. Ist. Entomol. Univ. Pavia* 1:1–35.

Pavan, M., Dazzini-Valcurone, M. 1976. Sostanze di difesa dei lepidotteri. *Pubbl. 1st Entomol. Agr. Univ. Pavia* 3:3–23.

Pavan, M., Ronchetti, G. 1955. Studi sulla morfologia esterna e anatomia interna dell'operaia di *Iridomyrmex humilis* Mayr e richerche chimiche e biologiche sulla iridomyrmecina. *Atti Soc. Ital. Sci. Nat. Mus. Civ. Stor. Nat.* 94:379–447.

Payne, O.G.M. 1916. On the life-history and structure of *Telephorus lituratus* Fallen. (Coleoptera). *J. Zool. Res.* 1:4–32.

Pearson, D.L. 1989. What is the adaptive significance of multicomponent defensive repertoires? *Oikos* 54:251–253.

Pesce, H., Delgado, A. 1971. Poisoning from adult moths and caterpillars. In *Venomous Animals and Their Venoms III.* W. Bücherl, E.E. Buckley, eds. 119–156 pp. Academic, New York. 537 pp.

Peschke, K. 1983. Defensive and pheromonal secretion of the tergal gland of *Aleochara curtula.* II. Release and inhibition of male copulatory behavior. *J. Chem. Ecol.* 9:13–31.

Peterson, A. 1948. Larvae of Insects. Part I. *Lepidoptera and Plant Infesting Hymenoptera.* Edwards, Ann Arbor. 315 pp.

Peterson, S.C., Johnson, N.D., LeGuyader, J.L. 1987. Defensive regurgitation of allelochemicals derived from host cyanogenesis by eastern tent caterpillars. *Ecology* 68:1268–1272.

Picarelli, Z.P., Valle, J.R. 1971. Pharmacological studies on caterpillar venoms. In *Venomous Animals and their Venoms. Vol. III.* W. Bücherl, E. E. Buckley, eds., 103–118. Academic, New York. 537 pp.

Pluot-Sigwalt, D. 1983. Les glandes tégumentaires des Coléoptères Scarabaeidae: répartition des glandes sternales et pygidiales dans la famille. *Bull. Soc. Entomol. Fr.* 88:597–602.

Post, D.C., Jeanne, R.L. 1983. Venom: source of a sex pheromone in the social wasp *Polistes fuscatus* (Hymenoptera: Vespidae). *J. Chem. Ecol.* 9:259–266.

Post, D.C., Mohamed, M.A., Coppell, H.C., Jeanne, R.L. 1984. Identification of ant repellent allomone produced by social wasp *Polistes fuscatus* (Hymenoptera: Vespidae). *J. Chem. Ecol.* 10:1799–1807.

Prestwich, G.D. 1979. Chemical defense by termite soldiers. *J. Chem. Ecol.* 5:459–480.

Prestwich, G.D. 1984. Defense mechanisms of termites. *Annu. Rev. Entomol.* 29:201–232.

Prestwich, G.D. 1988. The chemicals of termite societies (Isoptera). *Sociobiology* 14:175–191.

Prop, N. 1960. Protection against birds and parasites in some species of tenthredinid larvae. *Arch. Neerl. Zool.* 13:380–447.

Quennedey, A. 1975. Morphology of exocrine glands producing pheromones and defensive substances in subsocial and social insects. In *Pheromones and Defensive Secretions in Social Insects,* C. Noirot, P.. Howse, G. Le Masne, eds., 1–21. IUSSI, Dijon, France. 248 pp.

Quennedey, A. 1984. Morphology and ultrastructure of termite defense glands. In *Defensive Mechanisms in Social Insects,* H. Hermann, ed., 151–200. Praeger, New York. 259 pp.

Quennedey, A., Deligne, J. 1975. L'arme frontale des soldats de termites. I. Rhinotermitidae. *Insectes Sociaux* 22:243–267.

Quiroz, A.D. 1978. Venoms of Lepidoptera. In *Arthropod Venoms,* S. Bettini, ed., 555–611. Springer-Verlag, Berlin. 977 pp.

Qureshi, S.A., Ahmad, I. 1970. Studies on the functional anatomy and histology of the repellent gland of *Poekilocerus pictus* (F.) (Orthoptera: Pyrgomorphidae). *Proc. Roy. Entomol. Soc. Lond.* (A) 45:149–155.

Read, D.P., Fenny, P.P., Root, R.B. 1970. Habitat selection by the aphid parasite *Diaeretiella rapae* (Hymenoptera: Braconidae) and hyperparasite *Charips brassicae* (Hymenoptera: Cynipidae). *Can. Entomol.* 102:1567–1578.

Remold, H. 1962. Über die biologische Bedeutung der Duftdrüsen bei den Landwanzen (Geocorisae). *Z. Vergl. Physiol.* 45:636–694.

Remold, H. 1963. Scent glands of land-bugs, their physiology and biological function. *Nature* 198:764-768.

Renner, K. 1970. Über die ausstülpbaren Hautblasen der larven von *Gastroidea viridula* De Geer und ihre ökologische Bedeutung (Coleoptera: Chrysomelidae). *Beitr. Entomol.* 20:527-533.

Ritter, F.J., Brüggeman-Rotgans, I.E.M., Verkuil, E., Persoons, C.J. 1975. The trail pheromone of the Pharaoh's ant *Monomorium pharaonis:* Components of the odour trail and their origin. In *Proc. VII Congr. IUSSI, Dijon, France,* 99-103.

Robinson, M.H. 1969. The defensive behavior of some orthopteroid insects from Panama. *Trans. Roy. Entomol. Soc. Lond.* 121:281-303.

Roncadori, R.W., Duffey, S.S., Blum, M.S. 1985. Antifungal activity of defensive secretions of certain millipedes. *Mycologia* 77:185-191.

Roth, L.M. 1945. The odoriferous glands in the Tenebrionidae. *Ann. Entomol. Soc. Am.* 38:77-87.

Roth, L.M., Alsop, D.W. 1978. Toxins of Blattaria. In *Arthropod Venoms, Handbook of Experimental Pharmacology,* S. Bettini, ed., 48:465-487. Springer-Verlag, New York. 977 pp.

Roth, L.M., Stay, B. 1958. The occurrence of *para*-quinones in some arthropods, with emphasis on the quinone-secreting tracheal glands of *Diploptera punctata* (Blattaria). *J. Insect Physiol.* 1:305-318.

Rothschild, M. 1961a. A female of the crimson speckled footman (*Utetheisa pulchella* L.) captured at Ashton Wold. *Proc. Roy. Entomol. Soc. Lond.* 26:35-36.

Rothschild, M. 1961b. Defensive odours and Müllerian mimicry among insects. *Trans. Roy. Entomol. Soc. Lond.* 113:101-121.

Rothschild, M. 1985. British aposematic Lepidoptera. In *The Moths and Butterflies of Great Britain and Ireland,* J.H. Heath, A.M. Emmet, eds., 2:9-62. B.H. and A. Harley, Essex, England.

Rothschild, M. 1986. The red smell of danger. *New Scientist* 111(1524):34-36.

Rothschild, M., Haskell, P.T. 1966. Stridulation of the garden tiger moth, *Arctia caja* L., audible to the human ear. *Proc. Roy. Entomol. Soc. Lond.* (A) 41:167-170.

Rothschild, M., Moore, B.P., Brown, W.V. 1984. Pyrazines as warning odour components in the Monarch butterfly, *Danaus plexippus,* and in moths of the genera *Zygaena* and *Amata* (Lepidoptera). *Biol. J. Linn. Soc.* 23:375-380.

Roubik, D.W., Smith, B.H., Carlson, R.G. 1987. Formic acid in caustic cephalic secretions of stingless bee, *Oxytrigona* (Hymenoptera: Apidae). *J. Chem. Ecol.* 13:1079-1086.

Sands, W.A. 1982. Agonistic behavior of African soldierless Apicotermitinae (Isoptera: Termitidae). *Sociobiology* 7:61-72.

Scheffrahn, R.H., Gaston, L.K., Nutting, W.L., Rust, M.K. 1986. Chemical heterogeneity of soldier defensive secretions in the desert subterranean termite *Amitermes wheeleri. Biochem. Syst. Ecol.* 14:661-664.

Schildknecht, H. 1957. Zur Chemie des Bombardierkäfers. *Angew. Chem.* 69:62.

Schildknecht, H. 1970. The defensive chemistry of land and water beetles. *Angew. Chem.,* Int. Edit. Eng. 9:1–19.

Schildknecht, H., Berger, D., Krauss, D., Connert, J., Gehlhaus, J., Essenbreis, H. 1976. Defense chemistry of *Stenus comma* (Coleoptera: staphylinidae). LXI. *J. Chem. Ecol.* 2:1–11.

Schildknecht, H., Birringer, H., Maschwitz, U. 1967. Testosterone as protective agent of the water beetle *Ilybius.* (Part 26 of Protective Substances of Arthropods). *Angew. Chem.,* Int. Edit. Eng. 6:558–559.

Schildknecht, H., Holoubek, K. 1961. Die Bombardierkäfer und ihre Explosionschemie. V. Mitteilung üeber Insekten-Abwehrstoffe. *Angew. Chem.* 73:1–7.

Schildknecht, H., Maschwitz, U., Wenneis, W.F. 1967. Neue stoffe aus dem wehrsekret der diplopodengattung *Glomeris.* Über Arthropoden-Abwehrstoffe. XXIV. *Naturwissenschaften* 54:196–197.

Schildknecht, H., Maschwitz, U., Winkler, H. 1968. Zur Evolution der Carabiden-Wehrdrüsensekrete. *Naturwissenschaften* 55:112–117.

Schildknecht, H., Siewerdt, R., Maschwitz, U. 1967 Über Arthropodenabwehrstoffe XXIII. Cybisteron, ein neues Arthropoden-Steroid. *Justus Leibigs Annln. Chem.* 703:182–189.

Schildknecht, H., Tacheci, H., Maschwitz, U. 1969. 4-Pregnen-15 α ,20β-diol-3-on im Wehrsekret eines Schwimmkäfers. XXXVIII. Mitteilung uber Arthropoden-Abwehrstoffe. *Naturwissenschaften* 56:37–38.

Schildknecht, H., Weis, K.H. 1962. Über die chemische Abwehr der Aaskäfer. XIV. Mitteilung über Insektenabwehrstoffe. *Z. Naturforsch.* 17B:452–455.

Schmidt, G.H., Krempien, W., Johannes, B. 1987. Studies on the secretion of the prothoracic epidermal gland in *Acrotylus patruelis* (Insecta: Saltatoria; Acrididae). *Zool. Anz.* 219:357–368.

Schmidt, J.O. 1982. Biochemistry of insect venoms. *Annu. Rev. Entomol.* 27:339–368.

Schmidt, J.O. 1986. Chemistry, pharmacology, and chemical ecology of ant venoms. In *Venoms of the Hymenoptera,* T. Piek, ed., 425–508. Academic. London.

Scudder, G.G.E., Moore, L.V., Isman, M.B. 1986. Sequestration of cardenolides in *Oncopeltus fasciatus:* morphological and physiological adaptations. *J. Chem. Ecol.* 12:1171–1187.

Scudder, S.H. 1876. Odoriferous glands in Phasmidae. *Psyche* 1:137–140.

Selander, R.B. 1960. Bionomics, systematics, and phylogeny of *Lytta,* a genus of blister beetles (Coleoptera: Meloidae). *Illinois Biol. Monog.* 28:1–295.

Smith, E.L. 1970. Biosystematics and morphology of Symphyta. II. Biology of gall-making nematine sawflies in the California region. *Ann. Entomol. Soc. Am.* 63:36–51.

Staddon, B.W. 1979. The scent glands of Heteroptera. *Adv. in Insect Physiol.* 14:351–418.

Staddon, B.W. 1986. Biology of scent glands in the Hemiptera-Heteroptera. *Ann. Soc. Entomol. France* 22:183–190.

Staddon, B.W., Thorne, M.J., Knight, D.W. 1987. The scent glands and their chemicals in the aposematic cotton harlequin bug, *Tectocoris diophthalmus* (Heteroptera: Scutelleridae). *Aust. J. Zool.* 35:227–234.

Stamp, N.E. 1984. Interactions of parasitoids and checkerspot caterpillars *Euphydryas* spp. (Nymphalidae). *J. Res. Lepid.* 23:2–18.

Stamp, N.E. 1986. Physical constraints of defense and response to invertebrate predators by pipevine caterpillars (*Battus philenor*:Papilionidae). *J. Lepid. Soc.* 40:191–205.

Stay, B. 1957. The sternal scent gland of *Eurycotis floridana* (Blattaria: Blattidae). *Ann. Entomol. Soc. Amer.* 50:514–519.

Stein, G. 1967. Über den Feinbau der Duftdrüsen von Feuerwanzen (*Pyrrhocoris apterus* L., Geocorisae). Die 2. Larvale Abdominaldrüse. *Z. Zellforsch.* 79:49–63.

Strong, F.E. 1967. Observations on aphid cornicle secretions. *Ann. Entomol. Soc. Am.* 60:668–673.

Sulc. 1949. On the repugnatorial stink glands in the beetles of the genus *Cantharis,* Coleoptera. *Bull Int. Acad. Tcèque Sci.* 50:79–100.

Suzuki, T., Haga, K., Kuwahara, Y. 1986. Anal Secretion of Thrips. I. Identification of Perillene from *Leeuwenia pasanii* (Thysanoptera:Phlaeothripidae) *Appl. Ent. Zool.* 21:461–466.

Swynnerton, C.F.M. 1915. Birds in relation to their prey: Experiments on wood-hoopoes, small hornbills and a babbler. *J.S. Afr. Ornith. Union* 2:32–108.

Swynnerton, C.F.M. 1919. Experiments and observations bearing on the explanation of form and colouring 1908-1913. *J. Linn. Soc.* 33:203–385.

Tannert, W., Hien, B.C. 1973. Nachweis und Funktion eines "Versammlungsduftstoffes" und eines "Alarmduftstoffes" bei *Blaps mucronata* Latr. 1804 (Coleoptera: Tenebrionidae). *Biol. Zentralbl.* 92:601–612.

Tschinkel, W.R. 1969. Phenols and quinones from the defensive secretions of the tenebrionid beetle, *Zophobas rugipes.* *J. Insect Physiol.* 15:191–200.

Tschinkel, W.R. 1975a. A comparative study of the chemical defensive system of tenebrionid beetles: chemistry of the secretions. *J. Insect Physiol.* 21:753–783.

Tschinkel, W.R. 1975b. A comparative study of the chemical defensive system of tenebrionid beetles. Defensive behavior and ancillary features. *Ann. Entomol. Soc. Am.* 68:439–453.

Tschinkel, W.R. 1975c. A comparative study of the chemical defensive system of tenebrionid beetles. III. Morphology of the glands. *J. Morphol.* 145:355–370.

Usher, M.B., Balogun, R.A. 1966. A defence mechanism in *Onychiurus* (Collembola, Onychiuridae). *Entomol. Mon. Mag.* 102:237–238.

Uvarov, B. 1966. *Grasshoppers and Locusts.* Vol. I. Cambridge University Press, London. 481 pp.

Uvarov, B. 1977. *Grasshopper and Locusts. Vol. II.* Centre for Overseas Pest Research, London. 613 pp.

Verhoeff, K.W. 1917. Zur Entwicklung, Morphologie und Biologie der Vorlarven und Larven der Canthariden. *Arch. Naturgesch.* 83(A2):102–140.

Vidari, G., Bernardi, M., Pavan, M., Ragozzino, L. 1973. Rose oxide and iridodial from *Aromia moschata* L. (Coleoptera: Cerambycidae). *Tetrahedron Lett.* 41:4065–4068.

von Euw, J., Fishelson, L., Parsons, J.A., Reichstein, T., Rothschild, M. 1967. Cardenolides (heart poisons) in a grasshopper feeding on milkweeds. *Nature* 214:35–39.

Vosseler, J. 1890. Die Stinkdrüsen der Forficliden. *Arch. Mikrosk. Anat.* 36:565–578.

Vosseler, J. 1893. Den zweiten Vortrag, betreffend Biologische Mitteilungen über einige Orthopteren aus Oran. *Jh. Ver. Vaterl. Naturk. Württ* 49:87–95.

Wallace, J.B., Blum, M.S. 1969. Refined defensive mechanisms in *Chrysomela scripta. Ann. Entomol. Soc. Am.* 62:503–506.

Wallace, J.B., Blum, M.S. 1971. Reflex bleeding: A highly refined defensive mechanism in *Diabrotica* larvae (Coleoptera: Chrysomelidae). *Ann. Entomol. Soc. Am.* 64:1021–1024.

Wallbank, B.E., Waterhouse, D.F. 1970. The defensive secretions of *Polyzosteria* and related cockroaches. *J. Insect Physiol.* 16:2081–2096.

Waterhouse, D.F., Wallbank, B.E. 1967. 2-Methylene butanal and related compounds in the defensive scent of *Platyzosteria* cockroaches (Blattidae: Polyzosteriinae). *J. Insect Physiol.* 13:1657–1669.

Weatherston, J., MacDonald, J.A., Miller, D., Riere, G., Percy-Cunningham, J., E., Benn, M.H. 1986. Ultrastructure of exocrine prothoracic gland of *Datana ministra* (Drury) (Lepidoptera: Notodontidae) and the nature of its secretion. *J. Chem. Ecol.* 12:2039–2050.

Weatherston, J., Percy, J.E. 1969 Studies on physiologically active arthropod secretions. III. Chemical, morphological, and histological studies on the defense mechanism of *Uroblaniulus canadensis* (Say) (Diplopoda: Julida). *Can. J. Zool.* 47:1389–1394.

Weatherston, J., Percy, J.E. 1978a. Venoms of Coleoptera. In Arthropod Venoms, *Handbook of Experimental Pharmacology,* S. Bettini, ed., 511–554. Springer-Verlag, Berlin. 977 pp.

Weatherston, J., Percy, J.E. 1978b. Venoms of Rhyncota (Hemiptera). In Arthropod Venoms, *Handbook of Experimental Pharmacology,* S. Bettini, ed., 489–509. Springer-Verlag, Berlin. 977 pp.

Weatherston, J., Percy, J.E., MacDonald, L.M., MacDonald, J.A. 1979. Morphology of the prothoracic defensive gland of *Schizura concinna* (J.E. Smith) (Lepidoptera: Notodontidae) and the nature of its secretion. *J. Chem. Ecol.* 5:165–177.

Werner, F. 1935. Pedipalpen. In: *Klassen und Ordnungen des Tierreichs,* H.G. Bronn, ed., 5(4):317–490.

Wheeler, J.W., Blum, M.S. 1973. Alkylpyrazine alarm pheromones in ponerine ants. *Science* 182:501–503.

Wheeler, J.W., Happ, G.M., Araujo, J., Pasteels, J.M. 1972. γ Dodecalactone from rove beetles. *Tetrahedron Lett.* 46:4635–4638.

Whelan, P.I., Weir, T.A. 1987. Skin lesions caused by *Paederus australis* Guérin-Méneville (Coleoptera, Staphylinidae). *J. Aust. Entomol. Soc.* 26:287–288.

Whitman, D.W. 1982. Grasshopper sexual pheromone: a component of the defensive secretion in *Taeniopoda eques. Physiol. Entomol.* 7:111–115.

Whitman, D.W. 1988. Allelochemical interactions among plants, herbivores, and their predators. In *Novel Aspects of Insect-Plant Interactions,* P. Barbosa, D.K. Letourneau, eds., 11–64. John Wiley, New York.

Whitman, D.W., Billen, J.P.J., Alsop, D., Blum, M.S. (Unpublished). Anatomy, ultrastructure and functional morphology of the metathoracic tracheal defense glands of the grasshopper *Romalea guttata.*

Whitman, D.W., Blum, M.S., Jones, C.G. 1985. Chemical defense in *Taeniopoda eques* (Orthoptera: Acrididae); role of the metathoracic secretion. *Ann. Entomol. Soc. Am.* 78:451–455.

Whitman, D.W., Jones, C.G., Blum, M.S. (Unpublished). A comprehensive survey of the actual and potential predators of the chemically defended grasshoppers *Taeniopoda eques* and *Romalea guttata.*

Wiklund, C., Järvi, T. 1982. Survival of distasteful insects after being attacked by naive birds: a reappraisal of the theory of aposematic coloration evolving through individual selection. *Evolution* 36:998–1002.

Williams, F.X. 1917. Notes on the life-history of some North American Lampyridae. *N.Y. Entomol. Soc.* 25:11–33.

Witthohn, K., Naumann, C.M. 1987. Cyanogenesis—a general phenomenon in the Lepidoptera? *J. Chem. Ecol.* 13:1789–1809.

Woodring, J.P., Blum, M.S. 1963. The anatomy and physiology of the repugnatorial glands of *Pachydesmus crassicutus* (Dipolpoda). *Ann. Entomol. Soc. Am.* 56:448–453.

Woodring, J.P., Blum, M.S. 1965. The anatomy, physiology and comparative aspects of the repugnatorial glands of *Orthocricus arboreus* (Diplopoda: Spirobolida). *J. Morph.* 116:99–108.

Wright, R.H. 1982. *The Sense of Smell.* CRC Press, Boca Raton, Fla., 236 pp.

Youdeowei, A., Calam, D.H. 1969. The morphology of the scent glands of *Dysdercus intermedius* Distan (Hemiptera: Pyrrhocoridae) and a preliminary analysis of scent gland secretions of fifth instar larvae. *Proc. Roy. Entomol. Soc. Lond.* (A)44:38–44.

Young, A.M., Blum, M.S., Fales, H.M., Bian, Z. 1986. Natural history and ecological chemistry of the neotropical butterfly *Papilio anchisiades* (Papilionidae). *J. Lep. Soc.* 40:36–53.

Yuasa, H. 1922. A classification of the larvae of the Tenthredinoidae. *Ill. Biol. Mon.* 7:1–172.

Recycling Plant Natural Products for Insect Defense

M. DEANE BOWERS

Introduction

Arthropods in general, and insects in particular, are well known for the variety of chemical compounds included as part of their defensive arsenal (Blum 1981; Brower 1984; Rothschild 1985). These defenses include venomous stings and bites, urticating hairs, defensive secretions and sprays, repulsive aromas, deterrent tastes, and toxins. In many of these cases, the insect manufactures the defensive product in its own body, often in a specialized gland or with a group of glandular cells. In the case of some unpalatable and toxic insect species, however, they do not produce their own chemical defense at all, but rather take advantage of compounds produced by the plant species on which they feed. These unpalatable insects may "recycle" certain compounds (figure 13.1) by sequestering them during larval or adult feeding and by storing them in the hemolymph, cuticle, or in some cases in specialized organs. These compounds may then render the insect unpalatable or toxic to potential predators.

Plants produce a wide variety of chemical compounds, allelochemicals, which appear to function primarily as a defense against herbivory (Fraenkel 1959, 1969; Rosenthal and Janzen 1979), although they may serve other functions in the plant as well (Seigler and Price 1976; Robinson 1974; Del Moral 1972). These compounds include alkaloids, mustard oils, flavonoids, terpenes and sesquiterpenes, cucurbitacins, phenolics, and many others (see Rosenthal and Janzen 1979). Although generally not thought to be important in the primary metabolism of the plant (but see Seigler 1977; Robinson 1974), these compounds are often found in relatively large amounts, sometimes as much as 5 to 10 percent of the plant's dry weight. Many of these plant natural products are toxic or deterrent to most insects, but some adapted specialists may feed with impunity on plants containing these compounds. Because of these toxic and deterrent effects against both vertebrates and invertebrates, some plant natural products are particularly well suited to being recycled by specialist insect herbivores for use in defense against their own predators. However, of the tens of thousands of plant natural products known (Haslam 1986), only relatively few have been shown to be used in such a way (table 13.1, figure 13.1).

Unpalatable insects that sequester chemical compounds from their hostplants and use them as an antipredator defense usually specialize on one or a few closely related plant species or genera that produce the compounds that render them unpalatable. For example, danaid butterflies specialize on plants that contain cardenolides (Ackery and Vane-Wright 1984), and checkerspot butterflies in the genus *Euphydryas* specialize on plants containing iridoid glycosides (Bowers 1980, 1981, 1983). Deroe and Pasteels (1982) found that aposematic chrysomelids are less polyphagous than species which are cryptic. There may be exceptions to this generalization, however, such as the lubber grasshopper, *Romalea guttatus* (Romaleidae), which is extremely general in its feeding habits, warningly colored, and unpalatable to predators (Jones et al. 1987). In general, such host plant specialization by unpalatable insects, as by other specialist insects, allows the herbivore to synchronize its life history with that of the plant and to fine-tune its physiology to cope with plant defensive compounds, potentially by sequestering them.

In some cases, predators and parasitoids of unpalatable insects may in turn sequester potential defensive compounds from their hosts. For example, the tachinid fly, *Zenilla adamsonii* was found to contain cardenolides acquired from its host, the monarch butterfly, *Danaus plexippus*, reared on the milkweed, *Asclepias curassavica* (Reichstein et al. 1968). In addition, the predatory insects, *Coccinela undecimpunctata* (Coccinellidae) and a lacewing, *Chrysopa* sp. (Chrysopidae), contained cardiac glycosides apparently obtained from their aphid prey, *Aphis nerii*, which had fed on oleander (*Nerium oleander*) which contained cardiac glycosides (Rothschild, et al. 1973). Despite these earlier reports, detailed investigation is just beginning in this fascinating area of tritrophic level transfer

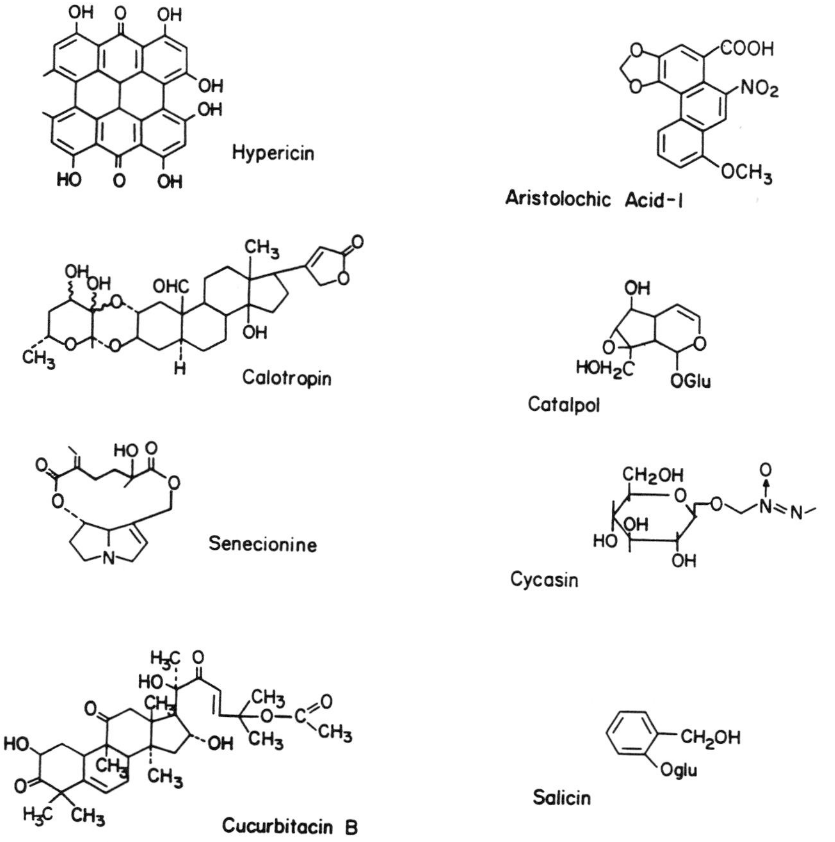

Figure 13.1   Some plant natural products that are sequestered by insects, which are then rendered unpalatable.

and effects of plant natural products (Barbosa and Saunders, 1986; Barbosa, et al., 1986; Duffey et al. 1986). Future research in this area will certainly prove rewarding.

This review will focus on four aspects of the use of plant natural products as insect defenses: first, a brief consideration of the importance of plant allelochemicals for insect herbivores; second, the possible fates of ingested plant allelochemicals, with a focus on processes of sequestration; third, the implications of individual chemical variation of unpalatable insects and their host plants for the deterrence of potential predators; fourth, what does consideration of the above topics say about the evolution of the ability to sequester plant natural products and the evolution of unpalatability.

Table 13.1. Orders and representative species of insects which sequester plant allelochemicals for use in their defense.

Insect order	Example	Compound(s) sequestered	Host plant	References
Orthoptera	*Poekilocerus bufonius* (Pyrgomorphidae)	Cardenolides	Various Asclepiadaceae	von Euw et al. 1967
	Zonocerus variegatus (Pyrgomorphidae)	Pyrrolizidine alkaloids	*Crotalaria* (Euphorbiaceae)	Bernays et al. 1977
	Zonocerus elegans (Pyrgomorphidae)	Cannabinoids[1]	*Cannabis sativa* (Moraceae)	Rothschild et al. 1977
Hemiptera	*Aphis nerii* (Aphididae)	Cardenolides	*Asclepias currassavica* and *Nerium oleander*	Rothschild et al. 1970
	Oncopeltus fasciatus (Lygaeidae)	Cardenolides	Various Asclepiadaceae	Duffey and Scudder 1972
	Lygaeus kalmiae (Lygaeidae)	Cardenolides	Various Asclepiadaceae	Duffey and Scudder 1972
	Neacoryphus bicrucis (Lygaeidae)	Pyrrolizidine alkaloids	*Senecio* sp.	McLain and Shure 1985
	Diabrotica bulfeata (Chrysomelidae)	Cucurbitacins	Various Cucurbitaceae	Ferguson and Metcalf 1985
	Diabrotica undecimpunctata howardii (Chrysomelidae)	Cucurbitacins	Various Cucurbitaceae	Ferguson and Metcalf 1985
	Diabrotica virgifera virgifera (Chrysomelidae)	Cucurbitacins	Various Cucurbitaceae	Ferguson and Metcalf 1985
	Acalymna vittatum (Chrysomelidae)	Cucurbitacins	Various Cucurbitaceae	Ferguson and Metcalf 1985
	Phratora vitellinae (Chrysomelidae)	Salicylaldehyde	*Salix* sp. (Salicaceae)	Pasteels et al 1983
	Chrysomela tremulae (Chrysomelidae)	Salicylaldehyde	*Populus trichocarpa* (Salicaceae)	Pasteels et al 1983
Neuroptera	*Chrysopa carnea* (Chrysopidae)	Cardenolides[2]	—	Rothschild et al. 1973

Table 13.1. *(Cont'd.)*

Order	Species (Family)	Compound	Host plant (Family)	Reference
Diptera	*Zenilla adamsoni* (Tachinidae)	Cardenolides[3]	—	Reichstein et al. 1968
Coleoptera	*Tetraopes oregonensis* (Cerambycidae)	Cardenolides	Various Asclepiadaceae	Isman et al. 1977
	Chrysolina brunsvicensis (Chrysomelidae)	Hypericin	*Hypericum hirsutum* (Guttiferae)	Rees 1969
	Dibolia borealis (Chrysomelidae)	Iridoid glycosides	*Chelone glabra* (Scrophulariaceae)	Bowers and Puttick, unpublished data
	Coccinella undecimpunctata (Coccinellidae)	Cardenolides[2]	—	Rothschild et al. 1973
Hymenoptera	*Hyposoter exiguae* (Ichneumonidae)	A-tomatine[4]	—	Campbell and Duffey 1979
	Tenthredo grandis (Tenthredinidae)	Iridoid glycosides	*Chelone glabra* (Scrophulariaceae)	Bowers and Puttick, unpublished data
	Microplitis sp. (Braconidae)	Pyrrolizidine alkaloids[5]	—	Benn et al 1979
	Neodiprion sertifer (Diprionidae)	Mono- and sesquiterpenes[5]	*Pinus* spp. (Pinaceae)	Eisner et al. 1974
Lepidoptera	*Danaus plexippus* (Nymphalidae)	Cardenolides	Various Asclepiadaceae	Reichstein al. 1968
	Euphydryas phaeton (Nymphalidae)	Iridoid glycosides	*Chelone glabra* (Scrophulariaceae)	Bowers and Puttick 1986
	Euphydryas anicia (Nymphalidae)	Iridoid glycosides	Various Scrophulariaceae	Stermitz, et al. 1986
	Battus philenor (Papilionidae)	Aristolochic acids	*Aristolochia* spp. (Aristolochiaceae)	Rothschild et al. 1970
	Pieris brassicae (Pieridae)	Mustard oils	Various Cruciferae	Aplin et al. 1975
	Eumaeus atala (Lycaenidae)	Cycasin	*Zamia floridana* (Cycadaceae)	Rothschild et al. 1986, Bowers and Larin, 1989
	Seirarctia echo (Arctiidae)	Cycasin	*Zamia* sp. (Cycadaceae)	Teas et al. 1966
	Tyria jacobaeae (Arctiidae)	Pyrrolizidine alkaloids	*Senecio jacobaea* (Compositae)	Aplin et al. 1968
	Eloria noyesi (Lymantriidae)	Cocaine	*Erythroxylum coca* (Erythroxylaceae)	Blum et al. 1981

Table 13.1. *(Cont'd.)*

Insect order	Example	Compound(s) sequestered	Host plant	References
	Xanthopastis trimals (Noctuidae)	Amaryllidaceae alkaloids	*Ficus* sp. (Moraceae)	Rothschild 1972
	Meris alticola (Geometridae)	Iridoid glycosides[6]	*Penstemon virgatus* (Scrophulariaceae)	Stermitz et al. 1988
	Neoterpes graeflaria Geometridae)	Iridoid glycosides[6]	*Penstemon barbatus* (Scrophulariaceae)	Stermitz et al. 1988
	Syntomeida epilais (Ctenuchidae)	Cardenolides	*Nerium oleander* (Apocynaceae)	Rothschild 1972
	Ceratomia catalpae (Sphigidae)	Iridoid glycosides[6]	*Catalpa* sp. (Bignoniaceae)	Bowers and Puttick 1986
	Amblyptiiia (Platyptiia) pica (Pterophoridae)	Rhexifoline[7]	*Castilleja rhexifolia*	Roby and Stermitz 1984

NOTE: These examples include species in which the author indicated, or the type of compound suggested, that the allelochemicals served a defensive purpose for the insect.

1. From *Cannabis sativa*, not a normal host plant
2. Sequestered from prey, *Aphis nerii*, not from a plant
3. Determined on the basis of digitalislike activity on the frog heart
4. Sequestered from the host, *Heliothis* (Lepidoptera)
5. Sequestered from the host, *Nyctemera annulata* (Arctiidae)
6. In larva only, absent or in very small amounts in adult
7. A pyridine monoterpene alkaloid

Plant Allelochemicals and Insects

The diversity of natural products produced by plants is immense, and a multitude of excellent references have been devoted to this topic (e.g., Hegnauer 1964–1973; Gibbs 1974; Rosenthal and Janzen 1979; Blum 1981). Humans have used these compounds as drugs and medicines for centuries. It is not surprising that they also have dramatic effects on the insects feeding upon plants that contain them.

Allelochemicals, or plant secondary compounds, were initially so called because of their presumed role as the metabolic waste disposal system of plants (Whittaker and Feeny 1971). Beginning with Fraenkel (1959, 1969) and Ehrlich and Raven (1964), and now generally accepted, the major role ascribed to these compounds is that of a plant defense against herbivory and attack by pathogens. However, this may not be the only role that such compounds play in the plant's physiology. For example, many groups of allelochemicals show a relatively high rate of turnover within the plant, suggesting that they are not merely inert end products (Robinson 1974; Seigler 1977), but may also function in the primary metabolism of the plant. Seigler (1977) suggests several "primary" roles of "secondary" compounds: a source of some limiting material such as nitrogen or carbon, hormones or other regulators, or UV-screens (Del Moral 1972). More recently, it has been suggested that plant secondary metabolism serves to maintain the components of primary metabolism when normal substrates cannot be exploited (Bu'Lock 1980, in Haslam 1986).

The effectiveness of plant allelochemicals as a defense against vertebrate (Freeland and Janzen 1974; Bryant 1980; Bryant and Kuropt 1980) and invertebrate (Bernays and Chapman 1978; Rosenthal and Janzen 1979; Blum 1981; Visser and Minks 1982; Ahmad 1983; Futuyma and Slatkin 1983; Hedin 1983; Bell and Carde 1984) herbivores, fungal pathogens (Deverall 1977; Harbone and Ingham 1978; Bell 1981), bacteria (Harborne and Ingham 1978), and other plants (Rice 1979) is well documented. However, herbivores and pathogens may breach the plant's defenses, and even, as in the case of unpalatable insects, usurp the compounds for use in their own defense.

The specific effect of a particular chemical compound on a phytophagous insect is a function of many attributes of the insect and the plant. For example, synergistic effects of other allelochemicals in the plant

(Berenbaum 1985; Kubo and Hanke 1985), drought or water stress undergone by the plant (Rhoades 1983), and facultative synthesis (Haukioja and Niemala 1977; Ryan 1979; Karban 1983; Valentine et al. 1983) may all contribute to the efficacy of a particular defense. On the other hand, the health, prior feeding experience (Jermy et al. 1968), and age of the insect may all influence an insect's response to plant allelochemicals. Plant allelochemicals have been shown to act as feeding deterrents or toxins to generalist and nonadapted specialist insects (e.g., Burnett et al 1974; Berenbaum 1978; Blau et al. 1978; Bernays and DeLuca 1981; Miller and Feeny 1983). In contrast, these same substances are consumed with no ill effects by adapted specialist insects which may use these compounds as feeding or oviposition cues (e.g., Vershaffelt 1910; Chambliss and Jones 1966; David and Gardner 1966a,b; Schoonhoven 1972; Bowers 1983, 1984; Pereyra and Bowers 1988). Some allelochemicals, notably nonprotien amino acids (Rosenthal 1983), phenolics (Bernays and Woodhead 1982), and salicin (Pasteels et al 1983) may be used as nutrient sources for some specialist insects.

Potential Fates of Ingested Allelochemicals

Unpalatable insects are a small subset of specialist insect herbivores. Although many insect species are known to specialize on plants that contain very toxic chemical compounds, only some of these insects reroute the plant chemicals for use in their own defense (table 13.1). Feeding on a plant that contains chemical compounds that could be recycled for insect defense does not necessarily indicate sequestration and use of those compounds for defense. Some insect species may manufacture their own defensive compounds de novo or from precursors in the host plant (Pasteels et al. 1984). Other species metabolize and/or eliminate these compounds. The biochemistry of sequestration, metabolism, or elimination of such compounds is poorly understood (Duffey 1980; Blum 1981, 1983). In only a few cases have the fates of particular compounds been followed in insects feeding on plants containing them, and quantification of the ultimate fate of what is ingested (i.e., metabolic by-products as well as sequestration and/or elimination) requires use of such techniques as radioactive labeling (e.g., Bull et al. 1984).

The several possible fates of plant natural products after insect ingestion are detailed below. Briefly, four primary fates may befall such a chemical compound after an insect consumes it: (1) it may be eliminated intact (Self et al. 1964a,b): (2) it may be used as a precursor to a pheromone or defensive compound (Schneider et al. 1975; Connor et al. 1981); (3) it may be metabolized in some way (Rothschild 1972; Blum 1983); or (4) it may be sequestered and used for the insect's defense (Rothschild 1972; Roeske et al. 1976; Duffey 1980; Nishio 1980; Blum 1981). Some combination of these fates is also possible.

ELIMINATION

Some insect larvae may eliminate ingested compounds relatively intact. A classic example is *Manduca sexta* (Sphingidae), the larvae of which feed on tobacco and rapidly excrete the nicotine (Self et al. (1964a,b). Although Self et al. (1964a,b) found no evidence of metabolic conversion, Barbosa and Saunders (1985) found that small amounts of nicotine (2 percent or less) were sequestered by the larvae, and that most of that was metabolized into cotinine. Study of other systems as well have indicated that the fate of an ingested plant allelochemical may not be limited to a single avenue. For example, Blum et al. (1981) found that larvae of *Eloria noyesi* (Lymantriidae), which are monophagous on *Erythroxylum coca* (Exythroxylaceae), eliminate most of the cocaine, the primary alkaloid in the leaves of this plant, virtually unchanged. However, small traces of this compound were found in the adult, indicating that there is some sequestration of the cocaine (Blum et al. 1981). Larvae of *Junonia coenia* (Nymphalidae) and *Ceratomia catalpae* (Sphingidae) sequester some of the iridoid glycosides ingested during larval feeding into the hemolymph, but also eliminate iridoid glycosides in the frass (Bowers and Puttick 1986). Thus, although elimination of an ingested natural product may be the primary fate, a combination of fates is also possible: some of the compound may also be metabolized or sequestered (Rothschild 1972; Blum 1981).

PHEROMONE PRODUCTION

Some ingested plant allelochemicals may be used as precursors in the biosynthesis of pheromones. Connor et al. (1981) found that the mating pheromone of *Utetheisa ornatrix* (Arctiidae), hydroxydanaidal, was synthesized from pyrrolizidine alkaloids that were sequestered from the host plants, *Crotalaria* spp. (Fabaceae), during larval feeding. When larvae were fed on a pinto bean diet that did not contain these alkaloid precursors, the adults contained only a minute amount of hydroxydanaidal, which probably was derived from compounds put into the eggs by the ovipositing mother (Connor et al. 1981). These adults reared on pinto beans were less successful at mating than their *Crotalaria*-reared counterparts. In addition, pinto bean-reared moths were palatable to spiders, but those containing pyrrolizidines were unpalatable and were rejected (Eisner 1980). Pyrrolizidines are thus important both as pheromone precursors and defensive compounds in *U. ornatrix*.

The adult males of many species of danaid butterflies also ingest pyrrolizidine alkaloids from various plant species in the family Boraginaceae, notably the genus *Heliotropium* (Schneider et al. 1975; Edgar et al. 1979). The alkaloids are metabolized to hydroxydanaidal and some similar compounds, which are aphrodisiac pheromones used during courtship of these butterflies (Edgar and Culvenor 1974, 1975; Bernays et al. 1977). These compounds may also serve a defensive function in danaids and other lepidopterans that ingest them (Ackery and Vane-Wright 1984).

METABOLISM

Many allelochemicals are metabolized before being eliminated or sequestered (Brattsten 1979a; Blum 1983). Most allelochemicals are lipophilic and thus are difficult for organisms, including insects, with water-based excretory systems to eliminate. Such lipophilic compounds tend to accumulate in various lipid-containing membranes and tissues, and over time the continued accumulation of relatively small amounts may reach toxic levels (Brattsten 1979a). Many insect enzyme systems attack foreign chemicals. In general, these systems convert foreign compounds to more water-soluble, or hydrophilic, compounds by oxidizing, reducing, or hydrolyzing each compound, and then, in some cases, by conjugating this product with sugars, sulfates, phosphates, or other hydrophiles to form a water-soluble end product that can then be excreted (Brattsten 1979a).

The primary enzyme systems involved in the metabolism of foreign compounds in insects are the mixed function oxidases, or MFOs. Brattsten (1979a) describes three characteristics of MFOs which make them well suited for dealing with numerous kinds of allelochemicals: (1) they catalyze a variety of oxidative reactions which produce more polar products which then can be conjugated or excreted; (2) they are fairly nonspecific, accepting many different kinds of compounds as substrates; and (3) they can be induced by the entrance of foreign compounds into the system, and thereby rapidly respond to ingested allelochemicals (Brattsten et al. 1977). In insects, high MFO activity is associated with the fat body (often a site for the accumulation of lipophilic toxins) and tissues associated with the digestive tract (Krieger et al. 1971; Brattsten 1979a,b; Brattsten et al. 1980). Although scientists have primarily studied the action of these enzymes in insects in response to insecticides (e.g., Wilkinson 1983; Terriere 1984), recent work has shown that these enzymes are also important in insect detoxification of plant allelochemicals (Brattsten et al. 1977; Brattsten et al. 1980; Brattsten 1979a,b; Yu 1982, 1983; Yu et al. 1979; Terriere 1984), and these enzymes may be critical in the ability of insects to feed on plants containing various allelochemicals.

SEQUESTRATION OF PLANT ALLELOCHEMICALS

A variety of unpalatable insects sequester their defensive compounds from their host plants (table 13.1, figure 13.1). Probably the best-studied system in this regard is that of insects that feed on cardenolide-containing milkweeds (Asclepiadaceae), but other systems are becoming increasingly well documented and understood, including those of insects that feed on plants containing iridoid glycosides (see below), azoxyglycosides (Rothschild et al. 1986; Bowers and Larin 1989), pyrrolizidines (McLain 1984; McLain and Shure 1985; Boppre 1986) and cucurbitacins (Gould and Massey 1984; Ferguson and Metcalf 1985; Metcalf 1986). The amount and kind of defensive chemicals present in a putatively unpalatable insect may determine its degree of unpalatability and thus its potential for protection from predators. Variation in host plant chemistry, as well as in the ability of the insect to sequester these compounds, will also be critical in determining the amount of chemical protection conferred by a particular group of chemical compounds.

The Biochemistry of Sequestration

In an excellent review of the phenomenon of sequestration, Duffey (1980) synthesizes a great diversity of literature that bears on many aspects of this process. He describes three phases in the process of sequestration of plant allelochemicals (as well as insecticides and other xenobiotics): (1) absorption by the gut; (2) transport from the gut to the hemolymph and then transport in the hemolymph; (3) deposition in organs and other sites of storage. The dynamics of each of these phases is dependent on the lypophilicity/hydrophilicity of the compound in question, the compound's partition coefficient, the molecular weight of the compound, the energy requirements of each of these phases, and the availability of that energy (Duffey 1980). One of the very few natural systems in which this has been investigated is sequestration of cardenolides by the milkweed bug, *Oncopeltus fasciatus* (Lygaeidae), where cardenolides appear to be sequestered differentially on the basis of the family of genus and their partition coefficient (Isman et al. 1977; Duffey et al. 1978). Other groups of plant allelochemicals sequestered by insect herbivores need to be investigated in a similar manner.

For sequestration of a particular compound to occur, the compound must not be attacked by detoxifying enzymes and must be transported out of the gut to the sites of sequestration. Specialist insects, which are coping with a limited diversity of allelochemicals, are predicted to have a less active detoxification system than generalist insects which must cope with a suite of varied chemical defenses (Krieger et al. 1971; Brattsten et al. 1977). In addition, however, specialist insects that sequester allelochemicals must prevent autotoxicity of these compounds in some way. This may be accomplished by isolating the compounds in certain glands (Morrow et al. 1976; Duffey and Scudder 1974; Pasteels et al. 1984) or by shunting them to the cuticle (Brower and Glazier 1975; Nishio 1980). However, many allelochemicals abound in the hemolymph, where they contact a variety of internal organs (Duffey 1980; Blum 1981). How autotoxicity is prevented in such instances is unknown, but is certainly an area of fruitful investigation.

As discussed throughout this chapter, several systems have been studied with regard to the phenomenon of sequestration of plant allelochemicals. However, one of the most critical and interesting questions surrounding this phenomenon has seldom been addressed: that is, in a group of insect species feeding on plants containing a particular group of allelochemicals, why do some insect species sequester these compounds or a subset of these compounds while others do not, or sequester a different subset? The phenomena of differential sequestration, selective sequestration, and comparative sequestration have been documented in a variety of systems (Aplin et al. 1968; Aplin and Rothschild 1972; Rothschild et al. 1975; Roeske et al. 1976; Rothschild and Reichstein 1976; Isman et al. 1977; Nishio 1980; Cohen and Brower 1983; Bowers and Puttick 1986), yet there is still relatively little understanding of what is going on at a physiological and biochemical level (Duffey 1980).

Sites of Sequestration

Storage of plant allelochemicals in specialized glands or organs is an efficient means of concentrating the compounds as well as of isolating them from potentially vulnerable internal organs. Larvae of the sawfly, *Neodiprion sertifer* (Diprionidae), feed on the needles of pine (*Pinus silvestris*) and sequester monoterpenes and sesquiterpenes into diverticular pouches of the foregut (Eisner et al. 1974). These stored compounds can then be discharged in response to predator or parasitoid attack, and have been shown to be effective deterrents to ants and spiders (Eisner et al. 1974). Several species of Australian sawflies in the family Pergidae, which specialize on *Eucalyptus* species, also store monoterpene and sesquiterpene oils from their host plants into such diverticular pouches (Morrow et al. 1976). The composition of this oil is essentially identical to that extracted from the leaves. Although some components of the leaf oil were found in the midgut contents and fecal pellets, these were only a subset of those available in the leaf and stored in the foregut pouch. Feeding experiments with mice, birds, and ants showed that this discharge was an effective deterrent (Morrow et al. 1976). The means by which these defensive compounds are extracted from the leaf material and stored in the foregut diverticulum are unknown (Morrow et al. 1976). Two lepidopteran species in the genus *Myrascia* (Oecophoridae) sequester oils from their host plants in the family Myrtaceae (Common and Bellas 1977). They also selectively sequester these oils in a foregut diverticulum and regurgitate them when disturbed (Common and Bellas 1977).

Regurgitated gut fluid, although not confined to isolated glands or organs, is used by many insect species as a defense against predators (Nishio 1980; Brower 1984; Blum 1978; Stamp 1982; Cornell et al. 1987). This fluid may contain defensive chemicals derived from ingested plant material. Nishio (1980) found that the regurgitant of larvae of *Danaus plexippus* (Danainae) fed on *Asclepias humistrata* (Asclepiadaceae) contained a high concentration of cardenolides. Larvae of *Euphydryas phaeton* and *E. chalcedona* (Nymphalinae) will regurgitate in response to disturbance, and this fluid contains iridoid glycosides (Bowers and Puttick unpublished data) compounds which are important in the unpalatability of these species. Larvae of *Hemileuca lucina* (Saturniidae) will also regurgitate in response to disturbance (Cornell et al. 1987), although the presence of plant-derived allelochemicals in the regurgitant of this species has not yet been determined. Many grasshopper species are well known for their ability to "spit." This gut-derived liquid may contain allelochemicals from the host plant which are toxic to both vertebrate and invertebrate predators (Freeman 1968; Eisner 1970).

The milkweed bug, *O. fasciatus*, sequesters cardiac glycosides from its milkweed host plants (Duffey and Scudder 1972; Scudder and Duffey 1972; Vaughan 1979). In the adult, most of the sequestered cardenolide is found in the dorsolateral space, which is specialized for cardenolide storage (Duffey and Scudder 1974; Scudder et al. 1986).

Most unpalatable insects which derive their unpalatable qualities from chemicals in their host plants do not store these compounds in specialized structures, but rather in the hemolymph and cuticle (Blum 1981). Many species of insects in at least seven orders sequester plant allelochemicals, thus rendering themselves unpalatable to their own predators (table 13.1). Although in only a few cases have the anatomical sites of sequestration been identified (Brower and Glazier 1975; Nishio 1980; Cohen and Brower 1983; Cohen 1985), it appears that these defensive compounds are found primarily in the hemolymph, cuticle, and in the case of nonpolar compounds, the fat body (Blum 1981, 1983).

In many studies of insect sequestration of plant allelochemicals, the entire animal is extracted and tested, but this procedure does not allow separation of gut contents from compounds which pass out of the gut and into the hemolymph, that is, those compounds which are actually sequestered. Often studies only report that an animal contains the compounds, not where in the insect they occur. In several instances, however, the hemolymph has been assayed separately from the rest of the animal (e.g., Brower and Glazier 1975; Blum et al. 1981; Nishio 1980; Ferguson and Metclaf 1985). Primarily cardiac glycosides have been well studied with regard to their distribution in insects (Duffey and Scudder 1974; Brower and Glazier 1975; Nishio 1980; Scudder et al. 1986), and the work of Nishio (1980) is notable in this regard.

Nishio (1980) investigated the sequestration of cardenolides in two lepidopteran species fed on *Asclepias humistrata,* a milkweed species very rich in cardenolides: *Danaus plexippus* (Nymphalidae) and *Cycnia inopinatus* (Arctiidae). In *C. inopinatus,* cardenolides were sequestered into the hemolymph and maintained at very high levels throughout larval and pupal development. Elimination of cardenolides during larval development occurred mainly via the larval exuviae, which were extremely rich in cardenolides. Very little cardenolide was found in the gut. In the adult of *C. inopinatus,* cardenolides were distributed relatively equally among wings, head, thorax, and abdomen (Nishio 1980). *Danaus plexippus* showed different patterns of cardenolide sequestration and processing (Nishio 1980). Much of the cardenolide content of monarch larvae was in the gut fluid. These cardenolides then ended up in the hemolymph and scales of the adult, making these the richest concentration of cardenolides, whereas the flight muscles were the lowest. Larval exuviae of *D. plexippus* were similar to those of *C. inopinatus* in being rich in cardenolides (Nishio 1980). In an earlier study on *D. plexippus,* Brower and Glazier (1975) found that different cardiac glycosides were concentrated to different degrees in different parts of the body. They found that the wings had the highest concentration of cardiac glycosides, and the thorax the least. In addition, they found that the cardenolides in the wings, although overall in highest concentration, were composed of the least emetic compounds, whereas those in the abdomen, although not in as high a concentration as in the wings, were the most emetic of the range found in the butterfly (Brower and Glazier 1975). Thus there may be substantial variation in the amounts of defensive compounds found in different body parts, as well as in the patterns of sequestration exhibited by different species of insects, which may be related to patterns of predation on those species (Brower and Glazier 1975).

COMBINATION OF FATES

Sequestration of plant allelochemicals may involve metabolism of the compounds prior to storage in the appropriate tissue. In addition, there may be selective sequestration of a subset of the allelochemicals available in the food of a herbivorous insect. Thus the array of allelochemicals sequestered by a herbivorous insect may be different from that found in the host plant (Rothschild 1972; Rothschild et al. 1972; Rothschild et al. 1979; Blum 1983; Gardner and Stermitz 1988). The cardenolides found in milkweed plants and the herbivores feeding on those plants again provide the best-studied examples. For example, *O. fasciatus* and the larvae of the monarch butterfly metabolize the nonpolar cardenolides, digitoxin and uscharidin, respectively, to more polar cardenolides which are readily sequestered (Duffey and Scudder 1972; Duffey et al. 1978; Seiber et al. 1980). Another example is found in two species of chrysomeline larvae which ingest salicin from their host plants, *Salix* or *Populus* spp. (Salicaceae) (Pasteels, et al. 1983). The larvae derive their defensive compound, salicylaldehyde (figure 13.1) from hydrolysis of salicin in their defensive glands. Salicylaldehyde is an effective defense against ants. The glucose can then be used as a nutritional source (Pasteels et al. 1983).

One group of compounds may meet three possible fates: sequestration, elimination, and metabolism. The work of Gardner (1987; Gardner and Stermitz 1988) on sequestration of iridoid glycosides by the butterfly *Euphydryas anicia* (Nymphalidae) showed that such is the case for these compounds (figure 13.2). The fate of a particular compound appeared to be related (at least in part) to its chemical structure (figure 13.2). Gardner identified the iridoid glycosides in the host plants of *E. anicia, Besseya alpina,* and *Castilleja integra* (Scrophulariaceae). Of nine iridoid glycosides found in the host plants, only three (aucubin, catalpol, and macfadieno-side) were sequestered and found in the butterfly. A set of esters of catalpol, veronicoside, verproside, and isovanillylcatalpol were apparently metabolized into catalpol. A feeding experiment using an artificial diet into which isovanillylcatalpol was incorporated showed that larvae metabolized the isovanillylcatalpol into catalpol, which was sequestered, and isovanillic acid, which was excreted (Gardner and Stermitz 1988). A third group of iridoid glycosides in the host plants mussaenoside, methylshanzhiside, and 8-epiloganic acid, were excreted in the larval frass. Analyses of other species of *Euphydryas* (Bowers, Fixman, Janzen, L'Empereur, Seewald, unpublished data) have revealed similar patterns: of a diverse array of dozens of iridoids found in the host plants of these insects, only aucubin, catalpol, and macfadienoside were sequestered. Esters of catalpol were apparently hydrolyzed to catapol, and other iridoids were excreted. This system thus provides an example of the multiplicity of fates that may result with a single group of plant allelochemicals.

Comparative Processing of Plant Allelochemicals by Insects

Different insect species feeding on plants containing the same group of allelochemicals may treat these compounds very differently. For example, *Tyria jacobeae* (Arctiidae) larvae fed on ragwort, *Senecio jacobaeae* (Compositae), sequestered the alkaloid seneciphylline, which occurred in the leaves as the N-oxide (Rothschild et al. 1979). In contrast, the grasshopper *Zonocerus variegatus* (Pyrgomorphidae) appeared to convert most of the pyrrolizidine alkaloid, monocrotaline, found in the host plant, *Crotalaria* sp., to its N-oxide before sequestration (Bernays et al. 1977).

Many insect species feed on plants known to contain unpalatable or toxic allelochemicals, yet they do not evince any of the characteristics typical of unpalatable insects, suggesting that they do not sequester such compounds from their host plants (Rothschild 1972; Marsh and Rothschild 1974). In addition, different species of aposematic insects may vary substantially in their ability to sequester plant allelochemicals (Rothschild 1972; Isman et al. 1977; Blum 1981; Cohen 1985). Finally, different individuals of a single insect species may show substantial variability in what particular chemicals and how much of those chemicals they sequester (Brower et al. 1975; Rothschild et al. 1975; Gardner and Stermitz 1988).

SEQUESTERED IRIDOID GLYCOSIDES

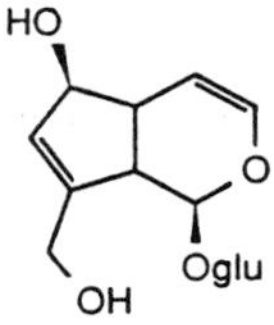

Aucubin

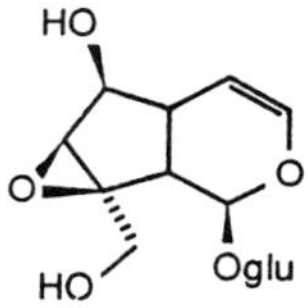

Catalpol

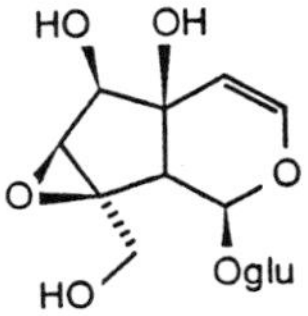

Macfadienoside

METABOLIZED IRIDOID GLYCOSIDES

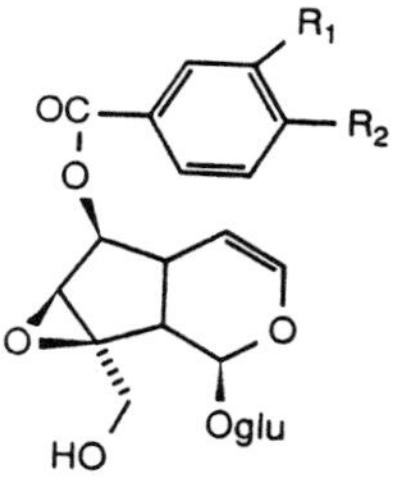

Veronicoside $R_1 = R_2 = H$
Verproside $R_1 = OH, R_2 = H$
Isovanillylcatalpol $R_1 = OH, R_2 = OCH_3$

ELIMINATED IRIDOID GLYCOSIDES

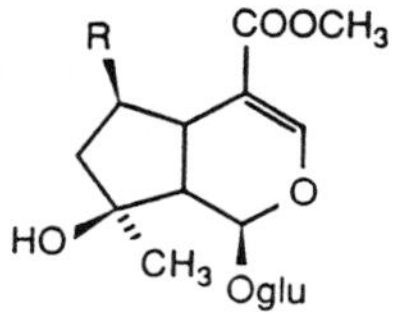

Mussaenoside $R = H$
Methyl Shanzhiside $R = OH$

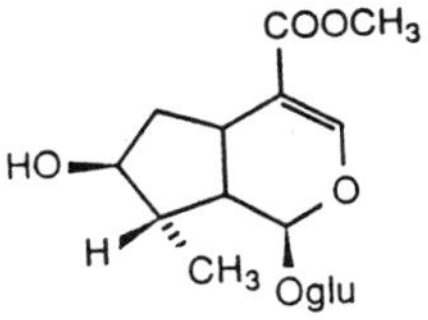

8-epiloganic Acid

Figure 13.2   Iridoid glycosides that are sequestered, eliminated, and metabolized by members of the lepidopteran genus *Euphydrays* (Nymphalidae).

Perhaps most interesting are those insects which feed on toxic plants yet are characteristically cryptic, or species, typically Lepidoptera, in which the larval stage is aposematic and the adult is cryptic (Rothschild 1972; Marsh and Rothschild 1974; Bowers and Puttick 1986).

As previously discussed, the systems of insects feeding on plants containing cardenolides are probably best studied with regard to differential processing of plant allelochemicals (Isman et al. 1977; Rothschild et al. 1975; Nishio 1980; Blum 1983; Cohen 1985). Isman et al. (1977) examined the cardenolide content of eight species of insects that feed on milkweed (*Asclepias*) in North America. They found that one aposematically colored beetle, *Labidomera clivicolis* (Chrysomelidae), which is orange and black, did not contain any cardenolides when fed on *Asclepias incarnata*. Other species of aposematic milkweed specialists, such as *Chrysochus cobaltinus* (Chrysomelidae) and *Tetraopes tetrophthalmus* (Cerambycidae), showed a great deal of variation in total cardenolide content, from none being detected to fairly substantial amounts. They also found that two cryptic herbivore species, *Scolops abnomis* (Dictyopharidae: Homoptera) and *Melanoplus devastator* (Acrididae: Orthoptera), did not contain any cardenolides. *Scolops abnormis*, however, as a plant sap feeder, may not be exposed to the cardenolides.

The fates of iridoid glycosides have been studied in a guild of herbivorous insects that specialize on plants containing these compounds (Bowers and Puttick 1986). These insects exhibit a range of feeding strategies, from generalist to specialist, and different predator avoidance strategies, from cryptic and palatable to warningly colored and unpalatable (figure 13.3). The fates of iridoid glycosides ingested during larval feeding differed in the species studied. They were sequestered through to the adult stage in unpalatable and aposematic checkerspot butterflies of the genus *Euphydryas* (Nymphalidae). In contrast, they were selectively sequestered by aposematic larvae of the moth *Ceratomia catalpae* (Sphingidae), but eliminated in the meconium (the waste products accumulated during the pupal stage) upon emergence, and thus the cryptic adults were devoid of these compounds. They were found in larvae and pupae, but not adults, of the palatable butterfly, the buckeye, *Junonia coenia* (Nymphalidae). These lepidopterans are all specialists on iridoid glycoside-containing plants, and the larvae of *Euphydryas* species, *J. coenia*, and *C. catalpae* use the compounds as feeding cues (Bowers 1983, 1984; Nayar and Fraenkel 1963). The *Euphydryas* species feed on plants in five families, all of which contain iridoid glycosides: Scrophulariaceae, Plantaginaceae, Caprifoliaceae, Oleaceae, and Valerianaceae (Jensen et al. 1975). *Junonia coenia*

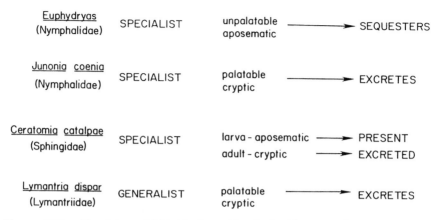

Figure 13.3   The fates of iridoid glycosides in lepidopteran herbivores with different feeding strategies and different predator avoidance strategies.

feeds on many of the same plant species as the *Euphydryas,* and has been recorded as using plants in four families: Scrophulariaceae, Plantagin-aceae, Verbenaceae, and Acanthaceae (Bowers 1984). *Ceratomia catalpae* is monophagous on species of *Catalpa* (Bignoniaceae). In contrast, the gypsy moth, *Lymantria dispar* (Lymantriidae), a generalist species, did not store iridoid glycosides, but eliminated them in the frass (although some may also be metabolized) (Bowers and Puttick 1986). Thus the fate of iridoid glycosides in these four lepidopteran herbivores is related to the feeding strategies and predator avoidance strategies that they exhibit (figure 13.3).

A variety of plant and insect species that specialize on iridoid glycoside-containing plants have been examined for the presence of these compounds using thin-layer chromatography and gas chromatography. For example, the putatively warningly colored black flea beetle, *Dibolia borealis* (Chrysomelidae), a specialist on *Chelone glabra* (Scrophulariaceae) and a few other iridoid glycoside-containing plants (Parry 1974; Haw-thorne 1978), sequestered iridoid glycosides (Bowers and Puttick, unpub-lished data). The sawflies, *Macrophya nigra* and *Tenthredo grandis* (Tenthred-inidae), which feed on *C. glabra* (Stamp 1984), sequestered iridoid glycosides in the larval stage, but adults have not yet been tested (Bowers and Puttick, unpublished data). These larvae are warningly colored black and white and are unpalatable and emetic to birds (Bowers 1980). How-ever, pupae of the tortricid moth, *Endothenia hebesana* (Tortricidae) whose larvae are seed predators of *C. glabra* (Spencer 1969; Stamp 1986) did not contain iridoid glycosides (Bowers and Puttick unpublished data).

Stermitz and co-workers (Harris et al. 1986; Stermitz et al. 1986, 1988) have examined other species of Lepidoptera that specialize on iridoid glycoside-containing plants. *Euphydryas anicia* (Nymphalidae), which feeds on various plant species in the Scrophulariaceae, Plantaginaceae, and Caprifoliaceae, contains iridoid glycosides in amounts as high as 8 percent dry weight (Stermitz et al. 1986; Gardner and Stermitz 1988). The larvae of two species of *Penstemon*-feeding (Scrophulariaceae) geometrids, which are waringly colored black and white, sequester iridoid glycosides; but the adults, which are cryptic, are essentially devoid of these compounds (Stermitz et al. 1988) (table 13.1). *Platyptilia pica* (Pterophoridae), which feeds on certain *Castilleja* species, is small and cryptic and did not sequester iridoid glycosides (Harris et al. 1986). Thus the fates of plant natural products may differ substantially in different species of herbivores feeding on plants containing those compounds. For potentially defensive compounds such as iridoid glycosides, warning coloration and associated characteristics that appear to advertise unpalatability may be good clues as to the fates of such compounds.

The Importance of Variation

The recent development and implementation of analytical chemical techniques such as high performance liquid chromatography, gas-liquid chromatography, gas chromatography-mass spectroscopy, and radioactive labeling have been catalytic to the study of the chemical ecology of plant-insect interactions. Of particular importance to the topic of insect sequestration of plant allelochemicals, these techniques have revealed dramatic variation in the allelochemical composition of plants and insects. In plants, this variation may be evident among different individuals within a species (Langenheim et al. 1978; Brower et al. 1982; Rodman and Chew 1980), among different organs of an individual plant (Brower et al. 1982; Chambliss and Jones 1966; Langenheim et al. 1978; Lincoln et al. 1982), and even within individual leaves (Whitham 1983; Zucker 1982). This variation may be qualitative, that is, related to what particular compounds are present, as well as quantitative, related to how much of particular compounds are present. For insects which sequester such compounds, the kind and amount of these compounds present in the host plant may determine the relative concentration of these compounds in the insects, and hence the degree of chemical defense and potentially, protection from predators.

Among insects, variation in the sequestration of plant natural products occurs among different insect species which feed on the same plant species (Dixon et al. 1978; Nishio 1980; Cohen and Brower 1983), among individuals of a single insect species which feed on different plant species (e.g., Brower et al. 1972; Isman et al. 1977; Bowers 1980), and among individuals of a single species which feed on the same plant species (e.g., Nishio 1980; Isman et al. 1977; Gardner and Stermitz 1988). In addition, there may be substantial variation from one developmental stage to the next: as larvae grow, they may sequester increasingly large amounts of plant allelochemicals; alternatively, compounds sequestered during larval feeding may be lost in the adult stage (e.g., figure 13.3). Several studies have also shown differences among males and females of the same species in the amounts and kinds of allelochemicals that are sequestered (Marsh and Rothschild 1974; Stermitz et al. 1986).

Such variation may be crucial to both the plant and the insect. Individual plants with more allelochemicals or a more variable allelochemical array may be better protected from insect predation (Coley 1983; Dolinger et al. 1973; Breedlove and Ehrlich 1968). Plant parts with more allelochemicals may be less acceptable as food for herbivorous insects (Feeny 1970; Lincoln et al. 1982); thus the feeding patterns of insects may be determined by the variation in the allelochemical content of their food plants (Whitham 1983; Lincoln et al. 1982). Insect species which sequester plant allelochemicals to use in their own defense may increase their unpalatability by feeding on individual plants or plant parts which have a high allelochemical content. Chemical variation among and within host plants may affect the dynamics of insect populations, as in Müllerian mimicry rings (Gilbert 1984). Thus the phenomenon of automimicry, previously discussed for only a few species (e.g., *D. plexippus* and *E. phaeton* [Brower et al. 1972; Bowers 1980, 1981], is probably an important factor in populations of many unpalatable insect species.

The Evolution of Unpalatability

The use of unpalatability as a defense strategy of insects has been documented in a variety of species. However, in only a few cases has the basis of this unpalatability been determined or the potential role of host plant chemistry been unraveled. Moreover, only rarely have host plant chemistry, insect processing and putative chemical defense, and predator response to a putative chemical defense been examined in a single system. An examination of all three levels is necessary for understanding the importance, or lack thereof, of plant natural products in the dynamics of these interactions. Within this three-trophic-level framework, there are several areas that may be particularly productive for future research. The first is to continue to examine qualitative and quantitative variation in plant allelochemicals, and the importance of this variation for unpalatable insects. For example, if an unpalatable insect species is physiologically efficient at sequestering defensive compounds from its host plant, chemical variation among different individual host plants may be less important than for a species that is less efficient. In a less efficient species, preference for, and the ability to choose, individual plants that are already relatively high in their concentrations of potential defensive compounds may be critical in the degree to which the insect is protected from potential predators. Such factors may affect the population dynamics of both the unpalatable insect and the host plant. A study of the insect physiological processess involved in sequestration and the efficiency of this process, coupled with an examination of insect host choice as related to host plant chemistry, would add to our understanding of the importance of such factors in the evolution of the ability to sequester plant natural products.

The evolution of unpalatability and the ability to manufacture or sequester defensive compounds constitute a second area of potential study. Such evolutionary questions can be addressed by a comparative approach, for example, by comparing related taxa that do and do not sequester host plant chemicals for use in their own defense, with a view to understanding similarities and differences in their physiology, ecology, and behavior. This approach may identify those features that characterize taxa with the ability to sequester defensive chemicals and perhaps provide insight into the evolution of those features. A related, but potentially more powerful, approach is to couple phylogenetic analyses of taxa that exhibit variation in their ability to sequester defensive chemicals, or in their exhibition of aposematic coloration and behaviors, with a study of the chemistry, physiology, and behavior of those taxa. A phylogeny may provide the framework on which can be placed information on plant chemistry, insect processing capabilities, and insect coloration, with a view to understanding the evolution of those characters (e.g., Sillén-Tullberg 1988). The collaboration of systematists with chemists, physiologists, and chemical ecologists could be extremely productive in providing insight into the evolution of unpalatability and its associated adaptations.

This manuscript has benefited from comments by Gillian Puttick, James Carpenter, Kathryn Burgess, Theodore Sargent, and Nancy Stamp. Supported by NSF grant BSR-8307353 to M.D. Bowers.

References

Ackery, P.R., and R.I. Vane-Wright. 1984. *Milkweed Butterflies.* New York: Cornell University Press.

Ahmad, S. (ed.). 1983. *Herbivorous Insects: Host-seeking Behavior and Mechanisms.* New York: Academic Press.

Aplin, R.T., M.H. Benn, and M. Rothschild. 1968. Poisonous alkaloids in the body tissues of the Cinnabar Moth (*Callimorpha jacobaeae* L.). *Nature* 219:747-748.

Aplin, R.T., and M. Rothschild. 1972. Poisonous alkaloids in the body tissues of the Garden Tiger Moth (*Arctia caja* L.) and the Cinnabar Moth (*Tyria (=Callimorpha) jacobaeae* L.). In A. de Vries and E. Kochva (eds.), *Toxins of Animal and Plant Origin, Vol. 2.* London: Gordon and Breach. Pp. 579-595.

Aplin, R.T., R. d'Arcy Ward, and M. Rothschild. 1975. Examination of the large white and small white butterflies (*Pieris* spp.) for the presence of mustard oils and mustard oil glycosides. *J. Ent. (A)* 50:73-79.

Barbosa, P., and J.A. Saunders. 1985. Plant allelochemicals: linkages between herbivores and their natural enemies. *Rec. Adv. Phytochem.* 19:107-137.

Barbosa, P., J.A. Saunders, J. Kemper, R. Trumbule, J. Olechno, and P. Martinat. 1986. Plant allelochemicals and insect parasitoids: Effects of nicotine on *Cotesia congregata* (Say) (Hymenoptera: Braconidae) and *Hyposoter annulipes* (Cresson) (Hymenoptera: Ichneumonidae). *J. Chem. Ecol.* 12:1319-1328.

Bell, A.A. 1981. Biochemical mechanisms of disease resistance. *Ann. Rev. Plant Physiol.* 32:21-81.

Bell, W.J., and R.T. Carde (eds.). 1984. *Chemical Ecology of Insects.* Sunderland, Mass.: Sinauer Press.

Benn, M.H., J. DeGrave, C. Gnanasundersam, and R. Hutchins. 1979. Host-plant pyrrolizidine alkaloids in *Nyctemera annulata* Boisduval: their persistence through the life-cycle and transfer to a parasite. *Experientia* 35:731-732.

Berenbaum, M. 1978. Toxicity of a furanocoumarin to armyworms: a case of biosynthetic escape from insect herbivores. *Science* 201:532-533.

_____. **1985.** Brementown revisited: interactions among allelochemicals in plants. *Rec. Adv. Phytochem.* 19:139-169.

Bernays, E.A., and R.F. Chapman. 1978. Plant chemistry and acridoid feeding behavior. In J.B. Harborne (ed.), *Biochemical Aspects of Plant and Animal Coevolution.* New York: Academic Press. Pp. 99-141.

Bernays, E.A., and C. DeLuca. 1981. Insect anti-feedant properties of an iridoid glycoside: ipolamiide. *Experientia* 37:1289-1290.

Bernays, E.A., J.A. Edgar, and M. Rothschild. 1977. Pyrrolizidine alkaloids sequestered by the aposematic grasshopper, *Zonocerus variegatus. J. Zool.* 182:85-87.

Bernays, E.A., and S. Woodhead. 1982. Plant phenols utilized as nutrients by a phytophagous insect. *Science* 216:201-202.

Blau, P.A., P. Feeny, L. Contardo, and D. Robson. 1978. Allylglucosinolates and herbivorous caterpillars: a contrast in toxicity and tolerance. *Science* 200:1296-1298.

Blum, M.S. 1978. Biochemical defenses of insects. In M. Rockstein (ed.), *Biochemistry of Insects.* New York: Academic Press. Pp. 465-513.

_____. **1981.** *Arthropod Defenses.* New York: Academic Press.

_____. **1983.** Detoxification, deactivation, and utilization of plant compounds by insects. In P. Hedin (ed.). *Plant Resistance to Insects.* Washington, D.C.: American Chemical Society. Pp. 265-275.

Blum, M.S., L. Rivier, and T. Plowman. 1981. Fate of cocaine in the lymantriid *Eloria noyesi,* a predator of *Erythroxylum coca. Phytochemistry* 20:2499-2500.

Boppré, M. 1986. Insects pharmacophagously utilizing defensive plant chemicals (pyrrolizidine alkaloids). *Naturwissenschaften* 73:17-26.

Bowers, M.D. 1980. Unpalatability as a defense strategy of *Euphydryas phaeton* (Lepidoptera: Nymphalidae). *Evolution* 34:586-600.

_____. **1981.** Unpalatability as a defense strategy of western checkerspot butterflies (*Euphydryas,* Nymphalidae). *Evolution* 35:367-375.

_____. **1983.** Iridoid glycosides and larval hostplant specificity in checkerspot butterflies (*Euphydryas,* Nymphalidae). *J. Chem. Ecol.* 9:475-493.

_____. **1984.** Iridoid glycosides and host-plant specificity in larvae of the Buckeye butterfly, *Junonia coenia* (Nymphalidae). *J. Chem. Ecol.* 10:1567-1577.

Bowers, M.D., and Larin, Z. 1989. Acquired chemical defense in the lycaenid butterfly, *Eumaeus atala. J. Chem. Ecol. 15:1133-1146.*

Bowers, M.D., and G.M. Puttick. 1986. The fate of ingested iridoid glycosides in lepidopteran herbivores. *J. Chem. Ecol.* 12:169-178.

Brattsten, L.B. 1979a. Biochemical defense mechanisms in herbivores against plant allelochemicals. In G.A. Rosenthal, and D. Janzen (eds.), *Herbivores: Their Interaction with Plant Secondary Metabolities.* New York: Academic Press. Pp. 200-270.

_____. **1979b.** Ecological significance of mixed-function oxidations. *Drug Metab. Rev.* 10:35-58.

Brattsten, L.B., S.L. Price, and C.A. Gunderson. 1980. Microsomal oxidases in midgut and fat-body tissues of a broadly herbivorous insect larva, *Spodoptera eridania* Cramer (Noctuidae). *Comp Biochem. Physiol.* C 66:231-237.

Brattsten, L.B., C.F. Wilkinson, and T. Eisner. 1977. Herbivore-plant interactions: mixed-function oxidases and secondary plant substances. *Science* 196:1349-1352.

Breedlove, D.E., and P.R. Ehrlich. 1968. Plant-herbivore coevolution: lupines and lycaenids. *Science* 162:672–673.

Brower, L.P. 1984. Chemical defense in butterflies. In R.I. Vane-Wright and P.R. Ackery (eds.), *The Biology of Butterflies.* Royal Entomological Society Symposium 11. New York: Academic Press. Pp. 109–134.

Brower, L.P.,M. Edmunds, and C.M. Moffitt. 1975. Cardenolide content and palatability of a population of *Danaus chrysippus* butterflies from West Africa. *J. Ent. (A)* 49:183–196.

Brower, L.P., and S.C. Glazier. 1975. Localization of heart poisons in the Monarch butterfly. *Science* 188:19–25.

Brower, L.P., P.B. McEvoy, K.L. Williamson, and M.A. Flannery. 1972. Variation in cardiac glycoside content of monarch butterflies from natural populations in eastern North America. *Science* 177:426–429.

Brower, L.P., J.N. Seiber, C.J. Nelson, S.P. Lynch, M.M. Holland. 1984. Plant-determined variation in the cardenolide content, thin-layer chromatography, and emetic potency of monarch butterflies, *Danaus plexippus,* reared on the milkweed *Asclepias speciosa* in California. *J. Chem. Ecol.* 10:601–639.

Brower, L.P., J.N. Seiber, C.J. Nelson, S.P. Lynch, and P.M. Tuskes. 1982. Plant-determined variation in the cardenolide content, thin-layer chromatography profiles, and emetic potency of Monarch butterflies, *Danaus plexippus,* reared on the milkweed, *Asclepias eriocarpa,* in California. *J. Chem. Ecol.* 8:579–633.

Bryant, J.P. 1980. Phytochemical deterrence of snowshoe hare browsing by adventitious shoots of four Alaskan trees. *Science* 213:889–890.

Bryant, J.P., and P. Kuropat. 1980. Selection of winter forage by subarctic browsing vertebrates: the role of plant chemistry. *Ann. Rev. Ecol. Syst.* 11:261–285.

Bull, D.L., G.W. Ivie, R.C. Beier, N.W. Pryor, and E.H. Oertli. 1984. Fate of photosensitizing furanocoumarins in tolerant and sensitive insects. *J. Chem. Ecol.* 10:893–911.

Burnett, W.C., S.B. Jones, Jr., T.J. Mabry, and W.G. Padolina. 1974. Sesquiterpene lactones— insect feeding deterrents in *Vernonia. Biochem. Syst. Ecol.* 2:25–29.

Campbell, B.C. and S.S. Duffey. 1979. Tomatine and parasitic wasps: potential incompatability of plant-antibiosis with biological control. *Science* 205:700–702.

Chambliss, O.L., and C.M. Jones. 1966. Cucurbitacins: specific insect attractants in Cucurbitaceae. *Science* 153:1392–1393.

Cohen, J.A. 1985. Differences and similarities in cardenolide contents of Queen and Monarch butterflies in Florida and their ecological and evolutionary implications. *J. Chem. Ecol.* 11:85–103.

Cohen, J.A., and Brower, L.P. 1983. Cardenolide sequestration by the dogbane tiger moth (*Cycnia tenera;* Arctiidae). *J. Chem. Ecol.* 9:521–532.

Coley, P.D. 1983. Herbivory and defensive characteristics of tree species in a lowland tropical forest. *Ecol. Mon.* 53:209–233.

Common I.F.B., and T.E. Bellas. 1977. Regurgitation of host-plant oil from a foregut diverticulum in the larvae of *Myrascia megalocentra* and *M. bracteatella* (Lepidoptera: Oecophoridae). *J. Aust. Ent. Soc.* 16:141–147.

Connor, W.E., T. Eisner, R.K. Vander Meer, A. Guerrero, J. Meinwald. 1981. Precopulatory sexual interaction in an arctiid moth (*Utetheisa ornatrix*): role of a pheromone derived from dietary alkaloids. *Behav. Ecol. Sociobiol.* 9:227–235.

Cornell, J.C., N.E. Stamp, and M.D. Bowers. 1987. Developmental change in aggregation, defense and escape behavior of buckmoth caterpillars, *Hemileuca lucina* (Saturniidae). *Behav. Ecol. Sociobiol.* 20:383–388.

Crankshaw, D.R., and J.H. Langenheim. 1981. Variation in terpenes and phenolics through leaf development in *Hymenaea* and its possible significance to herbivory. *Biochem. Syst. Ecol.* 9:115–124.

David, W.A.L., and B.O.C. Gardner. 1966a. The effect of sinigrin on the feeding of *Pieris brassicae:* larvae transferred from various diets. *Ent. Exp. Appl.* 9:95–98.

_____. **1966b.** Mustard oil glucosides as feeding stimulants for *Pieris brassicae* larvae in a semi-synthetic diet. *Ent. Exp. Appl.* 9:247–255.

Del Moral, R. 1972. On the variability of chlorogenic acid concentration. *Oecologia* 9:289–300.

Deroe, C., and J.M. Pasteels. 1982. Distribution of adult defense glands in chrysomelids (Coleoptera, Chrysomelidae) and its significance in the evolution of defense mechanisms within the family. *J. Chem. Ecol.* 8:67–82.

Deverall, B.J. 1977. *Defence Mechanisms of Plants.* Cambridge: Cambridge University Press.

Dixon, C.A., J.M. Erickson, D.N. Kellett, and M. Rothschild. 1978. Some adaptations between *Danaus plexippus* and its food plant, with notes on *Danaus chrysippus* and *Euploea core* (Insecta: Lepidoptera). *J. Zool. Lond.* 185:437–467.

Dolinger, P.M., P.R. Ehrlich, W.L. Fitch, and D.E. Breedlove. 1973. Alkaloid and predation patterns in Colorado lupine populations. *Oecologia* 13:191–204.

Duffey, S.S. 1980. Sequestration of plant natural products by insects. *Ann. Rev. Ent.* 25:447–477.

Duffey, S.S., M.S. Blum, M. Isman, and G.G.E. Scudder. 1978. Cardiac glycosides: a physical system for the sequestration by the milkweed bug. *J. Insect Physiol.* 24:639–645.

Duffey, S.S., K.A. Bloem, and B.C. Campbell. 1986. Consequences of sequestration of plant natural products in plant-insect-parasitoid interactions. In D.J. Boethel and R.D. Eikenbary (eds.) *Interactions of Plant Resistance and Parasitoids and Predators of Insects.* Chichester, England: Ellis Horwood Ltd. Pp. 31–60.

Duffey, S.S., and G.G.E. Scudder. 1972. Cardiac glycosides in North American Asclepiadaceae, a basis for unpalatability in brightly colored Hemiptera and Coleoptera. *J. Insect Physiol.* 18:63–78.

_____. **1974.** Cardiac glycosides in *Oncopeltus fasciatus* (Dallas) (Hemiptera: Lygaeidae). I. The uptake and distribution of natural cardenolides in the body. *Can. J. Zool.* 52:283–290.

Edgar, J.A., M. Boppré, and D. Schneider. 1979. Pyrrolizidine alkaloid storage in African and Australian danaid butterflies. *Experientia* 35:1447–1448.

Edgar, J.A., and C.C.J. Culvenor. 1974. Pyrrolizidine ester alkaloids in danaid butterflies. *Nature* 248:614.

_____. **1975.** Pyrrolizidine alkaloids in *Parsonsia* species (family Apocynaceae) which attract danaid butterflies. *Experientia* 31:393–394.

Ehrlich, P.R., and P.H. Raven. 1964. Butterflies and plants: a study in coevolution. *Evolution* 18:576–608.

Eisner, T. 1970. Chemical defense against predation in Arthropods. In E. Sondheimer and J.B. Simeone (eds.), *Chemical Ecology.* New York: Academic Press. Pp. 157–217.

_____. **1980.** Chemistry, defense and survival: case studies and selected topics. In M. Locke (ed.), *Insect Biology in the Future.* New York: Academic Press. Pp. 847–878.

Eisner, T., J.S. Johnessee, J. Carrel, L.B. Hendry, and J. Meinwald. 1974. Defensive use by an insect of a plant resin. *Science* 184:996–999.

Eisner, T., and Y.C. Meinwald. 1965. Defensive secretion of a caterpillar (*Papilio*). *Science* 150:1733–1735.

Feeny, P.P. 1970. Seasonal changes in oak leaf tannins as a cause of spring feeding by winter moth caterpillars. *Ecology* 51:656–681.

Ferguson, J.E., and R.L. Metcalf. 1985. Cucurbitacins: plant-derived defensive compounds for diabroticites (Coleoptera: Chrysomelidae). *J. Chem. Ecol.* 11:311–318.

Fraenkel, G. 1959. The raison d'etre of secondary plant substances. *Science* 121:1466–1470.

_____. **1969.** Evaluation of our thoughts on secondary plant substances. *Ent. Exp. Appl.* 12:473–486.

Freeland, W.J., and D.H. Janzen. 1974. Strategies in herbivory by mammals: the role of secondary compounds. *Am. Natur.* 108:269–289.

Freeman, M.A. 1968. Pharmacological properties of the regurgitated crop fluid of the African migratory locust, *Locusta migratoria* L. *Comp. Biochem. Physiol.* 26:1041–1049.

Futuyma, D.J. 1983. Evolutionary interactions among herbivorous insects and plants. In D. Futuyma and M. Slatkin (eds.), *Coevolution.* Sunderland, Mass.: Sinauer Press. Pp. 207–231.

Futuyma, D.J., and M. Slatkin (eds.). 1983. *Coevolution.* Sunderland, Mass.: Sinauer Press.

Gardner, D.W. 1987. Iridoid glycoside chemistry of some *Castilleja* and *Besseya* plants and their hosted checkerspot butterflies. Ph.D. dissertation. Colorado State Universtiy, Fort Collins, Colorado.

Gardner, D.W., and F.R. Stermitz. 1988. Hostplant utilization and iridoid glycoside sequestration by *Euphydryas anicia* (Lepidoptera: Nymphalidae). *J. Chem. Ecol.* 14:2147–2168.

Gibbs, R.D. 1974. *Chemotaxonomy of Flowering Plants.* Montreal: McGill-Queens University Press.

Gilbert, L.E. 1984. The biology of butterfly communities. In R.I. Vane-Wright and P.R. Ackery (eds.), *The Biology of Butterflies.* Symposium of the Royal Entomological Society of London 11. New York and London: Academic Press. Pp. 41–54.

Gould, F., and A. Massey. 1984. Cucurbitacins and predation of the spotted cucumber beetle, *Diabrotica undecimpunctata howardi. Ent. Exp. Appl.* 36:273–278.

Harborne, J.B., and J.L. Ingham. 1978. Biochemical aspects of the coevolution of higher plants with their fungal parasites. In J.B. Harborne (ed.), *Biochemical Aspects of Plant and Animal Coevolution.* London: Academic Press. Pp. 343–405.

Harris, G.H., F.R. Stermitz, and W. Jing. 1986. Iridoids and alkaloids from *Castilleja* hostplants for *Platyptilia pica* (Lepidpotera: Pterophoridae): rhexifoline content of *P. pica. Biochem. Syst. Ecol.* 14:499–504.

Haslam, E. 1986. Secondary metabolism: fact and fiction. *Nat. Prod. Rep.* 1985:217–249.

Haukioja, E. and P. Niemala. 1977. Retarded growth of a geometrid after mechanical damage to leaves of its host tree. *Ann. Zool. Fenn.* 14:48–52.

Hawthorne, W.R. 1978. Some effects of different *Plantago* species on feeding preference and egg laying in the flea beetle *Dibolia borealis* Chev. (Chrysomelidae). *Can. J. Zool.* 56:1507–1513.

Hedin, P.A. (ed.) 1983. *Plant Resistance to Insects.* Washington D.C.: American Chemical Society.

Hegnauer, R. 1964–1973. *Chemotaxonomie der Pflanzen.* Vols. 1–6. Basel and Stuttgart: Berkhauser Verlag.

Isman, M.B., S.S. Duffey, and G.G.E. Scudder. 1977. Cardenolide content of some leaf-and stem-feeding insects on temperate North American milkweeds (*Asclepias* spp.). *Can. J. Zool.* 55:1024–1028.

Jensen, S.R., B.J. Nielsen, and R. Dahlgren. 1975. Iridoid compounds, their occurrence and systematic importance in the angiosperms. *Bot. Not.* 128:148–180.

Jermy, T., F.E. Hanson, and V.G. Dethier. 1968. Induction of specific foodplant preference in lepidopterous larvae. *Ent. Exp. Appl.* 11:211–230.

Jones, C.G., T.A. Hess, D.W. Whitman, P.J. Silk, and M.S. Blum. 1987. Effects of diet breadth on autogenous chemical defense of a generalist grasshopper. *J. Chem. Ecol.* 13:383–399.

Karban, R. 1983. Induced responses of cherry trees to periodical cicada oviposition. *Oecologia* 59:226–231.

Krieger, R.I., P.P. Feeny, and C.F. Wilkinson. 1971. Detoxification enzymes in the guts of caterpillars: an evolutionary answer to plant defense. *Science* 172:579–581.

Kubo, I., and F.J. Hanke, 1985. Multifaceted chemically based resistance in plants. *Rec. Adv. Phytochem.* 19:171–194.

Langenheim, J.H., W.H. Stubblebine, D.E. Lincoln, and G.E. Foster. 1978. Implications of variation in resin composition among organs, tissues and populations in the tropical legume *Hymenaea. Biochem. Syst. Ecol.* 6:299–313.

Lincoln, D.E., T.S. Newton, P.R. Ehrlich, and K.S. Williams. 1982. Coevolution of the checkerspot butterfly *Euphydryas chalcedona* and its larval food plant, *Diplacus aurantiacus:* Larval response to protein and leaf resin. *Oecologia* 52:216–223.

McKey, D. 1979. The distribution of secondary compounds within plants. In G.A. Rosenthal and D.H. Janzen (eds.), *Herbivores: Their Interaction with Secondary Plant Metabolites.* New York: Academic Press. Pp. 55–133.

McLain, D.K. 1984. Coevolution: Mullerian mimicry between a plant bug (Miridae) and a seed bug (Lygaeidae) and the relationship between hostplant choice and unpalatability. *Oikos* 43:143–148.

McLain, D.K., and D.J. Shure. 1985. Hostplant toxins and unpalatability of *Neacoryphus bicrucis* (Hemiptera: Lygaeidae). *Ecol. Ent.* 10:291–298.

Marsh, N., and M. Rothschild. 1974. Aposematic and cryptic Lepidoptera tested on the mouse. *J. Zool.* 174:89–122.

Metcalf, R.L. 1986. Coevolutionary adaptations of rootworm beetles (Coleoptera: Chrysomelidae) to cucurbitacins. *J. Chem. Ecol.* 12:1109–1124.

Miller, J.S., and P. Feeny. 1983. Effects of benzylisoquinoline alkaloids on the larvae of polyphagous Lepidoptera. *Oecologia* 58:332–339.

Morrow, P.A., T.E. Bellas, and T. Eisner. 1976. *Eucalyptus* oils in the defensive oral discharge of Australian sawfly larvae (Hymenoptera: Pergidae). *Oecologia* 24:193–206.

Nayar, J.K., and G. Fraenkel. 1963. The chemical basis of host selection in the catalpa sphinx, *Ceratomia catalpae* (Lepidoptera: Sphingidae). *Ann. Ent. Soc. Am.* 56:119–122.

Nelson, C.J. J.N. Seiber, and L.P. Brower. 1981. Seasonal and intraplant variation of cardenolide content in the California milkweed, *Asclepias eriocarpa,* and the implications for plant defense. *J. Chem. Ecol.* 7:981–1010.

Nishio, S. 1980. The Fates and Adaptive Significance of Cardenolides Sequestered by Larvae of *Danaus plexippus* (L.) and *Cycina inopinatus* (Hy. Edwards). Ph.D. dissertation. University of Georgia. University Microflims.

Parry, R.H. 1974. Revision of the genus *Dibolia* Latreille in America north of Mexico (Coleoptera: Chrysomelidae). *Can. J. Zool.* 52:1317–1354.

Pasteels, J.M., M. Rowell-Rahier, J. Braekman, and D. Daloze. 1984. Chemical defences in leaf beetles and their larvae: the ecological, evolutionary and taxonomic significance. *Biochem. Syst. Ecol.* 12:395–406.

Pasteels, J.M., Rowell-Rahier, J.C. Braeman, and A. Dupont. 1983. Salicin from hostplant as precursor of salicylaldehyde in defensive secretion of Chrysomeline larvae. *Physiol. Ent.* 8:307–314.

Pereyra, P., and M.D. Bowers. 1988. Iridoid glycosides as oviposition stimulants for the Buckeye, *Junonia coenia* (Nymphalidae). J. Chem. Ecol. 14:917–928.

Rees, C.J.C. 1969. Chemoreceptor specificity associated with choice of feeding site by the beetle *Chrysolina brunsvicensis* on its foodplant *Hypericum hirsutum*. *Ent. Exp. Appl.* 12:565–583.

Reichstein, T., J. von Euw, J.A. Parsons, and M. Rothschild. 1968. Heart poisons in the monarch butterfly. *Science* 161:861–866.

Rhoades, D.F. 1983. Herbivore population dynamics and plant chemistry. In R.F. Denno and M.S. McClure (eds.), *Variable Plants and Herbivores in Natural and Managed Systems.* New York: Academic Press. Pp. 155–220.

Rice, E.L. 1979. *Allelopathy.* New York: Academic Press.

Robinson, T. 1974. Metabolism and function of alkaloids in plants. *Science* 184:430–435.

Roby, M.R. and F.R. Stermitz. 1984. Pyrrolizidine and pyridine monoterpene alkaloids from 2 *Castilleja* plant hosts of the plume moth, *Platyptilia pica. J. Nat. Prod.* 47:846–853.

Rodman, J.E. and F.S. Chew. 1980. Phytochemical correlates of herbivory in a community of native and naturalized Cruciferae. *Biochem. Syst. Ecol.* 8:43–50.

Roeske, C.N., J.N. Seiber, L.P. Brower, and C.M. Moffitt. 1976. Milkweed cardenolides and their comparative processing by monarch butterflies (*Danaus plexippus* L.). *Rec. Adv. Phytochem.* 10:93–167.

Rosenthal, G.A. 1983. L-canavanine and L-canaline: protective allelochemicals of certain leguminous plants. In P.A. Hedin (ed.), *Plant Resistance to Insects.* Washington, D.C.: American Chemical Society. Pp. 279–290.

Rosenthal, G.A., and D.H. Janzen. 1989. *Herbivores: Their Interaction with Plant Secondary Metabolites.* New York: Academic Press.

Rosenthal, G.A., D.H. Janzen, and D.L. Dahlman. 1977. Degradation and detoxification of canavanine by a specialized seed predator. *Science* 196:658–660.

Rothschild, M. 1972. Secondary plant substances and warning colouration in insects. In H.F. Van Emden (ed.), *Insect/Plant Relationships.* Symposium of the Royal Entomological Society, No. 6. New York: John Wiley and Sons. Pp. 59–83.

_____. **1985.** British aposematic Lepidoptera. In J. Heath and A.M. Emmet (eds.), *The Moths and Butterflies of Great Britian and Ireland.* Essex, England: Harley Books. Pp. 9–62.

Rothschild, M., R.T. Aplin, P.A. Cockrun, J.A. Edgar, P. Fairweather, and R. Lees. 1979. Pyrrolizidine alkaloids in arctiid moths (Lep.) with a discussion on host plant relationships and the role of these secondary plant substances in the Arctiidae. *Biol. J. Linn. Soc.* 12:305–326.

Rothschild, M., R.J. Nash, and E.A. Bell. 1986. Cycasin in the endangered butterfly, *Eumaeus atala florida. Phytochemistry* 25:1853–1854.

Rothschild, M., and T. Reichstein. 1976. Some problems associated with the storage of cardiac glycosides by insects. *Nova Acta Leopoldina. Suppl.* 7:507–550.

Rothschild, M., J. von Euw, and T. Reichstein. 1972. Aristolochic acids stored by *Zerynthia polyxena* (Lepidoptera). *Insect Biochem.* 2:332–343.

Rothschild, M., J. von Euw, and T. Reichstein. 1970. Cardiac glycosides in the oleander aphid, *Aphis nerii. J. Insect Phys.* 16:1141–1145.

Rothschild, M., J. von Euw, and T. Reichstein. 1973. Cardiac glycosides in a scale insect (*Aspidiotus*), a ladybird (*Coccinella*) and a lacewing (*Chrysopa*). *J. Ent. (A)* 48:89–90.

Rothschild, M., M.G. Rowan, and J.W. Fairburn. 1977. Storage of cannabinoids by *Arctia caja* and *Zonocerus elegans* fed on chemically distinct strains of *Cannabis sativa. Nature* 266:650–651.

Ryan, C.A. 1979. Proteinase inhibitors. In G.A. Rosenthal and D.H. Janzen (eds.), *Herbivores: Their Interaction with Plant Secondary Metabolites.* New York: Academic Press. Pp. 599–618.

Schneider, D., M. Boppré, H. Schneider, W.R. Thompson, C.J. Borak, R.L. Petty, and J. Meinwald. 1975. A pheromone precursor and its uptake in male *Danaus* butterflies. *J. Comp. Physiol.* 97:245–256.

Schoönhoven, L.M. 1972. Plant recognition by lepidopterous larvae. *Symp. Roy. Soc. Lond.* 6:87–99.

Scudder, G.G.E., and S.S. Duffey. 1972. Cardiac glycosides in the Lygaeinae (Hemiptera: Lygaeidae). *Can. J. Zool.* 50:35–42.

Scudder, G.G.E., L.V. Moore, and M.B. Isman. 1986. Sequestration of cardenolides in *Oncopeltus fasciatus:* morphological and physiological adaptations. *J. Chem. Ecol.* 12:1171–1187.

Seiber, J.N., P.M. Tuskes, L.P. Brower, and C.J. Nelson. 1980. Pharmacodynamics of some individual cardenolides fed to larvae of the monarch butterfly (*Danaus plexippus* L.). *J. Chem. Ecol.* 6:321–339.

Seigler, D. 1977. Primary roles for secondary compounds. *Biochem. Syst. Ecol.* 5:195–199.

Seigler, D., and P.W. Price. 1976. Secondary compounds in plants: primary functions. *Am. Natur.* 110:101–105.

Self, L.S., F.E. Guthrie, and E. Hodgson. 1964a. Adaptation of tobacco hornworms to the ingestion of nicotine. *J. Insect Physiol.* 10:907–914.

———. **191964b.** Metabolism of nicotine by tobacco feeding insects. *Nature* 204:300–301.

Sillén-Tullberg, B. 1988. Evolution of gregariousness in aposematic butterfly larvae: a phylogenetic analysis. *Evolution* 42:293–305.

Sillén-Tullberg, B., C. Wiklund, and T. Järvi. 1982. Aposematic coloration in adults and larvae of *Lygaeus equestris* and its bearing on mullerian mimcry: an experimental study on predation on living bugs by the great tit, *Parus major. Oikos* 39:131–136.

Spencer, K.A. 1969. *The Agromyzidae of Canada and Alaska. Mem. Ent. Soc. Can.* 64:3–311.

Stamp, N.E. 1982. Behavioral interactions of parasitoids and Baltimore checkerspot caterpillars (*E. phaeton*). *Environ. Ent.* 11:100–104.

———. **1984.** Effect of defoliation by checkerspot caterpillars (*Euphydryas phaeton*) and sawfly larvae (*Macrophya nigra* and *Tenthredo grandis*) on their hostplants (*Chelone* sp.). *Oecologia* 63:275–280.

———. **1986.** Availability of resources for predators of *Chelone* seeds. *Am. Midl. Natur.* 117:265–279.

Stermitz, F.R., D.R. Gardner, F.J. Odendaal, and P.R. Ehrlich. 1986. *Euphydryas anicia* utilization of iridoid glucosides from *Castilleja* and *Besseya* (Scrophulariaceae) hostplants. *J. Chem. Ecol.* 12:1459–1468.

Stermitz, F.R., D.R. Gardner, and N. McFarland. 1988. Iridoid glycoside sequestration by two aposematic *Penstemon* feeding geometrid larvae. *J. Chem. Ecol.* 14:435–441.

Teas, H.J., J.G. Cyson, and B.R. Whisenant. 1966. Cycasin metabolism in *Seirarctia echo* Abbot and Smith (Lepidoptera: Arctiidae). *J. Ga. Ent. Soc.* 1:21–22.

Terriere, L.C. 1984. Induction of detoxication enzymes in insects. *Ann. Rev. Ent.* 29:71–88.

Valentine, H.T., W.E. Wellner, and P.M. Wargo. 1983. Nutritional changes in host foliage during and after defoliation, and their relation to the weight of gypsy moth pupae. *Oecologia* 57:298–302.

Vaughan, F.A. 1979. Effect of gross cardiac glycoside content of seeds of common milkweed, *Asclepias syriaca*, on cardiac glycoside uptake by the milkweed bug, *Oncopeltus fasciatus. J. Chem. Ecol.* 5:89–100.

Verschaffelt, E. 1910. The cause determining the selection of food in some herbiviorous insects. *Proc. Acad. Sci. Amsterdam* 13:536–542.

Visser, J.H., and A.K. Minks (eds.). 1982. *Proceedings of the 5th International Symposium on Insect-Plant Relationships.* Wageningen (the Netherlands): Pudoc.

von Euw, J., L. Fishelson, J.A. Parsons, T. Reichstein, and M. Rothschild. 1967. Cardenolides (heart poisons) in a grasshopper (*Poekilocerus bufonius* (Klug 1802) (Pyrgomorphinae)) feeding on milkweeds (Asclepiadaceae). *Nature* 214:35–39.

Whitham, T. 1983. Host manipulation of parasites: within-plant variation as a defense against rapidly evolving pests. In R.F. Denno and M.S. McClure (eds.), *Variable Plants and Herbivores in Natural and Managed Systems.* New York: Academic Press. Pp. 15–41.

Whittaker, R.H., and P.P. Feeny. 1971. Allelochemicals: chemical interactions between species. *Science* 171:757–770.

Wiklund, C., and T. Järvi. 1982. Survival of distasteful insects after being attacked by naive birds: a reappraisal of the theory of aposematic coloration evolving through individual selection. *Evolution* 36:998–1002.

Wilkinson, C.F. 1983. Role of mixed-function oxidases in insecticide resistance. In G.P. Georghiou and T. Saito (eds.), *Pest Resistance to Insecticides.* New York: Plenum Press.

Yu, S.J. 1982. Induction of microsomal oxidases by host plants in the fall armyworm, *Spodoptera frugiperda* (J.E. Smith). *Pestic. Biochem. Physiol.* 17:59–67.

_____. **1983.** Induction of detoxifying enzymes of allelochemicals and hostplants in the fall armyworm. *Pestic. Biochem. Physiol.* 19:330–336.

Yu, S.J., R.E. Berry, and L.C. Terriere. 1979. Host plant stimulation of detoxifying enzymes in a phytophagous insect. *Pestic. Biochem. Physiol.* 12:280–284.

Zucker, W.V. 1982. How aphids choose leaves: the role of phenolics in host selection by a galling aphid. *Ecology* 63:972–981.

CHAPTER 14

Hymenopteran Venoms: Striving Toward the Ultimate Defense Against Vertebrates

JUSTIN O. SCHMIDT

In a contest with a vertebrate, an insect usually loses. Insects, by being small relative to vertebrate predators, are constantly challenged with the problem of how to engage in necessary activities yet not be eaten while doing so. The common insect defenses of biting, kicking, and scratching are usually ineffective against the grasp of a vertebrate; the vertebrate is simply too overpowering and its integument is too tough to be easily penetrated or damaged. One group of insects, the aculeate Hymenoptera, particularly the social Hymenoptera, overcame this problem mainly by developing a new and effective weapon, venom delivered with a sting. Among insects, the hymenopteran sting is unique because it provides a means of penetrating the tough vertebrate integument and injecting a potent blend of toxic and/or algogenic (painful) chemicals. These chemicals often startle and punish the potential predator and allow the sting bearer to escape or to drive the predator away. Driving large predators from the nest area is especially crucial for social insects, whose often large colonies filled with immobile, edible progeny represent a tempting food cache.

The aculeate Hymenoptera are a large insect group (over seventy thousand species worldwide [O'Toole 1986]; seven thousand in the U.S. and Canada [Krombein et al. 1979]) consisting of the true wasps, the ants, and the bees. Most are predators of one sort or another, or are pollen and nectar feeders. All female aculeate Hymenoptera have sting apparatus which is essentially a modified ovipositor. It no longer functions as an egg-laying tube; instead it acts as a biological syringe that injects venom, the modified secretion of accessory glands to the ovipositor. Because the sting and venom were no longer necessary for egg laying, they were acted upon by natural selection and modified into their present state as potent, effective weapons for prey capture or defense. In this chapter I describe the defensive value and uses of the sting, and present evidence demonstrating how the sting and venom combine to form a defensive weapon par excellence against vertebrate predators.

Venom From a Prey's Perspective

Virtually all organisms have predators. Their ways of dealing with predators and potential predators provide a showcase of structure and strategy. From a prey's perspective, predators many times larger than itself have always presented a special problem. Perhaps the most effective of the usual insect defenses against the grasp of large predators are chemical defenses. These allomones, however, are most effective when discharged onto sensitive tissues—the eyes, nose, and mouth—of the predator and typically have low effect when discharged onto the protective integument of a vertebrate predator. Venomous animals, including stinging Hymenoptera, have one distinct defensive advantage over nonvenomous prey—their venoms. A sting-venom system provides the means for a tiny aculeate hymenopteran such as a two-milligram fire ant (*Solenopsis invicta*) to make an impact on a human or other large mammal, a size difference of at least seven orders of magnitude.

In this chapter, I focus on stinging Hymenoptera (the Aculeata) as prey and on vertebrates as predators. Arthropod predators are omitted from discussion because hymenopteran venoms are, for the most part, ineffective against them. Furthermore, the other defenses (i.e, mandibles, kicking, protean escape, etc.) employed by aculeate Hymenoptera against arthropods are usually little different from those used by nonstinging prey. There are some notable exceptions: the venoms of the fire ants (*Solenopsis* spp.), thief ants (*Monomorium* and *Solenopsis* (*Diplorhoptrum*) spp.), and *Wasmannia auropunctata* are exceedingly effective against many arthropod adversaries (Wilson 1976; B. Hölldobler 1973; Blum et al. 1980; K. Hölldobler 1928; Howard et al. 1982). These specialized situations will not be discussed further (see Schmidt 1986 for a review of their venoms and uses).

VENOMS, GREGARIOUSNESS, AND SOCIALITY

Without effective means of defense, groups of insects are especially vulnerable to vertebrate predators. A group of hundreds or thousands of individuals, each of whom individually possesses no effective defense, is a potential food bonanza and an open invitation for vertebrates. If each individual within a group possesses some attributes of defensive value against vertebrates, then aggregation will be selected for. In such situations, the defensive potentials of the individuals synergize one another to the extent that the group as a whole is likely to be safer for its individual members than if they were dispersed (see Chapter 11 by Vulinec, this volume). When groups of stinging Hymenoptera mount a mass defensive attack, the predator's attention and efforts cannot simultaneously focus on all of the attackers. This confusion increases the chances that one or more of the attackers will deliver a successful sting. Attacks en masse appear to be effective means in driving away predators and can be of value even when some of the attackers have no further damaging potential, such as honey bees that have already lost their stings (J.O. Schmidt, unpublished).

Without venoms, it is unlikely that social Hymenoptera would exist because of the almost insurmountable problem of vertebrate predation. Unlike termites, social Hymenoptera usually do not possess effective topical allomones or, with a few exceptions among the ants, mandibles. Moreover, those ants with the most effective allomones and mandibles and lacking defensive venoms are derived from ancestors that possessed potent stings (Taylor 1978).

INCREASED ECOLOGICAL OPPORTUNITIES AS A RESULT OF VENOMS

The two major ecological advantages of possessing a vertebrate-deterrent venom are the opportunity to evolve sociality and the ability to exploit heretofore unavailable niches. Venoms are a key means by which social Hymenoptera defend their nests from vertebrate predators. Once defense against vertebrates is achieved, advanced sociality becomes an evolutionary option.

An effective defense is also of value to the individual hymenopteran while foraging and away from the nest. Without the ability to sting, any hymenopteran that spends much time in open habitats during the day is courting the attention and possible predation by visually hunting vertebrates. An effective sting allows bees and wasps to exploit, while in full view of many birds, such rich sources of food as floral nectar and pollen; allows wasps to actively and conspicuously search vegetation and the ground for their prey; and allows ants to patrol plants and open soil in their search for food. Sometimes sociality and the sting combine to further enable niche exploitation. For example, sociality confers increased ability to effectively thermoregulate body temperature. Thermoregulation allows the exploitation of floral and insect food sources at ambient temperatures too low for most solitary species and improves defensive movements. Examples of such thermoregulating species are honey bees, bumblebees, and social wasps (Heinrich 1979a,b; Seeley and Heinrich 1981; Gibo et al. 1974).

The Physiological and Pharmacological Basis of Venom Effectiveness

Venoms exhibit a dazzling diversity of defensive properties: they cause pain, mortality, and tissue damage; they can be distasteful; and they can induce allergic hypersensitivity.

PAIN

Pain is the most noted and widespread defensive property of insect venoms—noted because pain usually attracts one's attention, and widespread because pain induction is a powerful means of defense. Pain is the body's early warning system that indicates that tissue damage has occurred, is occurring, or is about to occur. Organisms have evolved to react quickly to pain and to thereby prevent or minimize the potential damage to their bodies. Without such a response, the organism is at risk of incurring serious damage which, in turn, is likely to reduce its overall fitness. Predators experiencing sudden, unexpected pain tend to respond in a manner advantageous to their potential prey: retreat, defensive evasion, and startle responses, including mouth gaping. Sting pain thus often allows the venomous insect to stop an attack and escape unharmed. If the venomous insect is social, the pain often stops attak on its nest and the brood therein.

Pain is simply a sensory response transmitted to higher nervous centers. In itself, it is not actually damage. Therefore pain is an ideal system for prey organisms to exploit for their own benefit. Normally pain and potential or actual damage are coupled, but with insect venoms decoupling is possible. For example, the venom can induce great pain yet be essentially nondamaging to a vertebrate predator. Examples of such venoms include those produced by tarantual hawks (*Pepsis*) and mutillid wasps (*Dasymutilla*). This use of venom-induced pain is a "trick" played on a potential predator, a form of Batesian mimicry. It is mimicry because the venom's action—pain—does not actually indicate damage potential, yet frequently elicits responses by the targeted predator as if damage were eminent. One advantage to the prey of such a system is that a painful venom might be easier to evolve than a truly damaging venom. Like the more usual color-based Batesian mimicry, damage mimicry is not a perfect defense, and occasionally its defensive value is overcome. For example, bears and beekeepers have learned that honey bee stings are painful yet nondamaging (in most cases). Hence, both "learn to ignore" the pain and proceed with robbing the colony of its food stores.

Pain is elusive. It is a sensation that depends on a great many factors. The pain induced by the same stimulus varies from situation to situation and from individual to individual. It also depends upon such factors as the species and individuals involved, their age and size, their physiological (and possibly psychological) states, their hunger states, and the time of day. Measuring levels of pain is one of the most difficult of medical and scientific endeavors. Most pain assays are long and subjective procedures based on human responses to questionnaires (Melzak 1975; Corson and Schneider 1984). Pain in animals is even more difficult to quantify than in man. Some of the most frequent assays involve foot-lifting responses by rodents (Chapman et al. 1985), assays that best measure the abilities of pharmaceuticals to antagonize the pain response to heat.

In spite of the difficulty in measuring pain, its effectiveness as a defensive agent against vertebrate predators can be semiquantitatively measured. This is done for venomous Hymeoptera stings by ranking the pain on a scale from 0 to 4. By this means a hierarchy of venom algogenicity and thereby defensive value can be obtained. The scale is based on a level of 2 for the pain from a sting by the common honey bee, *Apis mellifera*, with 4 being the greatest-known insect sting pain, and 0 being unable to penetrate the human skin. The results of a survey of venom pain produced by stinging insects are presented in table 14.1. These results were derived from the personal experiences of the author and his associates, and also from numerous stung individuals interviewed in the field. Any sting which induces a pain level of 2 or more has clear defensive value against humans and probably most other large vertebrates. A sting with a pain

Table 14.1. Relative pain induced in humans by envenomation by various stinging Hymenoptera.

Family	Species	Relative immediate sting pain	Duration of pain	Reference[1]
Scoliidae	Various	0-1	Short	a
Pompilidae	*Pepsis formosus*	4	2-5 min	a
	Other species	2-3	Short	a
Mutillidae	*Dasymutilla klugii*	3	Short-30 min	a
	D. lepeletierii	2	Short-30 min	a
	Small species	1-2	Short	a
Eumenidae	*Monobia quadridens*	2	—	b
Vespidae				
Stenogastrinae	*Eustenogaster luzonensis*	3	—	b
Polistinae	*Agelaia panamensis*	3	Many min	b
	Apoica pallens	2	2-5 min	a
	Brachygastra mellifica	2	2-5 min	a,b
	Metapolybia docilis	0-1	Short	b
	Mischocyttarus angulatus	1	Short	b
	M. atrocyaneus	1	Short	b
	M. costaricensis	1	Short	b
	M. flavitarsus	1-2	2-5 min	a
	Parachartergus fraternus	2	2-5 min	a
	Polistes annularis	3	5-10 min	a
	P. arizonensis	2-3	4-10 min	a
	P. canadensis	2-3	4-10 min	a
	P. dorsalis	2	—	b
	P. exclamans	2	—	b
	P. fuscatus	2	2-5 min	a
	P. infuscatus	3	5-10 min	a
	P. instabilis	2	2-5 min, residual pain 1-2 h	a
	P. metricus	2-3	—	b
	Polybia diguetana	0-1	—	b
	P. occidentalis	1	Short	a,b
	P. rejecta	2	2-4 min	a
	P. sericea	2	2-5 min	a
	P. simillima	2	—	b
	Ropalidia flavobrunnea	1	Short	b
	R. horni	1-2	Short	b
	R. nigrescens	1-2	Short	b
	R. sp.	1-2	1-3 min	a
	Synoeca septentrionalis	3-4	1 hr	a
Vespinae	Dolichovespula maculata	2	3-4 min	a
	Paravespula flavopilosa	2	4-10	a
	P. maculifrons	2	4-10 min	a,b
	P. pensylvanica	2	4-10 min	a
	Vespa mandarinia	2	4-10 min	a
	Vespula squamosa	2	4-10 min	a
Formicidae				
Myrmeciinae	Myrmecia nigripes	2	2-5 min	a
	M. pyriformis	2,2-3	—	c

Table 14.1 *(Cont'd.)*

Family	Species	Relative immediate sting pain	Duration of pain	Reference[1]
Ponerinae	*Diacamma* near *rugosum*	2	2–10 min	a
	Dinoponera grandis	2	2–10 min	a
	Ectatomma quadridens	1–2	—	a
	E. tuberculatum	2	—	a
	Odontomachus haematodus	2	4–10 min	a
	O. infandus	3	—	b
	O. simillimus	2	—	b
	Pachycondyla apicalis	2	4–10 min	a
	P. villosa	2	4–10 min	a
	Paraponera clavata	4	Intense 3–5 hr, less to 24 hr	a
Pseudomyrmecinae	*Pseudomyrmex mexicanus*	1	2–5 min	a
	P. nigrocinctus	1–2	2–5 min	a
	P. triplarinus	2	—	b
Ecitoninae	*Eciton burchelli*	1–2	2–5 min	a
	E. haematum	1	—	b
Myrmicinae	*Manica bradleyi*	1–2	—	a
	Myrmica hamulata	1–2	1–4 hr	a
	Pogonomyrmex (most of 20 species)	3	Intense 1–4 hr, less to 12 hr	a
	Solenopsis geminata	1–2	2–5 min	a,b
	S. invicta	1–2	2–5 min, prolonged local reaction	a
	S. xyloni	1	2–5 min	a
Sphecidae	Most species	0–1	Short	a
Apoidea	Small bees in general	0–1	Short	a
Anthophoridae	*Centris pallida*	1–2	Short	a
	Diadasia rinconis	1–2	Short	a
	Habropoda pallida	1	Short	a
	Xenoglossa angustior	1	Short	a
	Xylocopa virginia	2	Short	a
	X. magnifica	2–3	5–10 mim	a
Colletidae	*Crawfordapis luctuosa*	1	Short	a
Apidae	*Apis cerana*	2	2–10 min	a,b
	A. mellifera	2	4–10 min	a,b
	A. dorsata	2	4–10 min	a
	Bombus sonorus	2	2–5 min	a

[1]a = Schmidt et al. 1984; Schmidt 1986; J.O. Schmidt, unpublished; b = Starr 1985, A pain scale; Starr personal communication; c = de la Lande et al. 1965 and Lewis and de la Lande 1967.

level of 0 ot 0–1 has little defensive value against large vertebrates and is probably effective mainly against small vertebrates. Most stinging species with these low levels of venom pain are either small solitary species or small individuals from small colonies of social wasps or ants (the latter not listed on the table). Pain ratings of 1 and 1–2 are intense enough to be of general defensive value against many vertebrates, but mainly so if the vertebrate is not especially hungry at the time of encounter. Most species whose venoms produce 1 or 1–2 pain levels are solitary species, or social species whose colony biomass is not too large. Neither category represents a great nutritional discovery for a potential vertebrate predator. Most stinging species whose venoms produce pain levels of 2 or more are social species which have a large nest investment to defend. There are a few exceptions in the form of solitary species whose stings are also extremely painful. The life-styles of all these solitary species are such that they are almost constantly in view of vertebrate predators and susceptible to attack. Examples of these include *Pepsis* and other spider wasps, species that spend a great deal of time searching the ground or vegetation for their spider prey, all the while under the watchful eyes of birds and lizards; mutillid wasps, long-lived flightless species that also spend a deal of time searching the ground for burrows of their prey and within sight and reach of lizards and birds (Schmidt 1978); and carpenter bees (*Xylocopa*), large long-lived, usually black, bees that would appear to present easy prey for large insectivorous birds.

There is a general consensus that bee, wasp, and ant stings are used in defense and are effective against vertebrates. Actual studies to show that stinging Hymenoptera are avoided or that their stings are effective are surprisingly few: most investigators simply assume this to be the case. In studies demonstrating that Hymenoptera are avoided by vertebrate predators (Poulton 1887; Marshall and Poulton 1902; Mostler 1935; Cott 1940; Brower and Brower 1962; Schmidt and Blum 1977; Evans and Waldbauer 1982), the actual reasons that the venoms were deterrent was not addressed, perhaps because their pharmacological and toxinological properties were unknown and the venoms were just assumed to be harmful. Alternatively, it was assumed that the pain alone was the cause of the deterrence. To date, no thorough studies have determined exactly why and how insect venoms deter vertebrate predators. Part of the problem involves separating the various venom actions from one another. It could be hypothesized that pain is the main driving deterrent because it portends the later damage. As mentioned earlier, however, damage need not occur, even locally, for pain alone to be effective. As an example, the venom of *Dasymutilla occidentalis,* a conspicuous mutillid wasp, is essentially nonlethal and contains few active enzymes (based on those of the sister species *D. lepeletierii* and *D. klugii;* Schmidt et al. 1986), yet it is very algogenic. Local names for this species include *cow killer* and *mule killer.* In experimental trials involving a variety of predators, including four species of lizards and one each of a bird and a rodent, all the predators with one exception were repelled by the wasp. In the most definitive example of sting pain effectiveness, four gerbils (*Meriones shawi*) attacked the mutillids, were stung, and retreated while vigorously scratching their stung mouths. Two of the four gerbils never attacked again, two attacked a second time, and one of these successfully ate the insect (Schmidt and Blum 1977). It might be noted that the successful attacker had not eaten for forty-eight hours and persevered in the attack despite the stings. This example demonstrates that in most cases a painful venom that lacks damaging physiological activities is highly effective in stopping an attack.

VENOM LETHALITY

Pain in a venom has the advantage of providing immediate feedback to the assailant that the victim can be dangerous. Thus minimal predator learning is necessary for the prey's defenses to work. However, immediate feedback to the predator is not required for a venom to be effective over the long term. Vertebrate predators are capable of learning and associating later adverse effects with the act that induced those affects (Mühlmann 1934; Islam 1979; Palmerino et al. 1980; Nicolaus et al. 1983). Thus, to induce vertebrate learning and future avoidance, an insect venom need only cause delayed injury. Since the individual that causes the damage to the vertebrate is often killed and eaten, this defensive attribute is mainly of value for social species in which individual acts of altruism serve to protect closely related colony nestmates.

The ability of venoms to produce injury and tissue damage is of great defensive value for social insects. Without injury or damage, venom pain alone might be discovered to be harmless, and attacks on the nest would continue until successful. In attacks on a social insect nest, a predator is usually stung and retreats. At this point the sharp immediate sting pain starts to decrease, but the damaging effects begin to become apparent. Gross symptoms of venom damage can include such features as sickness and lethargy resulting from neurotoxins, or blood erthrocyte destruction (which lowers oxygen-transporting abilities and might cause kidney failure), skin and muscle necrosis, swelling to the extent of impairing vision, nose or tongue function, or mobility of various body parts, and death. Any of these effects are maladaptive to the predator: it is less able to discover and obtain food, to detect and avoid its own predators, and to successfully compete for mates and produce progeny. Such damaging effects can be associated by the predator with the stings and the attack on the nest of the stinging insects. As a result, future encounters with individuals from the nest of that species are likely to be avoided.

The extreme of injury is death. To kill a predator can be viewed as the ultimate defense. The argument can be presented that death precludes any possibility of learning on the part of the predator or its kin and therefore might be less effective a deterrent than simply educating the predator to stay clear. Although there might be some appeal to this argument, predator death is advantageous to the prey simply because the death eliminates from the predator gene pool an individual who has genetic tendencies to mount extreme predatory attacks (in spite of early warnings or the numerous stings it has received). By eliminating such an individual from the gene pool, the remaining individuals in the population have been selected for less intense attack behavior and more readily stimulated avoidance behavior. Such selection is clearly advantageous for the stinging insect in that not only is its own fitness improved, but the survival of its progeny, kin, and descendants, all of whom are likely to live in the same general area, will be increased.

Unlike pain, lethal damage can be easily measured and precisely quantified. The most direct measure of a venom's damaging potential is its lethality, or LD_{50}. Venom lethality is best analyzed by comparing various venoms against one uniform vertebrate predator model organism. This approach allows for direct comparisons of the lethal potency of venoms. Of course, the use of such a model system does omit the discovery of relationships between various prey and their specialized predators, but it provides a good starting point for future analyses of predator-prey relationships.

Table 14.2 is a list of lethalities to mice of the venoms from 28 genera of stinging Hymenoptera. For convenience, genera containing solitary species are listed first and are followed by those containing social species. The first point of note is that, with one exception, all nine solitary species, but only two of the thirty-six individually listed social species have LD_{50} values greater than 20 mg/kg. At the generic level, only one out of eight solitary genera versus eighteen out of the twenty social genera have a venom lethality less than 20 mg/kg. These data suggest that lethal activities in venoms are more important for social hymenopterans than for solitary species.

Table 14.2. Lethality of hymenopterous venoms to mice.

Family	Species	LD$_{50}$	µg venom/sting	LC	Reference[1]
Scoliidae	*Crioscolia flammicoma*	> 63	29	< .46	h
Pompilidae	*Pepsis formosus*	65	2,500	38	b
Mutillidae	*Dasymutilla klugii*	71	420	5.9	a
Sphecidae	*Sphecius grandis*	46	220	4.8	h
Halictidae	*Nomia heteropoda*	25	22	0.88	h
Anthophoridae	*Diadasia rinconis*	76	32	0.42	b
	Xenoglossa angustior	12	23	1.9	h
	Xylocopa varipuncta	33	390	12	h
	X. (Koptortsoma) sp.	21	240	11	h
Vespidae Polistinae	*Brachygastra mellifica*	1.5	70	47	h
	Parachartergus fraternus	5.3	200	38	h
	Polistes arizonensis	2.0	170	85	h
	P. canadensis	2.4	140	58	h
	P. comanchus navajoe	5.0	200	40	c
	P. flavus	3.8	270	71	h
	P. infuscatus	1.3	190	146	h
	P. tepidus	7.7	180	23	h
	Polybia rejecta	16	60	3.8	h
	Ropalidia (Icarielia) sp.	14	60	4.3	h
	Ropalidia flavobrunnea	5.9	40	6.8	h
	Synoeca septentrionalis	3.0	270	90	h
Vespinae	*Paravespula flavopilosa*	15	80	5.3	a
	P. maculifrons	9	60	6.7	a
	P. pensylvanica	11	70	6.4	b
	Vespa luctuosa	1.6	430	270	f
	V. mandarinia	4.1	1,100	270	f
	V. simillima	3.1	420	140	f
	V. tropica	2.8	770	280	f
	Vespula squamosa	3.5	100	29	a
Formicidae Myrmeciinae	*Myrmecia nigriceps*	7.3	130	18	h
Ponerinae	*Diacamma* near *rugosum*	7.0	55	7.0	h
	Ectatomma quadridens	6.5	120	18	a,h
	E. tuberculatum	1.7	130	76	a,h
	Odontomachus infandus	33	70	2.1	e
	Odontoponera transversa	> 29	55	< 1.9	h
	Pachycondyla villosa	7.5	130	17	h
Pseudomyrmecinae	*Pseudomyrmex mexicanus*	8	16	2.0	d
	P. nigrocinctus	1.9	4.2	2.2	h
Ecitoninae	*Eciton burchelli*	10	90	9.0	a,h

Table 14.2. *(Cont'd.)*

Family	Species	LD$_{50}$	µg venom/ sting	LC	Reference[1]
Myrmicinae	*Manica bradleyi*	6.1	14	2.3	h
	Pogonomyrmex maricopa	0.125	25	200[2]	h
	P. magnacanthus	0.71	9	11[3]	h
	Pogonomyrmex ($\bar{x}$ = 20 spp.)	0.66	19	29	g,h
Apidae	*Apis cerana*	3.1	43	14	h
	A. dorsata	2.8	220	79	h
	A. mellifera	2.8	150	54	h

[1] a = Schmidt et al. 1980; b = Schmidt 1986; c = Schmidt 1983; d = Schmidt et al. 1984; e = Schmidt et al. 1986, Comparative enzymology; f = Schmidt et al. 1986, Hornet venoms; g = Schmidt and Blum 1978; h = J.O. Schmidt, unpublished.

[2] Most lethal of 20 species of *Pogonomyrmex*

[3] Least lethal of 20 species of *Pogonomyrmex*

The killing power of an insect venom can be further refined quantitatively. The lethal action of a venom depends upon two factors: the lethality of the venom and the amount of venom delivered. Obviously, if either value is low, the ability of defensive stings to kill is low. The term *Lethal Capacity* (LC) describes the killing power of an insect sting. It is determined as

$$LC = \frac{\text{µg venom per stinging insect}}{\text{µLD}_{50}\ (\text{g/g})}$$

and equals the weight of an envenomed animal which would receive one median lethal dose of venom when stung by one average insect. Although not without problems, the LC value of an insect venom provides a convenient means of quantifying the ability of an insect venom to kill another organism and allows comparisons among venoms. Obviously, LC values will vary with the susceptibility of the particular target species to the venom. Moreover, because not all of an insect's venom is necessarily delivered during the stinging process, LC values are maximum values. Although the absolute values of the LCs might be higher than occur as a result of an actual sting, the value of LC for comparisons among stinging species remains, assuming different species deliver about the same percentage of their venom during stinging.

In evolutionary terms the same general hypothesis that natural selection should favor the development of more lethally active venoms in social than solitary species should apply to LC as it does to lethality. The LC values from table 14.2 for the nine solitary species range from 0.42 to 38 with an average of 8.4 g/sting. For the thirty-six listed social species, the LC range is ~1.9 to 280, with an average of 59.2 g/sting. On the basis of averages for genera, the means for the eight solitary genera are 8.0 versus 35.7 g/sting for the twenty social genera. It should be further noted that all of the solitary species analyzed have very large individuals, often over 300 mg in mass, whereas all but one of the ants and many of the social wasps are relatively small. These data suggest that, overall, social Hymenoptera have experienced much stronger selection pressure for the evolution of highly life-threatening venoms than have solitary Hymenoptera.

NONLETHAL TISSUE DAMAGE

Nonlethal damage induced by a venom is much more difficult to quantify than lethal damage. This is because death can be measured exactly, but such features as edema (swelling), hemorrhagic damage, and gross metabolic dysfunction are more difficult, and often impossible, to measure. The ability to produce such damages must, however, have defensive value. Again the venom-damaged individual is placed at a disadvantage compared to its normal state and is likely to associate the damaged state with its predatory action toward the stinging insect or its nest. As with lethality and lethal capacity, venom-induced damage would be expected to be greater as a result of stings by social species than by solitary species.

One in vitro method of measuring venom tissue damage that is simple and quantitative involves measuring the ability of venoms to lyse red blood cells. This activity, as measured in hemolytic units (HU) per mg venom, is shown for a variety of stinging insects in table 14.3. One ml of blood from a typical vertebrate contains enough erythrocytes for approximately 15–20 HU, and about 5–9 percent of a vertebrate body mass is typically blood (Schmidt-Nielsen 1979). As can be seen, most of the venoms of the social wasps are profoundly damaging to blood cells. Venom of the ants *Pogonomyrmex*, *Pseudomyrmex*, and *Platythyrea* and the honey bee *Apis* are also highly hemolytic. Only two venoms of solitary species were investigated, and neither of them was particularly active toward blood cells. Preliminary investigations of several other species of solitary bees and wasps indicate that they too have venoms with low hemolytic activity (J.O. Schmidt, unpublished).

As in the case of the lethal action of a venom, the overall damaging power of a venom depends on both the activity of the venom and on the amount of venom available. In table 14.3 the amounts, when known or estimated based on values from congenerics, of venom possessed per

Table 14.3. Direct hemolytic activities of hymenopterous venoms to mouse erythrocytes.

Family	Species	HU/mg sting	μg venom/ sting	HU/sting
Mutillidae	*Dasymutilla lepeletierii*	4	—	~1.2
Anthophoridae	*Xylocopa virginica*	25	210	5.2
Formicidae				
Ponerinae	*Dinoponera grandis*	103	860	89
	Ectatomma quadridens	86	120	10
	E. tuberculatum	36	130	4.7
	Odontomachus haematodus	28	~70	~2.0
	Pachycondyla apicalis	70	~130	~9.1
	Paraponera clavata	10	180	1.8
	Platythyrea cribrinoidis	305	330	100
Pseudomyrmecinae	*Pseudomyrmex mexicanus*	405	16	6.5
Ecitoninae	*Eciton burchelli*	13	90	1.2
Myrmicinae	*Pogonomyrmex badius*	480	12	5.8
	P. barbatus	850	32	27
Vespidae				
Polistinae	*Apoica pallens*	64	150	9.6
	Brachygastra bilineolata	280	—	—
	Polistes annularis	725	~200	~145
	P. comanchus navajoe	1,000	200	200
	P. infuscatus	12,000	190	2,300
	Polybia sericea	1,450	100	140
Vespinae	*Paravespula maculifrons*	405	60	24
	P. pensylvanica	570	70	40
	Vespa orientalis	435	—	—
	Vespula squamosa	1,500	100	150
Apidae	*Apis mellifera*	270	150	40

[1]One hemolytic unit is the amount of test venom needed to release the hemoglobin from 50% of the cells in a 1 ml solution of washed erythrocytes incubated in 0.87% NaCl saline buffered to pH 7.2 with 0.01 M Tris (hydroxymethyl) aminomethane and with the cell concentration adjusted to yield an absorbance of 0.8 at 545 nm when 100% lysed.

SOURCE: Data from Schmidt et al. 1984, Bernheimer et al. 1980, 1982, and J.O. Schmidt, unpublished.

individual are listed. The combination of this figure and the hemolytic activity allows the calculation of the total erythrocyte damaging potential of a sting, a value listed as hemolytic units per sting (HU/sting). In terms of HU/sting, many of the venoms are profoundly active. Notable are the venoms of *Polistes infuscatus* and its near relative *Polistes comanchus navajoe* with 2,300 and 200 HU/sting, respectively, and *Vespula, Polybia,* and *Platythyrea* (150, 140, 100 HU/sting, respectively). These data support the idea that many hymenopterous venoms have defensive value in part because of their ability to damage the predator, in this case via its oxygen transport system and kidneys.

NOISOME TASTE

Not all hymenopterous venoms need to be injected into a potential predator to be effective. Some venoms can act in a fashion similar or identical to classical allomones, that is, by being topically active. Many predators will release a potential prey when allomones are discharged onto their sensitive mouth or eye tissues. Liepelt (1963) was the first observer to postulate that venoms can be of defensive value by virtue of possessing a nasty taste (Mostler's 1935 results provided some suggestion that venom, might possess deterrent taste; but his overall conclusions confused, rather than clarified the situation). No subsequent studies have followed this initial observation and no experimental data have been collected to determine if in fact the noisome tastes of venoms are actually of defensive value. With these limitations in mind, I present the following personal observations about the tastes of various venoms. The venoms of *Dinoponera grandis, Pachycondyla obscuricornis, P. apicalis, Odontomachus hematodus, Synoeca septentrionalis, Vespa luctuosa, Apis cerana, Bombus sonorus,* and *Xylocopa varipuncta* are very bitter. Those of *D. grandis, Ectatomma tuberculatum, P. obscuricornis, P. apicalis, Pogonomyrmex rugosus, S. septentrionalis, Parachartergus fraternus, A. cerana,* and *X. varipuncta* taste hydrolytic or "corrosive" and leave a "burning" sensation in the mouth. The venoms of *D. grandis* and especially *E. tuberculatum* are also "hot and spicy." The venoms of *Crioscolia flammicoma, Centris pallida, Agapostemon* sp., *Peponapis pruinosa, Crawfordapis luctuosa, Paraponera clavata,* and *Eciton burchelli* have no profound tastes to humans. These subjective evaluations of sporadically analyzed venoms indicate that nasty-tasting venoms are widely distributed throughout the ants and are present in at least some bees and social wasps. Exactly how frequently venoms are noisome is unknown and presents an interesting topic for future research. The actual value of these offensively tasting venoms in defense against vertebrate predators is another topic worthy of investigation.

VENOM ALLERGY

Is venom allergenicity of defensive value? This question cannot be answered with a clear yes or no. Even more difficult to answer is the question of whether the allergenicity of hymenopterous venoms is a direct product of natural selection or simply the result of the inherent biochemical nature of venom. Since no direct evidence can be brought to bear on these questions, I will simply present a few observations. First, among humans (the only species for which data are available) an estimated 1–4 percent of the population is hypersensitive to social wasp and bee venoms, many to a life-threatening degree (Herbert and Salkie 1982; Golden et al. 1982; Zora et al. 1984). Second, the venom of honey bees, *Apis mellifera*, is especially prone to cause large local reactions in humans following stings subsequent to the first (Graft et al. 1982). The first datum might not seem particularly high; but when viewed in relation to the infrequent nature of human envenomations by stinging insects, it looks more impressive. Moreover, the frequency of allergy among those individuals (beekeepers) who are frequently stung has been reported to be between 9 and perhaps 42 percent (Yunginger et al. 1978; Bousquet et al. 1982; Bell and Hohlbohm 1983). The value to an insect of being able to induce allergic reactions in a predator is obvious: an allergic (anaphylactic) attack not only abruptly halts the predator's attack, but will also traumatize that individual, who is unlikely again to intentionally encounter similar insects. The incidence of death in humans due to venom allergy is only one in seven million (Parrish 1963; Barnard 1973), so death itself would be expected to play only a minor role in the defensive value of venom allergy.

Large local reactions to hymenopterous stings are debilitating because they severely curtail muscle and joint movement in the affected area. In humans, for example, often little movement is possible in the wrist and fingers for 24 to 72 hours after a sting to the wrist or hand. Albeit temporary, such impairment is certain to reduce foraging and predator escape abilities and is likely to be a factor in the predator's future decisions about whether to attack the species again. The fact that large local reactions only affect repeat offenders (those stung on two or more occasions) also selectively affects those individuals that are more likely to attack in the future.

To summarize the defensive value of venom allergenicity, all that can be stated now with certainty is that, whether or not selection has operated on hymenopterous venoms to increase their allergenicity, the possession of allergenic properties cannot harm the defender, and will probably benefit it.

Venoms and Other Defenses

Venom use is generally the last line of defense for aculeate Hymenoptera, and one whose use has the greatest risks. To avoid or delay the use of the sting, aculeates often use a variety of other defenses (Starr 1985, Enabling mechanisms; see Starr, chapter 15, this volume, for detailed discussions of alternatives to stinging in social wasp defenses).

CRYPSIS

Crypsis is among the major defenses utilized by aculeate Hymenoptera. Many individual aculeates are conspicuous when seen on the wing, but when at rest and in subdued light their broken color patterns can appear cryptic. All nests of aculeate Hymenoptera are made of neutral colored material (if visible) and are cryptic. The cryptic nature of social wasp nests is evident to the majority of humans who, when traveling through vegetation, first become aware of a nearby nest by the attack by its inhabitants.

ALLOMONES

Allomones are little used by wasps and most bees for defense. Notable exceptions are the stingless bees (*Trigona, Melipona*) that use effective, often vesicating, allomones in place of stings to defend against large predators (Blum 1966; Smith and Roubik 1983; Francke et al. 1983). Ants are the major aculeate group that has evolved a high degree of effective use of allomones for defense. Many of the primitive ponerine ants produce prodigious quantities of pyrazines that appear to function primarily as allomones (Wheeler and Blum 1973; Duffield et al. 1976; Longhurst et al. 1978; Brophy et al. 1983; Fales et al. 1984; Hermann et al. 1984). Many other species of stinging ants produce various short chained ketonic components in their mandibular glands and these often function both as alarm pheromones and allomones (Ghent 1961; reviewed in Hermann and Blum 1981). 4-Methyl-3-heptanone, the major mandibular gland component of *Pogonomyrmex*, is repellent to predacious fire ants (*Solenopsis invicta*) and is probably repellent by both odor and taste to vertebrates (J.O. Schmidt, unpublished). Two entire subfamilies of ants, the Formicinae and Dolichoderinae, lack functional sting apparatuses. Most, if not all, members of these subfamilies are veritable arsenals of chemical warfare materials. The formicines contain powerful formic acid, the strongest of the aliphatic fatty acids, plus hydrocarbon surfactants and other compounds such as terpenes that function well as chemical defenses (reviewed in Blum and Hermann 1978a; Schmidt 1986). The dolichoderines contain a variety of complex secretions, often including aldehydes and ketones (reviewed in Blum and Hermann 1978b). These allomones are effective defenses against both vertebrate and invertebrate predators, but are probably used principally against arthropod predators including other ant species.

PHEROMONES

Pheromones are of defensive value against vertebrates primarily by their ability to alarm and recruit other individuals to aid in the defense. Mass attack of a predator is usually much more effective than individual attack. Alarm pheromones are used both to alert nestmates rapidly of the danger and to direct them to the predator. In honey bees mandibular gland components including 2-heptanone are responsible for increasing the arousal level of fellow guards (Shearer and Boch 1965; Boch et al. 1970), and sting based pheromones, including isopentyl acetate plus a dozen or so others (Blum et al. 1978; Collins and Blum 1983), not only lower the threshold for attack, but also act as an olfactory beacon to direct attackers to the spot where a nestmate successfully inserted her sting in the predator (Maschwitz 1964). Alarm pheromones serve almost identical functions among a great many species of ants (Blum 1969). Yellowjackets of the genus *Paravespula* also have sting based alarm pheromones. Unlike the pheromone in the honey bee, their pheromone is actually contained in the venom itself and is readily detected as a sweet, almost floral odor by humans who have aroused a colony sufficiently to induce its members to squirt venom toward their faces (J.O. Schmidt, unpublished). The alarming ability of this pheromone, that is, it's ability to draw defenders out of the colony, is striking (Maschwitz 1964; J.O. Schmidt, unpublished). The pheromone consists of water soluble spiroketals, compounds identified by Francke et al. (1978) who did not realize the compounds they isolated were alarm pheromones. Our own attempt to demonstrate the alarm nature of the venom spiroketals failed due to the difficulty of synthesizing the four diasteriomers of the compound and the fact that unnatural enantiomers apparently mask the activity of the natural enantiomer (J.O. Schmidt and M.S. Blum, unpublished). Nevertheless, the effectiveness of the attack of a *Paravespula* colony attests to the value of the rapid alarm pheromone based defensive warning.

APOSEMATISM

Aposematic animals advertise that they are noxious and/or can retaliate against an attacker, or they mimic such an animal (see Guilford, chapter 2, this volume). Many aculeate Hymenoptera are classical examples of aposematic insects. Most yellowjackets and hornets (Vespinae) contain brightly colored contrasting patches of yellow, red, orange, or white on a base color of brown, black, tan or yellow. The vespid sub-family Polistinae contains about 800 species, many of which have contrasting bright color patches on a dark background. *Synoeca,* a genus whose species have particularly potent stings (table 14.1) consists of individuals colored a conspicuous irridescent blue-black and with red-dish mandibles.

Some bees are aposematically colored. Most bumble bees have bright patches of yellow, red, or white pubescence superimposed on the black base color of the body. Carpenter bees, *Xylocopa* spp., are often shiny black in color, and most orchid bees (*Euglossa, Eulaema*) are colored any of a number of brilliant or iridescent colors. All of these groups are capable of delivering powerful stings to humans (Schmidt 1986; Starr 1985, A pain scale; Dressler 1979; R.E. Silberglied, personal experience).

Solitary wasps, especially those with large individuals, are often aposematically colored. Among these are members of the Mutillidae, whose 8000+ species are often adorned with contrasting colors of red, orange, yellow, and white on a black, rust, or tan base color; the Scoliidae, which are often yellow, orange, red, or white on black or tan; the Pompi-lidae, which are often iridescent blue-black with or without bright red, orange or yellow; the Eumenidae, which frequently have yellow or white patches on a dark background; and some Sphecidae that are splashed with yellows, reds and iridescent blues. Like the other brightly colored aculeates discussed above, many of these particular solitary wasps posses powerfully algogenic venoms.

The presumed benefit of aposematism to all of these groups of Hymenoptera is the protective value that conspicuousness confers: verte-brate predators, either innately or by learning, associate these colored insects with danger (Coppinger 1970; Rubinoff and Kropach 1970; Smith 1977; Schuler 1982; see Guilford, chapter 2, this volume).

TOUGH INTEGUMENT AND AGILITY

A venom apparatus is effective only if it can penetrate the target animal. To do so, the aculeate must survive the predatory attack at least long enough to deliver the sting. Like many toxic and aposematic butter-flies (Cott 1940), many stinging Hymenoptera possess tough integuments. Perhaps the most extreme example of this and probably the most armored and impenetrable of the arthropods are the Mutillidae. Females of *Dasy-mutilla occidentails,* a large red-on-black mutillid wasp, possess the most crush resistant bodies of any tested insects (Schmidt and Blum 1977). Undoubtedly the pronotum of some large weevils or other beetles can withstand more force than can any part of *D. occidentalis,* but the weakest points of these beetles are almost certainly weaker than the analogous mutillid part. For example, the forces to crush either the head or the abdomen of *D. occidentalis* were always greater than half that required to crush the thorax (the hardest part); whereas the forces to crush the abdomens of weevils and other beetles were many times less than that to crush the weevil pronotum (Schmidt and Blum 1977; J.O. Schmidt, unpublished). Aside from its extreme hardness, the remarkable feature of the mutillid's integument is its uniformity of hardness. In particular, all sclerites on *D. occidentalis* are closely fitting (those of the abdomen have powerful contracting muscles to prevent anything slipping between the plates) and overlap so completely that no membrane is ever exposed. This overlap and lack of exposed membranes is well demonstrated by the inability of spiders, such as the black widow (*Latrodectus mactans*), to deliver a killing bite to a small mutillid wasp (*Dasymutilla vesta*). Despite long biting attempts, including at the femor-tibial joint, spiders failed to penetrate anywhere on the body of the silk ensnared wasp (J.O. Schmidt, unpublished). Lizards and mantids could not crush or penetrate the cuticle of *D. occidentalis* and rodents could penetrate only with great difficulty (Schmidt and Blum 1977).

Although not as hard as mutillid wasps, many other aculeate Hymenoptera also posses tough integuments. Scoliid and tiphiid wasps, many vespids, carpenter bees, and a variety of ants (most of the Ponerinae, leaf-cutters of the Attinini, *Pogonomyrmex,* etc.) also have hard integuments. One obvious advantage to all of these species in having a hard integument is the time sparing factor that it confers upon them in their attempts to sting or bite the attacker.

Agility is extremely beneficial for a stinging hymenopteran. Many of the Hymenoptera with the most potent stings are also agile. Included are the mutillid wasps, species that have coiled and exceptionally long mobile stings (Hermann 1968); the spider wasps (Pompilidae), that have very flexible abdomens, petioles and sting apparatuses; and many ants that have long flexible petioles joining the thorax and abdomen. The petiole is actually a hallmark of aculeate Hymenoptera—and this flexible joint greatly increases the ability of the insect to point its sting in the direction of its target. The combined integumental strength and hardness and body flexibility are almost certainly key factors in allowing the sting to be an effective defensive weapon for the Aculeata.

Venom Limitations and Predator Factors

Major defensive limitations of venoms are their potential inability to penetrate the integument of the predator, the potential lack of effect on the predator once penetration is successful, and the ability of some vertebrates to overcome the defensive sting and, possibly, to specialize on stinging Hymenoptera. Major predator factors affecting venom effectiveness are predator behaviors and predator hunger.

PREDATOR INTEGUMENT

Most hymenopteran stings are incapable of penetrating the sclerotized integument of arthropod predators because the predator's integument and the sting are both of sclerotized cuticle and have roughly the same hardness. Available sites for sting penetration are mainly the soft, usually intersegmental, areas that are frequently tough and difficult to penetrate with the generalized stinging motions made by the attacked aculeate. Many vertebrates also possess integuments difficult to penetrate. Feathers and thick hair render access to covered parts difficult for most hymenopterans. Further, their sting apparatuses are often too short to reach the skin below the protective covering. This problem sometimes limits the areas susceptible to being stung to those around the eyes, nose, mouth, ears and the sparsely covered underparts. Even the accessible areas on the head are sometimes covered with dense short hairs or feathers, and the eye, nose, and ear openings sometimes can be closed to attack. The integuments of many lizards are hard and difficult for stings to penetrate, and those of amphibians are rubbery and tough. Perhaps the most frequently encountered vulnerable part of a vertebrate predator's body is the oral area, and in this area a sting must be placed quickly to be effective.

CONFLICTING VENOM ROLES: DEFENSE VERSUS OFFENSE

A problem with some stings as defenses against vertebrates is their possible ineffectiveness after venom delivery is accomplished. This problem is especially acute for small solitary wasps. However, these organisms do, have the advantage that their solitary natures and small size tend not to attract a great deal of vertebrate attention. One of the reasons solitary wasp venoms might be ineffective once delivered to a predator is a conflict

of venom role. The venoms of most solitary wasps are nonlethal paralyz-
ing fluids intended for inactivating their prey while maintaining it alive as
a food source for the wasp's larvae. A venom that kills the prey could be
seriously disadvantageous: rotting meat might not be a suitable food for
the larvae. To be effective against a vertebrate, however, a venom often
must be damaging or have lethal potential (see earlier): thus the obvious
conflict. A possible solution to the problem has evolved in at least one
family, the Pompilidae. These spider wasps possess highly painful
venoms (to vertebrates), yet venoms devoid of lethal activity (see earlier).
Why this solution to the prey and predator problems has arisen only once
(or possibly a second time in the Bethylidae) is open to speculation.

PREDATOR RESISTANCE TO VENOMS

Predator resistance to hymenopterous venoms is a rare but serious
problem encountered by stinging Hymenoptera. Some vertebrate predators have either learned to "ignore" stings or are physically "insensitive"
to them. Examples include bears, honey badgers, and honey buzzards,
which attack honey bee nests and eat the contents, and racoons, skunks,
bears, hedgehogs, and feral and domestic pigs, which readily consume
yellowjacket, hornet, and paper wasp nests (Walker et al. 1975; Cobb 1979;
Edwards 1980; MacDonald and Matthews 1981; Akre and Reed 1984; Akre
and MacDonald 1986). Toads and frogs seem to be physiologically resistant to the effects of many stinging insect venoms. Cott (1940) in some of
his pioneering studies demonstrated that toads, *Bufo bufo,* near the entrances of bee hives would frequently eat and be stung by bees over
several consecutive days without ill effects. Hilse (1986) recorded numerous stings in the throats of *Bufo marinus* and 152 honey bees in the
stomach of one large toad. I have personally fed *Bufo americana* up to nine
worker yellowjackets, *Paravespula maculifrons,* within a ten minute period
and observed no ill effects in the toads. The toads were clearly stung, as
shown by their mouth gaping and eye retracting motions after eating
each worker yellowjacket, behaviors not exhibited when nine male yellowjackets were fed, one after each worker, to the toads (J.O. Schmidt,
unpublished).

Physiological resistance by specialized vertebrate predators to the
venoms of their prey is a subject open for investigation. Resistance by
some mammals to snakes is well known and partially physiologically
investigated (Perez et al. 1978; Minton and Minton 1982; de Wit and
Weström 1987; 1982; Poran et al. 1987; Tomihara et al. 1987). Philippine

spine-tailed swifts, *Chaetura gigantea,* have been reported to contain as many as four hundred detached honey bee stings in their mouths and gizzards and are almost certainly resistant to the bee venom (Morse and Laigo 1969, as cited in Fry 1983).

A system we are currently investigating is the predator-prey relationship between horned lizards and harvester ants. Horned lizards are specialist predators that often consume 90 percent or more of their food as ants. Although the ants sometimes overwhelm the lizards through mass biting and stinging attacks (Milne and Milne 1950; R.R. Snelling, personal communication; W.C. Sherbrooke, personal communication) the lizards are remarkably resistant to the attacks and stings of the ants. When challenged with harvester ant venom, *Phrynosoma douglassi* and *P. cornutum* were hundreds of times more resistant to the lethal effects of the venom than were mice (P.J. Schmidt et al. 1989; P.J. Schmidt and J.O. Schmidt, 1989). That this resistance was not inducible (i.e., immunologically mediated) is demonstrated by the resistance of naive juvenile *P. douglassi* taken from a habitat free of *Pogonomyrmex.* The exact nature of this resistance factor is unknown, but it is present in the blood of the horned lizards, as demonstrated by the ability of small quantities of *Phrynosoma* plasma to neutralize the lethal effects of 2.5 times a median lethal dose of *Pogonomyrmex* venom to white mice. The physiological resistance of *Phrynosoma* to *Pogonomyrmex* venoms is evidently a specifically evolved phenomenon, as is indicated by the lack of ability of the *Phrynosoma* plasma to protect mice from the lethal effects of three snake venoms (*Crotalus adamanteus, Vipera russelli, Naja naja atra*) and the honey bee (*Apis mellifera*) (P.J. Schmidt et al. 1989).

PREDATOR BEHAVIOR

Vertebrates are capable of learning, and many learn to avoid being stung by their prey. Bee eaters (Meropidae), birds that feed extensively on stinging bees and wasps, have learned to capture flying aculeates, mash their heads and abdomens into a substrate to kill them and cause them to expel their venoms, and then swallow them headfirst (Fry 1969; reviewed: Fry 1983). Shrikes, *Lanius* spp., have also learned to capture bees and wasps and frequently capture so many that they impale the excess on spines in their larder (figure 14.1).

Skunks, *Mephitis mephitis,* are known by North American beekeepers for their fondness for honey bees. Skunks successfully feed on the bees by attacking in the night and early hours of the morning, a time when the

Figure 14.1   Honey bees (*Apis mellifera*) impaled on prickley pear cactus (*Opuntia* sp.) spines in the larder of a shrike (*Lanius* sp.).

ambient temperatures are low and activity inside the hive is at a minimum. The skunks scratch at the hive entrance just enough to slowly draw out the few guard bees. These are quickly eaten as they emerge. The skunk continues scratching and waiting for bees to slowly come out until it has eaten as much as desired (Storer and Vansell 1935; Caron 1978). By using this behavior, the skunk usually avoids a mass attack by the bees while obtaining a meal derived from crawling individuals that can be handled a few at a time.

Some rodents have learned yet another means of dealing with stinging insects. Gerbils (*Meriones shawi*), when confronted with a stinging wasp, adapt a characteristic behavior observed only when stinging prey are encountered. Instead of simply grabbing the prey and consuming it in the usual fashion, stinging insects are grabbed and continually and quickly rotated with the fore paws. The gerbil meanwhile makes quick cutting bites into the prey until it is immobilized and defenseless. By this means the aculeate's sting can rarely be successfully brought into play and the gerbil obtains a meal (J.O. Schmidt, unpublished).

Tamanduas (*Tamandua tetradactyla*), pangolins (*Manis* spp.), and anteaters (*Myrmecophaga tridactyla*) are mammals that specialize on termites and ants. They have evolved specialized sticky protrusible tongues that not only rapidly entrap the aculeate prey, but also render the stinging motions generally ineffective. In addition to their rapid feeding behavior, which gives their prey little time to attempt to sting, these mammals are protected by fur and skin that are exceedingly difficult to penetrate.

PREDATOR HUNGER

One of the experimentally poorly investigated areas of predation studies is, somewhat surprisingly, the importance of hunger on predator behavior (see Ernsting and Van der Werf 1988 for literature). Hunger is undoubtedly an important factor in the risk-taking decision processes of a predator. A well-fed predator is unlikely to attempt to eat a prey that either offers a difficult challenge to overcome or is noxious in some fashion. Hungry predators are more motivated, less choosy, and more likely to take risks, such as being stung, in order to obtain food. The relative hunger of predators is a likely explanation for the presence of many aposematic and distasteful species present in tropical rain forests during the wet season, a time when many alternative prey are available, and why they are proportionately scarce during the dry season, when alternative prey are rare (Poulton 1908; Haviland 1926). Despite the obvious importance of predator hunger as a factor influencing the outcomes between encounters of predators with noxious prey, little empirical data are available to help quantify the importance of this hunger. The obvious problems involving the difficulty of measuring hunger aside, we know that under conditions of strong hunger animals will attempt to kill and eat otherwise unacceptable or dangerous prey. For example, starving humans from western cultures have been known to eat rats, a food source never previously considered (Falk 1962).

Hunger can be crucially important to the success of the sting as a defense. A hungry vertebrate is much less likely to be deterred by stings from bees, ants, and wasps than a recently or partially fed animal. For example, the small- to medium-sized species of toads used in the now famous tests of mimicry involving honey bees and their syrphid fly mimics (in which some toads were stung by bees and subsequently refused both model and mimic), were not exceedingly hungry (Brower and

Brower 1962). Moreover, in that study, sixteen of the twenty-two experimental toads repetitively ate honey bees, presumably in spite of the stings. Cott (1940) reported similar observations. Toads in the author's lab and those used by colleagues were "lean and hungry." These toads readily ate—and were stung by—yellowjackets (*Paravespula maculifrons* and *Vespula squamosa*) and honey bees, and also ate a variety of allomonally protected prey, including spirobolid and polydesmid millipedes, centipedes, and scorpions (*Vejovis* sp.). Other investigators have also reported that hungry anurans consume large numbers of honey bees (reviewed by Morse 1978). The conclusions from these studies are that the ultimate defensive value of the sting and the outcome of encounters with predators can be highly dependent on the hunger and nutritional state of the predator.

Conclusion

Venoms are not a defensive panacea for stinging Hymenoptera. However, in evolutionary and present contexts, they have been the next best thing. Hymenopterous venoms have given their possessors the ability to explore and exploit many new habitats that otherwise would be closed or risky to them because of potential vertebrate predators. The success of the ants, wasps, and bees in dominating many of the world's habitats, including tropical rain forests and thorn-scrubs, deserts, temperate woodlands, and into arctic zones attests to the defensive value of having evolved effective stings and venoms. The sting and venom have provided a key enabling mechanism for these small organisms to defensively counter the predatory actions of most vertebrates. Hymenopterous venoms owe their defensive utility primarily to their abilities to be delivered through the vertebrate integument and into sensitive tissues, where their activities of pain, tissue damage, and lethality can occur. Secondary defensive values of venoms include their frequent repellent tastes and abilities to induce allergy. Vertebrate-effective venoms have also provided the basis for the evolution of aposematism, a defensive warning system, and have removed a major obstacle to gregariousness and the evolution of sociality in the Hymenoptera.

I thank many individuals throughout the world for their assistance in locating and obtaining Hymenoptera for study, and Christopher Starr, Stephen Buchmann, David Evans, and Patricia Schmidt for manuscript reviews and many helpful suggestions.

References

Akre, R.D., and J.F. MacDonald. 1986. Biology, economic importance and control of yellow jackets. In *Economic Impact and Control of Social Insects* (S.B. Vinson, ed.), pp. 353–412. Praeger: New York.

Akre, R.D., and H.C. Reed. 1984. Vespine defense. In *Defensive Mechanisms in Social Insects* (H.R. Hermann, ed.), pp. 59–94. Praeger: New York.

Barnard, J.H. 1973. Studies of 400 Hymenoptera sting deaths in the United States. *J. Allergy Clin. Immunol.* 52:257–264.

Bell, T.D., and D.F. Hahlbohm. 1983. Hymenoptera allergy: clustering in beekeeping households. *Ann. Allergy* 50:356.

Bernheimer, A.W., L.S. Avigad, and J.O. Schmidt. 1980. A hemolytic polypeptide from the venom of the red harvester ant, *Pogonomyrmex barbatus. Toxicon* 18:271–278.

Bernheimer, A.W., L.S. Avigad, J.O. Schmidt, and J.S. Ishay. 1982. Proteins in venoms of two wasps, *Polistes comanchus navajoe* and *Vespa orientalis. Comp. Biochem. Physiol.* 71C:203–207.

Blum, M.S. 1966. Chemical releasers of social behavior. VII Citral in the mandibular gland secretion of *Listrimelitta limao. Ann. Ent. Soc. Am.* 59:962–964.

Blum, M.S. 1969. Alarm pheromones. *Annu. Rev. Ent.* 14:57–80.

Blum, M.S. and H.R. Hermann. 1978a. Venoms and venom apparatuses of the Formicidae: Myrmeciinae, Ponerinae, Dorylinae, Pseudomyrmecinae, Myrmicinae, and Formicinae. In *Anthropod Venoms, Handb. Exp. Pharm. Vol. 48* (S. Bettini, ed.), pp. 801–869. Springer-Verlag: Berlin.

Blum, M.S. and H.R. Hermann. 1978b. Venoms and venom apparatuses of the Formicidae: Dolichoderinae and Aneuretinae. In *Arthropod Venoms, Handb. Exp. Pharm. Vol. 48* (S. Bettini, ed.), pp. 871–894. Springer-Verlag: Berlin.

Blum, M.S., H.M. Fales, K.W. Tucker, and A.M. Collins. 1978. Chemistry of the sting apparatus of the worker honeybee. *J. Apic. Res.* 17:218–221.

Blum, M.S., T.H. Jones, B. Hölldobler, H.M. Fales, and T. Jaouni. 1980. Alkaloidal venom mace: offensive use by a thief ant. *Naturwissenschaften* 67:144–145.

Boch, R., D.A. Shearer, and A. Petrosavits. 1970. Efficacies of two alarm substances of the honey bee. *J. Insect Physiol.* 16:17–24.

Bousquet, J., Y. Coulomb, M. Robinet-Levy, and F.B. Michel. 1982. Clinical and immunological surveys in beekeepers. *Clin. Allergy* 12:331–342.

Brophy, J.J., G.W.K. Cavill, and R.K. Duke. 1983. Volatile constituents in a methylene chloride extract of a ponerine ant, *Rhytidoponera aciculata* (Smith). *Insect Biochem.* 13:503–505.

Brower, J.V.Z., and L.P. Brower. 1962. Experimental studies of mimicry. 6. The reaction of toads (*Bufo terrestris*) to honeybee (*Apis mellifera*) and their dronefly mimics (*Eristalis vinetorum*). *Am. Nat.* 96:297–307.

Caron, D.M. 1978. Marsupials and mammals. In *Honey Bee Pests, Predators, and Diseases* (R.A. Morse, ed.), pp. 227–256. Cornell Univ. Press: Ithaca, N.Y.

Chapman, C.R., K.L. Casey, R. Dubner, K.M. Foley, R.H. Gracely, and A.E. Reading. 1985. Pain measurement: an overview. *Pain* 22:1–31.

Cobb, F.K. 1979. Honey buzzard at wasps' nest. *Br. Birds* 72:59–64.

Collins, A.M., and M.S. Blum. 1983. Alarm responses caused by newly identified compounds derived from the honeybee sting. *J. Chem. Ecol.* 9:57–65.

Coppinger, R.P. 1970. The effect of experience and novelty on avian feeding behavior with reference to the evolution of warning coloration in butterflies. II reaction of naive birds to novel insects. *Am. Nat.* 104:323–335.

Corson, J.A., and M.J. Schneider. 1984. The Dartmouth pain questionnaire: an adjunct to the McGill pain questionnaire. *Pain* 19:59–69.

Cott, H.B. 1940. *Adaptive Coloration in Animals.* Methuen: London.

Dressler, R.L. 1979. *Eulaema bombiformis, E. meriana,* and Mullerian mimicry in related species (Hymenoptera: Apidae), *Biotropica* 111:144–151.

Duffield, R.M., M.S. Blum, and J.W. Wheeler. 1976. Alkypyrazine alarm pheromones in primitive ants with small colonial units. *Comp. Biochem. Physiol.* 54B:439–440.

Edwards, R. 1980. *Social Wasps: Their Biology and Control.* Rentokil Ltd.: East Grinstead, W. Sussex.

Ernsting, G., and D.C. van der Werf. 1988. Hunger, partial consumption of prey and prey size preference in a carabid beetle. *Ecol. Ent.* 13:155–164.

Evans, D.L., and G.P. Waldbauer. 1982. Behavior of adult and naive birds when presented with a bumblebee and its mimic. *Z. Tierpsychol.* 59:247–259.

Falk, S.L. 1962. *Bataan: The March of Death.* Norton: New York.

Francke, W., G. Hindorf, and W. Reith. 1978. Methyl-1,6-dioxospiro[4,5]decanes as odors of *Paravespula vulgaris* (L). *Angew. Chem. Int. Ed. Engl.* 17:862.

Francke, W., W. Schröder, E. Engles, and W. Engles. 1983. Variation in cephalic volatile substances in relation to worker age and behavior in stingless bee, *Scaptotrigona postica. Z. Naturforsch.* 38C:1066–1068.

Fry, C.H. 1969. The recognition and treatment of venomous and non-venomous insects by small bee-eaters. *Ibis* 111:23–29.

_____. **1983.** Honeybee predation by bee-eaters, with economic considerations. *Bee World* 64:65–78.

Ghent, R.L. 1961. Adaptive refinements in the chemical defense mechanisms of certain Formicinae. Ph.D. Dissertation, Cornell Univ.: Ithaca, N.Y.

Gibo, D.L., H.E. Dew, and A.S. Hajduk. 1974. Thermoregulation in colonies of *Vespula arenaria* and *Vespula maculata* (Hymenoptera: Vespidae). II. The relation between colony biomass and calorie production. *Can. Ent.* 106:873–879.

Golden, D.B.K., M.D. Valentine, A. Kagey-Sobotka and L.M. Lichtenstein. 1982. Prevalence of Hymenoptera venom allergy. *J. Allergy Clin. Immunol.* 69(1, Part 2):124.

Graft, D.F., K.C. Schuberth, A. Kagey-Sobotka, K.A. Kwiterovich, L.M. Lichtenstein, and M.D. Valentine. 1982. Large local reactions following Hymenoptera stings in children. *J. Allergy Clin. Immunol.* 69(1, Part 2):124.

Haviland, M.D. 1926. Forest, Steppe and Tundra. Cambridge Press: Cambridge.

Heinrich. B. 1979a. Thermoregulation of African and European honeybees during foraging, attack and hive exits and returns. *J. Exp. Biol.* 80:217–229.

_____. 1979b. Bumblebee Economics. Harvard Univ. Press: Cambridge, Mass.

Herbert, F.A., and M.L. Salkie. 1982. Sensitivity to Hymenoptera in adult males. *Ann. Allergy* 48:12–13.

Hermann, H.R. 1968. The hymenopterous poison apparatus. IV. *Dasymutilla occidentalis* (Hymenoptera: Mutillidae). *J. Georgia Ent. Soc.* 3:1–10.

Hermann H.R., and M.S. Blum. 1981. Defensive mechanisms in the social Hymenoptera. In *Social Insects, Vol. 2* (H.R. Hermann, ed.), pp. 77–197. Academic Press: New York.

Hermann, H.R., M.S. Blum, J.W. Wheeler, W.L. Overal, J.O. Schmidt, and J.-T. Chao. 1984. Comparative anatomy and chemistry of the venom apparatus and mandibular glands in *Dinoponera grandis* (Guerin) and *Paraponera clavata* (F.) (Hymenoptera: Formicidae: Ponerinae). *Ann. Ent. Soc. Am.* 77:272–279.

Hilse, B. 1986. Survey of cane toads and their effect on the bee population. *Australasian Beekeeper* 88:261–262.

Hölldobler, B. 1973. Chemische Strategie beim Nahrungserwerb der Diebsameise (*Solenopsis fugax* Latr.) und der Pharaoameise (*Monomorium pharaonis* L.). *Oecologia* 11:371–380.

Hölldobler, K. 1928. Zur Biologie der deibischen Zwergameise (*Solenopsis fugax*) und ihrer Gäste. *Biol. Zentralbl.* 48:129–142.

Howard, D.F., M.S. Blum, T.H. Jones, and M.D. Tomalsky. 1982. Behavioral responses to an alkylpyrazine from the mandibular gland of the ant *Wasmannia auropunctata*. *Insectes Soc.* 29:369–374.

Islam, S. 1979. Severe conditioned taste aversion elicited by venom of Russell's viper. *Experientia* 35:1205–1207.

Krombein, K.V., P.D. Hurd, Jr., and D.R. Smith. 1979. *Catalog of Hymenoptera in America North of Mexico*, Vol. 3. Smithsonian Institution Press: Washington, D.C.

de la Lande, I.S., D.W. Thomas, and M.J. Tyler. 1965. Pharmacological analysis of the venom of the 'bulldog' and *Myrmecia forficata. Proc. 2nd Int. Pharmacol. Meet, Prague* 9:71-74.

Lewis, J.C., and I.S. de la Lande. 1967. Pharmacological and enzymic constituents of the venom of an Australian bulldog ant *Myrmecia pyriformis. Toxicon* 4:225-234.

Liepelt, W. 1963. Zur Schutzwirking des Stachelgiftes von Bienen und Wespen gegenüber Trauer-fliegenschnöpper und Gartenrotschwanz. *Zool Jb. Physiol.* 70:167-176.

Longhurst, C., R. Baker, P.E. Howse, and W. Speed. 1978. Alkylpyrazines in ponerine ants: their presence in three genera and the caste-specific behavioural responses to them in *Odontomachus troglodytes* Santschi. *J. Insect Physiol.* 24:833-837.

MacDonald, J.F., and R.W. Matthews. 1981. Nesting biology of the eastern yellowjacket, *Vespula maculifrons* (Hymenoptera: Vespidae). *J. Kansas Ent. Soc.* 54:433-457.

Marshall, G.A.K., and E.B. Poulton. 1902. Five years' observations and experiments (1896-1901) on the bionomics of South African insects, chiefly directed to the investigation of mimicry and warning colours. *Trans. Ent. Soc. Lond.* 1902:287-584.

Maschwitz, U. 1964. Gefahrenalarmstoffe und Gefahrenalarmierung bei Sozialen Hymenopteren. *Z. Vergl. Physiol.* 47:596-655.

Melzak, R. 1975. The McGill pain questionnaire: major properties and scoring methods. *Pain* 1:277-299.

Milne, L.J., and M.J. Milne. 1950. Notes on the behavior of horned toads. *Am. Midland Nat.* 44:720-741.

Minton, Jr., S.A., and M.R. Minton. 1981. Toxicity of some Australian snake venoms for potential prey species of reptiles and amphibians. *Toxicon* 19:749-755.

Morse, R.A. 1978. Amphibians (frogs and toads). In *Honey Bee Pests, Predators, and Diseases* (R.A. Morse, ed.), pp. 210-215. Cornell Univ. Press: Ithaca, N.Y.

Morse, R.A., and F.M. Laigo. 1969. The Philippine spine-tailed swift, *Chaetura dubia* McGregor as a honey bee predator. *Philipp. Ent.* 1:138-143.

Mostler, G. 1935. Beobachtungen zur Frage der Wespenmimikry. *Z. Morph. Ökol. Tiere* 29: 381-454.

Mühlmann, H. 1934. Im Modellversuch künstlich erzeugte Mimikry und ihre Bedeutung für den 'Nachahmer'. *Z. Morph. Ökol. Tiere* 28:259-296.

Nicolaus, L.K., J.F. Cassel, R.B. Carlson, and C.R. Gustavson. 1983. Taste-aversion conditioning of crows to control predation on eggs. *Science* 220:212-214.

O'Toole, C. 1986. *The Encyclopedia of Insects.* Facts On File Pub.: New York.

Palmerino, C.C., K.W. Rusiniak, and J. Garcia. 1980. Flavor-illness aversions: the peculiar roles of odor and taste in memory for poison. *Science* 208:753-755.

Parrish, H.M. 1963. Analysis of 460 fatalities from venomous animals in the United States. *Am. J. Med. Sci.* 245:129–141.

Perez, J.C., W.C. Haws, V.E. Carcia, and B.M. Jennings III. 1978. Resistance of warm-blooded animals to snake venoms. *Toxicon* 16:375–383.

Poran, N.S., R.G. Coss, and E. Benjamini. 1987. Resistance of California ground squirrels (*Spermophilus beecheyi*) to the venom of the northern pacific rattlesnake (*Crotalus viridis oreganus*): a study of adaptive variation. *Toxicon* 25:767–777.

Poulton, E.B. 1887. The experimental proof of the protective value of colour and markings in insects with reference to their vertebrate enemies. *Proc. Zool. Soc. Lond.* 1887:191–274.

————. **1908.** Essays on Evolution, 1889–1907. Oxford Press: Oxford.

Rubinoff, I., and C. Kropach. 1970. Differential reactions of Atlantic and Pacific predators to sea snakes. *Nature* 228:1288–1290.

Schmidt, J.O. 1978. *Dasymutilla occidentalis:* a long-lived aposematic wasp (Hymenoptera: Mutillidae). *Ent. News* 89:135–136.

————. **1983.** Hymenopteran envenomation. In *Urban Entomology: Interdisciplinary Perspectives* (G.W. Frankie and C.S. Koehler, eds.), pp. 187–220. Praeger: New York.

————. **1986.** Chemistry, pharmacology, and chemical ecology of ant venoms. In *Venoms of the Hymenoptera* (T. Piek, ed.), pp. 425–508. Academic Press: London.

Schmidt, J.O., and M.S. Blum. 1977. Adaptations and responses of *Dasymutilla occidentalis* (Hymenoptera: Multillidae) to predators. *Ent. Exp. Appl.* 21:99–111.

————. **1978.** A harvester ant venom: chemistry and pharmacology. *Science* 200:1064–1066.

Schmidt, J.O., M.S. Blum, and W.L. Overal. 1980. Comparative lethality of venoms from stinging Hymenoptera. *Toxicon* 18:469–474.

————. **1984.** Hemolytic activities of stinging insect venoms. *Arch. Insect Biochem. Physiol.* 1:155–160.

————. **1986.** Comparative enzymology of venoms from stinging Hymenoptera. *Toxicon* 24:907–921.

Schmidt, J.O., S. Yamane, M. Matsuura, and C.K. Starr. 1986. Hornet venoms: lethalities and lethal capacities. *Toxicon* 24:950–954.

Schmidt, P.J., and J.O. Schmidt. 1989. Harvester ants and horned lizards: predator-prey interactions. In *Special Biotic Relationships in the Arid Southwest* (J.O. Schmidt, ed.), pp. 25–51. Univ. New Mexico Press: Albuquerque.

Schmidt, P.J., W.C. Sherbrooke, and J.O. Schmidt. 1989. The detoxification of ant *(Pogonomyrmex)* venom by a blood factor in horned lizards *(Phyrnosoma). Copeia* 1989:603–607.

Schmidt-Nielsen, K. 1979. *Animal Physiology: Adaptation and Environment.* Cambridge Univ. Press: Cambridge.

Seeley, T.D., and B. Heinrich, 1981. Regulation of temperature in the nests of social insects. In *Insect Thermoregulation* (B. Heinrich, ed.), pp. 159–234. John Wiley: New York.

Shearer, D.A., and R. Boch. 1965. 2-Heptanone in the mandibular gland secretion of the honey-bee.*Nature* 206:530.

Smith, S.M. 1977. Coral-snake pattern recognition and stimulus generalization by naive great kiskadees (Aves: Tyrannidae). *Nature* 265:535–536.

Smith, B.H., and D.W. Roubik. 1983. Mandibular glands of stingless Bees (Hymenoptera: Apidae): Chemical analysis of their contents and biological function in two species of *Melopona J. Chem. Ecol.* 9:1465–1472.

Starr, C.K. 1985a. A simple pain scale for field comparison of hymenopteran stings. *J. Ent. Sci.* 20:225–232.

Starr, C.K. 1985b. Enabling mechanisms in the origin of sociality in the Hymenoptera—the sting's the thing. *Ann. Ent. Soc. Amer.* 78:836–840.

Storer, T.I., and G.H. Vansell. 1935. Bee eating proclivities of the striped skunk. *J. Mammal.* 16:118–121.

Taylor, R.W. 1978. *Nothomyrmecia macrops:* a living-fossil ant rediscovered. *Science* 201:979–985.

Tomihara, Y., K. Yonaha, M. Nozaki, M. Yamakawa, T. Kamura, and S. Toyama. 1987. Purification of three antihemorrhagic factors from the serum of a mongoose (*Herpestes edwardsii*). *Toxicon* 25:685–689.

Walker, E.P., F. Warnick, S.E. Hamlet, K.I. Lange, M.A. Davis, H.E. Uible, and P.E. Wright. 1975. *Mammals of the World 3rd Ed.* Johns Hopkins Press: Baltimore, Md.

Wheeler, J.W., and M.S. Blum. 1973. Alkylpyrazine alarm pheromones in ponerine ants. *Science* 182:501–503.

Wilson, E.O. 1976. The organization of colony defense in the ant *Pheidole dentata* Mayr (Hymenoptera: Formicidae). *Behav. Ecol. Sociobiol.* 1:63–81.

de Wit, C.A. 1982. Resistance of the prairie vole (*Microtus ochrogaster*) and the woodrat (*Neotoma floridana*), in Kansas, to venom of the Osage copperhead (*Agkistrodon contortrix phaeogaster*). *Toxicon* 20:709–714.

de Wit, C.A., and B.R. Weström. 1987. Venom resistance in the hedgehog, *Erinaceus europaeus:* purification and identification of macroglobulin inhibitors as plasma antihemorrhagic factors. *Toxicon* 25:315–323.

Yunginger, J.W., R.T. Jones, K.M. Leiferman, B.R. Paull, P.W. Welsh, and G.J. Gleich. 1978. Immunological and biochemical studies in beekeepers and their family members. *J. Allergy Clin. Immunol.* 61:93–101.

Zora, J.A., M.C. Swanson, and J.W. Yunginger. 1984. How common is unrecognized Hymenoptera venom allergy in the general population? *J. Allergy. Clin. Immunol.* 73(1 Part 2):139.

Holding the Fort:
Colony Defense in Some Primitively Social Wasps

Christopher K. Starr

Introduction

The social wasps, in the formal sense, are the vespid subfamilies Vespinae, Polistinae, and Stenogastrinae, together forming a monophyletic group (Carpenter 1982, in press) of about eight hundred known species. With two known exceptions (Matthews in press), all social wasps are within this group, and with only very few possible exceptions (personal observation), all members of the group are social. The variety of their social organization can be reduced to a small number of fundamental patterns, in which two variables are of particular importance (Jeanne 1980):

1. In all known stenogastrines and virtually all polistines, the reproductive females (queens) and nonreproductive females (workers) are indistinguishable by external physical features. The vespines have departed from this pattern, in that queens are almost always distinct.

2. Primitively, a new colony is founded by a queen or group of queens alone (*independent founding*). In one known vespine species (Matsuura 1985) and about three lineages of polistines, on the other hand, founding queens are accompanied by workers, a departure known as *swarm founding*.

The subject of this chapter is the antipredator defenses of those species which are primitive for these two characters, the majority of polistines (comprising the genera *Polistes*, *Mischocyttarus*, *Belonogaster*, *Parapolybia*, and part of *Ropalidia*) and all known stenogastrines. For convenience, I will call them collectively "primitive social wasps." The greater part of my facts are drawn from *Polistes*, the only primitive social genus with a significant presence in the north temperate zone and the one most extensively studied to date.

THE NATURE OF THE COLONY AND SOCIAL DEFENSE

Primitive-social wasps occupy a special place in the study of social evolution. Along with certain bees (Michener 1974), they stand just over what has been called the "eusociality threshold" (Oster and Wilson 1978) and so seem to hold the key to understanding how insect sociality arose and arises. Some theoretical treatments (e.g., Orlove 1975) explicitly take *Polistes* as a model of primitive sociality, and in many others (e.g., Craig 1982, 1983) *Polistes* nesting biology seems to serve as an implicit standard for setting realistic assumptions. Among the important features of these and other primitive social wasps are the following:

1. Small colony size. The total number of adults is often less than one hundred at its peak, and very few species ever have colonies of one thousand adults. This sets them apart from such advanced social insects as honey bees, stingless bees, termites, and most ants.

2. Functional monogyny, except in *Belonogaster*. Fertile queens tend to be intolerant of each other and come into conflict until all but one are reduced to nonreproductive, workerlike status. In some species the founding group characteristically consists of a single queen, so that colonies are monogynous from the start.

3. With the emergence of the first workers, queens stop almost all colony-maintaining activities. Again, *Belonogaster* is exceptional.

4. A simple uncovered nest. In independent-founding polistines this nest characteristically consists of a single open brood comb (figures 15.1a,b, 15.2). In many stenogastrines the nest is not especially comblike, but it is always of comparable simplicity

Figure 15.1 Nests of (a) *Mischocyttarus labiatus,* (b) *Ropalidia marginata,* (c) *Parischnogaster mellyi,* (d) *Eustenogaster luzonensis,* and (e) *Polybia diquetana,* to show gross structure.

Figure 15.2   Comb face of *Mischocyttarus* sp., showing nest pulp smeared on the two pupal caps.

(figure 15.1c,d). Vespines and almost all swarm-founding polistines, on the other hand, build a covering envelope around the comb(s) (figure 15.1e) or nest in a preexisting cavity.

In most of this book defense is an individual, personal affair, the defender and defended being one. Such is not the case here. The main object of all interesting defense reactions in social insects is the immature members of the colony, or brood, while the main agent of defense is the workers. Personal defense is not substantially different in solitary and social insects; it is in brood-defense that the innovations appear.

The evolution of social life is a contradictory phenomenon associated both with new opportunities and new problems (e.g., Alexander 1974). Our understanding of the nature and interplay of these in insects is still at an early stage. For example, there is still no plausible explanation why all *Polistes* spp. are social, and our insight into why *any* of them should be social is not much better. I have argued elsewhere (Starr 1985b) that in primitively social insects the general problems are necessarily much more important than the general opportunities, so that sociality is closed to all lineages without special solutions. The main problem cited is the attractiveness of the concentrated brood-mass to new classes of predators and parasites.

The title of this chapter is taken from the metaphor of the social insect colony as a fortified factory with the dual task of maximally producing and defending new colony members (Oster and Wilson 1978). We will take production as a given and concern ourselves only with how primitive social wasp colonies keep what they have made.

THE ENEMIES OF PRIMITIVE SOCIAL WASPS

Enemies of primitive social wasps are conveniently divided into three groups: (a) insect brood parasites and parasitoids, (b) social insect predators, and (c) vertebrate predators.

Unlike the colonies of many vespines and swarm founders (Spradbery 1973; Richards 1978; Edwards 1980), those of primitive social wasps usually seem to support very few commensals, including parasites and parasitoids. The most extensive work on this subject has been with some New World *Polistes* (Nelson 1968, 1971). A recent compilation of records of parasitoids of polistine brood (Makino 1985) shows representatives of a broad taxonomic range, but with just four genera standing out: the hymenoptera *Dibrachys* (Pteromalidae), *Pachysomoides* (Ichneumonidae), and *Elasmus* (Eulophidae), and the moth *Chalcoela* (Pyralidae). Although no systematic comparison has yet been done, there seem to be very large, unexplained geographic differences in the impact of these and similar insects. Defense against parasites and parasitoids is largely outside the scope of this book. I will just note that the single general tactic among primitive social wasps is apparently to remain constantly vigilant and to physically repulse any foreign insect approaching the nest. Even where parasites and parasitoids are a serious menace, the wasps rarely have any other tactic of note. In comparison with some of their antipredator adaptations, this is a surprisingly crude response. The parasites and parasitoids, for their part, seem to rely on stealth to enter brood cells, avoiding engagement with adult wasps.

Two quite different types of social insect predators stand out. In much of Asia, hornets (*Vespa* spp.) prey heavily on social wasps and bees (Sakagami and Fukushima 1957; Matsuura 1984; Yamane 1984; R. Gadagkar, personal communication; personal observation). This is especially true of the widespread *V. tropica*, which in parts of Japan preys exclusively on independent-founding polistines and in tropical Asia attacks both these and stenogastrines. Hornets are not native to Africa, Australia, or the New World.

Ants are ubiquitous, and their role as predators of other social insects has long been evident. Jeanne (1975) in particular has emphasized the importance of predation pressure from ants in the evolution of social wasps. The unremitting nature of this pressure can hardly be overstated. Some other natural enemies are locally absent or insignificant, but social wasps throughout the world coexist with large numbers of ants which would quickly eat their brood if permitted. Extant species are those which have solved this problem, and some of the solutions are known.

Observations of vertebrate predation on primitive social wasps are fragmentary, but they suffice to show that the predators are usually birds. In North America the blue jay (*Cyanocitta cristata*) and summer tanager (*Piranga rubra*) are frequent predators of *Polistes* and *Mischocyttarus* brood (Rau 1941; Litte 1979; Strassmann 1981b; D.L. Gibo and J.W. Krispyn, personal communications).

A vertebrate predator's approach to a wasp colony cannot very well be that of a parasite or parasitoid. In most cases it will be larger than the entire colony, so stealth is of limited value. Plain frontal force will be perfectly effective where it is worth the hazards. It is generally assumed (e.g., Jeanne 1975) that vertebrates search visually for wasp nests.

In these respects, hornets much more resemble vertebrates than ants. An individual hornet is much bigger than the wasps or bees she attacks, and because of her relatively hard, thick cuticle she probably has little to fear from most prey species workers. It is not yet known how hornets locate nests. My impression from often watching *V. tropica* searching among foliage is that a combination of vision and smell at close quarters is involved, in the manner of wasps searching for solitary prey. Although they are social insects, hornets are not known to mount coordinated mass attacks on primitive social wasp colonies.

The search and attack of ants are necessarily very different from those of hornets, as indicated by three factors:

1. Worker ants do not fly, so that search must be a slow, thorough affair, not a quick scan.

2. Most ants rely little on vision. The compound eyes of workers are usually markedly reduced and in army ants are often lost entirely (Schneirla 1971; Gotwald 1982).

3. Ants are almost always smaller than wasps, so that a worker by herself cannot attack effectively. Consequently, they

depend on communication with colony mates (recruitment) and mass attack.

There is now strong evidence that in the New World ants are a more serious problem for social wasps in the tropics than in the temperate zones. A gradient of increasingly rapid discovery and exploitation by ants of wasp larva baits has been shown from the northern United States to equatorial South America (Jeanne 1979b). We may expect a similar trend between Europe and tropical Africa and between northern and southern Asia, but this prediction might be mistaken. Both the New World army ants (Ecitoninae) and Old World army ants (Dorylinae) are almost entirely tropical (Schneirla 1971; Watkins 1976; Gotwald 1982). The importance of ecitonines in the life economy of Neotropical wasps is well established (Richards and Richards 1951; Jeanne 1975, 1982a; Chadab 1979; Chadab-Crepet and Rettenmeyer 1982), but it is much less apparent that dorylines have a comparable impact in Africa (W.H. Gotwald, personal communication) or Asia (Wilson 1964; personal observation). At the same time, the importance of ants as a whole in these regions is not doubted.

The prevailing judgement, then, is that ants are the main predators of tropical social wasps, especially in the New World, that hornets are important in south and east Asia, and that vertebrates take on increasing importance away from the tropics (Jeanne 1975; Turillazzi 1984). In addition, many features of nest structure are best interpreted as adaptations to lessen the impact of predation by ants (Jeanne 1975). In what follows I examine the known and supposed defense of primitive social wasps against these three classes of predators. It is convenient to distinguish *primary defenses,* which operate whether an enemy is present or not, from *secondary defenses,* which only come into play under provocation (Edmunds 1974).

Primary Defense

THE IMPORTANCE OF NOT BEING SEEN

The most fundamental antipredator defense must be to remove oneself from all predation attempts, and primitive social wasps show some marked adaptations in this direction. The habit of most stenogas-trines and a few independent-founding polistines of nesting in dim, recessed places undoubtedly gives a degree of concealment, though it is not known that this is an ultimate cause of nest site choice. At least for humans, visual search is still reasonably effective for finding such wasp colonies. Even a moderate lowering of the light level, however, can decrease resolution and rob such predators as hornets and birds of much of the advantage of color vision (Endler 1978, 1986).

Even if the nest is visible, it will not necessarily be perceived, and the nests of many species are strongly cryptic. Stenogastrine nests are usually uniformly brown and very often of a shape to suggest the vines, root ends, dead leaves, or clods of earth which tend to abound in their nest sites (personal observation). My overall assessment of stenogastrine nests is that they are excellently designed not to attract attention. A similar tendency, though less pronounced, is found among *Mischocyttarus*. The nests of some species are elongate in a manner which cannot serve economy of materials or structural strength, but which produces a resemblance to a vine or twig. Among more normally comblike nests, some are of a shape and color to suggest dead leaves. In the most extensive treatment of *Mischocyttarus* nests to date, Zikán (1949) suggested that the considerable between-species variation is itself a concealing device, preventing predators from forming any general search image. A very few *Polistes* and *Ropalidia* species also have twiglike nests.

Pupal caps provide another evidence of evolved crypticity. Stenogastrine larve do not spin a complete cocoon, and any pupal cap is made by adults from nesting material. In polistines, though, the cocoon includes a strong, silk pupal cap which can be brightly white, so that a series of unadorned caps increases the nest's conspicuousness. This fact explains the habit of many species (I have especially noticed it in *Mischocyttarus* and independent-founding *Rapolidia*) of adding dabs of nest pulp to finished caps (figure 15.2). On the other hand, vespines and almost all swarm-founding polistines, whose cells are concealed by an envelope, use no such adornment (R.L. Jeanne, personal communication; personal observation). The peculiar chartreuse silk of *Polistes sagittarius funebris* may also serve to camouflage the nest among foliage, though to my eyes it is such a lurid color as to be rather ineffective.

Why do *Polistes* so rarely depart toward the cryptic? A simple and plausible answer is that they are large, and large size militates against not being seen. This answer may be too simple, though, as even small-bodied *Ropalidia* are very often brightly colored, as are a great many *Polistes*, and even large-bodied *Mischocyttarus* usually are not (personal observation). I have suggested elsewhere (Starr 1985b) that dependence on crypticity as a main tactic limits colony size.

The shape and color of wasps and their nests are probably of no apparent significance in escaping from ants. It is probably little exaggeration to say that ants search very widely and any nest will in time come within the scope of their search. This is not to say, though, that all nest sites are equal, and a well-chosen one may very rarely be visited by ants. Ants are above all the mistresses of the ground layer and the lower trunks of trees, which certainly accounts for the observation that wasps almost never nest there. Nests on leaves and secondary branches are more secure than those on trunks and primary branches (Jeanne 1975, 1979b). Similarly, the tips of palm trunk thorns are a favored nest site of *Mischocyttarus* species in the Corcovado National Park of Costa Rica (figure 15.1a). Where the density of thorns is high the total walking distance for a thorough search is tremendously increased. Thus, even if an ant could be certain that there was a nest somewhere on the trunk, it might not be worthwhile to search. The same consideration may explain why some *Parischogaster* species in the Philippines nest at the tips of roof thatch (Williams 1928; personal observation). This tactic is analogous to the classic trick of the leprechaun, sworn not to remove the marker on the sheaf above a pot of gold, of placing an identical marker on every other sheaf in the field. My casual observations in Corcovado suggest that army ants largely bypass thorny palms. The habit of many New World *Polistes* and *Mischocyttarus* of nesting under the eaves of buildings may spring from a similar cause, since such sites are relatively secure from ants (Jeanne 1979b).

NARROW APPROACHES AND CHEMICAL BARRIERS

Before the widespread use of gunpowder, the very narrowness of London's alleys was of major defensive importance. It forced invaders to advance in single file, so that a single superior swordsman could hold an alley against any number of foes. Most stenogastrines achieve a similar effect by nesting on such substrates that the walking approach is very narrow and can be defended by a single wasp (figure 15.1c,d). A good example of a primary defense enhanced by secondary defense. The independent-founding polistines have freed themselves from the need to nest in such places by building their own narrow approach, the petiole (figure 15.1a,b). This is in large part of a dense and very strong substance, almost certainly on oral secretion, with the advantage of allowing the petiole to remain thin as the comb grows (Jeanne 1975).

It seems unlikely, though, that a wasp can block the passage of army ants, no matter how narrow the petiole, and this may well be true of other ants which scout and advance in mass. Rather, the petiole may allow the wasp (a) to stop any single foragers, and (b) to prevent those species which lay odor trails from reaching the nest and gaining an occasion to recruit colony mates. Nests of *Mischocyttarus mexicanus* and *flavitarsis*, for example, are rarely invaded by ants. Any lone ant approaching the petiole is grasped and thrown from the plant, so that she cannot recruit the large numbers which might overwhelm the wasps (Litte 1977, 1979).

A great many independent-founding polistines are known to apply on the petiole a volatile substance from an abdominal gland, Vecht's organ, and it is probable that all of them do. In one species each of *Mischocyttarus, Polistes,* and *Ropalidia* this substance has been shown to have an ant-repellent effect (Jeanne 1970; Post and Jeanne 1981; Kojima 1983b), and two lines of indirect evidence leave little doubt that this is its function throughout the group:

> 1. The behavior of applying the ant repellent (rubbing) has been observed in many other *Mischocyttarus, Polistes,* and *Ropalidia* (Corn 1972; Hermann and Dirks 1974; Darchen 1976; Litte 1979; Turillazzi and Ugolini 1979; Kojima 1982; Dew 1983; Raposo-Filho 1983; personal observation), as well as in *Belonogaster* (Marino-Piccioli and Pardi 1970) and *Parapolybia* (Kojima 1983a; personal observation).

> 2. An extensive comparative study has shown the Vecht's organ to be well developed in all studied independent-founding polistines, but absent or strongly reduced in swarm founders (Jeanne et al. 1983).

The secretion has been studied chemically only in *Polistes fuscatus* (Post et al., Identification, 1984). Although rubbing is mainly a primary defensive tactic, it is not exclusively so. Two *Polistes* species are known to rub more when ants are near the nest (Turillazzi and Ugolini 1979; Post and Jeanne 1981), and this is likely also in other species as well.

Among the Stenogastrinae, putative chemical ant guards are known only from some *Eustenogaster* and *Parischogaster* species (Pagden 1958; Turillazzi and Pardi 1981; Ohgushi et al. 1983; personal observation). These are quite different from those of polistines and certainly evolved separately. They take the form of a visicid white band or set of bands

Figure 15.3   (a) Sticky ant guard above nest of undescribed *Parischnogaster* nr. *nigricans;* (b) putative physical ant guards above nest of *P. strandi.*

around the approach to the nest (figure 15.3a). Unlike in polistines, the substance is readily visible and lasts for several days without replenishment. It is emitted at the tip of the abdomen (Turillazzi and Pardi 1981; Ohgushi et al. 1983; M.H. Hansell, personal communication) and may come from the Dufour's gland.

For many years there was only indirect evidence that these bands in fact function as ant guards, but the white substance is now known to repel at least some ants (Turillazzi and Pardi 1981; Turillazzi 1985). This repellency would seem to have a different basis from that of the volatile chemicals of polistines. Ants appear to find the substance distasteful (Turillazzi 1985), but why should that inhibit them from walking over it? It may be that it is irritating to have it on their feet, akin to having sticky fingers. It was long ago suggested (Jacobson 1935) that the ant guard substance and the similarly appearing substance which all stenogastrines put on eggs and young larvae are the same, and Turillazzi (1985) gives further reason to expect this. Chemical analysis should soon render this idea certain, as well as suggest a mechanism for the ant repellent effect.

There is no reason to believe that repellency must be especially powerful in order to turn back approaching scout ants. Lacking contrary indications, we may assume that (a) an exploring ant cannot perceive the colony before reaching it, (b) there is nothing about the substrate to suggest that a nest should be there in particular, and (c) the repellent substance itself gives no such information. In that case, scouts should lack motivation to cross even a mildly repellent barrier. I suggest that ant guards simply mimic the volatile or sticky plant exudates which ants must often encounter.

Chemical brood defense need not be equally prevalent at all stages of the colony cycle. In the very vulnerable founding stage, *Ropalidia fasciata* rubs with increasing frequency as the brood matures, that is, as its value increases (Kojima 1983b), and in three *Polistes* species the frequency drops with the emergence of the first workers (Turillazzi and Ugolini 1979; Post and Jeanne 1981; Turillazzi 1984). Individual rubbing frequency is less in *R. fasciata* in larger foundress groups (Kojima 1983b). These last two observations are consistent with the idea that primary defense has a lesser role when more defenders are available.

It is unclear whether similar trends prevail for stenogastrine ant guards. Their durability makes it impractical to use application rate as a test, but in at least some species the size of the ant guard can vary considerably. Turillazzi and Pardi (1981) report increasing size as the nest ages in *Parischnogaster nigricans*. Table 15.1 shows the relationship between the state of the ant guard and the numbers of adults females, adult males, and brood in a closely related species. The ant guard does not vary significantly with any of the colony composition variables according to a one-way analysis of variance, but the Kruskal-Wallis H-test shows it varying with brood size (p<.01). In the field I interpreted a weak ant guard as one which had lapsed through lack of maintenance, since some abandoned nests have a similar trace of the substance. It now appears rather to be one which has not been brought to full size, consistent with the idea that it is expensive to produce and so is strengthened as brood size increases.

Some few stenogastrines build pulp structures with the appearance of physical ant guards (Williams 1919; Pagden 1958, 1962) (figure 15.3b).

HIDING BEHIND BIG BROTHER

Several relatively vulnerable animals are known to gain protection through close association with species better equipped to defend against a common enemy. Richards (1978) and Turillazzi (1984) have reviewed apparent cases of this tactic among social wasps. It is not surprising that it is not widespread, given the necessary conditions:

    1. The association must be such that an attack on one is perceived as an attack on both.

    2. The protector's defense against the common enemy must be a retaliation, not just a retreat or primary defense.

    3. The protector must tolerate the protected.

Nonetheless, several *Mischocyttarus* and *Polistes* species nest in association with swarm-founding *Polybia* wasps (Myers 1935; Corn 1972; Windsor 1971; Gorton 1978; Starr 1988) (figure 15.2e) or pugnacious ants (Zikán 1949; Herre et al. 1986). The statistical association is far from random, and it seems certain in each case that it is the primitive social wasps which nest with the *Polybia* or ants, and not the other way around. There is good reason to believe that the former, with their exposed brood and small colonies, gain protection through proximity to their neighbors, though attempts to demonstrate this idea have not always succeeded (Starr, 1988).

    Of the three conditions noted above, the last must be the most demanding. At least in the tropics, a wasp should find it easy to locate large, aggressive colonies of arboreal wasps or ants which will not tolerate the approach of a potential predator. But will they tolerate the primitive social wasp and her colony mates? The answer probably hinges on whether the potential protectors leave the nest to attack small, slowly moving objects which do not actually touch the nest. For example, noted instances of aggression by *Polybia* species against associated *Mischocyttarus immarginatus* are few and mild (Gorton 1978; personal observation). As a further indication, I have never found *Polistes* or independent-founding *Ropalidia* associated with the swarm founder *R. flavobrunnea*. This species is abundant in much of its range, where it builds large nests in accessible places and so would seem a prime candidate for a protector species. Yet it is so extremely aggressive, often attacking a slow-moving person at a distance of two meters or more, that it probably will not tolerate any animal near its nest. This illustrates the contradictory nature of the tactic of hiding behind Big Brother and probably accounts for its rarity.

    A somewhat similar tactic is seen in the tendency of *Polistes erythrocephalus* in some areas to tolerate tettigoniid grasshoppers resting very close to the nest (Downhower and Wilson 1973). The grasshoppers are thought to gain protection while they serve as sentinels for the wasps, warning of approaching large animals.

ADAPTATIONS OF THE COLONY CYCLE

The idea has been around for some time that if social insects cannot repulse or deceive an enemy, or escape from it in space, they can perhaps escape in time. Two largely incompatible forms of such escape have been proposed for primitive social wasps:

> 1. Colony growth in some species is remarkably slow. Jeanne (1975) suggested that these species may be adapted to spread out production so that there is little vulnerable brood at one time. In case of predation, the adults can refound with relatively little loss.

> 2. In some species colony growth does not go far before reproductives are reared and the colony disperses. It has been suggested that this increases the probability that the colony reproduces before it is destroyed by army ants (Jeanne 1975; Richards and Richards 1951; Turillazzi 1984).

The trouble with these hypotheses is that neither has been rigorously modeled, so their assumptions are not explicit. Each rests upon the contradiction—which is at the heart of insect sociality—between increased production and defending what has been produced. It is far from obvious, in the first instance, how a decrease in production might be favored by thus having less to lose. And for a given level of production, is there any reason that selection should favor hedging one's bets? The most that can be said in this latter regard is that (a) attacks by some army ants appear roughly cyclical in Neotropical rain forests (Chadab 1979), and (b) colonies of some *Polistes* species are increasingly susceptible to parasitism as they grow (Jeanne 1979a, 1982a; Strassmann 1981a,b). On the other hand, predation is for some a greater problem in the founding stage (Jeanne 1982a; Turillazzi 1984). In the absence of well-worked-out models, I am skeptical that social wasps adjust the colony cycle defensively.

The Irresistible Intruders

It has long been a truism that the worst enemies of social insects are

Table 15.1. Numbers of adult females, adult males, and brood in thirty active colonies of *Parischnogaster unicuspata* with ant guards in three conditions.

Condition of ant guard	Median Number of females	Median number of males	Median number of brood
Absent	2 (range 1–2) n = 6	0 (all 0) n = 6	4 (range 3–10) n = 7
Weak	1 (range 1–6) n = 15	0 (range 0–8) n = 15	7 (range 1–14) n = 14
Strong	2 (range 1–3) n = 7	0 (range 0–13) n = 7	8 (range 4–23) n = 4

NOTE: A weak ant guard is visible only as a trace, while a strong one is substantial (figure 15.3. All observations from Aborlan, Palawan, Philippines, during April 1984.

social insects. The particular importance of New World army ants (Ecitoninae) and hornets (*Vespa* spp.) for primitive social wasps is noted above, and their geographic distribution would seem to explain a curious observation on the nesting habits of independent-founding polistines. Although these very commonly nest under the eaves of buildings and on other human-made structures in the Neotropics, at least in Southeast Asia they only very rarely do so (personal observation). As noted above, such nest sites are relatively free of ants, including army ants. On the other hand, they must be relatively exposed to such visual hunters as hornets.

We have already seen that primitive social wasps have at their disposal various primary defensive tactics against predators. Against army ants and hornets these tactics must usually consist of nesting outside areas of likely contact. What can the wasps do to turn back an attack if either of these enemies locates the nest? It appears that they can do almost nothing: "We believe that army ants can successfully raid all species of neotropical Polistinae except species living in association with some [exceptionally pugnacious] ants" (Chadab-Crepet and Rettenmeyer 1982). Adult wasps make almost no attempt to repulse either army ants (Chadab 1979; Chadab-Crepet and Rettenmeyer 1982) or hornets (Matsuura 1984; R. Gadagkar, personal communication). Rather, their response is limited to fleeing in time and regrouping after the attack. In this way they usually lose all brood and the nest but save themselves and maintain social cohesion, so that they can found a new colony without delay. Neotropical polistines show special adaptations for such a salvage operation.

It remains to be seen whether Oriental polistines and stenogastrines have evolved comparable contingency tactics.

Secondary Defense Against Vertebrates

STINGING, THE LAST RESORT

The most characteristic feature of the aculeate hymenoptera, including wasps, is a specialized venom apparatus derived from the ovipositor and its associated glands. The biological study of venoms is still young, and we have only recently begun to reach confident conclusions about their roles in antipredator defense (Schmidt, this volume). Stinging by social wasps and bees is usually treated as directed mainly against vertebrates, an apparently sound assumption. Although they will attempt to sting insect intruders, this seems usually ineffective, especially against ants. Vertebrates are probably usually much easier to sting, on account of our large size and a relatively penetrable skin. Stinging may in fact be regarded as an exceptionally powerful antivertebrate tactic which may well have been instrumental in facilitating the evolution of sociality (Starr 1985b; but see also Kukuk et al. 1989 and Starr 1989).

THREATS

To call the sting an effective antivertebrate measure is not to suggest that it should be used lightly. Any close encounter with an adversary larger by an order of magnitude or more is a risky business. Stinging should thus be seen as a backup measure to be used in extermity, not as a standard first response. Analogously, although it is perfectly obvious that in human society "political power grows out of the barrel of a gun" (Mao 1965), any regime aiming for stability keeps the gun loaded but fires it as little as possible. Wasps should prefer any tactic which can repel the intruder without direct contact.

The conspicuous alert reactions of *Polistes* colonies to the approach of humans have often been noted (Weyrauch 1928; Rau 1930; Spieth 1948; Yoshikawa 1963; West-Eberhard 1969; Corn 1972; Hermann et al. 1975; Turillazzi 1984). All species appear to respond to disturbances below the attack threshold with several stereotyped behaviors. In order to identify behavior peculiar to this particular context, I compared that of disturbed and undisturbed colonies of two North American *Polistes* species. Between the two species, eleven such behaviors were identified (see Appendix): alert posture, wing raise, wing flip, wing buzz, wing flutter, leg wave, abdomen bend, antennate air, retreat, flee, and attack. Excluded from these is abdomen pumping, the rhythmic telescoping of segments to shorten and lengthen the abdomen. Although this has been called a response to provocation (Weyrauch 1928; Hermann and Blum 1981) and would seem well suited as a threat, it is also frequent in undisturbed wasps and apparently just as intense.

Leaving aside retreat, flee, and attack, what are the functions of these responses? Some, especially the alert posture, have previously been charactrized simply as "defensive" (West-Eberhard 1969; Darchen 1976; Litte 1979) or more specifically as "threats" (Schmitt 1920; Hermann et al. 1975). If they are not just a preparation exercise or sign of general agitation, such responses must be signals to colony mates (alarm) and/or the intruder (threats).

Threats are a class of agonistic behavior occurring between flight and attack and arising out of the conflict between the two (Hinde 1970; Brown 1975). They say, "If you continue this provocation, I shall attack." Of the eight responses, antennating the air has no apparent deterrent value and most likely is purely sensory (J. Engel and J.E. Klahn, unpublished). There is good evidence, though, that the other seven are in fact threats. The context is exactly that in which threats arise, and they appear well suited to convey the message just quoted. As a strong prima facie indication of this, to a human observer they can present a very potent warning. A group of wasps going quickly and largely simultaneously from at-rest (see Appendix) to the alert posture, with wings raised, legs waving, and the often bent abdomen probing vigorously (figure 15.4) is an impressive spectacle. The raising of many folded wings resembles the erection of spines on a porcupine, and the other movements add to the menacing appearance. The less common wing flip and wing flutter are likewise good candidates for visual signals, while wing buzz is the only one which is notably noisy.

In addition to their abstract conspicuousness, some of these behaviors have the effect of drawing attention to particular features of attack. The alert posture, wing raise, and leg wave are suggestive of takeoff from the nest, and abdomen bend suggests stinging. If they appear similar to other vertebrates, as seems likely, these behaviors constitute deimatic display (Edmunds 1974), the wasp's way of showing her teeth.

It is a short step from noting the resemblance between such responses and features of attack to suggesting that this is their evolutionary origin, and Marino-Piccioli and Pardi (1970:200-01) stated that similar behaviors in *Belonogaster grisea* have "the obvious significance of intention movements of an attack flight." Intention movements indicate a motivational conflict and appear with reduced intensity or frequency or in incomplete form (Hinde 1970; Brown 1975; Smith 1977). If they are to function as signals, though, they must not be muted or abbreviated, but the opposite, that is, they must evolve into displays (Brown 1975; Smith 1977). At least three putative threats of *Polistes* give evidence of just such a transformation:

1. Undisturbed wasps leaving the nest pass quickly through a stance quite like the alert posture. Under provocation this is intensified. Not only may it be held for some seconds, but the wasp is usually raised more strongly from the nest.

2. Wing raise is a necessary beginning of flight. Like the alert posture, though, in undisturbed wasps it comes right before take-off. Sustained wing raise is not simply continuous readiness to fly, since the wings are usually not lowered even when the wasp turns away from the provoker, retreats, or is not in a good position to take flight.

3. In about half of their undisturbed takeoffs, *P. annularis* and *exclamans* show perceptible movement similar to leg wave, though never as pronounced. This most likely functions in freeing the forelegs from the nest.

Before finally accepting that the alert posture, movements of the wings and forelegs, and abdomen pump function as attack threats, let us consider a last alternative. Might these behaviors instead carry a threat to flee by saying "I have seen you; it is futile to try to catch me" (B. Hölldobler, personal communication)? In that case the focus of defense shifts from the brood to the adults, and a successful flee threat saves both predator and adult wasps some trouble. The apparent origin of the alert posture, wing raise, and leg wave is also consistent with this interesting hypothesis, but other observations are not:

1. Abdomen bend, apparently originating as intention movements of stinging, often occurs along with these others.

2. The behaviors often precede attack. The fact that they may precede fleeing in no way vitiates their supposed character as attack threats.

3. We would expect to find flee threats especially in wasps disturbed away from the nest. Yet I have provoked a great many foraging *Polistes* of four species without seeing any of the more ritualized responses.

The hypothesis is also inconsistent with what is known of the focus of specialized defense in social insects, that is, it serves to protect the brood rather than the adults.

It has been my pleasure to provoke colonies of fifteen *Polistes* species in various parts of the world. All display a similar repertory of well-developed threats, evidently a regular feature of the genus. Does this generalization to entend other primitive social wasps? We can start by dismissing the stenogastrines in this regard. Not only has no stenogastrine ever attacked me (or anyone else, as far as I know), but I have never perceived anything suggestive of a threat. On the other hand, each of the six behaviors characterized as a threat in *Polistes* is also known from other social wasps, including independent-founding polistines (table 15.2). Can we infer from this that these others respond much like *Polistes* to a graded provocation? No. Especially in swarm-founding polistines, I have failed to find comparably organized threat displays, even though I have provoked healthy colonies of seven genera. The very fierce *Synoeca septentrionalis* shows consistent, conspicuous responses, but these are undirected and not evidently adapted as threats.

The contrast with other independent founders is not so sharp, but more instructive. One can often elicit *Polistes*-like responses from *Mischocyttarus* and independent-founding *Ropalidia*, but in no case has a consistent display been shown. Hermann and Chao (1984) imply that *M. mexicanus* resembles *Polistes* in this respect, but own observations of this species indicate a feeble, inconsistent, and much briefer set of responses which is far from impressive. The various other *Mischocyttarus* and *Ropalidia* species which R.L. Jeanne (personal communication) and I have provoked with this question in mind are much like *M. mexicanus*. There is some suggestion that *Belonogaster* species respond like *Polistes* (Roubaud 1916; Marino-Piccioli and Pardi 1970), but this requires confirmation.

Why does *Polistes* stand out among primitive social wasps in this regard? Phylogenetic inertia can be discounted, since the primitive movements are present in other genera, where they could presumably evolve

Table 15.2. Examples of the occurrence in other social wasps of behaviors regarded as threats in *Polistes*.

Behavior	Species	Reference
Alert posture	*Mischocyttarus drewseni*	Jeanne 1972
	M. flavitarsis	Litte 1979
	M. mexicanus	Personal observation
	Ropalidia cincta	Darchen 1976
	R. gregaria	Personal observation
	R. revolutionalis	A.W. Hook, personal communication
	Protopolybia scutellaris	Naumann 1970
Wing raise	*Belonogaster grisea*	Marino-Piccioli and Pardi 1970
	Mischocyttarus drewseni	Jeanne 1972
	M. mexicanus	Hermann and Chao 1984; Personal observation
	Ropalidia gregaria	Personal observation
	R. revolutionalis	A.W. Hook, personal communication
	Metapolybia docilis	Personal observation
	Polybia emaciata	Personal observation
	Protopolybia scutellaris	Naumann 1970
	Ropalidia flavobrunnea	Personal observation
	R. nigrescens	Personal observation
Wing buzz	*Mischocyttarus drewseni*	Jeanne 1972
	M. flavitarsis	Litte 1979
	Polybia diguetana	J.H. Hunt, personal communication
	P. occidentalis	J.H. Hunt, personal communication
	Protopolybia scutellaris	Naumann 1970
	Dolichovespula maculata	Personal observation
	Dolichovespula sp.	Weyrauch 1935
Wing flutter	*Mischocyttarus mexicanus*	Hermann and Chao 1984
Leg wave	*Belonogaster grisea*	Marino-Piccioli and Pardi 1970
	Mischocyttarus mexicanus	Hermann and Chao 1984; Personal observation
	Ropalidia revolutionalis	A.W. Hook, personal communication
	Polybia emaciata	Personal observation
Abdomen bend	*Mischocyttarus drewseni*	Jeanne 1972
	Protopolybia scutellaris	Naumann 1970

*Primitive social species.

into displays. It may simply be that, because *Polistes* are larger and/or more robust, any threats from them will be easily perceived and persuasive. There is much to recommend this hypothesis, though none of it is conclusive. Of the few *Mischocyttarus* and *Ropalidia* species so far tested for

Table 15.3. Incidence of particular threats preceding attack in five North American *Polistes* species.

Threat	Species				
	annularis	*dorsalis*	*exclamans*	*fuscatus*	*metricus*
Wing raise	**204** (97%)	**21** (95%)	**56** (100%)	**10** (100%)	**55** (98%)
Wing flip	4	5	0	0	17
Wing buzz	8	2	0	0	11
Wing flutter	2	0	**37** (66%)	0	4
Leg wave	**203** (97%)	**13** (59%)	**44** (79%)	**9** (90%)	**46** (82%)
Abdomen bend	**173** (82%)	5	**47** (84%)	4	**40**(71%)
Total trials	**210**	**22**	**56**	**10**	**56**

NOTE: Where incidence of a threat exceeds 50 percent, the figure is given in boldface. For a given species, the set of these frequent threats is defined as the *threat array*. For example, the threat array of *P. annularis* is wing raise, leg wave, and abdomen bend. The alert posture is not especially informative for present purposes and so is omitted.

I provoked colonies as described in the appendix and recorded for each individual which threats appeared before an attack. Individuals which did not attack within three minutes are discounted. In order to record the threat repertory as completely as possible, I also discount individuals attacking in the first fifteen seconds of graded provocation.

sting pain, none ranks as high as *Polistes* species (Starr 1985a). On the other hand, *Ropalidia* are about as stout as *Polistes,* are often colorful, and the larger ones are about the same size as the smaller *Polistes* species. Unless their colonies are always small, we should expect the largest colorful *Ropalidia* species to threaten. If they do not, it will mean that we really have little idea why *Polistes* do.

Polistes is the outstandingly generalized genus of social wasps. As presently understood, their threat displays are their only specialized feature.

THE NATURE OF THE THREAT ARRAY AND SEQUENCE IN *POLISTES*

Although all studied *Polistes* species respond to provocation with strong threats, they do not all respond alike. Leaving aside differences in the form of a given threat, we find that it is not equally prominent in different species. Table 15.3 shows the relative frequency of six threats in five North American species. Defining the set of frequent threats as the *threat array* (see note to table 15.3), we find wing raise and leg wave among the array in each species, wing flutter and abdomen bend in some species, and wing flip and wing buzz in none of the five.

Although different threats tend to continue together under sustained provocation, they often do not begin together but at differing stages of provocation. If this pattern is consistent for a given species, it will give rise to a characteristic *threat sequence*. As it happens, the five threat arrays derived from table 15.3 include few elements which can physically interfere with each other, thus precluding an important constraint on the form of the sequence. The exception, in *P. exclamans*, is that wing flutter evidently requires that the wings be raised. Wing flip and wing buzz, found in a significant minority of trials in *P. metricus*, seem to require that the wings be down. As seen in table 15.4, for any pair of threats in each array, it is quite predictable which will arise first (Chi-square, $p < .01$ in each case). Table 15.5 shows the resulting threat sequences. Post, Downing, and Jeanne (1984) show a partial corroboration of the sequences for *P. exclamans* and *fuscatus*.

How is it that threat arrays are structured into predictable sequences? Lehner(1979) has congently discussed causes of nonrandom behavior sequences, but for present purposes I prefer to derive hypotheses from an analogy with ecological succession (Horn 1981). Figure 15.5 illustrates three possible causal bases for the threat sequence. We can readily dispose of the idea that the sequence is a fixed action pattern. This pattern requires that a given threat appear only after the one which characteristically precedes it, yet we see in table 15.4 that threats sometimes appear out of turn. The second hypothesis is that threats arise independently of each other, the sequence simply being due to differing release thresholds. If the sequence is a Markov process, on the other hand, there is a certain constant probability that a given threat will follow a given other threat. A fixed action pattern could be seen as a special case of this process, in which all probabilities are 0 or 1.

To choose between these last two hypotheses, let us turn to those occasional trials in which a threat which is characteristically neither first nor last arises ahead of its usual position. The independent thresholds hypothesis predicts that the next threat will be the one which would have come next if the out-of-place threat had not moved ahead. The Markov process hypothesis, on the other hand, predicts that the next will be the threat which usually succeeds the out-of-place threat.

Three types of such exceptions were frequent enough to allow tests (figure 15.6). In each of these the outcome is unambiguous. For example, in thirty-seven out of thirty-eight trials with *P. annularis* in which wing raise came first, rather than the usual leg wave, the next threat was leg wave (figure 15.6a). This is consistent with the hypothesis

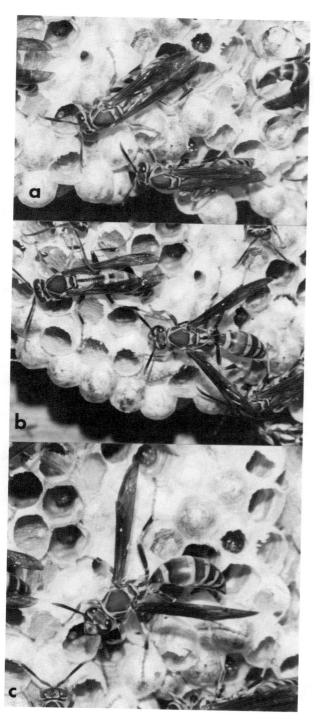

Figure 15.4 *Polistes* threat behaviors illustrated by *P. exclamans.*

Table 15.4. Relative precedence of members of the threat array in five North American *Polistes* species, from pairwise comparisons of threats

Threat pair	Species				
	annularis	*dorsalis*	*exclamans*	*fuscatus*	*metricus*
Wing raise: **wing flutter**			100:0		
Wing raise: **leg wave**	56:232	43:4	172:6	13:0	49:10
Wing raise: **abdomen bend**	144:32		167:8		53:5
Wing flutter: **leg wave**			5:83		
Wing flutter: **abdomen bend**			1:90		
Leg wave: **abdomen bend**	227:7		42:87		28:14

NOTE: The left side of each ratio is the number of trials in which the first threat of the pair preceded the second; the right side is the number of trials in which the opposite occurred. In 288 trials with *P. annularis*, for example, wing raise preceded leg wave 56 times, and leg wave preceded wing raise 232 times.

Data are from the same trials as used for table 15.3 and also include trials in which there was no attack within the (maximum three minutes) provocation. Good temporal separation was not always obtained. The state of the abdomen is often not clear when the wings are down, so I counted abdomen bend as preceding wing raise if it was already bent when the wings were raised. Otherwise, ties are discounted. When the provocation was properly gradual, wing flutter began clearly after wing raise.

that threats arise independently at differing thresholds and inconsistent with a Markov process (Chi-square goodness-of-fit test, p. < .01). Two similar tests with *P. exclamans* (figure 15.6b,c) support this conclusion.

Why are threats sequenced? As noted above, physical constraints probably have little to do with it. Present evidence does not definitely reject the null hypothesis that a given threat has to arise at some point, and if the provocation is sufficiently gradual it will not do so at exactly the same moment as another, yet the hypothesis is inconvincing on two grounds. First, the sequence is so predictable. In each of the fourteen pairwise comparisons in table 15.4 one threat has a precedence tendency over the other of at least 2:1, and a majority shows a 10:1 tendency. We customarily think of such strong patterns as the product of natural selection.

Second, a putative selective basis is readily apparent. A repertory of several independent threats permits signals of graded intensity, such

Table 15.5. Threat sequence in five North American *Polistes* species.

Species	Threat sequence
annularis	leg wave ➛ wing raise ➛ abdomen bend
dorsalis	wing raise ➛ leg wave
exclamans	wing raise ➛ abdomen bend ➛ leg wave ➛ wing flutter
fuscatus	wing raise ➛ leg wave
metricus	wing raise ➛ leg wave ➛ abdomen bend

NOTE: Based on table 15.4. Explanation in text.

that any two are stronger together than either is alone. If these are combined in a consistent fashion which a potential intruder can learn, the communication goes beyond that allowed by random combinations. Anyone familiar with dogs has noticed the fine gradations in their threats and can tell reasonably well how close one is to attacking.* Similarly, an experienced *Polistes* watcher can work close to the wasps with little danger of being attacked unaware. Armed with knowledge of the threat sequence, one can even, in the manner of a lion tamer, provoke colonies of a familiar species close to attack without eliciting attack.

It is much less apparent why species should differ in their threat arrays and sequences, but nesting habit and body coloration give some suggestions. As mentioned above, wing buzz is the only apparently auditory threat known from *Polistes*. In the five species treated, it is commonest in *P. metricus,* which tends to nest in dimmer places, and I have often become aware of colonies from hearing the buzz. If this is significant, wing buzz should be even more prominent in those few species which characteristically nest in enclosed, dark spaces. Second, threats tend to call attention to particular body parts; for example, leg wave calls attention to the forelegs, while wing raise exposes the abdomen, and abdomen bend renders it more conspicuous. The three species with each of these displays in the array differ in the brightness of the forelegs and/or abdomen, and where there are differences in array or sequence we might expect them to

*"All these signals of threat may be combined in different intensities, so that you can literally see how aroused the dog is and you can also predict with great certainty what his next move may be" (Fox 1972).

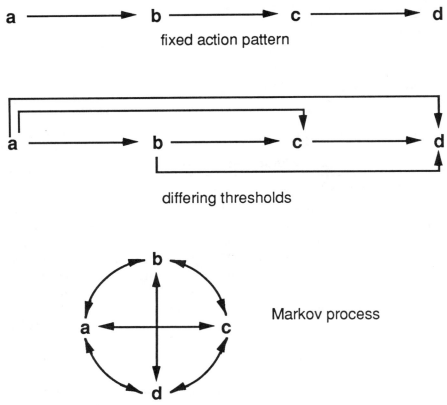

Figure 15.5   Three hypothetical causal bases for the *Polistes* threat sequence.

correlate with color differences. Tables 15.3 and 15.4 corroborate this prediction. Still, the null hypothesis that the system of threats bears no relation to either of these factors has not proven easily falsifiable, and it remains to be seen how it will stand up to a broad systematic test.

FAKING IT: AUTOMIMETIC THREATS OF MALE *POLISTES*

"If we were to ascribe human qualities to *Polistes* males, we would have to call them greedy, stupid and cowardly. Their courage does not extend beyond empty threats."* The parasitic nature of social insect males

*"Wenn wir den *Polistes*-Männchen menschliche Eigenschaften zusprechen müssten, dann würden wir sie feig, dumm und geil nennen. Ihr Mut reicht nur zur Schreckstellung." (Schmitt 1920:p. 221).

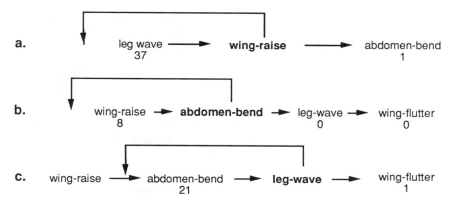

Figure 15.6   Distribution of threats immediately following a threat arising ahead of its usual position (*Polistes annularis* and *P. exclamans*).

has been noted since the time of Aristotle (König 1896), and cases of apparent male work or altruism are unusual enough to excite special interest (e.g., Hunt and Noonan 1979). A major problem in studying male work is that even where it is observed it is very infrequent. The one known exception in primitive social wasps is defensive work, since disturbed males in many species may resemble females in their subattack responses (Steiner 1932; Marino-Piccioli and Pardi 1970; Litte 1979; Hook and Evans 1982). Such threats are necessarily bluff because males have no venom apparatus. The rich, reliable threat array of *Polistes* presents us with a special opportunity for the study of male altruism.

A male who threatens like a female is defending brood which almost certainly are not his own, while almost certainly putting himself at personal risk. *Polistes* species differ widely in their degree of sexual dimorphism, particularly color dimorphism *(dichromism)*. In *P. annularis,* for example, it is difficult to tell the sexes apart, while in *P. metricus* and *fuscatus* they are readily distinguished even from a distance (table 15.6).* If species likewise differ substantially in the participation of males in their colonies' threat displays, this difference introduces the testable prediction that *males will threaten more in species with less sexual dichromism.*

Results from four North American species strongly uphold this prediction (table 15.7). The threat tendencies of *P. metricus* and *fuscatus* are not significantly different, a necessary outcome of small sample size in the latter, but all other species pairs differ significantly (Chi-square test,

---

*Sexual dichromism shows some definite taxonomic trends within the aculeates, especially in the tendency of males in some groups to have pale facial markings. These trends remain puzzling, inasmuch as we have little idea why males should or should not resemble females.

p.< .025) in the expected direction. The utility of threat tendency as an index of male altruism renders this question much more tractable than in the past and gives promise of allowing confident comparison among individuals, colonies, and species.

A male aculeate grasped in the fingers will usually make persistent, realistic pseudostinging motions, striking with the end of his abdomen. Such an imitation of real stinging motions by females is an unexceptional form of automimicry (Brower, Brower, and Corvino 1967; Brower, Pough, and Meck 1970) which I will call "solitary automimicry, to distinguish it from the social automimicry of males participating in a threat display on the nest.

Social automimicry in wasps differs radically from solitary auto-mimicry in at least two ways:

1. As noted, its evident function is in brood defense, rather than personal defense, and there is good reason to consider it altruistic.

2. Theoretical formulations of automimicry (Brower et al. 1970) do not apply to social automimicry. The difference lies in the sample taken by the predator, which will bear no simple relationship to the model-to-mimic ratio (i.e., the sex ratio) of the population or even the colony. A predator at the nest cannot very well sample individuals, only colonies, leaving little opportunity to learn discrimination or estimation of the ratio. In addition, only females will actually attack, and thus will give a biased estimate.

Organizing the Social Defensive Response

Is the response to intruders organized at the colony level, or is it simply the sum of independent individual responses? The best that we can do at present is to outline some ways that primitive social wasps might organize their response and to expose our slight knowledge and considerable ignorance of whether they actually do.

DIVISION OF LABOR

It is nearly unavoidable that there will be a certain division of labor within the worker caste, since this division requires only that individuals

Table 15.6. Sexual dichromism values for four North American *Polistes* species.

	Maximum value	Species			
		annularis	*exclamans*	*metricus*	*fuscatus*
Face	2	0	0.67	1	0.67
Dorsal	2	0	0	0	0.50
Side	2	0	0	0	0.67
Ventral	1	0	0.17	0.67	0.50
Total	7	0	0.84	1.67	2.33

NOTE: Each sub total is the product of (a) the weight given the body region, based on approximate prominence when in the alert posture with the wings raised, and (b) color difference between females and males in that region, in which yellow = 0, red = 1/3, brown = 2/3, and black = 1. An overall value of 7 would require that one sex be all yellow and the other all black. The body regions shown are condensed from a finer division into fourteen parts small enough that each has one predominant color (Starr 1981). Data for each species are from twenty females and twenty males from northeast Georgia.

have differing biases toward various colony-maintaining tasks. This tells us nothing, though, of how the tasks are divided, the casual basis for division, or how finely tuned it is, and since Steiner's (1932) early start there has been little progress in this question in primitive social wasps. The little that we have learned (Yoshikawa 1963; Dew and Michener 1981; Strassmann et al. 1984; Gadagkar and Joshi 1982, 1983, 1984) suggests a weakly age-based division of labor with weak individual specialization. Gadagkar and Joshi (1982, 1983) identified three worker subcastes in *Ropalidia*

Table 15.7. Male threat tendencies in four North American *Polistes* species.

	Species			
	annularis	*exclamans*	*metricus*	*fuscatus*
Sexual dichromism (from table 15.6)	0	0.84	1.67	2.33
Number of trials	19	19	19	3
Total males tested	74	65	86	9
Males threatening	50 (68%)	31 (48%)	2 (2%)	0

NOTE: All colonies are from similar farmland habitat in northeast Georgia, and each had at least one larva and a female: male ratio of at least unity. I provoked each colony until every male had either threatened or fled, for a maximum of three minutes. Any trial in which no female attacked is discounted, because it seems unreasonable to expect males to defend when even females do not. Earlier trials showed no difference between female and male threat repertoires. A male was scored as having threatened if, while facing me, he clearly wing-buzzed, wing-fluttered, leg-waved, or abdomen-bent. Wing raise seemed an unreliable index, since it often appeared in males which performed no other threat and stood their ground poorly.

marginata. Surprisingly, one of them (fighters) shows a strong tendency both to threaten the observer and to fight within itself, but no other specialization. The suggestion (the data are insufficient to call it more) is that (a) there is a rather indiscriminately aggressive subcaste in *R. marginata,* and (b) this gives rise to the defensive subcaste, insofar as one exists. On the other hand, the comparable subcaste in *R. cyathiformis* seem to specialize in aggression among themselves but not toward the observer (Gadagkar and Joshi 1982, 1984).

The first difficulty in comparing individual defensiveness is that natural intrusions are rare. Even with artificial provocation, the investigator may be reluctant to remain when the wasps begin to attack, and many wasps may not attack. The existence of a structured threat array in *Polistes* proffers a solution to these problems. Nonattacking workers can still show several levels of defensiveness, according to their response up to a certain point: (a) flee, (b) remain but no threat, (c) only the first threat, (d) only the first two threats, etc. Individuals responding at the same level can be further ranked according to the time sequence in which they reach that level. The utility of such a ranking in the study of division of labor rests in large part on the assumption that threat readiness is a good index of attack readiness. I tested this assumption in *P. annularis* by comparing the sequence in which marked wasps showed a given threat with the sequence in which they attacked during the same trial, with four to sixteen wasps in twelve to twenty-one trials for each of leg wave, wing raise, and abdomen bend. Each threat showed a significant correlation (Spearman rank correlation coefficient, $p < .01$) for the cumulative trials, though only a minority of trials was individually significant. At least in this species, then, the threat sequence can serve in analyzing the defensive division of labor. It will require a substantial data set, though, since even female threats appear to contain a large element of bluff.

ALARM

Alarm is the communication of a shared danger. To show that it exists we need only find a correlation between the responses of an individual which perceives an intrusion and one which does not. In the swarm-founding *Synoeca septentrionalis,* for example, a small number of wasps usually stand looking out through the nest hole, presumably guarding. A silent visual disturbance will commonly bring not only these wasps rushing aggressively out onto the nets envelope, but also several colony mates which could not possibly have perceived the disturbance (personal observation).

Alarm has been inferred in primitive social wasps in all three sensory modalities: mechanical, visual, and chemical. A wasp flying suddenly off the nest to attack might well jar or scrape it in such a way as to alert colony mates, as has been inferred in *Polistes* species (Hermann et al. 1975; West-Eberhard 1969). Inasmuch as there are commonly workers resting on the nest where they cannot see the observer, it should be easy to demonstrate such alarm, yet I have consistently failed to find it. An alarm signal, in order to work, must be rare, and wasps fly off the nest many times a day. Besides, a signal emitted only at the moment of attack would seem to come too late to be efficacious. On the other hand, there is good reason to believe that some mechanical signals, such as the pulsed vibrations from wing buzz, do in fact have such a function in independent-founding polistines (Freisling 1943; Corn 1972; Jeanne 1972; Darchen 1976). It is in fact hard to see how wing buzz might *not* shake the nest or how colony mates might *not* perceive this rare signal through their feet. Alarm by substrate vibration has also been adduced among vespines (Weyrauch 1935) and swarm-founding polistines (Naumann 1970; Chadab 1979).

Do wasps also communicate alarm visually? In the case of large intruders, there is a priori reason to doubt it, since a wasp which can see a signaling colony mate should also see the intruder. I have consistently failed to find any such alarm in *Polistes* species. Several times I have seen wasps fail to react while the rest of the colony was in uproar but they themselves were blocked from seeing me, and then react vigorously when I moved into view. On the other hand, if the intruder is inconspicuous the value of a visual signal is potentially much different. In three *Polistes* species, workers which had not seen a small parasitoid near the nest have been observed to wing-flip and move about agitatedly after colony mates began wing-flipping (West-Eberhard 1969; personal observation). In those species which do not commonly wing-flip at large intruders, this can function not only in alarm but more precisely in enemy specification, such as is known from swarm founders (Chadab-Crepet and Rettenmeyer 1982).

Chemical alarm is known from a great many social insects, but these are almost exclusively those with large, complex colonies. It has been experimentally shown that in at least some *Polistes* species venom acts as an alarm pheromone when it is released in stinging (Jeanne 1982b; Post, Downing, and Jeanne 1984). There have also been hints that it is released into the air before attack (Rau 1939; Jeanne 1972; Post, Downing, and Jeanne 1984), but this has resisted experimental corroboration. The distinction is important, as this latter tactic would be much more sophisticated, allowing transmission of the signal earlier in the provocation and without direct contact with the enemy. Given the large selfish component in the behavior of even worker wasps, we should expect strong selection for just such relatively safe signals. It is puzzling that they do not exist or are so subtle.

COORDINATED ATTACK

Is the colony's attack response, as distinguished from attack readiness, in any way organized? Does the summed response of different alerted workers, for example, show a particular time pattern? In some *Polistes* species it does in at least a crude way, through social facilitation by pheromones released in stinging. Again, it would be much better if such facilitation came earlier, so that many individuals attacked at once. Two stimuli suggest themselves as possible defense-coordinating signals: the sight of the first wasp flying to attack, and the vibration of the nest as she takes off. Note that neither seems to function in giving early warning, but either would seem well suited to release attack by wasps already alerted and oriented.

Is there any indication that such coordination exists? As stated above, this section deals more with ignorance than knowledge, and we have only some tantalizing suggestions. In particular, when *P. annularis* are provoked, the first attacks commonly come from a large group of wasps at apparently the same moment (H.R. Hermann, personal comunication; personal observation). This can occur even under very gradually elevated provocation, especially with large colonies. It is hard to believe that such mass attack is an illusion or the result of an identical attack threshold in different individuals. If such coordination can be statistically demonstrated, its cause should be a tractable problem.

Conclusion: Is There a Common Defense Strategy?

Small colony size in primitive social wasps poses important constraints on the evolution of defensive measures. Since colonies are without workers at the start of the colony cycle, this is a very hazardous time. Even later they are never very large; therefore, the sorts of tactics evolved in such taxa as formicine and mymicine ants, highly social bees, and termites are largely outside their list of options. Their outstanding defensive adaptation remains the sting. Given these basal considerations and what we have seen of particular defense mechanisms, is there a coherent defense strategy of primitive social wasps as a whole? This is not to ask whether we can identify a plan followed without exception, but it does mean that any such exceptions would require explanation if the strategy is to be regarded as real. As a first approximation, I propose five cardinal defensive rules:

1. Be inconspicuous if you can
    a. Keep the nest and adults inconspicuous, to avoid notice by vetebrates and hornets.
    b. To avoid notice by ants, nest in little-traveled places. Where possible, nest at the end of one of a great many similar projections. This is wide open to experimental test.
    c. Keep the nest and brood as odorless as possible. This predicts that wasps will avoid prey with strong odors which could become incorporated into brood. It also predicts that ant repellent chemicals will not be distinctive from an ant's point of view; if they were they would become kairomones advertising the colony's presence. I expect all ant guards to smell to ants like commonly encountered plant exudates.

2. In the founding stage, play it socially safe.
    a. Be pleometrotic if conflicts of interest can be resolved, so that there is always someone on guard.
    b. If haplometrotic, stay at the nest as much as feasible, even if this retards colony growth.

3. Play it personally safe, that is, almost always value yourself above the brood. Have no suicidal defensive features. No primitive social wasp is expected to have well-developed barbs on the sting lancets, such as could frequently lead to sting autotomy (Hermann 1971; Hermann and Blum 1981). This is not a very daring prediction, as it has already been corroborated in many stenogastrines and independent-founding polistines (E.A. Macalintal and C.K. Starr, unpublished).

4. Narrow the approach to the nest.
   a. Choose or build a very narrow passage which can be guarded by a single wasp.
   b. Make this passage physically or chemically inhibitory.

5. To the degree that you can retaliate, advertise this ability. All species with reasonably painful stings which cannot consistently nest cryptically are expected to have a colorful dorsum. Relatively large (forewing length not much below about 9.0 mm), colorful, independent-founding *Ropalidia* species are expected to threaten in a manner similar to *Polistes*.

Right at the outset there are evident violations of these rules and conflicts among them. For example, Japanese *Polistes* break rule 2a, and most stenogastrines break rule 4b, apparently unnecessarily. Rule 1a conflicts rather strikingly with rule 5. Fine-tuning of this approximation, if it is called for, will require that such anomalies be reconciled with more primary differences between taxa.

The treatment of *Polistes* threats is adapted from my doctorial thesis under Henry R. Hermann at the University of Georgia. Thanks to numerous Georgia farmers and the National Parks Service of Costa Rica for access to prime wasp habitat; to Tony Barroso, Jung-tai Chao, Henry Hermann, Junichi Kojima, Henry Schoenig, and Lorna Tuanggang for field assistance; to Bert Hölldobler, Jim Hunt, Rudolf Jander, Bob Jeanne, Joan Krispyn, Bob Matthews, Charles Michener, and John Wenzel for discussion and criticism; to Gabby Vallar and Luke Moortgat for statistical advice; and to Maite Miguel for volunteer typing. Support for materials came from the Department of Entomology of the University of Georgia, Francis Starr, and a grant-in-aid from Sigma Xi, and for travel from the National Science Foundation of the United States through the Entomological Society of America.

References

Alexander, R.D. 1974. The evolution of social behavior. *Ann. Rev. Ecol. Syst.* 5: 325–83.

Brower, L.P., Brower, J.V.Z., Corvino, J.M. 1967. Plant poisons in a terrestrial food chain. *Proc. Natl. Acad. Sci. USA* 57: 893–98.

Brower, L.P., Pough, F.H., Mech, H.R. 1970. Theoretical investigations of automimicry. I. Single trial learning. *Proc. Natl. Acad. Sci. USA* 66: 1059–66.

Brown, J.L. 1975. *The Evolution of Behavior.* New York: W.W. Norton. 761 pp.

Carpenter, J.M. 1982. The phylogenetic relationships and natural classification of the Vespoidea (Hymenoptera). *Syst. Entomol.* 7: 11–38.

_____. **In press.** Phylogenetic relationships and the origin of social behavior in the Vespidae. In *The Social Biology of Wasps,* ed. K.G. Ross, R.W. Matthews. Ithaca, N.Y.: Cornell Univ.

Chadab, R. 1979. Early warning cues for social wasps attacked by army ants. *Psyche* 86: 115–23.

Chadab-Crepet, R., Rettenmeyer, C.W. 1982. Comparative behavior of social wasps when attacked by army ants or other predators and parasites. In *The Biology of Social Insects,* ed. M.D. Breed, C.D. Michener, H.E. Evans, 270–74. Boulder, Colo.: Westview.

Corn, M.L. 1972. Notes on the biology of *Polistes carnifex* (Hymenoptera: Vespidae) in Costa Rica and Colombia. *Psyche* 79: 150–57.

Craig, R. 1982. Evolution of eusociality by kin selection: the effect of inbreeding between siblings. *J. Theor. Biol.* 94: 119–28.

_____. **1983.** Subfertility and the evolution of eusociality by kin selection. *J. Theor. Biol.* 100: 379–97.

Darchen, R. 1976. *Ropalidia cincta,* guêpe sociale de savane de Lamto (Côte-d'Ivoire) (Hym. Vespidae). *Ann. Soc. Ent. France (NS)* 12: 579–601.

Dew, H.E. 1983. Division of labor and queen influence in laboratory colonies of *Polistes metricus* (Hymenoptera: Vespidae). *Z. Tierpsych.* 61: 127–40.

Dew, H.E., Michener, C.D. 1981. Division of labor among workers of *Polistes metricus* (Hymenoptera: Vespidae): laboratory foraging activities. *Ins. Soc.* 28: 87–101.

Downhower, J.F., Wilson, D.E. 1973. Wasps as a defense mechanism of katydid. *Am. Midl. Nat.* 89: 451–55.

Edmunds, N. 1974. *Defence in Animals.* Harlow, Essex: Longman. 357 pp.

Edwards, R. 1980. *Social Wasps: Their Biology and Control.* East Grinstead, Sussex: Rentokil. 398 pp.

Endler, J.A. 1978. A predator's view of animal color patterns. In *Evolutionary Biology,* vol. 11, ed. M.K. Hecht, W.C. Steere, B. Wallace, 319–364. New York: Appleton-Century-Crofts.

Endler, J.A. 1986. Defense against predators. In *Predator-Prey Relationships,* ed. M.E. Feder, G.V. Lauder, 109–134. Chicago: Univ. Chicago.

Fox, M.W. 1972. *Understanding Your Dog.* New York: Coward, McCann. 240 pp.

Freisling, J. 1943. Zur Psychologie der Feldwespe. *Z. Tierpsychol.* 5: 439–63.

Gadagkar, R., Joshi, N.V. 1982. A comparative study of social structure in colonies of *Ropalidia.* In *The Biology of Social Insects,* ed. M.D. Breed, C.D. Michener, H.E. Evans, 187–91. Boulder, Colo.: Westview.

_____. **1983.** Quantitative ethology of social wasps: time-activity budgets and caste differentiation in *Ropalidia marginata* (Lep.) (Hymenoptera: Vespidae). *Anim. Behav.* 31: 26–31.

_____. **1984.** Social organization in the Indian wasp *Ropalidia cyathiformis* (Fab.) (Hymenoptera: Vespidae). *Z. Tierpsychol.* 64: 15–32.

Gorton, R.E. 1978. Observations on the nesting behavior of *Mischocyttarus immarginatus* (Rich.) (Vespidae: Hymenoptera) in a dry forest in Costa Rica. *Ins. Soc.* 25: 197–204.

Gotwald, W.H. 1982. Army ants. In *Social Insects,* vol. 4, ed. H.R. Hermann, 157–254. New York: Academic.

Hermann, H.R. 1971. Sting autotomy, a defensive mechanism in certain social Hymenoptera. *Ins. Soc.* 18: 111–20.

Hermann, H.R., Barron, R., Dalton, L. 1975. Spring behavior of *Polistes exclamans* (Hymenoptera: Vespidae: Polistinae). *Ent. News* 86: 173–78.

Hermann, H.R., Blum, M.S. 1981. Defensive mechanisms in the social Hymenoptera. In *Social Insects,* ed. H.R. Hermann, 2: 77–197. New York: Academic.

Hermann, H.R., Chao, J.T. 1984. Nesting biology and defensive behavior of *Mischocyttarus (Monocyttarus) mexicanus cubicola* (Vespidae: Polistinae). *Psyche* 91: 51–65.

Hermann, H.R., Dirks, T.F., 1974. Sternal glands in Polistine wasps: Morphology and associated behavior. *J. Georgia Ent. Soc.* 9: 1–8.

Herre, E.A., Windsor, D.M., Foster, R.B. 1986. Nesting associations of wasps and ants on lowland Peruvian ant-plants. *Psyche* 93: 321–30.

Hinde, R.A. 1970. *Animal Behavior.* New York: McGraw-Hill. 876 pp. 2nd. ed.

Hook, A.W., Evans, H.E. 1982. Observations on the nesting behaviour of three species of *Ropalidia* Guérin-Mèneville (Hymenoptera: Vespidae). *J. Aust. Ent. Soc.* 21: 271–75.

Horn, H.S. 1981. Succession. In *Theoretical Ecology,* ed. R.M. May, 253–71. Oxford: Blackwell Scientific. 2nd ed.

Hunt, A.N., Hermann, H.R. 1970. The hymenopterous poison apparatus. X. *Polistes annularis* (Hymenoptera: Vespidae). *J. Georgia Ent. Soc.* 5: 210–16.

Hunt, J.H., Noonan, K.C. 1979. Larval feeding by male *Polistes fuscatus* and *Polistes metricus* (Hym.: Vespidae). *Ins. Soc.* 26: 247–51.

Jacobson, E. 1935. Aanteekenigen over Stenogastrinae. *Ent. Meded. Ned.-Indië* 1: 15–19. (Translated in: *Sphecos* no. 16: 16–19, 1988).

Jeanne, R.L. 1970. Chemical defense of brood by a social wasp. *Science* 168: 1465–66.

_____. **1972.** Social biology of the neotropical wasp *Mischocyttarus drewseni*. *Bull. Mus. Comp. Zool.* 144: 63–150.

_____. **1975.** The adaptiveness of social wasp nest architecture. *Quart. Rev. Biol.* 50: 267–87.

_____. **1979a.** Construction and utilization of multiple combs in *Polistes canadensis* in relation to the biology of a predaceous moth. *Behav. Ecol. Sociobiol.* 4: 293–310.

_____. **1979b.** A latitudinal gradient in rates of ant predation. *Ecology* 60: 1211–24.

_____. **1980.** Evolution of social behavior in the Vespidae. *Ann. Rev. Ent.* 25: 371–96.

_____. **1982a.** Predation, defense, and colony size and cycle in the social wasps. In *The Biology of Social Insects,* ed. M.D. Breed, C.D. Michener, H.E. Evans, 280–84. Boulder: Westview.

_____. **1982b.** Evidence for an alarm substance in *Polistes canadensis*. *Experientia* 38: 329–30.

Jeanne, R.L., Downing, H.A., Post, D.C. 1983. Morphology and function of sternal glands in polistine wasps (Hymenoptera: Vespidae). *Zoomorphology* 103: 149–64.

Klahn, J.E. 1979. Philopatric and nonphilopatric foundress associations in the social wasp *Polistes fuscatus*. *Behav. Ecol. Sociobiol.* 5: 417–24.

Kojima, J. 1982. Notes on rubbing behavior in *Ropalidia gregaria* (Hymenoptera: Vespidae). *New Ent.* 31: 17–19.

_____. **1983a.** Occurrence of the rubbing behavior in a paper wasp, *Parapolybia indica* (Hymenoptera, Vespidae). *Kontyû* 51: 158–59.

_____. **1983b.** Defense of the pre-emergence colony against ants by means of a chemical barrier in *Ropalidia fasciata* (Hymenoptera, Vespidae). *Jap. J. Ecol. 33: 213–23*.

König, C. 1896. Was wussten die alten Griechen und Römer von den Wespen und Hornissen? *Illus. Wochenschr. Ent.* (1896): 261–66.

Kukuk, P.F., Eickwort, G.C., Raveret-Richter, M., Alexander, B., Gibson, R., Morse, R.A., Ratnieks, F. 1989. Importance of the sting in the evolution of sociality in the Hymenoptera. *Ann. Ent. Soc. Amer.* 82: 1–5.

Lehner, P.N. 1979. *Handbook of Ethological Methods.* New York: Garland STPM. 403 pp.

Litte, M. 1977. Behavioral ecology of the social wasp, *Mischocyttarus mexicanus. Behav. Ecol. Sociobiol.* 2: 229–46.

_____. **1979.** *Mischocyttarus flavitarsis* in Arizona: Social and nesting biology of a polistine wasp. *Z. Tierpsychol.* 50: 282–312.

Makino, S. 1985. List of parasitoids of polistine wasps. *Sphecos* no. 10: 19–25.

Mao Zedong 1965. Problems of war and strategy. In *Selected Works,* vol. 2. San Francisco: China Books.

Marino-Piccioli, M.T., Pardi, L. 1970. Studi sulla biologia di *Belonogaster* (Hymenoptera, Vespidae). I. Sull'etogramma di *Belonogaster griseus* (Fab.). *Monit. Zool. Ital., NS Suppl.* 3: 197–225.

Matsuura, M. 1984. Comparative biology of the five Japanese species of the genus *Vespa* (Hymenoptera, Vespidae). *Bull. Fac. Agric. Mie. Univ.* no. 69: 1–131.

_____. **1985.** Life history of the nocturnal vespine, *Provespa anomala. Sumatra Nat. Study (Ent.),* pp. 27–36.

Matthews, R.W. In press. Evolution of social behavior in sphecid wasps. In *The Social Biology of Wasps,* ed. K.G. Ross, R.W. Matthews. Ithaca, N.Y.: Cornell Univ.

Michener, C.D. 1974. *The Social Behavior of the Bees: A Comparative Study.* Cambridge, Mass.: Harvard Univ. 404 pp.

Myers, J.G. 1935. Nesting association of birds with social insects. *Trans. Roy. Ent. Soc. Lond.* 83: 11–22.

Naumann, M.G. 1970. The nesting behavior of *Protopolybia pumila* in Panama (Hymenoptera: Vespidae). Ph.D. thesis, Univ. Kansas 182 pp.

Nelson, J.M. 1968. Parasites and symbionts of nests of *Polistes* wasps. *Ann. Ent. Soc. Amer.* 61: 1528–39.

_____. **1971.** Nesting habits and nest symbionts of *Polistes eythroceophalus* Latreille (Hymenoptera: Vespidae) in Costa Rica. *Rev. Biol. Trop.* 18: 89–98.

Ohgushi R., Sakagami, S.F., Yamane, S., Abbas, N.D. 1983. Nest architecture and related notes of stenogastrine wasps in the province of Sumatera Barat, Indonesia (Hymenoptera, Vespidae). *Sci. Rep. Kanazawa Univ.* 28: 27–58.

Orlove, M.J. 1975. A model of kin selection not invoking coefficients of relationship. *J. Theor. Biol.* 49: 289–310.

Oster, G.F., Wilson, E.O. 1978. *Caste and Ecology in the Social Insects.* Princeton: Princeton Univ. 352 pp.

Pagden, H.T. 1958. Some Malayan social wasps. *Malay. Nat. J.* 12: 131–48.

_____. **1962.** More about *Stenogaster. Malay. Nat. J.* 16: 95–102.

Pardi, L., Turillazzi, S. 1982. Biologia delle Stenogastrinae. *Atti. Accad. Naz. Ital. Entomol. Rendic.* 30: 1–21.

Post, D.C., Downing, H.A., Jeanne, R.L. 1984. Alarm response to venom by social wasps *Polistes exclamans* and *P. fuscatus* (Hymenoptera: Vespidae). *J. Chem. Ecol.* 10: 1425–33.

Post, D.C., Jeanne, R.L. 1981. Colony defense against ants by *Polistes fuscatus* (hymenoptera: Vespidae) in Wisconsin. *J. Kansas Ent. Soc.* 54: 599–615.

Post, D.C., Mohamed, M.A., Coppel, H.C., Jeanne, R.L. 1984. Identification of ant repellent allomone produced by the social wasp *Polistes fuscatus* (Hymenoptera: Vespidae). *J. Chem. Ecol.* 10: 1799–1807.

Raposo-Filho, J.R. 1983. Dinâmica da hierarquia social em colônias de *Mischocyttarus (Monocyttarus) extinctus* Zikán, 1935 (Vespidae—Polistinae). DSc thesis, Julio de Mesquita Filho State Univ. 138 pp.

Rau, P. 1930. Life history notes on the wasp *Polistes annularis. Can. Ent.* 62: 119–20.

————. **1939.** Studies in the ecology and behavior of *Polistes* wasps. *Bull. Brooklyn Ent. Soc.* 34: 36–44.

————. **1941.** Birds as enemies of Polistes wasps. *Can. Ent.* 73: 196.

Richards, O.W. 1978. *The Social Wasps of the Americas, Excluding the Vespinae.* London: British Museum (Natural History). 580 pp.

Richards, O.W., Richards, M.J. 1951. Observations on the social wasps of South America (Hymenoptera: Vespidae). *Trans. Roy. Ent. Soc. Lond.* 102: 1–170.

Roubaud, E. 1916. Recherches biologiques sur les guêpes solitaires et sociales d'Afrique. La genèse de la vie sociale et l'évolution de l'instinct maternel chez les vespides. *Ann. Sci. Nat.* (10) 1: 1–160.

Sakagami, S.F., Fukushima, K. 1957. Some biological observations on a hornet, *Vespa tropica* var. *pulchra* (Du Buysson), with special reference to its dependence on *Polistes* wasps. (Hymenoptera). *Treubia* 24: 73–82.

Schmitt, C. 1920. Beiträge zur Biologie der Feldwespe (*Polistes gallicus* L.). [Part 3]. *Z. Wiss. Insektenbiol.* 16: 221–30.

Schneirla, T.C. 1971. *Army Ants: A Study in Social Organization.* San Francisco: Freeman. 349 pp.

Smith, W.J. 1977. *Behavior of Communicating.* Cambridge, Mass.: Harvard Univ. 545 pp.

Spieth, H.T. 1948. Notes on a colony of *Polistes fuscatus hunteri* Bequaert. *J. New York Ent. Soc.* 56: 155–69.

Spradbery, J.P. 1973. *Wasps.* Seattle: Univ. Washington. 408 pp.

Starr, C.K. 1981. Defensive tactics of social wasps. Ph.D. thesis, Univ. Georgia. 108 pp.

_____. **1985a.** A simple pain scale for field comparison of hymenopteran stings. *J. Ent. Sci.* 20: 225–32.

_____. **1985b.** Enabling mechanisms in the origin of sociality in the Hymenoptera: the sting's the thing. *Ann. Ent. Soc. Amer.* 78: 836–40.

_____. **1988.** The nesting association of the social wasps *Mischocyttarus immarginatus* and *Polybia* spp. in Costa Rica. *Biotropica.* 20: 171–173.

Starr, C.K. 1989. In reply, is the sting the thing? *Ann. Ent. Soc. Amer.* 82: 6–8.

Steiner, A. 1932. Die Arbeitsteilung der Feldwespe *Polistes dubia* Kohl. *Z. Vgl. Physiol.* 17: 101–52.

Strassmann, J.E. 1981a. Evolutionary implications of early male and satellite nest production in *Polistes exclamans* colony cycles. *Behav. Ecol. Sociobiol.* 8: 55–64.

_____. **1981b.** Parasites, predators and group size in the paper wasp, *Polistes exclamans. Ecology* 62: 1225–33.

Strassmann, J.E., Meyer, D.C., Matlock, R.L. 1984. Behavioral castes in the social wasp, *Polistes exclamans* (Hymenoptera: Vespidae). *Sociobiology* 8: 211–24.

Turillazzi, S. 1984. Defensive mechanisms in *Polistes* Wasps. In *Defensive Mechanisms in Social Insects,* ed. H.R. Hermann, 33–58. New York: Praeger.

_____. **1985.** Function and characteristics of the abdominal substance secreted by wasps of the genus *Parischnogaster* (Hymenoptera Stenogastrinae). *Monit. Zool. Ital. (NS)* 19: 91–99.

Turillazzi, S., Pardi, L. 1981. Ant guards on nests of *Parischnogaster nigricans serrei* (Buysson) (Stenogastrinae). *Monit. Zool. Ital. (NS)* 15: 1–7.

Turillazzi, S., Ugolini, A. 1979. Rubbing behavior in some European *Polistes* (Hymenoptera Vespidae). *Monit. Zool. Ital. (NS)* 13: 129–42.

Watkins, J.F. 1976. *The Identification and Distribution of New World Army Ants (Dorylinae: Formicidae).* Waco, Tex: Baylor Univ. 101 pp.

West-Eberhard, M.J. 1969. The social biology of polistine wasps. *Misc. Publ. Mus. Zool. Univ. Michigan* 140: 1–101.

Weyrauch, W.K. 1928. Beiträge zur Biologie von *Polistes. Biol. Zentralbl.* 48: 407–27.

_____. **1935.** *Dolichovespula* and *Vespa.* Vergleichende Übersicht über zwei wesentliche Lebenstypen bei sozialen Wespen. Mit Bezugnahme auf die Frage nach der Fortshrittlichkeit tierischer Organisation. I. *Biol. Zentralbl.* 55: 484–524.

Williams, F.X. 1919. Philippine wasp studies. II. Descriptions of new species and life history studies. *Bull. Expt. Stn. Hawaiian Sugar Planters' Assoc. (Ent.)* 14: 19–184.

————. **1928.** The natural history of a Philippine nipa house, with descriptions of new wasps. *Phil. J. Sci.* 35: 53–118.

Wilson, E.O. 1964. The true army ants of the Indo-Australian area (Hymenoptera: Formicidae: Dorylinae). *Pacif. Insects* 6: 427–83.

Windsor, D.M. 1972. Nesting association between two neotropical polybiine wasps (Hym., Vespidae). *Biotropica* 4: 1–3.

Yamane, S. 1984. Nest architecture of two Oriental paper wasps, *Parapolybia varia* and *P. nodosa*, with notes on its adaptive significance (Vespidae, Polistinae). *Zool. Jb. Syst.* 111: 119–41.

Yoshikawa, K. 1963. Introductory studies on the life economy of polistine wasps. II. Superindividual stage. 2. Division of labor among workers. *Jap. J. Ecol.* 13: 53–57.

Zikán, J.F. 1949. O gênero *Mischocyttarus* Saussure, (Hym.: Vespidae), com a descrição de 82 espécies novas. *Bol. Pargue Nac. Itatiáia* 1: 1–251.

APPENDIX

In order to identify behaviors arising when *Polistes* are disturbed by vertebratres, I repeatedly provoked colonies of five Nearctic species and compared their behavior with that when they were apparently unaware of me. All observations are from ergonomic-stage colonies during warm afternoons. Provocations consisted of waving a net or my hand near the nest and occasionally tapping the nest or substrate. In order to elicit the full range of responses, each provocation started out very mild and became increasingly violent until a large fraction of the colony had either attacked or fled. The bulk of observations was recorded on video or movies, supplemented with tape-recorded and hand written notes. Rates of wing flutter and leg wave were measured by slow-down video playback and frame-by-frame movie analysis.

Eleven behaviors were unambiguously associated with disturbed colonies. Some of these also appeared significantly often in unprovoked colonies when a foreign insect was nearby, though much less than under provocation (except for wing flip in some species). Otherwise, each of the eleven was seen rarely or never. All are strong departures from the at-rest posture, in which the wasp is pressed motionless against the nest with the wings down (figure 15.4a). My more casual observations of other species have not added to the following list.

1. *Alert posture.* Facing the intruder, body raised up on the mid- and hindlegs, usually with the front part of the body well elevated and forelegs raised away from the nest (figure 15.4b,c). This posture is mainly interesting as a basis on which other behaviors can be built.
2. *Wing raise.* Wings, still folded, raised up off the abdomen and spread apart (figure 15.4b,c). Usually they are raised at about a 30° angle with about 90° separating them. In *P. annularis* and some others, though, they may be more spread at the sides than raised. I treat this as a variant of the same behavior.
3. *Wing flip.* A discrete wingbeat motion, often repeated, beginning and ending with the wings at rest.
4. *Wing buzz.* A short burst of wingbeats lasting a fraction of a second. This seems close in form to wing flip, and the distinction between them is not always clear in the literature. This is the only one of the eleven behaviors which produces an audible sound, often quite noticeable.
5. *Wing flutter.* Wings in the raised position (figure 15.4b,c) fluttered at very low amplitude. The mean flutter rate in *P. exclamans* is 10.3 cycles/sec (SD = 2.8; 5–41 cycles measured in each of thirty trials).
6. *Leg wave.* Body in the alert posture, forelegs vibrated synchronously, usually at the femur-tibia joint (figure 15.4c).
7. *Abdomen bend.* The abdomen (more precisely the gaster, but the distinction need not detain us) is arched, the tip pointing toward the nest surface or to the side (figure 15.4c). The abdomen as a whole may also be flexed upward and/or in motion. Side-to-side motions of the tip are common, and in *P. annularis* there is often a nasty downward probing of the tip.
8. *Antennate air.* The antennae, pointed forward, are tapped downwards in discrete strokes, about 1–2/sec. The head is held away from the nest surface, so that the antennae do not tap it.
9. *Retreat.* A backing away or sideways walk to the far side of the nest, so that the wasp largely disappears from view. It can be accompanied by any of the above behaviors.
10. *Flee.* Fly off the nest away from the provoker. In order to distinguish this from attack, I took care to allow a flight direction which was clearly away from me.

11. *Attack.* Fly off the nest at the provoker. There are clearly two different forms: (a) true attack, with attempt to sting, and (b) bluff attack, turning short of direct contact. In practice the distinction was usually lost, since I found it convenient to respond to attack of whichever kind with true fleeing.

List of Contributors

David W. Alsop, Department of Biology, Queens College, Flushing, NY 11367, USA

Murray. S. Blum, Department of Entomology, University of Georgia, Athens, GA 30602, USA

M. Deane Bowers, Department of Environmental Population, and Organismic Biology, University of Colorado, Boulder, CO 80309, USA

Malcolm Edmunds, School of Applied Biology, Lancashire Polytechnic, Preston PR1 2TQ, UK

David L. Evans, Franklin Park Zoo, Franklin Park, Boston, MA 02121, USA

James H. Fullard, Department of Biology, Erindale College, University of Toronto, Mississauga, Ont. L5L 1C6, Canada

Tim Guilford, Animal Behaviour Research Group, Department of Zoology, South Parks Road, Oxford OX1 3PS, UK

Robert C. Lederhouse, Department of Entomology, Michigan State University, East Lansing, MI, 48824, USA

Michael H. Robinson, National Zoological Park, Smithsonian Institution, Washington, DC 20008, USA

Scott K. Sakaluk, Department of Biological Sciences, Illinois State University, Normal, IL 61761, USA

Theodore D. Sargent, Department of Zoology, University of Massachusetts, Amherst, MA 01003, USA

Justin O. Schmidt, Southwestern Biological Institute, 1961 W. Brichta, Tucson, AZ 85745, USA

Werner Schuler, Zoological Institute, University of Göttingen, Berliner Strasse 28, D-3400 Göttingen, Germany

Christopher K. Starr, Department of Horticulture, University of Georgia, Athens, GA 30602, USA

George W. Uetz, Department of Biological Sciences, University of Cincinnati, Cincinnati, OH 45221, USA

Kevina Vulinec, Department of Ecology and Evolution, University of Chicago, Chicago, IL 60637, USA

Douglas W. Whitman, Department of Biological Sciences, Illinois State University, Normal, IL 61761, USA

Subject Index

Author Index